MAGILL'S
LITERARY ANNUAL

1983

MAGILL'S LITERARY ANNUAL

1983

Essay-Reviews of 200 Outstanding Books
Published in the United States during 1982

With an Annotated Categories Index

Volume One
A-Med

Edited by
FRANK N. MAGILL

SALEM PRESS
Englewood Cliffs

LIBRARY OF CONGRESS CATALOG CARD NO. 77-99209
ISBN 0-89356-283-1

FIRST PRINTING

PRINTED IN THE UNITED STATES OF AMERICA

PREFACE

BEGINNING with these two volumes, *Magill's Literary Annual* will undergo a change in contents. Articles dealing with history, general biography, current affairs, and political science will no longer appear here but will be published separately in a single volume covering one hundred individual works under the title *Magill's History Annual*. This change will enable the staff to expand the number of new works reviewed for history-oriented readers from the usual seventy or eighty to a full hundred each year. The change will also make possible an increase of perhaps one-third in the general literature titles covered in the regular two-volume literary annual, which will continue to feature two hundred titles, all for general readers. Although general biography reviews will now appear in the history volume, literary biographies will continue to be included in their appropriate place: the two-volume literary annual.

The staff philosophy since 1954 has been to evaluate critically each year a given number of major examples of serious literature published during the year that are likely to be of more than passing general interest. Not all selections have been timeless works by any means, but the effort, nevertheless, continues. Individual critical articles for the first twenty-two years were collected and published in *Survey of Contemporary Literature* in 1977. A similar procedure will eventually be followed for articles published after 1977.

The record of a contemporary critical response to a work in the context of its own time—rather than a retrospective view at some remote vantage point in the future—often offers some permanent advantages, which idea has been the theory behind Salem's yearly surveys since 1954. Selections for these annuals usually include works that have been recognized by the major prize selection committees as well as landmark works that are representative of, say, a new literary trend (the post-Modernist novel) or characterized by unique insights (Rachel Carson's *Silent Spring*, 1962).

Those two hundred works represented in the 1982 Annual are drawn from the following categories: fiction, 84; poetry and drama, 23; literary criticism and literary history, 14; essays, 21; literary biography, 19; autobiography, memoirs, diaries, and letters, 32; and miscellaneous, 7.

As usual, fiction absorbs the major share of space in *Magill's Literary Annual*, accounting for 42% of the titles covered. The year 1982 was a good year for fiction, many excellent novels having appeared during the year, but the tenor of most of the major works seemed to lean toward despair and loss of the human connection rather than toward romantic satisfaction. Margaret Atwood's *Bodily Harm* is a typical example of such a work. The novel paints a bleak picture of the possibility of satisfactory human connectiveness and ends on a sterile note. Little hope for improvement springs from Ann Beattie's *The Burning House*, five stories that approach the ultimate in hopelessness. There is, however, a different tone in *The Color Purple*, Alice Walker's moving and highly praised epistolary novel which ends in total victory for the protagonist as a human being. The book won the Pulitzer Prize and the American Book Award for Fiction in 1983.

Lighter in tone also is *Cadillac Jack*, Larry McMurtry's social satire featuring a rover, a womanizer, a collector, and a trader all wrapped up in one free-floater on the make. Jack is unstable in his human relationships but is representative of today's restless society. With *Bech Is Back*, John Updike gives readers more of Henry Bech, first introduced in *Bech: A Book* (1970). Bech, too, is restless, at least psychologically, but he makes several efforts at commitment. Only Updike knows whether Bech will be back again, but the fact that, after thirteen years, Henry finally finished his novel *Think Big*, may be a clue.

Stanley Elkin, in *George Mills*, offers an odd novel that traces several generations of losers, doomed by fate, or so they think, until the present George finally realizes that "The fault, dear Brutus, is not in our stars, but in ourselves. . . ." The book won the National Book Critics Award for Best Fiction of 1982. Other outstanding novels of 1982 include *A Bloodsmoor Romance* by Joyce Carol Oates, with a partly science-fiction plot line, not vintage Oates but interesting and imaginative; John A. Williams' *!Click Song*, which depicts the struggle of a young writer to gain recognition against great odds; and Graham Greene's *Monsignor Quixote*, a modern-day novel of Spain, very clever and without a hint of the "Greene thriller" so many of his readers are likely to expect from Greene. Also during the year, Saul Bellow published *The Dean's December*, a thoughtful novel, as usual, but not one of his best.

In addition to Ann Beattie's volume, two other short-story collections should be noted here. Prolific writer V. S. Pritchett published *Collected Stories*, an excellent volume from a finished artist whom Walter Allen has called the finest British writer of stories since D. H. Lawrence. Now, seventeen years after his death, Evelyn Waugh's *Charles Ryder's Schooldays and Other Stories* has appeared. This volume is a welcome posthumous publication of the title story; the other entries are not new.

A novella ends the career of John Cheever. *Oh What a Paradise It Seems*, his final volume, is a nostalgic farewell from one whose books told us how it is and, sometimes, how it should be.

As usual, poets were busy in 1982, with some new talents breaking into the limelight. Katha Pollitt won the National Book Critics Circle Award with her first poetry collection, *Antarctic Traveller*. She obviously is a fine young talent. Critic Henry Taylor reports: ". . . Pollitt is very good indeed. She has a sharp and loving eye for details. . . ." Another bright new poetic talent worth watching is Brad Leithauser, whose *Hundreds of Fireflies* has drawn praise from many sources; and a good poet who seems to be getting better all the time is William Matthews, whose volume *Flood* appeared in 1982. In *Our Ground Time Here Will Be Brief*, Maxine Kumin offers her sensitive and attractive poems—even the title is clever—revealing, among other things, the longing of the poet for a permanent, status quo condition with friends and family. *The Man in the Black Coat Turns* is Robert Bly's latest volume. Though the poet has lost his youthful fire, the mature artist still is no less engaged with his muse. John Haines's *News from the Glacier* is filled with beautiful language and striking images; for example, a paean to nature (of the mating season: "a voice, and someone to answer") celebrates the universal connection. Such examples abound.

An unusual number of good literary biographies appeared in 1982. F. W. J. Hemmings' *Baudelaire the Damned* is a highly competent biography of the dark-visioned poet whose masterpiece, *Flowers of Evil*, epitomized the decadence he so admired. Judith Thurman's *Isak Dinesen* presents an intimate biography of the superior short-story writer who prevailed with her talent in spite of her appalling personal life. In *Thomas Hardy*, Michael Millgate provides an excellent study of the great poet and novelist whose own life was in some ways as arid as that of his gloomiest literary creation. *Kafka*, an excellent study by Ronald Hayman, is very persuasive in its revisionist suggestions. In *Camus*, Patrick McCarthy also does not hesitate to alter the image of his subject when necessary, for he presents Camus as vulnerable and insecure at times. *Katherine Anne Porter*, by Joan Givner, is the authorized biography of a superlative short-story writer who lived as romantically as the women about whom she wrote. In this study, the biographer emphasizes the life more than the writings, and properly so. With John Halperin's *Gissing*, a fine but unfortunate writer is at last about to receive some deserved recognition. One of the most ambitious and interesting biographical works of the year is Nicholas Delbanco's *Group Portrait*. This illustrated volume is an interrelated study of Joseph Conrad, Stephen Crane, Ford Madox Ford, Henry James, and H. G. Wells, all of whom lived within a few miles of one another in southern England at the same time and reacted among themselves as artists through this unique opportunity for ideological exchanges.

Diaries, letters, memoirs, and essays provided much interesting reading in 1982. Hilda Doolittle's *The Gift* offers excellent images of H. D.'s childhood, sparked by the London Blitz and her perceptive interpretations of the human condition. Here is distilled art by a sensitive poet. Also recommended is Janice S. Robinson's *H. D.: The Life and Work of an American Poet.* Another memoir, Nobel Prize-winning Patrick White's *Flaws in the Glass*, is an emotionally deep and intellectually honest self-revelation. *The Diary of Virginia Woolf, Vol. IV: 1931-1935*, edited by Anne Olivier Bell, appeared during the year. It is interesting, informal, revealing, and filled with withering asides: perfect Woolf fare.

The Letters of Gustave Flaubert, selected, edited, and translated by Francis Steegmuller, was issued in 1982. This is the second of two volumes and carries the correspondence right up to the year of the great novelist's death. In 1982, Leslie Marchand edited *Lord Byron*, which provides a good selection of letters and journals. Byron is seldom tiresome. In *Pound/Ford*, the literary friendship of Ezra Pound and Ford Madox Ford is recorded through their correspondence and the connecting commentary of editor Brita Lindberg-Seyersted. In William Golding's essays in *A Moving Target*, readers encounter some good thought wrap-ups of a fine novelist at age seventy-two, a writer who won the 1983 Nobel Prize in Literature. For political and literary history, Herbert R. Lottman offers a study of the political engagement of eight French literary figures during the 1930's and 1940's, a time of turmoil that assaulted the sensibilities of millions locked in despair.

I wish to thank the many hands, and minds, that have been engaged in the preparation of these two volumes. All of us join in the hope that the exegeses here provided will serve users well.

FRANK N. MAGILL

LIST OF TITLES

                                                          page

Agon: Toward a Theory of Revisionism—*Harold Bloom* 1
Ah, But Your Land Is Beautiful—*Alan Paton* 6
Aké: The Years of Childhood—*Wole Soyinka* 10
All That Is Solid Melts into Air: The Experience of
    Modernity—*Marshall Berman* 15
Antarctic Traveller—*Katha Pollitt* 20
Argot Merchant Disaster: Poems New and Selected, The —
    George Starbuck 25
Atlantic High: A Celebration—*William F. Buckley, Jr.* 29
Aunt Julia and the Scriptwriter—*Mario Vargas Llosa* 34
Autumn—*A. G. Mojtabai* 39

Barthes Reader, A—*Roland Barthes* 44
Baudelaire the Damned: A Biography—*F. W. J. Hemmings* 49
Bech Is Back—*John Updike* 53
Beyond the Pale and Other Stories—*William Trevor* 57
Bloodsmoor Romance, A—*Joyce Carol Oates* 61
Bodily Harm—*Margaret Atwood* 65
Boy Scout Handbook and Other Observations, The—*Paul Fussell* 70
Braided Lives—*Marge Piercy* 75
Bronx Primitive: Portraits in a Childhood—*Kate Simon* 80
Burning House, The—*Ann Beattie* 86

Cadillac Jack—*Larry McMurtry* 90
Camus—*Patrick McCarthy* 96
Chain of Voices, A—*André Brink* 101
Charles Ryder's Schooldays and Other Stories—*Evelyn Waugh* 105
Chinese Insomniacs: New Poems, The—*Josephine Jacobsen* 110
Chosen Poems, Old and New—*Audre Lorde* 113
Circles on the Water: Selected Poems—*Marge Piercy* 119
!Click Song—*John A. Williams* 124
Clinging to the Wreckage: A Part of Life—*John Mortimer* 127
Collected Stories—*V. S. Pritchett* 131

page

Collected Stories of Isaac Bashevis Singer, The—*Isaac Bashevis Singer* 135
Color Purple, The—*Alice Walker* 139
Consoling Intelligence: Responses to Literary Modernism, The— *David Kubal* 144
Correspondence of Boris Pasternak and Olga Freidenberg, 1910-1954, The—*Boris Pasternak* and *Olga Freidenberg*............ 147
Correspondence of Thomas Carlyle and John Ruskin, The— *Thomas Carlyle* and *John Ruskin* 153
Cosmic Code: Quantum Physics as the Language of Nature, The—*Heinz R. Pagels* 156
Country Between Us, The—*Carolyn Forché* 161
Crimes of the Heart—*Beth Henley*....................................... 165

Dancing Girls and Other Stories—*Margaret Atwood* 169
Deadeye Dick—*Kurt Vonnegut* 174
Dean's December, The—*Saul Bellow*.................................... 179
Diary of Virginia Woolf, Vol. IV: 1931-1935, The— *Virginia Woolf* 185
Different Seasons—*Stephen King* 189
Dinner at the Homesick Restaurant—*Anne Tyler* 194
Distant Relations—*Carlos Fuentes* 200
Down the River—*Edward Abbey* 205
Duncan's Colony—*Natalie L. M. Petesch*............................... 210
Dutch Shea, Jr.—*John Gregory Dunne*.................................. 216

Early Diary of Anaïs Nin, Vol. II: 1920-1923, The—*Anaïs Nin* 220
Emerson in His Journals—*Ralph Waldo Emerson* 224
Empire of Signs, The—*Roland Barthes*................................... 230
Eternal Curse on the Reader of These Pages—*Manuel Puig*............ 235

Family Installments: Memories of Growing Up Hispanic— *Edward Rivera*... 240
Fate of the Earth, The—*Jonathan Schell* 244
Feel of Rock: Poems of Three Decades, The—*Reed Whittemore*....... 250
Fiction and Repetition: Seven English Novels—*J. Hillis Miller*......... 253
Flaws in the Glass: A Self-Portrait—*Patrick White* 257
Flood: Poems—*William Matthews*.. 262
Four Wise Men, The—*Michel Tournier* 267

George Mills—*Stanley Elkin* 273
Gift, The—*H.D.* 278

page

Gissing: A Life in Books—*John Halperin* 283
Glass Face in the Rain, A—*William Stafford* 288
God's Grace—*Bernard Malamud* 291
Grace Abounding—*Maureen Howard* 296
Grammatical Man: Information, Entropy, Language,
    and Life—*Jeremy Campbell* 301
Great Code: The Bible and Literature, The—*Northrop Frye* 306
Greeting: New & Selected Poems, The—*R. H. W. Dillard* 309
Group Portrait: Joseph Conrad, Stephen Crane, Ford Madox
    Ford, Henry James, and H. G. Wells—*Nicholas Delbanco* 312
Growing Up—*Russell Baker* 317

Hannah Arendt: For Love of the World—*Elizabeth Young-Bruehl*..... 322
Happy to Be Here—*Garrison Keillor* 326
H. D.: The Life and Work of an American Poet—
    Janice S. Robinson 331
Headbirths: Or, The Germans Are Dying Out—*Günter Grass* 336
Her Victory—*Alan Sillitoe* 340
Hometown—*Peter Davis* 344
Hundreds of Fireflies—*Brad Leithauser* 348

Imaginary Crimes—*Sheila Ballantyne* 353
Isak Dinesen: The Life of a Storyteller—*Judith Thurman* 358

Joke, The—*Milan Kundera* 363
Journals of Sylvia Plath, The—*Sylvia Plath* 367

Kafka: A Biography—*Ronald Hayman* 372
Katherine Anne Porter: A Life—*Joan Givner* 376
Killing Ground, The—*Mary Lee Settle* 381

Last Stands: Notes from Memory—*Hilary Masters* 386
Left Bank: Writers, Artists, and Politics from the Popular
Front to the Cold War, The—*Herbert R. Lottman*...................... 390
Letters of Gustave Flaubert, 1857-1880, The—*Gustave Flaubert*........ 395
Letters to Ottla and the Family—*Franz Kafka*......................... 401
Levitation: Five Fictions—*Cynthia Ozick*............................... 405
Life of John Berryman, The—*John Haffenden*......................... 410
Living by Fiction—*Annie Dillard* 413
Lord Byron: Selected Letters and Journals—*George Gordon
    Byron, Baron Byron* 418
Loser, The—*George Konrád* 423

page

Mailer: A Biography—*Hilary Mills* 428
Making of the Representative for Planet 8, The—*Doris Lessing* 432
Malgudi Days—*R. K. Narayan* 436
Man in the Black Coat Turns, The—*Robert Bly* 439
Mantissa—*John Fowles* 443
Marco Polo, If You Can—*William F. Buckley, Jr.* 447
Margin of Hope: An Intellectual Autobiography, A—
    Irving Howe 451
Me Again: Uncollected Writings of Stevie Smith—*Stevie Smith* 458
Meditation, A—*Juan Benet* 464
Memoirs of a Space Traveler: Further Reminiscences
    of Ijon Tichy—*Stanislaw Lem* 469
Mickelsson's Ghosts—*John Gardner* 475
Midnight Clear, A—*William Wharton* 480
Monolithos: Poems, 1962 and 1982—*Jack Gilbert* 484
Monsignor Quixote—*Graham Greene* 489
Mosquito Coast, The—*Paul Theroux* 496
Mother and Two Daughters, A—*Gail Godwin* 501
Moving Target, A—*William Golding* 506

Nabokov's Fifth Arc: Nabokov and Others on His
    Life's Work—*J. E. Rivers* and *Charles Nicol* 511
Names, The—*Don De Lillo* 515
Namesake—*Michel Goldberg* 518
New Islands and Other Stories—*María Luisa Bombal* 523
News from the Glacier: Selected Poems, 1960-1980—*John Haines* 527
Night Thoughts of a Classical Physicist—*Russell McCormmach* 532
No Fond Return of Love—*Barbara Pym* 536
No Place on Earth—*Christa Wolf* 540
Nobody's Angel—*Thomas McGuane* 544
Noël Coward Diaries, The—*Noël Coward* 549

Obasan—*Joy Kogawa* 554
Oh What a Paradise It Seems—*John Cheever* 558
One Way to Spell Man—*Wallace Stegner* 563
Orality and Literacy: The Technologizing of the Word—
    Walter J. Ong 568
Ordeal by Labyrinth: Conversations with Claude-Henri
    Rocquet—*Mircea Eliade* 572
Our Ground Time Here Will Be Brief—*Maxine Kumin* 577
Outline of Sanity: A Biography of G. K. Chesterton, The—
    Alzina Stone Dale 582

LIST OF TITLES

page

P. G. Wodehouse: A Biography—*Frances Donaldson* 587
Philosophy in the Twentieth Century—*A. J. Ayer* 592
Pieces and Pontifications—*Norman Mailer* 597
PM/AM: New and Selected Poems—*Linda Pastan* 603
Poets in Their Youth: A Memoir—*Eileen Simpson* 608
Polish Complex, The—*Tadeusz Konwicki* 611
Portage to San Cristóbal of A. H., The—*George Steiner* 616
Pound/Ford: The Story of a Literary Friendship—*Ezra Pound*
    and *Ford Madox Ford* 621
Purple Decades: A Reader, The—*Tom Wolfe* 626

Rabbis and Wives—*Chaim Grade* 630
Realistic Imagination: English Fiction from Frankenstein
    to Lady Chatterley, The—*George Levine* 635
Rebel Angels, The—*Robertson Davies* 641
Red Smith Reader, The—*Walter W. ("Red") Smith* 645
Regina—*Leslie Epstein* 650
Robert Lowell: A Biography—*Ian Hamilton* 654
Rogue's March—*W. T. Tyler* 659

Sabbatical: A Romance—*John Barth* 665
Sacred Journey, The—*Frederick Buechner* 670
Samurai, The—*Shusaku Endo* 674
Scenes of Childhood and Other Stories—*Sylvia Townsend Warner* 679
Schindler's List—*Thomas Keneally* 684
Science Observed: Essays Out of My Mind—*Jeremy Bernstein* 689
Science of Goodbyes, The—*Myra Sklarew* 694
Second American Revolution and Other Essays (1976-1982),
    The—*Gore Vidal* 700
Second Life of Art: Selected Essays, The—*Eugenio Montale* 705
Secret Symmetry: Sabina Spielrein Between Jung and
    Freud, A—*Aldo Carotenuto* 709
Seizure of Power, The—*Czeslaw Milosz* 713
Selected & New Poems: 1961-1981—*Jim Harrison* 718
Selected Letters: The Personal Correspondence,
    1844-1877—*Karl Marx* and *Friedrich Engels* 722
Selected Poems—*Galway Kinnell* 726
Selected Poems—*John Frederick Nims* 730
Selected Stories—*Robert Walser* 734
Shiloh and Other Stories—*Bobbie Ann Mason* 739
Shoeless Joe—*W. P. Kinsella* 742
Short Stories of Thomas Hardy, The—*Kristin Brady* 747

page

Soldier's Play, A—*Charles Fuller*.. 751
Somewhere a Master: Further Hasidic Portraits and Legends—
    Elie Wiesel 756
Souls and Bodies—*David Lodge* 761
Stuff of Sleep and Dreams: Experiments in Literary
    Psychology—*Leon Edel*.. 765
Susan Sontag Reader, A—*Susan Sontag*................................. 769

Teaching a Stone to Talk: Expeditions and Encounters—
    Annie Dillard 773
Terrible Twos, The—*Ishmael Reed* 778
Terrorists and Novelists—*Diane Johnson*................................ 783
These the Companions: Recollections—*Donald Davie* 787
13th Valley, The—*John M. Del Vecchio*.................................. 791
This Quiet Dust and Other Writings—*William Styron*................... 796
This Was Harlem: A Cultural Portrait, 1900-1950—
    Jervis Anderson.. 800
Thomas Hardy: A Biography—*Michael Millgate*....................... 806
To See You Again—*Alice Adams* 811
Tolstoi in the Sixties—*Boris Eikhenbaum* 816
Tolstoi in the Seventies—*Boris Eikhenbaum* 821
Torch in My Ear, The—*Elias Canetti* 827
Truants: Adventures Among the Intellectuals, The—
    William Barrett 833
Tugman's Passage, The—*Edward Hoagland*............................. 836
Twice Shy—*Dick Francis* 841
2010: Odyssey Two—*Arthur C. Clarke* 844

Uncivil Liberties—*Calvin Trillin* 849
Unsuitable Attachment, An—*Barbara Pym*.............................. 855

Visions from San Francisco Bay—*Czeslaw Milosz* 860

Wait for November—*Hans Erich Nossack*............................... 864
Waking—*Eva Figes* 869
War Within: From Victorian to Modernist Thought in the
    South, 1919-1945, The—*Daniel Joseph Singal*..................... 873
Watchfires—*Louis Auchincloss*.. 878
What Was Literature? Class Culture and Mass Society—
    Leslie Fiedler 884
When Things of the Spirit Come First: Five Early Tales—
    Simone de Beauvoir 890

page

Whisper to the Earth: New Poems—*David Ignatow* 894

White Plague, The—*Frank Herbert* 900

Why Can't We Live Together Like Civilized Human Beings?—
  Maxine Kumin 903

Wider Sea: A Life of John Ruskin, The—*John Dixon Hunt* 908

Woman and the Demon: The Life of a Victorian Myth—
  Nina Auerbach 913

Women of Brewster Place: A Novel in Seven Stories, The—
  Gloria Naylor 918

Woods, The—*David Plante* 923

Writers and Friends—*Edward Weeks* 928

Young Rebecca: Writings of Rebecca West, 1911-1917, The—
  Rebecca West 932

TITLES BY CATEGORY

———

ANNOTATED

                                                                        page

FICTION.. xix

POETRY.. xxvi
DRAMA

LITERARY CRITICISM xxviii
LITERARY HISTORY

ESSAYS xxx

LITERARY BIOGRAPHY xxxii

AUTOBIOGRAPHY xxxiv
MEMOIRS
DIARIES
LETTERS

MISCELLANEOUS.. xxxvii

FICTION

page

Ah, But Your Land Is Beautiful—*Alan Paton* 6

A novel of life in South Africa under apartheid, showing the ill-effects of that policy on men and women of all races

Aunt Julia and the Scriptwriter—*Mario Vargas Llosa* 34

A deceptively realistic fiction in which an autobiographical episode serves as a pretext to write a story about how and why a writer writes

Autumn—*A. G. Mojtabai* 39

This short novel expresses the consciousness of a sixty-six-year-old man, a recent widower, in his confrontation with loneliness and its alternatives as autumn approaches in a summer resort town

Bech Is Back—*John Updike* 53

A compilation of seven interwoven short stories, this work focuses on the consciousness of an aging and unproductive writer, while satirizing the contemporary literary scene and humorously capturing the decadence and inanity of modern life

Beyond the Pale and Other Stories—*William Trevor* 57

A collection of twelve short stories characterized by a high degree of narrative skill and a wide range of characters and themes

Bloodsmoor Romance, A—*Joyce Carol Oates* 61

Members of an eccentric Pennsylvania family illustrate the concerns of nineteenth century America through their fantastic adventures

Bodily Harm—*Margaret Atwood* 65

A powerful but somewhat melodramatic account of a young Canadian woman's encounters with various kinds of "bodily harm"

Braided Lives—*Marge Piercy* 75

A feminist poet traces the friends and incidents that shaped her coming of age as a working-class student in college on a scholarship during the 1950's

Burning House, The—*Ann Beattie* 86

The modern struggle for identity involves a reconciliation between love and freedom, a fulfillment which seems impossible for the characters in these stories

Cadillac Jack—*Larry McMurtry* 90

Narrated by the title character, a roving antique dealer, Larry McMurtry's eighth novel probes the tribulations of modern love and marriage against a background of deft and often hilarious social satire, dealing in particular with current morals and manners in the nation's capital

page

Chain of Voices, A—*André Brink* 101
The inherent tensions of slavery, exacerbated by ironic misunderstandings, cause a slave revolt in South Africa in 1825

Charles Ryder's Schooldays and Other Stories—*Evelyn Waugh* 105
Apart from the title story, self-contained but probably an incomplete part of a projected longer work that Waugh never issued during his lifetime, this collection of short stories and sketches originally was published in 1936 under a different title

!Click Song—*John A. Williams* 124
A black novelist traces his struggles in the world of publishing

Collected Stories—*V. S. Pritchett* 131
Twenty-nine stories by one of England's masters of the genre

Collected Stories of Isaac Bashevis Singer, The—
    Isaac Bashevis Singer 135
A compilation of the best work produced by an outstanding contemporary master of short fiction

Color Purple, The—*Alice Walker* 139
An epistolary novel in which poor, ugly, uneducated Celie reveals the horrors, drudgeries, and ecstasies of her life in rural Georgia

Dancing Girls and Other Stories—*Margaret Atwood* 169
Fourteen short stories that deal with various subtle and complex relationships between men and women

Deadeye Dick—*Kurt Vonnegut* 174
Rudy Waltz, at age fifty, reviews his life from the age of twelve, when he accidentally shot and killed a pregnant woman

Dean's December, The—*Saul Bellow* 179
A tale of two cities contrasting the chaos, violence, and moral decay of liberal America with the warmth and caring of people in a repressive totalitarian state

Different Seasons—*Stephen King* 189
A collection of four novellas, each associated with a different season, demonstrating that King's prowess and versatility are not confined to the horror genre

Dinner at the Homesick Restaurant—*Anne Tyler* 194
A novel which portrays the emotionally difficult relationships of three children to their mother and to one another

Distant Relations—*Carlos Fuentes* 200
A narrative of the strange experiences of the Comte de Branly with the descendants of the Heredias, a family in colonial Mexico

LIST OF TITLES BY CATEGORY

page

Duncan's Colony—*Natalie L. M. Petesch*............................... 210

A short novel which tells of the establishment and dissolution of a communitarian society dedicated to surviving a nuclear holocaust and provides a strong sense of the failings of twentieth century American life

Dutch Shea, Jr.—*John Gregory Dunne*................................... 216

A once-successful attorney tries to make some sense of the chaos of his life

Eternal Curse on the Reader of These Pages—*Manuel Puig*............ 235

A novel consisting almost entirely of dialogue between two seemingly very different men who come to be related in a kind of mutual dependence that resembles that of self and double

Four Wise Men, The—*Michel Tournier* 267

Each of the three wise men tells the story of his journey to pay tribute to the Christ-child, but the longer story of a legendary fourth wise man enriches the mythic significance of the event

George Mills—*Stanley Elkin* 273

Written in five parts and set in various locales and historical periods, the novel traces the misadventures of a long line of George Millses, who claim to be fated to lead second-rate lives but who in fact doom themselves because they prefer their extraordinary fate to ordinary human life

God's Grace—*Bernard Malamud* 291

An ironic post-Armageddon history of God's new chosen people, told from the point of view of the last surviving human

Grace Abounding—*Maureen Howard* 296

A four-part novel which chronicles the intellectual and emotional development of Maude Lasser, a widow with a teenage daughter

Happy to Be Here—*Garrison Keillor*................................... 326

Five stories dealing with the arts and media, baseball, political phenomena, and contemporary styles

Headbirths: Or, The Germans Are Dying Out—*Günter Grass* 336

On a Third World lecture tour, Günter Grass develops ideas for a screenplay about a touring German couple

Her Victory—*Alan Sillitoe*... 340

A psychological novel which deals with the quest for liberation of three principal characters by focusing on their separate histories, their current interrelationships, and their attempts to achieve victory over the forces that have determined and shaped their present situations of emptiness and loneliness

Imaginary Crimes—*Sheila Ballantyne*................................... 353

A woman comes to terms with her difficult childhood

xxi

page

Joke, The—*Milan Kundera*.. 363

A narrative fugue on the futilty of man's attempt to use sex to avenge a wrong done
him fifteen years earlier and, in general, on the frailty of man's strongest emotions and
most compelling illusions

Killing Ground, The—*Mary Lee Settle* 381

A search for a pattern of death that ends in a discovery of life

Levitation: Five Fictions—*Cynthia Ozick*................................... 405

A collection of three novellas and two short stories, each involving a departure from
reality into pure fantasy or an altered past

Loser, The—*George Konrád* 423

The work of a deeply reflective historical consciousness which explores a wide range
of both personal and political experience in postwar Hungary

Making of the Representative for Planet 8, The—*Doris Lessing* 432

Unspecified but natural causes bring about climatic changes that render an alien planet
uninhabitable, dooming all who live there

Malgudi Days—*R. K. Narayan*.. 436

Thirty-two stories, most of which have been culled from two previous collections,
that create a gentle, often satirical, but loving portrait of the populace of Malgudi—
ranging from holy men to businessmen, from beggars to students, from housewives to
saints, and including several very distinctive animals

Mantissa—*John Fowles* 443

A playful attempt to articulate the complex relationship between a writer and his muse

Marco Polo, If You Can—*William F. Buckley, Jr.* 447

In the fourth of Buckley's espionage novels, Blackford Oakes returns as the pilot of
a U-2 which lands in Russia just before the Paris peace talks between Dwight D.
Eisenhower and Nikita Khrushchev in 1960

Meditation, A—*Juan Benet*.. 464

A novel which re-creates, through a series of disparate remembrances, the fate of two
families in post-Civil War Spain

Memoirs of a Space Traveler: Further Reminiscenses
of Ijon Tichy—*Stanislaw Lem*....................................... 469

A collection of satiric science-fiction stories, related to one another by narrator and
theme

Mickelsson's Ghosts—*John Gardner*....................................... 475

A discursive novel which treats the various breakdowns—marital, professional, financial, and mental—of a man who eventually renews his faith in himself and others and
who learns the redemptive power of forgiveness, love, and human community

LIST OF TITLES BY CATEGORY

page

Midnight Clear, A—*William Wharton* 480

The six young survivors of a special college army reservist squad struggle to survive during the terrible winter of 1944 in France, discovering along the way their own vulnerability as men and the essential similarities and differences between them and their elusive enemy

Monsignor Quixote—*Graham Greene* 489

A picaresque novel that parallels Cervantes' Don Quixote de la Mancha *in its account of the travels and adventures of a Catholic priest and a Communist politician around contemporary Spain*

Mosquito Coast, The—*Paul Theroux* 496

This realistic novel, which relates the experiences of an eccentric New England inventor who uproots his family and emigrates to Honduras to begin a new life, explores the paradoxes inherent in the American search for moral and technological absolutes

Mother and Two Daughters, A—*Gail Godwin* 501

A study of three women from a small North Carolina city who are able to grow and thrive with change, despite having been shaped and limited by a rigid social structure

Names, The—*Don DeLillo* 515

A witty, ambitious account of the fragmented lives of multinational businessmen in the Third World and of the mysterious cult that one of them, the narrator, seeks to understand

New Islands and Other Stories—*María Luisa Bombal* 523

A remarkable collection of stories, most of which are appearing for the first time in English translation, by one of the most important Latin American women writers of the twentieth century

Night Thoughts of a Classical Physicist—*Russell McCormmach* 532

A physics professor, whose career and life are ending, reflects on the ending of the old social order, the forthcoming end of the German Reich, and the end of the classical physics to which he has devoted his life

No Fond Return of Love—*Barbara Pym* 536

A comedy of romantic errors that chronicles the experiences of two spinsters who seek to change their circumstances by researching the life of a notable litterateur

No Place on Earth—*Christa Wolf* 540

An account of an imagined meeting between the famous German author Heinrich von Kleist and a minor German poet Karoline von Günderrode, both of whom, in real life, committed suicide

Nobody's Angel—*Thomas McGuane* 544

This modern-day, ironic Western traces the efforts of Patrick Fitzpatrick, a former army officer now approaching middle age, to reestablish connections with his heritage and to discover some purpose in a life he finds increasingly meaningless

page

Obasan—*Joy Kogawa* 554

A record of the Japanese experience in Canada during and after World War II, as told by a young girl whose family was uprooted and exiled to camps far from the Pacific Coast

Oh What a Paradise It Seems—*John Cheever* 558

In this fable, the pollution and reclamation of a pond serve as a metaphor for man's spiritual waywardness and his desire for spiritual salvation; man's task is to affirm the world as a sign of the spirit—that is, to connect the realms of matter and spirit—if he is to satisfy his deepest longings for light and wholeness

Polish Complex, The—*Tadeusz Konwicki* 611

An oblique meditation on Polish history and the Polish character

Portage to San Cristóbal of A. H., The—*George Steiner* 616

This work approaches the Holocaust and its aftermath through a fiction about the discovery of Adolph Hitler, a discovery that reveals the latent power of his personality and his ideas and exposes a troubled world that still has not learned to accept responsibility for the Holocaust or for the conditions that have perpetuated much of its evil

Rabbis and Wives—*Chaim Grade* 630

Three novellas which focus on the everyday concerns, the moral conflicts, and the religious yearnings of Jews in Lithuania between the two world wars

Rebel Angels, The—*Robertson Davies* 641

An engrossing and witty tale of discoveries, scholarly and personal, mixing academic and Gypsy environments

Regina—*Leslie Epstein* 650

With almost overwhelming odds against her, the protagonist frantically struggles to come to terms with existence in contemporary society

Rogue's March—*W. T. Tyler* 659

A drama of world politics and intrigue where people attempt to understand and control events but instead set in motion a "rogue's march" of perplexity, confusion, and disorder

Sabbatical: A Romance—*John Barth* 665

A novel about the narrative process by which Fenwick Turner (a writer) and Susan Seckler (a reader) try to decide on their future and to construct their novel

Samurai, The—*Shusaku Endo* 674

The story of a Japanese voyage to the New World and beyond, and of the spiritual trials faced by two men of dissimilar cultures

Schindler's List—*Thomas Keneally* 684

Oskar Schindler, a factory owner, saves the lives of his Jewish workers in World War II Poland and Czechoslovakia

LIST OF TITLES BY CATEGORY

page

Seizure of Power, The—*Czeslaw Milosz* 713
A fictionalized account of the last days of the Nazi occupation of Poland and the early years of the postwar Communist regime

Selected Stories—*Robert Walser* 734
These forty-two stories of comic despair, most of them told in the first person, deal with the desires, alienation, and self-effacements of Prufrockian characters who long for their place in a world they fear

Shiloh and Other Stories—*Bobbie Ann Mason* 739
A collection of short stories about ordinary people, written with extraordinary clarity, grace, and compassion

Shoeless Joe—*W. P. Kinsella* 742
A whimsical metafiction concerning an Iowa farmer who loves baseball with a religious fervor

Souls and Bodies—*David Lodge* 761
In this clever, entertaining, and occasionally poignant novel, the author examines Catholicism in a period of traumatic change by tracing the fortunes of ten Catholics from their college days at the University of London in the 1950's to the 1970's

Terrible Twos, The—*Ishmael Reed* 778
A Christmas Carol for modern times, The Terrible Twos is arranged, following the Charles Dickens story, into two sections—Christmas Past, 1980, and Christmas Future, 1990

13th Valley, The—*John M. Del Vecchio* 791
A story of the Vietnam War and the men who fought in it, a fictionalized account of an actual operation in which the author took part

To See You Again—*Alice Adams* 811
A collection of stories portraying upper-middle-class people in pursuit of, or in flight from, love

Twice Shy—*Dick Francis* 841
In this tensely exciting thriller based on his expert knowledge of horse racing, Dick Francis writes about a computerized betting system and the desperate men who will do anything to get the computers working for them

2010: Odyssey Two—*Arthur C. Clarke* 844
As a mixed Russian and American crew keeps a rendezvous with the abandoned spaceship Discovery, the derelict's captain, transfigured by a superior alien race, returns to the solar system to help new intelligence develop on Jupiter's satellite, Europa

Unsuitable Attachment, An—*Barbara Pym* 855
A subversive and richly comic treatment of a plot drawn from the storehouse of romance—the story of an unmarried woman in her early thirties who falls in love with a darkly handsome and "unsuitable" younger man

page

Wait for November—*Hans Erich Nossack*............................... 864
*Through an adulterous love affair, the protagonist is exposed to and possessed by
another world beyond the realm of the known world*

Waking—*Eva Figes* 869
*A spare narrative evoking seven crucial stages in the life of a nameless narrator whose
experience is representative of that of countless women*

Watchfires—*Louis Auchincloss*... 878
*The usual Auchincloss psychological portraitures, centered upon the upper levels of
society and politics where public policy decisions are made*

When Things of the Spirit Come First: Five Early Tales—
    Simone de Beauvoir 890
*Stories written in the 1930's which foreshadow Beauvoir's philosophy as expressed
in her mature works*

White Plague, The—*Frank Herbert* 900
A novel about the effects of a gender-specific plague which strikes only women

Why Can't We Live Together Like Civilized Human Beings?—
    Maxine Kumin.. 903
*By exploring the relationships between husbands, wives, lovers, parents, and children,
these stories examine the human need to inflict pain on others and the resiliency with
which people face their sorrows*

Women of Brewster Place: A Novel in Seven Stories, The—
    Gloria Naylor.. 918
*Like the Irish and Italian tenants who came before them, these black daughters of
Brewster Place find among themselves reasons for pride and ways to survive*

Woods, The—*David Plante*... 923
*This three-part novel shows the protagonist, a young college student, in the process
of learning about himself and life*

POETRY
DRAMA

Antarctic Traveller—*Katha Pollitt*... 20
*This distinguished first collection of forty poems received the National Book Critics
Circle Award for Poetry in 1983*

Argot Merchant Disaster: Poems New and Selected, The—
George Starbuck.. 25
*To a generous selection from three decades of earlier work, Starbuck adds seventeen
new poems; all display superior craftsmanship*

LIST OF TITLES BY CATEGORY

page

Chinese Insomniacs: New Poems, The—*Josephine Jacobsen* 110
 A collection of forty-nine poems by a poet's poet, technically polished and intellectually penetrating

Chosen Poems, Old and New—*Audre Lorde* 113
 An excellent selection of Lorde's poems that chart her development over thirty years and demonstrate the insufficiency of ideological categories for approaching the moral intensity and psychological complexity of her work

Circles on the Water—*Marge Piercy* 119
 A poet's selection of her poems, which presents everyday events to everyday readers for their use and appreciation

Country Between Us, The—*Carolyn Forché* 161
 This volume, Forché's second book of poems, largely addresses political themes and clearly establishes its author as one of the strongest poetic voices of her generation

Crimes of the Heart—*Beth Henley* 165
 A warm, funny, compassionate play about a "bad day" in the lives of three zany Southern sisters

Feel of Rock: Poems of Three Decades, The—*Reed Whittemore* 250
 A wry account of how the suburban temperament contends with disorder

Flood: Poems—*William Matthews* 262
 This new collection of verse marks a major advance in the development of an increasingly major talent

Glass Face in the Rain, A—*William Stafford* 288
 A volume of almost a hundred poems appearing for the first time in book form

Greeting: New & Selected Poems, The—*R. H. W. Dillard* 309
 An analysis of the nature of dreams and imagination and of their relationship to art and human sexuality

Hundreds of Fireflies—*Brad Leithauser* 348
 Strength of perception and ease of formal control characterize this first collection by a young poet

Man in the Black Coat Turns, The—*Robert Bly* 439
 A new collection of poems from one of America's most prolific poets, who continues to make public his mystic, visionary world

Monolithos: Poems, 1962 and 1982—*Jack Gilbert* 484
 Eighty-one poems, including the best from Gilbert's 1962 Yale Series of Younger Poets collection, Views of Jeopardy, *and fifty-five more recent poems reflecting the poet's extended travels and long residence abroad*

page

News from the Glacier: Selected Poems, 1960–1980—*John Haines*..... 527

A retrospective selection from five previous volumes of verse by a writer who has quietly established himself as one of America's finest contemporary poets

Our Ground Time Here Will Be Brief—*Maxine Kumin*................. 577

New and selected poems which explore issues of loss and separation, human depravity, and the saving nature of ritual

PM/AM: New and Selected Poems—*Linda Pastan* 603

A selection from the author's four previous collections, together with new poems that reveal the rich literary possibilities of the commonplace

Science of Goodbyes, The—*Myra Sklarew* 694

All the goodbyes in this book are so many little deaths, but the science is a matter of coming alive again without illusion and without the need for fixity

Selected & New Poems: 1961–1981—*Jim Harrison* 718

A catalog of rural events and of the poet's difficulties with women, drink, despair, and death

Selected Poems—*Galway Kinnell* 726

An evolving record of the poet's life as a physical and sentient process

Selected Poems—*John Frederick Nims* 730

A morally informed presentation of human desire and loss

Soldier's Play, A—*Charles Fuller*... 751

The destructive effects of racial hatred, bigotry, and hypocrisy are dramatized in this powerful, complex "whodunit" about the murder of a black noncommissioned officer on a Southern Army base

Whisper to the Earth: New Poems—*David Ignatow* 894

Sixty-five poems, varying in form from lyric and prose to dialogues, but unified by recurring images and by a concern for the relationship between the self and the impersonal nature which exists outside the human mind

LITERARY CRITICISM
LITERARY HISTORY

Agon: Toward a Theory of Revisionism—*Harold Bloom*   1

Cabalistic explorations toward a theory of revisionism as a critical stance, Bloom's work advances a Gnostic and Cabalistic view of literary composition and critical reading

Consoling Intelligence: Responses to Literary Modernism,
   The—*David Kubal* 144

Essays on important nineteenth and twentieth century writers, which stress the vital relationship between art and moral growth

LIST OF TITLES BY CATEGORY

page

Fiction and Repetition: Seven English Novels—*J. Hillis Miller* 253
Miller's collection of insightful studies on a selection of nineteenth and twentieth century novels is a useful introduction to Deconstructive analysis, illustrating some of the advantages and limitations of this important modern critical methodology

Great Code: The Bible and Literature, The—*Northrop Frye* 306
In this first of two projected volumes, Northrop Frye analyzes the Bible as the most important influence in the imaginative tradition of Western art and literature

Left Bank: Writers, Artists, and Politics from the Popular
  Front to the Cold War, The—*Herbert R. Lottman* 390
A study of the rise and fall of the "engaged" French writers of the period between 1930 and 1950 against the background of political movements which shaped their work and gave their ideas prominence

Living by Fiction—*Annie Dillard* 413
An idiosyncratic, conversational analysis of the metaphysics of modern fiction

Me Again: Uncollected Writings of Stevie Smith—*Stevie Smith* 458
A diverse collection of poems, essays, reviews, stories, letters, and a radio play, including many previously unpublished pieces, emphasizing Stevie Smith's barbed humor and intelligent skepticism

Orality and Literacy: The Technologizing of the Word—
  Walter J. Ong 568
A study of the oral nature of language, the contrasts between oral and literate cultures, and the profound implications of orality-literacy contrasts for a history of consciousness

Realistic Imagination: English Fiction from Frankenstein
  to Lady Chatterley, The—*George Levine* 635
A scholarly investigation of the realistic tradition in the nineteenth century novel which highlights the characteristics of the genre and the way in which methods used by novelists to break away from the conventions of older traditions became conventions themselves, thus generating the modern reaction against Realism

Short Stories of Thomas Hardy, The—*Kristin Brady* 747
An appreciative critical study of Thomas Hardy's short stories, placing them in relation to the development of the short story in the late nineteenth century

Truants: Adventures Among the Intellectuals, The—
  William Barrett 833
A narrative of the author's involvement in the New York literary scene, chiefly in the years following World War II, together with a retrospective evaluation of the political and aesthetic concerns of that era

War Within: From Victorian to Modernist Thought in the
  South, 1919-1945, The—*Daniel Joseph Singal* 874
A cultural study of the shift in the South from Romanticism to Realism, from innocence to awareness, focused on the years between the two world wars

page

What Was Literature? Class Culture and Mass Society—
Leslie Fiedler 885

A spirited inquiry into the Establishment practice of dividing literature into "high" and "low" ("compulsory" and "optional"), defending the proposition that popular culture produces and recognizes excellence in such works as Uncle Tom's Cabin, Gone with the Wind, *and* Roots

Woman and the Demon: The Life of a Victorian Myth—
Nina Auerbach... 914

Radically revising the pervasive Victorian ideal of woman as the selfless, compliant "Angel in the House," Auerbach depicts that image as the culture's defensive response to an alternate, unarticulated myth: woman as a transcendent and demoniac force, capable of infinite change

ESSAYS

Barthes Reader, A—*Roland Barthes*..................................... 44

A selection spanning Barthes's oeuvre and comprising meditations on a great variety of subjects, including literature, film, and photography

Boy Scout Handbook and Other Observations, The—*Paul Fussell* 70

A collection of essays and reviews commenting on American life and values, British and American literary figures, travel, and World War II

Down the River—*Edward Abbey* 205

A collection of miscellaneous environmental essays and reflections on the pleasures of rafting on the rivers of the American West

Empire of Signs, The—*Roland Barthes*................................. 230

A series of brief meditations on Japanese culture as a source of sign production

Fate of the Earth, The—*Jonathan Schell* 244

A collection of three long essays that detail the process and consequences of a nuclear holocaust, argues humanity's cause against those who would jeopardize it with nuclear war, and finally offers a plea for a new world order based on total nuclear disarmament

Me Again: Uncollected Writings of Stevie Smith—*Stevie Smith* 458

A diverse collection of poems, essays, reviews, stories, letters, and a radio play, including many previously unpublished pieces, emphasizing Stevie Smith's barbed humor and intelligent skepticism

Moving Target, A—*William Golding* 506

A collection of sixteen lectures, reviews, and travel articles delivered and published during the past two decades by the Nobel Prize-winning author

LIST OF TITLES BY CATEGORY

page

Nabokov's Fifth Arc: Nabokov and Others on His
Life's Work—*J. E. Rivers* and *Charles Nicol*....................... 511

Essays about the life and work of Vladimir Nabokov, including two brief pieces by Nabokov previously unpublished in the United States

One Way to Spell Man—*Wallace Stegner*............................... 563

A collection of essays written over a period of roughly three decades, concerning a variety of subjects such as regionalism, ecology, history, literature, the writing process, growing up—all presented through the eyes of a Westerner

Pieces and Pontifications—*Norman Mailer* 597

A compilation of Mailer's essays and interviews from various journalistic sources, covering chiefly the middle 1970's in the case of the essays ("pieces"), but stretching back to the late 1950's and forward to the early 1980's in the case of the interviews ("pontifications")

Purple Decades: A Reader, The—*Tom Wolfe* 626

A collection of feature articles, chapters, sections from books, and vignettes from Wolfe's previous volumes, illustrated by the author

Red Smith Reader, The—*Walter W. ("Red") Smith* 645

After Red Smith, long recognized as one of America's finest sportswriters, died early in 1982, a colleague on The New York Times *assembled 128 of the columns Smith had written for that newspaper and, earlier, for the* St. Louis Star, The Philadelphia Record, *and* The New York Herald Tribune

Science Observed: Essays Out of My Mind—*Jeremy Bernstein* 689

A wide-ranging collection of essays by one of America's preeminent science-writers— accessible, often playful, yet never sacrificing accuracy for ease of explanation

Second American Revolution and Other Essays (1976-1982),
The—*Gore Vidal*.. 700

A collection of provocative, always clever, and at times brilliant essays concerning literature, sexual mores, and the American political scene

Second Life of Art: Selected Essays, The—*Eugenio Montale*........... 705

The first substantial collection of essays to appear in English translation by the Nobel Prize-winning poet

Stuff of Sleep and Dreams: Experiments in Literary
Psychology—*Leon Edel*.. 765

A collection of essays which demonstrates and justifies the application of psychology and of psychoanalytical concepts to the study of literature

Susan Sontag Reader, A—*Susan Sontag*................................ 769

A retrospective collection of essays, fiction, and an interview

Teaching a Stone to Talk: Expeditions and Encounters—
   Annie Dillard 773
   *A series of meditations, purportedly focusing on the natural world, but in reality
   emphasizing the relationship between the human and the Divine; these meditations
   highlight religious experiences in which the narrator completely loses self*

Terrorists and Novelists—*Diane Johnson* 783
   *Essays and reviews by a contemporary novelist and biographer focus on reality, truth,
   and ethics*

This Quiet Dust and Other Writings—*William Styron* 796
   *Though not a major work, William Styron's first book of nonfiction is an interesting
   and important companion to his fiction, with biographical sidelights and background
   information on several of his novels*

Tugman's Passage, The—*Edward Hoagland* 836
   *A collection of thirteen personal essays and thirty "seasonal editorials" originally
   published in magazines and newspapers between 1976 and 1981*

Uncivil Liberties—*Calvin Trillin* 849
   An amusing collection of brief essays which first appeared as columns in The Nation

Visions from San Francisco Bay—*Czeslaw Milosz* 860
   *Essays on the spiritual character of California as experienced by an émigré from
   Eastern Europe and as symptomatic of the crisis in Western civilization*

Young Rebecca: Writings of Rebecca West, 1911-1917, The—
   Rebecca West 932
   A selection of periodical essays and one story by a radical feminist

LITERARY BIOGRAPHY

Baudelaire the Damned: A Biography—*F. W. J. Hemmings* 49
   *In this important biography of the great nineteenth century French poet, critic, and
   translator, the sources of Baudelaire's malaise are traced to his complex relationship
   with his mother and to his tenaciously held notion of suffering from the curse of
   damnation*

Camus—*Patrick McCarthy* 96
   *An account, intended for the general reader, of the troubled life of the French-Algerian
   author*

Gissing: A Life in Books—*John Halperin* 283
   *A carefully detailed biography, emphasizing the connections between George Giss-
   ing's life and the characters, opinions, attitudes, and events in his novels*

LIST OF TITLES BY CATEGORY

Group Portrait: Joseph Conrad, Stephen Crane, Ford Madox
  Ford, Henry James, and H. G. Wells—*Nicholas Delbanco* 312
  An exploration of the relationships among five important writers who lived in south-eastern England at the turn of the century

Hannah Arendt: For Love of the World—*Elizabeth Young-Bruehl*..... 322
  A biography of one of the foremost political philosophers of the twentieth century, a woman as fascinating as she was brilliant, a thinker as controversial as she was profound

H. D.: The Life and Work of an American Poet—
  Janice S. Robinson 331
  An analysis of the interrelationship between the life and work of an American poet and novelist

Isak Dinesen: The Life of a Storyteller—*Judith Thurman*.............. 358
  A complete and very readable biography of the great Danish writer Isak Dinesen, based on previously unavailable sources, outlining Dinesen's life and personal difficulties and discussing the tales for which she is best known

Kafka: A Biography—*Ronald Hayman*.................................. 372
  A brief but sharply detailed and persuasive biography of Franz Kafka that illuminates the social background of his writing

Katherine Anne Porter: A Life—*Joan Givner* 376
  Katherine Anne Porter's chosen biographer has provided a well-balanced account of the life of one of America's finest artists in fiction

Life of John Berryman, The—*John Haffenden*......................... 410
  An account of the difficult and often painful life on one of America's most important recent poets and men of letters

Mailer: A Biography—*Hilary Mills* 428
  This is the first work to investigate thoroughly the career of Norman Mailer, an American novelist, and while it will serve very well as the basis for further explorations of his life and work, it devotes insufficient attention to the significance of his writing and thereby obscures the central importance of his place in American literature

Nabokov's Fifth Arc: Nabokov and Others on His
  Life's Work—*J. E. Rivers* and *Charles Nicol*...................... 511
  Essays about the life and work of Vladimir Nabokov, including two brief pieces by Nabokov previously unpublished in the United States

Outline of Sanity: A Biography of G. K. Chesterton, The—
  Alzina Stone Dale 582
  An outstanding biography, in which a brilliant English writer is seen in the context of his time

P. G. Wodehouse: A Biography—*Frances Donaldson* 587
  A biography of the famous novelist and humorist that attempts to give a more complete portrayal of the man and a more serious estimate of his work than heretofore available

Robert Lowell: A Biography—*Ian Hamilton* 654
  A chronological study of Lowell's life and works which includes previously unpublished material

Thomas Hardy: A Biography—*Michael Millgate* .... 806 .
  A new biography of Thomas Hardy reveals with penetrating insight and appreciation the life and accomplishments of one of England's greatest modern authors

Tolstoi in the Sixties—*Boris Eikhenbaum* 816
  An analysis of the influences on Tolstoy's ideas and works during the 1860's

Tolstoi in the Seventies—*Boris Eikhenbaum* 821
  An analysis of the influences on Tolstoy's ideas and works during the 1870's

Wider Sea: A Life of John Ruskin, The—*John Dixon Hunt* 908
  This scholarly biography highlights the major events of Ruskin's life and demonstrates the relationship between the writer's life and his major works

AUTOBIOGRAPHIES
MEMOIRS
DIARIES
LETTERS

Aké: The Years of Childhood—*Wole Soyinka* 10
  A highly imaginative autobiography which covers the first eleven years in the life of the Nigerian writer Wole Soyinka, emphasizing his dramatic initiation into the exotic, stimulating, and sometimes paradoxical world of adults and the established social ways surrounding him

Atlantic High: A Celebration—*William F. Buckley, Jr.* 29
  A record, with many flashbacks and tangents, of the voyage of the racing-ketch Sealestial *crewed by the author, his six companions, and a professional crew of four, from the Virgin Islands to Marbella, Spain*

Bronx Primitive: Portraits in a Childhood—*Kate Simon* 80
  A noted travel writer's recollections of her girlhood as a Jewish immigrant living in the Bronx

Clinging to the Wreckage: A Part of Life—*John Mortimer* 127
  The autobiography of the English novelist, playwright, screenwriter, and lawyer

LIST OF TITLES BY CATEGORY

Correspondence of Boris Pasternak and Olga Freidenberg,
1910-1954, The—*Boris Pasternak* and *Olga Freidenberg*........... 147
More than four decades of letters exchanged between Olga Freidenberg and her cousin Boris Pasternak reveal Freidenberg to be a notable author in her own right

Correspondence of Thomas Carlyle and John Ruskin, The—
Thomas Carlyle and *John Ruskin* 153
The correspondence of two of the most prominent Victorian men of letters

Diary of Virginia Woolf, Vol. IV: 1931-1935, The—
Virginia Woolf.. 185
Virginia Woolf continues a very busy life of writing, socializing, and traveling, and she records her impressions, her moods, and her views of her writing

Early Diary of Anaïs Nin, Vol. II: 1920-1923, The—*Anaïs Nin* 220
In this second volume of Anaïs Nin's early diaries, the writer emerges from her sheltered adolescence to attend Columbia University, to work as a model, and to fall in love with her future husband

Emerson in His Journals—*Ralph Waldo Emerson* 224
A new, one-volume edition of Emerson's journals selected and edited from the Harvard edition of Emerson's Journals and Miscellaneous Notebooks

Family Installments: Memories of Growing Up Hispanic—
Edward Rivera.. 240
An autobiographical account of a young Puerto Rican's youth and education in Spanish Harlem, and of his family and friends

Flaws in the Glass: A Self-Portrait—*Patrick White* 257
These candid sketches of times and places and people in the life of the Nobel Prizewinning novelist are suffused with a depth of emotion and intellectual honesty that elevates them to the level of literature

Gift, The—*H. D.* 278
A distinguished poet's recollections of her childhood seen from the perspective of war-ravaged London during the Blitz

Growing Up—*Russell Baker*... 317
Winning the 1983 Pulitzer Prize for Autobiography, this is the story of the early life of a prize-winning columnist

Journals of Sylvia Plath, The—*Sylvia Plath* 367
Selected journal entries which include Sylvia Plath's thoughts on her prose and poetry

Last Stands: Notes from Memory—*Hilary Masters* 386
A search for identity, place, and meaning through memories

Letters of Gustave Flaubert, 1857-1880, The—*Gustave Flaubert*........ 395
The second of two volumes which includes representative correspondence by one of the world's greatest novelists and letter-writers

Letters to Ottla and the Family—*Franz Kafka*.......................... 401
A collection of letters written largely to Kafka's favorite sister, Ottla; all but a handful of the letters were written between 1917, when Kafka suffered the first hemorrhage in his lungs, and 1921

Lord Byron: Selected Letters and Journals—*George Gordon
Byron, Baron Byron* 418
A one-volume collection of letters and journal excerpts drawn from Marchand's twelve-volume Murray-Harvard edition of Byron's letters and journals

Margin of Hope: An Intellectual Autobiography, A—
Irving Howe 451
Recollections of Irving Howe's years as a Trotskyist radical, his rise to prominence as a New York intellectual, his work as an interpreter of Yiddish culture, and his battles as an advocate of democratic socialism

Namesake—*Michel Goldberg*... 518
A memoir of the author's search for his own identity as a French nonpious Jew and as the son of a victim of the Nazi Holocaust

Noël Coward Diaries, The—*Noël Coward* 549
The diaries of one of Britain's most famous entertainers and playwrights trace his career and friendships from the height of World War II until his knighthood by Queen Elizabeth II in 1969

Ordeal by Labyrinth: Conversations with Claude-Henri
Rocquet—*Mircea Eliade*... 572
A transcription of conversations between Mircea Eliade and Claude-Henri Rocquet concerning Eliade's life and works; Eliade's essay "Brancusi and Mythology" is also included

Poets in Their Youth: A Memoir—*Eileen Simpson*...................... 608
A leisurely reminiscence of life among American writers and poets in the years immediately following World War II

Pound/Ford: The Story of a Literary Friendship—*Ezra Pound
and Ford Madox Ford* 621
This volume reveals the literary relationship of the poet Ezra Pound and the novelist Ford Madox Ford through their letters, supplemented by their writings about each other and by the editor's connecting narrative

Sacred Journey, The—*Frederick Buechner* 670
The first volume of the highly selective two-volume autobiography of a novelist and writer of popular theology, a spiritual memoir concentrating on the working of God in his life

Scenes of Childhood and Other Stories—*Sylvia Townsend Warner* 679
Autobiographical sketches by an outstanding British short-story writer, essayist, and novelist

Secret Symmetry: Sabina Spielrein Between Jung and
Freud, A—*Aldo Carontenuto* 709
The story of the Russian psychoanalyst Sabina Spielrein (1885-1937?) and her complicated relationship with both Carl G. Jung (1875-1961) and Sigmund Freud (1856-1939)

Selected Letters: The Personal Correspondence,
1844-1877—*Karl Marx* and *Friedrich Engels* 722
A selection and translation into English of the personal correspondence of Marx and Engels, emphasizing their personal friendship

These the Companions: Recollections—*Donald Davie* 787
The reminiscences of a contemporary poet and literary critic, which include his experiences with some of the most prominent writers and critics of the last fifty years

Torch in My Ear, The—*Elias Canetti* 827
An introspective, subtly rendered autobiography of the intellectually decisive years in the career of a major European writer

Writers and Friends—*Edward Weeks* 928
A memoir of Edward Weeks's twenty-eight-year tenure as editor of The Atlantic

Young Rebecca: Writings of Rebecca West, 1911-1917, The—*Rebecca West* 932
A selection of periodical essays and one story by a radical feminist

MISCELLANEOUS

All That Is Solid Melts into Air: The Experience of   15
Modernity—*Marshall Berman* ....
An effort to restore a sense of history to the experience of modernity

Cosmic Code: Quantum Physics as the Language of Nature,   156
The—*Heinz R. Pagels* ....
A largely nonmathematical account of the developments in physics, particularly quantum physics and the physics of subatomic particles, during the twentieth century

Grammatical Man: Information, Entropy, Language,   301
and Life—*Jeremy Campbell* ....
A history of the development of information theory and an analysis of its relationship with and contribution to contemporary physics, biology, linguistics, philosophy, and psychology

Hometown—*Peter Davis* 344
A subjective portrait of the social tensions facing several families and individuals in Hamilton, Ohio, detailing their lives in the contexts of work, education, play, crime, and politics, and climaxing in the trial of a popular teacher charged with public indecency

Philosophy in the Twentieth Century—*A. J. Ayer* 592
A history of twentieth century philosophy, written from the point of view of a British analytical philosopher, that focuses on American pragmatism and analytic philosophy

Somewhere a Master: Further Hasidic Portraits and Legends—   756
   Elie Wiesel ....
Reflections on the lives and teaching of past Masters of Hasidic Judaism, with strong implications for the problems and needs of today

This Was Harlem: A Cultural Portrait, 1900-1950—   800
   Jervis Anderson ....
An anecdotal history of Harlem from its development as an Afro-American community through the Harlem Renaissance to its decline as a cultural center at midcentury, concentrating on the people and places that contributed to its distinctive and influential style

CONTRIBUTING REVIEWERS FOR 1983 ANNUAL

Michael Adams

Andrew J. Angyal

Edwin T. Arnold

Peggy Bach

Dean Baldwin

Olga Liberti de Barrio

Paul A. Bateman

Carolyn Wilkerson Bell

Gordon N. Bergquist

Gerhard Brand

Peter Brier

Jeanie R. Brink

Daniel J. Cahill

Gordon W. Clarke

John J. Conlon

Mark Conroy

Leon V. Driskell

Elizabeth Elchlepp

Robert P. Ellis

John W. Evans

John P. Ferré

Daniel Mark Fogel

Margot K. Frank

Sam Frank

Faith Gabelnick

Kristine Ottesen Garrigan

Georg Gaston

Leslie E. Gerber

Scott Giantvalley

Robert Gish

Sidney Gottlieb

Peter W. Graham

William E. Grant

Gary L. Harmon

Terry Heller

Greig E. Henderson

Erwin Hester

John L. Howarth

Philip K. Jason

Judith L. Johnston

Carola M. Kaplan

Joanne Kashdan

Steven G. Kellman

Henderson Kincheloe

Angelika Kuehn

Elizabeth Johnston Lipscomb

Mark McCloskey

Margaret McFadden

Willis E. McNelly

David Madden

Kathleen Massey

Augustus A. Mastri

Charles E. May

Laurence W. Mazzeno

Walter E. Meyers

Jim W. Miller

Sally Mitchell

Leslie Mittleman

Robert A. Morace

Katharine M. Morsberger

Robert E. Morsberger

Carole Moses

Keith Neilson

Stella Nesanovich

Michael P. Parker

David B. Parsell

Bruce D. Reeves

Ann E. Reynolds

Michael S. Reynolds

David Rigsbee

Mary Rohrberger

Carl E. Rollyson, Jr.

Dale Salwak

David N. Samuelson

Roberta Sharp

T. G. Shults

Jan Sjåvik

Gilbert Smith

Lynne Davis Spies

Michael Sprinker

Rae H. Stoll

Christina Stough

Charles Johnson Taggart

Daniel Taylor

Henry Taylor

William B. Toole III

John N. Wall, Jr.

Craig Werner

James L. W. West III

Melinda W. West

Mary C. Williams

John Wilson

James A. Winders

MAGILL'S
LITERARY ANNUAL

1983

AGON
Toward a Theory of Revisionism

Author: Harold Bloom (1930-   )
Publisher: Oxford University Press (New York). 336 pp. $22.00
Type of work: Essays, lectures, and addresses

Cabalistic explorations toward a theory of revisionism as a critical stance, Bloom's
work advances a Gnostic and Cabalistic view of literary composition and critical reading

Stately and prolific, Harold Bloom, one of America's foremost literary critics and theorists has, in this collection of essays, lectures, and addresses, made considerable progress in demystifying himself. Bloom writes with relish of his own inner agon in a difficult and sometimes perplexing but brilliant and rewarding study that has for its object an examination of the possibilities of applying Gnostic and Cabalistic thought to the interpretation of literature. Preparatory to anything else about Bloom's work, it is important to realize that for him, the art of criticism has no language but that of the individual critic.

Bloom initiates his readers into an agonistic, Gnostic world of revisionism through his own particularly "ferocious alphabet," as Denis Donoghue has recently termed it when he classified Bloom among the "epireaders" of modern criticism. In this book, however, Bloom departs from the school of Jacques Derrida, from his Yale colleagues such as Geoffrey Hartman and J. Hillis Miller, and from such advocates of the "reader response" party as Stanley Fish and Susan Horton to form a majority of one clearly outside what he calls the "Deconstruction Road Company." His avowed purpose in this work is to write a provisional prolegomenon and a partial exploration of the theory of revisionism he hopes to write. So, in his introduction, "A Prelude to Gnosis," he calls this study in revisionism the work of a Jewish Gnostic (fully aware of the oxymoronic nature of that designation), a sectarian whose thought is strained through Friedrich Nietzsche, Giambathsta Vico, and Gershom Scholem, as Cynthia Ozick has suggested in *Art and Ardor* (1983). To this list one must add Ralph Waldo Emerson, one of Bloom's intellectual progenitors. Central to this work and to Bloom's still unfolding thought is his conviction that the Emersonian American religion of competitiveness is at the base of American literature and the uniquely American criticism he seeks to establish.

In seeking to establish his own brand of criticism and to find a voice, Bloom has, over several years, been providing a new critical vocabulary to buttress his highly personal responses to literary works, responses that have caused much consternation and no little antipathy in the critical world. His vatic vocabulary, while still expanding with each new lecture and essay, does have some major fixed elements. One of his givens is that the reading of a text and any consequently produced critical response is a misreading or misprision and cannot be otherwise, as each reader implicitly or overtly asks the question Walter Pater asked in his preface to *Studies in the History of the Renaissance* (1873) about what a work means "to me." A deep reading or "strong misreading" is a lively and welcome agon between the reader and the author's text as the critic attempts to usurp what the author has written, to usurp, "A place, a stance, a fullness, an illusion of identification or possession." The act of writing in the post-Miltonic era is also, according to Bloom, an anxiously influenced misprision of earlier literary works, since later writers, conscious of their literary predecessors and impressed with a lively sense of their own posteriority (Bloom's "belatedness"), attempt, by allusion and trope, to usurp strong anterior texts. In this respect, Bloom is not far from the poetic intention of the pre-Miltonic Edmund Spenser and other writers of Renaissance dynastic epic who sought to "overgo" Vergil.

The whole notion of usurpation is an intriguing one that is not without unexpected precedent. Michael Levey in a recent book on Walter Pater (*The Case of Walter Pater*, 1978) follows the lead of Thomas Wright's *Life of Walter Pater* (1907), where Wright spoke of the young Pater as assuming, by turns, the identities of the writers and artists of whom he wrote. This is very close to T. S. Eliot's sentiment that one cannot criticize a writer to whom one has never fully surrendered. Levey, Wright, and Eliot prefigure the sort of usurpation through strong misprision Bloom advocates. In Wright's case, the strong misreading is a surprising treatment of a writer who seriously explored Gnosticism and continues to exert a profound influence upon Harold Bloom.

The fifteen chapters of *Agon* treat of a wide variety of writers and works that range from the Hellenistic Gnostic Valentinius to Sigmund Freud, William Blake, Emerson, Walt Whitman, Wallace Stevens, Hart Crane, John Ashbery, John Hollander, and David Lindsay. In connection with David Lindsay's fantasy novel *A Voyage to Arcturus* (1920), Bloom also engages in a high misprision of his own novel, *The Flight of Lucifer* (1979), which he somewhat slights in a catchy trope by saying it reads as though Walter Pater were writing *Star Wars*. Vastly ambitious in scope and necessarily uneven, *Agon* is held together by the pervasive presence of Bloom's mind at work and by his multifaceted but single-minded quest after revisionism as he consistently makes clear that the American difference in criticism is Harold Bloom's American difference: the subject of the work is not just Bloom's revisionism, it is Bloom himself.

In his first chapter, "Agon: Revisionism and Critical Personality," Bloom initially defuses his critics while welcoming their criticism: from his perspective, they will become wise if they but persist in their folly. This inviting challenge is followed by three self-clarifying notions about interpretation. First, he perceives no differences between the language of poetry and the language of criticism, despite the fact that he continues to find critical vocabularies for which poetry yields no precedents. Second, although he finds inadequate a rhetoric that analyzes tropes synchronically, his own rhetorics of rhetoric fall short of being diachronic: this is a major factor in the Gnostic dilemma. Third, he continues to return to ostensibly incompatible models for interpreting poems, Gnostic catastrophe creations, and Freudian conflicts of heightened emotional ambivalence. These three notions translate, as Wallace Stevens would have said, into pages of illustrations. From his considerably abstruse discussion of Gnostic and Cabalistic misprision, an antithetical criticism, a "breaking of the vessels" (*Shevirath ha-Kelim*) emerges that involves a diachronic rhetoric rooted in Bloom's sense of the Emersonian American difference in poetry and criticism that marks American thought of the last hundred years. This diachronic rhetoric is at the base of his notion of belatedness and of his idea that poetry is, in effect, criticism.

Gnosis as a way of knowing, reading, and interpreting forms the basis of Bloom's second chapter, "Lying Against Time," in which he elaborates several of the points made in the first chapter, points about usurpation and misprision as usurpation and the stance of belatedness as having Gnosticism as its essence and Valentinianism as its quintessence. In his discussion of catastrophe creation based on his reading of Valentinius, the Cabala, and the poetry of William Blake, Bloom drives steadily toward the hypotheses that a theory of poetic creativity must also be a catastrophe theory and that artistic creation is both a creation of catastrophe and by catastrophe. This sort of catastrophic thinking is common to the Gnostic texts and the Cabala; Bloom also finds it typical of Freud's thought about the genesis of drives.

Both of Bloom's chapters that focus upon Freud, one of which concerns the Sublime relative to catastrophic creationism and one of which considers Freud's concepts of defense and the poetic will, build upon concepts Bloom established early in the text. Here Bloom makes several important points, among them that Freud is so strong a writer that he contains every available mode of interpretation; thus, there can be no true or correct reading of Freud. Another is that Freud has written this century's only major contribution to the aesthetics of the Sublime. A third concerns Bloom's obsessions with anteriority and belatedness as the precursor Freud adumbrates them. Still another posits Freud as the author of high Romantic crisis-poems in prose. These views of Freud, some of which are not wholly original with Bloom, are filled with potential controversey as well as exciting speculation.

When he is discoursing on Emerson and Whitman, Bloom's virtuosity truly shines through. His celebration of Emerson as the founder of American religion and the American Orpheus contains the dogma Bloom uses to measure all other attempts to create an American religion: "it cannot become the American religion until it first is canonized as American literature." Thus, he dispenses with what he terms the American heresies. An additional insight into Emerson that Bloom's Gnosticism provides is the distinction that while

Emerson's Gnosis is unquestionable, he has nothing much in common with historical Gnosticism. This Gnosis has for one of its primary characteristics the ability to see and, as Bloom has it, to see earliest—to usurp. In singing of Whitman, Bloom characterizes the voice the poet projects by saying quite simply that Whitman *is* the American Sublime and then provides some extraordinarily acute reading of the poetry.

American Orphism is also at play in the quite brief section Bloom devotes to Wallace Stevens and, to a greater extent, in his study of Hart Crane's poetry and poetic religion. Crane, in this strong misreading, becomes a poet of supreme negative transcendence as his religious stance moves from Orphism to what Bloom finds is, after all, Gnosticism. Like Whitman and Crane, John Ashbery comes under Bloom's formulation of the American Sublime and enters, full-blown, into what the critic regards as the true canon of poetry on the strength of "Tapestry." Like the essay on Ashbery—which contains fine speculative passages on the meaning of canonical poetry and the strength of poetry that is, upon its reception, immediately canonical—the essay on John Hollander's *Spectral Emanations* (1978) treats Hollander's work as a superb "breaking of the vessels" that Bloom proclaims one of the central achievements of his generation.

In his last chapter, Bloom reiterates his notions about the American difference in poetry and criticism by using telling examples from Whitman, Stevens, and Ashbery. Though it is brief, his "coda" turns the reader back upon the whole text that has preceded it and reinforces Bloom's assertion of revisionism as the necessary angel of true American thought. The chapter preceding this coda is both atypical of the rest of the volume and yet deeply related to it. Its title, "Free and Broken Tablets: The Cultural Prospects of American Jewry," speaks to Bloom's own cultural prospects and prospect of culture. In it, he raises, in the context of a public address, the fundamental question of all writers and critics who assume public roles with prophetic voices—the question of the transmission of culture. This question is of prime importance not only for American Jewry but also for all Americans who live in a lapsarian culture that has lost its text-centeredness. This address, worth more than all but a handful of the thousands of commencement addresses reverberating through the stadia and halls of America each year, is a plea and a hope for an American renaissance that will bring a return of the Book.

In all, and despite the undeniable difficulty of Bloom's language and of his dialectic, *Agon* cannot simply be dismissed as arcane but ought to achieve an important place in the canon of Bloom's own continuing debate with himself and his quarrel with the critical world. He provides extraordinary insight into the writers and works he discusses and into his own attempt to explicate both poetry and the process of criticizing poetry.

John J. Conlon

Sources for Further Study

Choice. XIX, April, 1982, p. 1060.
Criticism. XXIV, Summer, 1982, p. 297.
Library Journal. CVI, December 15, 1981, p. 2394.
The New Republic. CLXXXVI, February 17, 1982, p. 31.
The New York Times Book Review. LXXXVII, January 31, 1982, p. 8.
Times Literary Supplement. July 30, 1982, p. 811.
Virginia Quarterly Review. LVIII, Summer 1982, p. 79.
Yale Review. LXXII, Autumn, 1982, p. 116.

AH, BUT YOUR LAND IS BEAUTIFUL

Author: Alan Paton (1903-   )
Publisher: Charles Scribner's Sons (New York). 271 pp. $12.95; paperback $5.75
Type of work: Novel
Time: 1952-1958
Locale: South Africa

A novel of life in South Africa under apartheid, showing the ill-effects of that policy on men and women of all races

> Principal characters:
> PREM BODASINGH, a clever young Indian woman
> ROBERT MANSFIELD, a white liberal
> HUGH MAINWARING, a liberal activist, in love with Prem Bodasingh
> JAN WOLTEMADE FISCHER, an Afrikaner leader
> GABRIEL VAN ONSELEN, a bureaucrat in the Justice Department
> EMMANUEL NENE, a Zulu landowner, a political activist

Ah, But Your Land Is Beautiful, like the earlier works of Alan Paton, reveals the author's great love for his native land and its people. He writes of a grand part of the world, a country of which visitors say, "Ah, but your land is beautiful." For Paton, however, the well-meant praise for South Africa, especially Natal, where the novelist resides, has a fearsome irony: while the land is undeniably beautiful, the lives its people lead are full of prejudice, of stress, of fear, and even of terror. Each individual, regardless of race, has to learn how to live within the stringent regulations of apartheid. Each person has to decide whether to accept the policies of segregation or to strive to change them. Conflicts arise and not only between groups of people—the whites, the blacks, the Indians, and those of mixed race known in South Africa as "Coloured." Conflicts grow among the members of each group, too. Further, conflicts arise within the individual and must be mastered, lest they destroy the person in whom they occur.

Paton has divided his novel into six chronological sections. The first section deals with the Defiance Campaign which arose in 1952. In part, it is the story of Prem Bodasingh, an eighteen-year-old Indian girl who insists on defying the rules that forbid her to use the Durban Municipal Reference Library because she is not white. Again and again, quietly but firmly, she enters the library, to be arrested, to be imprisoned, to risk having her chances for an education ended. She does this to demonstrate the injustice of a rule which prevents her, an outstanding student in her secondary school, from using the library's resources. The novelist uses her as a striking example of how people in South Africa tried to change the policies of the government. Her efforts were, at the time, seemingly without success. During the Defiance Campaign, rioting occurred, people were killed, and hundreds more suffered injuries. The government, in answer to the situation, stiffened the punishments for lawbreaking with intent to protest apartheid. Africans and Indians cooperated in the campaign, but the leaders had to call off the efforts because of the harm coming to their own people and the whites who helped them.

The second portion of the novel relates how people who worked for the government found themselves caught, as it were, in a cleft stick. The ruling Nationalist Party and its regulations placed them in conflict with the government if they did not share the Afrikaner views. To illustrate the problems of these people, Paton relates the difficulties facing the white, English-speaking headmaster of a school for whites, who wishes to have his students compete with students from a nonwhite school in athletics and debate. Paton also shows the difficulties of the black headmaster of a school for blacks. The two administrators only wish to help their students, but to do so becomes impossible for them; the political conditions interfere with the goals of education. Given both courage and an independent income, a person can leave teaching and enter politics to fight as a leader of the Liberal Party, as the white headmaster, Robert Mansfield, does. Without resources, the black headmaster can only try to survive professionally until retirement.

The division between whites and blacks is not the only line of tension in South Africa. Paton shows vividly how the events of history have pitted the white descendants of Dutch settlers against the people of English-speaking ancestry. In part, this conflict is rooted in the defeat of the Afrikaners in the Boer War of almost a century ago. The Afrikaners came to have political power once again and have remembered bitterly how they were "outside" for many years. The conflict between Afrikaner and Britisher has its roots in religion as well. For the Afrikaner, the policies of apartheid have the blessing of his church, as he and his coreligionists interpret the Bible. For them, the separation of the races is a mandate from heaven which must be honored. Opposing the Afrikaner view is the more democratic, nonracist attitude of the Anglican Church, to which most of the English-speaking white people adhere. The Anglican leaders of the 1950's openly, even rigorously, opposed the concept of apartheid and its consequences. Finally, Afrikaners are divided from their English-speaking countrymen by their language itself, an offshoot of Dutch.

These diverse racial and ethnic tensions are given focus in the lives of Paton's characters, most vividly in the fate of Dr. Jan Woltemade Fischer, an Afrikaner leader held in high esteem by his fellows. He is a public figure, a bureaucrat, and a church leader, a man high in the Justice Department, where he helps make and enforce the policies and practices of apartheid. He is acclaimed by political leaders, by theologians, and by university leaders. Unfortunately, he is attracted to a Zulu girl, the daughter of a black policeman. The white man importunes the girl again and again, until she agrees to meet him under cover of darkness in a public park. In the park, the man falls victim to his own beliefs. Caught in an "immoral act" with a woman of another race, he is tried for violation of the Immorality Acts. Found guilty at his trial, he is sentenced to death, on the basis that an offense against the Immorality Acts is treason against his nation. Unable to face life, even until an official execution, Dr. Fischer commits suicide.

Violence was part of life in South Africa in the 1950's. Paton writes, for example, of a nun, a medical doctor who devoted her life to helping sick black people. The doctor encounters an angry black mob and is killed by the rioters, who also burn her body and car. When the flames die down, members of the mob cut off pieces of her flesh and eat it. Whites, too, turned to violence, and Paton describes violent acts directed against other whites who disagree with apartheid, as well as against blacks and Indians.

The final section of the novel is entitled "Into the Golden Age." The title is in reference to a new political era, with a new prime minister of South Africa to lead the nation into a promised land, as viewed by Afrikaner Nationalists. The new leader sees a wonderful era for the sections of the country set aside for the various racial groups. While the Afrikaners see this partitioning and segregation as proper for a nation, the liberals of all races and religions disagree.

Part of the fascination of this novel is Paton's narrative method. While dialogue has a large part in that method, his most striking and successful device—particularly effective in revealing character—is his use of letters, which are juxtaposed with the narrative proper. There is an unforgettable series of poison-pen letters written by an Afrikaner woman who signs her venomous epistles as a "Proud White Christian Woman." Also memorable is a parallel series of letters sent in the name of The Preservation of White South Africa League. The latter, as it turns out, are the work of a German Nazi who took refuge in South Africa after World War II. More subtle, and wonderful in their revelation of character, is a series of long letters written by Gabriel Van Onselen, an official in the Justice Department, to an aunt who lives on a farm in rural Natal. He is the voice of the Afrikaner movement in both politics and religion; he, too, shares the troubled mind of the other characters. He knows, though he tries to deny it, what a troubled land it is in which he dwells.

Through the persons who speak within his pages, both the real personages and the fictional characters, Alan Paton gives the reader an insight into what it is like to live in an officially divided society. Paton has been perhaps the best-known twentieth century interpreter of life in South Africa for readers in America. Although he despises the yoke of apartheid, Paton persuades his readers that he tells the truth about all South Africans.

Gordon W. Clarke

Sources for Further Study

The Atlantic. CCXLIX, April, 1982, p. 110.
Commonweal. CIX, May 21, 1982, p. 310.
Christian Science Monitor. March 12, 1982, p. B1.
Library Journal. CVII, March 15, 1982, p. 651.
The New Republic. CLXXXVI, March 24, 1982, p. 35.
New Statesman. CII, November 27, 1981, p. 22.
The New York Times Book Review. LXXXVII, April 18, 1982, p. 7.
Newsweek. XCIX, March 15, 1982, p. 73.
Saturday Review. IX, April, 1982, p. 59.
Times Literary Supplement. November 20, 1981.

AKÉ
The Years of Childhood

Author: Wole Soyinka (1935-   )
Publisher: Random House (New York). 230 pp. $14.95
Type of work: Autobiography
Time: 1934-1944
Locale: Nigeria

A highly imaginative autobiography which covers the first eleven years in the life of the Nigerian writer Wole Soyinka, emphasizing his dramatic initiation into the exotic, stimulating, and sometimes paradoxical world of adults and the established social ways surrounding him

Principal personages:
WOLE SOYINKA, a young boy, later to become a gifted writer
BEERE, a radical female leader and an inspiration to him
DIPO, Wole's younger brother
ESSAY, Wole's gentle father, who taught him to love books
FOLASADE, Wole's baby sister, who died when she was one year old
WILD CHRISTIAN, Wole's passion-filled mother

As a Nigerian writing in the English language, Wole Soyinka was forced to work in relative obscurity for a long time. As his body of work grew, however, so did his reputation, and today he is looked upon as Nigeria's foremost exponent of Afro-European literature. It is even safe to say that he has now become a kind of one-man cultural force in his native land, with the sort of international influence only writers of genuine greatness can affect or claim.

Soyinka's primary achievements lie in the field of drama. He was a leader in the birth and development of an authentic Nigerian theater, and he has written several plays which, grounded in native culture, have a universal appeal and impact. His body of poetry is less accessible, particularly to a reader unfamiliar with African history and culture. At his best, however, Soyinka writes the kind of verse which stirs the imagination and conscience, whatever one's background happens to be. In the area of fiction, Soyinka's contribution to modern literature is less certain. Always experimenting with the possibilities of assimilating the aesthetic and cultural approaches of both the African and Western worlds, he seems not yet to have found a natural way to do this in his novels. Thus, perhaps his venture into fictive autobiography may have been at least partly brought on by this strategic frustration. Whatever first prompted him to consider writing *Aké: The Years of Childhood*, composing the book must have been especially gratifying artistically, since it provided him with a traditional format in which he could resolve the technical problems which have marred his fiction.

Soyinka's novels have been persistently troubled with meandering or uncertain form and with cultural ambiguity or confusion. In *Aké*, Soyinka combines a chronological direction with a dramatic strategy of a child's step-by-step, or crisis-by-crisis, initiation into intelligent awareness. This approach, which contrasts favorably with the narrative strategies of his fiction, provides his account with the kind of unfolding, fateful quality essential to an initiation story. As for the problem of cultural ambiguity, it seems to be resolved less in a technical than in a cunningly imaginative way. Soyinka still has not learned to join his various cultural cross-references with the harmony he desires, yet this seems to matter less in *Aké* than in Soyinka's novels, mainly because here, one is seeing everything through the eyes of a very young boy. Being so young, the boy is often not quite clear about the life which surrounds him. When such confusion reflects cultural matters, it seems a natural consequence of youth. Thus, the occasional bewilderment and allusive ambivalence only add to the dramatic perception of a young mind struggling (and not always succeeding) to understand a confusing world.

In addition, *Aké* is a successful book because it unites all of Soyinka's most characteristic strengths. The story features many descriptive sections which rise with a poetic power of insight and richly suggestive meaning. The passages of dialogue, always vivid and energetic, carry forward Soyinka's thematic concerns. The language throughout is consciously chosen to reflect the imaginative, direct, and rhythmic qualities of folk art at its best. Above all, *Aké* is distinguished by its narrative intelligence—an intelligence at once charming, angry, satirical, intensely observant, and profoundly moral.

The story begins when Soyinka is about three years old, in the mid-1930's, a time when the European influence was felt in Africa, but not to the extent that the old ways were seriously threatened. To emphasize this point, Soyinka describes Aké and the surrounding area where he grew up in terms which stress its mixture of lyrical extravagance and powerful mystery—the appropriate tone for introducing a memoir. By establishing this tone at the start, however, Soyinka also means to introduce a bitterly nostalgic theme, the theme of the death of faith. As Soyinka will make increasingly plain in the story, the boy's gradual loss of the sense of magic anticipates a society's religious decadence. While the boy grows in intellectual awareness, and his eyes see the world more and more clearly, he is less and less puzzled and frightened by the various native superstitions, mystical rituals, or inherited beliefs. This is as it should be, except that as a result, there is a loss of that wonder which distinguishes a child—or a society which values religious mystery more than sophistication.

An exceedingly precocious child, Soyinka took it upon himself one day to go to school when he was not yet three years old. This event, described with great warmth and self-deprecating humor, is one of the most charming parts of the book, but, charm aside, it is also important for revealing Soyinka's lifelong obsession with learning. Growing up in a parsonage compound where his father ran the Christian grammar school, Soyinka felt the influence of books and people who love books. His father, referred to as "Essay," was the most important person during Soyinka's formative years. He was the kind of remote, eccentric man who responds to a son more with bemusement than with open affection, but as a kindly, droll, contemplative figure who loved learning and truth, Essay proved to be ideal as his son's primary teacher. If Soyinka did not exactly follow in his father's footsteps, he was destined to begin his life's journey in the classroom by his father's gentle example.

The influence of Soyinka's mother was also great, but in a different way. Significantly, Soyinka calls her "Wild Christian." Unlike her husband, she was an intense person driven by mercurial passions. While her husband's response to the Bible and to Christian teachings was temperate and somewhat academic, Wild Christian's was fundamentally aggressive and passionate. This emotionalism marked her life as a whole and was often directed toward her family. For young Soyinka, this passion was something to fear; Wild Christian's mood could turn from tenderness to violence at a moment's notice and, it seemed to the boy, without reason. Thus, because of her example, Soyinka began to perceive the irrational strains in the adult world and to anticipate entering adulthood with some dread.

When Soyinka was still four years old, he left the compound alone for the first time to follow a passing parade, a representative panorama of the native society which existed outside the walls of the Christian home. This is the most exhilarating portion of the book. One is made to feel the child's sense of wonder in discovering a new world on his own. Passing through the streets in the wake of the parade, he sees those things which make up a vital society. Not everything he sees is beautiful or pleasant—the scene is at times ugly and personally threatening—yet it offers so much energy and variety that the boy is transported, and the reader senses that this experience was the inception of Soyinka's truly African life.

The next major event in young Soyinka's life was the most poignant. Before she was even one year old, Folasade, Soyinka's sister, came down with a mysterious illness. She was taken to the hospital, and she returned with her little body encased in plaster. After this, the infant cried now and then, but often she lay awake for long periods of time, staring silently. Faced by the unavoidable loss of a loved one, Soyinka at this time barely senses the enormity of death. When, however, Folasade dies on her first birthday, and Soyinka sees her laid out in a white dress covering her plastered body, he bursts into tears. They are instinctive tears of understanding of the cruelest fact of life, and they indicate the premature gravity of the boy's vision.

After this painful experience, Soyinka lost some of his merriment, boisterous optimism, and innocent self-confidence. Then, his self-esteem suffered a direct blow when he erupted one day against his younger brother, Dipo.

Teased by adults about his bookishness and tormented by Dipo's aggressively physical behavior, he suddenly lashes out. As he does, he blacks out, and when he regains his senses, he discovers that he has been furiously battering his younger brother. After realizing what he has done, Soyinka suffers a feverish guilt which leads him toward self-examination. What was behind his outburst, he wonders. He concludes that, in a way, he had decided to strike out at the torments of life, but that this was nevertheless inexcusable. However life might treat him in the future, he resolves to control the demons of self-pity and violent retribution which he has discovered in himself.

When it appears that his father is about to die, Soyinka has his next great crisis, faced once again with the painful reality of the death of a loved one. This time, though, he is old enough to understand the added factors of personal upheaval and temporal insecurity. If his father really dies, what will happen to the family and their well-being? To worry about such things while one is ten years old seems to be an unfair burden. Therefore, when Essay has a talk with Soyinka about how he expects his son to carry on as "the man of the house," the consequence is not surprising. Under the enormous pressure of approaching mature responsibilities, Soyinka comes down with a high fever which lasts for three days. He survives, and so, ironically, does his father, but even if his father is not about to die yet, Soyinka has been forced to agonize about the future of his family. Consequently, much of the magical innocence of childhood has been lost forever.

Toward the end of the story, Soyinka, now about eleven years old, becomes peripherally involved in a political uprising—a women's revolt which began by attacking local taxes and ended by challenging a whole social structure which depended on female subservience. This protest movement—which started with trying to resolve the problem of a lack of social graces among newlywed natives—grew into a populist uprising because of two factors: resentment against social injustice had been festering for many years, and there were people who were ready to take great personal risks for the cause. The primary leader of the movement, a woman named Beere, was closely connected with the Soyinkas, and young Soyinka thus had the chance to observe the cause and the leader from a privileged position. What he saw changed his life's direction. Implicitly, the story ends with Soyinka looking to Beere as his final example and guide just before he leaves home to enter Government College. Once Soyinka reached manhood, the evidence is that he was always willing to take risks for just social causes. Perhaps this was his inevitable destiny, but it is apparent that as a woman of high principle and courage, Beere served as Soyinka's primary model of political conscience.

In tracing his young life from the onset of magical awareness to the point where he is on the verge of accepting the serious and conflicting demands of the adult world, Soyinka has made a major contribution to the literature of childhood. *Aké* is not a perfect book. There are times when one could wish for a clearer sense of thematic progression, for example, and a fuller development of some of the Yoruban customs and beliefs. One could most certainly wish for a more thorough job of editing, since the book is marred both by basic writing errors and by printer's errors. Ultimately, however, one comes away from *Aké* with the hope that Soyinka will offer grateful readers another imaginative installment of his life.

Georg Gaston

Sources for Further Study

The Atlantic. CCL, September, 1982, p. 95.
Economist. CCLXXX, August 1, 1981, p. 74.
Library Journal. CVII, August, 1982, p. 1454.
Los Angeles Times Book Review. October 31, 1982, p. 6.
The New York Review of Books. XXIX, October 21, 1982, p. 3.
The New York Times Book Review. LXXXVII, October 10, 1982, p. 7.
Newsweek. C, November 1, 1982, p. 87.
Times Literary Supplement. February 26, 1982, p. 228.
World Literature Today. LVI, Summer, 1982, p. 561.

ALL THAT IS SOLID MELTS INTO AIR
The Experience of Modernity

Author: Marshall Berman (1940-   )
Publisher: Simon and Schuster (New York). 384 pp. $17.50; paperback $6.95
Type of work: Political science

An effort to restore a sense of history to the experience of modernity

Marshall Berman, who teaches at City College and City University of New York, has written an intriguing history of a dominant theme in Western thought—or, perhaps more accurately, a dominant Western attitude or mood: the ambivalence toward the idea of progress or development. In an analysis of the work of writers ranging from Johann Wolfgang von Goethe to Fyodor Dostoevski to Dylan Thomas, and with forays into architecture, Berman has discerned the nature of modernism to be the tension between the will toward social and physical change and the desire for social and physical stability. "To be modern," says Berman,

> is to be both revolutionary and conservative: alive to new possibilities for experience and adventure, frightened by the nihilistic depths to which so many modern adventures lead, longing to create and hold on to something real even as everything melts.

To be modern, says Berman, is to live in perpetual tension between personal and social development and decay, but to be modern*ist* is to be at home in this environment. Berman wants to make modernists of his readers; he wants them to feel at home in the world in which they live. For this reason, he argues, it is crucial to understand contemporary modernism as the product of two earlier modern periods, represented by, among others, Goethe and Karl Marx.

Goethe's *Faust* (1808, 1832), one of the first major treatments of the themes of modernism, is set up in three stages: Faust the dreamer, the lover, and the developer. In the first stage, Faust awakens in the middle of the night, tempted to commit suicide because he realizes that he belongs to the privileged class and is free to engage in esoteric pursuits while most people are trapped by a stagnant society. His despair about his remoteness from the rest of humanity is relieved when he hears church bells, which remind him of his childhood and the memories and feelings that he had suppressed. He remembers that he and his father had worked as physicians among the poor, but that their efforts had been futile, even destructive, so he had withdrawn from practicing medicine to engage in a solitary intellectual quest. Only now does he realize that self-fulfillment cannot be solitary, and he wants to unite his intellectual life with life in the world. He also learns that creation necessitates destruction and that he must risk physical, emotional, and financial ruin if he is to find self-fulfillment. The theme of the first stage, then, is the desire for authentic human existence.

Faust's new mind-set makes him less self-preoccupied and more sensitive to others. He becomes self-confident, and with the help of stylish clothes and drugs that make him feel and look years younger, he becomes attractive. He soon seduces Gretchen, a poor young girl from a small town. She loses her virginity and her naïveté and focuses all of her passion upon Faust. At first, he is delighted with her development and newfound self-respect, but Gretchen's intensity scares him, and he leaves town to participate in an orgy of sex, drugs, and heady conversation. He returns, however, when he hears that Gretchen's family and village have turned against her. Faust kills Gretchen's brother in a fight, and when Gretchen is condemned to death for bearing Faust's illegitimate child, he sneaks into the prison to rescue her. Gretchen refuses to go, because she senses that Faust no longer loves her, and she dies. From his involvement with Gretchen, Faust learns that if he wants to help others to grow, then he must take responsibility for their development or be responsible for their destruction. Faust the lover shows that change necessitates struggle and destruction.

In Faust's third and final metamorphosis, his dreams and loves are transformed into strategies of economic development. Standing by the sea, watching its endless tossing, he decides to channel the water for the sake of human productivity. He strikes a bargain with the emperor: he will solidify the monarch's power in return for complete freedom to develop the coastal region. Faust organizes workers for the rapid industrial transformation of the coast and is very pleased that the intense, systematic labor stirs the stagnant economy. When a virtuous old couple refuse to move from their seashore house to make way for the developers, Faust orders them removed by any means. When Faust discovers that his orders resulted in the murder of the couple and the burning of their house, he becomes outraged and sad, even though he refuses to accept responsibility. Faust's sadness belies his usefulness, however, so he dies. He had obliterated the old ways, but he was not totally modern himself—he retained a residue of former values; thus, he stood in the way of the modern processes that he initiated.

Goethe's *Faust* shows that transformation—modernism—envelops the entire physical, social, and moral world. This work, according to Berman, is representative of the beginning of modernism, a period from the early sixteenth century to the end of the eighteenth century. The second phase of modernism, which extended from the revolutionary 1790's until the end of the nineteenth century, was marked by a sense of change in personal, social, and political life as well as by the sense of living simultaneously in modern and premodern worlds. Those who lived in this second epoch of modernism had memories of the world before modernism while living in a world that was completely modern. Berman says that this period yielded the clearest definitions of modernism, the classic being Karl Marx's vision in the *Kommunistisches Manifest*

(1848; *Communist Manifesto*):

> All fixed, fast-frozen relations, with their train of ancient and venerable prejudices and opinions, are swept away, all newformed ones become antiquated before they can ossify. All that is solid melts into air, all that is holy is profaned, and men at last are forced to face with sober senses the real conditions of their lives and their relations with their fellow men.

In Marx's view, the modern world is permeated by the paradoxes of continuous change. In order to maintain their position of control, capitalizing upon and liberating the human thrust toward development, the bourgeoisie continuously revolutionize production and social relations. Thus, the bourgeoisie are what Berman calls the prime movers of modernity. Products are purposefully made to become obsolete so that there will be a demand for newer, more profitable products that will need to be replaced by newer, more profitable products. This cycle of continuous development, manufacture, and replacement ensures high profits and, hence, the power of the bourgeoisie. Even catastrophes are useful in that they provide even more opportunity for production and replacement. The workers are taught to value the idea of development in support of this capitalistic system, but they are free to develop themselves only in ways that are profitable. The essential ingredient of destruction, however, will lead to capitalism's demise. Change is continuous and universal; therefore, even the social hierarchy is not exempt from the engines of change. The bourgeoisie may see themselves as the guardians of social order, but the revolutions they have set in motion will not bypass them. Capitalist social relations will, like everything else, crumble. Capitalism will give way to Communism, at which time individuals will begin to develop in concert. The bourgeoisie will be hoist with their own petard.

Marx does not explain, however, why Communism itself will not be destroyed and replaced by some other social, economic, and political form. If everything changes, why does the overthrow of capitalism stop the process? Berman suggests that Marx described the present and the near future in terms of his insight into contemporary modernism, but then resorted to a premodern view when he discussed the millenium of Communism.

The third phase of modernity, still in progress, is exemplified by the work of architect and developer Robert Moses. By the turn of the twentieth century, modernism had enveloped the world, which had become a mosaic of modern fragments. Modernism continued at full tilt, but the sense of premodernism which Marx and his contemporaries knew so well had disappeared. Today's modernism lacks a sense of heritage and a foundation for values.

Berman uses Moses as an archetype of contemporary modernism, an era of development for development's sake. Moses built beaches, highways, parks, and bridges; among his most notable achievements was the renovation of New York City's Central Park. To oppose his construction, he argued, was to oppose progress. "There's a little discomfort and even that is exaggerated," he remarked while he was building the Cross-Bronx Expressway, a project which displaced some sixty thousand residents and, in effect, led to the ruin of the Bronx. In the 1920's and 1930's, Moses built in order to enhance city living, but by the 1950's, when his power had grown virtually unchecked, he had lost that ostensible humaneness and built thruways for the suburbs that all but destroyed large numbers of urban neighborhoods. Moses had become a classic twentieth century modernist, building in spite of rather than for humane goals. "When you operate in an overbuilt metropolis," he said, "you have to hack your way with a meat ax."

All That Is Solid Melts into Air argues a position that is well worth heeding: a historical perspective is necessary to understanding the contemporary world. Berman, who has grounded his argument in centuries of texts, has presented a history of modernism that demands attention. The dialectic of destruction and construction, or progress, has, says Berman, in four centuries redesigned the world but is now out of control because of its lack of regard for history. Modernism can be a menace because it denies its own past.

While Berman has reconstructed a perceptive, three-stage history of modernism, he has given few clues as to how modernism works. He has shown the character of modernisms past and present, but he has not shown why and how the worlds of Goethe and Marx led to the world of Robert Moses. Without knowing how one era led to another, one is still at the mercy of modernism. One becomes like an alcoholic who knows he has a problem but does not know why. He might be able to alter some of the symptoms by a sheer act of will, but without understanding how his mind works, he cannot channel his energies in a different, and perhaps more constructive, way. Berman has shown that modernism has taken certain forms in the past, but not *how* and *why* it has done so.

Reading about modernism is a little like reading about warfare: no matter how long any given book is, it is not long enough. Berman discusses modernism in terms of architecture and literature; he could have written instead about modern politics or modern music or modern communications. His choices are both wise and arbitrary. *All That Is Solid Melts into Air* is thus insightful but not definitive, necessary but not sufficient, interesting but not wholly satisfying. Nevertheless, Berman has provided a historical perspective on an elusive cultural current, and so has served an end far more humane than does the subject that he describes.

John P. Ferré

Sources for Further Study

The Atlantic. CCXLIX, January, 1982, p. 84.
Choice. XIX, May, 1982, p. 1224.

Commentary. LXXIII, April, 1982, p. 74.
Commonweal. CIX, November 19, 1982, p. 636.
Library Journal. CVII, April 1, 1982, p. 734.
Nation. CCXXXIV, January 30, 1982, p. 118.
The New Republic. CLXXXVI, January 6, 1982, p. 37.
The New York Review of Books. XXIX, March 4, 1982, p. 27.
The New York Times Book Review. LXXXVII, February 14, 1982, p. 9.
Newsweek. XCIX, January 25, 1982, p. 78.

ANTARCTIC TRAVELLER

Author: Katha Pollitt (1949-   )
Publisher: Alfred A. Knopf (New York). 60 pp. $11.50; paperback $5.95
Type of work: Poetry

This distinguished first collection of forty poems received the National Book Critics Circle Award for Poetry in 1983

In 1982, Alfred A. Knopf published the sixth and seventh volumes in their new poetry series. These volumes turned out to be the most successful first collections to have appeared in many years. *Antarctic Traveller* is number seven in the series; number six, Brad Leithauser's *Hundreds of Fireflies* (1982), is reviewed elsewhere in this volume. Both collections were nominated for the National Book Critics Circle Award, and *Antarctic Traveller* received the award.

Katha Pollitt is acquainted with the techniques of traditional metrics and works within them when subject, occasion, or mood demands; she is perhaps more at home in the kind of open form or free verse which has itself become nearly traditional. It is a kind of free verse in which appreciation for line-breaks must be purely a visual experience, unavailable to one who only hears the poems; it seems designed to encourage matters of line and stanza to withdraw into the background, so that imagination and word choice, for example, may come to the fore. Most of the time, this approach works well for Pollitt, but it poses a few problems. One problem is that the strongly metrical poems in this book tend to be the best, so that one wonders whether metrical writing is the most effective way Pollitt has of forcing herself to pay prolonged attention to each line of a poem. This impression is borne out by the realization that the handful of underachieved poems, those that went in to fill out the book to a decent length, are all unmetrical. Every book of poems is likely to contain a few poems that found their way in only because there was room for them; the poet strives to eliminate these, but finally the desire to get a book finished overcomes the poet's perceptions of that which is passable but inferior. That is not a serious problem. The problem here is that Pollitt somehow suggests by the shape and arrangement of the book that free verse is significantly easier to write than metrical verse—as of course it is, unless one is doing one's best.

When she is doing her best, metrically or not, Pollitt is very good indeed. She has a sharp and loving eye for details that can convey the speaker's attitude, not only toward the thing observed, but also toward the world in general. She understands the many ways in which living and loving are difficult and necessary.

The arrangement of these poems is generally intelligent and effective: two longer sections framing a brief central section. The first part of the book is chiefly concerned with moods of loneliness, or desire for the unattainable, or the isolation one feels in the city. The middle section, "Five Poems from Japanese Paintings," takes the poet out of herself toward the poems of the third section, in which the lives of others are imagined, sometimes with moving empathy, sometimes with humor.

Three of the strongest poems in the first section are "Ballet Blanc," "Archaeology," and "Chinese Finches." Each of these draws on unusual, even exotic, subject matter to illuminate experiences which will be familiar to many readers. "Ballet Blanc" is a brilliant evocation of the way a member of the audience at a ballet may become so involved in the beauty of the production, the surroundings, that she begins to imagine herself the center of attention:

> You glow, you sway,
> it's as though the audience were dancing too
> and with a last, stupendous tour jeté
> turned for a solo suddenly to *you*
>
> and you become the Duke, the Queen, Giselle,
> and waltz in a whirl of white through the painted grove,
> your gestures as extravagant as tulle,
> as wild as nineteenth-century hopeless love.

After the ballet, however, as the enraptured person goes home, things begin to change back, unnoticed:

> You float upstairs and into bed
>
> and into dreams so deep you never hear
> how all night long that witch, your evil fairy,
> crows her knowing cackle in your ear:
> *Tomorrow you will wake up ordinary.*

The balance here between the speaker of the poem and the "you" is delicate and important; this is not one of those many recent poems in which "you" stands for "I." In the last stanza of this poem, the speaker knows something that the "you" does not.

"Archaeology" is probably the best-known poem in this collection; Pollitt may possibly have begun to regret that it is excerpted in the jacket copy, since most of the earlier reviews of the book have fastened upon it for further quotation. It is indeed a splendid poem. Its epigraph is a statement by Jonathan Galassi: "Our real poems are already in us and all we can do is dig." That epigraph is the only insistent pointer to the metaphor the poem explores; the poem itself may be taken on the literal level as a description of the hopes, disappointments, and triumphs of archaeological excavation. The last few lines of the poem give it its metaphoric resonance; the use of the word *invent* is crucial:

> Pack up your fragments. Let the simoom
> flatten the digging site. Now come
> the passionate midnights in the museum basement
> when out of that random rubble you'll invent
> the dusty market smelling of sheep and spices,
> streets, palmy gardens, courtyards set with wells
> to which, in the blue of evening, one by one
> come strong veiled women, bearing their perfect jars.

The writing here is exquisite; the lines hover purposefully over blank verse, but do not settle on it, and the accidental rhymes do not intrude. The sound of the lines is uncannily reminiscent of Richard Wilbur's style in such long poems of his as "Walking to Sleep" or "The Mind-Reader," but this recognition does not diminish the poem's effectiveness, since the style in question is plain enough to be available to anyone who has the skill to use it. Finally, the least effective part of the poem is its epigraph, which seems to reduce the poem's metaphoric versatility; one is almost sorry to be told that this is a poem about poetry, when it could so easily be equally suggestive of other laborious and rewarding pursuits, from carpentry to psychotherapy.

"Chinese Finches" effects a similar escape from its immediate setting, which is the apartment of a pair of quarrelsome lovers who have given themselves a bamboo cage containing a pair of Chinese finches. Around the cage, the lovers' lives revolve toward dissolution, while the birds remain suggestive of something calmer and more lasting. Pollitt's skillful descriptions, here and in other poems such as "Failure" and "Turning Thirty," make various interiors— furniture, wallpaper, and so on—wonderfully evocative of states of mind and emotion.

By contrast, "Five Poems from Japanese Paintings" are slightly less engaging, on the whole, than most of the poems in this book. They contain flashes of brilliance, but there is a self-consciousness about them, as if the business of the poet were to fasten on an object and wring significance from it.

The third section opens with a sequence of five "Vegetable Poems," which produce decidedly the opposite effect. Here again, five items are set out for contemplation, but the self-consciousness is gone, and instead one finds a serious wit, a profound playfulness. The single sentence of "Eggplant" is typical of what these poems can do:

> Like a dark foghorn in the yellow kitchen
> we imagine the eggplant's
> melancholy bass
> booming its pompous operatic sorrows
> a prince down on his luck

preserving among peasants
an air of dignified, impenetrable gloom
or Boris, dying,
booming, *I still am Tsar.*

This is splendidly visualized, and yet one looks in vain for a sense of inevitability about the lengths of the lines; this is one of those poems in free verse which seems to have been tossed off, at least where meter is concerned; everything is left to the ingenious images. In so slight a poem, perhaps that is enough, but having seen what Pollitt can do with lines when she feels inclined to work at them, one wishes that she felt so inclined a little more often.

In two or three cases, the free verse poems in this final section do manage to defy attempts at improving the line-breaks. One poem, "Two Fish," like several of the poems discussed earlier, demonstrates that Pollitt is at ease when rearranging the traditional expectations of established forms. "Two Fish" is technically a sonnet; one of its lines is a trimeter, yet it is clear that Pollitt has departed from certain metrical expectations in full knowledge of the effect produced. There are times when a near-sonnet takes fuller advantage of the tradition behind it than would a flawless exemplification of the form.

The last two poems in the collection rise again to the level of Pollitt's best. "Seal Rock" and the title poem are remarkable for the apparent ease with which they handle large themes. In the first of these two poems, the speaker considers the change that seems to have come over the seals in recent years; they no longer come at night to the dock "behind Arthur's Gift Shop and General Store," but remain aloof, providing no new fuel for the legends surrounding them: that they have "floated this drowner, nudged that skiff off rocks." Now, as the speaker passes their rock in a ferry, people lean from the railings to glimpse the seals, whose barking evokes only squeaking boat pulleys and the cries of sea gulls. "They are no Sirens, we only weekend trippers./ Whatever their language, they are not speaking to us." The realistic approach of this poem is almost stern; in its declaration of human separateness from "the natural world," it is somewhat reminiscent of Robert Frost's "Come In," or Brewster Ghiselin's "Vantage," though it does not aspire to the Olympian tone of those two poems.

The title poem of the collection, "To an Antarctic Traveller," addresses someone who has been to Antarctica and will soon return to a round of cocktail parties and questions. The speaker senses that the traveler's tolerance for the daily temperate world will have been lessened by the experience of having seen "the ego glinting at the heart of things." The second of the poem's two parts contains an interesting paradox: the traveler's name has been given to an Antarctic mountain, but the named mountain disappears into mist, into surrounding whiteness, as the traveler lifts off in an airplane. One thinks of

Horace, or of William Shakespeare's "Not marble, nor the gilded monuments." To paraphrase the ending of the poem, it is possible to write one's name on the world itself and still be assured of oblivion. In the face of that knowledge, Katha Pollitt has written with strength and grace.

Henry Taylor

Sources for Further Study

Georgia Review. XXXVI, Summer, 1982, p. 438.
Library Journal. CVII, January 1, 1982, p. 96.
Ms. XI, September, 1982, p. 94.
Nation. CCXXXIV, March 20, 1982, p. 342.
The New Republic. CLXXXVI, April 14, 1982, p. 37.
The New York Times Book Review. LXXXVII, March 14, 1982, p. 17.
Poetry. CXLI, December, 1982, p. 170.
Virginia Quarterly Review. LVIII, Summer, 1982, p. 92.

THE ARGOT MERCHANT DISASTER
Poems New and Selected

Author: George Starbuck (1931-   )
Publisher: Little, Brown and Company (Boston). 119 pp. $12.95
Type of work: Poetry

To a generous selection from three decades of earlier work, Starbuck adds seventeen new poems; all display superior craftsmanship

The three subtitles of the sections of Wallace Stevens' *Notes Toward a Supreme Fiction* (1942) make the following stipulations concerning poetry: "It must be abstract. It must change. It must give pleasure." The first of these, when applied to the work of George Starbuck (or any excellent poet, for that matter), needs some qualification in the light of Ezra Pound's dictum: "Go in fear of abstractions." To "be abstract" is not necessarily to toss abstract ideas around, but possibly to exist as an object for contemplation, somehow beyond the subject and even the theme of the poem. Starbuck's poems are abstract in the way that Andrew Wyeth argues that some of his paintings are abstract; they are of the world, about it, and they are themselves. They change, not only in the usual sense of development over the years, but even as one looks at them; and they give enormous pleasure.

The selected poems in *The Argot Merchant Disaster* are taken from three of Starbuck's five previous books: *Bone Thoughts*, the 1960 volume in the Yale Series of Younger Poets; *White Paper* (1966), whose tone is dominated by poems of satire and protest concerning issues of the 1960's; and *Desperate Measures* (1978), in which Starbuck demonstrates his skills with metrical invention and gamesmanship. The selection of new poems is placed at the beginning of the book, but it makes more sense in considering a book of this kind to begin with the earliest poems.

In his introduction to *Bone Thoughts*, Dudley Fitts expresses his admiration for Starbuck's ability, not only to work within traditional forms, but also to make them his own, to do something with them other than merely to obey their rules. Certainly there are spectacular examples of this skill here; perhaps the best known of these is "A Tapestry for Bayeux." Metrically, the poem may be described thus: it is in two sections of equal length, each section being composed of six stanzas of thirteen lines each; each line is a single dactylic foot. The first section, "Recto," describes a battle scene from World War II; "Verso" employs the idea that a tapestry's reverse side is hung with thread-ends and describes the battle from the other side, in terms of wires from exploded switchboards and fibers from exploded men. The tension between the subject and the wit is considerable, but the thread is strong.

Stevens also stipulated that poetry "must change," and this poem changes in a startling way. It is difficult to imagine what might prompt a reader to examine the first letters of all the lines, in search of an acrostic, because the even-numbered lines are indented, and capitalization appears only according to prose rules. The acrostic is there nevertheless, and says: "Oscar Williams fills a need but a monkey ward catalog is softer and gives you something to read. We treasure his treasuries most every pominem our remarks are uncouth or unjust or ad hominem." As is appropriate to a poem whose two sections are called "Recto" and "Verso," the two sentences in the acrostic are contradictory. That they rhyme, and that they contain precisely the same number of letters, and that they are so skillfully concealed along the left edge of this poem, is a remarkable demonstration of versifying skill and patience.

The range between playfulness and solemnity in this first book is wide, but Starbuck broadened it further when he confronted the subject matter of the 1960's. *White Paper* contains poems of genuine outrage, under the firm control of Starbuck's technical mastery; it also contains *jeux d'esprit* of considerable skill, but of such slight substance that pleasure in them diminishes with successive readings.

In the first category, for example, there is "Of Late," which recalls the horror of one man's protest of the American involvement in Vietnam:

"Stephen Smith, University of Iowa sophomore, burned what he said was his draft card"
and Norman Morrison, Quaker, of Baltimore Maryland, burned what he said was himself.
You, Robert McNamara, burned what you said was a concentration of the Enemy Aggressor.

The poem repeats variations on the second line, presenting evidence of Morrison's deranged mental state. The poem ends movingly and angrily:

Norman Morrison, Quaker, of Baltimore Maryland, burned and was burned and said
all that there is to say in that language.
Twice what is said in yours.
It is a strange sect, Mr. McNamara, under advice to try
the whole of a thought in silence, and to oneself.

Anger, poetic skill, and restraint combine here effectively; the technical skill is unobtrusive. Part of the reason for this is that Starbuck, unlike certain of his contemporaries, did not suddenly develop a social conscience during the 1960's; his first book contains a number of somber reflections on war and the possibility of thermonuclear disaster.

At the opposite end of the scale of "seriousness," one finds in this collection some smart-aleck slang versions of well-known poems. At their worst, they are momentarily funny; at their best, they make satirical comments on the drug culture: "Little Boy Blue come blow./ Can't Man; learning a new instrument./ What's with the old one? Where'd you get the new one?/ Found it in a haystack Man." Clever as this verse is, it does not meet the standard which Starbuck has long since established for himself. When he sets to work on a "slight" poem, a performance in what might be called "light verse," he is capable of astonishingly dextrous rhymes, puns, echoes of statelier poems, and an overall finish which is beyond the skill of most contemporary poets.

Starbuck probably achieves his maximum versifying brilliance in the third section of his earlier poems. In *Desperate Measures*, for example, he begins with a kind of shaggy Arab story, "The Sad Ballad of the Fifteen Consecutive Rhymes." Starbuck constructs an entertaining and, at times, plausible little story of Amantha Roin, a poetess and teacher of creative writing, and her infatuation with a student, the Sheik of Serendip. He endures her severe verse exercises, she languishes in his presence, until at last, driven mad by the difficulty of "A narrative/ In stanza form containing/ At least fifteen consecutive/ Rhymes," he comes to her wielding his Damascus blade.

This section also contains some fourteen double-dactylic verses, and five clerihews. The double-dactyl, invented several years ago by Anthony Hecht and John Hollander, is a poem of eight lines, the fourth and eighth lines rhyming. All the lines except the rhyming ones are double-dactylic; the rhyming lines cut off the two unstressed syllables of the second foot. The first line must be a nonsense phrase, such as "pocketa-pocketa"; the second must be someone's double-dactylic name; the fifth must be a single double-dactylic word. Clearly, only a finite number of such poems can be written, but Starbuck's cleverness is such that he makes one wonder whether he could not go on producing these things indefinitely. At the conclusion of the selection of clerihews and double-dactyls, there is a poem of 124 lines, "Falling Asleep over Scott," which takes maximum advantage of the discovery that Sir Walter Scott's Waverley novels are thickly populated with double-dactylic names: "Who in the name of the/ Quasihistorical/ *Sent* me this houseful of/ Metrical freaks?" The poem appears to lavish more effort and attention on the double-dactylic problem than is likely to be expended again.

Some readers will probably object that poetry is serious, and that Starbuck wastes too much time and ingenuity on incidentals. This is a narrow and humorless complaint, arising from the dubious conviction that poems in this late era emerge under a shadow of extinction and ought to reflect that gloomy fact. Certainly these are troubled times, fraught with problems which gifted speakers ought to address, but to imagine excellence, even at the level of the double-dactyl, and to create it, is a responsible poetic act; furthermore, Starbuck does not restrict himself to games. In his introduction to *Bone Thoughts*, Dudley Fitts characterizes Starbuck as "a man awake in the nightmare of our day."

The new poems, in the first section of this book, bear out this statement. Once again, Starbuck has extended his range. The second poem in the book is among his longest and funniest, but the style of the humor depends less on wordplay and intricate metrics than on the style of the stand-up comic, building gags on the foundation of earlier ones. "Magnificat in Transit from the Toledo Airport" begins, "The world has a glass center./ I saw the sign for it./ TOLEDO, GLASS CENTER OF THE WORLD." The poem goes on, noting the existence of the numerous cities that each claim to be the "Athens of the Midwest," and rambles along toward a joyful conclusion: "Merciful Muchness, Principle of Redundance,/ Light of the World converted at every turn,/ the world *is* too much for us, wait and see!"

This last line is only one example of something characteristic of Starbuck; he echoes lines from other poems with pleasant aptness, and sometimes with outrageous irreverence. At other times, though, Starbuck manages a blend of sparkling technique and deep feeling, as when, at the end of one of his best new poems, he reveals himself emotionally to the reader. "The Universe Is Closed and Has REMs" is an extended meditation on the prospect of annihilation, and it is suffused with dark humor, but these lines from the conclusion explain much:

> I take my task as to record
> At close hand, for the glory of no Lord,
> Delight of no posterity, some part
> Of what it was to take the world to heart
> . . . .
> Tell the whole shebang I love it,
> And buck the odds, and hope, and give it my
> Borrowed scratched-up happy hello-goodbye.

There is much more in these poems than has been mentioned or described. *The Argot Merchant Disaster* is a splendid collection.

Henry Taylor

Sources for Further Study

Booklist. LXXVIII, August, 1982, p. 1501.
Library Journal. CVII, September 15, 1982, p. 1758.
Los Angeles Times Book Review. October 31, 1982, p. 8.
The New York Times Book Review. LXXXVIII, February 15, 1983, p. 15.
Publishers Weekly. CCXXII, July 23, 1982, p. 131.

ATLANTIC HIGH
A Celebration

Author: William F. Buckley, Jr. (1925-   )
Publisher: Doubleday & Company (Garden City, New York). Illustrated. 262 pp.
   $22.50
Type of work: Travelogue and memoir
Time: May-June, 1980
Locale: The Atlantic Ocean

A record, with many flashbacks and tangents, of the voyage of the racing-ketch
Sealestial *crewed by the author, his six companions, and a professional crew of four.*
from the Virgin Islands to Marbella, Spain

> *Principal personages:*
>   WILLIAM F. BUCKLEY, JR., author, editor, and chief organizer of
>   the voyage
>   RICHARD M. "DICK" CLURMAN, a former chief of correspondents
>   for *Time/Life*
>   EVAN "VAN" GALBRAITH, a United States diplomat
>   ANTHONY "TONY" LEGGETT, a New York banker
>   DANIEL "DANNY" MERRITT, a sailing companion of the Buckley
>   family
>   REGINALD "REG" STOOPS, a plastics engineer and long-time sailing
>   companion of Buckley
>   CHRISTOPHER LITTLE, a professional photographer

William F. Buckley, Jr., wears many hats: editor, columnist, novelist, television personality, wit, and pundit. In *Atlantic High: A Celebration*, he puts on, for the second time, his captain's yachting cap. Ostensibly, the book is a record of a cruise in the chartered ocean yacht *Sealestial*, from St. Thomas in the Virgin Islands to Marbella in Spain, by way of Bermuda and the Azores. As crew and companions, Buckley had with him Richard Clurman, former chief of correspondents for *Time/Life* and now a private consultant; Evan Galbraith, a United States diplomat to France; Tony Leggett, a young New York banker; Danny Merritt, a friend of Buckley's son Christopher; Reginald Stoops, a plastics engineer and long-time sailing companion of Buckley; and Christopher Little, a professional photographer responsible for most of the photographs in the book. Clurman traveled only to Bermuda, and Galbraith left the ship in the Azores.

Both the voyage and the book are really an outgrowth and continuation of a similar 1975 voyage across the Atlantic and the resulting book, *Airborne: A Sentimental Journey* (1976). On that voyage, Galbraith, Merritt, and Stoops also accompanied Buckley. This voyage, however, is not merely a reprise of the earlier one. For one thing, the first voyage was made in Buckley's own ocean yacht *Cyrano*; this second cruise is made in the chartered *Sealestial* with its professional crew of four (who are rarely figured in the narrative).

Also on this voyage, there is a professional photographer, as well as, for the St. Thomas-Bermuda run, a motion-picture cameraman and a sound man, all for the purpose of enabling the group to finance the voyage. The idea was that the book which would result from the voyage, augmented by the work of a professional photographer, and a documentary film based on the group's experiences, would help pay the expenses. This note of planned financial calculation does tend to undercut the expected romance and pleasures of the sea and sailing.

Atlantic High is not really a book about sailing. While there are the requisite references to reefing and halyards and navigating and genoas, this is really a book about yachting, which is a very different thing. Yachting is a rich man's sport, and Buckley clearly moves in worlds unfamiliar to ordinary mortals. The *Sealestial* is equipped with a multitude of electronic devices and gadgets (a fair number of which do not work), including a stereo tape-player and an ice-maker. A well-stocked wine bin is an absolute necessity; a cook to produce succulent meals is another. The often sybaritic life aboard *Sealestial* bears little resemblance to the experiences of Sir Francis Chichester or Horatio Hornblower. Indeed, one is reminded of those people who go camping in the wilds and take along with them all the mechanical and electrical marvels of the modern American home.

Atlantic High, while full of many interesting and entertaining bits, remains a bit unfocused; there is really no climax. The ship does eventually reach its goal, but almost too easily. There are no real problems on the voyage, no emergencies (except almost running out of ice), no great pains to be endured or difficulties to overcome. There is, of course, no absolute requirement that every sailing voyage contain a brush with death, gales, and mystical insights into the eternal fascination of the deep. There is always a danger in confronting the sea, whether in an ocean liner or a racing ketch (*Sealestial* was about the same length as Columbus' *Pinta*), but the narration of such a confrontation is usually expected to have more pace to it, more point, more rising action than the shorebound reader is likely to find here.

The book is also structurally unbalanced. Actually, less than half of the work deals with the trip itself. The first three chapters deal, *inter alia*, with a cruise to Yucatan, a week's sail in the Fiji Islands, and a Christmas cruise in the Caribbean, where *Sealestial* was first chartered. As he had for the *Airborne* volume, Buckley required his companions to keep journals, portions of which he then abstracts for inclusion in the text. Along with these journal extracts, Buckley interlards one of his regular columns for the *National Review*, a brief article written for *Esquire*, a parody of a Suzy Knickerbocker column, a chapter on the contents of his mailbag, and two chapters on the problems of celestial navigation and the wonders of the Plath Navicomp computer. While certainly not a thing of shreds and patches, *Atlantic High* is at times a rather strange combination of bits and pieces.

To be sure, some of the bits and pieces are well worth having. The mock gossip column is hilarious in its own right, and a mock Platonic dialogue is both amusing and intellectually acute. To his credit, Buckley invites the reader to skip the chapter on how to handle the navigational computer if the reader is less than interested in such matters. The reader would be well advised *not* to skip the chapter, even if he or she does not wish to follow a string of mathematical calculations, because it is interesting and amusingly written. The following chapter on how to make mistakes in celestial navigation, and the consequences thereof, is even more entertaining. Then, too, the whole book is well-spiced with jokes, amusing anecdotes, and interesting tangents.

One of the greatest pleasures of the book is its sheer virtuosity, which also serves to unify the sometimes disparate elements. The style is the man, and the whole book is suffused with the style and wit that one has come to expect from Buckley. The knack of saying unpalatable things in a pleasant or even amusing way is of inestimable value to a political and social pundit; at the very least, it usually guarantees a hearing. Apart from a few mild digs at President Carter and at the reforms within the Roman Catholic Church, there are few unpalatable things here, and Buckley's sense of style never deserts him.

The book is not a succession of jokes; rather, Buckley can see the humorous or truly comic element in characters and situations. It is always the cast of mind, the point of view, and not mechanical manipulation that distinguish the true comic or satiric vision, and Buckley has these characteristics. He can be as severe or satiric about his own foibles and failings as about those of great institutions or of his own companions. One would not call this a jolly book, but a witty one, because the remarks so trenchantly expressed usually spring from a sense of principles and standards. In many ways, Buckley reminds the reader of Evelyn Waugh; though Buckley is usually more genial, the pleasures of *Atlantic High* are touched with enough Attic salt for full flavor.

On one level, the entire book is really about Buckley. In the relaxed atmosphere of the trip and its preparations, one sees Buckley in undress; his personality dominates the book. He adheres well to his announced purpose of giving the reader both practical and idiosyncratic experiences. One learns of his fascination with gadgets, his determination that he captain the affair, his fondness for vodka and grapefruit juice, his delight in his personal acquaintance with the wealthy, powerful, and famous. Scattered through the book are anecdotes, reminiscences, and personal insights about public figures such as David Niven, Howard Cosell, Ronald Reagan, the Viscountess Lambton, Charlie Chaplin, Barry Goldwater, the King of Spain, Milton Friedman, and Dinah Shore—to name only a few.

There is no doubt that Buckley is a pleasant fellow, a companion of choice. He can be a genial fellow, amused but forgiving about human weaknesses.

At the appropriate times, he can be animated and carefree. He has a great talent for making arrangements and a fondness for carrying them out. He is clearly a workaholic, with a great capacity for juggling a variety of concerns and projects, both personal and professional.

This recognition of the way in which the person and personality of Buckley bestrides the book leads to the real and dominant theme of the book: companionship. Companionship is something more than mere friendship, however close: it is the friendship of those engaged in a common duty or exploit. Companions are, almost by definition, compatible, and it is compatibility that Buckley sought first and above all in the planning of both the 1975 and 1980 voyages. His desire to have a professional photographer aboard was qualified by his concern that the chosen photographer fit in well with the other members of the enterprise; in the event, Buckley believed that he had made a good choice.

In the memo that Buckley wrote in an attempt to promote the idea of a documentary film, he called the enterprise "a venture in companionship at sea," and this, more than the sea or sailing or adventure or even simple escapism, is what the book is all about. In his prologue, Buckley makes this theme even more explicit: "It is required that you have aboard companions who take, and give, pleasure from refractions of every kind. Without them we lose what the social scientists so regrettably term 'the interfaces.' My conviction . . . is that the entirety of the experience grows out of the sea and the shared experience, the operative word here being 'shared.'"

The attention that Buckley devoted to the mixing of personalities paid off. All those aboard, at least in relation to the group in which they find themselves, are clubbable men. Some, as Buckley points out, are clearly helpers, and some are helpees. Each has individual personal concerns; each has particular strengths or talents valuable to the group. All are comfortable in one another's company, sharing a delight in the sea and in the give-and-take of close living.

Atlantic High, then, is an entertaining if undemanding work that is less about the sea and sailing than one might expect from the cover photo and jacket blurb. If one demands from books with such covers a sense of the romance and beauty of the sea, one will find it in *Atlantic High* more in the photographs than in the text.

Gordon N. Bergquist

Sources for Further Study

Booklist. LXXVIII, August, 1982, p. 1484.
Los Angeles Times Book Review. September 12, 1982, p. 2.

National Review. XXXIV, October 15, 1982, p. 1291.
The New York Times Book Review. LXXXVII, August 5, 1982, p. 6.
Publishers Weekly. CCXXII, July 16, 1982, p. 68.
Time. CXX, October 25, 1982, p. 82.
The Wall Street Journal. September 23, 1982, p. 34.

AUNT JULIA AND THE SCRIPTWRITER

Author: Mario Vargas Llosa (1936-   )
Translated from the Spanish by Helen R. Lane
Publisher: Farrar, Straus and Giroux (New York). 374 pp. $16.50
Type of work: Novel
Time: Several months in 1954
Locale: Lima, Peru

A deceptively realistic fiction in which an autobiographical episode serves as a pretext to write a story about how and why a writer writes

> *Principal characters:*
> MARITO OR VARGUITAS, an eighteen-year-old would-be writer
> AUNT JULIA, thirty-two years old, his "aunt" by marriage and his wife-to-be
> PEDRO CAMACHO, a successful, prolific, soap-opera scriptwriter
> JAVIER, Marito's friend and a literary critic
> PASCUAL, a member of the editorial staff at Radio Panamericana, where Marito and Pedro are employed

For about twenty years, the dreadful announcement that "the novel is dead" has been made with monotonous regularity, yet the corpse seems to be in good health, at least in Latin American narrative. A number of Latin American novelists—Mario Vargas Llosa prominent among them— have employed the self-conscious devices of metafiction in such a vital way that what in other writers is merely clever contrivance becomes, in their hands, humane, sympathetic, even humorous, appealing to the senses, the emotions, and the intellect alike.

Vargas Llosa's *Aunt Julia and the Scriptwriter* is unquestionably a metafiction—a fiction about fiction—and yet, like many contemporary Latin American novels, it escapes from the dead-end in which so many works in that genre are trapped. If literature has exhausted its possibilities so that it has to turn to itself to find a subject, Latin American writers still have the power to make of that very exhaustion a vehicle for an adventure of the human intellect, a means to tell a story. This has been the primary end of fiction from time immemorial, and now, even as the death of the novel is being proclaimed, Latin American writers show that they are still, above all, storytellers.

Aunt Julia and the Scriptwriter is divided into twenty chapters, of which the odd ones tell the autobiographical story of Marito while the even chapters narrate episodes of soap operas written, performed, and directed by Pedro Camacho, Marito's fellow-employee at Radio Panamericana. These two narrative planes are merged subtly and skillfully, so that the "real" reality—the story of Marito, based on the experience of the youthful Vargas Llosa—is constantly pervaded by the fiction, while the fictive reality of the soap-opera writer is invaded by the reality of Vargas Llosa's own life. This effective handling of the literary materials is part of the narrative, and the novel thus becomes an overt statement of the author's "literary ideology": the rigid organizational scheme on which the novel is based—that of a separation of life from fiction by devoting different chapters to each—is defeated by the novel's "literary logic." That is, literary language and techniques transform whatever they touch into a new dimension of reality, the fictive. Whether the subject matter of fiction is reality or dream, truth or lie makes no difference; once it falls within the limits of literary conventions, it is, inexorably, fiction.

Vargas Llosa's literary output comprises several novels, some of which have been translated into English. They include *La Ciudad y los perros* (1963; *The Time of the Hero*, 1966), *La Casa Verde* (1966; *The Green House*, 1968), and *Conversacion en la catedral* (1969; *Conversation in the Cathedral*, 1975). *Los Cachorros* (1976) and *Los Jefes* (1959) have appeared in translation combined under the title *The Cubs and Other Stories* (1979). Vargas Llosa—one of the chief figures in what has been termed the "boom" of Latin American narrative—is not only a novelist but also an essayist, scriptwriter, journalist, and literary critic whose work reveals a permanent concern with the means by which fiction can reflect reality. He concludes that fiction cannot give an image of reality by "direct enunciation" but by "transposition." This transposition or transference can be defined as the act by which fiction transforms, re-creates, and manipulates reality in order for it to become proper literary subject matter—fictional reality. In most of Vargas Llosa's novels, this transposition takes the form of various technical devices such as multiple narrative perspectives and interpolation of objective dialogue into interior monologues. These innovative techniques illustrate Vargas Llosa's permanent, almost obsessive concern for objectivity in the best Flaubertian style.

Aunt Julia and the Scriptwriter exhibits only some of these complexities, and the experienced Vargas Llosa reader may even be surprised at its simplicity. The linear narrative of the odd chapters recounts the romantic relationship that develops between Marito, a young aspiring writer, and Julia, a Bolivian divorcée, sister-in-law to one of Marito's many uncles. Certain that the family will raise havoc if they learn of the affair, they keep their romance clandestine, thus adding flavor to it, but, finally, they elope and get married. This episode drawn from Vargas Llosa's own life constitutes the main narrative line, and the other themes are woven around and into it—Marito's wish to become a writer, his attempts at writing stories, the cultural atmosphere of Lima in the 1950's, the story of Pedro Camacho and his subliterature, and some minor incidents and subplots. The simplicity of the language and the narrative technique, together with the smooth flow of the authorial voice, counterpoint the atrocious episodes of the soap operas, which include incidents of rape, incest, violent death, and several forms of perverse behavior. The contrast in language between Marito's narrative and the serials of Pedro

Camacho is also noticeable: in the soap-opera chapters, Vargas Llosa's language becomes ornate, cheaply fiery, full of clichés, and minutely descriptive.

These subtle distinctions behind the more overt ones and the unobtrusive way in which the two narrative strands draw together and finally merge, constitute the core of the novel, the real tale it tells. The gradual approximation of the different narrative levels until they finally and efficiently interact is made possible by what Vargas Llosa calls the technique of the *vasos comunicantes*: when the multiple and simultaneous structures fuse in a single reality, each brings to the narrative its own tensions, its own emotions, its own life-quality, so that they affect and transform one another. The originality of *Aunt Julia and the Scriptwriter* lies not merely in the use of converging narratives but also in Vargas Llosa's foregrounding of the device.

Analyzing this characteristic interplay between different levels of reality in several of Vargas Llosa's earlier novels, the critic José Miguel Oviedo has coined the term "dialogue-waves"—an excellent descriptive term for the movement back and forth, the action and reaction of the different realities. Though these "dialogue-waves" are not as complex in *Aunt Julia and the Scriptwriter* as they are in other Vargas Llosa novels, they appear simpler than they really are.

On the plane of the interaction between the two stories, the autobiographical and the fictional, Marito learns of Pedro Camacho the same day he meets Aunt Julia, so that the real and the fictive join and constitute a single narrative line. Julia herself says of their love affair that it is "A perfect subject for one of Pedro Camacho's serials." Finally, during their pilgrimage around Lima to find a mayor willing to marry them despite the fact that the groom is under age, Marito has a dream in which he finds himself "living through one of Pedro Camacho's recent catastrophes." These and other details are comments on the relative reality of life and of fiction: Pedro Camacho's serials are almost unbelievable in their complexity and absurdity, yet the reader is told that the autobiographical episode could be a proper subject for one of Camacho's soap operas. The logical conclusion is that life is also complex and absurd, that an individual life is but a story that a person creates for himself and for others.

In this regard, the novel provides an incident that in its humor and humanity is more telling and appealing than all theoretical explanations. When Marito needs money to get married, he goes to Genaro, Jr.—one of the owners of the radio station for which he works—with the following story: "I had sworn that I needed the money urgently to pay for a hernia operation my granny had to have, a plea that had left him unmoved. But then he suddenly said: 'All right, I'll give you the advance,' and then added with a friendly smile: 'But admit that it's to pay for your girlfriend's abortion.' I lowered my eyes and begged him not to give my secret away." In a sense, both stories are make-believe. In another, deeper sense, both are true because both are real acts of the imagination, true in their own terms, responding to a wider story, a frame story: life itself. Marito's tale suits his need for an explanation appropriate to the character he believes Genaro to be. Genaro's tale is his way of interpreting reality so as to make sense of it. Both are inventions, not lies.

The awareness that the relation between life and literature cannot be reduced to imitation, reflection, or objective representation but that it is of a more intimate nature, leads to an insight into another reality: the reality of the act of writing that Vargas Llosa develops along two intersecting lines—the story of his own attempts to write stories and the story of his creation, the scriptwriter, writing stories. While the "serious" aspiring writer Marito regards the transformation and re-creation of reality as a difficult task, an almost sacred undertaking the seriousness of which inhibits creation, the pseudowriter Camacho disposes of reality with an inexhaustible store of conventions and clichés—for him infallible devices that make creation possible and abundant.

Camacho is a parody of the novelist, and his portrayal gives Vargas Llosa an opportunity to mock the ambitions of realism in general and of his own realism in particular. Camacho says, "I write about life, and the impact of reality is crucial to my work." Later he adds, "I work from life; my writings are firmly rooted in reality," and "What is most important is the truth, which is always art, as lies, on the other hand, never are." An echo of these words is heard in the last pages of the novel, when Vargas Llosa tells of his own obsession with the idea that fiction should be realistic.

Camacho's obsession with reality and realism causes him to buy a map of Lima to locate his radio serials in the proper district according to subject. He also keeps "socio-psychologico-racial cards," uses names befitting his characters' statuses and professions, and wears, as he writes, disguises to fit the characters he is describing so as to identify "materially" with reality. How is it, then, that despite his immersion in reality, the melodramas he produces are but tragicomic caricatures of reality? How is one to account for the final mental collapse that causes him to lose track of his characters in the different stories until they all appear in a final bizarre parade of obsessive perversions? In the end, the fantasies he invents distort his life, but they also reflect the aberrations that haunt him. The split in his personality becomes obvious: the asceticism of his personal life is opposed by a morbid treatment of reality in his fiction. All his efforts to write "realistically" are to no avail; his own "demons"—as Vargas Llosa would call them—transform and deform reality.

Another detail deserves mention. The title of one of the stories Marito cannot write is "The Qualitative Leap." In Vargas Llosa's literary theory, this leap means the passage from a concrete, objective, verifiable reality to a fantastic, symbolic, oneiric one, a new dimension of reality beyond the objective and the subjective. The reader is discreetly led by the novelist from one dimension to the other until he crosses the mysterious boundary between both and accepts the marvelous as real, the incredible as credible. Camacho, a caricature of the novelist, fails; swallowed by his demons, he leaps into the chaos of his subjective reality. The true novelist—Vargas Llosa in this case— is driven by his demons but subjects them to the control of his art.

Olga Liberti de Barrio

Sources for Further Study

America. CXLVII, October 23, 1982, p. 237.
Christian Science Monitor. September 10, 1982, p. B3.
Library Journal. CVII, July, 1982, p. 1347.
Los Angeles Times Book Review. August 22, 1982, p. 1.
Nation. CCXXXVII, September 25, 1982, p. 281.
National Review. XXXIV, December 10, 1982, p. 1559.
The New Republic. CLXXXVII, August 16, 1982, p. 38.
The New York Times Book Review. LXXXVII, August 1, 1982, p. 1.
Newsweek. C, August 30, 1982, p. 65.
Time. CXX, August 9, 1982, p. 70.

AUTUMN

Author: A. G. Mojtabai (1938-   )
Publisher: Houghton Mifflin Company (Boston). 140 pp. $9.95
Type of work: Novel
Time: The present
Locale: A Maine coastal town

This short novel expresses the consciousness of a sixty-six-year-old man, a recent widower, in his confrontation with loneliness and its alternatives as autumn approaches in a summer resort town

> *Principal characters:*
> WILL ROSS, a retired accountant
> LIL HARMON, Will's friend, a widow
> DAVEY, Will's son, who telephones long distance
> A BOY, whom Will discovers asleep in a tree house

The main character of A. G. Mojtabai's fourth novel is an unusual protagonist. Aging heroes in literature are not new; one need only recall Sophocles' *Oedipus at Colonus* (401 B.C.), William Shakespeare's *King Lear* (1605), and the first great novel, *Don Quixote de la Mancha* (1605, 1615), by Miguel de Cervantes. Modern novels such as Ernest Hemingway's *The Old Man and the Sea* (1952) and Saul Bellow's *Mr. Sammler's Planet* (1970) continue to attest to the endurance and determination of old age. These books are likely to be regarded as inspirational by the young but perhaps contribute also to their impatience with the unheroic elderly who are more likely a part of their own experience. It is pleasant to think that one might develop into a grizzled hero, but clearly the older generation at hand does not often furnish authentic heroes.

A number of modern novels have as central characters older men and women who, far from striving for achievements of the sort usually reserved for the young, like Miguel de Cervantes' Don Quixote or Alfred, Lord Tennyson's Ulysses, resemble those more or less passive and exhausted characters who frequently helped fill in the background of earlier novels and added perhaps a spice of eccentricity. Now they step forward as leading, and often viewpoint, characters. Whereas Cervantes' and Hemingway's old men magnificently resisted their physical decline, older protagonists now are increasingly likely to occupy themselves with the more mundane business of coping and adjusting. Thus, the heroine of Angus Wilson's *Late Call* (1964) must endure the folly and then the death of her husband, take up residence in her son's deeply divided family, and accommodate herself to an alien suburban way of life. In James Gould Cozzens' *Morning, Noon and Night* (1968), a corporation president adjusts to reduce vitality and accomplishment. In May Sarton's *As We Are Now* (1973), a sensitive and intelligent woman endures confinement in a rural nursing home.

Will Ross, the protagonist of *Autumn*, is neither heroic questioner nor patient sufferer. A retired accountant of thrifty habits, he has secured the means to winter in Florida with the rest of the summer residents of the Maine seacoast, but chooses instead to remain in his summer cottage. Will's wife, Helen, is five months dead, and his son, Davey, has long since established his own family at a distance. Although Will frets about his health, his physician can find nothing to suggest that Will should relinquish his independent life-style. With quixotic disdain, Will rejects the role of typical senior citizen with its rounds of bingo and community sings.

Beyond braving the rugged winter weather and mitigating his loneliness, however, Will's challenge consists of little more than coping with the unambitious regimen he has set for himself: a daily bus trip to town for groceries, sessions on park benches with newpapers, and migration between the only two rooms of his house he wishes to inhabit. In his kitchen, he eats cheap prepared food out of tins and listens to the radio; in his bedroom, he spends largely sleepless nights. This old man's relationship with the sea begins and ends with daily observation.

The author has taken on the formidable challenge of presenting not only the viewpoint but also the consciousness of an essentially dull man with nothing to do. From the start, the reader is Will's confidant, but his confidences are laconic, elliptical, utterly commonplace: "I'm famished. . . . Can't taste anything. . . . Not a speck left." He took up accounting, he reveals, because he had no way with words. The task ahead of him is, in Robert Frost's words, "what to make of a diminished thing," but he seems disinclined to make much at all of his diminished life.

In the first of the three parts of the novel, he visits the grocery store, his physician, a restaurant, and the house of his comfortable widow friend, but he rejects involvement. The titles of the six chapters in the second part indicate the outcome of his choice of life-style: "Night," "Sunday," "Living Room," "Afternoon," "Evening," and "Fighting the Blues." He has not fallen from any great height, but he has nevertheless reached his nadir.

Although Will's imagination is wholly unliterary, he is living out his version of an American myth, his kindred spirits being all those socially inept and graceless individuals who, like Natty Bumppo, Captain Ahab, and Huckleberry Finn, scorn the social order and its amenities and prefer to go it alone or in the company of savages and pariahs. Lil Harmon stands ready to envelop him in domesticity, but Will's repugnance for "the pretty touches, those odds and ends, little glassies, doodads" of her home is pure Huck Finn. He avoids his own living room less because it reminds him of his wife than because it exudes her own brand of domesticity. Because he is fifty years older than Huck, he affects admiration for these womanly arts, but he betrays his real feeling in a simile: "cunning as spiders, they are."

At the beginning of part 3, a storm gives Will the opportunity to indulge his Natty-Huck-Ahab propensities. Unable to reach him on the telephone, Lil dispatches a repairman to his house. After determining that everything is in working order, the repairman notices the tree house Will's son built years ago in a pine tree in the yard and advises him to remove it as dangerous. Will curtly refuses this advice, for the solitary weathering of storms and the boy's unused tree house mark precisely the limits of the romance in Will's life. (His perfunctory courtship of Lil had been fumbling and ineffectual.) What he has just experienced and is now guarding from the world is an adventure in that tree house.

Davey is now thirty-six and has lost all interest in the tree house; his periodic long-distance calls to his father invariably end in arguments. For Will, how-ever, the tree house signifies their earlier, simpler relationship. When he decides to climb the fifty-foot ladder and visit the tree house, he confesses that he has not been up there "in a year or more." To Will, that is obviously a long time, but hardly to the reader—unless one takes into account that Will is an American primitive, a rugged individualist who, while contemptuous of social climbing, does not retire early from tree-climbing. After all, Natty Bumppo was tramping around the Western prairies at the age of eighty.

What Will has found—and left—in the tree house is a sleeping teenage boy, and when the repairman calls, Will wants nothing more than to get back and discover whether the boy is still there. Will's subsequent vigil over the still-sleeping boy is the climax of the book and his only approach to com-munion, the profundity of which it is left to the reader to measure. The boy attracts Will as no powdered and perfumed widow can. Although he is pre-sumably about the same age as Davey was when he built the lofty refuge, what draws Will most powerfully to him is that he is a runaway—in short, a Huckleberry Finn, a young noble savage unable to come to terms with society.

Mojtabai's interest in the psychology of aging and her sympathy for elders has previously informed her portraits of Dr. Alkavist, the founder of a sci-entific summer school in *The 400 Eels of Sigmund Freud* (1976), and of James Nirmal Roy, who in her last novel, *A Stopping Place* (1979), comes out of retirement to direct the search for a missing Muslim relic in a border city between Pakistan and India. Both of these novels, however, have a more conventional story to tell, with Alkavist seen from the point of view of the students and Roy sharing the spotlight of Mojtabai's omniscience with two other characters. *Autumn* also differs from her other novels in its stripping away of all evidences of the author's considerable intellectuality. She has risked flatness and even dullness for the sake of an intense focus on a common-place character who does not recognize and cannot analyze his own vague romantic aspirations.

Much more than these earlier novels, however, *Autumn* aspires to, and achieves, lyricism. Not permitted eloquence, Will reports un-self-consciously on the sights and sounds he takes in from his park bench: the town derelict with "socks dripping down loose around his ankles," the pigeons around his feet, "necks jiggling like ninety-year-olds," a passing black girl with "hair, all electric, standing up all over the place!" The reader feels acutely Will's terror when the girl mistakenly thinks that he, rather than the derelict, has directed a remark at her; the reader shares his frustration at being a member of a barely tolerated generation: "We're slow, we're clumsy, we clog the way." Staying out of the way, Will finds no compensation in his role as spectator of life: "I pass by like a shadow."

At home, within sight of the sea, Will waxes as poetic as his circumstances permit. "Broody weather: there's something afoot," he muses. "It's something in the speed and the shape of the waves, the way they're bent over. They're hurrying and they're crouched." On another occasion: "It's bleary out. Kind of bleak, air's kind of raw. The sea's gray this morning, the water clouded, color of flint or gun metal—or darker, the metal of bells." The lyrical high point is his sojourn with the boy in the swaying tree house: "How dark it is. My eyes so heavy arms so heavy hands so full they cannot hold. Touch me. Why is your hair so cold?"

Mojtabai's exclusive use of the simple present tense contributes to the immediacy of her portrait, as do her short chapters, averaging only five pages, which reduce to a minimum the necessity of generalizing time and forestall the exhaustion of Will's consciousness. The moments of less than a week's days and nights establish the parameters of his life.

"So many stories for growing up, and none for growing down," Will complains in an unavailing search for something to read. Is *Autumn* a book for "growing down"? It is a novel that will neither inspire nor console most people of Will's age, while younger readers may well find it unpleasantly prophetic. Its most appreciative audiences are likely to be readers of poetry and students of aging, for whom Will's unfocused but nevertheless fierce resistance to conventional gerontological wisdom may prove enlightening. Will has had sixty-six years in which to grow stubborn—that is, in which to become thoroughly himself, and although that self seems meager enough, Mojtabai has labored to make it an authentic self. Except for poets and painters, people with the leisure to know themselves and to look at the sea are those without any realizable ambitions to give tone and poise to their observations. Mojtabai has smuggled elements of the poet into a representative of that growing class of retired persons who have provided for themselves financially but not spiritually and so must choose between regimentation and any available residue of rugged individualism.

Will is in his autumn, a kind of suspended animation short of the "cold light" of the winter described in Archibald MacLeish's "Winter Is Another Country," a poem which the author has quoted as a preface. What would Will Ross's state be in another ten or fifteen years? Would his winter bring enlightenment? Would the recollection of the tree house adventure deepen his grasp on life or only his isolation?

Mojtabai has resisted the writing of easy, popular novels, and her fiction to date has occasioned more sincere but superficial praise than sustained critical attention. If she never writes the best-seller that, even in critical and academic circles, is often necessary to rescue a writer from comparative obscurity, it seems likely that the variety, craft, and intelligence of her work will still earn for her a respected place among later twentieth century novelists.

Robert P. Ellis

Sources for Further Study

Booklist. LXXVIII, July, 1982, p. 1423.
Library Journal. CVII, June 1, 1982, p. 1113.
Maclean's. XCV, September 6, 1982, p. 50.
The New York Times Book Review. LXXXVII, August 8, 1982, p. 1.
Newsweek. LVIII, September 6, 1982, p. 106.
Publishers Weekly. CCXXII, June 4, 1982, p. 60.

A BARTHES READER

Author: Roland Barthes (1915-1980)
Edited, with an introduction, by Susan Sontag
Publisher: Hill and Wang (New York). 495 pp. $20.00
Type of work: Essays

A selection spanning Barthes's oeuvre and comprising meditations on a great variety of subjects, including literature, film, and photography

At the time of his death in early 1980, Roland Barthes was undoubtedly the best-known French intellectual of his day and perhaps even the most highly regarded critic and theorist working within the confines of Western literary culture. A prolific writer whose favored form was the essay, Barthes differed from almost all of his predecessors as well as from most of his contemporaries in that he did not so much explore the writings of others as the processes of reading and writing themselves. Both his formulation of new principles for the reading of literature and his rejection of older notions of literary understanding are articulated in a manner which unites the best in critical and creative writing, the result being that the reader finds his mind enlivened at the same time as many of his, perhaps cherished, ideas are challenged.

Barthes did not attempt to build a theoretical system or to formulate principles which can be codified into a rigid approach to literature. Each of his successive texts can be regarded as a departure from the previous one rather than as an attempt at refining and consolidating previously advanced arguments. His work is not, however, lacking in internal consistency; it is possible to point to the presence of considerable unity while recognizing that fundamental differences exist, for example, between the earlier "Structuralist" and the later "post-Structuralist" stages of his literary production.

Barthes's intellectual development was late by modern standards. Born in 1915, he became ill with tuberculosis in 1934 and lived in sanatoriums several times during the next thirteen years. Profoundly influenced by Sartrean existentialism, he abhorred the essentialism of bourgeois culture. In his first book, the polemical *Le degré zéro de l'écriture* (1953; *Writing Degree Zero*, 1972) he consequently attacked established academic literary criticism, which he regarded as ahistorical and psychologically naïve, the work of scholars who were unwilling to acknowledge that their writings were founded on a certain ideology and who refused to accept the possibility that a text might have more than one correct meaning. Barthes rejected the established normative criticism, showing an interest not so much in the significance of individual works as in the process of signification itself.

Barthes's concern with the signifying process led him to perform a series of detailed analyses of various "languages," such as those of magazine illustrations, advertisements, newspaper articles, and films. The results of his studies are detailed in *Mythologies* (1957; English trans., 1972), where Barthes explains his conception of a structure of double-functioning in sign systems; one signification has the ability to generate a second one. Barthes treats myth, which in this context should not be confused with the kind of stories that are studied by anthropologists and folklorists, as a second-order signifying system where a linguistic or other cultural sign functions as a signifier to which a second signified attaches itself, thus producing the mythic sign. Barthes distrusts myth, for unlike the system of language, the system of myth does not generate its own meaning. History supplies the meaning which is embedded in myth, but—because the signifier in the mythical system is also a signified in a first-order signifying system and thus carries a certain meaning of its own in that capacity—the consumer of myth, while sensing this first-order meaning, will be inclined not to notice that the meaning of the myth (the second-order meaning) is dependent on somebody's intention. The message of the myth will therefore be taken as natural and true rather than as culturally determined. As most of the myths Barthes was dealing with were created by and served the interests of the bourgeoisie, *Mythologies* can be viewed as representing a further development of the antibourgeois stance manifested in *Writing Degree Zero*.

Barthes's reputation grew steadily during the 1960's, when he came to be regarded as one of the foremost members of the French structuralist movement. It is important to note, however, that he was never exclusively a structuralist; his intellectual interests were too broad to permit him to affiliate himself with one particular school. It is nevertheless appropriate to speak of a Structuralist phase in his work. The most important texts from this period are two essays and a book, "L'activité structuraliste" ("The Structuralist Activity"), *Éléments de semiologie* (1964; *Elements of Semiology*, 1967), and "L'Introduction à l'analyse structurale des récits" ("Introduction to the Structural Analysis of Narrative.")

"The Structuralist Activity," which regrettably was excluded from *A Barthes Reader* by its editor, Susan Sontag, is a brief, abstract, and frequently anthologized statement of what Structuralism is. It is neither a school nor a movement, Barthes says, but rather an activity: namely, man's attempt at discovering how meaning is generated. Inspired by the structural linguistics of Ferdinand de Saussure, the Structuralist dissects his object in order to identify those units which are capable of carrying meaning, after which he attempts to make manifest the rules by which these units function. This process entails the construction of a structure which is actually a simulacrum of the object which is being studied. The simulacrum thus constructed is not identical to the object itself, however, but shows how man has given meaning to that portion of his world which the object represents. In the final analysis, the object of Structuralist study thus becomes not the world as such but the processes by which man endows his world with meaning.

In his book *Elements of Semiology*, Barthes conducts a thorough theoretical investigation into the nature and possibilitites of a semiological science. The book demonstrates his dependence on Saussure for his basic model and conceptual vocabulary, but Barthes is original in his application of Saussure's concepts to signifying systems other than language, such as food and dress. Literary semiology, however, is not specifically dealt with until the essay "Introduction to the Structural Analysis of Narratives," which Barthes wrote as a preface to a special issue of the journal *Communications* in 1966 and the complete text of which has been included in *A Barthes Reader*. This essay has come to be regarded as one of the canonical texts of literary Structuralism.

The essay constitutes an indispensable contribution to literary Structuralism, as Barthes sketches a theory of narrative structure based on the linguistic model. The individual narrative can be treated as a large sentence, so that one may speak of narrative subjects and verbs. A central point of Barthes's theory is the idea that a narrative may be described on several levels: that of the narrative functions, or pieces of narrative which exist as correlates to other pieces of narrative; that of the actants, or characters as described by what they do; and the level of narration itself. The reader or listener understands a story not only by following it sequentially, or from beginning to end, but also by moving back and forth between the various narrative levels as the story unfolds. The greater portion of the essay is devoted to a detailed analysis and classification of the elements which are at play on each of these narrative levels. Barthes maintains that each level stands in a hierarchical relationship to the next level, and that the various elements on one level carry meaning not only because of their relationship to other elements on the same level, but also because they are integrated into a superior level. The highest level, that of narration, receives its meaning from the world, those other sign systems whose elements are other substances, as, for example, historical facts. The level of narration consequently serves as a diaphragm which closes off the narration, thus giving it a certain amount of unity, at the same time as the narration is brought into contact with the world and its systems of production and consumption.

It would therefore be a mistake to think of Barthes as a Formalist who removes his object of study from the domain of history. It is the case, however, that structural analysis of literature has tended to focus on the text itself, thus bypassing both the problems which are associated with the figure of the author and other concerns which are exterior to the text. Barthes's Structuralist phase came to an end in 1968, when he published another landmark essay entitled "La Mort de l'auteur" ("The Death of the Author"). Although Sontag did not include this pivotal essay in *A Barthes Reader*, she states in a prefatory note that she regrets the omission.

"The Death of the Author" marks Barthes's transition into what could be called his post-Structuralist phase. Like his countryman Jacques Derrida, he argues for a definition of writing that detaches the text from the figure of the author, which traditionally has been regarded as the guarantor of the text's meaning. Writing is, on the contrary, the destruction of every identifiable voice and every fixed point of origin, says Barthes; the text is orphaned in the sense that it is cut off from any fixed and generating consciousness. Rather than focusing attention on the author, Barthes prefers to locate the meaning of the text in the reader, who, however, is no more a fixed consciousness than the author. The real meaning of a text is to be found in its language, which is a textual field without beginning or end, and the reader is simply that function in the text which holds its various strands together. A text is nothing but the sum of a number of quotations from and relations to other texts. Barthes thus establishes the two cardinal post-Structuralist principles of textuality and intertextuality.

These two principles serve as a foundation for the final stage in Barthes's thought, that of his erotics of literature. The central texts relative to this development are *Le Plaisir de texte* (1973; *The Pleasure of the Text*, 1976), *Roland Barthes par Roland Barthes* (1975; *Roland Barthes by Roland Barthes*, 1977), and *Fragments d'un discours amoureux* (1977; *A Lover's Discourse: Fragments*, 1979). First, Barthes reiterates the idea that the principle of intertextuality extends to the selves of authors, readers, and critics, the result being that the human cogito has to be regarded as a sum of relations, influences, and codes, much as a piece of literature is thus composed. In the guise of an autobiography, *Roland Barthes by Roland Barthes* is an extended exercise in such a decomposition or deconstruction of the self. The highest form of interaction between mind and text, however, is found when the reader and the text interact in a manner which is similar to the sexual embrace of love, resulting in what Barthes designates with the French word *jouissance*. Literally translated as a full and satisfying pleasure, Barthes uses the word to reflect a literary experience which is analogous to the pleasure of an extended sexual climax. This is possible precisely because both mind and text are unbounded; in both, there is an absence of the final signified, which makes possible endless active interpretation. In a section of *The Pleasure of the Text*, Barthes terms the reader who is able to experience the text thus a hysteric, as opposed to obsessive, fetishistic, and paranoid readers, and *A Lover's Discourse* is a successful attempt at creating a monument to "hysterical" discourse.

What above all characterizes Barthes's work is his sense of intellectual adventure. Indeed, his latest work, cut off before fruition by his accidental death (he was struck by a van while crossing a street), gave evidence of yet another unpredictable metamorphosis—this time in the direction of mimesis, scorned by Structuralists and post-Structuralists alike. As a critic and a theorist, as a writer too protean to be comfortable with any theory, he created a legacy which undoubtedly will be a benefit to thoughtful people everywhere for generations to come. *A Barthes Reader* contains a representative selection from the texts which constitute that legacy.

Jan Sjåvik

Sources for Further Study

Commonweal. CIX, December 3, 1982, p. 666.
Library Journal. CVII, August, 1982, p. 1463.
Los Angeles Times Book Review. September 5, 1982, p. 3.
Nation. CCXXXV, November 20, 1982, p. 525.
The New Republic. CLXXXVII, october 11, 1982, p. 27.
The New York Times Book Review. LXXXVII, September 12, 1982, p. 1.
Newsweek. C, October 11, 1982, p. 106.
Publishers Weekly. CCXXI, June 11, 1982, p. 55.
Times Literary Supplement. December 10, 1982, p. 1372.

BAUDELAIRE THE DAMNED
A Biography

Author: F. W. J. Hemmings (1920-   )
Publisher: Charles Scribner's Sons (New York). 251 pp. $17.95
Type of work: Literary biography
Time: 1821-1867
Locale: France

In this important biography of the great nineteenth century French poet, critic, and translator, the sources of Baudelaire's malaise are traced to his complex relationship with his mother and to his tenaciously held notion of suffering from the curse of damnation

> *Principal personages:*
> CHARLES BAUDELAIRE, a French poet and critic
> CAROLINE ARCHENBAUT DEFAYIS AUPICK, the poet's mother
> JOSEPH-FRANÇOIS BAUDELAIRE, the poet's father
> JACQUES AUPICK, Caroline's second husband
> JEANNE DUVAL, the poet's mistress
> APOLLONIE SABATIER, another of the poet's lovers
> NARCISSE-DÉSIRÉ ANCELLE, the notary charged with administering
> the poet's fortune

F. W. J. Hemmings' title is not intended to be provocatively sensational, nor is it pejorative. The author's thesis is that Charles Baudelaire (1821-1867) believed himself to be—taking the precise sense of the word—damned. In a letter to his mother, Caroline Archenbaut Defayis Aupick, on December 4, 1854, the poet expressed this conviction succinctly: "In short, I believe that my life has been *damned* from the beginning, and that it is damned for ever" [Baudelaire's italics]. Hemmings argues that Baudelaire not only accepted as a demonstrable fact the curse of his "damnation," but also believed that his art was deeply influenced by a consciousness of doom. According to Hemmings, Baudelaire frequently uses the word "damnation" and its cognates to describe his condition, evidencing the circumstances of his own life as proof that he had been condemned—damned—while still on the earth.

In this masterful biography, Hemmings provides for the reader carefully selected patterns of events in Baudelaire's life to illuminate some of the dark areas in the French poet's psychology. Essentially a study of Baudelaire's mind rather than of his art, Hemmings' book, although not ignoring aesthetics, concentrates on two basic themes, often interwoven: that of Baudelaire's preoccupation with questions of election and damnation; and that of his mother's powerful impact upon his self-image of failure. These themes, sharply elaborated, form the pattern of a depressive personality. In nineteenth century language, Baudelaire's psychological state would have been called "morbid." Hemmings avoids judgmental terms. Instead, with compassion moderated by a sound understanding of human behavior, he shows how the poet allowed his own self-fulfilling curse of damnation to shape a life that was, though wretched by almost all materialistic standards, not without compensating artistic glory.

To be sure, other commentators have also been aware of Baudelaire's obsession with damnation. Jean-Paul Sartre interprets the poet's life-pattern as the result of conscious choice—indeed, existential choice—from options that might as well have provided other, more satisfactory results. Sartre notes that Baudelaire's selection was deliberate, urged by his deepest needs, and even when the poet failed to make choices, his passivity contributed to formulating a certain destiny. Hemmings goes beyond the observation of Sartre and other critics, to show that Baudelaire feared that his damnation was predestined. From his father's supposed sins (chief among them, from a Catholic point of view, his failure to abide by an early vow to remain a priest), Baudelaire may have assumed that the father's curse would fall as well upon the son. Hemmings points to the fact that the poet's father, François Baudelaire, had once worn a priest's cassock and that Charles habitually referred to himself as "the son of a priest." Not only was the poet suspicious of his father's conduct as a cause for damnation, but he also feared that his mother shared in the blame because she had consented to marry a former priest. In Hemmings' view, Baudelaire probably rationalized that the curse of misery which darkened his existence had originated with his parents' sins. Since he could not change the circumstances of his birth, the writer was bound to suffer the consequences of unatoned guilt.

A second theme of the biography, one that Hemmings treats as subordinate to that of Baudelaire's "damnation," is the impact of Caroline Aupick upon her son's behavior. Without question, this strong-willed, capricious, intelligent, parsimonious, ambitious woman influenced Baudelaire's personality perhaps more for evil than good. Yet Caroline was not without virtues. Although she was reticent in showing her affection, she loved her son dearly and brooded over his wayward progress, alternately cajoling and hectoring him. Baudelaire wrote letters of complaint, supplication, and confession to her, clearly valuing her good opinion, respecting her intelligence, and deferring to her system of values, though he would not—or could not—conform to them. Chief among Caroline's faults, both from Baudelaire's and an objective reader's point of view, was her narrow materialism. An attractive, ambitious woman in her youth, Caroline advanced her social position through two prudent marriages. Her first, to Baudelaire's father, who was thirty-four years her senior, lasted eight years, until his death from cancer. She was left with a six-year-old son and a comfortable but modest estate. Her second marriage, to Captain—later General—Jacques Aupick, provided much greater financial security. Although young Baudelaire never had a loving relationship with his stepfather, Aupick treated the child kindly, looked after his well-being, and tried to serve as a dignified role model during the youngster's troubled adolescent years. In turn, Baudelaire learned to respect his stepfather, but with cool reserve.

At the heart of Baudelaire's rebelliousness toward all types of authority was a chagrin that no one could appreciate his uniqueness. He insisted upon maintaining a special identity, no matter what it cost in social ostracism. To this end, in his early manhood he affected to wear flamboyant costumes that would mark him as a dandy. Although scrupulously clean and tidy, he roved the Bohemian underworld of Paris, choosing for his friends prostitutes as well as artists, opium addicts as well as people of culture. Of his lovers, the mulatto Jeanne Duval served as his source of both pain and joy, a scourge for his masochistic spirit and a companion whom he could treat as a social, if not sexual, equal. As Hemmings makes clear, Baudelaire's relationship with Jeanne was never exploitative on his side; in repayment for the meager sexual solace she could provide him, he offered loyalty and what little money he could afford. Years after she had separated from him, when, quite sick, she had lost her beauty, Baudelaire still cared enough for her to try to provide for her after his death. In this endeavor, however, as in many others, his mother frustrated him, refusing to honor her son's deathbed request to set aside a small allowance for his former mistress. Thus, from his youth to his last years, Baudelaire had to contend with parental disapproval.

In Hemmings' account, the relationship between mother and son was one of "truly monstrous morbidity." No matter how strong their seeming antipathies, they never remained out of touch with each other for long periods of time. Caroline kept all or most of Baudelaire's correspondence and, according to the biographer, "this series of 360 letters not only represents the fullest single source of information available to us concerning the wretched tribulations of his day-to-day existence, but in addition provides the elements of a case history, possibly unique in the literature of psychology." Hemmings does not probe deeply into this psychological aberration, but he offers the reader teasing clues that may help to answer some difficult questions. Why did Carolyn withhold from her son some scrap of recognition for his talents, which she acknowledged to others? She could not have been ignorant of how deeply he needed her approval. Certainly she shared with other people a private pleasure in his achivements, but rarely would she praise her son, rarely show him maternal tenderness, and to his constant pleas for money, her response was generally slow and grudging.

Questions about Baudelaire's part in the relationship are also difficult to answer. Why did he appear to punish himself by conduct that was both masochistic and self-advertising? Did he wish to punish his mother with his own degradation? Because she had striven so hard to become socially respectable, financially independent, and morally superior, did her son—perhaps out of some compulsive psychological need for revenge—controvert her expectations by destroying any hopes for genteel social acceptance, or for economic or moral stability? Had he "damned" himself to spite her? No doubt he blamed Carolyn for holding tight control, through his father's financial manager Narcisse-Désiré Ancelle, over his small inherited allowance. He would have been better off, he declared, if he had been permitted to deplete his father's provisions at once. Destitute, he might have been forced to fend for himself, but with the help of a meager allowance that sapped his ambition to succeed on his own, he managed to eke out a miserable life.

Hemmings provides clues to an understanding of Baudelaire's psychological maladies, even though he neglects to probe the sources with thorough analysis. The poet himself described his emotional block (which was also his artistic vision) as *spleen*—a word difficult to render, either in French or English. Baudelaire's "spleen" is a complex emotion: disgust, ennui, neurotic depression, velleity. Yet spleen shaped Baudelaire's art, a solace for his suffering. Through the flowers of evil, he could discover glory. As a biographer, Hemmings helps the reader to perceive the poet's suffering but fails to appreciate the poet's joy. That joy manifests itself primarily in his art. Against the tragic impression of this man's compulsive, self-fulfilling yearning for damnation is the counter-impression of his poetry (capably translated by Hemmings): a song of life, of victory over decadence.

Leslie Mittleman

Sources for Further Study

Library Journal. CVII, October 15, 1982, p. 1990.
Los Angeles Times Book Review. December 5, 1982, p. 11.
The New York Review of Books. XXIX, December 2, 1982, p. 16.
The New York Times Book Review. LXXXVII, November 21, 1982, p. 39.
The New Yorker. LVIII, October 18, 1982, p. 180.
Publishers Weekly. CCXXII, August 13, 1982, p. 65.
Spectator. CCXLIX, November 20, 1982, p. 27.
Times Literary Supplement. January 21, 1983, p. 68.

BECH IS BACK

Author: John Updike (1932-   )
Publisher: Alfred A. Knopf (New York). 195 pp. $13.95
Type of work: Novel
Time: The 1970's
Locale: Manhattan and Ossining, New York; Africa, Asia, Australia, Canada,
South America, Jerusalem, and Scotland

*A compilation of seven interwoven short stories, this work focuses on the conscious-
ness of an aging and unproductive writer, while satirizing the contemporary literary
scene and humorously capturing the decadence and inanity of modern life*

> *Principal characters:*
> HENRY BECH, a fifty-year-old Jewish writer who lives in Manhattan
> BEA LATCHETT COOK, Bech's girlfriend and later his wife, a resident
>   of suburban Ossining, New York
> NORMA LATCHETT, Bea's older sister and Bech's former mistress
> DONALD, Bea's preadolescent son from her first marriage
> ANN and
> JUDY, Bea's twin daughters, also from her first marriage
> PÈRE GIBERGUE, a Jesuit priest and archaeologist who serves as
>   Bech and Bea's guide in the Holy Land
> JIM FLAGGERTY, Bech's boyish and arrogant new editor at Vellum
>   Press in New York
> ELLEN, HANNAH, MOIRA, GLENDA, AND ARLENE, various young
>   women whom Bech meets in his travels and with whom he is
>   briefly infatuated

A realist noted for both the richness of his style and the satiric implications
of his fictional portraits of middle-class life and values, John Updike is one
of the most prolific and accomplished writers in contemporary America. Novelist, short-story writer, essayist, and poet, he is frequently grouped with John
Cheever and J. D. Salinger as a practitioner of *"The New Yorker* story," a
form known for its stylistic understatement as well as for the sparseness of
its plot. Updike's work is too varied, however, his style too evocative, to be
quickly labeled. In his numerous novels, he has experimented with many
subjects and created a widely divergent cast of characters. The hero of *Bech
Is Back*, an aging and unproductive Jewish novelist and intellectual, testifies
to Updike's range.

Ironically, Henry Bech, first introduced in *Bech: A Book* (1970), is the very
antithesis of his creator: far from being able to produce a book a year, as
Updike has, Bech struggles for more than thirteen years to write a new novel,
the immense and sloppy *Think Big*. In the meantime, he lives off royalties
from paperback reprints and honoraria from lectures and college readings.
As his creator's alter ego, Henry Bech is an effective satiric device for viewing
contemporary life and culture. He is the modern artist caught in what Updike
describes in the novel as "the tenor of meaninglessness in our late-twentieth-

century, post-numinous, industrial-consumeristic civilization."

In Bech's world, sex, literature, and religion have become decadent and empty—the victims of overexperimentation and liberation, commercial exploitation, and the insatiable craving of almost everyone for easy money. Touring Canada and Australia, Bech encounters attractive young women whose sexual arrangements confuse and bewilder him. Two, Hannah and Moira, share each other as well as a common boyfriend. On the literary scene, publishing firms have been swallowed up by huge oil companies and conglomerates, and the old committed and exciting writers have vanished. "Sexual display" has replaced "the noble tradition of social criticism" in American literature. Bech's own reputation is kept alive only because each large corporation that buys Vellum Press, his publisher, reprints his early novels in yet another paperback format in order to make a profit. The Church of the Holy Sepulcher in Jerusalem, which Bech unwillingly visits with his enthusiastic wife, is at once an architectural monster—so much so that the priest-guide who accompanies Bech and Bea hides his head in his hands—an object of commercial exploitation, and a bone of contention among various Christian sects. There, a fat Greek priest sips wine in a pew, then later hustles business selling blessed candles. At the Wailing Wall, where the Jewish Bech feels no link with the praying Hasidic Jews, lice infest the stones, while beverage and camera film signs mar the Via Dolorosa where Christ stumbled on his way to Calvary.

Throughout the novel, Bech is the recording consciousness for Updike's implicit cultural and social satire. Ironically, because Bech is himself driven by a concern for comfort and sex—a post-Modernist writer enamored of the life of the artist but not the hard work—his eye for the "irrelevant" details of corruption is all the more significant. As greedy and egotistical as the next man, Bech is made uncomfortable in the Middle East and the Third World countries he tours: his own consumeristic American identity is mirrored there, and he must repeatedly confront his own dissatisfaction and stagnation. In Kenya on a lecture tour, he agrees with a young African who tells Bech that his novels "are weeping, but there are no tears." As a Western observer of Third World suffering and political repression, Bech remains an outsider exempt from the need to change. Again, his role is to capture and unify the contrasts between Western decadence and Eastern chaos, contrasts that serve Updike's satiric ends. In Egypt, for example, Bech notices "the beggars" with "sores and upturned, blind eyes," rationalizes their pain as part of a "sacred hierarchy of suffering," then turns his attention to a pleasant afternoon of conversation and social drinking at the Royal Cricket Club. In Lagos, where people sleep in the streets, Bech dances in a nightclub, his attention riveted to his dance instructress' slinky waist. At the height of the Vietnam War, his purpose in Korea is to attend a conference on humor. Though a young Korean poet is clubbed before Bech's eyes for reciting political satire, Bech can mingle later with the literati, including a Japanese poet who has written more than one hundred poems about frogs. In the liberated and politically activist 1970's, literature, like religion, is free of social and moral significance.

Despite these serious underpinnings, *Bech Is Back* is not a polemical novel. At times, in fact, it is wildly comic, as evidenced in the episode involving Bech's conversation with the Japanese "frog" poet or in a later telephone conversation Bech has with the editor-in-chief of Vellum Press, a glib young woman whose speech is filled with publishing jargon shocking to the writer accustomed to a gentler era. As part of his literary satire, moreover, Updike has Bech receive "the Melville Medal" for being "that American author who has maintained the most meaningful silence." When *Think Big* does finally appear, Updike uses the opportunity to satirize the marketing strategy of modern publishers as well as parodying such writers as Gore Vidal, George Steiner, Benjamin DeMott, and Alfred Kazin. Parodies of reviews appropriate to each critic's style (and to the styles of various prominent literary periodicals) appear, complete with the critics' echoing of one another's words. Earlier in the novel, a satire of the scholar appears in the form of an Anglican priest who has prepared a concordance to Bech's works. Unlike the medieval monks who preserved culture through the laborious copying of manuscripts, this modern cleric has used a scanning computer and completed his task "in twelve minutes flat."

Other humorous attacks on the shallowness and decadence of modern existence include Updike's satire of middle-class suburban life and the New York cocktail party. While Bech's Third World tour leaves him insecure, the marriage he runs to is boring and inhibiting, a far cry from the freedom of his Manhattan bachelorhood. Bea, Bech's mistress-turned-wife, is a full-fledged WASP with all the characteristics of a nagging Jewish mother. On their tour of the Holy Land, she is indeed more Jewish than Bech in her enthusiasm for the historic sites, while he identifies with Scotland, the land of her ancestors. Bea is nevertheless able to drive Bech to complete *Think Big*, though the exercise is partly a retreat from life in Ossining, New York. There, life is complete with dogs, kids, cats, reggae music, citizen band radios, visiting housewives, and neighbors discussing insulation—people, animals, and objects Bech finds undetachable from their "illegible Westchester surroundings." In this chapter of *Bech Is Back*, Updike comes closest to re-creating his earlier novelistic portraits of middle-class life while offering also an implicit tribute to John Cheever, a resident of Ossining and another astute observer of married life.

The culmination of Updike's satire comes in the final section, a chapter entitled "White on White." The title refers to a cocktail party given in honor of an avant-garde photographer whose latest collection is entitled "White on White." Complete with albino fish in a huge tank, guests clad only in white, and a strikingly black bartender, the party captures the emptiness of contemporary life and the art scene. The host, a television producer who made his money on various game shows and whose current endeavor is female mud wrestling, has no knowledge of literature—his wife is the reader—though many of his guests are writers. Almost clairvoyant from the liquor he has imbibed, Bech becomes again a device for Updike's social and cultural observations about the inanity of modern life. He sees that the "white of this party" is a cover for the real sickness of the human body, a mask or "illusion" the writers and artists present. At the heart of the glamour, there is poverty, the real self of the writer. At the end, Bech is left wondering what "the point of fiction" is and feeling "not quite satisfied," for the scene he witnesses is somehow "unclean."

Structurally, *Bech Is Back* is loose, its cohesiveness a product mainly of Bech's consciousness. This weakness results from the novel's form, a compilation of seven short stories covering a span of about a decade in Bech's life. Four of these stories first appeared in separate publications—three in *Playboy*, one in *The New Yorker*. The novel consists of mere fragments in the life of Bech, yet this very fragmentation may be said to mirror the meaninglessness of life in twentieth century America. As an observer of modern life, no doubt Henry Bech will reappear, like Harry "Rabbit" Angstrom, as one of Updike's representative characters, what George Hunt in the June 21, 1975 issue of *America* has called "the quintessential postwar American adult: a man granted unlimited freedom of speech but without anything to say."

Stella Nesanovich

Sources for Further Study

The Atlantic. CCL, October, 1982, p. 103.
Christian Science Monitor. October 6, 1982, p. 14.
Commentary. LXXV, January, 1983, p. 55.
Los Angeles Times Book Review. October 24, 1982, p. 3.
The New York Times Book Review. LXXXVII, October 17, 1982, p. 1.
Newsweek. C, October 18, 1982, p. 67.
Time. CXX, October 18, 1982, p. 72.
Times Literary Supplement. January 14, 1983, p. 30.

BEYOND THE PALE AND OTHER STORIES

Author: William Trevor (1928-   )
Publisher: The Viking Press (New York). 256 pp. $12.95
Type of work: Short stories

A collection of twelve short stories characterized by a high degree of narrative skill and a wide range of characters and themes

William Trevor is among the select group of contemporary writers who have achieved distinction in both the short story and the novel. *Beyond the Pale and Other Stories*, his fourth collection of short stories, will undoubtedly contribute significantly to his stature as a writer in the United States as well as in Great Britain, where he is better known. Though he was born in Cork and educated in Dublin, Trevor has lived and worked in England for more than twenty years. Thus, it is not surprising to find that the majority of the stories in this collection—seven of the twelve—have an Irish or an Anglo-Irish provenance, nor is it surprising that all of the stories have been previously published in distinguished magazines or anthologies in either England or the United States.

Perhaps the outstanding stylistic feature of this collection is the high degree of narrative skill reflected in the stories. Trevor, like many of his great Irish predecessors in the genre, is first and foremost a storyteller, and the reader will become immediately and continuously engaged in almost all of these stories. Indeed, Trevor's narrative ability is so strong and sure that it overshadows minor flaws—particularly his tendency on occasion to push too hard for dramatic or ironic effect. His narrative mastery results, in part, from his sharp eye for, and economical use of, compelling realistic details in his descriptions of character, atmosphere, and place; it is, in larger measure, a result of his sense of pace and his artful use of point of view.

The collection is also distinguished by a wide range of characters, situations, and themes. Three of the stories—"The Blue Dress," "The Teddy-bears' Picnic," and "The Bedroom Eyes of Mrs. Vansittart"—focus in one way or another on psychological aberration. The journalist narrator of "The Blue Dress" gradually unveils a paranoia that has its roots in childhood misperceptions, accounts for the failure of his first marriage, and assumes monstrous dimensions in his interpretations of the character of his fiancée and her family. Normal behavior is evaluated through an abnormal vision so confident and apparently natural that, without ever being misled, the reader is almost seduced into accepting it.

Though grimmer and more shocking in impact, "The Teddy-bears' Picnic" is similar in structure to "The Blue Dress." The same kind of incremental revelation prepares the reader for a shocking climax. Though the reader may well be startled by the secret act of violence that disturbs a charming, tranquil setting, a little reflection will make it clear that the enormously self-centered young stockbroker on whom the story centers has been presented as a pathological personality.

"The Bedroom Eyes of Mrs. Vansittart" is the best of these three stories because of its deeper thematic resonance and broader ironic reverberations. On the one hand, the story blends the motif of marital exploitation with that of martyred love. On the other hand, it illustrates one of the main themes of William Shakespeare's *Julius Caesar* (1599-1600): in the words of Cicero, "Men may construe things after their fashion,/ Clean from the purpose of the things themselves." The genius of "The Bedroom Eyes of Mrs. Vansittart" lies in the manner in which the theme of misconstruction emerges from the relationship of Mrs. Vansittart and her husband. Because of a pure and almost selfless passion, she has dedicated her life to protecting him from the consequences of his childish sexual predilections and to playing out a role which satisfies his psychological masochism. As a result, she becomes the victim of malicious gossip while he elicits a kind of condescending concern and pity from their friends. It is important to note that the initial assumptions made by the reader about the nature of the marriage are shaped by characters whose imperfections of spirit are clearly, if subtly, delineated. The final revelation is made directly by Mrs. Vansittart herself and serves, through the reflection of a submerged sense of self, to make her more real and the nature of the situation itself more believable than it would be otherwise.

"Mulvihill's Memorial" is a satirical story skillfully tracing the set of circumstances which almost brought down a powerful, prestigious advertising firm as a result of one little man's unobtrusive attempt to counteract the artificiality and superficiality of the world in which he worked. Mulvihill, an obscure designer of labels, becomes an amateur filmmaker. In his compulsion to record reality, he moves from house-and-garden subjects to real-life pornography in an advertising executive office. By accident, his work falls into the wrong hands after his death, and Mulvihill thus has more impact on the firm than he had ever had in life. Though the story is weakened by the manner in which ironic retributive coincidence is compounded to the point of implausibility, it is noteworthy for the crispness of its narrative pace and, above all, for the power of its primary thematic point: the basic human need for truth.

"Beyond the Pale," which has pride of title in the collection, also juxtaposes an artificial, superficial vision of life with the real thing. The story deals with the characters and relationship of four middle-aged, upper-middle-class friends—a married couple, a bachelor, and a widow—who have for many years vacationed together at a charming lodge in Northern Ireland. As a result of a shocking incident at the lodge, the reader becomes aware of the apparent gulf that separates the serene life they lead from the passion, pathos, and horror of the Irish experience. Only Cynthia, the wife of the retired colonel, has the compassion and intelligence to respond appropriately to what has taken place. Her outrage at the snobbish insensitivity of her companions to the significance of the tragic event spurs her into speaking a truth about them which leads to the thematic heart of the story: If there are crimes against humanity outside the pale of civilization, there may also be comparable crimes in the sheltered lives of those who live within it.

Two stories which, in different ways, rely for their impact on blind or limited perspectives are "The Paradise Lounge" and "Mr. Tennyson." Both are stories of thwarted love. "Mr. Tennyson" describes the infatuation of a teenage girl, Jenny, for a middle-aged English teacher who had, several years before, engaged in a sordid affair with one of his students. His hopeless love for the former student who has outgrown him is paralleled both by Jenny's infatuation with him and the infatuation of Jenny's friend, Clive, with her. Jenny considers her friend's feeling for her silly but fails to see either herself or her teacher in the same mirror. The ironic conclusion of "The Paradise Lounge" is somewhat similar but perhaps has greater moral depth. A still beautiful elderly woman meets weekly with two old friends, a married couple, for the pleasant ritual of drinks and conversation. She and the husband, unknown to the wife, have been in love for years, but the relationship has not been consummated because of the constraints of village life and the more stringent moral code of the past. In the Paradise Lounge, she observes the meeting of two young people from out of town who have been having an affair. The old woman envies the freedom the young woman has been given by modern life, unaware that the young woman bitterly regrets what she has done. Passion has ebbed, and the affair is drawing to a close. The young woman knows that she will forever carry upon her conscience the stain of her secret guilt.

"Downstairs at Fitzgerald's" lacks the narrative drive of some of the other stories, but the dialogue and the delineation of character and place provide an evocative description of life in Dublin in the 1940's. In this moving rite-of-passage story, a young girl is confronted by a question that results in a sense of uncertainty concerning her identity and the significance of the happiest moments she had experienced as a child.

"The Time of Year" is also, at least indirectly, a rite-of-passage story; it deals with the impact that a childhood tragedy has had on the mind and personality of a young college student. Though the student finds herself unable to celebrate the season of Christmas because of its associations with this childhood tragedy, it becomes apparent that something good has come out of the shadows of that memory. Her thoughts and behavior at an academic Christmas party make it clear that she has acquired a habit of introspection that has led her to an understanding of herself and an insight into other people.

A similar note regarding the possible significance of adversity is sounded in "Sunday Drinks." A middle-aged suburban couple who, in effect, have lost a son to drugs, have been brought closer through their mutual suffering.

Their relationship stands in marked contrast to the marriages of the other couples who attend a weekly cocktail party.

Two of the finest stories in the collection are essentially character studies which reflect what William Wordsworth called "the still, sad music of humanity." "Being Stolen From" is a moving depiction of a middle-aged woman whose charitable character makes her an easy mark for both the calculated and the unintentional selfishness and thoughtlessness of others. As she makes the decision which will deprive her of the only love and joy she knows, one feels her suffering and marvels at her integrity of spirit. "Autumn Sunshine" is a brilliant, subtle study of the way in which one's interpretations and judgments can be shaped by one's deepest needs. A widowed Irish clergyman is confronted with evidence that strongly suggests that his youngest daughter, whom he loves deeply, is moving toward a life of terror and violence. The painful concern that he feels is, however, turned away by a vision of love out of his past which convinces him that his fears are groundless—although the reader knows them to be only too well-justified. This is perhaps the best story of the collection—remarkable in its stylistic finesse and its depth of implication.

Trevor's astringent vision is best-suited to the short story, where—in contrast to the novel—one can afford to hold one's characters always at a distance. The stories in *Beyond the Pale* show his cool art at its best.

William B. Toole III

Sources for Further Study

Encounter. LVIII, January, 1982, p. 49.
Library Journal. CVI, December 15, 1981, p. 2408.
The New Republic. CLXXXVI, February 22, 1982, p. 39.
The New York Times Book Review. LXXVII, February 21, 1982, p. 7.
Newsweek. XCIX, February 22, 1982, p. 74.
Saturday Review. IX, February, 1982, p. 59.
Times Literary Supplement. October 16, 1981, p. 1193.

A BLOODSMOOR ROMANCE

Author: Joyce Carol Oates (1938-   )
Publisher: E. P. Dutton (New York). 615 pp. $16.95
Type of work: Novel
Time: 1879-1900
Locale: Bloodsmoor, a valley in Eastern Pennsylvania

Members of an eccentric Pennsylvania family illustrate the concerns of nineteenth century America through their fantastic adventures

    Principal characters:
        JOHN QUINCEY ZINN, the father of a large family, and a gentleman
          inventor
        PRUDENCE KIDDEMASTER ZINN, his wife, mother of the Zinn
          daughters
        CONSTANCE PHILIPPA, the oldest daughter, who later becomes a
          son
        MALVINIA, another daughter and a famous actress
        OCTAVIA, another daughter, whose role is that of a wife and mother
        SAMANTHA, another daughter, who works as her father's laboratory
          assistant
        DEIRDRE, an adopted daughter and a spiritualist

    In her latest fiction, *A Bloodsmoor Romance*, the prolific Joyce Carol Oates forsakes the contemporary world in favor of an earlier and therefore more pliable setting. The classification of *A Bloodsmoor Romance* demands more words than thoughts, since its genre is not hard to recognize, only to name. It belongs to those few works that attempt to blend realism and fantasy by setting their action in a past that closely resembles the historical past, and by peopling their settings partly with fictional characters invented by the author and partly with characters who bear the names of historical men and women.

    Nevertheless, the author of such a work might well argue that if the books are not historically accurate in detail, then they are at least historically accurate in recapturing the "feel" of the time they depict. Such could well be Oates's justification, because her characters exemplify many of the more eccentric attitudes and interests of the nineteenth century and some of the common ones as well. For example, Oates's narrator is an elderly and sheltered virgin, who has little worldly knowledge; she exemplifies "ladylike" behavior and mores and is happiest when describing the dutiful, wifely life of Octavia Zinn or the conversion of Malvinia in middle age from stage-star to housewife. She has little sympathy with any attempt by the Zinn sisters to escape from the confines that society places on their lives. Her portrait is that of a type, so much so that the reader never even learns her name. She is a nineteenth century colored glass through which the reader can view the world that Oates has made.

    Oates has discovered that by setting a story in the past and by creating a narrator of that time, the author is free to invent a new world. That world, according to the author's intention, may be very much or very little like the historical past. In the case of *A Bloodsmoor Romance*, historical accuracy has not been followed. No one in the historical nineteenth century invented a working time machine; no one changed from a woman to a man by simply wanting to be one. The nineteenth century in *A Bloodsmoor Romance*, however, shares many of the interests of the real one, exploring those interests in the lives of the members of the Zinn family: spiritualism, the theater, the westward movement, experimental science, abnormal psychology, female sexuality, and the nature of marriage.

The first on this list, spiritualism and the occult, is portrayed in the life of Deirdre Zinn, the adopted daughter of John and Prudence. The sometimes outrageous comic tone of the book is well illustrated by Deirdre's being kidnaped by a mysterious stranger who flies a black balloon. One never learns much about the stranger, but the incident serves to introduce the first of several of the novel's characters who are modeled on historical figures. The balloonist deposits Deirdre on the lawn of the New York mansion of "Madame Elena Blavatsky." Like her historical counterpart, the Madame Blavatsky of the novel is the cofounder of the American Theosophical Society, a group which attempts to achieve contact beyond the grave. Madame Blavatsky has been traveling the world, holding séances and demonstrations of occult power. She takes Deirdre under her protection and sponsors the girl's entry into the world of spiritualism.

In Deirdre, the spirits find a natural soul; indeed, she has been haunted since childhood by at least three presences: a cruel older man, a sensual girl, and a weak old woman. It is questionable whether Deirdre is "possessed" by them in the usual sense of that word, but they do control her actions and her speech. The girl is never sure whether the spirits will allow her to speak, or what she will say under their control. They sometimes delude her, so that although she thinks she is being pleasant, she is in fact saying vicious things. Under Madame Blavatsky's tutelage, Deirdre becomes "Deirdre of the Shadows," and goes on tour.

The Zinn family, reading about the show, decides to attend to find out whether this Deirdre is their lost daughter, but the spirits intervene to make her unrecognizable to her family. She continues in her chosen work under the protection of her spirits, who also profit from the association; they become strong enough to destroy, both mentally and physically, the members of a team sent to investigate Deirdre's authenticity.

Another daughter, Malvinia, has a very different role from that of Deirdre. Interested in the theater since childhood, Malvinia, as a young woman, runs off with a troupe of actors. She becomes their leading lady, has a love affair with her leading man, and as a result, discovers a horrible secret: she likes sex. When the lights are out, Malvinia finds herself the victim of what she regards as a perversion; she calls her desire "the beast," and is humiliated by what she considers an unwomanly part of her character. Nevertheless, her attempts to "control herself" fail. Later, Malvinia achieves fame and meets "Mark Twain." The two fall instantly in love, and all goes well until the inevitable night when the lights are turned out and "the beast" appears. A horrified Twain flees from the frenzied woman. Much later, Malvinia is freed of her "burden" when she marries a clergyman who helps her to become the meekly compliant wife she wants to be.

Another side of female sexuality is shown in the gentle sister Octavia. Her only desire is to be a wife and mother, but although she knows how one becomes a wife, she does not know how one becomes a mother. She is willing to "do her wifely duty" but finds it difficult to get instruction. She searches diligently for information in books such as *The Wedding Day Book* by Katherine Lee Bates. (The historical Miss Bates wrote many books for young people, but the New England schoolteacher is best remembered for her poem "America the Beautiful.") The euphemisms of *The Wedding Day Book*, however, never supply the facts of reproduction to the young woman so earnestly scanning its pages. Octavia then consults her mother, but Mrs. Zinn scolds her and ends by advising her to do whatever her husband wants. Unfortunately, Octavia marries an aged man of unusual tastes. With no standard of comparison, the obliging Octavia allows herself to be trussed up in silken cords with a sack over her head, while the groom does odd things to her. She is finally rewarded with two babies on whom she lavishes love and care. When her babies and husband die, Octavia turns to a "higher calling," assuaging her grief in prayer and good works, and attending to her parents in their old age.

The complete nineteenth century family must have an inventor, and John Quincey Zinn, the father, fills this need. He becomes one of the brilliant but unknown great failures of science. Born the son of an itinerant Yankee peddler, Zinn saw his father tarred and feathered for selling useless patent medicines. Resolving not to share his father's fate, Zinn is very secretive about his work and reveals it only when it is ready for use. Unfortunately for his pocketbook, nothing is ever quite ready for use. One enduring quest is for a perpetual motion machine, and only Samantha, his assistant and daughter, has any confidence in his ability to create one. While working on this machine, Zinn invents the ballpoint pen and solar heating, sees no use for them, and forgets about them. He invents a time machine that works, but he destroys it after accidentally sending a pupil back in time to the year before the boy's birth. (The boy disappears; he did not exist then, hence he does not exist now. The boy's brothers, sent to fetch him home, forget why they have come.)

Although the household is poor, it is peaceful. This quiet vanishes, however, when Zinn is interviewed by a reporter from *The Atlantic*. The resultant notoriety leads Congress to subsidize Zinn to invent a new method of capital punishment. When he invents the electric chair, Samantha is so angered by this prostitution of her father's talents that she runs off with a young inventor.

America's westward movement is personified by the most fantastic of the sisters, the oldest daughter, Constance Philippa. Constance grows up believing that she will one day be married, and consequently, she prepares dozens of every type of household linen and readies a wardrobe for her wedding trip. She is no more prepared for what the wedding night will entail than Octavia, and she becomes increasingly nervous. Her groom is a middle-aged German visitor to Bloodsmoor, one who has paid a considerable price for the beautiful young Constance. When he finally gets into bed on the wedding night, he finds that Constance has run away with only the clothes on her back.

Constance changes into a man's suit and makes her way west. Posing as a man, she becomes a wrangler, a desperado, a deputy sheriff, and finally, a gambler in San Francisco. Her transformation into a man is complete, apparently physically as well as mentally, and it becomes appropriate to speak of Constance as "he." When he returns to Bloodsmoor, it is as "Philippe Fox," who represents himself as Constance's agent. Although some members of the family find Philippe suspiciously like Constance, they never grasp the full implication of the resemblance, and they continue to expect the eventual return of Constance to home and hearth. Philippe Fox's last act in Bloodsmoor is to rescue a childhood girlfriend from the attic where her husband has imprisoned her, after which the two disappear forever.

Women's suffrage, female authors, and the horrifying effects of tight lacing are among other concerns of the age pictured in the characters who people the Bloodsmoor valley. The Zinns and their friends proceed toward and into a new century, and their desires, needs, and interests are a microcosm of those of millions of others who shared their era. If that era is not exactly the same as the historical one, it nevertheless is interesting in its own right, and the two eras—fictional and historical—can illuminate and explain each other.

Walter E. Meyers

Sources for Further Study

Harper's Magazine. CCLXV, September, 1982, p. 67.
Library Journal. August, 1982, p. 1482.
Los Angeles Times Book Review. September 19, 1982, p. 1.
The New York Times Book Review. LXXXVII, September 5, 1982, p. 1.
The New Yorker. LVIII, September 27, 1982, p. 145. *Newsweek*. C,
    September 20, 1982, p. 91.
Time. CXX, October 4, 1982, p. 79.
West Coast Review of Books. VIII, November, 1982, p. 31.

BODILY HARM

Author: Margaret Atwood (1939-   )
Publisher: Simon and Schuster (New York). 266 pp. $14.50
Type of work: Novel
Time: The present
Locale: Toronto and the fictitious Caribbean islands of St. Antoine and Ste. Agathe

A powerful but somewhat melodramatic account of a young Canadian woman's encounters with various kinds of "bodily harm"

> Principal characters:
> RENATA "RENNIE" WILFORD, a journalist, a Canadian in her late twenties or early thirties
> JAKE, her former lover
> DR. DANIEL LUOMA, her surgeon
> PAUL, a middle-aged American drug smuggler
> LORA LUCAS, Paul's ex-mistress, an American who lives on St. Antoine

The violence that human beings inflict on one another and their isolation in an uncaring world are pervasive themes in Margaret Atwood's work. *Bodily Harm*, her fifth novel, is in many respects her bleakest, though it holds out some hope in the form of compassion to be shared by those who are victims of bodily harm in any form. The novel suggests that every person falls into this category. All are victims. There is no exemption, no escape for anyone.

Rennie Wilford, the central character, is a type who will be familiar to readers of Atwood's earlier novels—the university-educated young Canadian woman of Anglo-Saxon heritage who is mildly rebellious against the stuffy respectability of her past but far from free of its influences. She is a "lifestyles" journalist, writing about fast-food restaurants, "drain chain" jewelry, how to pick up men in laundromats—in short, about the surfaces of life. She left college in the early 1970's expecting to dedicate herself to causes, to honest explorations of serious issues, but she soon found herself drifting toward externals, concerned more with what protesters were wearing and eating than with the issues of their protests. She has successfully avoided making deep commitments to anything or anyone, even Jake, the man with whom she lives. Significantly, he too is a person connected chiefly to the surfaces of life; he makes his living as a planner of product packaging.

Rennie's comfortable, safe, impenetrable world of externals cracks when she discovers that she has breast cancer. Although her surgeon, Daniel Luoma, assures her that her mastectomy is successful, she reacts by withdrawing from Jake and seeing herself as both mutilated and incapable of feeling. Then, a few weeks after her operation, she returns to her apartment to find two policemen there, investigating the presence of an unknown intruder, a "face-less invader" who has made himself a cup of Ovaltine in her kitchen and left a coil of white rope lying on her bed. Unnerved by this inexplicable assault from outside, as well as by the equally inexplicable attack from her own body, she decides to escape. She flies to St. Antoine, a fictitious Caribbean island, where she believes she will, as a tourist, be "exempt" from involvement in the problems that plague her at home. She learns that no one is exempt from anything.

On the plane to St. Antoine, Rennie meets a native of the island, Dr. Minnow, who is a presidential candidate campaigning against the current dictator, Ellis, and a young man who is picturesquely known as the Prince of Peace. Later, she becomes acquainted with Lora, a rather brassy American expatriate, and Paul, a powerful drug smuggler. Through these three characters, Rennie becomes involved in island politics and is gradually sucked into a whirlpool of brutality. As she watches, horrors increase. A deaf-mute is beaten insensible. The decent patriot, Dr. Minnow, is assassinated. Dozens of citizens are tortured and mutilated in a brief political revolt. Yet, Rennie continues to try to detach herself from what is happening, to see herself as a tourist, one free to leave and to ignore the sufferings of others. Then, she and Lora are imprisoned by the government—under "suspicion," she is told. Even under these circumstances, she refuses to see reality. When Rennie realizes that Lora is prostituting herself in order to buy small luxuries from the prison guards, she scorns her for cheapening herself. She withholds her sympathy from her companion until Lora finally rebels against their captors and is battered into unconsciousness, perhaps death, by the guards. Only then does Rennie realize that she may never be free. She cannot escape bodily harm, whether it comes through her own cancerous cells or from faceless men outside.

The novel's ending seems deliberately ambiguous. Rennie is on a flight back to Canada, but it is a flight that is introduced in the future tense, as something that will happen. It may be a flight that exists only in Rennie's imagination. Through this ambiguity, Atwood suggests that the "reality" of Rennie's flight is ultimately irrelevant, since there is no escape or rescue for anyone. What is important is to accept one's involvement in death and violence and to reach out to others, as Rennie is finally able to do when she takes Lora's cold hand and holds it in her own, trying to draw her companion back into the world of the living.

Like Atwood's other novels, *Bodily Harm* is technically complex. Rennie's story is presented in fragments, sections that advance the plot alternating with flashbacks to her childhood, her operation, and her relationships with Jake and her doctor. While most of the book is narrated in the third person, there are several passages in the first person, headed "says Rennie" or "says Lora." These are presumably conversations that take place between the two in their damp, fetid, underground prison cell—Atwood offers the reader few clues. The disjointed segments of Rennie's history are unified by the author's always skillful handling of image patterns. Apparently insignificant details are woven into the novel time and time again until they take on major symbolic significance. Offhand comments become laden with irony in the light of later events: Rennie's mention of her childhood fear of being punished by being sent to the cellar, for example, and her revulsion at her first sight of Lora's hands with ragged fingernails, bitten to the quick.

Images of hands, in fact, constitute the most striking image-cluster in the book. Human ties are symbolized by physical touch; the loss of connections, by the withholding of contact. The first thing Rennie is conscious of as she comes out from under the anesthetic after her mastectomy is someone holding her hand—Daniel, her surgeon—and she promptly falls in love with him. She reflects several times that his soul is in his hands, the hands that preserve life for his patients. He is married and conscientious about his professional obligations; his feelings for Rennie are for the most part expressed in "some pretty frantic hand-holding." Conversely, when Jake leaves Rennie and the apartment they have shared, Rennie holds her own hands to keep them from trembling and makes no gesture of farewell. Her brief affair with Paul, the drug smuggler, begins as he grasps both her hands to pull her over a wall, and she reflects after their first night together, "He's touching her, she can still be touched."

Perhaps the most effective use of the image of hands is in Rennie's memory of her childhood horror of her senile grandmother, who would mourn plaintively that she could not find her hands, while the child Rennie could see them dangling lifelessly from her wrists. It is the recollection of her mother's reaching out reassuringly to grasp the pathetic old woman's hands that enables Rennie, finally, to clasp Lora's cold, nail-bitten hands in her own in an affirmation of their human kinship. On the real or imagined flight home, Rennie "can feel the shape of a hand in hers, both of hers, there but not there, like the afterglow of a match that's gone out. It will always be there now."

A second crucial cluster of images grows out of Rennie's cancer. Words commonly associated with the disease—"terminal," "malignant," "massive involvement"—are used first in connection with her illness. As the book progresses, they become attached to the violent events in which Rennie is embroiled. When Daniel, early in the story, reassures her that there is no "massive involvement" necessitating radical surgery, she reflects, "Massive involvement, . . . it's never been my thing." Later, when Paul suggests that she is getting too involved with him, the words come into her mind again. She chooses not to flee back to the cold gray winter in Toronto, however, and as a consequence finds herself massively involved in the political revolution and its aftermath. "Malignant," too, is a word charged with meaning— not only a word to diagnose her physical condition, but also a word to describe the expression on her landlady's face as she watches, with perverse pleasure, Rennie's arrest by the native policemen.

There is a strong vein of social satire in this novel, as in much of Atwood's other work. She first takes aim at the superficial complacency of a society in which men "package" products to appeal to consumers and women wear chains clipped from their bathtub stoppers if some magazine writer tells them that is chic. On a deeper level, she attacks the perverted faddishness that allows Rennie to say, "Outrage is out of date." Atwood seems to be attempting to shock her readers out of this kind of attitude, to arouse rage at the brutality that fills the daily newspapers. Her depiction of the political turmoil on St. Antoine and its sister island, Ste. Agathe, is a savage portrayal of the blindness of leaders of Western democracies, who do not take the trouble to learn the truth about the governments to which they send foreign aid. Rennie, the tourist who thinks she can avoid involvement in the violence that afflicts others, becomes a symbol of all the privileged Westerners who see themselves as tourists in the midst of horrors.

Paradoxically, the very setting that Atwood has chosen to make her point about contemporary politics and human responsibility may prevent many readers from taking her message seriously. Violent political upheavals in the Caribbean are hardly new in modern fiction, and the situation in which Atwood places her heroine is so improbable and chaotic that the reader is likely to adopt the complacent detachment the author deplores. Instead of recognizing Rennie's fate as emblematic of humanity's, one can easily dismiss it as exaggerated and unrealistic.

The melodramatic plot is not the only source of difficulty in the novel. Rennie herself is simply not a character in whose fate most readers will be greatly interested. Her coldness, her detachment, her unwillingness to go below the surfaces of life may be essential elements of the author's critique of contemporary society, but they are not characteristics that make a reader care deeply about what happens to her. In addition, none of the minor characters ever becomes quite real. Again, this may have been the author's intention. Most of the people and events are filtered through Rennie's consciousness, and she cannot see deeply into others. Yet the book seems filled with stereotypes: Elva, an old native woman with healing in her hands; Dr. Minnow, the martyred patriot; Paul, the enigmatic he-man, stimulated by danger; Lora, the fallen woman with the heart of gold. The setting, too, seems somewhat artificial. Atwood's Toronto and Griswold (Rennie's childhood home) ring true; her Caribbean islands, however carefully researched, have something of the air of the background of a prime-time television thriller.

There is much that is important and powerful in *Bodily Harm*. Atwood clearly feels the significance of what she is trying to say, and she has marshaled many of her gifts as poet and novelist to try to shatter her readers' illusions about their exemption from the horrors that plague the rest of humanity. Unfortunately, much of the power and subtlety of the work lies in images and details that become clear only on a second or third reading, and the plot and characters are not compelling enough to interest readers in reading the novel more than once. It is unfortunate, for Atwood is an extraordinarily talented writer, and her position is one that should be heard.

Elizabeth Johnston Lipscomb

Sources for Further Study

The Atlantic. CCXLIX, April, 1982, p. 110.
Commonweal. CIX, September 24, 1982, p. 506.
Library Journal. CVII, February 15, 1982, p. 471.
New Statesman. CIII, June 11, 1982, p. 31.
The New York Times Book Review. LXXXVII, March 21, 1982, p. 3.
Newsweek. XCIX, January 29, 1982, p. 71.
Saturday Review. IX, March, 1982, p. 62.
Times Literary Supplement. June 11, 1982, p. 643.

THE BOY SCOUT HANDBOOK AND OTHER OBSERVATIONS

Author: Paul Fussell (1924-   )
Publisher: Oxford University Press (New York). Illustrated. 284 pp. $15.95
Type of work: Essays

A collection of essays and reviews commenting on American life and values, British and American literary figures, travel, and World War II

The essays in Paul Fussell's *The Boy Scout Handbook and Other Observations* uphold high ideals of civilized conduct and recognize the depths of irrationality—evil, really—to which man can descend. For Fussell, civilization resides in strongly held ethical values, but also in order, in grace, in knowledge acquired by study and perception, and in the precise and accurate use of language. Irrational evil lies in every man and can manifest itself in the egotism of the individual or in the monstrous insanity of war. The essays suggest that the qualities of civilized man include compassion, sensitivity, breadth of knowledge, and a profound awareness of his own frailties. They also include a sense of irony that protects his sanity in a world which he perceives to be neither reasonable nor just.

In "My War," the final essay in this collection, Fussell focuses on his participation in World War II as the experience which transformed him, almost literally overnight, from a touchingly innocent nineteen-year-old, upper-middle-class college student into an infantry rifle platoon leader with profound skepticism about man's capabilities for reason and virtue. Although Fussell maintains that his experience as a foot soldier was the determining force of his life, even prompting him to sophisticate his sense of irony by enrolling in a course in Alexander Pope and Jonathan Swift when he entered graduate school after the war, surely his career as a teacher of eighteenth century English literature (he is John DeWitt Professor of English at Rutgers University) has also been a powerful influence on his tastes and values. The abiding attitudes of Pope, Swift, Samuel Johnson, Edmund Burke, and the other great eighteenth century writers are Fussell's attitudes too: a contempt for vague and sloppy language; a distrust of fanaticism; a fascination with paradox in individual character; a respect for order; a delight in the ideal of universal civilization, experienced in part through literature and travel; and, finally, a recognition that only a thin veneer masks human irrationality—and worse.

Among Fussell's previous books, *The Rhetorical World of Augustan Humanism: Ethics and Imagery from Swift to Burke* (1965) and *Samuel Johnson and the Life of Writing* (1971) reveal his interest in the relationship between man's ethical nature and the quality of his expression. *The Great War and Modern Memory* (1975), which won the 1976 National Book Award, the National Book Critics Circle Award for Criticism, and the Ralph Waldo

Emerson Award of Phi Beta Kappa, brilliantly explores the impact of World War I on the modern consciousness. *Abroad: British Literary Traveling Between the Wars* (1980) analyzes the phenomenon of travel and travel books in the 1920's and 1930's as expressions of a kind of celebration of life after World War I and a growing awareness of the threat of World War II. In all of his books, but especially in the last two, Fussell demonstrates his command of a vast amount of material, his ability to choose persuasively illuminating details, and his recognition of the cultural significance of certain kinds of writing which other critics have tended to overlook. Further, he writes with so much grace and wit that he makes his achievements look easy. The knowledge, perception, and wit of these earlier books are abundantly evident in *The Boy Scout Handbook and Other Observations*.

The essays in this collection appeared during the past fifteen years in *The New Republic*, *The New York Times Book Review*, *Harper's Magazine*, and similar periodicals. In many cases, the incentive for the essay was to review a book, but as Fussell remarks in "Being Reviewed," a "reviewer is writing an essay, and the book in question is only one element of his material." Besides the obligation to comment justly and accurately on the book he is reviewing, the reviewer also "has an obligation to be interesting." This obligation is one that Fussell discharges admirably, at least in part because of the wide range of his own interests. Although most of the essays are about books in one way or another, the five sections of the collection, entitled "Americana," "Hazards of Literature," "Going Places," "Britons, Largely Eccentric," and "Versions of the Second World War," offer a variety of topics that move in a rough progression from innocence to experience—from observations on the *The Offical Boy Scout Handbook* (1979) to an account of Fussell's ordeal in World War II, from Henry Ford's World War I Peace Ship to a discussion of the rhetoric of a German officer describing the destruction of the Warsaw ghetto, from William Carlos Williams' poignant sense of deficiency in not having had a liberal education to British poet Ivor Gurney's being driven mad by his experience of trench warfare in World War I.

Fussell's method in these essays is suggested by the last word in his title, *The Boy Scout Handbook and Other Observations*. He is a splendidly acute observer, with an excellent eye for the telling detail. "What We Look Like" and "The War in Black and White," two essays in which he "reads" photographs, calling attention to small but revealing items of dress and posture, perhaps demonstrate his talent as an observer most obviously, but this talent is apparent everywhere, whether he is assessing the footnotes in scholarly editions of Edgar Allan Poe and Walt Whitman, checking the list of books banned by the Union of South Africa, discovering the unexpected delights of travel, scanning letters from aggrieved authors in the *Times Literary Supplement*, or noting the revealing signs of class structure in the United States. When the observer is as acute as Fussell, it is hard not to agree with his comment in "Notes on Class" that perception is a "more trustworthy method" than any kind of quantitative analysis. The picture on the dust jacket, showing a boy scout, in the traditional wide-brimmed army field hat, holding a pair of binoculars, but looking over them to rely on his own keen-eyed vision, is an appropriate emblem for the book as a whole.

The Official Boy Scout Handbook itself is for Fussell a kind of moral touchstone, providing one of the few surviving popular expressions of classical ethics, implying the benefits of losing one's preoccupation with oneself while attending to work on behalf of the larger community. This kind of goodness contrasts markedly with the self-indulgent egotism that Fussell regards as characteristic of the modern world, variously manifested in the arrogance of Somerset Maugham, who, after a lifetime of courting publicity, directed that no biography of him be written; in the verbalized self-pity of May Sarton, blaming an unfriendly reviewer for her nervous anxiety and even physical illness; in the evasive rhetoric of Graham Greene, who seems to make a statement, but escapes into imprecision; and in the pomposities of authors writing to complain about the failure of reviewers to understand or appreciate their work—all manifestations of a self-concern at odds with the broader ethics of the *The Official Boy Scout Handbook*.

For Fussell, as for the great eighteenth century satirists, precise and accurate use of language is both a stylistic and a moral responsibility. Consequently, authors and books that fail to describe experience honestly and accurately are guilty of an ethical transgression as well as a literary one. The *Time-Life* history of World War II, for example, presents, in Fussell's view, a picture of the war that sugarcoats and exaggerates, relying on clichés and oversimplifications, ultimately falsifying not only war but also the realities of life itself. As one might expect, fictional treatments of war have a special propensity for falsification. Thus, although Fussell has high regard for the documentary portions of Herman Wouk's *War and Remembrance* (1978) and lauds Wouk for recognizing that interpreting World War II is the most crucial intellectual and moral problem of the modern era, he views the fictional story line of the novel as cliché-ridden and false in the manner of a Hollywood melodrama from the early 1950's.

A similar kind of sentimental dishonesty is evident in a recent edition of Booth Tarkington's *Penrod* (1914) that carefully purges racial epithets and evidence of condescension toward blacks, an expurgation that eliminates, along with the objectionable language, Tarkington's implicit condemnation of the characters who use it. Censorship of a more drastic kind is discussed in "Smut-Hunting in Pretoria," an essay on the effects of the Publications Act of 1974 in the Union of South Africa. As Fussell suggests, to describe the operation of this act is to satirize it: the act prohibits as "undesirable" the importation of books criticizing the Union's political and racial policies, of books implying a negative view of the military, and, in vast quantity, of books condemned as sexually provocative or unorthodox.

Several of the essays imply Fussell's scorn for pedantry, for scholarship which is pretentious or which lacks rigor and purpose. Scholarly editions of Poe and Whitman are condemned because they fail to supply an apparatus which makes these authors significant, or even accessible, to a new generation of readers. Similarly, the introductory essays in a literary atlas of the British Isles fail because of a lack of precision in information, because of shallowness in the mere listing of names and places, and, especially, because of the author's apparent failure to take into account the purpose of literature to interpret, rather than to transcribe, actuality. Irrelevant criticism of a different kind is, in Fussell's view, exemplified by Vladimir Nabokov's *Notes on Prosody* (1965), capriciously unorthodox in its terminology and inaccurate in the comparison it makes between English and Russian prosody.

Fussell's adverse criticism of these writers implies an ideal of what scholarship should accomplish, and this ideal is supplied in his essay on Marc Aurel Stein, a British archaeologist whose explorations of Central Asia began in 1900 and continued until his death in 1943. If Stein's vast knowledge, acquired through research and exploration, make him a model of intellectual curiosity, Samuel Schoenbaum, author of *Shakespeare's Lives* (1970), exemplifies another quality of ideal scholarship—the sympathetic understanding of the objects of his investigation. Thus, while Schoenbaum exposes the absurdities of writers who have extrapolated fanciful biographies of Shakespeare from random passages in his works and the small number of facts available about his life, he simultaneously sympathizes with the well-intentioned motives which drove them to their excesses.

Fussell himself demonstrates this combination of knowledge and the sympathetic recognition of human frailty throughout this volume, but nowhere more than in those essays in which he treats the painful process by which innocence is enlightened by experience. One apt example is his consideration of Henry Ford's naïve attempt to end World War I by going to Europe on his Peace Ship—an exercise in optimism that seems incredible to a generation whose consciousness includes not only World War I but World War II and the Holocaust as well. A darker, and more pathetic example of American innocence gone awry is Harry Crosby, a wealthy Boston aristocrat, emotionally scarred by World War I, who dedicated himself in monomaniacal ignorance to what he conceived to be art in Paris after the war, a life that culminated in his murder of his mistress and his suicide. Innocence is not exclusively an American quality: in reviewing H. Rider Haggard's diaries, Fussell notes Haggard's progress from a rather complacent view of World War I as a sort of moral tonic to a sense of despair at the enormous and tragic waste of young men that the war soon became.

The compassion that Fussell exhibits in these essays is a salient characteristic of his satire, and like any satirist he implies a moral and social norm—one that may seem surprisingly conservative, or perhaps even neoclassical. In "Notes on Class," Fussell suggests that an ideal of privacy, freedom, grace, and independence—perhaps even the concept of the gentleman—may be the motive force behind the American class system. In "A Place to Recuperate," he describes an imaginary but ideal resort, located perhaps on one of the Swiss or Italian lakes, where almost Edwardian amenities of dignity and service still obtain; here one could recuperate, indeed, from what he elsewhere calls the "formlessness and uniformity that is the modern scene." In "Waugh in His Letters," Fussell pays tribute to Evelyn Waugh's intense and rigorous sense of honor and, even more, to Waugh's embodiment of a vision of comic irony in meticulous prose.

There is something neoclassical, also, in Fussell's tastes in literature: he clearly regards nonfictional works such as biographies, memoirs, diaries, and letters as offering surer insights into human behavior than do novels; those novels that he does seem to regard most highly, such as Joseph Heller's *Catch-22* (1961) and Thomas Pynchon's *Gravity's Rainbow* (1973), perhaps emphasize a satiric vision over verisimilitude and realism; they may be the modern era's nearest approach to Jonathan Swift's *Gulliver's Travels* (1726). Paralleling his preference for nonfiction in literature is his interest in photographs, which he interprets with skill and insight; these too have for him a particular kind of truth.

Fussell's essays and reviews make witty and entertaining reading, but they should not be regarded as trivial because they are amusing or as ephemeral because they were often written as occasional pieces. The essays in *The Boy Scout Handbook and Other Observations* are reflections of the humanistic ideal that recognizes the depths of man's irrationality but still affirms the glories of his fragile civilization, which is based on a strong sense of ethics in conduct and a passionate devotion to clarity, wit, and elegance in language.

Erwin Hester

Sources for Further Study

Christian Science Monitor. September 10, 1982, p. B4.
Library Journal. CVII, August, 1982, p. 1463.
Nation. CCXXXVI, November 27, 1982, p. 565.
National Review. XXXIV, November 12, 1982, p. 1428.
The New York Times Book Review. LXXXVII, August 29, 1982, p. 6.
The New Yorker. LVIII, October 4, 1982, p. 151.
Publishers Weekly. CCXXI, June 25, 1982, p. 102.
The Sewanee Review. XC, October, 1982, p. R110.

BRAIDED LIVES

Author: Marge Piercy (1936-   )
Publisher: Summit Books (New York). 441 pp. $15.50; paperback $3.95
Type of work: Novel
Time: 1953 to the present
Locale: Detroit, Ann Arbor, New York

A feminist poet traces the friends and incidents that shaped her coming of age as a working-class student in college on a scholarship during the 1950's

> *Principal characters:*
> JILL STUART, a half-Jewish, half-Welsh girl from inner-city Detroit
> DONNA STUART, Jill's cousin and college roommate
> PEARL STUART, Jill's mother, the child of immigrants
> HOWIE DAHLBERG, a pre-medical student from Detroit
> MIKE LOESSER, a college poet
> PETER CRECY, a graduate student from Grosse Pointe, Michigan

Poetry, feminism, and political activism are the strands that have composed Marge Piercy's public life for the past twenty-five years. Her seventh novel, apparently more autobiographical than previous books, explores the experiences that mark Jill Stuart's passage into womanhood. Despite the book's autobiographical basis, it is not primarily personal; like many women's coming-of-age novels, it tells of entwined lives. Although Jill is essentially an outsider, many women of her generation passed through college in the 1950's and through first marriages in the 1960's to become the new feminists of the 1970's. Why were they not permanently misshapen by the enormous pressures toward conformity, the feminine mystique, the rigid sex roles, the massive lecture classes, the fraternity pins and cashmere sweater sets, the rush to achieve marriage before the end of four college years? Answering these questions, *Braided Lives* is political in the broadest sense: it not only traces the convictions that grow from personal experiences but also contains a political message for the 1980's.

Jill Stuart is able to forge an identity of her own, in part, because she is a chronic misfit. The Kazan-Jewish looks inherited from her mother do not suit the name that comes from her Welsh father. Very few white children attend her Detroit grade school—and the only other Jewish girl in her neighborhood is not one of them. (Brown-skinned Sarah Altweiler will, however, become important in the civil rights movement.) In high school, the rest of the A-track students are middle-class and socially exclusive; the girls from Jill's neighborhood hang out on street corners, get pregnant, and drop out of high school. In college, Jill is too poor, has the wrong clothes, takes the wrong courses (hard ones), and will never be rushed by sororities or dated by football players; in her vacation and part-time jobs, she is a college girl misplaced among working women. To the families of her men friends, she is from the wrong social class or of the wrong religion (usually both). Piercy does not, however, dwell on Jill's discomfort. The people who felt at home in Ann Arbor in the 1950's disappeared into corporations, suburbs, station wagons, and Valium—and some of the women did not discover their own worth until twenty years later, when their husbands replaced them with newer models. Because Jill does not fit and is too stubborn to make herself fit, she learns at a Midwest college during the conformist years how to examine, to ask questions, to care, and to take responsibility for making the world more tolerable.

Like many twentieth century women's books, *Braided Lives* deliberately collectivizes the center of interest. Some of the women treated in the novel are seriously damaged. Callie, pregnant before the end of high school, is sent to prison for shooting her husband with his own Police Special when he abuses their daughter. Theo is sexually victimized by the psychoanalyst her parents have enlisted to "cure" her lesbianism. Others survive, or rise again, or discover their own strength. Alberta Mann, who serves as Jill's model of a mature and politically aware woman in the 1950's, leaves her father's law firm to join another that specializes in domestic disputes. Piercy braids the threads of many stories into a political lifeline, a net that links the women who have touched at various points in the past.

Braided Lives thus admirably avoids the charge that feminism is a middle-class luxury. Piercy downplays adolescent emotional slights; she provides no guaranteed income to support her heroine in a search for self-realization, nor is Jill trapped and destroyed by the grind of poverty and circumstances beyond her control. She takes control, exercises options. Conscious of her position as outsider, she never unthinkingly adopts the standards of worlds into which she passes; she questions male values, bourgeois values, and the values of the intellectual elite.

The relationship between Jill and her roommate/cousin Donna Stuart is the book's central thread. The two are light and dark twins who may function as alternate sides of the same personality or alternate versions of the scholarship woman trying to make something of herself. Donna has an acceptably WASPish appearance and is thankful that the scholarship gives her in her college years the opportunity of finding a man who will supply the later life-style she craves. Donna is also sexually voracious, or at least constantly involved with her sexuality: as a freshman, she lies about her virginity; she confesses to having sex with her sister's husband, wears slinky clothes given to her by a married man, picks up a townie greaser who rapes her, flees from one involvement to another amid mounting webs of lies, false facades, and efforts to get money needed for abortions. What Donna seeks, however, is only peripherally linked to sex itself. Her sexuality is both an unpredictable appetite and a means to get from men something that she cannot achieve in her own right. Donna's cockiness covers a deep sense of inadequacy. She attaches herself to men with prestige or money because she despairs of having them otherwise. Nor is her ambition modest enough to be satisfied by the man she can get; she marries Peter Crecy and immediately begins trying to make him into something better. Toward the end of the novel, there is hope that she may be about to break out of her trap, although her weather-bunny and casting-couch entrance into the world of television reporting does not suggest that she is yet prepared to exercise her own power instead of borrowing it from men.

The book is inevitably concerned with sex and its consequences; it is about attaining womanhood in the days before the pill and legal abortion, when a woman needed a "married name" and a plain band from Woolworth's to persuade a doctor to fit a diaphragm. Surprisingly, there is relatively little of the typical late-adolescent romantic drama (questions about love, fantasies about proposals or propositions, fending off seductions and entrapments). Jill does not confuse sex with love. In all of her most intense relationships— particularly with Donna and with Howie—erotic attraction contributes to the emotional closeness, but sexual union is ultimately harmful. One of the reasons that Jill's adult energies are available for poetry, civil rights, the antiwar movement, and feminism is that her emotion and caring are not funneled into a single heterosexual attachment. Although Jill and Donna share sex in their early teens, *Braided Lives* is not about "repressed lesbianism." The more important issue is how women can be real friends at a time (both a particular historical time, and a personal time—late adolescence—when the nesting instinct is strong) that encourages them to measure their worth by masculine standards and that creates in them a strong need for men's love and recognition. Women must value other women, as well as feeling their pain, if feminism is to be meaningful. After Donna dies, Jill's love for her fuels an organization that effectively provides aftercare services for women who have illegal abortions.

All of the well-realized characters are women; the men—even Howie Dahlberg, Jill's long-time friend—are two-dimensional. The third dimension, which men lack, is caring. Jill's eldest brother lives across the state line to evade child support; her other brother (apparently killed by police) leaves two widows; Professor Donaldson, the history department's resident radical, ends his relationship with Alberta Mann rather than damage his career by marrying the daughter of Communists. Mike Loesser, Jill's first lover, earnestly tells her what to read and what to think; he also lets her know that her poetry is too inadequate to discuss. The campus political action group talks about abstractions in order to avoid passions. For Jill and the other women, however, feelings and friendship require action. Jill as an undergraduate will burglarize a warehouse to get money for someone's abortion, and Jill as an adult is still not interested in any abstract discussion of relative ethics. Piercy avoids argument and preaching; she expects her readers to transform emotions into political realizations.

The book's shape and message grow from its grounding in the present, which supplies Jill's mature voice and makes readers contribute to the making of meaning. Although most of the events occur between the spring of 1953 and the decade's end, the story begins in the present; the book is framed by the reader's recognition that the first-person narrator is a survivor, an author of some reputation, an activist, and a warm, competent, mature, and relatively contented woman. Thus, although the connections are never mechanical, readers see that the incidents Jill selects have shaped the attitudes and ethics important to her as an adult. Furthermore, the post-1960 events are not described in sequence or detail. Readers are required to fill in gaps, to know, for example, enough about the civil rights movement to guess what must have happened to Howie. Readers thus become part of the collective story; they are engaged within the braid of lives.

Because the narrative voice is that of Jill as an adult, the book tellingly reveals the slow transformation of her feelings about her mother. At the story's opening, Jill leaves the house after a stormy argument, and hardly a day passes without tension. Even in *Small Changes* (1973), Piercy's picture of mother-daughter relationships was still largely biased in favor of the daughters. Jill in the 1980's, however, is the age that her mother was during Jill's adolescence. The reader, with Jill, increasingly appreciates Pearl Stuart's cunning, her own radicalism, and the way that her life history makes her urge Jill toward marriage or a secretarial job for the sake of safety and security. The link is tempered by fire when Pearl reaches into her stock of female tradition and tells Jill how to abort herself. The relationship is never sentimentalized or uncomplicated; Jill and Pearl are different women, matured by different pasts. Nevertheless, they share essential values, and Jill's growing perception of their similarities is moving and convincing.

Jill's voice is the voice of Piercy the poet. Jill does not bore readers with extensive commentary or self-analysis. She has an attractive, clear-eyed cynicism and creates lucid phrases that communicate the exact taste of the moment. Even in self-mockery, she sees herself true. "I will go to Detroit and be good to my mother," she thinks, "and make her love me. I will come back and seduce Howie magically without his realizing I am seducing him: he will think it is his idea. I will find the money somewhere and save Donna. Everybody will love me, because I am good and indispensable." Behind the wry tone, Jill has put her finger on both the psychic and the moral roots of her political activism.

The reminders of the present also give the book its relevance. The most powerful scenes are dominated by the fear of pregnancy, the desperation to raise money in time, and the horrifying consequences of illegal abortions. Piercy, in the tradition of Harriet Beecher Stowe, arouses her readers' emotions for a purpose. The adult values of Jill and her comrades were created during the college years when they made choices and defined the emotions and ethics that guide their lives. The book speaks personally and vividly to women who shared some of Jill Stuart's experiences. More pointedly, it reminds all readers that thirty years have passed. If women were shaped by their experiences during the 1950's, so were men. The male undergraduates that Jill knew would not take responsibility for their sexuality, would not come up with money when women needed it. Pregnancy was a woman's problem, and she ought to keep her mouth closed; men deliberately avoided thinking about it. Without climbing on a platform, Piercy makes readers realize that the college boys of the 1950's are now men in their most influential years: they are judges, editors, legislators, and public officials. They make laws and social policy. The book's intense emotions require that women in the 1980's consider what laws the boys of the 1950's are likely to make regarding contraception, pregnancy, and abortion—for which, thirty years ago, they successfully denied responsibility and sympathy.

Sally Mitchell

Sources for Further Study

Books and Bookmen. July, 1982, p. 15.
Library Journal. CVII, January 1, 1982, p. 109.
Ms. X, June, 1982, p. 18.
The New Leader. LXV, January 25, 1982, pp. 18-19.
The New York Times Book Review. LXXXVII, February 7, 1982, p. 7.
The New Yorker. LVII, February 22, 1982, p. 128.
The Progressive. XLVI, July, 1982, p. 62.
Publishers Weekly. CCXX, December 11, 1981, p. 51.
Saturday Review. IX, February, 1982, p. 60.
Times Literary Supplement. July 23, 1982, p. 807.
Wilson Library Bulletin. LVI, March, 1982, p. 548.

BRONX PRIMITIVE
Portraits in a Childhood

Author: Kate Simon
Publisher: The Viking Press (New York). 179 pp. $13.95
Type of work: Autobiography
Time: The 1920's
Locale: The Bronx, New York

A noted travel writer's recollections of her girlhood as a Jewish immigrant living in the Bronx

> *Principal personages:*
> KAILA "KATE," the author
> YUKELE, Kate's father
> LONIA, Kate's mother
> KATE'S BROTHER
> KATE'S SISTER

To open the pages of *Bronx Primitive: Portraits in a Childhood* is to step back sixty years into the childhood world of the author, who arrived in New York as a four-year-old Jewish immigrant from Poland at the end of World War I. Kate Simon, best known for her travel books on England, Italy, Mexico, and New York, does an extraordinarily skillful job of re-creating both the atmosphere of the Bronx neighborhood in which she grew up and the perspective of her eight- to twelve-year-old self. Simon's combination of humor, pathos, realism, and honesty makes this a moving record of an era and of a young girl's struggle to grow up in a new world.

Simon begins her book with a tour of her neighborhood, the area around the Tremont El Station, near Crotona Park. She deftly depicts the major landmarks of her life there: P.S. 58, the public library, Mrs. Katz's candy store, two movie houses (one for regular Saturday afternoon entertainment, the other for special occasions), and a white blossoming tree on 179th street, a rare example of natural beauty which she considered her private possession. The center of this world was the family apartment on the top floor of a tenement on Lafontaine Avenue. Each room, as she describes it, takes on a character of its own. The bathroom is associated both with the carp that swam in the tub on Wednesdays and Thursdays before becoming Friday's dinner and with the lectures and whippings that her father administered there when she or her brother was disobedient. The kitchen was the center of family conversation, newspaper reading, and her mother's storytelling, often tinged with macabre humor. The living room, used only for visitors and for piano practicing, contained her mother's treasures, among them a tablecloth that was elaborately embroidered in pink and red roses and a marble bowl with tiny pigeons that rested in holes on the rim, providing endless fascination to Kate, who was considered careful enough to take them in and out.

Central to the book, appropriately subtitled "Portraits in a Childhood," are sketches of dozens of individuals whose lives touched the author's, some significantly, some lightly. She devotes a chapter to the neighbors who shared their fifth floor landing. The men, whose contact with the children was limited, are mentioned briefly; the women are described in more detail. At the time when her mother was preoccupied with the birth of her third child, Kate sought out Fannie Herman, "a skinny little sparrow, hopping, restless, a bewildered child in a strange room." Fannie was housebound, terrified by the street where her young son had been killed by a truck, bewildered by the "machinkele" her husband drove, and powerless to control her rebellious daughter, Tobie. Kate spent long hours teaching her to write her first name in large letters on the dusty piano top.

Next door to Fanny lived Mrs. Haskell, who "resembled a melting vanilla cone." Mrs. Haskell included her young friend Kate in her preparations for the end of the world, which was to come, she assured the child, on October 20. Kate felt sure no blond Christian God would save Jewish children, but she repressed her anxiety and watched with interest as Mrs. Haskell scrubbed everything in her house and purchased new white clothing from the faraway fantasy land of Macy's. When October 20 passed without incident, Mrs. Haskell invited Kate in for a Fig Newton and announced that God had told her she must be patient. From then on, Kate noted, they carefully avoided looking at each other when they met.

The third of the neighbors, Mrs. Silverberg, was for a time Kate's ideal of style and glamour, as well as the provider of delicious homemade cookies. Then she vanished, after a noisy night when she appeared on the landing covered with makeup and jewelry, shrieking about her affair with Rudolph Valentino. The memory of her, the author says, was forever after tied to the perplexing question of the boundary between madness and sanity.

Portrayed more briefly are many other neighborhood characters: Mrs. Santini, the Italian mother who persisted in chewing her babies' food in her own mouth before giving it to them; Mrs. Rabinowitz, who was reputed to be able to cast the evil eye on unsuspecting acquaintances; Dr. James, the elderly New England physician who quietly performed thousands of abortions on immigrant women to keep them from killing themselves with knitting needles and poisonous home remedies. Especially alluring to young Kate were the older girls, both Italian and Jewish, who were eager to share their often-spurious information about sex and childbirth with her. She greatly admired Helen Roth for being brave enough to fail a grade in school—something she herself would never have dared. Helen also acted as the provider of young female company for an elderly musician who fed his young guests cake and showed them pornographic pictures. Invited once to his Sunday morning "party," Kate left hastily, sure she did not want to be there, but equally sure this was not something to report to adults.

While each of these individuals made some contribution to Kate's education in the ways of the world, the dominant figures in her life were clearly her parents. Significantly, except in the one chapter devoted to their early life in Poland, she never calls them by name. They are simply "my mother" and "my father." In characterizing them, the author almost always keeps her vision limited to what she could have perceived as a child. They were presences in her life, rather than individuals bound up in their own problems. Yet on at least one memorable occasion, she had a fleeting glimpse into their separate existence. Onè evening, after a long period of silent quarreling, Kate found the apartment door uncharacteristically locked. Returning a little later, when the door was unlocked, she stumbled into one of the few moments of tenderness she relates in the book—her mother sitting in a chair with her feet in a pan of warm water, gently splashing her husband as he cut her toenails.

Battle was far more common than camaraderie for this strong-willed couple. Kate's father was the much-beloved, spoiled last child and only son of a prosperous Polish family. Married to satisfy his father's desire to see him settled, he left his pregnant wife and his one-year-old daughter Kaila (she became Kate when they arrived in America) and went to New York with visions of making a fortune. His daugher surmises that once there, he adopted a carefree bachelor existence that he was reluctant to give up when his family joined him as refugees from war-ravaged Europe. He was a good craftsman, a shoemaker, who provided a regular if not lavish income for his family, but he was also a domestic tyrant. Any slip in academic achievement or, worse, "wild" behavior in the neighborhood aroused his fury at both Kate and her mother, whom he considered much too permissive. He regularly launched into tirades in which he prophesied his daughter's moral degradation. She would become a "street girl," he raged. The role eventually began to take on a certain appeal for her.

The greatest strain between father and daughter came as Kate neared the end of elementary school. Her father cherished a dream of making her a concert pianist, and to that end, provided music lessons with the best teacher available, accompanyed her regularly to Sunday afternoon student recitals, and even purchased an expensive new piano. He wove elaborate schemes that took him and Kate on concert tours around Europe. He vowed to take her out of school at once so that she could begin to practice the obligatory six to eight hours a day. Kate, who loved school and recognized the limitations of her musical talents, was disturbed that his plans ignored the existence of her mother, brother, and sister, and she was prepared to defy him to the death if he insisted.

An undercurrent of resentment toward him runs throughout the book, surfacing most strongly near the end as the author reflects on her unpleasant experiences with two young relatives of her father, a man and a woman who stayed with the family on their arrival in America. Both of them, at separate times, slipped into the bed she shared with her brother, using her to satisfy their sexual urges. She resisted them silently, angrily, not wanting to cause the turmoil that would result if she appealed to her parents. Eventually, much later, she concluded that her light-sleeping father must have known what was going on. Yet in his value system, the family of his origin was more important than the family he had helped to create, and he apparently felt no need to protect his daughter.

Kate's relationship with her mother, though it had the usual tensions, seems to have been much more positive. Lonia Babicz—she, alone, is once given her full name—came from a larger, less prosperous family than that of her husband. She had little schooling but had educated herself in the ways of the world as the proprietor of a corset shop before she married in her early twenties. In New York, she became the neighborhood authority on many matters, encouraging Mrs. Santini to use more sanitary methods of feeding her babies, helping the hapless Fannie Herman clean house for Jewish holidays, responding to calls for help from others when children became ill. She took English lessons at the library and in many other ways provided for her daughter a model of self-sufficiency and competence.

Kate's reliance on her mother was severely shaken when Lonia was pregnant with Kate's younger sister. (Many years later, she told Kate that she had had this baby only because Dr. James had refused to perform another abortion; she had thirteen abortions—a startling insight into immigrant life at this time.) Kate found it hard to understand her mother's new and unfamiliar vulnerability and fatigue, and she had picked up just enough women's conversation to have bizarre visions of babies being ripped from their mothers' stomachs with "enormous black pincers, like those the iceman used to pull blocks of ice from his wagon." The trauma of lying in bed and hearing her mother's screams during the delivery, coupled with the understanding that her own birth had put her mother through the same agony, was so great that she refused to see either her mother or the baby for days after her sister was born. Once she discovered that her mother had not been horribly mutilated and the baby had no forceps-caused "ditch" in her head, however, they settled back into their family routine, Kate with another young sibling.

Neither the brother nor the sister is very distinctly characterized here; again, the author chooses not to use names. "My brother" was Kate's companion in forbidden escapades, like sailing along on roller skates behind passing trucks or trying to scale a rocky cliff in Crotona Park. He once, to her amazement, came to her defense with his fists, when a gang of bullies set upon her and her friends and began pulling up their skirts. Most of the time, however, he was a care and a burden. Even at four, she was expected to look after him on the trip to America; he was so emaciated that she had little trouble carrying him. Later, he caused her at least one moment of excruciating humiliation. While her mother was convalescing after the baby's birth, his teacher called Kate to his classroom and scolded her for allowing him to come to school with a dirty neck. This event so enraged her that she flung a knife at his head when they got home. Fortunately, she missed, but she received the worst whipping of her life as a result, and she could not explain her motives in her own defense. Her sister was also a responsibility, but she appears to have been a gentle child, and her providential sickliness during her first year provided Kate and their brother with one of the happiest weeks of their lives, a vacation on Coney Island that is described in memorable detail.

Simon's most moving and fully developed portrait is the self-portrait that emerges stroke by stroke throughout the book. The child Kate is seen as both vulnerable and tough, naïve and responsible beyond her years. There is a poignant description of her, at four, in a strange room somewhere in Europe. Her mother has gone to find food, and she is holding her brother on her lap, reassuring him that their mother will return, though she herself is terrified at the possibility of abandonment. The same fear returned in a more paralyzing form a year or two later in New York, when her father left the two children alone in front of a toy store window—to teach them not to lag behind. Rescue by her mother and explanations by her father did not erase the stark terror she had felt or her anger at being subjected to this experience: "I remembered and judged, accumulating a sort of Domesday Book on my father's deeds. He sensed and feared it, and it was that fear on which I battened, the tears he could not make me shed freezing as an ice wall between us."

To the outside observer, Kate was a model child. She did well in school, walked her brother to school, pushed her sister in her carriage and turned her over only once, even practiced the piano two hours a day and four on Sunday. Yet her internal life was much less serene. She was struggling against her father and simultaneously trying to identify herself as a female, to unravel the mysteries of sexuality that produced the babies and the hushed whispers among her mother's acquaintances. Since this was an era when parents and children avoided these subjects, she derived most of her information from the older girls in the neighborhood. What she learned shocked and disgusted her; she was so reluctant to become a woman that she bound her developing breasts so tightly with ribbons that her underarms bled. Yet she coped quite maturely with the stealthy, unwelcome attentions of her cousins, the barber who cut her hair, and an elderly neighbor, and she developed a normal, healthy crush on a glamorous, irresponsible Italian boy a year or two older than she. The last glimpse the author gives of her adolescent self is of a thirteen-and-a-half-year-old who saw herself "as desirable as Gloria Swanson, as steely as Nita Naldi, as winsome as Marion Davies . . . like them, invincible and immortal."

Bronx Primitive offers the reader many pleasures. It is a vivid, detailed, and authentic picture of what life was like for the Italian and Jewish immigrants who settled in the Bronx in the 1920's. It is even more appealing as the portrait of a courageous, resourceful child and her struggles to carve out an identity as a woman in a new society.

Elizabeth Johnston Lipscomb

Sources for Further Study

Library Journal. CVII, May 1, 1982, p. 883.
Ms. X, June, 1982, p. 80.
The New York Times Book Review. LXXXVII, May 23, 1982, p. 9.
The New Yorker. LVIII, May 10, 1982, p. 169.
The Sewanee Review. XC, October, 1982, p. R108.
Time. CXIX, April 19, 1982, p. 80.

THE BURNING HOUSE

Author: Ann Beattie (1947-   )
Publisher: Random House (New York). 256 pp. $12.95
Type of work: Short stories
Time: The late 1970's to the present
Locale: The East Coast

The modern struggle for identity involves a reconciliation between love and freedom, a fulfillment which seems impossible for the characters in these stories

Ann Beattie's characters live in a world where most of the old certainties no longer obtain. Values have been shaken, religious beliefs overthrown. The passivity of spiritual inertia threatens. Yet humankind has a history of readjusting its sights in the face of confusing change and moving ahead with new integrity. *The Burning House* deals with the passivity and aimlessness of a generation of men and women who have found that the values of an earlier time are out of place, worn down, no longer valid; some of the titles of these stories suggest their plight: "Afloat," "Waiting," "Like Glass," "Learning to Fall." Work brings no pleasure, even though many of the characters are professionals; the main focus in their toneless lives is overwhelming dispiritedness, a sort of structural fatigue that belies the drama of the title of the work: the house burns down around them.

Beattie's protagonists are without footholds. Friends *do* help one another, but the help is merely sustaining, not rehabilitating. In the title story, "The Burning House," Amy's marriage is falling apart. Although her house is full of friends whom she and her husband have known for years, these friends can offer no support, for their own lives are torn: Freddy, high on marijuana, can only offer to help with the housework; J. D., whose wife and child were killed in an accident, can only bandage Amy's bleeding finger. Her husband has a mistress, she has a lover, and the trivial conversation of avoidance continues endlessly.

The friends in "Jacklighting" have gathered to commemorate the birthday of a beloved companion who has died. None of them is able to concentrate on the reason why they have gotten together. The dead man, Nicholas, had defined life for them by seeing them through LSD trips and planning their vacations; now, the young girlfriend of Nicholas' brother says, "I don't get the feeling you people had another life." Each is incapable of mourning or of comforting the others, and the narrator, when she closes her eyes in a kind of tribute, sees nothing.

Children figure significantly in these stories. They are tight, tense, suspicious, selective, wise—in contrast to the adults, who are fearful, preoccupied, guilty, confused, and childish. In "Learning to Fall," Andrew, eight years old, is taken to the city by a friend of his mother. These two make the trip often, and the friend has known Andrew since his birth, yet the adult cannot love the child—he is not perfect. Slight damages caused by the impatient use of forceps have made him pitiable to this woman. She anticipates the time when Andrew will recognize that he is imperfect and become as self-conscious as adults inevitably must be. The boy clearly loves her and trusts her; he confides that his mother is learning to fall in her dancing class. She is learning to fall slowly and gracefully, a lesson she will pass on to her son: once one begins to fall, there is no stopping, so one must be as resourceful as possible. Perhaps this is a way out of the dilemma of stasis; a message of hope that Andrew will be in control.

In "Afloat," a sixteen-year-old visits her father. Each year, she brings a message from her mother which contains personal information recalling the life the parents shared ten years before. Annie is angry with her father because he never deigns to send a reply. Her anger, in fact, is quite positive in its energy compared to her father's distance.

Louise in "The Cinderella Waltz" directs her life as best she can around the childishness of adults: her mother, her father, and her father's lover. Louise's mother and her father's lover become confidantes of a sort, trying hard to be adult in a surrealistic way, while the child is the only one who dares to cry or to show anger. Bryce, in "Desire," misses his father when he is with his mother in Vermont and misses his mother when he is with his father in Pennsylvania. His father's live-in girlfriend plays with a toy fish in the bathtub and smokes marijuana. Bryce has never smoked marijuana and has planned already, at eight years of age, whom he will marry and where he will live. Certainly, his dreams are the same as those his elders saw pass away, yet his serious nature presages more moral conviction than his father can muster in his present relationship, where desire and anxiety are confused.

The children in *The Burning House* are like sad adults, and the adults are childlike, longing to be saved. In this world of psychic and social difficulties, drugs are used to blur the pain. Valium, marijuana, and liquor are used abundantly, but these painkillers merely induce a pervasive ennui.

In "Happy," a young, pregnant wife eyes her decanter full of drugs, yellow Valium, blue Valium, green Donnatol, and wonders if they will hurt the fetus. She does not really care, one feels, for she reveals her pregnancy by saying, "I wasn't trying not to get pregnant." Jake, of "Sunshine and Shadow," recalls his last acid trip: he had felt he was grounded, unable to move yet *needing* to move, knowing, "if he had taken off, he would have drifted not far from the ground, at a peculiar tilt, like the old man walking through air in the Chagall painting." Another character is asked if he is smoking marijuana in the office. "Not this time," he replies.

The loss of love is a pervasive theme in many of the stories. Ironically, the story "Happy" is about a marriage that does not even possess the energy to disintegrate. Husband and wife are like two strangers with no names and muted identities. There are no surprises. When a man dressed in a bear suit rings her doorbell to deliver a birthday message, the protagonist is unamazed, mildly irritated to have her depression interrupted. The details here minimize the drama: the notebook from which the bear reads his lines is marked "American Lit. from 1850"; a call to Los Angeles produces only familiar clichés; the present of a chocolate éclair is reduced to the brown stain of the frosting seeping through the bag "like dirt." When, at the end, the husband holds his wife and asks her to say, " I have a nice life," the words constitute merely a meaningless ritual, the fabric of which cannot possibly hold these people together.

Incorporeality defines the pregnant woman in "Girl Talk," who is conscious of her surroundings as if she has just surfaced from a long sleep: "I am really at some out-of-the-way beach house, with a man I am not married to and people I do not love, in labor." "Waiting" is about changing lives. Once husband and wife had the time to wait for precisely the right things to come into their lives. Now, John has left, last heard from in Berkeley, and Sally is at home selling the once-coveted life they shared, preparing to move "eventually." There is more than one refrigerator, a heavy, antique cupboard, permanent pieces of lives that no longer fit the aimless, drifting need to find something else onto which to hold. When the old dog, Hugo, fails to respond to his mistress' call, she is sure he is dead, yet she is unable to move to touch him. Instead, she sits on the lawn, tense with anxiety, immune to the caring inquiries of a delivery man and her best friend, Ray. When Hugo at long last arises and moves slowly toward her, there is no sigh of relief or cry of rejoicing: silent tears simply stream down her face—an affirmation of life only because what seems to have been taken away has been given back for awhile. Ray misunderstands her tears and comforts, "Anybody can take a trip." What can she do? Nothing. Nothing to resurrect the old life, nothing to define the new one.

In "Greenwich Time," a man spends nearly twenty-four hours trying to summon up enough directed animation to drive out to his remarried former wife's house and try to explain to her that he somehow had lost his son in the confusion of the situation and now wanted him back. When he finally overcomes his inertia, he cannot say what he wants to; it is as if he is moving in slow motion through a bad dream, eyelids unable to lift against the pressure of the horror. Nervous breakdowns, however, imply a certain amount of expended energy, and this character cannot complete his fall—he remains in suspended animation.

There are no answers. There are no templates to reshape lost forms. Everyone is changing, and any one of them could have been the first to cry. The story ironically entitled "Gravity" presents a character whose boyfriend is returning to his ex-girlfriend: "He opens the outside door with his key . . . and for a minute we're squeezed together in the space between locked doors.

I've called it jail. A coffin. . . . I've stood there and felt, more than once, the lightness of a person who isn't being kept in place by gravity, but my weightlessness has been from sadness and fear."

Sadness about the unexplained loss of past values; fear about the unknown quantities that lie ahead: characters treading water, afraid of drowning. Ann Beattie is under no illusions concerning the plight of the people in her stories. Writers reflect their times, and one hopes that Beattie's characters will grow up and out of their stagnation and dread and rediscover the ideal of individual fulfillment in whatever way lies ahead for her readers as well.

Kathleen Massey

Sources for Further Study

Library Journal. CVII, September 15, 1982, p. 1767.
Nation. CCXXXV, October 30, 1982, p. 441.
The New York Times Book Review. LXXXVII, September 26, 1982, p. 1.
Publishers Weekly. CCXXII, July 23, 1982, p. 128.

CADILLAC JACK

Author: Larry McMurtry (1936-   )
Publisher: Simon and Schuster (New York). 395 pp. $15.95
Type of work: Novel
Time: The present
Locale: Primarily Washington, D.C., and its environs

Narrated by the title character, a roving antique dealer, Larry McMurtry's eighth novel probes the tribulations of modern love and marriage against a background of deft and often hilarious social satire, dealing in particular with current morals and manners in the nation's capital

Principal characters:
"CADILLAC" JACK McGRIFF, a former athlete and rodeo-rider now in the antique trade
BOOG MILLER, a Texan political manipulator now based in Washington
BOSS MILLER, Boog's wife, a highly successful businesswoman
CINDY SANDERS, a young retailer from California
JEAN ARBER, a struggling antique dealer in the process of divorce
JIMMY ARBER, Jean's petulant but somehow charming husband
BEVERLY and
BELINDA ARBER, ages five and three, their daughters
COFFEE, known by her favorite drink, the latest of Jack's former wives
"UNCLE IKE" SPETTLE, age 110, who claims to have acquired at age nine the pair of boots that Billy the Kid was wearing when he died

Abandoning the large cast of recurring characters who have helped to populate all of his novels since *Moving On* (1970), Larry McMurtry in *Cadillac Jack* continues nevertheless to work the same social and psychological territory that has become familiar to readers of his recent fiction. Concerned as usual with the instability of human relationships in an increasingly rootless society, McMurtry offers as his narrator and viewpoint character one Jack McGriff, who, although a Texan by birth and allegiance, now claims no real home except for the lavishly equipped vintage Cadillac that carries him from coast to coast in search of rare collectibles and provides him with a convenient trade-name. Twice married and divorced at thirty-three, Jack still yearns for the rewards of love, marriage, and family; he is reluctant, however, to abandon the mobility that provides him with greater potential profits than those enjoyed by "stationary" dealers who must stock and maintain their own shops. Describing himself as a "scout," he functions professionally as a middleman between hard-to-find artifacts and avid collectors for whom cost is no object; in the process, he spares the reader few insights into the lives and personalities of the super-rich.

If *Somebody's Darling* (1978) is McMurtry's Hollywood novel, then *Cadillac*

Jack is his Washington novel, paying particular attention to the use and abuse of money and power in the nation's capital. It is not, however, in any real sense a "political" novel; although politicians and their hangers-on appear frequently, often portrayed in broad caricature (with such names as Khaki Descartes and Dunscombe Cotswinkle), it is clear that McMurtry's real interest lies not in politics but in the twists and turns of human behavior occasioned by the pursuit of love, sex, and material possessions. Washington hostesses, for example, are notable mainly for their amatory exploits, and one senior correspondent commands the narrator's attention primarily because of his overweening interest in truncheons, antique billy clubs of which he is presumably the leading American collector.

Indeed, McMurtry's choice of an antique dealer as his narrator-protagonist allows for thorough exploration of American acquisitiveness in one of its most prevalent current manifestations. Although a few of the collectors from whom Jack buys and to whom he sells have a genuine interest in what they collect, the vast majority value their accumulation of rare objects as mere status symbols, expressions of their often newfound purchasing power. Uniqueness, rather than beauty or intrinsic value, determines the asking price for artifacts often acquired for no better reason than to keep them out of the hands of others.

Skillfully blending psychological analysis with social observation, McMurtry places at the center of his novel the gross, boorish figure of "Boog" Miller, a transplanted Texan political manipulator who epitomizes the mindless collector's mentality that helps to keep Jack McGriff in business. It is on one of his trips to satisfy his apparently boundless greed that Jack finds himself drawn into the current social orbit of Boog and his wife Boss, in her own right a highly successful executive with a wide range of business interests. For Jack, the principal attraction is one Cindy Sanders, an upwardly mobile yet oddly insecure young Californian with three retail shops of her own. Throughout most of the novel, Jack surveys the prevailing social scene as Cindy's chosen escort, increasingly vulnerable to the woman's unconventional and potentially dangerous charm. At one party, he watches with mixed indignation and amusement as the carefully chosen, well-dressed guests attack the buffet table in a scene not unlike that to be observed in a zoo at feeding time; on another occasion, an elegant hostess casually places her two aging pug dogs on the banquet table where they proceed to wreak various kinds of havoc, incidentally devouring a portion of coq au vin left untouched by a talkative and absentminded legislator. "Now that *is* an upper-class thing," exclaims a Georgetown matron seated next to Jack.

For most of his career, McMurtry has been known for his portrayal of strong, often enigmatic female characters whose behavior continues to baffle the men with whom they occasionally become involved. In *Moving On*, for example, it is Patsy Carpenter and not her husband Jim whose quest for identity and sexual fulfillment animates the action of the novel; similarly, in *Cadillac Jack*, the narrator and title character serves mainly as a foil (and occasional plaything) for strong-minded women currently working out their destinies. Jack McGriff, like many of McMurtry's male characters, remains totally masculine yet emotionally immature, seemingly incapable of keeping the type of woman to whom he is habitually attracted. Even as he finds himself attracted to Cindy Sanders, and almost simultaneously to the petite but willful near-divorcée Jean Arber, Jack holds frequent and affectionate conversations with one of his former wives over the mobile telephone in his car. Partially illuminating the picture of Jack's love life is a long-lit torch for Boss Miller, whose mature beauty and seemingly effortless authority appear to represent Jack's eventual ideal. He has the common sense, however, to admire Boss from afar as she satisfies her own needs with a variety of lovers, including an Israeli poet known as Micah Leviticus who currently resides within the Miller household. Throughout the action, moreover, McMurtry leaves little doubt that Jack is the author of many of his own amatory misfortunes: although quick to fall in love, Jack is more than a little fickle himself, never quite able to decide what he really wants or expects from a woman, or from which one. By the time he appears ready to make up his mind, it is quite probably too late.

Embodying many of the current stereotypes concerning her home state of California, Cindy Sanders is nevertheless sufficiently credible as a character both to sustain Jack's interest and to symbolize much of the emptiness that McMurtry finds in contemporary American life. A former high-school homecoming queen, already quite successful in her chosen trade, Cindy plays the game of social one-upmanship with a determination that frequently betrays a nagging sense of insecurity. As elsewhere in McMurtry's fiction, liberation for women comes at high cost, often the cost of one's own humanity. Like Jill Peel, the troubled young artist of *All My Friends Are Going to Be Strangers* (1972) who reappears as a troubled Hollywood screenwriter by then in her late thirties in *Somebody's Darling*, Cindy Sanders is most dangerous to others precisely when she is least sure of herself, reaching out in what appears on the surface to be a bid for tenderness. Jack, in turn, is—like many McMurtry men—too prone to mistake vulnerability for the beginnings of affection.

Only slightly less dangerous to Jack's free-floating emotions is Jean Arber, née Tooley, a deceptively frail-looking woman who at thirty-five is attempting to achieve independence for herself and her two small daughters by opening an antique shop in one of the shabbier sections of suburban Washington. Predictably, she and Jack first meet at an auction, where he has just outbid her on a rare tripartite icon improbably "lotted" between such undesirables as old tires and garden tools. Pursuing the disappointed bidder in an attempt to cheer her up, Jack soon finds himself quite attracted to Jean and increasingly drawn into her disordered family life. Jean's pending divorce, it seems, has been very much her own idea; her husband Jimmy, an affable bearded sort who reminds Jack of a "human hamster," appears determined to prevent the rupture at all costs, and Jack, for his part, has difficulty believing Jean's assertions that Jimmy is considerably less lovable and friendly than he seems. Compounding the issue is Jack's developing friendship with the Arbers' two daughters, ages five and three, who soon awaken in the childless Jack a latent yearning for family. The younger girl, Belinda, makes a particular appeal to Jack; with her unpredictable clownlike ways, she often impresses him as a synthesis of all the women in his life, present, past and future. As it happens, Jack is still quite involved with Cindy at the time of his encounter with the Arbers; he is also deeply concerned about the welfare of his ex-wife, Coffee, who has recently changed her taste in lovers from Texas lawyers named Robert or Richard to an Italian drug trafficker named Emilio who apparently beats her.

Hailed in mid-career as the originator of the "urban Western," McMurtry in *Cadillac Jack* continues, despite the Washington setting, to evoke memorable images of the West, both old and new. Jack, for all his rootlessness, is quite readily identifiable as a Texan by his choice of imagery and diction as well as by his cowboy attire, his rodeo background, and his choice of mobile trademark. One typical McMurtry touch is Jack's recollection of Goat Goslin, a beat-up old rodeo-rider who, quite literally, died with his boots on; the Millers, meanwhile, continue to exemplify Texas high living and big spending regardless of their current residence, recalling many of the characters to be found in *Moving On* and *All My Friends Are Going to Be Strangers*. Both of Jack's former wives still live in Texas, and he frequently passes through the state on his trips in search of collectibles.

Perhaps not surprisingly, much of the antique traffic described in *Cadillac Jack* involves Western memorabilia, a new status symbol among nouveau-riche collectors. Heading the list of desirables, often with Jack's help, are cowboy boots both old and new, the newer ones made valuable by the silver, gold, and precious stones used in their decoration. In a major subplot concerning his relationship with Cindy Sanders, Jack helps Cindy to plan a major boot exhibit in the Washington area, of which the principal attraction will be the boots that Billy the Kid was wearing when Pat Garrett shot him. The boots, now in a bank vault, are the property of an old man of the sort that McMurtry excels in portraying: Uncle Ike Spettle, now 110 years old, witnessed the shooting as a nine-year-old boy and had the presence of mind to acquire the boots, which have since provided his main claim to fame. When Jack and Cindy visit him in New Mexico to arrange for exhibition of the boots, Uncle Ike reveals himself as a highly observant and outspoken old curmudgeon, receptive despite his age to Cindy's obvious charms. Later, Jack's quest for other display boots involves him briefly with the Twines, a wealthy Texas ranch couple with many valuable boots and a turbulent domestic life that may well erupt in violence. Jack, although resisting Josie Twine's sexual approaches, agrees to take her with him to Washington, where she soon joins the growing list of the Millers' semipermanent house guests.

Although the names are changed, along with certain details, the Twines and Uncle Ike are likely to appear familiar, as does Jack McGriff himself, to those readers already familiar with McMurtry's recent fiction. The Twines resemble many couples briefly glimpsed in *Moving On* and *All My Friends Are Going to Be Strangers*; Uncle Ike, too, has his counterparts in those two novels, self-sufficient oldsters who perhaps trace their ultimate ancestry to the archetypal figure of Homer Bannon in McMurtry's first novel, *Horseman, Pass By* (1961), best-known as the basis of the motion picture *Hud*. Jack, meanwhile, with his combined background in rodeo and in intercollegiate basketball, recalls many of the increasingly urbanized and mobile young Texans first encountered in *Moving On*. Indeed, the major difference between *Cadillac Jack* and McMurtry's earlier novels often appears to be in the author's tone; by comparison, for example, with *All My Friends Are Going to Be Strangers* (perhaps McMurtry's strongest novel to date, if not his most ambitious), the writing in *Cadillac Jack* appears at times too facile, the characterization at times too close to caricature. Still, the book is a considerable improvement over *Somebody's Darling* with its strained satire, or *Terms of Endearment* (1975), in which the author's apparently deepening pessimism all but precludes any possibility of humor.

Over the years, one of McMurtry's greatest weaknesses as a novelist has been his handling of point of view, particularly when attempting third-person narration. *The Last Picture Show* (1966), although justly acclaimed both as a novel and as a film, is severely flawed in the printed form by shifting points of view, with the omniscient narrator (or author) straining credibility as he attempts to speak for a variety of characters, communicating their innermost thoughts. A similar problem occurs, although with less severity, in *Moving On*, suggesting that McMurtry may well do his best writing when limited to the viewpoint of a single character who addresses the reader directly in the first person. As noted above, *All My Friends Are Going to Be Strangers* is probably McMurtry's finest novel to date, owing no small part of its success to the unifying character of its narrator-protagonist Danny Deck, ostensibly a soon-to-be-published first novelist. Jack McGriff, McMurtry's only first-person narrator since Danny, is nearly as successful in sustaining the reader's interest and attention, thanks in part to a similar sense of humor and of life's wry ironies. Jack's sense of humor, however, tends to be a bit broader than Danny's, bordering at times upon farce; of the two narrator-protagonists, it is Danny who, although presented at an earlier age, seems to have the more balanced and mature appreciation of life's possibilities.

At the very least, McMurtry's choice of characters, situations, and point of view in *Cadillac Jack* suggests that he is working his way back toward the type of thoughtful, engrossing, often highly amusing satire that characterizes the best of his earlier work, drawing power from his own roots in a West that has undergone most of its social change during McMurtry's own lifetime. No small part of the change, as McMurtry duly notes, has had to do with rapidly shifting sexual roles and the resulting effects upon contemporary love and marriage: indeed, at the end of the novel, it is hard to tell whether Jack McGriff's emotional immaturity is the cause or the effect of his frequent misadventures with the opposite sex. Even as his momentary hesitation between Cindy Sanders and Jean Arber appears to have cost Jack the love of both women, McMurtry appears to suggest that he may well be better off without either of them as he trains his sights on a yet-invisible future. Today's woman as seen by McMurtry, liberated in most respects save for her sexual needs and desires, is a most dangerous creature indeed; the male of the species, meanwhile, lags far behind the female in protective coloration and adaptive behavior.

David B. Parsell

Sources for Further Study

America. CXLVIII, March 5, 1983, p. 179.
Kirkus Review. L, August, 1982, p. 894.
Los Angeles Times Book Review. November 14, 1982, p. 1.
Nation. CCXXXV, November 20, 1982, p. 536.
National Review. XXXIV, November 26, 1982, p. 1492.
The New York Times Book Review. LXXXVII, November 21, 1982, p. 13.
Publishers Weekly. CCXXII, July 30, 1982, p. 63.
Village Voice Literary Supplement. October, 1982, p. 5.

CAMUS

Author: Patrick McCarthy (1941-   )
Publisher: Random House (New York). 359 pp. $17.95
Type of work: Literary biography
Time: 1913-1960
Locale: Algeria and France

An account, intended for the general reader, of the troubled life of the French Algerian author

> Principal personages:
> ALBERT CAMUS, a leading writer of the contemporary French renaissance in literature
> CATHERINE CAMUS, Camus' mother
> JEAN GRENIER, Camus' teacher in Algiers and a notable writer
> SIMONE HIÉ, Camus' first wife
> PASCAL PIA, an editor and an early influence on Camus
> FRANCINE FAURE, Camus' second wife
> JEAN-PAUL SARTRE, a dominant literary figure in postwar Paris
> MARIA CASARÉS, a Spanish actress and Camus' lover
> RENÉ CHAR, a major poet and Camus' neighbor in Provence
> MICHEL GALLIMARD, Camus' friend and publisher

Patrick McCarthy's biography appears as part of a recent revival of interest in the writings of Albert Camus. *Camus* begins and ends with references to the Nobel laureate's posthumous fate; while he remained generally respected in the United States, he had come to seem stale and antiquated to many Europeans. His drama was superseded by that of Samuel Beckett and Eugene Ionesco and his fiction by *le nouveau roman*. His ideals of clarity and measure were not congenial to the passionate intensity of the late 1960's, but subsequent disillusionment with secular absolutes has led some to champion Camus again as an exemplary voice of liberal moderation. McCarthy's book, following Herbert Lottman's *Albert Camus: A Biography* (1979), is the second study of Camus' life to have appeared in English in three years. It is admittedly indebted to Lottman's copious scholarly work for much of its information, but it attempts to provide a more widely accessible review of the renowned author's troubled life.

McCarthy's account is based on the premise that Camus' career is best understood within the context of Algeria, where, of mixed European ancestry, he was born and reared. Despite customary and exaggerated claims of American influence on *L'Étranger* (1942; *The Stranger*, 1946), McCarthy makes a case for that book as the great Algerian novel. He is intent on avoiding hagiography, and the Camus who emerges in these pages is not only a proletarian *pied noir* ill at ease among Parisian intellectuals but also a lofty moralist with feet of clay—inconstant as a lover, muddled as a thinker, and, ultimately, paralyzed as a writer. While convinced, despite weaknesses in the handling of plot and character, of the enduring value of the three novels Camus published before his death and of some of the lyrical essays, McCarthy finds many of the other texts as much an embarrassment to the reader as they were personally disastrous for their author.

Camus was shaped by Belcourt, the predominantly European, working-class suburb of Algiers in which he grew up. Camus' father died in World War I, when Camus was an infant. Catherine Camus, his impoverished, illiterate, and inaccessible mother, remained an exasperating challenge to him throughout his life. As portrayed by McCarthy, interwar Algeria was a lively, heterogeneous alembic for the future author. Its elemental landscape etched itself indelibly on his imagination. Algeria was a world of simple physical pleasures, where swimming was more urgent than metaphysics, and where violence was always lurking. Camus' first attack of tuberculosis, which was to plague him for the rest of his life, occurred when he was only sixteen; the effects of that dread disease, the loss of his father, the remoteness of his mother, and the anomalies of French Algerian society created in him a sense of alienation and a preoccupation with death. In an image suggesting the tough and savvy urchin, McCarthy repeatedly characterizes a mistrustful Camus, in Algeria and in Europe, as confronting the world with a compact boxer's stance.

McCarthy contends that Jean Grenier was the first great influence on the boy's career and one of the many surrogate fathers Camus sought. Grenier was an inspiring schoolteacher, who recognized and cultivated the young Camus' literary talents. Grenier was himself an ambitious and gifted writer, and later, as his former pupil began to acquire international acclaim, relations between the two became strained. Pascal Pia, Camus' editor when he worked for the newspaper *Alger-Républicain* in the late 1930's, likewise encouraged and then envied his protégé. As World War II approached, and Camus left Algeria, never again to live there, he had already established a pattern of simultaneous involvement in journalism, theater, politics, and belles lettres. He had also already married his first wife, Simone Hié, but as a result of her drug addiction and his constitutional inability to be faithful to any woman, divorce soon followed. In 1940, Camus married Francine Faure, and that marriage nominally survived prolonged separations, emotional turbulence, considerable philandering, and his passionate involvement with Spanish actress Maria Casarés that lasted more than fifteen years.

McCarthy describes Camus' literary oeuvre in terms of three cycles, three textual constellations, each clustering around one of the novels: *The Stranger*, *La Peste* (1947; *The Plague*, 1948), and *La Chute* (1956; *The Fall*, 1957). Camus began writing by probing the experience of oneness, and his first cycle, including *Noces* (1939; *Nuptials*, 1968), *Le Mythe de Sisyphe* (1942; *The Myth of Sisyphus*, 1955), and *Caligula* (1944), was created to bear stark witness to the individual's alienation within an inhuman universe. The second cycle—

The Plague, *L'État de siège* (1948; *State of Siege*, 1958), and *L'Homme révolté* (1951; *The Rebel*, 1953)—was, though scarcely more hopeful than the first, undertaken as a kind of declaration of freedom against this inhumanity. The third cycle—including *The Fall*, *L'Exil et le royaume* (1957; *Exile and the Kingdom*, 1958), and Camus' theatrical adaptations of works by Spanish, Russian, and American authors—is marked by a gloomy obsession with artistic sterility.

A problem confronting any literary biography is the disjuncture between life and art: how to avoid both a factitious exegesis of one by the other and a clumsy crosscutting between plot synopses and biographical episodes. McCarthy does not entirely succeed in creating a seamless web. Summary descriptions of the fictional worlds Camus created are abruptly and uncomfortably inserted within McCarthy's narrative of Camus' life, and attempts to provide the reader with background briefings, for example on French Algeria, further interrupt the story that McCarthy seems most eager to tell.

It is a story that acquires its greatest momentum with Camus' sojourn in France, out of journalistic ambition and concern for his health. The German invasion initially stranded Camus in the Massif Central, enforcing a lengthy separation from Francine in Algeria and reinforcing his sense of isolation. It was during this period that Camus worked on *The Plague*, the sophisticated narrative of rebellion against an indifferent cosmos that, when published after the war, ensured Camus' international fame and financial security. It, too, features a journalist, Rambert, who finds himself suddenly quarantined in a foreign land. During this period, Camus also began editorial work for the Gallimard publishing house and became an intimate of many leading Parisian intellectual figures. His troubled alliance with Jean-Paul Sartre also dates from the period when, alone in France, Camus, through his contacts in publishing, journalism, theater, and Left Bank café life, began to emerge as a literary celebrity. Camus and Sartre were simultaneously, in McCarthy's phrase, "becoming famous for giving glimpses of a godless, manless universe."

McCarthy is intent on dismantling the legend of Camus the Resistance warrior. He points out that, despite earlier opportunities, Camus did not become an active member of the Resistance until less than a year before the liberation of Paris. Nevertheless, his activity as an editor of the clandestine anti-Nazi newspaper *Combat* was of capital importance in determining the subsequent course of his career. The editorials he wrote for *Combat*, though bombastic, simplistic, and dogmatic, provided him the illusion of righteous, concerted struggle against the enemies of the Left. After the war, *Combat* lacked the same urgency and fell victim to latent tensions within its own ranks. Its loose coalition of anti-Nazis fragmented in bitter internecine quarrels once a common enemy was removed.

The most dramatic feud in the postwar Parisian cultural world developed between Sarte and Camus, erstwhile drinking companions and widely hailed as the dual leaders of the Existentialist movement. McCarthy makes it clear that between the Algerian Camus and the upper-middle-class Sartre, an intellectual from Normandy, there yawned a chasm of background, taste, and style already evident in the exhilarating days when both were first rising to prominence. The immediate occasion for the acrid public dispute was the publication, in 1951, of *The Rebel*. Though Camus invested substantial time and energy in this elaborate essay in political theory, it is often florid and misinformed—in McCarthy's assessment, "not merely his worst book but one that did him great harm." The critics were not kind to *The Rebel*, and when Sartre's magazine *Les Temps modernes* published a scathing attack by Francis Jeanson, Camus interpreted it as an act of personal betrayal by a trusted friend. The ensuing polemics, notable for their lack of charity, exposed Camus' intellectual shortcomings and exacerbated his feelings of isolation.

Further contributing to Camus' depression during the 1950's was a growing sense of guilt concerning his infidelities. Francine Camus, well aware of her husband's continuing affair with Maria Casarés and of his casual seductions of many other women, suffered a nervous breakdown in 1953. Moreover, the beginnings of the Arab uprising in Algeria particularly disturbed Camus, torn between France and Algeria and now at home in neither. He made repeated attempts to mediate among the violent factions, but, despite his moral authority, Camus saw himself powerless to effect a reconciliation between those who insisted on European domination of North Africa and those who would rid it of any French influence. He found himself forced to accept the role of passive spectator as calamity overtook his homeland.

It was during such despondency, when he was no longer able even to write, that Camus was awarded the Nobel Prize for Literature. He keenly felt the animosity of his rivals as well as the bitter ironies of public apotheosis at this stage in his life, and he was to feel mocked by the restrictive role of global celebrity. By the following year, Camus was, according to McCarthy, "a broken man," obsessed with his inability to write.

With his Nobel Prize money, Camus bought a house in the Provençal town of Lourmarin, near his friend René Char. There he began work on another novel, "Le Premier homme," which remains unfinished and unpublished. It was from Lourmarin that, in January of 1960, Camus accepted a ride back to Paris from his friend and publisher Michel Gallimard. When Gallimard's automobile crashed, killing both of them, it remained forever impossible to determine whether Camus had been on the verge of a creative resurgence or whether his death, at the age of forty-six, brought a melodramatic conclusion to a career in irreversible decline.

After his death, Camus' literary canonization was by no means assured, and the values of honesty, clarity, and moderation he espoused (without always exemplifying them) were neglected. It is a curiously tainted Camus who now emerges as a figure for ripened veneration. Thus, McCarthy can declare: "It is the unsaintly, anguished and curiously indifferent Camus who is the subject of this book."

Camus' life was marked by a dialectic between effusiveness and reticence. Indeed, as the acknowledged laureate of alienation, he was often tempted to enlist florid prose in the service of his reductive gaze. So, too, with his latest biographer, who is capable of oratorical flourishes about how Camus "mirrored the empty universe through his indifference" but who most often presents his case in spare, understated prose. McCarthy is guilty of occasional stylistic lapses, most frequently and vexingly when he misplaces or omits commas, and his incidental judgments ("Film directors like William Wyler and Orson Welles were preferred to better French directors like Carné and Clouzot") are not incontrovertible. Yet more effectively than the wealth of specialized studies available, *Camus* will revive the general reader's interest in the days and works of a remarkable twentieth century figure.

Steven G. Kellman

Sources for Further Study

America. CXLVII, December 18, 1982, p. 397.
Choice. XX, December, 1982, p. 587.
Library Journal. CVII, October 15, 1982, p. 1981.
Los Angeles Times Book Review. September 26, 1982, p. 3.
The New Republic. CLXXXVII, November 29, 1982, p. 33.
The New York Times Book Review. LXXXVII, September 12, 1982, p. 1.
The New Yorker. LVIII, December 20, 1982, p. 134.
Times Literary Supplement. May 7, 1982, p. 505.

A CHAIN OF VOICES

Author: André Brink (1935-   )
Publisher: William Morrow and Company (New York). 352 pp. $15.50; paperback
    $5.95
Type of work: Novel
Time: 1825
Locale: South Africa

The inherent tensions of slavery, exacerbated by ironic misunderstandings, cause a
slave revolt in South Africa in 1825

> *Principal characters:*
> GALANT, a slave
> OLD PIET VAN DER MERWE, a farmer and slave owner
> BAREND VAN DER MERWE, Old Piet's older son
> NICOLAAS VAN DER MERWE, Old Piet's younger son
> ALIDA VAN DER MERWE, the wife of Old Piet
> HESTER VAN DER MERWE, the wife of Barend
> CECELIA VAN DER MERWE, the wife of Nicolaas
> ABEL, a slave and a violinist

André Brink is a professor of Afrikaans-Dutch literature, internationally respected as a writer and political liberal. *A Chain of Voices* is indeed impeccably liberal but is admirably professional rather than professorial. In fact, the central problem of the novel is that, in presenting the conventional liberal universal wisdom on the issue of slavery in a manner that eschews pedantry, Brink frequently strays into the commonplace. Brink's primary audience may well be his fellow South Africans, for whom public expression of such conventional wisdom is rare, and, surely, those American readers shocked and amazed by *Roots* (1976) will be shocked and amazed by *A Chain of Voices*.

Despite the apparent political differences between the nineteenth century United States and the South Africa of 1825, one senses from *A Chain of Voices* the distinct universality of human nature. In 1825 South Africa had British "carpetbaggers" and half-hearted "Reconstruction" with Hottentotts freer than Bushmen, but not totally free. Slavery was abolished in 1834, and the Boer War (the South African equivalent of the American Civil War) was fought in 1842. A historical note included in the book would have been helpful to the reader.

Readers will see striking similarities of incident and symbol between *A Chain of Voices* and William Styron's *The Confessions of Nat Turner* (1967). The central problem is the same. It is superficially easier for contemporary authors and readers to depict and identify with rebellious slaves than with non-rebellious slaves and slave owners, but what may result is a sort of unwitting time travelogue in which an understandably irate contemporary man is trapped in a slave era as a slave and surrounded by stereotyped "white trash" racists, "Curse of Canaan" cracker-barrel theologians, "Uncle Toms," and worse. Both Styron and Brink rise above that problem in some impressive ways, but both sink into it from time to time.

A Chain of Voices presents an unsurprising range of attitudes toward slavery, developed in a multi-narrator series of monologues somewhat padded with too many traditional symbols of racial tension. The attitudes and situations are exacerbated by ironies of honest misunderstanding and mis-communication. The van der Merwe family *en famille* exists in a "cold comfort farm" situation that tends to write itself. Old Piet van der Merwe is a patriarchal Bible-reading bully who kidnaps a gentle city girl, Alida, as his bride. She has her own kind of strength and brings table manners and other amenities to the farm. Barend van der Merwe, the older son, becomes the image of his father, a bully and a coward, but is softer. Nicolaas van der Merwe, the younger son, has his mother's mixture of gentleness and iron will. It is a subtle irony, buried under more flamboyant ironies, that Old Piet's life is spared when the slaves revolt, because he has been brutally simple and honest while his sons are complex brutes who should know better than to mistreat slaves.

Cecelia van der Merwe, Nicolaas' wife, is seriously injured by the slaves but not killed. She has commonsense flashes of insight into the flaws of slavery and intimations of the slaves' humanity, but she fails to act positively and indulges in excesses of brutality. Hester van der Merwe, Barend's wife and a somewhat uncivilized lower-caste white woman, is a spiritual sister to the slaves. Her marriage is slavery and her rebellion is ongoing.

The slaves' wished-for identities run the gamut. There are those who have a self-conscious need for equality or a desire for freedom without equality; there are those who want better working conditions, those who want to be on the winning side, those loyal to whites, and those without attitudes.

The attitudes developed in the four parts of the novel begin with Galant's unrest as a subplot to the story of Old Piet and his sons and their wives. In the second part, the white marriages and taking of black mistresses intertwine with Galant's hopes and fears for his own prospects of marriage and children. The third part concerns the rebellion conspiracy. Part 4 depicts the rebellion itself.

These four parts are framed by the documents of indictment and verdict by the court trying the rebels. A careful reader will discover discrepancies between the court's assumptions and findings and the truth revealed in the novel. For example, the slaves found guilty on the evidence of stolen clothes in their possession were given clothes as a reward for their loyalty. The court's assumption that the lives of women and children were spared by the intervention of the black women is not true. They were, in fact, spared by Galant. Such misconceptions are found throughout the book.

The novel's four parts are subdivided into character monologues given by virtually every named adult character in the novel; the major characters have more turns and longer sections. Most of these monologues are linked by a kind of interlocked chain of chronology. The next character to speak is generally mentioned in the last part of a monologue, and he or she takes up as "old business" the matters that linked him or her to the previous narrator. A careful reader can develop a long list of events interpreted by multiple points of view, but the differences only serve to indicate major misunderstandings, and often they are merely redundant. Even subplot scenes get at least dual readings, and there is a compulsion to touch base with every named adult character, even when they have literally nothing to contribute.

Add to these problems the fact that the grammar and style do not vary much between characters, even from master to slave—dialect is not used beyond the unavoidable titles of South African usage—and the chain device becomes a gimmick which adds to the length of the novel, but not to its depth.

Communication from whites to whites and whites to blacks breaks down ironically beyond the demands of the institution of slavery or individual personalities. The most complex web of bungled communication follows from the mismatched marriages of the brothers, Barend and Nicolaas. Barend must take his wife Hester by force every time, throughout their marriage. Impotent with Cecelia, Nicolaas is able to have sex only with black women; in turn, Cecelia gets her sexual satisfaction by beating Lydia, Nicolaas' first concubine. Such confusion and dissatisfaction in relationships is rampant in the novel.

The central interweaving and repetition of the novel, however, is neither by plot, character, or chain of narration, but by symbol. Although there are too many symbols and some are traditional, universal, and commonplace, some are rich and new. For example, Galant desires to be married and have a child. He also wants to be literate and wear shoes. These are both literal needs and needs symbolic of the desire to be free. The richest symbol in this cluster is Galant's vision of printed letters that act as ants which eat his insides.

There are also secondary and indirect symbols of slavery and freedom in the novel. The richest of these is found in an episode where Abel, after playing his violin at a town on The Cape, loses it gambling, and Barend, his master, will not help him to retrieve it. The loss is devastating for Abel, for his violin gave him a sense of freedom.

A wealth of animal symbols in the book relate to sexual frustration, which in turn symbolizes slavery itself. Barend kills Hester's lamb; Galant feasts on sheep while Nicolaas is at The Cape. Frances du Toit, repulsive to women because of a facial birthmark, has sex with pigs. Slave lore explains nocturnal emissions as the result of sex with monstrous female "nightwalkers."

The rewards of exploring this rich symbolism are undercut by Brink's lack of confidence in the efficacy of his own devices. Unwilling to let the symbols stand on their own, he has characters identifying them and reflecting on them *as* symbols with a leaden explicitness.

The great reward of *A Chain of Voices* is that it awakens, or reawakens, deep thoughts about slavery and racism. Slavery works best when neither master nor slave sees the possibility of freedom; no single slave or master, no matter how great his intelligence and goodwill, can see "the big picture" while inhibited by the present reality of slavery.

A Chain of Voices is grist for an important mill. The fact that the major ideas of this novel are obtainable in other novels and documents does not diminish its importance as a reaffirmation that may be "new news" for a significant number of black and white readers.

T. G. Shults

Sources for Further Study

Christian Science Monitor. July 21, 1982, p. 17.
Commonweal. CIX, December 3, 1982, p. 660.
Library Journal. CVII, May 1, 1982, p. 903.
Listener. CVII, May 13, 1982, p. 26.
Maclean's. XCV, May 10, 1982, p. 58.
The New York Times Book Review. LXXXVII, June 13, 1982, p. 1.
The New Yorker. LVIII, July 19, 1982, p. 99.
Times Literary Supplement. May 14, 1982, p. 536.

CHARLES RYDER'S SCHOOLDAYS
AND OTHER STORIES

Author: Evelyn Waugh (1903-1966)
Publisher: Little, Brown and Company (Boston). 292 pp. $12.95; paperback $5.95
Type of work: Short stories
Time: Primarily the 1930's
Locale: Primarily Great Britain or the British colonies

Apart from the title story, self-contained but probably an incomplete part of a projected longer work that Waugh never issued during his lifetime, this collection of short stories and sketches originally was published in 1936 under a different title

The publication of any posthumous work by Evelyn Waugh is welcome, but the circumstances regarding *Charles Ryder's Schooldays and Other Stories*, issued sixteen years after the writer's death, are somewhat suspicious. A brief editorial notice accompanies the volume: "All stories excepting 'Charles Ryder's Schooldays' have appeared in a limited edition published in 1936 under the title *Mr. Loveday's Little Outing*." No other editorial comment appears, although the reader would like to know precisely when the stories were written, when or whether they were revised, and whether the author set great store by them. Furthermore, one would like more information about the single previously unpublished piece in the collection. The title story appears to be a fragment, consisting of fifty-one pages, of a longer work that was either incomplete at the time of the author's death or abandoned years earlier. Did Waugh intend the fragment to be a sequel to *Brideshead Revisited*, published in 1945, or to serve as a prefatory novel to that successful book? Certainly Charles Ryder is a major character in *Brideshead Revisited*, the narrator whose point of view controls the reader's perception of the theme, and the Charles Ryder of this fragment, although a young man in 1919 and a student in the Classical Upper Fifth at Spierpoint College, bears a strong resemblance to the similarly passive, introspective, sensitive (but older) artist of *Brideshead Revisited*.

Readers can find some answers to the questions raised by this collection in Christopher Sykes's chatty biography, *Evelyn Waugh* (1975). For example, one learns from Sykes that Waugh wrote most of these stories during 1931 and 1932, and that they were originally submitted to various magazines, including *Harper's Bazaar*. Waugh had written the rest of the stories, with the exception of the Charles Ryder piece, by 1934. The collection as a whole— minus that one fragment—was published in the middle of June, 1936, by Chapman and Hall, under the title *Mr. Loveday's Little Outing and Other Sad Stories*. According to Sykes, "The book enjoyed success in England and later on in the United States, where it was published in October. It kept Evelyn's reputation in the public eye but, except possibly for the title-story, added little to the reputation." Sykes's account appears to contradict that offered in the editorial notice to *Charles Ryder's Schooldays*, where the original volume is said to have appeared in a "limited edition."

A final question remains: Why did the present editors reissue under a new title a collection of stories, most of which were written fifty years previously and published as long ago as 1936? The answer is obvious to those who watched and enjoyed the superb 1982 BBC television presentation of *Brideshead Revisited*. Following the popular reception of the mini-series, the editors expected that readers would be interested in additional fiction relating to the characters or events of the 1945 novel. Indeed, when that book first appeared, it enjoyed the widest success of any of Waugh's novels—not even *A Handful of Dust* (1934) or *The Loved One* (1948) had greater sales. Although critical reception for the book was mixed, the public reaction was favorable enough to encourage M-G-M in 1947 to consider presenting a film version of the novel. M-G-M eventually dropped the project, possibly because of pressure from the Catholic Legion of Decency, whose members objected to the references to adultery, but for a while Waugh was excited by the prospects of such a film and even interviewed two possible directors. Perhaps between 1945 and 1947, Waugh began his "Charles Ryder's Schooldays"; certainly the style of the fragment is similar to that of the *Brideshead Revisited* period. Clearly, Waugh must have planned the story when another book describing the fortunes of Charles Ryder seemed appropriate.

As Waugh developed his story line, however, he probably came to the conclusion, after completing four chapters (or sections), that the material was not sufficiently promising. He could not sustain any genuine plot conflict, apart from Ryder's annoyance with several boys, especially O'Malley, or the mild opposition he endured from the House Tutor, Mr. Graves. In sum, the story progressed well stylistically, with the subdued elegiac tone that informs *Brideshead Revisited*, the close attention to detail, and the sharp eye for satire, but the plot—the plot was languishing. Waugh had the good sense to give up his exercise in nostalgia, and for present-day readers, the Charles Ryder fragment is more interesting for the light it throws upon Waugh's impressions of his own education, than for any additional significance that it brings to one's appreciation of the novel. In fairness to Waugh, his editors should have mentioned the circumstances regarding the acquisition of the manuscript. Had Waugh rejected the fragment as unworthy of his talents? Without editorial help, the reader will have to judge these matters for himself.

The same cautious approach is recommended in examining the rest of the stories of this volume. Some of the pieces are droll, some wickedly satirical, but others are quite flat—failures by any artistic standard. The pieces belong to a period of fairly early Waugh, stylistically resembling *Black Mischief* (1932) or *A Handful of Dust*. Indeed, two of the most interesting stories derive from these two books. "Incident in Azania," an amusingly ironic tale, is set in the same locale as *Black Mischief*. Waugh might have written the episode for a novel, although the material did not quite fit; or he might have composed the piece after the book was published. At any rate, the "incident" concerns Prunella Brooks's supposed kidnaping by a tribal chief or brigand named Joab, in the Azania highlands. As Waugh spins his narrative yarn, the reader perceives that Prunella, the well-bred, prissy daughter of the resident Matodi colonial, has connived to have herself "ransomed" as part of a scheme involving her confederate, Mr. Youkoumian, an Armenian adventurer. Waugh spoofs both the native Azanians and their English administrators, the former absurdly crude and the latter absurdly naïve.

The second piece deriving from Waugh's novels is entitled "By Special Request." It serves as an alternative conclusion to *A Handful of Dust*. Instead of the brilliant chapter 5 ("In Search of a City"), chapter 6 ("Du Côte de Chez Todd"), and chapter 7 ("English Gothic—III"), Waugh substitutes a new chapter 5, "The Next Winter," for the sake of his more queasy readers. Those familiar with *A Handful of Dust* will remember that the good-natured, but befuddled Tony Last has departed with Dr. Messinger to explore the Amazon in order to find the fabled Lost City of the jungle. His plans go awry: Dr. Messinger disappears in the upper waters, and Tony is rescued, then nursed back to health by the demented Mr. Todd, of mixed Pie-Wie Indian and Barbados ancestry. In his remote jungle compound, Mr. Todd, an illiterate, keeps Tony captive, forcing the hapless soul to spend the rest of his life reading aloud from the works of Charles Dickens. Waugh's alternative ending, "By Special Request"—perhaps a request from certain readers or editors who could not appreciate the malicious irony of the original version— is much shorter (twelve pages) and much less mordant. Tony has returned to England; his adulterous wife, Brenda, who has been jilted by her paramour, John Beaver, is now ready for a reconciliation. Beaver, in turn, has been smitten by Mrs. Rattery, the so-called Shameless Blonde, but she rejects his advances, so the doltish fellow has had to rejoin his mother in their interior decorating business, buying bric-a-brac from Berlin and Vienna. A few other familiar names from the novel turn up—Polly Cockpurse, Viola Chasm, Jenny Abdul Akbar, Jock Grant-Menzies—but Waugh makes little of them. By the end of the chapter, Tony has rented his own apartment in London, without advising Brenda, presumably to have the same freedom for mischief that she once had. The conclusion, although appropriately cynical, falls short of the original version, which at least allows the reader to pity the feckless Tony. Now he appears to be as heartless as most of the other characters in the book.

Other stories in the collection range in their effects from drollery to cruel satire. "Mr. Loveday's Little Outing" is an example of Waugh's more affectionate comedy, although it carries the expected nasty turn at the end. In a letter to his friend, W. N. Roughhead, Waugh describes the story as his "loony bin one," noting with satisfaction that it has "the best opening sentence I have seen for years." The sentence in question is: "'You will not find your father greatly changed,' remarked Lady Moping, as the car turned into the gates of the County Asylum." Typical of Waugh's prose, the sentence combines sophisticated nonchalance with a sudden, unsettling turn of thought. Originally titled "Mr. Cruttwell's Little Holiday," the story concerns a genial old "loony" who has been a trusted inmate of the asylum where he was committed after a single, capricious, insane act—an act of murder. Over the years, the doctors have come to respect him, and his fellow-inmates to love him. Angela Moping, a silly do-gooder, sympathizes with his captivity so much that she provokes the establishment to grant the kindly gentleman one brief "outing". Her petition is granted, and Mr. Loveday has a delightful day outside the asylum gates, and returns very grateful for his opportunity to taste freedom. Half a mile beyond the County Home for Mental Defectives, in a ditch, is the body of a young woman, obviously strangled to death. She is mute evidence of Mr. Loveday's amusements during his outing.

A story equally trivial in content, yet with the same high gloss of insouciant style is "On Guard," the tale of a young woman with a turned-up nose and of a pet dog jealous of her affection. Hector, the dog, was only a puppy when Millicent Blade received him as a token of love from one of her admirers, Beckthorpe. Beckthorpe soon disappeared into the backlands of Mombasa, but Hector remained, guarding Millicent's virtue and also his adoptive rights to hearth and home. No suitor could endure Hector's bark or bite, until Major Sir Alexander Dreadnought, a thick-skinned, determined gentleman, fell in love with Millicent's tilted nose and, ignoring the dog's mischief, laid seige to her. Hector had only one expedient. Since he could not frighten or dismay his mistress' lover, he bit off her charming nose. Without the proper tilt, Millicent's nose—and her person—was much less attractive to Sir Alexander and to any other caller, so they followed other noses; Hector had Millicent, hearth, and home all to himself. Waugh concludes his malicious anecdote by suggesting that the lady will remain unwed and, "like all spinsters she is accompanied everywhere by an aging lap-dog."

To present-day readers, this story and most of the others of the collection will seem curiously inconsequential, although they are surely well told. To readers of the 1930's, they probably seemed to be abrasive little satires on a generation of bored, fatuous, self-indulgent English and American snobs. To Waugh himself, they must have seemed somewhat mannered and exaggerated but basically realistic studies of the inanity he witnessed everywhere in genteel society. Even the intellectually vacuous story "On Guard" was modeled upon some elements of Waugh's experience: Sykes claims that the nose-proud young lady was fashioned after Maimie Lygon and her dog Grainger.

Because the modern reader's perspective differs from that of Waugh's generation, he will probably fail to appreciate some of the stories in this collection. Granted that Waugh's prose here is as finely controlled as in the major fiction of the 1930's, his subjects simply are no longer provocative. "Cruise" is a clever but unimportant sketch treating a series of letters from a fickle "young lady of leisure" to a friend. In "Period Piece," Lady Amelia, an elderly lady of leisure, likes to have her servant read aloud to her hot, sexy contemporary novels because the incidents in these books seem tame to her. "I invariably find modern novels painfully reticent," she opines. "Bella Fleace Gave a Party" concerns a socialite hostess who gives a party—but neglects to post the invitations. To her dismay, two guests, neither of whom had been on the list of invitations, arrive at the empty house. A day later, the hostess dies, presumably from chagrin.

In such stories, all of them period pieces, a modern-day reader can appreciate Waugh's meticulous craftsmanship, his timing—above all, his gift of spite. For the special quality which distinguishes Waugh's satire is not righteous anger, not indignation which lacerates the heart, but sudden, unexpected malice lurking within the sumptuous prose. At his best, Waugh could startle his readers, some to laughter, some to fury, but his gift was never softened by compassion. These stories, interesting because they preserve the style and steely temperament of Waugh's most creative period, still fall short. It was in the fuller scope of the novel that Waugh most effectively satirized the atrocities of twentieth century culture.

Leslie Mittleman

Sources for Further Study

Booklist. LXXIX, October 1, 1982, p. 191.
Library Journal. CVII, October 15, 1982, p. 2006.
Los Angeles Times Book Review. October 3, 1982, p. 3.
The New York Times Book Review. LXXXVII, November 14, 1982, p. 25.
Publishers Weekly. CCXXII, August 20, 1982, p. 56.
The Wall Street Journal. October 11, 1982, p. 20.

THE CHINESE INSOMNIACS
New Poems

Author: Josephine Jacobsen (1908-   )
Publisher: University of Pennsylvania Press (Philadelphia). 79 pp. $9.95; paperback
    $4.95
Type of work: Poetry

A collection of forty-nine poems by a poet's poet, technically polished and intellectually penetrating

Josephine Jacobsen's most recent book of poetry, *The Chinese Insomniacs: New Poems*, is her fifth volume of verse in a career which began with the collection *For the Unlost* in 1948. Hers has been a distinguished record: in addition to her poetry, she has published two books of criticism—one on Samuel Beckett, the other on Eugene Ionesco and Jean Genet, both in collaboration with William R. Mueller. She has also published three volumes of lectures, two of them growing out of her tenure as Poetry Consultant to the Library of Congress from 1971 to 1973. A 1979 collection of short stories, *A Walk with Rashid*, rounds out the record.

Jacobsen is a poet's poet. The verses in *The Chinese Insomniacs*—divided into three sections, entitled "Personae," "Poems," and "Notes Toward Time"— are tight and spare, technically polished, and intellectually penetrating. Time, love, and death are the subjects; Jacobsen confronts them as eternal riddles. Love is often a blessed solace in these poems. The poet must cease contemplating the mysteries of his own past and his approaching end, and turn instead to the present, where passionate or spiritual love can sustain him. Finally, the poet must move beyond time. "A date is only a mark on paper," Jacobsen writes in the title poem. "It has little to do with what is long."

That title poem, "The Chinese Insomniacs," introduces ideas which reappear throughout the collection. The poet is often alone in life, but in the companionable past he knows that he can find kindred spirits who, like him, once mused and brooded through the quiet hours. "It is good to know the Chinese insomniacs. How in 495 A.D., in 500 B.C., the moon shining, and the pine trees shining back at it, a poet had to walk to the window." From their restless thoughts, those poets fashioned works of art which have outlived them. They said "something difficult to forget, like music counts the heartbeat." They "made poems later out of fragments of the dark."

Two other poems in this collection pick up the idea in modern times. In "Rainy Night at the Writers' Colony," the poet lies awake and senses the presence of poets who, in other years, inhabited this same summer refuge. Dead poets "stalk the air, stride through tall rain and peer through wet panes where we sleep, or do not, here." Their presence does not frighten the living; rather, the past supports the endeavors of the present: "What they did, we know," but now "it is we who are here," we living poets who must master the same task, the same difficult feat of tricking sense out of obdurate language, reason out of the babel of disorder.

"Bulletin from the Writers' Colony" is the third of Jacobsen's poems on the subject. Here the poet figure is a more aggressive hunter after truth. The woods around the writers' colony are filled with deer hunters stalking game; their rifles crack, and one can spy their red shirts through the leaves. "Today winter's dog, autumn, snuffs through the leaves ahead of his master; who is ahead of his." Within the cabins of the artists' colony, however, there are other hunters who, each morning, enter "the jungle of the keyboard's teeth; the canvas riot of underbrush; the pencil's secretive wood." These hunters, like the poets in "Rainy Night," sense the immediacy of their predecessors: "On the wall past hunters' formal names are scratched on plaques: kilroy, le roi, was here." The poet-hunter's quarry is not slain; the artist must instead transfix his prey, preserve, and crystallize it, so that it will live after him. Winter stalks the poet in the colony as surely as it does the hunter outside, and "time's trick" will overtake both, but the poet, with luck and steady aim, may leave something behind.

Jacobsen suggests that the poet, in his search through time, must simultaneously escape from, and immerse himself in, the present. Life threatens to inundate him with everyday trivia. In "Notes Toward Time," she imagines that in a single night, free of insomnia, one may yet be buried: "While we slept debris has been emptied upon us: black hours like loops of undeveloped film have littered us, a pile beyond belief." "Help!" she cries. The means of escape are close: "There is a motion, make it with me and we are elsewhere, unscratched, silent as a leaf." Love—the immediate motion of sexual love, the eternal motion of spiritual love—offers the needed escape and sustenance. One can forget time, or cheat it. One is still *in* time, one must live with synchroneity, yet with a handless clock one is free of the tyranny of minutes and hours. In "The Clock," the poet learns to "move in space" where only "love's event and death's, notch times's face."

Perhaps the two most memorable poems in *The Chinese Insomniacs* are "Mr. Mahoney" and "Tears." The former is an eerie piece, set in a hospital where Mr. Mahoney, a dying patient, wanders in confusion through the night, seeking release in death. He cannot "find his room" quite yet, and pretty blonde nurses must pursue him through the corridors and steer him back to where he belongs, to his own Room 280. Though tranquilized, he still eludes them, and "at 2 A.M. in my dark 283 the wide door cracks and sudden and silently Mr. Mahoney's nutty face obtrudes." It is the face of death; it does not belong in Room 283 yet, and by noon of the next day Mr. Mahoney is gone, moved elsewhere. This poem is composed in pentameter quatrains, rhyming *abba*. Often the rhyme is fashioned with a room number—"Mahoney" with "280," "silently" with "283." The technique emphasizes how the sterile regimentation of the hospital, the antiseptic sweetness of the nurses, and the numbered order of the routine join and demand conformity. Death must stay in its room and not roam the halls at night. No one is ready to face it yet.

"Tears" should be the anthology piece of this collection, though it gains impact from its position at the heart of Jacobsen's book. Tears are eternal yet, paradoxically, temporary; grief is meaningless yet profound. Tears are exclusively human: Animals do not weep because they are not conscious of time. "Must we see the future," asks the poet, "in order to weep?" "Is that why the animals refuse to shed tears?" Tears are outside time and space, they evaporate: "They are a classless possession yet are not found in the museum of even our greatest city." Jacobsen's poem speaks of tears and reveals their essence: "Could tears not make a sea of their mass? It could be salt and wild enough; it could rouse storms and sink ships, erode, erode its shores: tears of rage, of love, of torture, of loss. Of loss." Tears are humanizing, and if one becomes perpetually "dry-eyed," one becomes like the animals—outside time, to be sure, but also beyond grief and love.

As a volume, *The Chinese Insomniacs* progresses from the contemplation of death, to the release of tears, and on to the solace of love. Through all the poems, one senses the poet's conception of her mission—to contemplate the riddles of death, time, and love, but not to solve them. She remains an insomniac, linked through her poetry to the past and the future, but able to escape occasionally to the blessed present, where love gives life some meaning, time is tricked a little longer, and death stays in its room.

James L. W. West III

Sources for Further Study

Commonweal. CIX, September 24, 1982, p. 502.
Library Journal. CVI, October 1, 1981, p. 1930.
Nation. CCXXXV, October 16, 1982, p. 371.
The New York Times Book Review. LXXXVII, April 19, 1982, p. 13.

CHOSEN POEMS, OLD AND NEW

Author: Audre Lorde (1934-   )
Publisher: W. W. Norton and Company. 115 pp. $12.95; paperback $5.95
Type of work: Poetry

An excellent selection of Lorde's poems that chart her development over thirty years and demonstrate the insufficiency of ideological categories for approaching the moral intensity and psychological complexity of her work

Audre Lorde introduces her *Chosen Poems, Old and New* with a statement that accurately reflects the complexity of her career: "Here are the words of some of the women I have been, am being still, will come to be. The time surrounding each poem is an unspoken image." Despite her emphasis on flexibility, however, critics almost always consign Lorde to some rigid category, usually that of "Afro-American Lesbian feminist." Unfortunately, this in turn leads to a glib dismissal of Lorde as a serious poet, a fact clearly reflected in her absence from all major anthologies of contemporary poetry other than those devoted entirely to the work of Afro-Americans and/or women. The moral intensity and psychological insight of *Chosen Poems*, which includes work from all of Lorde's previous collections except for the sequence *The Black Unicorn* (1978), argues persuasively for much wider recognition. As Lorde's introductory statement implies, she resists all pressures toward ideological rigidity, committing herself instead to the discovery of individual processes while recognizing that each provisional self is inevitably conditioned by the unstated and elusive premises of its historical context. In line with this emphasis, Lorde continually explores the limits and possibilities of various identities, traditional and innovative. The question she poses in "Change of Season" strikes near the core of her sensibility: "Am I to be cursed forever with becoming/ somebody else on the way to myself?" All views of Lorde exclusively in relation to Lesbian, feminist, or Afro-American poetry radically oversimplify her voice, which also has roots in Romantic and Modernist sensibilities.

To be sure, Lorde shares a great deal with poets such as Gwendolyn Brooks and Adrienne Rich who, like Lorde, have passed through several distinct phases of development. All three gradually developed an awareness that the political and the personal aspects of experience cannot be separated. Like those of Brooks and Rich, Lorde's early poems (written during the 1950's) concentrate on "universal" themes such as the destruction of childhood innocence by an oppressive environment. Lorde has never abandoned these concerns, but, beginning in the mid-1960's, she has begun to emphasize the relationship of personal problems to larger social and political forces. Rather than imitating her better-known contemporaries, Lorde has worked toward a synthesis of Brooks's and Rich's emphases on the racial and sexual dimensions of these larger forces, steadfastly refusing to elevate one concern over the other. She begins "Revolution Is One Form of Social Change" with an allusion to Malcolm X's question: "What does a racist call a black Ph.D.?" The answer is "nigger." Lorde pursues the implications of the question, concluding

> when he's finished
> off the big ones
> he'll just change
> to sex
> which is
> after all
> where it all began.

Refusing to participate in the divisiveness discussed by Angela Davis in *Women, Race and Class* (1981), Lorde, like other contemporary Afro-American writers such as David Bradley, recognizes the necessity of confronting racial and sexual oppression simultaneously.

Lorde's confrontation focuses on several crucial issues. First, she insists on the reality of the emotions, many of them violent and painful, generated by racial and sexual oppression. Second, she observes that the violence of the culture inevitably infects each individual, including herself. Frequently this generates a defensive retreat into rigid categories which, in the interest of a specious protection of self, circumscribe individual processes and distort communication. Finally, she recognizes that individuals frequently transmit this historically conditioned rigidity and defensiveness to their children, denying the children's growth and perpetuating the forces which generate the entire vicious cycle. Ultimately, Lorde insists that any hope for the future demands an acceptance of natural development, that of the self and that of the children.

Although Lorde shares some of these concerns with her contemporaries, her poetry suggests an affinity with Romantic and Modernist poets, most notably T. S. Eliot, William Wordsworth, and Walt Whitman. Eliot, who at first glance seems profoundly incompatible with Lorde's radical sensibility, nevertheless anticipated her use of myth as a mirror for contemporary experience. Ironically, Lorde's explorations of African and matriarchal mythologies in poems such as "The Winds of Orisha" and "To Marie, In Flight" (and at greater length in *The Black Unicorn*) can be seen as an application of Eliot's method to specific circumstances he never anticipated. Lorde draws more directly on the Wordsworthian motif of childhood as the emblem of higher wisdom destroyed by socially conditioned experience. She employed this motif especially frequently in early poems such as "Now That I Am Forever with Child," "What My Child Learns of the Sea," and "A Child Shall Lead"— which echoes Wordsworth's "Ode: Intimations of Immortality" in its concluding lines: "And I am grown/ past knowledge." Similarly, "Rites of Passage" provides an image of fathers "dying/ back to the freedom of wise children." For Lorde at this stage, the hope for rebirth rested on an essentially romantic dedication to the universal innocence that precedes the consciousness of patriarchal power.

As she has developed, however, Lorde has yoked Wordsworth's celebration of childhood to a vision of personal and social growth that recalls Whitman's exhortation to "destroy the teacher" ("Song of Myself," section 47). Like Whitman, Lorde refuses to provide simple answers, and instead offers her own development as a model for inspiration and criticism. Lorde's poem "Mentor" echoes Whitman's vision of unique individual processes interacting for mutual benefit: "I sing this for beacon now/ lighting us home/ each to our separate house." This recognition recurs in "Relevant Is Different Points on the Circle," where Lorde asks to be blessed with "my children's growing rebellion." She then extends her imagination to the Native American heritage, attempting to generate a synthesis reflecting her knowledge that "This is a country where other people live." Although her poetry frequently resembles Whitman's, Lorde never simply imitates him. Her poems, especially after 1969, express political anger much more intensely than Whitman's ever did. Placing her commitment to process in the context of a racist society, Lorde insists in the closing lines of "Teacher" that poetic visions, however idealistic, must contribute to social transformation or else become part of the oppressive machinery: "Promise corrupts/ what it does not invent."

Lorde incorporates these affinities and influences in a poetic voice that alternates between social didacticism ("Blackstudies," "Cables to Rage or I've Been Talking on This Street Corner a Hell of a Long Time") and conversational sympathy ("Martha," "To the Girl Who Lives in a Tree"). This essentially oral voice, which has changed only slightly over thirty years, to some extent masks the one weakness of Lorde's work, the relative absence of striking intensities of sound and image. Poems from her early volume *First Cities* (1968) differ from the "New Poems" included in *Chosen Poems* primarily in their optimism and personal emphasis rather than in any distinctive prosody. A typical Lorde poem from any period consists of relatively short free-verse lines, somewhat like those of Rich's work of the 1960's and 1970's, divided to emphasize the rhythm of speech or perception. While Lorde occasionally makes effective use of oratorical devices, she shows little interest in exploring the rhythms of Afro-American language or music in the manner of Sterling Brown or Langston Hughes. Without doubt, Lorde's most memorable lines and poems draw their power primarily from the quality of her emotional and intellectual insight rather than from technical brilliance as such.

Nowhere is the depth of Lorde's insight clearer than in her poems concerning children, especially, though not exclusively, the female children of Afro-American mothers. In her poems of the 1950's and early 1960's, Lorde focuses on her own childhood and the ambiguity of her relationship with her mother. Gradually, she turns to her own role as mother. Ultimately, Lorde seeks to contribute to the development of a liberating tradition which she images in "Generation" as a bridge purchased "with our mother's bloody gold." Resisting the temptation—faced by tradition-oriented poets as diverse as the Southern-Agrarian Donald Davidson and the Afro-American militant Amiri Baraka (LeRoi Jones)—to provide ideological manifestos that oversimplify history, Lorde refuses to romanticize the maternal tradition. In "Story Books on a Kitchen Table," for example, the persona confronts her mother's refusal to share her personal experience. In place of her pain, the mother offers fairy tales "where white witches rule." Lorde's description of the mother's attempt to force her daughter into an "ill-fitting harness of despair" emphasizes the failure of the dominant tradition to provide any mythology capable of clarifying the experience of women. Even in her meditation on "the vanished mother/ of a Black girl," however, Lorde identifies the potential for a tradition which encourages rather than denies growth. Following an image of her mother's "womb of pain," the persona invokes a regenerative rage: "anger re-conceived me." Other early poems, notably "Father, Son, and Holy Ghost," trace the mother's pain to its source in the patriarchal desire to "redefine each of our shapes." Adding to the unavoidable tension of Afro-American life, this sexual oppression generates the black mother's desire to protect her daughter by shielding her from reality. Nevertheless, Lorde clearly rejects all such attempts which condemn the daughters to the internal conflict described in "Prologue":

> whatever my mother thought would mean survival
> made her try to beat me whiter every day
> and even now the color of her bleached ambition
> still forks throughout my words.

The following lines, however, reveal Lorde's complex awareness that the very impulses she rejects also contribute to her ability to interact with the new generation of children: "but I survived/ and didn't I survive confirmed/ to teach my children where her errors lay." Summing up this ambivalence in "The Woman Thing," Lorde sees both acquiescence to the dehumanization of women and an indestructible strength born of suffering in her Afro-American female heritage: "the woman thing my mother taught me/ bakes off its covering of snow/ like a rising blackening sun."

"Black Mother Woman," originally published in the transitional volume *From a Land Where Other People Live* (1973), marks Lorde's symbolic transition from daughter to mother. After noting her mother's "deceitful longings" and "myths of little worth," the persona presents herself to her mother as "a dark temple where your true spirit rises." As resurrected Black Mother Woman, she vows to provide her own children a source of strength without denying them their own explorations. Nevertheless, the possibility of failure, personal and social, haunts Lorde in her role of mother. "To My Daughter the Junkie on a Train" conjures up the "nightmare of all sleeping mothers" and demands that, however weary from their own struggles, the mothers find strength to support the suffering children. Without this support—without access to tradition—the children will inevitably be infected by the violence of the culture. Recognizing both the threatening and the liberating potentials of maternal tradition, Lorde both hopes and fears that her children will "use my legends to shape their own language." Specifically, she imagines that they will "discard my most ancient nightmares/ where the fallen gods became demon/ instead of dust." Lorde's ambivalence involves, on the one hand, her fear that the children may discard the entire nightmare. If they do so, they will not recognize the demoniac nature of the fallen gods, implicitly rejecting their mother's pain. If, however, the children discard the nightmare *at the place where* the gods are becoming demons, they will see *only* the demoniac aspect of their adversary. Unable to dismiss the fallen gods/demons as insubstantial dust, the children will remain subject to their power, eventually succumbing to the rage and despair which lead the persona in the poem to the verge of suicide.

Against these pressures and fears, Lorde constructs rituals of resistance and courage. In "New York City," she repudiates the impulse to shield her children from the city's brutality:

> I submit my children
> . . . .
> to the harshness and growing cold to the brutalizations
> which if survived
> will teach them strength
> or an understanding of how strength is gotten

Significantly, she seeks to provide her children with an image of a mother in the *process* of becoming rather than *fait accompli*. Lorde realizes that submitting the children to "ritual scarifications" places each mother under an absolute obligation to love them "above all others save [herself]." Furthermore, it obliges her to repudiate the fallen gods unambiguously. In "Sacrifice," the persona seeks to "pull down statues of rocks from their high places" and refuses "to sleep/ even one night in houses of marble." The outcome of these rituals—which ultimately demand the sacrifice of personal desire—remains uncertain. What is certain is that the experiences of Lorde, of her mother, and of the battered women portrayed in "Need: A Choral of Black Women's Voices" must not be denied. Only when the pain and the anger find full acceptance, internal and external, will women, and others among the dispossessed to whom Lorde refers, be free to accept their mothers, their daughters, their potential selves, and ultimately their fathers and brothers and lovers. Only then will Lorde's words, from a poem entitled "Now," lose their ironic undertone:

> Woman power
> is
> Black power
> is
> Human power
> is
> always feeling.

For readers willing to view Lorde as a complex individual rather than as an example of Afro-American Lesbian feminism, *Chosen Poems* provides a chart of the processes, political and personal, necessary to change her dream into a reality which could nurture the children it now mocks and destroys.

Craig Werner

Sources for Further Study

Commonweal. CIX, December 3, 1982, p. 666.
Library Journal. CVII, June 15, 1982, p. 1227.
Publishers Weekly. CCXXI, May 14, 1982, p. 214.

CIRCLES ON THE WATER
Selected Poems

Author: Marge Piercy (1936-   )
Publisher: Alfred A. Knopf (New York). 320 pp. $17.50; paperback $8.95
Type of work: Poetry

A poet's selection of her poems which present everyday events to everyday readers for their use and appreciation

In an essay in the *New Republic* entitled "Beyond the Feminist Mystique," Benjamin Barber, a professor of Political Science at Rutgers University, identifies three stages in the development of the contemporary woman's movement. In the first stage, which began in the early 1960's, marriage and the nuclear family were regarded as patriarchal institutions that robbed women of their identity, making them little more than servants. Men were the enemy; children were a burden to be shared equally or avoided altogether. In the early 1970's, Barber contends, feminists shifted into a second stage, a period of reevaluation and "recantation." While marriage was still regarded as bondage, women acknowledged that they had work to do, too. Feminists of the 1970's argued that human beings are essentially androgynous—that women, like men, need to be strong, ambitious, and independent, avoiding petty emotionality, selfishness, and envy.

Recently, Barber suggests, feminists have moved into a third stage, in which it is permissible for women to acknowledge their limitations and their intrinsic differences from men: "Feminism in its third stage would seem to be pushing toward a full demystification of both the feminist and the feminine mystiques, in favor of a realistic appreciation of sexual differences, the constraints they place on us, and the plural virtues they make possible."

Poets have always been in touch with the political currents of their own times. They write out of the experience of the moment, with the perspective of history. They do not make great generalizations about history and ideology, but they express in their aesthetic the nature of the times. *Circles on the Water* chronicles the past fifteen years, approximately the same period that Barber surveys. Marge Piercy writes in her introduction that she selected these poems to make a pattern, to present a vision. From her seven books of poetry, she has selected more than 160 poems, from *Breaking Camp* (1968) to *The Moon Is Always Female* (1980). One is tempted to read Piercy's poems in the light of the three-stage developmental theory proposed by Barber, yet such an exercise merely reveals that the poet's sensibility eludes Barber's categories— as does the women's movement itself. Piercy's vision is complex, angry and loving, disillusioned and committed—throughout her work. She cherishes her individuality *and* her ability to love *and* her vulnerability. She eludes the stage-theory. Her book is, after all, entitled *Circles on the Water*.

The circle or cycle is an archetypal pattern representative of woman's consciousness, while stages, steps, and hierarchies reflect the masculine ethic of conquering and overcoming. In her introduction, Piercy emphasizes the synthesizing potential of poetry:

> A poem can momentarily integrate the different kinds of knowing of our different and often warring levels of brain, from the reptilian part that recognizes rhythms and responds to them up through the mammalian centers of the emotions, from symbolic knowing as in dreams to analytical thinking, through rhythms and sound and imagery as well as overt meaning.

The poem itself, like a weaving, pulls through the warp and woof of our humanity. The fiber that results is at once one piece and myriad pieces. A reader can focus on the fine aspects of a poem, find its elements and describe the minutiae of its construction; he can read it whole and pull in its emotional or political impact; he can accept it in the context of its time and allow it to speak for him. Writes Piercy, "My work is of a piece. . . . The voice is the same voice."

"The Sabbath of Mutual Respect," taken from Piercy's book *The Moon Is Always Female*, tries to encompass the choices women have made not only in recent times but also in all civilizations. Undermining the stage-theory of feminism, it accepts as sacred, noble, and worthy those choices—motherhood, lesbianism, professionalism, celibacy, martyrdom—which women have made now and in the past:

> When I consecrate
> my body in the temple of our history,
> when I pledge myself to remain empty
> and clear for the voices coming through
> I do not choose for you or lessen your choice.

The 1960's word "sisterhood" here takes on a strong contextual obligation, the obligation to choose and to learn from other sisters' choices, to be in touch with those who produce books and not children, or children and gardens but not cities or political parties. "Praise the lives you did not choose./ They will heal you, tell your story, fight/ for you."

The main focus in *Circles on the Water* is the paradox of joining and remaining apart. Each joining carries with it the danger of total merging, of becoming lost in another entity, in one's family, work, or history. The selected poems from the volume *To Be of Use* form the centerpiece of the entire collection. They contain the trajectory of what has come to be known as women's poetry, yet they transcend that limiting voice. There are the expected prosaic statements about the exploitation of women, but the tone of many of these poems is not the grim anger of Adrienne Rich, Robin Morgan, or Diane Wakoski. They are spare, descriptive, empathic, and even ironic.

Initially, Piercy is clearly in touch with the ways men and women are being exploited, but she also is sympathetic to their struggles as part of a larger historical/political context. She sees women hanging on to love, allowing themselves to be trained like bonsai trees ("A Work of Artifice"). She writes about Janice Joplin's need for loving, "the drug that hangs us and drags us down" ("Burying Blues for Janis"). She describes the "dishwater blond," the waitress who worked at the truck stop standing "behind the counter/ with a smile like an outsized safety pin/ holding [her] lips off [her] buck teeth" ("What You Waited For"). She playfully dissects the office worker who has lost her identity: "My hips are a desk./ From my ears hang/ chains of paper clips" ("Secretary Chant"). Men do not escape the microscope; Piercy describes how men have viewed her, especially when she thought she was being clever and intellectual: "When I brought my aerial maps of Sartre or Marx,/ they said, she is trying to attract our attention" ("In the Men's Room(s)"). She derides what she sees as men's practicalities ("The Thrifty Lover"), their rhetoric of community which really means self-enhancement ("A Shadow Play for Guilt"), and their ability to deify the patriarchal role:

> Plato sits on his right hand and Aristotle on his left.
> . . . .
> He is a good man: if you don't believe me,
> ask any god.
> He says they all think like him.

While these kinds of poems are concentrated in *To Be of Use*, they are found in the other volumes, too. Piercy allows these poems to happen; one is never finished with personal alienation or political narrowness. Yet staying only in that framework of hypersensitivity to oppression is itself oppressive ("Phyllis Wounded"). In an honest poem which is typical of Piercy's ability to acknowledge that human interchange, even if it is not pleasant, can be fruitful, she writes:

> Of course it all came apart
> . . . .
> We coalesced in the false chemistry of words
> rather than truly touching
> yet I burn cool glinting in the sun
> and my energy sings like a teakettle all day long.

What she celebrates in this poem and in others from other volumes ("Simple-Song," "Walking into Love," "Excursions, Incursions," "Smalley Bar," "Bridging") is at once a feeling of belonging and of being alone, recognizing the energy generated by the joining *and* the dislocation. She likes to embrace that attitude of engagement, the ability to roll up one's sleeves and plunge in without embarrassment or self-denigration. "The people I love the best," writes Piercy in "To Be of Use," "jump into work head first/ without dallying in the shallows/. . . . They seem to become natives of that element."

Joining, then, for Piercy, involves taking risks, and she addresses this special vision of joining in "Doing It Differently." With a candid voice, she unravels the challenges and the pitfalls: How easy it is to embrace old habits of relating to one another, how easy to merge physically and embrace the familiar body, rehearse the familiar yet tainted "rhetoric of tenderness." How easy to state "we will be equal . . . new man and new woman," and how difficult to examine and experience the underlying lack of connection. Yet all of these aspects of human interaction must be acknowledged:

> Periodic, earthy, of a violent tenderness
> it is the nature of this joining
> to remain partial and episodic
> yet feel total: a mountain that opens like a door
> and then closes
> like a mountain.

Piercy's recent volumes (from 1976 on) reflect her move to Wellfleet on Cape Cod. Many of these poems, such as "Homesick," "Seedlings in the Mail," and "Cod Summer," address the poet's recurring concerns in a new context. "Living in the Open," the title poem from the 1976 volume, elaborates the theme of honesty and clarity in joining. Here the "joining" extends to the poet's environment. These poems use natural images of squashes, apples, fish, and sand dunes. They celebrate the harvesting of nature's richness ("September Afternoon at Four O'Clock") and the spareness of vision which allows for the richness to come through: "The price of seeing is silence/ . . . On my arm a woodnymph lights probing/ me curiously, faintly, as she opens/ and closes the tapestried doors of flight" ("Intruding").

What human beings need above all, Piercy suggests, is openness and a sense of wonder. Men and women, together and separate, with different histories, different ways of constructing what is real, move in their circles on the water:

> I am the woman sitting by the river.
> I mend old rebellions and patch them new.
> . . . .
> I am the old woman sitting by the river scolding corpses.
> I want to stare into the river and see the bottom
> glinting like clean hair.
> I want to outlive my usefulness
> and sing water songs, songs
> in praise of the green brown river
> flowing clean through the blue green world.

Faith Gabelnick

Sources for Further Study

Booklist. LXXVIII, May 15, 1982, p. 1221.
Library Journal. CVII, July, 1982, p. 1329.
The New York Times Book Review. LXXXVII, August 8, 1982, p. 10.
Publishers Weekly. CCXXI, April 9, 1982, p. 48.

!CLICK SONG

Author: John A. Williams (1925-   )
Publisher: Houghton Mifflin Company (Boston). 430 pp. $13.95
Type of work: Novel
Time: The 1940's to the late 1970's
Locale: New York City, with occasional journeys across the United States and into
Spain, France, and Africa

A black novelist traces his struggles in the world of publishing

> *Principal characters:*
> CATO CALDWELL DOUGLASS, a black novelist
> ALLIS GREENBERG DOUGLASS, his Jewish wife
> GLENN DOUGLASS, Cato's son by a previous marriage
> MACK DOUGLASS, son of Cato and Allis
> PAUL CUMMINGS, born Kaminsky, a Jewish novelist, Cato's friend
> AMOS BOOKBINDER, a black editor, Cato's friend

"Who is that nigger?" is the unspoken question that haunts Cato Douglass, the protagonist and narrator of *!Click Song*, as he seeks to pursue a writing career and live undisturbed with his wife (who happens to be white) and his sons. This question does not merely reflect paranoia (of which Cato has his share); he really does have much to complain about in his treatment as a writer and as a black man.

!Click Song, named after a form of language surviving in African songs and in the conversation of some American blacks as a type of private communication, thoroughly details the struggles of the black American writer. The author of nine novels, John A. Williams clearly knows whereof he writes: the difficulties of getting published, reviewed, sold, read; the burden (familiar to all modern writers) of teaching college to support oneself while writing; the rivalries between writers who are friends; the conflicts between writing and allowing time for loved ones. Some of these problems are resolved more happily than others, yet Cato will not give in or give up, persevering in his writing and in his belief in himself. Others in the world of this novel are not so lucky. One black poet gains fame and acclaim only posthumously, after drinking himself to death. Another brilliant black writer dies a heroin addict, out of despair at not getting published. One black man does manage to succeed in the literary world, but only because he has passed for so long that not even Cato learns that he is black until they have known each other for many years.

The fellow-writer who has been Cato's closest friend—their friendship dates to their college days after World War II—is a white man, Paul Cummings. The importance which this relationship has had for Cato is clear from the beginning of the novel, when Cato learns of Paul's suicide. The novel is a long flashback from this event, with occasional returns to the present for Paul's funeral and for negotiations over Cato's latest book. Throughout this extended flashback, tracing Cato's career from the late 1940's to the present, the relationship between Cato and Paul provides a major motif, even when they are essentially estranged during the last decade of the novel's action and of Paul's life.

Cato and Paul build a relationship in which race is irrelevant, an intensely competitive friendship based on their shared desire to write. From their earliest efforts, it is clear that neither will be able simply to accept the other's successes without considering his own relative success. Although Cato is the first to sell a book, and indeed writes more and better fiction than does his friend (so he tells the reader), Paul outstrips him. He is, after all, white, and as Cato is often reminded at different stages in his career, books by black authors are not popular.

Black writers are caught in a double bind. They are advised to write about the black experience, and yet when they do so, they are then advised that such books do not sell enough copies to justify publishing expenses. Another constant source of frustration to Cato and his circle is the inevitable comparison of a new black writer with canonized black predecessors, rarely with white writers. When Cato's son Glenn publishes *his* first novel, he is acclaimed as potentially "another Wright, another Whittington, another Huysmans." If those last two names are unfamiliar, it is because they are Williams' own invention. Throughout the novel, Williams blends real names with fictitious ones, although the real-life writers never appear as characters. Williams adds another interesting touch transcending the limits of the text: he gives Cato a rather extraneous sexual encounter with a student at the college where he teaches, and she turns out to be Raffy Joplin, daughter and niece respectively of Ralph and Iris Joplin, the two leading characters of Williams' third novel, *Sissie* (1963).

While Cato's books are ignored, Paul's are successful, especially after he finally acknowledges his Jewish identity, hidden from even his closest friends under an Anglo-Saxon surname which he felt would be less restrictive than his own, Kaminsky. Cato perceives the irony in the acclaim which greets this revelation, a luxury he will never know because he can never disguise his skin color.

Cato never learns the reason for Paul's suicide, although it may have been caused in part by Paul's unhappy relationships. Ironically, Cato's wife was Jewish, while none of Paul's three wives were. Even though Cato is sustained by his wife's warmth and understanding, his frustrations nearly drive him to self-destruction. Various black men in this novel are pitted against one another rather than against a common enemy. Cato and his fellow black writers nurse bitter jealousies and resentments, and he and his heroin-addicted writer friend Ike nearly destroy each other in a bastion of white sophistication.

This scene is truly dramatic, but Ike, like Paul and most of the book's many other characters, is never fully realized because of the solipsistic limitations of Cato's first-person narration. Most of the dialogue, with attendant physical gestures, rings true, but many of the characters are mere stereotypes. One of Williams' representative types, however, does resonate: Amos Bookbinder, a black editor and Cato's most reliable friend. Although Bookbinder fails to admit that his power is limited or to acknowledge that his company is using him as a token black, he possesses an integrity that Cato only gradually comes to appreciate. The novel's climax is also its most appalling instance of black pitted against black. When Amos proposes to publish the novel that Cato's long-time publisher has just rejected, his company agrees—on the condition that he resign his position. When Cato discovers the terrible sacrifice Amos is making for him, he is shattered.

In *!Click Song*, Williams simply attempts to cover too much ground—the literary profession, racial conflict, family relationships, and the sociopolitical climate in America over some thirty years. Intensely autobiographical, the novel contains far too much undigested raw experience. There are brilliant passages depicting Cato's sometimes frenzied thought-processes, moving between dream and reality, but there are also frequent digressions on contemporary universities, teachers, and students; general living conditions in the 1970's; and assorted other matters presented in discussions that seem inappropriate in this context.

Williams' indictment of the publishing industry and his powerful account of the plight of the black writer deserve a wide audience, yet even here his argument is marred by a curious blind spot: in discussing black writers in *!Click Song*, he virtually ignores women. The acclaim recently won by black women writers such as Alice Walker, Toni Morrison, and Ntozake Shange is surely an encouraging sign. Whatever the role of feminism in their success, it is clear that such writers must be taken into account in any assessment of the current status of the black writer.

Scott Giantvalley

Sources for Further Study

Choice. XIX, July/August, 1982, p. 1563.
Library Journal. CVII, February 15, 1982, p. 476.
Los Angeles Times Book Review. May 9, 1982, p. 10.
The New York Times Book Review. LXXXVII, April 19, 1982, p. 12.
Publishers Weekly. CCXXI, February 19, 1982, p. 59.
Saturday Review. IX, April, 1982, p. 60.
Time. CXIX, April 12, 1982, p. 73.
West Coast Review of Books. VIII, May, 1982, p. 23.

CLINGING TO THE WRECKAGE
A Part of Life

Author: John Mortimer (1923-   )
Publisher: Ticknor & Fields (New Haven, Connecticut). Illustrated. 200 pp. $12.95
Type of work: Autobiography
Time: 1923-1982
Locale: England, Ireland, France, Italy, and Hollywood

The autobiography of the English novelist, playwright, screenwriter, and lawyer

> *Principal personages:*
> JOHN MORTIMER, a lawyer and author
> CLIFFORD MORTIMER, his father
> KATHLEEN MORTIMER, his mother
> PENELOPE MORTIMER, his first wife
> HENRY WINTER, his Oxford roommate

John Mortimer has been a successful writer in England for thirty-five years, turning out novels, plays, radio and television scripts, and screenplays for such films as Carol Reed's *The Running Man* (1963) and Otto Preminger's *Bunny Lake Is Missing* (1965). He is perhaps best known in America as the creator of the television series "Rumpole of The Bailey" and as the adapter for television of Evelyn Waugh's *Brideshead Revisited* (1945). His productivity as a writer is all the more remarkable when one considers that he has maintained a law practice at the same time. *Clinging to the Wreckage: A Part of Life* is his account of his dual careers and all that has influenced them. It is a witty, no-nonsense sort of memoir that Horace Rumpole himself might have written.

Mortimer writes in his opening paragraph that the distant past seems clearer to him than the events of ten years ago, and he presents the details of his childhood and adolescence more specifically and more movingly than those of his later years. He depicts his past with little nostalgia but with genuine affection for the boy he was; growing up in Henley, England, he was an only child who was not close to this parents and who had few friends.

As a child, Mortimer was taken to West End plays by his parents, and he became enthralled by the magic of the theater. He decided he wanted to be a musical comedy star who sported a silver-topped ebony cane and a monocle. With his young friend Bill Mann, who later became a music critic for *The Times*, he wrote and performed reviews and plays in his home. The most exciting event in his early years was his election by his classmates to play the leading role in his school's production of William Shakespeare's *Richard II* (1595-1596).

About the same time, Mortimer's father, a prominent probate and divorce barrister, went totally blind. This tragedy brought father and son closer together; the two took long walks, during which Mortimer's father told him Sherlock

Holmes stories and other stories he had read as a boy. The barrister continued his work, relying on his wife to lead him to court, write his petitions, and read him his briefs.

Mortimer went from preparatory school to Harrow, where he felt like a "long-term, good conduct prisoner." There, he developed enthusiasms for Lord Byron and William Wordsworth and wrote a novel about the school in the style of Aldous Huxley. When he informed his father of his ambition to become a writer, he was told that he would be better off in the law. For years, Mortimer's father continued to discourage his son's writing.

After Mortimer left Harrow, he was informed suddenly by his father that he would be going to Oxford and reading law. His father considered the law as enjoyable as doing *The Times* crossword puzzle or budding roses in his beloved garden. He assumed that his son would naturally share this passion for the law. Mortimer was not a serious student at Oxford and benefited from the school primarily because of the friends he made, especially Henry Winter, a pacifist who introduced him to classical music. With the "extraordinarily gentle firmness of his moral stance," Winter had a profound influence on his friend. As an adult, Mortimer felt "somehow guilty and corrupt" compared to Winter, who became a country doctor.

After leaving Oxford and failing his army physical because of poor eyesight, Mortimer joined the Ministry of Information, where he rose from fourth assistant director of documentaries to scriptwriter, experiencing finally the joy of being a professional writer. He had so much fun making films during the war that he felt guilty because of the sacrifices and suffering of so many of his countrymen during that time.

After the war, Mortimer published his first novel, *Charade* (1947), inspired by his film experiences. In 1949, he married his first wife, also a novelist, who brought with her four young daughters from a previous marriage. His father became even friendlier with these little girls than he had been with his own son. Mortimer is very reticent about the details of his marriage, neither attempting to re-create the period of love with which it must have begun nor describing how he and his wife got along during their twenty-three years together, which produced two more children. He is satisfied in saying that the marriage gradually disintegrated.

A year before he married, Mortimer was called to the bar, and he spent the next several years distressed by the conflict of his two professions. He looks back with amusement at himself during this time: "That serious, prematurely middle-aged figure in the wig and gown, or the bowler-hat and pinstripes." He believes that he became exactly "what my father had in mind, the ambitious barrister of the Probate, Divorce and Admiralty Division, the professional product of an English education." He is less amused by what his years as a divorce specialist taught him about the agonies of marriage, divorce, and loneliness; and he writes sadly of the barrister who could dissect other people's marriages but not his own.

Several important events changed Mortimer's life after he thought he had settled down as lawyer, novelist, husband, and father. The first was that, quite by accident, he abandoned fiction for drama and found his true writing voice. Plays such as *The Dock Brief* (1958), about an aging, unsuccessful barrister, were considerably more popular than his six novels had been.

Success as a playwright, money from writing scripts for both British and American films, and the accumulated depression from handling hundreds of divorces caused Mortimer to consider leaving the law. He changed his mind, however, when he went to Africa for Amnesty International and successfully defended the Nigerian writer Wole Soyinka against criminal charges brought about because of a political protest. Seeing how the Africans had adopted British legal practices, Mortimer "had the unoriginal thought that British law might, together with Shakespeare, Wordsworth, Lord Byron and the herbaceous border, be one of [Britain's] great contributions to the world. [He] decided not to abandon the law, but to try and practice it more interestingly." He did so by changing from divorce and probate to criminal law, frequently handling such censorship cases as the defense in 1967 of Hubert Selby, Jr.'s novel, *Last Exit to Brooklyn* (1964).

During this period, the tragic death of Henry Winter occurred. This kind, peaceful man shocked his longtime friend by murdering his mistress and then committing suicide. Mortimer was also deeply affected by his father's death, although he succeeded in understanding and appreciating their relationship while writing *Voyage Round My Father* (1970), one of his best plays. In creating this drama, he had difficulty distinguishing between the father he had known and the one he was inventing: "In giving him to other people I came, after a time, to lose him for myself." Gradually, shortly before her death, he developed a closer relationship with his mother, whom he had resented for the many sacrifices she had made for his father.

Mortimer writes affectingly and entertainingly about his parents, about his friend, Henry Winter, and about the celebrities he has known. He paints a sad portrait of actor Peter Sellers and a much brighter one of author Kenneth Tynan. Yet *Clinging to the Wreckage* is handicapped by his reluctance to reveal much about anyone still living. He is not very specific about the details of his offstage, out-of-court life. Much of the second half of the book consists of ruminations about matters such as the death penalty, the nature of French farce, and the decline of England since World War II.

One of the most enjoyable aspects of the book is its store of amusing anecdotes about minor characters in Mortimer's life: the woman who claimed to have been taught by Havelock Ellis to urinate standing up; the cook who had been engaged for thirty years while waiting for her fiancé's younger brother to die; Mortimer's Lesbian friends who rudely interrupted him while he was trying to lose his virginity; the client accused of attempted murder who said, "Your Mr. Rumpole could've got me out of this, so why the hell can't you?" Mortimer's attention to the details of other people's lives yields passages more interesting than most of his sparing self-revelations.

Michael Adams

Sources for Further Study

Library Journal. CVII, September 1, 1982, p. 1653.
Listener. CVII, March 25, 1982, p. 23.
New Statesman. CIII, April 2, 1982, p. 20.
The New York Times Book Review. LXXXVII, October 17, 1982, p. 12.
The New Yorker. LVIII, October 26, 1982, p.166.
Publishers Weekly. CCXXII, July 30, 1982, p. 67.
Times Literary Supplement. April 16, 1982, p. 431.
The Wall Street Journal. October 11, 1982, p. 20.

COLLECTED STORIES

Author: V. S. Pritchett (1900-   )
Publisher: Random House (New York). 520 pp. $19.50
Type of work: Short stories

Twenty-nine stories by one of England's masters of the genre

A prolific essayist, critic, biographer, travel writer, and novelist, V. S. Pritchett claims in the preface to *The Sense of Humour and Other Stories* (1956) that short fiction is the only writing that has given him great pleasure. Considering the critical acclaim he has received for his writing in all forms, this may seem an extraordinary statement, but there is no mistaking the care and love that Pritchett lavishes on his short stories. A writer of great subtlety and precision, he crystallizes each story to its essentials and polishes each phrase until the words gleam like precious stones. The result is writing of the utmost lucidity and economy, yet paradoxically of denseness and gravity as each word carries its full weight of significance. This tension between surface lightness and underlying complexity is perhaps responsible for the widely varying critical assessments of Pritchett's work. Dismissed by some critics as an entertainer, he has been praised by Walter Allen (*The Short Story in English*, 1981) as the finest British writer of stories since D. H. Lawrence. There are similar dichotomies in the characters about which he writes and the world they inhabit. Typically, his men and women are drawn from the lower strata of the middle classes: clerks, shopkeepers, housewives, pensioners, commercial travelers. They are at first glance ordinary and unremarkable, but beneath their mundane exteriors, nearly all of them are eccentric, slightly obsessed, a bit crazy. Similarly, the world in which they move is the workaday one of ordinary objects described in exact particularity. Suburban bungalows, London apartments, parks, city streets, shops, and gardens are delineated with a naturalist's precision and objectivity, yet there lurks at the heart of things a seediness and decay that betrays their outward appearance. These dualities result in stories that are at once conventional and entertaining, yet bizarre and deeply disturbing. Like his compatriot H. E. Bates, Pritchett believes that the short story more than the novel is the ideal literary form for the nervous and fractured twentieth century, and while his stories are somewhat limited in scope, it is easy to see why Pritchett feels as he does, for his short fiction offers a report on modern life that is both disturbing and heartening.

These qualities are visible throughout *Collected Stories* but difficult to illustrate, for Pritchett's narratives defy summary and brief analysis, so complex and intricate are their inner workings. A tale like "The Diver," for example, seems at first glance an ironic and amusing look at a young Englishman in Paris between the world wars. In a city that appears to him designed for sex, he maintains an embarrassing virginity, and while his ambition is to become a writer, he can formulate stories only in his head and then exclusively in French. Virginity and inarticulateness disappear finally in the company of the previously intimidating Mme. Chamson, to whom he tells a fantastic and violent lie about his first encounter with a naked woman, the wife of a shop-keeper he claims to have found strangled in her bed. Innocence, violence, danger, and lust unite in illicit passion, Mme. Chamson calling out, "Kill me. Kill me," as she draws the young man to her. The story has the structure of an elaborate joke, but its real subject is less the seduction of a young man than his discoveries regarding sex, power, and language. The youth creates Paris from the language he uses to describe it as surely as he conjures a fictitious self for Mme. Chamson to seduce. Out of language comes not only perception but also power, for as a young man with a past, he suddenly becomes a person of consequence, no longer the object of pity and ridicule. More contemporary in theme and mode is "The Lady from Guatemala," which features the editor of an influential newspaper, Julian Drood, who relates only to humanitarian issues and people in abstract masses and cannot connect with individuals. The lady from Guatemala is an ugly, stumpy poetess who follows him from city to city as he lectures, writing him poems, idolizing his bogus compassion, driving him nearly to despair by forcing him to confront her as a person. This is no morality play on the modern vice of emotional hollowness but an intricate study in passion, self-centeredness, isolation, and idealism. The gauzy world of newspaper crises and abstract issues inhabited by Julian Drood cannot come to terms with the personal and immediate one Miss Mendoza represents.

The divided self, the inability to connect and communicate, the lonely isolation of modern life: these are Pritchett's recurring themes. He develops them with great skill and variety. In "Handsome Is as Handsome Does," one meets a physically ugly couple bound to each other by the opposites that first attracted them and by the humiliations life has since inflicted. The husband is a bundle of frustrated inarticulateness, a self-made man, slow of wit and tongue, trying to bully the world into his image of it. His childless wife married beneath her class and now spends most of her time interpreting her husband's half-expressed utterances to the world. They are dull, almost lumpish people, but their pain is touching, their very drabness a mark of individuality. The divided self recurs in "The Fall," where it takes peculiar form in Mr. Peacock, who on the one hand jealously guards his private life (he cannot bear to see himself unclothed) behind a facade of music-hall accents, while on the other hand makes himself conspicuous by demonstrating repeatedly and publicly the technique of the stage fall. "Tea with Mrs. Bittell" brings a widow of established family into contact with a young man of the working class. She has no relationship with anything: her ancestral furniture has no sentimental or aesthetic value; her churchgoing lacks conviction; her prayers are to no

God; what social conscience she has derives from loneliness and a vague sense of duty. None of the stories in this vein, however, lacks compassion for its people, however misdirected and schizophrenic they may be. Pritchett engages the reader's sympathy, not his scorn. Through his characters, one is reminded that the modern world is a drab and dreary place where most people feel ill at ease, out of touch, alienated. Love, if it comes, is a welcome surprise, an unexpected—even unhoped for—reward or lucky accident. "The Spree" illustrates this with humor and gentleness, bringing together a widow and widower who by a series of unlikely chances find themselves sitting together on an organized coach tour.

It would be misleading, however, to focus exclusively on the pessimistic aspect of this collection, for Pritchett has a lively ironic wit. From the early stories, "The Saint" is a classic of droll humor, recounting an afternoon spent by a young man (reminiscent of the author himself) with a religious zealot whose creed rests on a single article: that evil cannot exist because a beneficent God could not have created it. To the youth, the reality of an overturned punt on a dirty river is enough to demolish his wavering faith in this sect. Much later in time and more complex in structure is "The Key to My Heart," a novella narrated by a young man whose attempts to recover a bad debt from the local gentry land him in the center of raucous and outlandish domestic quarrels. A more acerbic side of Pritchett's wit emerges in "The Skeleton," a brilliant study of old age, avarice, and emotional frigidity that manages to be both satirical and sympathetic.

Many readers will be drawn to Pritchett's astonishing skill in creating the pressure, texture, and feel of physical objects and events. "The Marvellous Girl" includes an extended passage in which the sensation of being trapped in a crowd is made exasperatingly real, but the tour de force of physical description is found in "Blind Love." Here, one is taken literally under the skin of Mr. Armitage, a blind lawyer, and his secretary Mrs. Johnson, whose body is disfigured by a large birthmark on her neck. There is a certain contrived quality in bringing together these two partial people to make a single whole, but this minor structural fault is more than outweighed by the force and clarity with which the author probes the nature of blindness. Nowhere is Pritchett's empathy more apparent than in this uncanny and moving story.

Collected Stories is a rich and varied selection of Pritchett's short fiction, but it is unfortunately not the representative collection one would anticipate. There are no inclusions from his first collection, *The Spanish Virgin and Other Stories* (1930), a decision Pritchett defends by saying that he was then still learning his craft. One purpose of a retrospective volume, however, is that it permits an overview of an author's growth and affords the pleasures of early, raw efforts that frequently delight by suggesting the genesis of a writer's mature powers. Admirers of Pritchett's stories will miss personal favorites such as "It May Never Happen" and "Aunt Gertrude," but such omissions are inevitable and hence excusable. Less understandable is the unbalance of the collection in favor of later stories. Eleven of the twenty-nine stories included here derive from *The Camberwell Beauty and Other Stories* (1974) and *On the Edge of the Cliff* (1979). An author cannot be faulted for wanting to call attention to his more recent ideas and development, for the tendency of critics to dwell on a few chestnuts from a writer's early years is well-known; nevertheless, a more even balance between old and new would make this a more representative volume. Of the remaining stories, most were previously collected in *Selected Stories* (1978), so that for many libraries, *Collected Stories* will seem almost superfluous. Pritchett deserves a genuinely representative and comprehensive collection of his best work.

This overlap is the only fault in a collection otherwise notable for a high level of excellence. Few readers will remain unmoved by the incisiveness of Pritchett's perceptions and the charity of his vision. Readers requiring the stimulation of daring new techniques may find these tales a bit tame and conventional, but only if they fail to look beneath the surface of Pritchett's deceptively simple approach, direct style, and natural, colloquial dialogue.

Dean Baldwin

Sources for Further Study

Christian Science Monitor. May 14, 1982, p. B1.
Harper's Magazine. CCLXV, August, 1982, p. 74.
Library Journal. CVII, April 15, 1982, p. 826.
Los Angeles Times Book Review. May 23, 1982, p. 1.
The New Republic. CLXXXVII, August 2, 1982, p. 30.
The New York Times Book Review. LXXXVII, May 30, 1982, p. 5.
Newsweek. XCIX, May 10, 1982, p. 85A.
Saturday Review. IX, May, 1982, p. 56.
Times Literary Supplement. June 25, 1982, p. 687.

THE COLLECTED STORIES OF ISAAC BASHEVIS SINGER

Author: Isaac Bashevis Singer (1904-   )
Translated from the Yiddish by Joseph Singer and others
Publisher: Farrar, Straus and Giroux (New York). 610 pp. $19.95
Type of work: Short stories

A compilation of the best work produced by an outstanding contemporary master of short fiction

Isaac Bashevis Singer is one of the great storytellers of this century, and he may well rank with the greatest storytellers of all time. His novels, short stories, and books for children have won many awards, culminating in the Nobel Prize for Literature in 1978.

In spite of the high esteem in which his works are held, Singer has been something of a problem for the world of literary criticism. He developed his art independently, and it does not fit easily into any convenient niche. There are those who consider him a modernist or a realist; others emphasize his preoccupation with the past and his frequent use of supernatural elements. He has been called a pessimist, but a strong religious quality permeates his work. Writers who defy classification and make themselves difficult to place in what is termed "critical perspective" are often ignored, and may constitute an endangered species. Singer's stature is such that he transcends this danger. An independent spirit, he has little sympathy with those who attempt to categorize writers and their work.

The fact is that, in spite of their seemingly contradictory nature, all the foregoing assessments are accurate. Singer has mastered an art as old as the human race, and he deals with fundamental aspects of the human condition. Thus, his stories are timeless, regardless of their setting. They contain most of the elements of folklore: ordinary people, a strong but not explicit sexual content, the intervention of the inexplicable, and a very deceptive simplicity.

Nearly all of the stories in this collection make use of the supernatural in some way. Upright citizens are led astray by evil spirits or bad angels, or they are possessed by demons; ghosts appear; premonition and telepathic communication occur frequently. Moreover, these events occur so naturally that they never seem out of place: curiously enough, they are somehow a part of the reader's own heritage, if not of the reader's experience.

It is reported that Singer, when asked whether he actually believed in his demons, replied that he did: he then referred to the various psychological explanations for such phenomena, adding that perhaps he believes in the demons too. His point will be sufficiently clear to the perceptive reader. Singer is interested in the sudden changes that occur in people, the alterations that result in uncharacteristic behavior. For most of the history of humanity, these vagaries have been attributed to supernatural intervention. In a more rational age, the answers have been sought in scientific contexts. Since the processes involved are still not well understood, there are times when these answers may seem to be mere substitutions in terminology, and not explanations at all. In actuality, *everyone* believes in demons—whether by that name or by another.

It is also likely that there are very few individuals who have never felt a premonition that proved to be accurate, never followed a hunch to their advantage, never sensed emotional or spiritual contact with another person who was distant in space or time, or who were never impelled into rash and uncharacteristic acts by some inner compulsion they were utterly unable to explain. The things lumped together in popular literature as unexplained phenomena are universally fascinating, still mysterious, and go back to the beginnings of mankind. These things, and their consequences, form the basis for many of Singer's tales.

Singer was born in Poland and emigrated to the United States in 1935. The stories generally considered his strongest works are those that depict the world of his childhood and youth: Jewish villages of Poland and life in the Warsaw ghetto. It is a world that no longer exists. The villages are gone, and most of their inhabitants perished in the Nazi death camps or vanished during the Stalinist purges. Singer occasionally mentions these horrors, but only in passing when one of his characters refers to them. He does not exploit the Holocaust, but treats it as an accepted fact of life. This attitude on his part has aroused strong criticism in Jewish circles.

One reason his tales are refreshing is that Singer, unlike many of his contemporaries, does not embrace causes in his writing: he does not believe it is the purpose of fiction to make social or political statements. His aversion to propaganda will in all probability insure his permanence. As he has observed, commentaries always become dated. It should be added that the majority of such efforts become dated very quickly.

The forty-seven stories in this volume represent roughly one-third of Singer's published work in short fiction, excluding his children's books. He indicates, in a brief introduction, that he has selected them himself and that he cherishes them all; it can be safely assumed that he considers them his best work. The reader is unlikely to disagree, for this is a most impressive collection.

Most of the selections tell of Jewish life in early twentieth century Poland. There are stories of devout scholars who go astray, of women possessed by demons, of evil spirits and devils, of ghosts malevolent and benign. In "The Gentleman from Cracow," the devil, disguised as a wealthy young nobleman, spreads wealth among the villagers in order to corrupt them and then drags them off to hell. In "Zeidlus the Pope," the evil one destroys a good man by playing on his vanity. "Henne Fire" is the story of a woman whose ungovernable temper is punished by fire: things around her ignite spontaneously, and she is ultimately destroyed by a conflagration that consumes only her body and leaves the objects surrounding her untouched. Singer has stated that he likes to write ghost stories, but these are by no means conventional ghost or demon stories: they are stories of things that happen to people. Even in this presumably enlightened age there are accounts, seemingly authentic and well-documented, of persons who have died precisely as Henne did.

These stories are not without their humorous sidelights. Because all the marriages are contracted by arrangement, matchmakers play a prominent part. In spite of their conscientious effort, they seem peculiarly inept. Singer's brides are often attractive and occasionally beautiful, but his bridegrooms are almost invariably the opposite.

Singer is no sentimentalist, but there is a certain tenderness in him. "Short Friday" tells of a devoted old couple, each of whom has dreaded death because then there would be no one left to care for the other. A good angel takes pity on them and causes them to die simultaneously. "The Letter Writer" is a moving tale of the interdependence among a solitary man, a mouse, and a lonely woman. "Joy" tells of a rabbi who despairs after his daughter's death and then finds grace after her spirit appears to him.

In some of these stories, which are never altogether the simple tales of folk tradition, the reader will discover those elements that have led some critics to consider Singer a modernist. The bad angels often masquerade as good angels, and the evil spirits often appear disguised as loved ones; the omens come from enigmatic sources. "A Crown of Feathers" is a good example. Singer's people are very much at the mercy of forces they do not understand. In "The Slaughterer," a man who cannot abide the sight of blood is appointed to perform the ritual sacrifices. Unable to overcome his phobia, he is mentally and physically destroyed by the dilemma in which he finds himself.

More in the modernist vein are stories set in another time and place, usually contemporary America. Seldom without a touch of the uncanny, they are often absurd or bizarre. "The Joke" is a prank with fatal consequences; in "The Séance," an elderly skeptic becomes lost in a medium's home and wets his pants while trying to find her bathroom in the dark; in "Brother Beetle," the narrator finds himself trapped naked on a roof while his girl of the moment entertains her mad lover; "A Quotation from Klopstock" is an anecdote told by a womanizer, in which one of his lovers dies in his bed. "The Bus" chronicles a tour in which all the participants are eccentric or worse; it becomes a nightmare for the narrator, and he does not quite escape from it.

Singer believes that the purpose of fiction is to entertain, and the short story is his preferred medium. He considers it a craft more demanding than other forms because it must move directly to its point and cannot allow itself the liberties that are permissible in a novel. In his introduction, Singer enumerates briefly the qualities that genuine literature must possess. As he says, they are all well-known and basic, but he perceives that too many contemporary writers are afflicted by a kind of literary amnesia and that the basics must be reemphasized. These principles are easily stated, less easily mastered. Singer's readers will find that he has mastered them all.

Singer also states in his introduction that the short story is not currently in vogue. This is not altogether the case, although it has received relatively little emphasis during the past two decades. One reason for its partial disappearance from the scene is the demise of a great many periodicals that served as vehicles for it, but there are still magazines, widely read, that publish shorter fiction. Many of Singer's own stories, for example, have appeared in *The New Yorker*. Several good collections by recognized authors have appeared in book form during recent years, and a reawakening of interest seems destined to occur. The form that such a revival might take remains to be seen.

Singer writes exclusively in Yiddish, a dying language, and all the stories in this volume have been translated from it. The translations are by many hands, but there are no perceptible differences in style or expression from story to story, and it is evident that Singer has monitored his translators with extreme care. There are readers familiar with Yiddish who believe that an inevitable loss of flavor has occurred in translation, but those who know Singer only in English should feel confident that the loss is minor. These stories are beautifully written and told by a master whose insight and fertility of invention are unexcelled by any other writer of this century. They possess all the magic that genuine and enduring literature must have.

The art of the storyteller, in its most vital and entertaining form, has been given a fresh impetus by Isaac Bashevis Singer. His is a remarkable achievement, and one that sets a new standard for future writers. He is at the same time an individualist in the best sense of the term. That he will have successful imitators or followers is most unlikely.

John W. Evans

Sources for Further Study

America. CXLVII, August 21, 1982, p. 97.
Christian Science Monitor. April 9, 1982, p. B4.
Library Journal. CVI, November 1, 1981, p. 2155.
The New York Times Book Review. LXXXVII, March 21, 1982, p. 1.
Newsweek. XCIX, April 12, 1982, p. 81A.
Saturday Review. IX, April, 1982, p. 59.
Time. CXIX, April 5, 1982, p. 74.
Times Literary Supplement. July 16, 1982, p. 761.

THE COLOR PURPLE

Author: Alice Walker (1944-   )
Publisher: Harcourt Brace Jovanovich (New York). 245 pp. $11.95
Type of work: Novel
Time: The period between the two world wars
Locale: The rural South (Georgia) and the interior of West Africa

An epistolary novel in which poor, ugly, uneducated Celie reveals the horrors, drudgeries, and ecstasies of her life in rural Georgia

Principal characters:
> CELIE, a poor, uneducated black woman, fourteen years old at the beginning of the novel
> NETTIE, her older sister, separated from Celie for most of the story by being a missionary in West Africa
> SHUG AVERY, Celie's husband's mistress, later her lover; a beautiful, popular blues singer
> SOFIA, Celie's stepdaughter-in-law, one of a family of amazonian sisters who use physical violence to protect themselves
> MR.—— (ALBERT), Celie's husband in a marriage arranged by Celie's stepfather; his first name never used by Celie

Alice Walker's latest fiction is a marvel of words, rhythms, cadences; a singing of faith in the strength and survival skills of black women; a testament to sisterhood; a tribute to a belief in humanity and a supreme being; an optimistic affirmation that people such as Celie will not merely survive, or "endure," like William Faulkner's Dilsey: they will joyfully prevail.

In structure, imagery, and theme, this novel speaks universals by narrating the richness and complexity of the lives of a community of black people—especially the women of that community—in the rural South in the 1920's and 1930's. Yes, there are differences—black/white, male/female, educated/uneducated, traditional African/American—and the novel does not gloss over those differences or belittle their importance in history and culture. The tone of the book at times is bitter about the experience of black people, in this country and in colonial Africa, but, as in all good fiction, the specificity of one woman's experience helps the reader to recognize commonalities—in being female, in being human—and is ultimately an affirmation of life.

The narrative form Alice Walker chooses gives this novel its special flavor, brings together the disparate plot elements, and augments the main themes. Unlike most epistolary novels, which have the effect of distancing the reader from the events mediated by the letter-writer, *The Color Purple* uses the letter form to bring the reader into absolute intimacy with the main character—poor, ugly, uneducated Celie, who, for more than two decades, reveals the horrors, drudgeries, and ecstasies of her life in rural Georgia. There is no authorial voice to intrude between Celie and the reader, and Celie's voice itself in her letters—in its lyrical, rhythmic black folk idiom—speaks in a continuous present. Speakers of black English often omit endings for past tense, third person singular present, and possessives; the same verb form is used for all tenses and persons. Celie's distinctive language draws the reader into the experience, allowing no distance between narrator and reader. This sense of intimacy is further enhanced by the fact that Celie writes all the letters of the first part of the novel to God, the only one she dares tell the horrors of her adolescent years: being repeatedly raped by the man she believes to be her father; of the two children, born to her before she is sixteen, given away by the same man; of being married off to a widower (who beats her unmercifully) with four unruly children; of her beloved sister, whom she helps escape from the lecherous eyes of this same husband, now believed dead or lost.

It is years after Nettie's disappearance when Celie receives a letter from her, and she then discovers that her husband, Mr.——, has been hiding Nettie's faithful and regular missives. The voice in the book has been Celie's so long that the reader is caught up short with a new narrator who speaks standard English (Celie's letters constitute more than half of the book). It is only after this point that Celie begins writing her letters to Nettie; this change corresponds with her growing disillusionment with God. The concluding letter again begins "Dear God." Now, reunited with her sister and children, reconciled with her husband and with her lover Shug, clear about her past and hopeful about her future, her faith restored in a God who is no longer a white man with blue eyes and white flowing hair but instead is a powerful, wonder-creating concept, she writes her final letter. It is more of a thankful prayer than a confession or supplication: "Dear God. Dear stars, dear sky, dear peoples. Dear Everything. Dear God."

The letters from Nettie provide important thematic parallels between the traditional Olinka society in West Africa (where Nettie and a black couple are Christian missionaries) and traditional black society in America. Three parallels are evident: the treatment of women (women in Olinka society are valued only in relation to men, as wives or mothers; Nettie, as a single woman, has no value); the ultimate helplessness of a traditional society in the face of colonial capitalist expansion (the Olinka land is literally destroyed to build a British rubber plantation); and, the failure of Christianity to meet the real needs of the people (the missionaries are powerless to stop the destruction of the society as the land is denuded of the essential roofleaf tree). Nettie's letters also provide essential plot information—Celie discovers that her real father had been lynched and thus that her children were not the result of incest—and they help in Celie's growth toward self-assertion and redemption. Still, the African letters are the weakest part of the book because the tone, not mitigated by the rhythmic cadences of Celie's voice, becomes preachy. The reader never identifies with the African characters in the way that he does in other fictional works portraying the breakup of traditional African society with the coming of the white man, such as Chinua Achebe's *Things Fall Apart* (1958). More important, the African subplot is not satisfactorily resolved in the novel. When the missionaries leave Africa to return to America, taking with them the wife of Celie's son Adam, the Olinka problems are simply dropped. The rounded fulfillment of Celie's life in the novel does not include the rest of the world. Facial scarification and clitoridectomy continue among the Olinka in a vain attempt to maintain a dying culture while the economic base of the society has been completely destroyed. Perhaps Walker leaves this thread untied to suggest the magnitude of the problems of developing nations, but in terms of the masterful plotting and structure of the novel, the omission is a defect.

The twin themes of the novel are those of redemptive love as a means of survival as well as an end in itself, and the beauty and necessity of female-bonding. Celie's survival strengths are her forgiving spirit and her ability to tell herself not to feel—when she has to. Other women in the book are more assertive but are also punished more for it. Sofia, for example, is nearly killed for sassing a white woman. It is Celie, survivor, who is the binder of wounds, the healer, the necessary ingredient in redemption. It is Celie who goes to the battered Sofia in jail, Celie who nurses Shug Avery back to health, Celie who helps Nettie get away, Celie who tames Mr.——'s children. Nevertheless, Celie learns from Shug and Sofia's fighting spirit; she finally tells Mr.—— to get out and has to be restrained from killing him when she discovers he has kept Nettie's letters from her. "You a lowdown dog is what's wrong, I say. It's time to leave you and enter into the Creation. And your dead body just the welcome mat I need." The reader wants to cheer—and Celie's family are all so surprised they "ain't chewed for ten minutes." Helped to a first sexual awakening by Shug Avery (her husband's mistress), Celie begins to become her own person, asserting her individuality through her love of color (purple) and her sewing ability. Always sewing for others—curtains, dresses, quilts—she begins to branch out creatively and ultimately opens her own business, Folkpants Unlimited, when she goes off to Memphis with Shug. Celie's pants, each pair carefully fitted and designed for the individual customer, are comfortable, beautiful, unrestraining. For male or female, her pants become the symbol of the redemptive love of the book. Celie dreams while sewing pants for Jack, Odessa's helpful and loving husband:

> They have to be camel. And soft and strong. And they have to have big pockets so he can keep a lot of children's things. Marbles and string and pennies and rocks. And they have to be washable and they have to fit closer round the leg than Shug's so he can run if he need to snatch a child out of the way of something. And they have to be something he can lay back in when he hold Odessa in front of the fire. . . .

All the strong characters in the book are women, and it is the women who are the catalysts for positive growth and change. Shug Avery's love for Celie persuades Mr.⸺ to stop beating Celie; Celie's assertiveness and anger mellow Mr.⸺ (by the end the two sit on the porch, companionably smoking pipes and sewing together, talking about their good times with Shug). Squeak, Sofia's husband's mistress, saves Sofia from prison death by allowing herself to be raped by the white prison warden—and then asserts her own individuality, becoming "Mary Agnes" and beginning to sing for a living. Even the white mayor's family is partially redeemed as Miss Eleanor Jane cooks special food for Sofia's sickly daughter. This female-bonding is essential in the book; it is the source of strength across class, age, and sometimes even racial lines. The women in *The Color Purple* are "sisters" even if they both love the same man. There is evidence throughout the novel that degrading treatment of women is not limited to a particular group or race; in one telling incident, black and white men join in mocking the nature of women. It is the women who plan Sofia's release, using the strategy and tactics of Br'er Rabbit, saying that the worst punishment for Sofia would be making her work for a white woman, that her life in prison was too soft; the men had suggested only useless violence—blowing up the jail. Neither living in traditional African society nor living in dominant white society makes the woman's situation any better, suggests *The Color Purple*. Women helping women is what is necessary for survival.

Both black and white critics have faulted Walker's portrayal of males, but this charge is open to dispute. The main male characters are full, rounded people, and not totally unsympathetic (except for Mr.⸺, whose conversion seems unrealistic). Odessa's husband Jack, missionary Samuel, and Celie's stepson Harpo are all interesting, redeemable characters.

The color purple itself becomes, along with Celie's sewing, the central symbol in the book. Suggestive of royalty, creativity, surprise, it becomes for Celie symbolic of the wonder of the creativity of God. The first new dress she owns (not a hand-me-down), she wants to be purple. Purple not available, she opts for blue. When, at the end, she finally has her own house, she sleeps in a room painted purple. The pants she sews for Sofia have one red leg, the other purple. Purple is also the symbolic color of lesbianism; Celie's passionate love for Shug Avery is one of the poignant centers of the plot. When Shug leaves her for a young man, Celie is so crushed she can only communicate to Shug by writing notes: "I pray to die, just so I don't never have to speak."

It is Celie's voice—her language, her style, her imagery—that is the strength of the book. Celie gradually begins to use more standard English, through her contact with Shug and through her correspondence with Nettie. By the end she says, "My hair is short and kinky"; earlier, she would have said, "My hair *be* short and kinky." By the end she is using more possessive endings: "any woman's body"; earlier, she omitted them: "her sister doctor over Macon." Celie does not lose all of her unique language, however, even when sewing assistant Darlene tries to change her speech patterns, because "peoples think you dumb" when you say "US." Celie responds: "Every time I say something the way I say it, she correct me until I say it some other way. Pretty soon it feel like I can't think. My mind run up a thought, get confuse, run back and sort of lay down." Walker is clearly opting for the importance of retaining what she calls "black folk English"—rather than the pejorative and racist term "dialect." In an interview with Gloria Steinem, Walker asserts that writing in this, her first language, came easily: "I remember feeling real rage that black people or other people of color who have different patterns of speech can't just routinely write in this natural, flowing way" ("Do You Know This Woman? She Knows You: A Profile of Alice Walker," *Ms.*, June, 1982).

Celie may be uneducated and naïve, but she is wonderfully perceptive, and her ability to "peg" a character in a phrase gives the reader some marvelous pictures. On Sofia: "Solid. Like if she sit down on something it be mash." On Shug Avery: "She look so stylish it like the trees all round the house draw themself up tall for a better look." Her idiosyncratic language is graphic and often poetic: "Both the girls bigged and gone"; "black plum nipples"; and "dress like a moving star." She can tell a story economically or draw it out for effect; parts of the book are uproariously funny. Anecdotes are told in a traditional storytelling setting, with a community of people participating, their reactions also recorded. In fact, the oral tradition is very strong in this book: the community of listeners—the extended family—is always very much in evidence, as in the long narrative told by Sofia about teaching her white mistress how to drive. That that community of listeners is always black and mostly female does not detract from the universality of the themes of redemptive love, strength in adversity, independence, and self-assertion through the values of community. Alice Walker's triumph here is in creating a unique set of people who speak to the *human* condition. *The Color Purple* won both the Pulitzer Prize and the American Book Award for fiction in 1983, honors richly deserved.

Margaret McFadden

Sources for Further Study

Boston Review. VII, October, 1982, p. 29.
Library Journal. CVII, June 1, 1982, p. 1115.
Nation. CCXXXV, September 4, 1982, p. 181.
The New York Review of Books. XXIX, August 12, 1982, p. 35.
The New York Times Book Review. LXXXVII, July 25, 1982, p. 7.
The New Yorker. LVIII, September 6, 1982, p. 106.
Newsweek. XCIX, June 21, 1982, p. 67.
Publishers Weekly. CCXXI, May 14, 1982, p. 205.

THE CONSOLING INTELLIGENCE
Responses to Literary Modernism

Author: David Kubal (1936-1982)
Publisher: Louisiana State University Press (Baton Rouge). 201 pp. $22.50
Type of work: Literary criticism

Essays on important nineteenth and twentieth century writers, which stress the vital relationship between art and moral growth

David Kubal died on January 1, 1982—several months before *The Consoling Intelligence* was published. Kubal taught in the English Department at California State University, Los Angeles, the "city college" or urban university of the central city. It serves the general Los Angeles community but draws the bulk of its enrollment from the minorities and returning, working students. Kubal confronted the alienating forces of modern life in the classroom. No idly popular theme to be exploited by poor imitators of literary modernism, alienation (in language, moral and personal expectations, and social awareness) was a daily challenge to his teaching of writing and the works of the modern literary masters. Like his great model, Lionel Trilling, of whom he writes so eloquently in *The Consoling Intelligence*, Kubal came to believe that literary modernism, in general, was nihilistic rather than humanistic. Instead of criticizing the moral and cultural alienation it recorded, modernism seemed to glorify alienation in the name of art and formalist aesthetics. Unlike Trilling, who in the 1960's simply noted the dilemma of the humanist professor married to texts that undermine the values he professes, Kubal boldly suggests that the writers in the pantheon of literary modernism—Gustave Flaubert, Fyodor Dostoevski, Friedrich Nietzsche, D. H. Lawrence, and T. S. Eliot, among others—should defer to, or at least share the stage with, another group of moderns. These constitute a kind of secondary tradition, a tradition more closely identified with reason, cultural values, and moral compassion; they include Jane Austen, John Keats, Matthew Arnold, Sigmund Freud, Henry James, Saul Bellow, Philip Larkin, John Fowles, George Orwell, and Trilling.

Kubal's insistence that "humane centers" are more important to the integrity of literature than the dirge of alienation, questions some of the central assumptions of contemporary literary theory. The relativism of literary structures and the unraveling of cultural and generic modes that characterize the shift from Structuralism to Deconstructive Criticism are the intellectual descendants of the literary modernism that provide no sustenance for the spirit, no possibility of sanctuary. His answer to those who would dismiss his humanist critique as being naïve, traditionalist, and anti-intellectual is straightforward: Look at the modern writers who are not above the ordinary. Consider the writers who offer consolation; who prefer to engage a reader's affection rather than his skepticism; who prefer to be seen as sympathetic rather than as detached; who not only ask one to think but also know that one must believe in something. These are the writers, Kubal shows, who provide an alternative.

Comparing Jane Austen's conclusion to *Emma* (1815), which he calls a "dream of personal and social peace," with the concluding scenes of Shakespearean comedies, Kubal bases his case for a tradition of "humane centers" in literature on historical connections as rich as those which fed F. R. Leavis' idea of *The Great Tradition* (1948). It is important to note, however, how Kubal's interests differ from those of his great predecessor. Leavis insisted that Austen, James, Joseph Conrad, and Lawrence all contributed to the intensification of English moral consciousness; that their narrative and style promoted Arnoldian "high seriousness." Kubal does not take issue with Leavis (there are no explicit references to him in *The Consoling Intelligence*), but he is less interested in the contributions of literary art to consciousness, even of a moral nature. What intrigues Kubal is the Keatsian "soul-making" power of great literature, its ability to engage a reader's spiritual nature in a manner that both rivals and supplements what many would simply call religious feeling. It is that aspect of Arnold's legacy that Kubal stresses; he himself is consoled by Arnold's trust that the "modern self could extend its freedom, increase its powers of delight, and still find relative security."

Avoidance of complexity—social, psychological, political, or moral—is anathema to Kubal. Consolation or "security" have nothing to do with escape or isolation. He praises Henry James and Diana Trilling for insisting that despite its searing and alienating character, urban civilization provides the modern self with its greatest opportunity, and he eloquently demonstrates the consoling power of ordinary bourgeois experience in Freud and Orwell. It is Lionel Trilling, however, who moves Kubal to his strongest argument for the consoling power of literature itself. Just before he died in 1975, Trilling was working on an essay entitled "Why We Read Jane Austen." Kubal observes that Trilling was demonstrating the fact that "literature still exists to teach and console us." Indeed, notes Kubal, Trilling argues that even if literature does *not* grant power over life (and here Trilling and Kubal are both questioning Leavis' grand claims for literature), nevertheless "it can make it possible, by putting us in contact with the past, to think of ourselves as other than we are, to even permit us to imagine ourselves 'becoming' other than we are." The interpenetration of complexity with freedom is central to Trilling, and Kubal reverently appropriates the idea for his own purposes:

Defined by culture as we conceive ourselves to be, we can yet derive a moral pleasure, an ease from the discontents of our minds, by perceiving those options, knowing that at another time at least, a novelist, like Jane Austen, could dramatize what we are not, even perhaps what we can never be. It is a simple kind of consolation, conferring an ordinary sort of autonomy, but nonetheless one providing a release from the omnipotence of the present. Yet, as Trilling so often said, it was in just such ordinary pleasures we achieve so much dignity. Nothing could be more instructive about the nature of Lionel Trilling's thought than that he should happen to conclude by making these modest claims for the mind and art.

Nothing could be more persuasive of Kubal's own insistence that literature can console the modern temperament than *his* last chapter, a discussion of three major contemporary writers: Saul Bellow, John Fowles, and Philip Larkin. These two novelists and one poet have been recognized as philosophical and conservative in spirit by other critics, but by bringing them together, Kubal seems to uncover the real secret of their appeal. They rise above the black humor, cynicism, and hatred of history characteristic of so much contemporary fiction and poetry; their case for art is less self-assured than that of the great moderns (James Joyce, William Butler Yeats, Lawrence), and indeed they seem to revive some of the values of the nineteenth century. Bellow's hero, Charley Citrine, in *Humboldt's Gift* (1975) yearns for "an act of simplification . . . accompanied by an exercise of the imagination designed to . . . counteract 'the world's distraction.'" His friend Humboldt's last message gives him the key: "'The imagination must not pine away. . . . It must assert again that art manifests the inner powers of nature.'" Philip Larkin's poetry reveals "with unembarrassed simplicity a gratitude for the physical world." John Fowles's hero Daniel Martin discovers finally that compassion transcends genius, intellect, good luck or bad. Martin, the screenwriter, cannot write his true work of art, a novel, until he has learned that there is "no true compassion without will, no true will without compassion."

Kubal has written a beautiful book, something that cannot easily be said about books at any time. It is so not only because of the tough-minded hope that burns on every page but also because Kubal's style joins lucidity and gravity in such a happy blend that he charms his readers to his message. He writes like an angel because he thinks and feels like a man. Everything about this book challenges us to reexamine our tepid humanism and rise to the wisdom of our literary heritage. Kubal should have the last word:

> No one would now dare assert that literature and criticism can alone resurrect Atlas or any other buried god. That was the claim of the Prometheans of modernism; and if anything of their genius has been discredited that certainly has. Still, with a generous piety these arts, too long enamored of the awful truths, can at least begin to tell us the ordinary ones of how our strength is derived from our heritage and our nature; and how in sympathy and compassion our imaginations have dreamed of centers of human love— and then willed them into existence.

Peter Brier

Sources for Further Study

No listing.

THE CORRESPONDENCE OF BORIS PASTERNAK
AND OLGA FREIDENBERG
1910-1954

Authors: Boris Pasternak (1890-1960) and Olga Freidenberg (1890-1955)
Translated from the Russian by Elliott Mossman and Margaret Wettlin
Edited, with an introduction, by Elliott Mossman
Publisher: Harcourt Brace Jovanovich (New York). Illustrated. 365 pp. $19.95
Type of work: Letters
Time: 1910-1954
Locale: Primarily Leningrad and Moscow

More than four decades of letters exchanged between Olga Freidenberg and her cousin Boris Pasternak reveal Freidenberg to be a notable author in her own right

The Correspondence of Boris Pasternak and Olga Freidenberg: 1910-1954 (*Perepiska*, 1981; English translation, 1982) is Olga Mikhailovna Freidenberg's letter to the world. It is a powerful letter, indeed. Freidenberg preserved correspondence with her noted cousin—Russian poet, novelist, and translator, Boris Leonidovich Pasternak—through more than four decades of war, social upheaval, and political repression. Extracts from Freidenberg's unpublished diary fill in gaps in the correspondence. Elliott Mossman has organized the letters into ten chapters and provided each with an introduction, which is followed by excerpts from Freidenberg's retrospective diary and the letters themselves, arranged chronologically.

Both born in 1890, the cousins were members of a talented and aristocratic family. Leonid Osipovich Pasternak, Boris' father, was an Impressionist painter who also held a degree in law; Rosa Kaufman Pasternak, Boris' mother, was a concert pianist. Olga Freidenberg was born to another musician, Anna Osipovna Freidenberg (née Pasternak), and Mikhail Fedorovich Freidenberg, an inventor and publisher. As children, the young cousins saw each other only occasionally, but in the summer of 1910, when the two families vacationed together at a Baltic resort, a new relationship began, one which precipitated their correspondence and influenced the intellectual development of both of these romantic, gifted young people. Pasternak, whose inclinations toward philosophy, music, and poetry were strongly asserting themselves, believed himself in love with his cousin. At the time, Freidenberg claimed only filial affection for her cousin and rejected him as a lover. Over the years, the memory of that summer continued to be a source of poetic inspiration for the two, who recognized a bond closer than blood in their mutual love of art. Long after the halcyon days by the Baltic, ill and near death, Freidenberg wrote to Pasternak about her deep affection for him and about "what it means for a person to experience the singular joy of recognizing his *kinship* (literally that) to art."

The hiatus in correspondence of almost a decade after 1913 is filled to a certain extent by editorial comments and by illustrations such as that of Freidenberg as a nurse during World War I. After the chaos of war and revolution, the correspondence resumed in the early 1920's. At about the same time, Pasternak dedicated one of his early volumes of poetry, *Sestra moya zhian* (1922; *My Sister, Life: The Summer of 1917*), to Freidenberg.

By this time, women were allowed to attend Russian universities, and against her father's wishes, Freidenberg seized an opportunity to study the classics, folklore, and philology at Petersberg University. Developing into a passionate scholar, she defended her first dissertation in 1924 and her second in 1928. Despite suffering extreme financial hardship following her father's death, Freidenberg continued with original scholarly research for several years as an ostracized scholar. Unexpectedly, in 1932, she was selected to organize a new department of classical philology at the Leningrad Institute. Without benefit of prior teaching experience, she rose to the challenge of planning courses and selecting a staff. Among the political pressures she faced was a request that she raise grades for children of blue-collar workers and lower them for those of white-collar people. Freidenberg made herself politically vulnerable by refusing to do so. Despite her always precarious political status, she successfully defended her doctoral dissertation in 1935 to become the first Soviet woman to earn the doctorate degree. The dissertation was published as *Procris* (1936; *The Poetics of Plot and Genre: Classical Period*), only to be confiscated by the Soviet authorities after three weeks and critically attacked in *Izvestia*.

Letters written while Freidenberg was trying desperately to establish a career express her occasional resentment that Pasternak had not been able to keep his promises to help her secure a position. Exempted from military service because of a childhood leg injury, Pasternak had become well-known in Russia as a poet and translator in the 1920's. His letters to Freidenberg from Moscow do not give the detailed accounts of events that her diary and letters provide, and, indeed, she may have been unaware of the extent to which he was under both personal and political stress in the decade between the wars. When Pasternak's first marriage ended in the early 1930's, his half-grown son, Evgeny Borisovich (Zhenya) stayed with his mother. Pasternak remarried and fathered another son. He was concerned about his parents and sisters, who had gone to Germany for his mother's health in the early 1920's, but the Pasternaks in Germany escaped the Holocaust of World War II by moving to Oxford, England. Despite Stalin's capricious favor, which saved him from the fate of many of his contemporaries, Pasternak himself suffered persecution about such matters as the interpretation of his poetry and for acts such as his refusal to sign a death warrant. In 1935, Pasternak's mental and physical exhaustion led to a prolonged illness.

At that time, Pasternak was more thoroughly acquainted with political harassment than was his cousin, but the next year, the furor over the confiscation of her book imperiled her. The diary eloquently tells of the intrigue surrounding her appeal to Stalin, who she at first believed would intercede for her to overrule some petty underling. Her appeal jeopardized her further, and she was summoned to the Kremlin to be assured by a Soviet censor that her book had not been confiscated. The experience replaced Freidenberg's earlier confidence with the belief that "only for idealists is existence determined by consciousness. For dialectical materialists it is determined by the pointed finger." After Freidenberg's trip to Moscow, Pasternak wrote a letter on her behalf to an editor of *Izvestia*, pointing out that the book contained nothing to earn censorship. This editor, however, had suddenly fallen into political disfavor, and it was fortunate for Freidenberg that Pasternak's letter was never published. Eventually the furor subsided, but her book was not on the shelves as the Soviet official had assured her it was. The experience left her without illusions:

> Stalin chopped off the head of the Soviet people: their revolutionary intelligentsia. . . .
> My soul has never recovered from the trauma of the prisonlike knell of the Kremlin chimes
> striking the midnight hour. . . . The midnight chimes sounded particularly sinister when
> they followed on the terrible words, "The sentence has been carried out."

Only months later, the purges struck all too close, with the arrest and death of Sasha Freidenberg, Olga's somewhat eccentric brother. Heartbroken, she packed quantities of food and clothing in a desperate unsuccessful attempt to provide for her brother in the prison where she believed he would be taken. The arrest caused bitter division in the family. Olga's mother believed that Boris' brother, Alexander, should have been able to intercede for Sasha as the younger Pasternak had recently become a member of the Soviet secret police.

Those provisions which Freidenberg so desperately assembled in her futile attempt to save her brother probably accounted for her and her mother's survival of the unspeakable privations of the siege of Leningrad. Freidenberg's gift for understated yet expressive description is nowhere more evident than in her account of that siege, which she and her mother endured from its beginning in the summer of 1941 throughout its torturous nine hundred days. Her diary captures the horror of the bombing:

> I was shaken by the very strangeness of an attack from the air, of murder out of the skies.
> I lay there unable to understand, to accept this strange new life, these strange people,
> two tyrants throwing themselves at each other's throats, these factories making explosives,
> these bombs being thrown into beds where people lie sleeping, children and old folks
> among them.

Freidenberg and her mother did make one unsuccessful attempt to leave the city with other residents but were forced to endure that terrible winter of

1942 with its subzero temperatures. The ordeal inflicted a terrible toll on Freidenberg's health, but she did survive scurvy and other immediate effects of deprivation; her mother, however, died in 1944. Ironically, city residents were prohibited from speaking of starvation, much less writing of it. Through it all, Freidenberg continued writing on folklore, Homeric similes, and epic structure.

Freidenberg's inside view of history during those months makes unforgettable reading, yet the experience robbed her of heart as well as health. After the war, she lost interest in the university but continued to work there until the government allowed her to retire. She still desired to see her scholarly work published and likened its suppression to a "bleeding wound." Not long before her death, Freidenberg wrote in her diary with bitterness about her dilemma: "Everyone knows by this time that it is forbidden to engage in scholarly research. To introduce original ideas, to cite or make references to scholarly works, to pose genuine problems, is the equivalent of being caught in a political crime."

Pasternak's letters to Freidenberg were often necessarily circumspect during these times, and the two eventually used code words in attempting to avoid censorship of their personal correspondence. During the war, Pasternak at first remained in Moscow, but later he was evacuated along with other writers to Christopol. He occupied himself primarily with translations, especially of William Shakespeare, and wrote a play of his own. Mossman gives a quotation from Pasternak's play, which "invokes the plight of a Hamlet," and explains why Pasternak destroyed all but two scenes from it: "In the atmosphere of Stalinist, wartime Russia and the context of Eisenstein's and Prokofiev's film *Ivan the Terrible*, which substituted a new idol for Peter the Great, Pasternak's play would surely have been grounds for swift response." Mossman explains also that one scene from the play appears near the end of *Doctor Zhivago* while the other surviving scene involves a character later to appear in that novel. Pasternak's remarks to Freidenberg about his now-celebrated novel, on which he worked for more than a decade, begin early in 1946: "Your words about immortality were just right. This is the theme, or rather the primary mood of the prose I am now writing." Later in the same year, he gave further insights into his intentions in *Doctor Zhivago*:

> I have already told you I am writing a long novel in prose. It is, in fact, my first real work. In it I want to convey the historical image of Russia over the past forty-five years, and at the same time I want to express in every aspect, of the story—a sad, dismal story, worked out in fine detail, ideally, as in a Dickens or Dostoyevsky novel—my own view on art, the Gospels, the life of man in history, and much more. . . . The mood of the piece is set by my Christianity, somewhat different and wider in scope than Quaker or Tolstoyan Christianity, deriving from various aspects of the Gospels in addition to the ethical aspect.

Olga Freidenberg died on July 6, 1955. She did not live to see the publication of *Doctor Zhivago*, but she did read the manuscript in 1948 and responded enthusiastically to its "grandeur" and "scope." Neither did she live to know that the novel earned the Nobel Prize for Literature in 1958, but as early as November, 1954, she wrote Pasternak asking about rumors that he had won a Nobel Prize. He replied that the same rumors were heard in Moscow, and that they were bringing unwelcome attention to him from the bureaucracy.

Curiously, another Olga, Olga Ivinskaya, became an important part of Pasternak's life in the late 1950's. He referred to her obliquely in a letter to Freidenberg of August, 1949, as "a deep new attachment," and more directly four months later: "My friend and your namesake, about whom I wrote you not long ago, fell upon base times and has been transported to a place similar to the one where Sasha was." Olga Ivinskaya, the inspiration for Lara in *Doctor Zhivago*, twice suffered arrest and imprisonment, once before and once after Pasternak's death in 1960, because of her relationship with him. Those events are now documented in Ivinskaya's *A Captive of Time* (1978), a book which adds a posthumous chapter to Pasternak's life.

Clearly, Freidenberg adds an important chapter to her cousin's biography; even the best Pasternak biography to date, Guy de Mallac's *Boris Pasternak: His Life and Art* (1981), devotes only a line to her. As Pasternak himself did not keep letters or drafts, credit for the fact that this correspondence is now available to the reading public goes to Freidenberg and her archivist's instincts for preserving the correspondence and providing the diary, both of which are now in Oxford. Although the editor does not explain how these documents reached England, Pasternak's parents and sisters lived there after they fled Nazi Germany. It seems reasonable to speculate that Mashura Markova (née Maria Alexandrovna Margulius), a cousin who was with Freidenberg at the time of her last hospitalization and who administered the estate, must somehow deserve credit for getting the manuscripts to Oxford. Belatedly, the world is coming to know some of Freidenberg's scholarship; most notably, the synthesis of her life's work, *Image and Concept* (1978), has finally been published in Moscow. Her correspondence with her gifted cousin is valuable not only for its contribution to Pasternak studies but also for its testimony to her lifelong commitment to art.

Roberta Sharp

Sources for Further Study

Christian Science Monitor. October 8, 1982, p. B2.
Economist. CCLXXXIV, September 18, 1982, p. 108.
Library Journal. CVII, June 1, 1982, p. 1092.
Los Angeles Times Book Review. August 22, 1982, p. 8.

National Review. XXXIV, April 16, 1982, p. 434.
The New York Review of Books. XXIX, August 12, 1982, p. 3.
The New York Times Book Review. LXXXVII, June 27, 1982, p. 1.
Time. CXX, August 9, 1982, p. 70.
Times Literary Supplement. October 1, 1982, p. 1053.

THE CORRESPONDENCE OF THOMAS CARLYLE AND JOHN RUSKIN

Authors: Thomas Carlyle (1795-1881) and John Ruskin (1819-1900)
Edited by George Allan Cate
Publisher: Stanford University Press (Stanford, California). 251 pp. $28.50
Type of work: Letters

The correspondence of two of the most prominent Victorian men of letters

In the eyes of twentieth century readers, Thomas Carlyle and John Ruskin share the reputation of Victorian sage. Hidden behind their beards, they seem to dominate the nineteenth century, prophets in tandem. They were, in fact, separated by a generation, and Ruskin came to look up to Carlyle as a father figure. Indeed, in later years, after his own father died, Ruskin actually addressed Carlyle as "Papa." Ruskin first read Carlyle in 1841, became interested in him between 1843 and 1847 after correcting his initial bias against what he felt was the older man's "bombast," and met him sometime between 1847 and 1850. Carlyle's fierce moralism stood in contrast to Ruskin's aestheticism; Carlyle's tracts urged moral and social reform, while Ruskin's *Modern Painters* (Vol. I, 1843; Vol. II, 1846) and *The Seven Lamps of Architecture* (1849) dealt exclusively with art and theories of beauty. At the same time, however, Ruskin was still under the religious influence of his parents and very much the Evangelical sectarian; Carlyle was liberal, broad, the preacher of a secular faith.

Thus, from the start, they shared a deep concern for humanity. Ruskin's aesthetics and Carlyle's morality were the two sides of one face: modern humanism. Carlyle was excited by Ruskin's "expression," his intrinsic "poetry." The author of "The Hero as Prophet" recognized in the younger man a vehicle for the corrective voice of inspired "Nature," one more revelation of spirit in the world. Carlyle perceived and encouraged the moral bent of Ruskin's mind. Gradually, the philosopher of beauty became a social critic and moral reformer. The movement from *Modern Painters* through *The Stones of Venice* (1851) to *Unto This Last* (1860) is clear to the most cursory reader; one sees a believer in art turning into a believer in the absolute necessity of a morally inspired social reform. Carlyle's attack on the selfishness of the merchant class in *Past and Present* (1843) is repeated with vigorous sublimity in Ruskin's challenge to the merchant in *Unto This Last*: Give your life, as the soldier would his, in order to "provide" for the common welfare. One can trace in the correspondence between the two men precisely this development in Ruskin—so much so that one could argue that Ruskin may very well be Carlyle's greatest achievement. In his "infinite variety"—as art historian, aesthetic philosopher, social reformer, and more—Ruskin stands as an embodiment of *all* the heroes Carlyle had celebrated in *On Heroes, Hero-Worship, and the*

Heroic in History (1841).

Yet, it was precisely Ruskin's range and facility that proved his greatest weakness, a weakness that the singular mind of Carlyle was quick to detect. As late as 1865, a good fifteen years into their friendship and correspondence, Carlyle praised Ruskin's *The Ethics of the Dust* (1866) as a "shining performance," but the next day Carlyle wrote to his brother John that although he found Ruskin's dialogue

> well-informed and correct . . . it twists "symbolically" in the strangest way, all its Geology into Morality, Theology, Egyptian Mythology (with fiery darts at Political Economy, etc!)—pretending not to know whether the forces and destinies and behaviors of crystals are not very like those of men! Wonderful to behold. Apart from this sad weakness of "backbone" the Book is full of admirable talent; with such a faculty of "expression" in it (or of picturing what is meant) as beats all living rivals.

While not faint praise, this has a patronizing air. Carlyle obviously felt that Ruskin was a kind of showman or "performer," acting out the right things, a projector of images rather than ideas. Carlyle did not trust Ruskin's symbolizations. The older man's standards for symbolic organicism were high, as anyone who remembers the chapter on "Symbols" in *Sartor Resartus* (1836) can testify. Ruskin's symbolic imagination was ultimately facile in Carlyle's eyes. Ruskin invited this kind of judgment because he was constantly contradicting himself. Wavering between classical and romantic values in his aesthetics—"delicate" uniformity one day, "grotesque" detail the next—Ruskin was not considered a consistent thinker. This impression was strengthened in later years when Ruskin succumbed increasingly to attacks of insanity. In reference to Ruskin's encroaching madness, Carlyle urged him to garner his strengths: "you have a great work still ahead, and will gradually have to gird yourself up against the 'heat of the day' which is coming on for you—as the Night too is coming. Think valiantly of these things."

Throughout the whole correspondence, Ruskin is largely deferential to Carlyle, except in one important instance. Carlyle had said to him privately that the streets of London were so filled with bestial types that he did not feel safe on his walks. Ruskin put this into print, and Carlyle was incensed, particularly because he already had a bad press reputation for his purported contempt of the people. He insisted that Ruskin retract his statement. It was, said Carlyle, a distortion of what he had actually said. Ruskin demurred; Carlyle fumed. Ruskin's misplaced sense of honor and fact was evidence of his growing removal from practical affairs, from reality itself. It also confirmed Carlyle's intuition that Ruskin could not distinguish clearly between fact and symbol. Eventually, Carlyle showed great forbearance in the whole matter— not one of his characteristic virtues.

After Carlyle's death, Ruskin was drawn into the controversy regarding the posthumous publication of Carlyle's *Reminiscences* (1881) by James

Anthony Froude, Carlyle's "official" biographer. Carlyle's niece, Mary Aitken Carlyle, objected to the picture it gave of her uncle as a sometimes brutally frank and always harshly honest observer of life and people. Ruskin tried to pacify Mary Aitken and their mutual friend, the American scholar Charles Eliot Norton, who had taken up Mary's cause by publishing his edition of the Carlyle-Emerson correspondence (1883), which gave a more benign impression of Carlyle than did Froude's book. Finally, however, Ruskin's fidelity to Carlyle's own integrity, which had served as a personal and literary model for Ruskin for more than thirty years, forced him to champion Froude and urge Aitken and Norton to desist in their vain attempts to launder the legacy of a man too great to submit to their idea of propriety. Ruskin, despite his own mental deterioration, proved that he had learned to respect his friend's love of "fact."

This edition contains 199 letters, 114 of them published for the first time. The actual Carlyle-Ruskin correspondence consists of 154 letters, and the remaining forty-five letters printed here are "ancillary" letters to and from Carlyle and Ruskin and members of their families. George Allen Cate has supplied a detailed and useful introduction.

Peter Brier

Source for Further Study

Times Literary Supplement. October 22, 1982, p. 1153.

THE COSMIC CODE
Quantum Physics as the Language of Nature

Author: Heinz R. Pagels (1939-   )
Publisher: Simon and Schuster (New York). Illustrated. 370 pp. $17.50;
   paperback $4.50
Type of work: Essays

A largely nonmathematical account of the developments in physics, particularly quantum physics and the physics of subatomic particles, during the twentieth century

"I think that the universe is a message written in code, a cosmic code, and the scientist's job is to decipher that code." That is Heinz Pagels' answer to the question "What is the universe?" and in this book, Pagels takes his readers on a cryptographer's quest into the basic structure of the universe.

The book is divided into three parts, or rather two parts and a short coda. The first part, "The Road to Quantum Reality," traces the development of the quantum theory of the atom from 1900 to 1982; the second part of the book, "The Voyage into Matter," takes the reader from molecules to atoms to nuclei to hadrons and leptons and on to quarks and gluons, which, for the present at least, are the components of ultimate reality. In the concluding section entitled, "The Cosmic Code," Pagels philosophizes on the nature of the search and lays down the rules for "Laying down the Law." This ambitious undertaking is carried out with such clarity, enthusiasm, and conviction that the reader is carried along through the maze of difficult concepts without hesitation. Pagels is clearly delighted to be a participant in the recent triumphs of quantum physicists in understanding the code.

The year 1905 was a remarkable one for the development of physics. In that year, in *Annalen der Physik*, Albert Einstein published three papers which were to revolutionize physics. One was on the special theory of relativity; one was on statistical mechanics—an explanation of Brownian motion, the random movements of pollen grains observed under a microscope when they are suspended in a liquid or gas, resulting from the impact of the randomly moving atoms or molecules in the fluid. This explanation convinced a few diehard opponents of the atomic theory. The third, and the only one which Einstein himself thought revolutionary, was on the photoelectric effect. In it, Einstein used Planck's quantum hypothesis of 1900, but went beyond it to hypothesize that light itself was quantized into particles.

It is ironic that, although he himself in one of these papers provided an important contribution to a field of physics which depends on statistical interpretation and in another originated a quantum theory which would lead to a description of the world in nondeterministic terms, Einstein was never able to give up a belief in a causally determined universe. Einstein said, "I cannot believe that God plays dice." Pagels characterizes Einstein as "The Last

Classical Physicist," and throughout the book shows how modern theories are not concerned with whether God plays dice, but with how the dice-playing God plays the game.

Relativity theory is not a threat to a causally deterministic universe, and Einstein spent his later years searching unsuccessfully for a unified field theory which would link gravitation, which is explained by the theory of general relativity, with the other physical forces. There is further irony in the fact that in recent years, theoreticians have had some success with field theories which unify three of the four fundamental interactions—the electromagnetic, the weak, and the strong interactions—although not gravitation, but these theories are firmly rooted in the quantum indeterminism which Einstein could not accept.

After devoting his first two chapters to Einstein and relativity, Pagels turns his attention to a more or less historical account of what he calls "The Road to Quantum Reality." The phenomena of the subatomic world can only be explained in terms which seem bizarre, exhibiting what Pagels calls "quantum weirdness," to the everyday sensibility. Similar difficulties, though perhaps not to the same extent, attend an understanding of the world of enormous speeds and great distances where the theory of relativity, with its own kind of weirdness, holds sway. This is not really surprising. Both relativity and quantum physics predict classical results for phenomena on a human scale, a scale with distances ranging only from about a tenth of a millimeter to a few thousand kilometers and speeds of up to a few hundred kilometers per hour. Man's direct perceptual experience is limited to this range, so that there is no real reason to be astonished at the quantum weirdness on the subatomic scale. Yet such astonishment persists, and perhaps this makes the quantum reality all the more fascinating.

The author does not gloss over difficulties in this account of the development of quantum theory, and he presents quite detailed nonmathematical descriptions of the mathematics involved. These descriptions, for example that of the development of the matrix mechanics of Max Born, Camille Jordan, Werner Karl Heisenberg, and Paul Dirac, seem elegant to one who is familiar with the mathematics. It is, however, hard to estimate how much will be conveyed to the intelligent reader who has no knowledge whatsoever of matrix algebra.

Pagels leads his readers through Schrödinger's equation to Born's interpretation of the wave function (actually the square of the wave function) as expressing the probability of finding a particle at a particular point in space. This was, in Pagel's words, "the birth of the God who plays dice and the end of determinism in physics." The personalities and styles of the major figures illuminate the story: Heisenberg, who formulated the uncertainty principle, liked to express physical intuitions mathematically; Niels Bohr, who originated the principle of complementarity, was concerned with explaining the nature of the new quantum reality and emphasized the idea that one cannot verify the quantum world without taking into account that he inevitably alters the object of his scrutiny by merely observing it. Together, Heisenberg and Bohr provided the "Copenhagen interpretation."

Pagels approaches "quantum weirdness" through the concept of randomness, and an interesting digression into cryptography leads into a persuasive argument about some of the philosophical objections that have been raised to the concept of a dice-playing God. Modern nondecipherable codes consist of two completely random sequences, the message and the key, neither of which contains any information. The information lies solely in the cross-correlation between the two sequences. A correlation between two quantum particles can be established in an interaction between them, and this relationship between their motions continues even after they are separated by a large distance. A measurement on one of them, removing the quantum indeterminacy, would thus appear to determine the state of the remote one, thus violating the principle of local causality, but in the same way in which the cipher and the key are both random, the two distant events are still random sequences. What has been changed instantaneously by the measurement is the cross-correlation between the two events, and this is not a local object attached to the distant quantum.

Pagels concludes this section of the book with a refusal to accept as exclusive explanations any easy versions of quantum reality, seeing them as examples of the principle of complementarity. After an account of a fantasy sequence of a reality marketplace with merchants offering alternative views, Pagels concludes: "What quantum reality is, *is* the reality marketplace. The house of a God that plays dice has many rooms. We can live in only one room at a time, but it is the whole house that is reality."

In the second part of the book, Pagels provides an account, again largely chronological in organization, of the exploration through the use of larger and larger particle accelerators into the world of smaller and smaller particles. Forty years ago, physicists postulated that the atom consisted of a nucleus, made up of protons and neutrons, with surrounding electrons. There were pions, which glued the protons and neutrons together, and photons, or light quanta, which were involved in the electromagnetic interaction. There were a few others—the neutrino, whose existence was inferred from properties of radioactive beta-decay; the muon, with no clearly explicable role (I. I. Rabi is quoted as saying "Who ordered that?"); and the antiparticles such as the positron.

In the current picture, however, protons and neutrons are no longer fundamental particles. The ultimate building blocks are two sets of indivisible particles called leptons and quarks. The leptons are the negatively charged electron and its associated electron neutrino; the muon, similar to the electron but 207 times heavier, and its associated muon neutrino; and the tauon, similar but even fatter, with 3,491 times the electron's mass, and its tau neutrino. All of these have corresponding antiparticles. Since only the electron and its neutrino seem to be necessary to build atoms, Rabi's question is most apt.

The quarks come in six kinds or "flavors": up, down, strange, charmed, bottom (or beauty), and top (or truth); the existence of the top quark is inferred but not yet experimentally confirmed. The peculiar terminology arises from the special kind of sense of humor with which physicists are frequently afflicted. Each of these flavors comes in three "colors" (not really colors, of course, but merely some distinguishing characteristics so labeled), and each has its antiparticle. The quarks, first proposed by Murray Gell-Mann— and by George Zweig independently in 1963—have fractional electronic charges: plus two-thirds for the up quark; minus one-third for the down quark. (These two quarks are the only ones needed to make protons and neutrons.) They have masses ranging from approximately twice the electron mass for the up quark and six electron masses for the down quark to about nine thousand for the bottom quark and presumably more for the top quark.

The quarks combine to make a class of particles called hadrons, of which the proton and the neutron are the common ones. There may be an infinite number of hadrons, most of them having extremely short lives. There are two subsets of hadrons: the mesons, which have integral numbers of units of spin and are made up of two quarks each (the pion consists of a down quark and an up antiquark); the baryons have half integral spin numbers—one half, three halves, and so on—and are each made up of three quarks. (A proton consists of two up quarks and a down quark.)

Then there are the gluons, which, in the relativistic quantum field theories, hold the primary particles together. Each of the four quantum interactions between particles has its own corresponding gluon. In order of increasing strength, they are the gravitational interaction, which couples to the mass of the particles, with its gluon the graviton; the weak nuclear interaction, which couples to the "flavor" charges of the quarks, through weak gluons; the electromagnetic interaction, which couples to electric charges, for which the familiar photon is the gluon; and the strong nuclear interaction, which holds together the quarks through the mediation of the "colored" gluons coupling to the "color" charges of the quarks.

This seems a very complex picture, but it is less complicated than the model which obtained before the existence of quarks was postulated. Then, the apparently limitless proliferation of observed hadrons seemed to require a very complex taxonomy, leading Enrico Fermi to comment that, if he had known that this was where nuclear physics was heading, he would have studied zoology. The development in models of particle structure over the past thirty years has been somewhat similar to the development in models of atomic and nuclear structure which explained the regularities in Dmitri Mendeleev's periodic table of the elements in the latter part of the nineteenth century.

These developments, through which Professor Pagels skillfully guides his readers, require theories which make use of extremely sophisticated mathematics, and it is a remarkable achievement for him to convey at least some of the elegance of modern quantum field theories to the nonmathematical reader.

Physicists tend to use metaphors drawn from mountain climbing—indeed, mountain climbing is a common pastime among them—and Professor Pagels is no exception. After guiding his readers with remarkable skill, enthusiasm, and encouragement, up to the highest peaks and ridges of modern physical theory and through some very challenging rock climbs, he leaves them with a dream of falling, but a euphoric one, in which he is in touch with the cosmic code, "the order of the universe." It will be interesting to look at the topography of ultimate physical reality when Professor Pagels or one of his successors writes a similar guide twenty or thirty years from now.

John L. Howarth

Sources for Further Study

Antioch Review. XL, Summer, 1982, p. 371.
Choice. XX, November, 1982, p. 464.
Library Journal. CVII, February 15, 1982, p. 442.
Nature. CCXCVI, April 8, 1982, p. 503.
The New York Times Book Review. LXXXVII, March 7, 1982, p. 6.
Saturday Review. IX, March, 1982, p. 65.
Scientific American. CCXLVII, September, 1982, p. 53.
Sky and Telescope. LXIII, May, 1982, p. 481.

THE COUNTRY BETWEEN US

Author: Carolyn Forché (1948-   )
Publisher: Harper & Row, Publishers (New York). 59 pp. $11.50
Type of work: Poetry

This volume, Forché's second book of poems, largely addresses political themes and clearly establishes its author as one of the strongest poetic voices of her generation

Carolyn Forché's first book of poems, the highly praised *Gathering the Tribes*, was published in 1976 in the Yale Series of Younger Poets. Her second book, *The Country Between Us*, was the Lamont Poetry Selection for 1981. *The Country Between Us* makes extraordinary demands of its readers, not because Forché organizes her poems in obviously complicated ways nor because her language is obscure or esoteric, but because her subjects are extraordinarily painful: political torture and murder, powerlessness, the psychic damage to those who survive as witnesses to atrocity, and the difficulty of orienting oneself in a world in which grotesque injustice and suffering are the stuff of the nightly news. The reader may recoil from the recorded pain or, alternatively, put up defenses against Forché's strong poems, dodging their hard meanings with exaggerated attention to her purposely inconspicuous craft or with disproportionate emphasis on her lapses into falseness or self-indulgence.

The first section of *The Country Between Us* draws on Forché's two years as a journalist in El Salvador. A key poem in this section, "The Colonel," is in fact not a "poem" at all: Forché is reduced to the most banal prose to describe her dinner with a Salvadoran Colonel who, after the rack of lamb and good wine, spills from a grocery sack many human ears on the dinner table: "I am tired of fooling around he said. As for the rights of anyone, tell your people they can go fuck themselves." In "The Colonel," Forché confronts in unadorned prose the brutal reality out of which she has made poetry. The poems tell of a labor leader cut to pieces, of prisoners sexually mutilated: "the naked are tied open/ and left to the hands of those who erase/ what they touch." Hundreds die because of a slip of the tongue, and numberless people simply vanish. In California, thinking of the vanished of El Salvador, Forché says that their cries "might take years to get here," but not, one must add, to reach the minds and hearts of those who read Forché's powerful poems on behalf of the victims of torture and murder in Central America.

In the second section of the volume, the focus widens. The poet writes of a young man from Prague who has been imprisoned for ten years for toasting Alexander Dubček. She writes of loneliness and the deep insatiable yearning of long-gone or imperfectly realized loves: a love recalled by an old woman on a train coming into Detroit, for example, and a love between strangers on a train near Bucharest ("We have, each of us, nothing./ We will give it to each other"). She writes also of the dispossessed and forlorn of America, of a childhood boyfriend, Joseph, whose spirit has been blasted by service in Vietnam and whose life is now a drab dead-end in the steel-mill town in Northern Michigan where they grew up; and of Victoria, a girlfriend of her youth, who has not escaped, as the poet has, to Paris among many other places, but who lives in a trailer "in the snow near our town" with a husband (Joseph?) "returned from the Far East broken/ cursing holy blood at the table."

The third and final section of *The Country Between Us* is a single long poem called "Ourselves or Nothing." It is a meditation on the scathing pain of a lover who spent years writing a book about the Holocaust. The subject evokes "all the mass graves of the century's dead." We ourselves, Forché says, are doomed if we do not reach out to the murdered, for if we remain insulated from their reality we are not human but subhuman:

> There is a cyclone fence between
> ourselves and the slaughter and behind it
> we hover in a calm protected world like
> netted fish, exactly like netted fish.
> It is either the beginning or the end
> of the world, and the choice is ourselves
> or nothing.

The word "nothing" reverberates throughout this volume, echoed in poem after poem—"nothing" also sounds resonantly throughout Forché's first book, *Gathering the Tribes*. This insistent awareness of nothingness is balanced by Forché's tenderness, her understated affirmations of love and of political heroism, and her resilient faith—never stated, but implicit throughout *The Country Between Us*—that to make poems is to defy sheer negation, the more so when the poems are witnesses to inhumanity and to the defiant, astonishing persistence of humanity—the persistence, that is, of ourselves.

Forché's language in these new poems is at times intense and metaphoric, yet the poet retains control in large part because her tone is more often than not flatly journalistic. With such a dominant tonality, moreover, the color of the poet's language cools, the sound becomes less musical. "This is the ring/ of a rifle report on the stones" ("The Memory of Elena") is lovely in its muted alliteration (compare Wilfred Owen's appropriately harsher and more strident "only the stuttering rifle's rapid rattle"), dramatic in its strong dactylic beat, and witty in its play on the meanings of "report." The tautly governed craft of the lines is not obtrusive; the poet is not calling attention to herself or to her command of her medium. Her ability to understate material that in the hands of a lesser writer would be vulgarly sensational validates her authority. Carolyn Forché is the rare poet who can speak persuasively of the unspeakable.

Forché does pay a price, however, for the powerful restraint of the verse in *The Country Between Us*. The phrase "the ring/ of a rifle report" exemplifies the language of Forché's collection at its most musical, its most frisky. Forché's journalistic tone may be dictated by her difficult subject matter, yet one must also concede that the language of this second book is less lively than that of her first. There are thematic links between the two books, particularly in the poems about love and about the talismanic figure of Anna (Forché's Uzbek grandmother) and also in the reverberation through both works of the word "nothing," but the language of the new poems is by contrast drier, slacker, and simply duller. The loss is palpable, even if on balance one finds abundant recompense in the increased range, philosophical depth, and emotional power of this rapidly maturing poet.

The Country Between Us has received the sort of media attention generally reserved for best-selling novels, and it has often been described as "a book of poems about El Salvador," a highly misleading summary, as these lines from the conclusion of the volume suggest:

> In the mass graves, a woman's hand
> caged in the ribs of her child,
> a single stone in Spain beneath olives,
> in Germany the silent windy fields,
> in the Soviet Union where the snow
> is scarred with wire, in Salvador
> where the blood will never soak
> into the ground, everywhere and always
> go after that which is lost.

What or where, then, one must finally ask, is the country between us? Perhaps the country is any country, "between us" because of the power of nationality and nationalism to divide us from one another; perhaps "the country" is a trope for our humanity, "between us" because it is what we share in spite of all divisions; perhaps "the country" is the poetry that unites poet and reader in a community of feeling and insight. Forché's poetry does so unite. She is still gathering the tribes, but under much greater burdens and at far higher risk than before. The satisfying complexity of the title of *The Country Between Us* is one among many tokens of her success.

Daniel Mark Fogel

Sources for Further Study

American Book Review. V, November, 1982, p. 24.
Georgia Review. XXXVI, Winter, 1982, p. 911.
Library Journal. CVII, March 1, 1982, p. 552.
Los Angeles Times Book Review. May 23, 1982, p. 16.

Ms. XI, September, 1982, p. 94.
The New York Times Book Review. LXXXVII, April 18, 1982, p. 13.
Time. CXIX, March 15, 1982, p. 83.
Virginia Quarterly Review. LVIII, Autumn, 1982, p. 133.

CRIMES OF THE HEART

Author: Beth Henley (1953-   )
Publisher: The Viking Press (New York). 105 pp. $12.95; paperback $4.95
Type of work: Drama
Time: October 23-24, five years after Hurricane Camille
Locale: The MaGrath sisters' home in Hazlehurst, Mississippi

A warm, funny, compassionate play about a "bad day" in the lives of three zany Southern sisters

> *Principal characters:*
> LENNY MAGRATH, the oldest MaGrath sister, unmarried and thirty years old
> MEG MAGRATH, a flirtatious would-be singer, twenty-seven years old
> ZACKERY BOTRELLE, a local politician
> BABE MAGRATH, his twenty-four-year-old wife
> DOC PORTER, Meg's former boyfriend
> CHICK BOYLE, the sisters' bossy first cousin
> BARNETTE LLOYD, a young attorney

Crimes of the Heart, Beth Henley's Pulitzer Prize-winning first play, is about attempted murder, suicide, attempted suicide, failure, insanity, seduction, interracial sex, sexual inhibition and frustration, blackmail, political corruption, personal vengeance, self-deception, death by stroke, death by lightning, and caticide.

This catalog of disasters suggests either pure farce or extravagant melodrama. In fact, *Crimes of the Heart* is neither, although it has elements of both. As in farce, the catastrophes come upon the characters so rapidly and bizarrely that one never quite takes them seriously; from the beginning, it is clear that the characters will eventually emerge from their difficulties more or less intact. Yet they are not the stick figures of the typical farce; they are believable, colorful, sympathetic—if slightly grotesque—human beings, to whose feelings, needs, and frustrations viewers can relate. For all of the play's complicated and, at times, almost frenzied activity, *Crimes of the Heart* is basically about communication, courage, endurance, and, above all, love. As the title indicates, the real crimes in the play are not Babe's shooting of her husband, or Meg's "injuring" of Doc Porter, or mother's murder of the family cat; the real crimes are the betrayal of self and the refusal to love which have long haunted the characters and which have been overshadowed by the more mundane crises of the moment.

Each of the MaGrath sisters has, in a different way, made a mess of her life. The oldest, Lenny, having remained at home to nurse their aged, chronically ill grandfather, has fallen under the domination of Chick Boyle, a bossy cousin. Emotionally inhibited and sexually frustrated, the almost virginal

Lenny (she had "done it once") looks forward to a similarly barren future. The adventurous middle sister, Meg, after a disastrous affair with a local boy which left him with a permanent limp (he remained with her during Hurricane Camille and was pinned under a falling roof), ran off to Hollywood to become a singer—only to fail and be committed to a mental hospital. The youngest sister, Babe, has married Zackery Botrelle, a prominent businessman and politician, but that, too, has turned out badly. It is Babe's shooting of Botrelle in the stomach ("I aimed for his heart"), because "I didn't like his looks," that has forced this reunion on the sisters. Hovering over their personal failures is the enigmatic, frightening suicide of their mother. As Meg describes it, she hanged herself in the cellar after "a real bad day," first hanging the family cat for company. The dramatic question of the play is, Will the sisters be able to get through their own "real bad day?"

They not only do so, but they more or less come to terms with their own failures and tentatively set new, more positive directions for themselves. Babe's crisis and Meg's failure stimulate Lenny to venture out of her shell. She finally stands up to Chick, kicking her out of the house, and then reestablishes contact with her "one time" boyfriend, who seems overjoyed to hear from her, and not at all distressed by the fact that Lenny's "shrunken ovary" will make childbearing impossible.

Babe's problems are more complex than Lenny's and demand much more contrived solutions. While it is likely that Zackery's treatment of her accounts for—perhaps even justifies—Babe's assault on him, her situation is further complicated by her sexual involvement with a fifteen-year-old black youth ("I was so lonely . . . he was so, so good"), an affair unfortunately recorded on film by detectives working for her suspicious sister-in-law. Babe's rescue comes at the hands of Barnette Lloyd, a young, Harvard-trained lawyer, who takes her case because "she sold me a pound cake at a bazaar once," and because he has a "personal vendetta against Zackery Botrelle" (for reasons never stated). In the end, the lawyer manages to neutralize the evidence of Babe's sexual adventures with proof of Botrelle's political and financial corruption. Although Babe's precise fate is left in suspense, it is clear that some kind of deal will be made to resolve and suppress the crisis with as little damage and publicity as possible.

Meg is the most interesting and complicated of the sisters. She has neither refused to face life, like Lenny, nor has she made bad choices, like Babe; but, having pushed herself to her limit, she suffered a nervous breakdown. Returning home after hospitalization, she treads a precarious line between stability and collapse. Her reunion provokes not only the revelation of her Hollywood failure but also revives the issue of her affair with Doc Porter, the man whom she left a "cripple." Porter is not physically crippled—he merely has a slight limp "that adds rather than detracts from his quiet, seductive quality"—but in another sense, at least in the minds of the MaGrath sisters, he has been crippled by Meg. After the injury and her desertion, he gave up his ambition to become a doctor and became a house painter instead. In fact, Meg wonders if she has created an emotional cripple, but, upon meeting him again, she discovers, much to her surprise, that he has married, settled down, and seems quite contented. Her failure to reanimate their relationship provokes a curious response from Meg: she is pleased with herself and honestly happy for him.

> MEG: . . . he didn't ask me. He didn't even want to ask me. . . . Why aren't I miserable. Why aren't I morbid! I should be humiliated! Devastated! . . . But for now it was . . . just such fun. I'm happy. I realized I could care about someone. I could want someone. And I sang! I sang all night long! I sang right up into the trees! But not for Old Granddaddy. None of it to please Old Granddaddy!

Indeed, the character of Old Granddaddy is one of the central elements in the play, and his imminent death signals the new freedom that awaits the girls. On the most practical level, his death will free Lenny from the burden of caring for him, and, more important, it will free all of the sisters from the psychological bondage he has imposed on them. It was he who took them in after their mother's suicide, and his "strength" has constantly been contrasted with her weakness. It was he who put the idea in Lenny's head that her "shrunken ovary" would make her unacceptable to men. It was he who fostered Meg's illusion that she had a great future as a singer, spoiling her as a child and favoring her above her sisters until she was incapable of coping with the real world into which he then sent her. Finally, it was he who established the social environment that coerced Babe into her expedient, disastrous marriage to Zackery Botrelle.

All of these various story lines and themes come together in the marvelous birthday-party scene that ends the play, and when all of the plot complications are resolved—Lenny's call to her boyfriend completed, Chick dismissed from the house, Meg's revelation disclosed, Babe's case approximately resolved and her comical suicide averted—the three sisters sit down to consume a huge birthday cake in Lenny's honor—one day late. Although not fully articulated, Lenny's "wish" summarizes the final mood of the play.

> LENNY: Well, I guess it wasn't really a specific wish. This—this vision just sort of came into my mind.
> BABE: A vision? What was it of?
> LENNY: I don't know exactly. It was something about the three of us smiling and laughing together.
> BABE: Well, when was it? Was it far away or near?
> LENNY: I'm not sure; but it wasn't forever; it wasn't for every minute. Just this one moment and we were all laughing.
> BABE: Then, what were we laughing about?
> LENNY: I don't know. Just nothing, I guess.
> MEG: Well, that's a nice wish to make.

Crimes of the Heart clearly fits into the Southern gothic tradition with its echoes of Flannery O'Connor, Eudora Welty, and, at times, Tennessee Williams. The characters are at once believable people and comical grotesques. Their pain is real, and their eccentricities and absurdities—for all of the zany humor they provide—are tied to real pain. The idea of a horse being killed by lightning is amusing, but Lenny's grief over the horse's death is genuinely moving. A suicide pact between a human and a cat is ludicrous, yet the anguish that prompted Mrs. MaGrath to carry it out is quite believable. It seems improbable that a woman would shoot her husband, then make lemonade, drink three glasses, and offer one to her victim, who lies bleeding on the floor, yet in Henley's hands, such a woman is not only real but also sympathetic. Henley convinces audiences of the validity of these characters by creating a special world in which such behavior is the norm; her own love for this world and its inhabitants is infectious.

Part of Henley's secret is in her language. She has a playwright's instinctive sense of the rhythm of dramatic speech. Each of her characters has a distinctive voice, yet these individual voices blend easily into an impressive verbal medley. The accents are unmistakably Southern, but the "y'alls" are muted in favor of colloquial rhythms and carefully selected words and phrases, producing an effect that is both regional in flavor and universal in implication.

In terms of plotting, Henley's skill in balancing and manipulating her many complex plot lines is remarkable, especially in a first play. As improbable as the situations in the play may sound in summary, they are linked so deftly and proceed so rapidly that questions of strict plot logic will rarely trouble an audience. As Henley herself said in a recent interview:

> My plays aren't realistic. They're born of images of real events. I really can't write about reality. I don't know what my plays are. They're just filtered through the mind, or the heart, or somethin', and that's how they come out. They're real to me. They're real because they come from somethin' real.

Crimes of the Heart followed a curious path to success: it won the Pulitzer Prize *before* opening on Broadway, although the play had enjoyed a most impressive string of successes throughout the United States prior to its November, 1981, opening on Broadway. After its Broadway debut, *Crimes of the Heart* won the New York Drama Critics Circle Award as the best American play of the 1980-1981 season, as well as a nomination for the 1982 Tony Award for best play.

Keith Neilson

Sources for Further Study

Los Angeles Times. V, April 16, 1983, p. 1.
New York Theater Critics Reviews. 1981, p. 136.

DANCING GIRLS AND OTHER STORIES

Author: Margaret Atwood (1939-   )
Publisher: Simon and Schuster (New York). 240 pp. $14.95
Type of work: Short stories
Time: The late 1960's and 1970's
Locale: Various points in Ontario, Canada, especially Ottawa, and Boston or
    Salem, Massachusetts

Fourteen short stories that deal with various subtle and complex relationships between men and women

Dancing Girls and Other Stories is Margaret Atwood's sixth book of fiction, having been preceded by five novels: *The Edible Woman* (1960), *Surfacing* (1972), *Lady Oracle* (1976), *Life Before Man* (1980), and *Bodily Harm* (1982). Atwood has also published more than ten volumes of poetry, beginning with *Double Persephone* (1961), and a critical study, *Survival: A Thematic Guide to Canadian Literature* (1972).

Atwood's fiction reflects the old truth that a writer should write about what he knows best. Her stories and novels, set in the places where she grew up and was educated, relate the tics and traumas of mostly young men and women of the sort Atwood has known well. She was born in Ottawa, Ontario, Canada, in 1939, and pursued her education in both Canada and the United States, beginning with a B.A. from the University of Toronto in 1961, continuing with a graduate degree from Radcliffe in 1962, doing further graduate work at Harvard and at Trent University, from which she received a D. Litt. in 1973, and ending with an LL.D. from Queens University in 1974. She has worked as a cashier and as a waitress, as a writer of market research and of film scripts, as a college teacher of English, an editor, a critic, a novelist, and a poet. Along the way, she has obviously paid close attention to the awkward manner in which men and women grope and stumble about in one another's lives.

Dancing Girls and Other Stories probes some of the important themes treated in Atwood's five novels: the brutalizations and victimizations of love; the possibilities for metamorphosis of the personality; the nature and effect of power in human relationships and in the natural world; the continuum between human and animal, the human being and nature; and the instinct for survival. A recurring motif which links a number of these themes is the failure of men and women to communicate on a personal level, particularly when the individual couple is or has been in love. As Atwood writes in a poem entitled "True Romance": "It isn't sex that's the problem, it's language. Or/ Maybe love makes you deaf, not blind." Language frequently betrays Atwood's characters; the wonder is that any relationships survive. An enduring relationship, indeed, is rare in Atwood's fiction.

"The Man from Mars," the first story in the collection, is the first of many in which a female protagonist survives an unsatisfactory relationship with a man. Christine is the third of three daughters, a college-age girl with a "chunky reddish face" and "big bones"; she could "not possibly ever be beautiful even if she took off weight." She does not attract invitations for dates, but one fine day, an Oriental, "the man from Mars" of the title, asks her for directions to the economics building. She helps. He announces that he will come to her home for tea. Out of politeness, she complies, partly to please her mother. Time passes, during which he leaves the city, then returns. He tracks Christine on campus, jogging with her, joining her at lunch. Her friends begin to think of her as mysterious. She had never been mysterious before, only open, considered by her contemporaries to be "a plodder," a "plain one," "helpful and a hard worker"—and to her male friends, "the one who could be relied upon." The man chasing her is, in spite of his peculiarities, "still a man." Other men look her over again and begin to ask her out. "In the bathtub she no longer imagined she was a dolphin; instead she imagined she was an elusive water-nixie, or sometimes, in moments of audacity, Marilyn Monroe." The police pick up the "man from Mars," however, and he is soon deported: in Montreal, he had pursued the Mother Superior of a convent, a woman of about sixty. Christine is not special. Her "aura of mystery fades," and her life returns to its mediocre pattern. She gets fatter, has headaches, and takes to reading nineteenth century novels.

   Like many of Atwood's women, Christine is pathologically passive, a victim, one to whom "things happen." Other stories reveal the possibility of escaping from this passive role. In "Betty," when the narrator was seven years old and spending the summer in "a tiny wooden cottage" upstream from Sault Sainte Marie, she recalls meeting the older Betty. One of two daughters, the narrator recounts watching couples who lived nearby, thinking that one of the men "was a murderer" and that the other, Betty's husband, Fred, was so attractive. The narrator recalls that her mother was "livelier when he was around" and that her father drank beer with him and talked. Fred was attractive and likable but "didn't seem to make any efforts to be nice to people." She realizes that she cannot remember what Fred looked like—but that the inconsequential, deferential, kind Betty is easy to remember, "down to the last hair and freckle." Still, everyone loved Fred, and no one loved Betty, in spite of the fact that Betty was "always either smiling or laughing" and that she was always doing nice things for people. Predictably, Fred left Betty, perhaps for another woman, and Betty had a nervous breakdown. Four years later, the narrator met Betty again: She "smelled strongly of Lily of the Valley," used too much rouge to hide the "masses of tiny veins under her skin," and was working as an executive secretary, devoting herself to her boss as she had once devoted herself to Fred. She seemed "in a way, quite happy," but as the narrator asks, "What right had Betty to be cheerful?" Soon after this meeting, Betty became uncharacteristically aggressive; she had developed a brain tumor and died in the hospital two months later. The narrator contemplates; she sees herself abandoned "by a succession of Freds" who choose "vivacious girls" like her sister. She decides that Betty's final outburst of anger was one "of protest against the unfairness of life. That anger, I knew, was my own, the dark side of that terrible and deforming niceness that had marked Betty like the aftermath of some crippling disease." Others stop calling the narrator "a nice girl and started calling me a clever one, and after a while I enjoyed this."

"Under Glass" illustrates the continuum Atwood sees between nature and human beings. The narrator, a young woman in love with a young man who has recently cheated on her, admires some greenhouse plants that "look like stones, their fleshy lobed leaves knuckle-sized and mottled so that they blend perfectly with the pebbles." By the end of the story, she wonders "how long it takes, how they do it." She is busy trying to be like the stones around her, unnoticeable and accommodating. Apparently, she has recently been released from the hospital and is "feeling better." She goes to her lover's apartment, finding him hung over and discovering that her girlfriend has slept with him the night before. "It was her idea," he says, and "I was drunk." The narrator carefully keeps her murderous thoughts to herself. She sees the future and thinks of herself "picking up his dirty socks and cigarette butts . . . grunting away at the natural childbirth exercises while he's off screwing whatever was propped against him when he hit the mystic number of drinks." She begins to think of herself as "a place not a person." The nearest she can come to expressing her anger physically is to throw the rose she bought for him into the trash. He wants her to accept him and his "nervous tics," but she wants "to tell him now what no one's ever taught him, how two people who love each other behave, how they avoid damaging each other, but I'm not sure I know." They talk. "He kisses my fingers; he thinks we have all been cured. He believes in amnesia, he will never mention it again." She is of a different mind, but she still wants him. She will become like the flowers she admires: " . . . little zeros, containing nothing but themselves; no food value, to the eye soothing and round, then suddenly nowhere." Like so many of Atwood's stories, "Under Glass" is about the defensive maneuvers women take to survive in a world they believe they cannot change. What they often sacrifice is a part of themselves.

Dancing girls are women who perform for the pleasure of men, and Atwood's women are frequently cast in that role. Even the men in her stories sometimes assume this role, becoming "performers." The story "Dancing Girls" itself invokes the image of such girls only in passing. Told in the third person, the story recounts the experience of Ann, a graduate student in urban design who goes to Toronto to study. She lives in a boardinghouse inhabited by a succession of foreign students, with whom, as an "outsider," she feels a certain kinship. Her own character repressed, or simply never developed, she observes the succession of graduate students in the rooming house—a group of mathematicians from Hong Kong, a Frenchman studying cinema, a girl from Turkey studying comparative literature. The landlord, Mrs. Nolan, is domineering, noisy, and quaint, asking her foreign students at one point to don their "native costume" to come to a party; no one but Ann attends.

Ann has followed her father's advice to *"Finish what you start . . . I didn't and look what happened to me."* Her "first real boyfriend, beefy, easygoing Bill Decker . . ." was the one with whom she had "spent a lot of time parked on side streets, rubbing against each other through all those layers of clothes." She had "known this was not something she could get too involved in." Her relationships with "men since then" have been the same: *"Circumspect."* Early in the story, a young man, apparently Middle Eastern, moves next door to her apartment. She notices every detail about him, down to his "prosaic brown shoes" and a set of scars, tattoo marks, "running across each cheek." She "sympathized with his loneliness, but she did not wish to become involved in it, implicated by it. She had enough trouble dealing with her own." She wonders, as months go by, "Who was he, and what was happening to him?" She figures, "he was in exile, he was drowning . . . but there was nothing she could do. . . . All you could do for the drowning was to make sure you were not one of them." Instead she busies herself with her design for a shopping complex, a safe enclave for her mind and body. One night, she returns home to find that her mysterious Middle Eastern neighbor is having a party, with friends and drinking, she concludes from the sounds. She locks herself in and barricades the door. Later, she hears Mrs. Nolan shouting, there is a clattering on the stairs, and the front door bangs. In the morning, she learns that Mrs. Nolan has evicted the roomer, keeping his few belongings. He is homeless, possibly insane from the solitude of exile.

Mrs. Nolan, outraged by the roomer's having two friends and three dancing girls in for a Dionysian romp of a party, sends the Middle Easterners into the street before her broom. She was satisfied that she "had done something very brave." In his empty room, they find a pile of liquor bottles, and in another, all the trash accumulated during his stay. Ann begins to wonder about the conditions that produced such an outcome, feeling great sympathy for the Middle Easterner. She sees Mrs. Nolan from his point of view: "What would these cold, mad people do next?" Her "childish regret" is that she had not seen the dancing girls. Apparently, Atwood sees them as a sort of counterbalance to the loneliness in the Middle Easterners' lives. They are part of the natural order, about which Ann needs to learn more before she continues her career in urban design. Ann may indeed be learning, for as the story ends, she is planning a community, the design of which suggests a balance between nature and culture: "She must learn more about animals." Atwood suggests here and throughout the collection that we must all learn more about animals, especially the human animal that we are.

Atwood's fiction is full of such well-crafted imagery, imagery which vividly realizes the interior life of her protagonists. Beneath the ironic surface of her portraits of representative women—recording their muted existential losses and gains, their subtle, inconspicuous adjustments to make life as agreeable as possible, though agreeable it cannot be—there is unappeasable anger and a call to change.

Gary L. Harmon

Sources for Further Study

Library Journal. CVII, September 15, 1982, p. 1767.
Los Angeles Times Book Review. October 17, 1982, p. 3.
New Statesman. CIV, November 12, 1982, p. 33.
The New Republic. CLXXXVII, September 20, 1982, p. 40.
The New York Times Book Review. LXXXVII, September 19, 1982, p. 3.
The New Yorker. LVIII, October 4, 1982, p. 146.
Publishers Weekly. CCXXII, July 16, 1982, p. 62.
Times Literary Supplement. January 7, 1982, p. 23.

DEADEYE DICK

Author: Kurt Vonnegut (1922-   )
Publisher: Delacorte Press/Seymour Lawrence (New York). 240 pp. $14.95
Type of work: Novel
Time: 1932-1982
Locale: Midland City, Ohio

Rudy Waltz, at age fifty, reviews his life from the age of twelve, when he accidentally shot and killed a pregnant woman

> Principal characters:
> RUDY WALTZ, the protagonist; one of Vonnegut's bemused pilgrims
> OTTO WALTZ, his father, a flamboyant would-be painter
> FELIX WALTZ, Rudy's older brother
> CELIA HOOVER, "once the most beautiful girl in town"

Kurt Vonnegut, at age sixty-one, may be among "America's last generation of novelists," as he himself said in *Palm Sunday: An Autobiographical Collage*, his 1981 collection of autobiographical speeches, plays, and essays. Although he is a member of the World War II "family" of novelists, his work is unlike anyone's before or since. With each book, he donates a memorable character, setting, or object that becomes part of the American language for many readers: Ilium, New York, in *Player Piano* (1952); Malachi Constant, the American millionaire, in *The Sirens of Titan* (1959); "The White Christian Minuteman" newspaper in *Mother Night* (1961); Bokonon in *Cat's Cradle* (1963); the Rosewater Foundation in *God Bless You, Mr. Rosewater: Or, Pearls Before Swine* (1965); Billy Pilgrim and the marvelous planet Tralfamadore in *Slaughterhouse-Five: Or, The Children's Crusade* (1969); the Nobel Prize-winning science-fiction writer Kilgore Trout in *Breakfast of Champions: Or, Goodbye Blue Monday* (1973), who also appears in *Jailbird* (1979) with Walter F. Starbuck; Wilbur Daffodil-11 Swain, King of Manhattan and tenant of the vacant Empire State Building in *Slapstick* (1976); and Rudy (Rudolph) Waltz and Midland City, Ohio, in *Deadeye Dick*.

These novels may be called postrealistic. They do not imitate life. They are metaphorical, larger than life in implication, blending fiction with fact, fantasy with reality. *Jailbird*'s Walter F. Starbuck complains that "nobody who is doing well in this economy ever even wonders what is really going on." Presumably, those who purchase a $14.95 copy of *Deadeye Dick* qualify as "doing well." If so, Vonnegut's target is well-chosen for his message, which, as he has said in an interview, is to cause his readers "to stop hating and start thinking." If Kilgore Trout is Vonnegut's alter ego, his aim is "to be the eyes and ears and conscience of the Creator of the Universe." To these ends, Vonnegut uses irony and satire to imply a larger vision of bleakness—bleakness beneath the veneer of material prosperity. *Deadeye Dick* forces readers to confront the emptiness, loneliness, and craziness of contemporary life.

As in previous novels, Vonnegut's attention in *Deadeye Dick* focuses on the lack of "common decency" in American life. Even love does not accomplish what humaneness can for the quality of life. In his introduction to *Slapstick*, Vonnegut makes this point explicitly:

> Love is where you find it. I think it is foolish to go looking for it, and I think it can often be poisonous.
> I wish that people who are conventionally supposed to love each other would say to each other, when they fight, "Please—a little less love, and a little more common decency."

Such reasonable advice is almost impossible to accept. Hatefulness, cruelty, insistence on legal recourse, unswerving attention to "manners" and "good taste" all prevent one from acting with common decency. The search for such wisdom, difficult to acquire even in Rudy Waltz's fifty years, is at the center of *Deadeye Dick*.

Rudy, like Billy of *Slaughterhouse-Five*, is one of Vonnegut's bemused pilgrims, victimized and then rendered into a kind of recording intelligence— neutered, passive, alone. A chronological account misrepresents Vonnegut's alogical, fragmented narrative, but the effort helps the reader to understand some of the author's critical concerns. Still, the reader must, after disentangling the narrative, recall the discontinuity, essential to Vonnegut's vision of contemporary American life. Rudy tells his story, and the reader learns that he was born in 1932 in Midland City, Ohio. He is fifty years old at the time of his story in 1982. At the age of twelve, he accidentally fires a bullet that hits a pregnant woman between the eyes while she is vacuuming a second-story room eight blocks away. The young "murderer" thereafter bears the nickname Deadeye Dick, and his life is complicated by many undeserved hardships.

Although Rudy does not go to jail, his father, Otto Waltz, a painter who does not paint but whose means of support comes from a large fortune from a chain of drugstores managed by relatives, does go to jail. Lawsuits by the dead woman's family deplete the Waltz fortune, and Rudy becomes a servant and a cook for his reunited parents, who have never learned how to do anything. Eventually, he becomes a pharmacist and writes a one-act play, *Katmandu*, which lasts one night on Broadway. Later, he and his brother Felix, a reformed methaqualone addict and former NBC president, are in Haiti when a neutron bomb (whether accidentally or intentionally is unclear) kills all of the people of Midland City but leaves the buildings and machinery unharmed. Rudy's father, dies in a blizzard, muttering "Mama." His mother— "Mama"—dies from tumors caused by a radioactive mantelpiece. Which American myth does this story follow? Rudy is no Runaway Male. He has no Good Companion, and the only wilderness is his little patch of civilization. Surely, this is the myth of home as hell; home as America; home as Midland

City; home as the place where he is born and grows up with his parents and brother. In no way is his life satisfactory.

Vonnegut lets Rudy take the reader to an end that is also a conclusion. The last lines are apocalyptic: "You want to know something. We are still in the Dark Ages. The Dark Ages—they haven't ended yet." Like medieval cosmology, sophisticated modern notions of "the order of things" mask the essentially accidental nature of reality. Rudy, recalling that his father had bought one of Adolph Hitler's paintings in their student days when not buying it might have meant the end of Hitler, says that such an accident "is my principal objection to life." His father's purchase of Hitler's painting allowed Hitler to survive and come to power and cause World War II. Rudy's mother meets her end by being too close to a radioactive mantelpiece. His father, Otto, becomes a worthless good-for-nothing because Otto's mother, "on the basis of almost no evidence whatsoever," is convinced that he has artistic talent and hires a tutor who turns him into "a Good Time Charley" by the time he is eighteen. She also sends Otto to Vienna to art school, where he meets Hitler and lives life as a fraud. None of this would have been possible if his family had not become wealthy more or less by accident: they became owners of a chain of drugstores as a result of the success of a quack medicine called "Saint Elmo's Remedy," which contained such exotic ingredients as grain alcohol, opium, and cocaine.

Deadeye Dick is full of accidents; even the book's central incident is an accident: Rudy's shooting of a pregnant woman. Indeed, the book is also full of "loaded guns": Saint Elmo's Remedy, which makes undeserving people wealthy, thus giving them the power to impose their ignorance on others; the neutron bomb which, perhaps accidentally, explodes outside Midland City and kills all of its inhabitants; Otto Waltz's purchase of Hitler's painting, which ensured Hitler's survival; the radioactive mantelpiece that kills Rudy's mother; the deep voice of Rudy's brother Felix, which makes him president of his class, a radio announcer, and eventually president of NBC—which in the end makes him unhappy, for he has risen above his level; and finally, the beauty of Celia Hoover, "once the most beautiful girl in town," which attracts boys, though she does not want them, and which eventually causes her suicide when she eats Drāno. Once the idea of chance comes to the reader's consciousness, the book becomes much richer than it first appears to be.

Even the narrative seems to flow in an "accidental"—that is, aimless— manner. Plot is irrelevant in this example of postrealist storytelling. Vonnegut reflects the reality of a world of disorder, one in which no one knows the plot, through the consciousness of a single disturbed character. Logic, unity, rational order—these are concepts that belong to an older sense of the world. At one time, the complicated plot in which each situation resolves itself was a way to view the world. Readers more or less believed in some kind of destiny or fate that created order from chaos. One's fortunes followed from one's character. Realistic fiction presupposed chronological time as the medium of the plotted narrative, the individual psyche was the subject of its characterizations, and concrete reality was the basis for its description. A number of contemporary writers—among them Kurt Vonnegut, John Barth, Ronald Sukenick, Gilbert Sorrentino, Thomas Pynchon, and Donald Barthelme—do not accept these premises. As Ronald Sukenick has put it, "Reality doesn't exist, time doesn't exist, personality doesn't exist. God was the omniscient author, but he died; now no one knows the plot." Instead of literature, Sukenick says, the domain of the conventional well-made novel, is "reading and writing, which are things we do, like eating and making love, to pass the time, ways of maintaining a considered boredom in face of the abyss." Similarly, *Deadeye Dick* suggests that "reality" is itself a fiction—a fiction which people employ to pass the time until they die.

Vonnegut's emphasis on the ludicrous and the grotesque—on life as "slapstick"—is characteristic of post-Modern American fiction and points up a crucial distinction between post-Modernism and the Existentialist literature of the absurd. In the fiction of Albert Camus—and in many "existentialist" American novels of the 1950's—the notion of the absurd was invested with a kind of dignity, a heroism of consciousness. The Existential antihero replaced action with consciousness, and millions of readers were grateful for this new mythopoeic vision. It was a way of saving human dignity in the face of the abyss, a way of saving oneself in the face of a civilization that had gone bad in the teeth.

In *Deadeye Dick*, by contrast, the absurd becomes grotesquely accidental, blackly comic and stripped of its aura. Rudy embodies no heroism of consciousness in his attempts to bring order to the wretched mess of his life, yet Vonnegut suggests that his pathetic strategies are representative of the way that all men—including the novelist himself—cope with a world of accident. Rudy turns painful memories into plays; that way he can remove himself somewhat from his experience. He is also something of a chef, and readers by the millions, including many reviewers, have been puzzled by the many recipes scattered through the book: "Eggs a la Rudy Waltz," "Sauerbraten a la Rudolph Waltz, R.Ph.," and "Mary Hoobler's Chitlins," for example. Why has Vonnegut included these recipes? They are all part of Rudy's effort to bring order and coherence and control into a life that lacks such essential ingredients. Vonnegut implies that his readers, too, had best have some good recipes handy to provide at least a semblance of order.

Gary L. Harmon

Sources for Further Study

Christian Science Monitor. December 3, 1982, p. B3.
Los Angeles Times Book Review. October 31, 1982, p. 1.

Nation. CCXXXV, November 13, 1982, p. 500.
National Review. XXXIV, September 3, 1982, p. 1092.
The New York Times Book Review. LXXXVII, October 17, 1982, p. 1.
The New Yorker. LVIII, November 8, 1982, p. 170.
Publishers Weekly. CCXXII, August 20, 1982, p. 58.
Time. CXX, October 25, 1982, p. 82.
West Coast Review of Books. VIII, November, 1982, p. 36.

THE DEAN'S DECEMBER

Author: Saul Bellow (1915-   )
Publisher: Harper & Row, Publishers (New York). 312 pp. $13.95; paperback $3.95
Type of work: Novel
Time: The early 1980's
Locale: Chicago and Bucharest, Rumania

A tale of two cities contrasting the chaos, violence, and moral decay of liberal America with the warmth and caring of people in a repressive totalitarian state

Principal characters:

ALBERT CORDE, the protagonist, a middle-aged Dean of Students at a Chicago university, a journalist and a former newspaperman

MINNA, Corde's Rumanian-born wife, an astronomy professor and eminent scientist

VALERIA RARESH, Minna's mother, the family matriarch and a former Minister of Health in Bucharest

TANTI GIGI, Valeria's younger sister and Minna's aunt, a semi-invalid who manages Valeria's household after her sister has suffered a stroke

MIHAI PETRESCU, former *Chef de Cabinet* for Valeria, a minor officer in the secret police in Rumania

IOANNA, concierge at the Bucharest flat of Valeria and Tanti Gigi, also a police informant

TRAIAN, nephew of Ioanna, a driver for the Rumanian government police

ELFRIDA, Corde's only sister, a widow who lives in Chicago

MASON ZAEHNER, Elfrida's son and Corde's only nephew, a campus radical and dropout

MAX DETILLION, Corde's cousin, a lawyer defending a man accused of murdering a university student

ALEC WITT, Provost of the university where Corde is Dean of Students

In his ninth novel, Nobel laureate Saul Bellow combines journalistic realism with fictional characters, composites "from several individuals and from imagination," and a largely fictional plot, "portions" of which, the novelist admits in a headnote, "are derived from real events." As in Bellow's earlier novels, the hero is an intelligent, thoughtful man who seeks some sort of "human agreement" and whose consciousness forms the arena for a wrestling match with the issues of contemporary existence. Here, he encounters urban decay, random violence, political corruption and repression, and a general loss of value or meaning in life. Unlike those earlier novels, however, *The Dean's December* lacks humorous episodes—with few exceptions—as well as comic, if troubled and suffering characters. It is a slowly paced novel of ideas whose significant episodes gain meaning primarily through their effect on the central character, Albert Corde—a journalist, former newspaperman, and Dean of Students at an unnamed Chicago university.

The Dean's December is set in two contrasting major world cities: Chicago and Bucharest, Rumania. The former represents a troubled urban center of liberal, materialistic America. A city governed by a powerful, corrupt political machine and crippled by brutal, senseless crime, debilitating poverty and fear, and moral apathy on the part of its citizens, Chicago is a mirror for the problems confronting modern democratic society. It is a demoralized place without a fixed ideology, excessively concerned with technological advancement at the expense of men's souls. Believing primarily in progress, its people fail to perceive reality or to acknowledge the *"horrible"* existence of the underclass. To Albert Corde, Chicago is "the contempt center of the U.S.A.," a place where one must be pragmatic and "tough" in order to survive, qualities Corde himself lacks. In such a world, communication and warmth are virtually nonexistent. Even family members—Corde and his nephew and Corde's cousin Max—are enemies. Bucharest, in contrast, is filled with "warmhearted people," representatives of the "old Europe," who help one another survive despite the repression of their society. A dark and gloomy capital of a totalitarian government which sets "the pain level" for its citizens—forcing them to cope with a harsh reality—Bucharest is bitterly cold, but only in the physical sense. Here, emotion and intellect, humanism and science have not been severed. Doctors in a hospital intensive care unit where Corde's mother-in-law is dying light candles for the old woman. In this world where freedom of speech is denied—the apartment where Corde and his wife, Minna, stay is bugged by the government—faith and love thrive. Indeed, recognition of this fact, a rediscovery of those qualities which make life both meaningful and moral, is one principal consequence of Albert Corde's psychological journey—as well as of his literal one from Chicago to Bucharest.

Supported with vivid descriptions of the life of Chicago's underclass—tenement horrors, heroin addiction, child abuse, arson, rape, and murder—and with visual and tactile impressions of Bucharest's earthquake-damaged buildings and bitter cold, the novel depicts Corde's confrontation with several deaths. There is the death of a young student at the Chicago university where Corde is dean, an apparent murder involving a black prison parolee and a prostitute; the murder of a young white woman in Chicago after repeated rape by a deranged killer; and the terminal illness and death of his mother-in-law, Valeria Raresh, which brings Corde to Rumania. Each death precipitates a metaphorical descent into hell, a descent which culminates with Corde's going below the chapel of a crematorium in Bucharest in order to identify the body of Valeria moments before it is consumed in a huge furnace.

In Chicago, Corde must identify the body of the murdered student on a sweltering summer night. To do so, he must descend into the dark, polluted streets of Chicago, reeking of "sewer gases" and "hot sulfur" from a United States Steel plant. Agonized over the violence of prison life and the existence of the Chicago underclass, Corde writes a series of emotionally charged and politically volatile articles for *Harper's*, alienating him from the unctuous provost of his university by creating controversy for the school. To gather material for these articles, Corde visits the slums of Chicago: stifling public hospital wards, a detoxification center for heroin addicts, tenement buildings with menacing hoodlums, and the dark and violent tiers of the Cook County Jail. He even attempts to interview Spofford Mitchell, the man accused of raping and murdering a young housewife but is able to speak only with the public defender, who tells Corde that Mitchell is housed in solitary confinement, in a hole in the basement of the prison. Each interview, each trip— recorded in the novel through a series of flashbacks, many generated by mail Corde receives in Rumania from the United States, and the reproduction of long passages from the *Harper's* articles—is another figurative descent into hell, another confrontation with the brutal reality of life. Each episode is presented in vivid detail with images that evoke the landscape of hell.

At the center of *The Dean's December*, inseparable from the plot and the major conflicts, is Albert Corde. He moves through the work observing each event in detail, defining its components, weighing its significance, assigning motives to the participants, analyzing their behavior, and moving finally to a major insight or epiphany. This method of filtering everything through Corde's ruminative intelligence slows the novel's pace considerably, one of the book's major weaknesses, and focuses the plot on Corde himself rather than on the outcome of the Chicago murder trial, the consequences for the accused, or the death of Valeria and the fate of her extended family. Because major moral issues arise concerning the ways in which these people are treated, there is an incompleteness about the novel's development, yet not an inappropriate one. Bellow's focus is directed toward the limitations and inadequacies of modern consciousness.

From the beginning of the novel, Corde appears as a "hungry observer," noting the differences between himself as an administrator and the Communist general with whom he and Minna must deal in order to visit the paralyzed Valeria. He records the discomforts of life in a Communist nation—the inadequate lighting and heat, the difficulties of getting food—and ruminates about the controversy he has left behind in Chicago. Since virtually all of the present action in the novel occurs in Bucharest, with the Chicago episodes handled through memory, Corde's intelligence is the vehicle through which the novel's structure and episodes are integrated. His responses to death, to the literal and figurative "red hell" into which his soul has strayed, are the focus of the novel. Perhaps more important, he is the thread—an image used in the novel— linking Western democratic man to Eastern European consciousness and experience, which are represented by Minna, Corde's Rumanian-born wife, her mother, and her extended family.

In contrast to the humanist Corde, Minna is a scientist, an astronomer. Educated in the United States, she was saved from living under a Communist regime by her mother's quick action in sending her abroad years before the novel opens. Minna, however, has not renounced her Rumanian citizenship, a source of problems for her after returning to visit her dying mother. She feels a deep attachment to her mother and to the extended family of cousins and colleagues who gather at the old matriarch's home. Tanti Gigi, Valeria's sister, and these numerous cousins and colleagues are deeply attached to Valeria as is Minna and together they form a helpful community skillful in unraveling bureaucratic red tape. They form a sharp contrast to life in the United States, where even Corde's only sister, Elfrida, has difficulty sympathizing with her brother.

Indeed, parallels exist for virtually every family member. For example, Minna's ancient cousin, Dincutza, hobbles about helping Corde while Tanti Gigi is too busy with funeral arrangements to provide assistance; while Corde's own cousin, Max Detillion, not only defends the accused murderer in the Chicago trial concerning the death of the university student but also uses the trial's publicity to build his own law practice, and he openly attacks his cousin in court. In another example, the Rumanian concierge's nephew, Traian, is invaluable in making the necessary arrangements for Valeria's cremation and funeral with bureaucratic officials; in contrast, Corde's only nephew, Mason, is an antagonistic, unsympathetic campus radical battling his uncle over the murder trial. Repeatedly, Corde is struck by the manner in which the members of Valeria's extended family, though many possess double loyalties in order to survive, form a cooperative, humane community unlike anything he has experienced in the United States. Ioanna, the concierge, although a police informant, is also a loyal friend to Valeria and is deeply grieved by her death; so also is Mihai Petrescu, a former assistant to Valeria, now a Communist Party watchdog and member of the secret police who, Corde realizes at Valeria's funeral, has quietly battled the Communist police generals but met defeat. Lacking "personal rights," these people have not abdicated "the claims of feeling." Even the "secret agents" among Valeria's extended family "mourn their adoptive mother."

Significantly, at the beginning of the novel, Corde appears as the American intellectual, the American dean and husband accompanying his wife to discuss visitation policies with the secret police general who also supervises the hospital where his mother-in-law lies ill. In these early descriptions, as if to emphasize Corde's intellectual side, Bellow focuses on his "wide head," which moves forward on a narrow neck as the Dean listens. He is well-read—indeed, he "reads far too much"—and is conversant with a variety of literary works and philosophies. Yet Bellow is careful also to indicate early that Corde is neither an academician nor a purely intellectual being. For one thing, he feels out of place as dean, a position he took because of his need to resign from his foreign correspondent's post to return to his hometown to study and read. His *Harper's* articles on Chicago's underclass are embarrassingly emotional and, hence, repellent to the cool Provost, Alec Witt. Corde's response to the death of the student is, moreover, one of "excessive" sorrow. Even as a journalist, Corde identifies with the poetic, particularly with the poet Rainer Maria Rilke, who also sought to communicate effectively with others. Corde has the poet's temperament, his humanistic concern, his eye for detail, and his sensitivity to language and all forms of life. Confined to his wife's old rooms in Bucharest—for Minna fears he will be arrested for selling American dollars if he goes out—Corde becomes a silent observer of life around him, including even the beautiful houseplants Tanti Gigi provides for him.

On his journey, Corde moves increasingly to a recognition of the need for human cooperation, illustrated by Valeria's extended family, and hope for man's survival. His Chicago research had stirred this awareness, but his response has been anger. His *Harper's* articles are an attack on Chicago, not expressions of love. Corde's recognition must come in Rumania, at the crematorium where he must place his faith in cousin Dincutza to guide him through the procedures for identifying the body, and, earlier, at the hospital where Corde risks telling Valeria on her deathbed that he loves her, an action that sets the dials of the hospital's life-support machines spinning. Speaking from his heart—his name is French and means "heart-shaped"—Corde commits an act of faith. He has not previously felt that Valeria trusted or accepted him; in fact, it is only at the end of the novel that Minna tells him that he did the right thing and that Valeria thought well of him.

By making such a man the central intelligence of *The Dean's December*, Bellow focuses on the uncertainty of life, the cloudiness of moral issues, the ambiguity of relationships. While the novel lacks comic relief and is too slowly paced, it is, in the final analysis, a stirring book about the human soul, a work that suggests, through Corde's journey, that the solutions to the problems of modern life—moral decadence, urban crime and poverty, political corruption and repression—are not new social programs or political revolutions. The solutions rest with human sympathy and "personal humanity" of the kind which Corde finds in Rumania and with a balance of reason and emotion, of science with faith.

Stella A. Nesanovich

Sources for Further Study

America. CXLVI, February 20, 1982, p. 136.
The Atlantic. CCXLIX, February, 1982, p. 78.
Christian Science Monitor. January 15, 1982, p. B2.
Harper's Magazine. CCLXIV, February, 1982, p. 62.
Nation. CCXXXIV, January 30, 1982, p. 117.

The New York Times Book Review. LXXXVII, January 10, 1982, p. 1.
The New Yorker. LVIII, February 22, 1982, p. 120.
Saturday Review. IX, February, 1982, p. 73.
Time. CXIX, January 18, 1982, p. 77.

THE DIARY OF VIRGINIA WOOLF
Volume IV: 1931-1935

Author: Virginia Woolf (1882-1941)
Edited by Anne Olivier Bell, assisted by Andrew McNeillie
Publisher: Harcourt Brace Jovanovich (New York). 402 pp. $19.95
Type of work: Diary
Locale: England, France, Italy, Greece, Holland, and Germany

Virginia Woolf continues a very busy life of writing, socializing, and traveling, and she records her impressions, her moods, and her views of her writing

Principal personages:
VIRGINIA STEPHEN WOOLF, a novelist and essayist
LEONARD WOOLF, her husband, an author, publisher, and social critic
VANESSA BELL, her sister, an artist
CLIVE BELL, Vanessa's husband, an art critic
ROGER FRY, an art critic
THOMAS STEARNS ELIOT, an American-born poet, critic, and dramatist
DUNCAN GRANT, an artist
JOHN MAYNARD KEYNES, an economist
VITA SACKVILLE-WEST, a poet and novelist

"Lady L. a now shapeless sausage, & Mrs. Hunter, a swathed satin sausage, sat side by side on a sofa. Ethel stood at the piano in the window . . . conducting with a pencil. There was a drop at the end of her nose." The passage might have been taken from one of Virginia Woolf's novels, but is actually part of her diary record of her attendance as one of a small audience at a music rehearsal in a "vast" English mansion. The entry is representative of the mastery of laconic, descriptive detail and satiric bite that lend so much interest to the fourth volume of one of the most celebrated diaries of the twentieth century.

The fourth volume of Woolf's diary covers the years from 1931 to 1935. During this time, she published her sixth novel, *The Waves* (1931); a volume of essays, *The Common Reader: Second Series* (1932); and *Flush* (1933), a brief, whimsical biography of Elizabeth Barrett Browning's dog. She also worked intermittently for more than three years on her long, complex novel *The Years*, the publication of which was delayed by illness until 1937. Many diary entries concern the difficulties she had in writing *The Years*, which she originally intended to be "an Essay-Novel, called the Pargiters—& it's to take in everything, sex, education, life &c.; & come, with the most powerful and agile leaps, like a chamois across precipices from 1880 to here & now."

The manuscript would undergo many changes and revisions before it was published. As late as December, 1935, Woolf asked herself whether "the last revision of the last pages" of *The Years* was really the "last revision." The novel-essay portion, under the original title *The Pargiters* (1977), would be published separately forty years after the novel first appeared.

Virginia Woolf was the brilliant daughter of a distinguished scholar and critic, Leslie Stephen. At thirty, she married Leonard Woolf, an intellectual Jew who fortunately understood her manic-depressive temperament and was able to help her channel her energies during her manic periods and guard against unwelcome intrusions during the times when she suffered from violent headaches, exhaustion, or depression.

In her novels, Woolf writes from a variety of perspectives. Intentionally avoiding the limitations of the omniscient point of view or the even more strictly limited first-person approach to narration, she prefers to shift perspectives often. Thus, she enters the minds of various characters and yet at times draws back, as what a critic has called "the narrative consciousness," to comment on the characters or to offer general observations.

In the diary, Woolf also uses, whether consciously or not, much of the variety of approach found in the novels. There are quick shifts among straight reportage, gossipy comment, descriptive characterization, display of pique or anger, confession of regret or remorse, self-examination, and thoughtful observation. The imagination which created the carefully revised fiction reveals itself in the privacy of the diary and is unrestricted by any attempt to craft the writing into "literature."

As in earlier volumes of the diary, Woolf often comments on or describes her changing moods. "Lord, how I suffer!" she writes. "What a terrific capacity I possess for feeling with intensity." In a metaphoric description of a surge of emotion on one occasion, she suggests both mental and physical turbulence: "the galloping horses in my heart the night before last . . . it was a terrific effort, holding on to the reins."

She sometimes tries to understand or analyze what is happening to her. After a two-day stay in bed, she asks, "what are these sudden fits of complete exhaustion? . . . I think the effort to live in 2 spheres: the novel [*The Pargiters*]; & life is a strain. . . . I only want walking & perfectly spontaneous childish life with L. & the accustomed when I'm writing at full tilt: to have to behave with circumspection & decision to strangers wrenches me into another region; hence the collapse." This passage, like many others, hints at Woolf's recognition and appreciation of the important part which "L." played in providing for her a sense of security and comfort in a marriage which was to last nearly twenty-nine years.

One frequently wonders how Woolf managed to publish as much as she did. She and her husband had numerous family members to be visited or to be entertained in their home. There were many friends for whom social time must be allotted. There were parties, the theater, and concerts to be attended. Because the Woolfs ran a small publishing house, the Hogarth Press, they both had to read manuscripts, and often they needed to entertain or at least talk with authors about writings submitted. Woolf, in addition to her writing for publication and her diary keeping, was a voluminous letter writer. Time out from work on articles, essays, or books was taken also for numerous short trips as well as for several long tours on the Continent. Yet, often in bursts of energy, Woolf completed her writing, and she anticipated more to come. "I am so oppressed," she writes in June, 1935, "by the thought of all the books I have to write that my head is like a bursting boiler."

The Woolfs' circle of friends and acquaintances expanded greatly from 1915, when she began the diary, through 1930, the year with which Volume III of the published diary closed. During the period recorded in Volume IV, she was made increasingly aware of the toll of the years: people she had long known were dying, one after another. Arnold Bennett succumbed to typhoid fever, and his death left her sadder than she had supposed it would, since he had, as a critic, "abused" her, and she had answered him in kind. Lytton Strachey, who had been one of her cherished friends for many years, died after a long, painful illness, and the intensity of her emotion left her numb. Dora Carrington, with whom the homosexual Strachey had lived, committed suicide less than two months after his death, and the Woolfs argued over why she killed herself, Virginia Woolf blaming Strachey for having "absorbed" Dora while her husband considered Dora's suicide merely "histrionic."

Woolf herself had first attempted suicide at thirteen following her mother's death. She made a second attempt when she was thirty-one, after a breakdown following the completion of her first novel. The reader of the diary, knowing that Woolf would, within a few years, drown herself during a spell of deep depression, sees somber portents in remarks she makes after the deaths of other people, whether natural or self-induced. After Strachey dies and Dora threatens to kill herself, Woolf casually states, "Suicide seems to me quite sensible." Yet, when Dora carries out her threat, she just as casually comments, "I am glad to be alive and sorry for the dead: cant think why Carrington killed herself."

She is troubled, though, after the death of Roger Fry, another close friend, whose biography she would later write. She thinks of her own future extinction and, "A fear . . . came to me, of death. Of course I shall lie there too before that gate, & slide in; & it frightened me. But why?"

A reminder of the earlier suicide attempts comes to Woolf when her sister-in-law accidentally injures herself by banging her head against a car door, and Woolf explodes in anger. In a moment, though, she is stabbed by remorse as she stamps away "with gloom & pain constricting my heart; & the desire for death in the old way all for two . . . careless words."

Woolf's views of her writing were affected by her moods and by the particular work on which she was occupied. While engaged on one of the essays in *The Common Reader: Second Series*, she exclaims, "Lord, how tired one gets of one's own writing." She rejoiced that, when she had let the printer have the manuscript, she could then have "a fling into fiction & freedom." *Flush* was the "easy indolent writing" she turned to for relief from the more intense concentration required by the essays. She also escaped temporarily from some of the agony of composing *The Waves* by "fleeing" to *Flush*, which she regarded as mere light entertainment, in contrast to her serious novels.

Woolf was at times depressed by unfavorable criticism of her writing. After reading Hugh Walpole's review of *The Waves*, she found herself "trembling under the sense of complete failure." There must have been a compensating satisfaction, however, when she noted five months later that ten thousand copies of the novel had been sold.

She comforted herself some time afterward that she very soon recovered from both praise and blame. Thus, after Wyndham Lewis had mocked her style in an essay, she read it, later reread it, decided there was perhaps some justification in what he had written, and then remarked that the Lewis "illness" had lasted only two days.

Volume IV of the Woolf diary is, like the earlier volumes, indispensable for an understanding of her art and of the woman who created it. The editors have provided very useful supplements to the diary itself in the extensive footnotes, the appendix of biographical outlines, and the excellent index.

Henderson Kincheloe

Sources for Further Study

The Atlantic. CCL, August, 1982, p. 94.
Christian Science Monitor. August 4, 1982, p. 15.
Economist. CCLXXXII, March 20, 1982, p. 97.
History Today. XXXIII, February, 1983, p. 60.
Listener. CVII, March 11, 1982, p. 20.
New Statesman. CIII, March 19, 1982, p. 30.
The New York Times Book Review. LXXXVII, July 11, 1982, p. 3.
The New Yorker. LVIII, September 6, 1982, p. 107.
Times Literary Supplement. June 25, 1982, p. 701.

DIFFERENT SEASONS

Author: Stephen King (1947-   )
Publisher: The Viking Press (New York). 527 pp. $16.95
Type of work: Novellas

A collection of four novellas, each associated with a different season, demonstrating that King's prowess and versatility are not confined to the horror genre

Different Seasons is a collection of four novellas slightly related by a seasonal motif, only one of which—"The Breathing Method"—can be loosely termed a "supernatural horror story." This foray into realistic or "mainstream" fiction has lured some critics into suggesting that *Different Seasons* represents King's bid for "wider recognition," an attempt to shed his title as "King of the Horror Writers," but King claims he is quite content to be "typed" as a horror story writer. The three "non-horror" entries in *Different Seasons* are different simply because his creative imagination happened to take him—temporarily— out of his usual territory.

The four novellas which make up *Different Seasons* were composed at different times, each following the completion of a novel: "The Body" was written after *Salem's Lot* (1975), "Apt Pupil" after *The Shining* (1977), "Rita Hayworth and the Shawshank Redemption" after *The Dead Zone* (1979), and "The Breathing Method" after *Firestarter* (1980), although the novellas bear little resemblance to the longer works that preceded them.

As the title indicates, the book is organized around the seasons, with each section bearing an appropriate subtitle. Thus, the first novella, "Rita Hayworth and the Shawshank Redemption," is subtitled "Hope Springs Eternal," and it is indeed the most hopeful narrative in the book or, for that matter, in all of King's work. The story chronicles the career and ultimate escape of Andy Dufresne, a convict falsely imprisoned for life, as told by Red, a not-so-innocent inmate and friend. Andy's history is that of a self-possessed man whose courage and tenacity enable him to deal with adverse circumstances, to insist on his humanity under even the most dehumanizing of conditions, and, ultimately, to emerge victorious from his ordeal.

A mild-mannered banker in his pre-prison days, Dufresne seems an unlikely candidate for heroism, but his courage and shrewdness gradually earn him the narrator's admiration and trust. Dufresne fights off homosexual attacks by the prison "sisters," although beaten in the process, but his more characteristic strategy is to manipulate both his captors and his fellow prisoners through a judicious use of his small "cash store" and, more important, by his shrewd insights into the minds and needs of those around him. He parlays a chance opportunity to give a guard some tax advice into a series of "services" for the staff that he trades for favors, protection, a more comfortable lifestyle, and a private cell where he can, uncharacteristically, gaze at the lifesize poster of Rita Hayworth (and, subsequently, of Marilyn Monroe, Jayne Mansfield, Hazel Court, Raquel Welch, and Linda Ronstadt) that adorns the wall of his cell. Dufresne's manipulations backfire, however, and his chance for vindication and freedom is squelched by the prison warden because he has simply become too valuable to lose. Thwarted by the institution he has manipulated, Dufresne finally makes good on an escape that has been years in preparation.

Escape, rather than rescue or parole, is the appropriate fate for Andy Dufresne. To conclude the story on a fully hopeful note, Dufresne arranges for the final "redemption" of his friend Red. "Rita Hayworth and the Shawshank Redemption" is a cleverly executed, moving narrative that stimulates and excites the reader without a hint of the weird. If it has a fault, it is that, having given his readers an uncharacteristically happy ending, King savors it too much, carrying it out too long and in too much detail.

No such criticism can be made of the second tale, "Apt Pupil," subtitled "The Summer of Corruption," the bleakest and the least effective of the four novellas. The failure of this story is doubly unfortunate because the idea behind it is most original and provocative. Todd Bowden, "the total all-American kid," a typical California teenager, confronts Alfred Denker, an aged Geman recluse, with his discovery of Denker's true identity. In reality, Denker is Kurt Dussander, a Nazi war criminal in hiding, once the *Unterkommandant* of the Patin death camp. Bowden threatens Dussander with exposure, demanding not money, but a detailed, firsthand account of the German atrocities and Dussander's part in them. To Todd, Dussander is not a villain, but a kind of exotic hero. Dussander is irritated, even horrified, by Todd's request ("You are a monster," he tells the boy), but he has no choice: the oral history commences.

The first half of "Apt Pupil" is an engrossing study in progressive corruption, as the relationship between the boy, fascinated by evil-as-fun, and the old survivor, long numb to his own decadence, grows and changes both of them. The boy's power over the man gradually gives way, as he is infected by the depravity he has released; the old man's defenses slowly disintegrate and he rediscovers his taste for evil. In the end, the old man dominates the boy, but neither can control the corruption the boy's curiosity and perverse make-believe have set in motion. As a study in depravity, "Apt Pupil" is very provocative, but as a story it fails because King cannot resolve the conflict on the psychological level. Prodded by their mental deterioration, both Todd and Dussander become mass murderers in a manner that seems almost gratuitous. At the same time, Dussander's identity—and, therefore, Todd's complicity—is suddenly threatened by a fortuitous coincidence. Thus, physical gore replaces psychological violence and plot contrivance substitutes for characterization. Despite its most promising beginning, "Apt Pupil" is, finally, unconvincing and disappointing.

"The Body" is the earliest and, in terms of technique, the crudest of the novellas, but it also resonates with charm and force. Clearly the most personal of the stories, it was stimulated by an incident in King's own boyhood. At the age of four, King probably witnessed a playmate being hit by a train, although he has no conscious recollection of the incident (he has taken his mother's word for it; the incident is mentioned in *Danse Macabre*, 1981). Although very grim at the center, "The Body" is laced with a nostalgia for the freedom, camaraderie, and, with qualifications, innocence of boyhood in a manner somewhat reminiscent of one of King's favorite predecessors, Ray Bradbury. Indeed, "The Body" could be called King's *Dandelion Wine* (1957). The two works are celebrations of boyhood and sad introductions to the pains and limitations of adulthood, with the central motif of each being the boy-protagonist's first real confrontation with mortality.

The two works also emphasize the differences between these two masters of dark fantasy. The boyhood landscape of *Dandelion Wine* is seen through a soft, sentimental filter, however sad the book's thematic center, and even the fact of death only hovers at the novel's edge, never becoming much more than a poetic abstraction. "The Body," however, is about a corpse, a solid mass of dead, rotting, slug-infested flesh that had been a living boy, the same age as that of the protagonist. This concrete physical reality permeates the story, qualifying and darkening King's homage to youthful hope and exuberance.

"The Body" recounts the pilgrimage of twelve-year-old Gordon Lachance and three friends to recover the body of a teenage boy hit by a train and left in an undeveloped Maine woods near King's fictional town of Castle Rock. Lachance is telling the story from the viewpoint of an adult—a successful writer of horror fiction—looking back on the primary formative experience of his boyhood. To underscore the horror-writer identification, King even inserts two of his own crude apprentice works in the body of the novella, a gimmick that would seriously damage a more formal, polished narrative but does not seem overly awkward or intrusive in this exercise in dark nostalgia.

As the boys struggle through their difficult, sometimes comic trek into the woods, beset by natural and human barriers, including a harrowing brush with death on the train trestle, they also struggle with themselves—their fears, insecurities, confusions—and with one another. Second to the mortality theme in the story is the notion of boyhood camaraderie, a kind of pure, elemental companionship made more intense by its necessarily transitory quality. Two of the boys, Lachance and Chris Chambers (the product of a deprived, quasi-criminal background), come to understand this; the other two, Teddy Duchamp and Vern Tassio, remain blissfully ignorant, despite their terrifying shared experiences. In the end, after their arduous, dangerous trek, they are confronted by a gang of older boys, led by Chris's older brother, and subsequently beaten badly for their challenge. Thus, they are forced to confront human injustice and brutality as well as natural mortality. Perhaps the saddest insight of all comes when Gordon realizes that he must desert his boyhood friends in order to avoid the traps laid for them and achieve his own potential—a potential which, the reader knows, he has achieved, but at a considerable price.

If "The Body" is a relatively crude early story, "The Breathing Method," subtitled "A Winter's Tale," is the most well-crafted; it is, in fact, probably the most polished story that King has written to date. Despite nods in the direction of Peter Straub, Jorge Luis Borges, and even Henry James, "The Breathing Method"—the one "supernatural" story in the volume—is thoroughly original in conception and execution.

"The Breathing Method" is actually two stories, the first an open-ended narrative about a mysterious men's club at 149B East Thirty-fifth Street in New York City where a select, yet oddly assorted group of professional men meet for fine food, drink, low-key socializing, reading, and storytelling. The second story is an account by one of the members, an aged doctor, of the strangest event in his life.

One night, the narrator of the story, David Adley, is taken by his boss, without warning or ceremony, to the club and there left to his own devices. Although not really invited back, he returns to the club and is accepted. He establishes a regular routine over a number of years, enjoying his marginal participation in the club's casual activities and utilizing its facilities, especially the well-stocked library. A number of odd details, however, make him uneasy: excellent books that are unknown beyond the club library, mysterious rooms upstairs that are never visited, and Stevens, the club's enigmatic manager. This mysterious atmosphere prepares the reader for the club's favorite activity, the telling of stories. Although there are bits and pieces of several stories given, they only warm the reader up for the primary tale, "The Breathing Method."

This tale is told by Emlyn McCarron, an aged doctor, about an incident that occurred during the first years of his practice. The "breathing method" is a technique similar to the Lamaze method that McCarron offers to all of his pregnant patients as part of their prenatal training. He teaches it to Sara Standfield, an unwed mother-to-be, as he prepares her for the delivery of her unplanned but fiercely desired child. The story climaxes in the harrowing delivery of the child; the "breathing method" becomes a crucial element in a fantastic finale that is both unexpectedly gruesome and emotionally satisfying.

The "breathing method" story is a potent, provocative one, featuring two remarkable characters, a progressively engrossing situation, and a most adroit, unexpected turn in the plotting, yet it is unlikely that the story would retain anything like its present power were it deprived of its setting. The elegant, mysterious, vaguely threatening club, with Stevens, its strange, quiet, all-knowing manager, its library of unknown masterpieces, and its "corridors and corridors" of upper rooms, creates an atmosphere of otherworldly apprehension that gives the inner story a ready-made tension. The contrast between the sedately mysterious club atmosphere and the realistic story of a strong-willed unwed mother's struggle to have her child in spite of social ostracism and economic hardship, only to see a perverse fate threaten her at the end, gives the story its special impact.

The year 1982 was very active for Stephen King; it was one in which he established himself even more solidly as the most popular and important contemporary writer of dark fantasy. In addition to *Different Seasons*, a second work, *The Gunslinger*—probably his most enigmatic work—was published in a beautifully illustrated limited edition by a small specialty publisher. King's collaboration with film director George Romero (*Night of the Living Dead*, 1968, *Dawn of the Dead*, 1979) resulted in the release of *Creepshow*, scripted by King and featuring him in one episode and his young son, Joey, in another. A comic book version followed the film. Critics began to notice King's work as well, and two critical books about King appeared in 1982: *Fear Itself: The Horror Fiction of Stephen King*, a collection of thirteen essays by various hands, the most interesting of which is King's own autobiographical article "On Becoming a Brand Name"; and *Stephen King: A Reader's Guide*, by Douglas E. Winter, a short, perceptive overview of King's career, especially good on the relationship between his life and his work. In addition, at least two new King books are slated for 1983: the Stephen King phenomenon continues unabated.

Keith Neilson

Sources for Further Study

Library Journal. CVII, August, 1982, p. 1481.
Los Angeles Times Book Review. August 29, 1982, p. 7.
The New York Times Book Review. LXXXVII, August 29, 1982, p. 10.
Publishers Weekly. CCXXI, June 18, 1982, p. 64.
Time. CXX, August 30, 1982, p. 87.

DINNER AT THE HOMESICK RESTAURANT

Author: Anne Tyler (1941-   )
Publisher: Alfred A. Knopf (New York). 303 pp. $13.50
Type of work: Novel
Time: 1910-1980
Locale: Baltimore, Maryland

A novel which portrays the emotionally difficult relationships of three children to their mother and to one another

> *Principal characters:*
> PEARL TULL, a mother of three children
> CODY, Pearl's older son
> EZRA, Pearl's favorite child
> JENNY, Pearl's daughter
> BECK TULL, Pearl's husband

One of Anne Tyler's most appreciative reviewers, John Updike, writes that Tyler seems to "accept the belief, extinct save in the South, that families are absolutely, intrinsically interesting." Updike is right about Tyler's acceptance, if mistaken about the belief's near extinction. Her great subject is not sexuality but maternity, not romantic love but ties between parents and children. Far from viewing the family as trivial, she has long been fascinated by the complex feelings of those who are bound to one another by the most profound and intimate physical obligations. Mothers must feed their offspring's hunger for affection and security; siblings must compete; children must inevitably be hurt by the estrangement of their parents from each other. In *Dinner at the Homesick Restaurant*, Tyler illuminates all of these mundane domestic truths, bringing to bear on them her power to make the ordinary seem astonishing, the astonishing seem ordinary.

Her story begins with a mother, Pearl Tull, and takes up, one by one, the lives of Pearl's three children, and of their children after them. At the novel's beginning, Pearl is ill; in its last chapter, her family has gathered for a meal after her funeral. Through Pearl's recollections during her final illness, the reader learns that at thirty she married Beck Tull, a traveling salesman with a social background inferior to her own. Pearl knew from the beginning that Beck was unreliable, a "slangy, loud-voiced salesman peering at his reflection with too much interest when he tied his tie in the mornings, combing his pompadour tall and damp and frilly and then replacing the comb in a shirt pocket full of pencils, pens, ruler, appointment book, and tire gauge, all bearing catchy printed slogans for various firms." Sure enough, one day, Beck, like so many of Tyler's characters, embarks on a "thirty-five-year business trip," leaving Pearl, angry and frightened, to support their three young children.

The oldest child, Cody, is a troublemaker. Pearl does not seem to realize that Cody secretly wonders whether it was something he did that made his father leave, nor does she perceive that Cody is conscious of her favoritism toward his younger brother Ezra. These two worries motivate behavior in Cody that Pearl considers difficult and mean; still, handsome, dark-haired Cody is a hero as well as a villain. His success in business, like his obsession with winning at Monopoly, arises from a need for the absent Beck's approval. Similarly, the tricks he plays on Ezra—culminating in the theft of Ezra's finacée—are motivated by Cody's knowledge that Ezra is Pearl's favorite.

Ezra, his hair seeming "formed of layers of silk in various shades of yellow and beige," is indeed a lovable child, "so sweet and clumsy it could break your heart." His affectionate nature allows him to accomplish effortlessly what Cody cannot achieve by force. Innocent and dreamy, Ezra moves placidly through Tyler's story, playing his recorder and drawing others to him. He likes people to get along with one another, and as he grows into adulthood, he soothes and supports those he cares about by preparing special food for them: hot milk with honey and cinnamon, a "consoling" pot roast, a gizzard soup that can alter the "whole perception of the day." After a brief and unsuccessful stint in the Army, he returns to Baltimore to work in and eventually to own the Homesick Restaurant, where total strangers can "'come just like to a family dinner . . . and everything will be solid and wholesome, really homelike.'" Ezra so willingly accepts the events that occur in his life that he does not oppose even the loss of Ruth, the country cook with whom he falls in love, to the fiercely competitive Cody.

Jenny, the youngest of Pearl's three children, is an orderly and conscientious child, a hard-working perfectionist who earns straight A's and who, as she enters adolescence, begins a perpetual series of odd diets. Thrice married, she becomes a pediatrician and stepmother to a family of six. Jenny treats all these children generously, but she remains emotionally distant. When not surrounded by children, she experiences "an echoing, weightless feeling, as if she lacked ballast. . . ." Jenny's preoccupation with thinness provides a thematic counterweight to Ezra's inclination to nurture others. Her characteristic gesture of covering her mouth with her hand is related to the numb lips she associates with a nightmare about Pearl: "her mother laughed a witch's shrieking laugh; dragged Jenny out of hiding as the Nazis trampled up the stairs; accused her of sins and crimes that had never crossed Jenny's mind. Her mother told her, in an informative and considerate tone of voice, that she was raising Jenny to eat her."

Jenny's dream reveals that she and her brothers are well aware of their mother's deep ambivalence toward them. Although Pearl is a strong-willed and efficient woman, she is terrified by the awesome responsibility of supporting her children by herself. In their neediness, they often seem to her like "parasites," yet she cares for them dutifully, worrying over them through illnesses and enjoying their physicality as babies, their smell and shape, their weight against her shoulder. Like most parents, Pearl does the best she can.

Unable to alter either her personality or her circumstances, she sometimes attributes the family's conflicts to fate: "She feels that everything has been assigned, has been preordained; everyone must play his role." At other times, she takes the responsibility upon herself: "Pearl believes . . . that her family has failed. . . . There is no one to accept the blame for this but Pearl herself, who raised these children single-handed and did make mistakes. . . ." Her mistakes are serious ones—a fierce protectiveness that keeps her children from having friends, inexplicable and violent rages, physical abuse. Pearl's inept mothering leads to an apparently endless succession of emotional difficulties for her children and grandchildren. When Jenny finds herself abusing her own daughter, she asks herself, "Was this what it came to—that you never could escape? That certain things were doomed to continue, generation after generation?"

The question Jenny raises is central to the novel. If Tyler's subject here is the family, her themes revolve around the intricately connected issues of inevitability and responsibility. Pearl's vacillation between blaming fate and blaming herself suggests that *Dinner at the Homesick Restaurant* explores questions about causality that are no less baffling for being so familiar. What makes families unhappy? Can people change, or must they remain forever in the clutches of the neuroses they have inherited? Is human behavior inevitable, or can human choices affect it? Does character create circumstances, or do circumstances create character? In the treatment of such heavy thematic material, a writer less accomplished than Tyler might well have lapsed into abstractions or descended to sentimentality, but Tyler never makes a false move. She may put a simple formula into the mouth of a character, as when Jenny remarks that there is "no need to blame adjustment, broken homes, bad parents" for one's difficulties. "You have to overcome your setbacks," Jenny says; "You can't take them too much to heart." The cost of Jenny's adjustment, however, is thrown into relief by her stepson Slevin who, seeing a photograph of Jenny as a child, observes that she looks like the victim of a concentration camp. Slevin, whose own mother has left him, angrily rejects the idea that people can move beyond the emotional damage done to them by their parents. In considering this damage, Tyler is wise enough not to offer either her characters or her readers easy platitudes or quick assignments of blame. Instead, by dropping the detail that Pearl has requested as her funeral hymn a number called "We'll Understand It All By and By," Tyler insists on the painful, mysterious complexities of the relations between parents and children.

Among these complexities, and integral to the workings of Tyler's novel, are her characters' attitudes toward eating. As Cody observes midway through the novel, food has an "inexplicable, loaded meaning" in all their lives. Pearl is a "nonfeeder." On the literal level, her preparations for meals consist mainly of opening cans, and her terrible rages against her children most often take place at the dinner table. Less literally, food represents love. Because Pearl "disapprove[s] of neediness in people," she is unable to give her children the psychological nourishment they need. Cody sees that his brother and sister respond differently to this emotional starvation: Ezra becomes a "feeder" who makes friends with his customers and who tries repeatedly to get his family together for dinner at the Homesick Restaurant, while both Jenny and her daughter Becky are afflicted with anorexia nervosa. What is remarkable about Tyler's handling of this food motif is that it is worked unobtrusively into the texture of the story, yet it accumulates enormous force. The same artlessness characterizes the novel's repeated references to scars and wounds. Pearl has herself been hurt; on her forehead she bears a scar that looks like a crease, "the mark of a childhood accident." An acquaintance of the Tull children also has a mark on his forehead, "as deep as if someone has pressed an ax blade there." When Beck leaves, Pearl becomes a wound, "a deep, hollow hole, surrounded by shreds of her former self." These and other details subtly and masterfully reinforce the novel's theme of emotional damage.

The damage is literal as well as symbolic. Although the line of Tyler's narrative obscures the motivation for Beck Tull's departure, it is apparently precipitated by a bizarre incident which occurs when the Tulls are on an outing, the only occasion in the novel when the entire family is present. Beck has bought an archery set and has insisted that the family go shooting. Through a series of mishaps, an arrow strikes Pearl, and the infection and allergic reaction that ensue nearly kill her. The arrow incident, one of the most significant events in the Tull family's collective history, is, like the rest of their story, presented in pieces: one version is told from Pearl's point of view, a second version concentrates on Cody, a third and fourth explain Ezra's and Beck's perceptions of the event. It is not until the reader has heard all four versions that the incident's significance begins to emerge. Multiple points of view are exactly right for this material. The variety of perspectives demonstrates that events with psychological importance can be seen and interpreted in more than one way, depending on who is doing the seeing and interpreting; further, the multiple points of view realistically conceal and complicate the characters' motivation. Since each character is presented from all directions, as well as from within, it is impossible for the reader to take sides, to reject one character or make alliance with another. Instead, each must be contemplated fully, and, ultimately, with sympathy. Partly because Tyler stays in the third person, she is able to shift her story's angle of narration without sacrificing clarity or smoothness; the novel's exposition is orderly, its transitions are seamless. The apparent effortlessness of the book's surface belies the rich texture of its underlayers, and the effect of this tension on the reader is immensely satisfying.

Dinner at the Homesick Restaurant is also remarkable for its chronological structure. Tyler arranges the novel's ten chapters so as to enrich the book's meaning and intensify its emotional impact. Moving about in time, Pearl dominates the first chapter, Cody the second, Jenny the third, and Ezra the fouth. In chapter 5, the narrative voice becomes more omniscient as Tyler tells the story of how Cody steals Ruth from Ezra; if there is a weakness in the novel, it is the improbability of Ruth's capitulation. Each of the remaining five chapters is assigned to a single character. Differentiation among the characters' stories is achieved more by adjustments in content than by alterations in the narrative voice. That voice remains Tyler's own. As usual, she writes in a matter-of-fact, witty, intimate tone that conveys affection for her characters even while skewering their faults. All the other marks of Tyler's distinctive style are here too: the familiarity with the cadences of Southern speech; the ironic use of proper names (Pearl's deathbed is an "everyday, ordinary Posturepedic"); the precise use of simile (a baby's croupy cough is "like something pulled through tightly packed gravel") and of metaphor (Barbara Pace serves "as a kind of central switchboard for ninth-grade couples").

While the stylistic delights of *Dinner at the Homesick Restaurant* recall a number of Tyler's previous novels, her latest novel most closely resembles in its mood and impact the beautiful and somber *Celestial Navigation*, published in 1974. Not only is Ezra reminiscent of the artist Jeremy Pauling, but Tyler also explicitly links the two works. Ruth, the woman Ezra loves and Cody marries, stays for a while at Mrs. Pauling's boardinghouse, and Jeremy himself appears in the background, "a pale, pudgy man [who] stood gazing into an open refrigerator." In both books, the characters are so flawed that their natural growth is stunted, and yet, precisely because of their imperfections, Ezra, Jenny, Cody, and even Pearl shock the reader with their familiarity. During Pearl's illness, she has Ezra read to her from a diary she kept seventy years before: *"I went out behind the house to weed,"* Pearl had written, *"and all at once thought, Why I believe that at just this moment I am absolutely happy. . . . I saw that I was kneeling on such a beautiful green little planet. I don't care what else might come about, I have had this moment. It belongs to me."* Pearl Tull is not a bad woman. Scarred by the events of her own growing up, left by Beck to fend for herself, she has done her best with her children. As Beck observes at the novel's conclusion, "My family wasn't so much . . . but it's all there really is, in the end."

Tyler leaves the complicated issue of Pearl's culpability unresolved because there is no resolving it. Still, it is all too clear that her children are hurt by her inability to feed them as they need to be fed. *Dinner at the Homesick Restaurant* is a magnificent novel because it evokes sympathy not only for the children but also for Pearl herself. In this moving book, Anne Tyler has at last articulated a theme worthy of her prodigious stylistic gifts.

Carolyn Wilkerson Bell

Sources for Further Study

Christian Science Monitor. July 9, 1982, p. 14.
Library Journal. CVII, February 15, 1982, p. 476.
Ms. X, June, 1982, p. 75.
The New York Times Book Review. LXXXVII, March 14, 1982, p. 1.
The New Yorker. LVIII, April 5, 1982, p. 189.
Newsweek. XCIX, April 5, 1982, p. 72.
Saturday Review. IX, March, 1982, p. 62.
Time. CXIX, April 5, 1982, p. 76.
Times Literary Supplement. October 29, 1982, p. 1188.

DISTANT RELATIONS

Author: Carlos Fuentes (1928-   )
Translated from the Spanish by Margaret Sayers Peden
Publisher: Farrar, Straus and Giroux (New York). 225 pp. $11.95
Type of work: Novel
Time: The early 1980's
Locale: Mexico, the Caribbean, and Paris

A narrative of the strange experiences of the Comte de Branly with the descendants of the Heredias, a family in colonial Mexico.

> *Principal characters:*
> CARLOS FUENTES, the narrator, a fictional novelist bearing the author's name and elements of his identity
> COMTE DE BRANLY, an elderly man who tells the story that forms the novel
> HUGO HEREDIA, a Mexican Creole and famous archaeologist
> LUCIE HEREDIA, his wife, killed in a plane crash with their son, Antonio
> VICTOR HEREDIA, the twelve-year-old son of Hugo and Lucie
> VICTOR HEREDIA, a Frenchman and a "distant relation" of the Mexican Victor Heredia
> ANDRÉ HEREDIA, his twelve-year-old son
> ETIENNE, Branly's chauffeur

Carlos Fuentes first became well-known in the English-speaking world with the publication in 1964 of the translation of his novel, *The Death of Artemio Cruz* (originally published in Spanish as *La Muerte de Artemio Cruz* in 1962). *Distant Relations* (originally published in Spanish as *Una familia lejana*, 1980) is his eighth novel to appear in English. Although it is quite different in style and technique from *The Death of Artemio Cruz* and from Fuentes' extraordinarily complex *Terra Nostra* (1977), its concerns are similar to those evident in all of Fuentes' novels. The Comte de Branly in *Distant Relations* reconstructs an elaborate story that evokes his entire life experience. In similar fashion, Artemio Cruz remembers his life as he dies, drawing together all the experiences and cultural influences in a narrative that parallels the changing states of awareness of the dying man. *Terra Nostra* develops a vast interpretation of Hispanic culture through a fantastic manipulation and re-creation of the history of Spain from the seventeenth century to the eve of the year 2000. In each of Fuentes' novels, there is an attempt to derive from the cultural heritage a key to an understanding of human experience.

In *Distant Relations*, this heritage is the Mexican pre-Colombian and colonial experience, with the influence of the Spanish and the French reflected in the principal characters—the Mexican Creole Hugo Heredia, the French Victor Heredia, and the aristocratic French Branly. As in most of Fuentes' fiction, the relationships are not clearly delineated. There is a strange continuity to human experience that defies complete understanding, yet which emerges gradually from the intricate genealogy of the Heredias and the Comte de Branly.

The bloodlines lead back to the early nineteenth century in La Guaira, where Mademoiselle Lange, the daughter of an enterprising French merchant, married Francisco Luis de Heredia, a Spanish colonial hidalgo, each thinking erroneously that the other had money. From that unhappy marriage based on deception was born a son. Subsequently, Heredia delivered his French wife to the local brothel, where she conceived another son by the captain of a French force passing through Mexico. The story that Branly relates to the narrator, based on his experience in the home of the French Victor Heredia and in spite of the century and a half since the La Guaira incident, is that the son born to Heredia and Mme. Lange is the French Victor Heredia, while the son of the French captain and Mme. Lange is Branly himself. As several characters had earlier replied to Branly when he proclaimed that all this was impossible, "we have no memory but what we recall." What is remembered is what is true.

Branly's testimony is an elaboration of the concept that the limits of experience are determined by what is remembered, and that rationality imposes its own limits on what the mind will recall. Thus, the complex irrational relationships that surface throughout the novel are rejected and suppressed. Hugo Heredia and his son Victor play a game of searching in the telephone book of each city that they visit for someone with their same name. As they do, they uncover the irrational "distant relations" that create a maze of parallels and coincidences. The Heredia whom they meet in Monterrey, who promises Hugo the return of his dead son and wife, is reincarnated in the Victor Heredia whom they find in Paris. The portrait of the woman in white in the Paris mansion is at once Mme. Lange and Lucie, the dead wife of Hugo. Hugo Heredia, married to the French woman Lucie, is Francisco Luis de Heredia married to Mme. Lange, and their son Victor is the Victor Heredia of the Paris mansion, or his son André. The mysterious detainment and abuse that the French aristocrat Branly suffers at the hands of André and the two Victor Heredias is an ironic inversion of the colonial experience of the Mexicans at the time of the French occupation.

The entire experience that Branly reconstructs in his afternoon of talking to the narrator is a kind of game. As Hugo and his son lure Branly into the trap set by the Heredia in Monterrey, they create a scenario for the playing out of a series of cultural metaphors. The psychological struggle that emerges between Branly and the French Victor Heredia is a struggle of the Old World against the New, of the aristocracy against the nouveau riche, of the conquerer against the conquered.

The friendship that immediately develops between the Mexican child Victor Heredia and André has a sinister quality, made manifest in the scene in which

Branly discovers them engaged in homosexual intercourse in his Citroën. The two boys, the Mexican and the French, are transformed into one being, representing the union of the past and the present. Their single, transformed self appears in the figure of the waiter serving Branly and the narrator in the elegant Automobile Club de France as the Comte weaves his tale of mysterious relationships. In the final scene of the novel, the narrator discovers the remains of the two boys, now fetuses shriveled up like old men, floating in the "sperm-colored scum" of the swimming pool of the club, the pool in which Branly almost drowned while the waiter moved stealthily across the catwalk high above the water.

The most significant difference between Fuentes' recent fiction and his early works such as *The Death of Artemio Cruz* is his interest in the supernatural embedded in the context of the everyday experience of supposedly normal, rational human beings. Artemio Cruz's experience is rendered through a stream of consciousness that allows for considerable distortion of rational reality. The history narrated by Branly, however, is a sort of elegant ghost story which works remarkably well up to a point. As long as Branly talks, which he does through three-fourths of the novel, the story is credible. The narrative is the intricate rambling of an eighty-year-old man, a personal testimony that may at times seem implausible. This implausibility, however, does not detract from the credibility of the story that the *narrator* is transmitting to the reader—the story of an old man inventing a story that is entertaining, mysterious, though not necessarily true in its entirety. He is, in effect, creating a novel of his own life.

In the final chapters, however, the narrator begins to relate his own experience after hearing Branly's story, and the hocus-pocus does not succeed. It is difficult to accept the supernatural as reported by the narrator as an eyewitness, perhaps because he *is* the narrator and has established himself throughout as a skeptical, sane observer of Branly's eccentric testimony. The conversion of the narrator into a witness for the fantastic is too abrupt to be convincing.

The dust jacket of *Distant Relations* proclaims the novel as "already hailed throughout Latin America as his most personal." The reason is clear—the very strong identification between the fictional narrator and the "real" novelist. Branly calls the narrator alternately "Fuentes" and "Carlos," and makes reference to his self-imposed exile from Mexico first in Buenos Aires, then in France. Unlike the "real" Fuentes, however, the "Fuentes" of his narrative did not return to Mexico, publish his first books there, and become an interpreter of the Mexican experience. As the narrator says, "it was not like that. . . . I am not that person." That, suggests Branly, is his other, contiguous life.

Branly goes on to say that a narrative, or a life, is a set of propositions chosen from an infinite number of possibilities, always incomplete and always contiguous with other histories and other stories. To a great extent, *Distant Relations* is a novel about the nature of narrative. Branly invents the narrative, which the narrator—a "fictional" novelist named Carlos Fuentes—reinvents in the form of an autobiographical account of his experience with an old man in the Automobile Club de France. Branly claims that there is a condemnation visited on the last person to know the truth of what happened to the Heredias. He divests himself of that truth by re-creating it for the narrator, who in turn seeks absolution in the transmission of the truth through the text.

The truth consists of the continuity of European culture in the New World, and the return of that culture, impregnated with the unbridled vitality and sensuality of pre-Columbian America, to the Old World. The Heredias pass from Spain and France to America and back to France. Fuentes, as well as other writers mentioned in the text (Alexandre Dumas, Jules Supervielle, Isidore Ducasse, Jose María de Heredia, Jules Laforgue) migrate from South America to France to establish themselves in the refined Western cultural tradition. Throughout the migration, the processes of conquering and being conquered, of affirming and denying traditional values, are played out and reflected metaphorically in the lives of Hugo Heredia, Victor Heredia, the other Victor Heredia, and André Heredia. As the unwitting witness to this pageant of cultural history, Branly perceives the truth of his own existence and his own heritage.

The scene that initiates Branly's adventure with the Heredias is the key to the truth of the colonial experience. Young Victor finds an artifact, a perfect sphere, in the ruins of Xochicalco. He breaks it into two halves and hurls one away into the ravine because its mysterious heat burns his hands. His father—the archaeologist, who reveres the past embodied in the artifact—strives to rejoin the halves of that perfect sphere. So the history of Victor and André—finally joined together as representatives of the present Heredias and the past, colonial Heredias—synthesizes the disparate cultures of the New World and the Old.

Although most of the novel is the complex history of Branly's experience, in the final chapters it becomes the story of the narrator's transformation as he comprehends the mystery of his own heritage. The mystery, however, is never resolved entirely. It is only partially deciphered through a sort of Proustian association of diverse elements and experiences, such as the recurrence of the madrigal in the Mexican night, in Branly's childhood experience in the Parc Monseau, and in the mansion of the French Heredia.

Distant Relations is indeed a personal novel, but not because it describes the individual experience of Carlos Fuentes. Rather it explores the complex cultural milieu of the New World, manipulated and distorted by the European tradition, transformed into what it is today.

Gilbert Smith

Sources for Further Study

America. CXLVII, July 24, 1982, p. 59.
Library Journal. CVII, March 15, 1982, p. 649.
Nation. CCXXXIV, January 16, 1982, p. 57.
New Statesman. CIV, July 9, 1982, p. 23.
The New York Times Book Review. LXXXVII, March 21, 1982, p. 3.
Saturday Review. IX, March, 1982, p. 62.
Times Literary Supplement. July 9, 1982, p. 739.
Virginia Quarterly Review. LVIII, Autumn, 1982, p. 131.

DOWN THE RIVER

Author: Edward Abbey (1927-   )
Publisher: E. P. Dutton (New York). Illustrated. 242 pp. $13.95; paperback $6.95
Type of work: Essays

A collection of miscellaneous environmental essays and reflections on the pleasures of rafting on the rivers of the American West

As essayist and environmental spokesman for the American Southwest, Edward Abbey has effectively publicized the need to protect the deserts and wilderness areas of his adopted region. In works such as *Desert Solitaire* (1968), he has written eloquently of the beauty of the desert environment; in his latest book, *Down the River*, he shifts his attention to the rivers and canyons of the American West, using the occasion of a series of river-rafting trips on the Green and San Juan rivers in southeast Utah and the Tatshenshini in Alaska and the Canadian Yukon for a series of outdoor sketches and wide-ranging essays on a variety of environmental topics. Many of these essays and articles originally appeared separately in magazines elsewhere, but Abbey has skillfully woven them together here, using the central thematic motif of the river voyage. His narrative models include Henry David Thoreau's *A Week on the Concord and Merrimack Rivers* (1849) and Mark Twain's *The Adventures of Huckleberry Finn* (1884) as well as the numerous journals and accounts of the mountain men and early explorers of the West. "For twenty years now I've been floating rivers," he says in the preface. "Always downstream, the easy and natural way. The way Huck Finn and Jim did it, La Salle and Marquette, the mountain men, Major Powell, and a few hundred others," he continues.

Parts of the book are written in journal format, with daily entries and reflections as Abbey's group floats downstream through the canyons of the Green or San Juan rivers. Henry David Thoreau is the guiding spirit through many of these adventures, as Abbey blends quotations and excerpts from Thoreau's *Journals* (1906) and from *Walden* (1854) with truculent comments on contemporary environmental problems in the West: dams, lumbering, strip-mining, urban sprawl, missile silos, military bases, and nuclear weapons plants all come under the attack of his acerbic pen. Abbey reveals his atavistic sensibility in his love of wildness and adventure, and his dislike of crowds, urbanization, and development. Like a latter-day Huck Finn or a Jack Kerouac character, he is happiest when he is on the move, far from the reach of civilization or responsibility, drifting downstream away from the pollution and congestion of the overcrowded and crime-ridden cities that he detests.

"In wildness is the preservation of the world," Abbey reminds his readers, quoting again from Thoreau. Throughout the book, he equates freedom with the wilderness of the unspoiled river canyons and national forests of Arizona,

Utah, and New Mexico. Outdoor recreation, he asserts, is one of the last truly open and democratic activities available in America's increasingly regimented, urbanized, technological society. Perhaps this is hyperbole, but Abbey certainly has a point about the value of the wilderness for the renewal of the human spirit. Running rivers become for him a symbol of the unrestricted freedom of the American frontier that has largely been lost. He compares the relaxed freedom of his "river rat" companions with the uptight corporate and government types engaged in the armaments business and in environmental destruction. In between lyrical descriptions of running rapids, camping, and enjoying the spectacular Western scenery, Abbey offers his own brand of iconoclastic environmental philosophy—part hippie, part anarchist, part preservationist, and part Native American. Not surprisingly, the Reagan Administration receives his particular scorn, but as he explains, both superpowers are equally committed to "technology, the ever-expanding economy . . . industrialism, militarism, centralized control—the complete domination of nature and human beings." He contrasts the bold, free, and unexploitative spirit of the American Indians with the acquisitive, capitalist mentality that counts scenic and wilderness areas only as potential "resources" to be "developed" with dams, missile bases, strip mines, or timber-cutting. True to his frontier spirit, Abbey even objects to the permits and restrictions used by the Park Service to limit access to some of the most popular rivers for rafting and canoeing. Wild rivers are not "resources," he protests, but are "part of nature's bloodstream." Yet even he is forced to acknowledge that without some kinds of restrictions, their wild and scenic qualities would quickly be destroyed through overuse. His style of confrontational journalism is effective in calling attention to environmental disputes, but less effective perhaps in suggesting ways to resolve them.

The essays in *Down the River* are divided into four sections—"Thoreau and Other Friends," "Politicks and Rivers," "Places and Rivers," and "People, Books, and Rivers"—linked together by the river motif and by Abbey's eclectic style. In part 1, he tries to imitate Thoreau's extravagant, witty, hyperbolic style, and the result often seems forced and contrived. Later in the book, he shifts to a more typically "Western" style of brash, tall-tale humor, coarse jocularity, and boisterous exuberance, interspersed with lyrical and evocative descriptive passages celebrating the natural beauty of the river and canyon landscapes. His blend of coarse, good-natured humor and gruffness fits the free and easy company of his "river rat" companions and the relaxed style of their river voyages, as they float and drift with the currents past rapids and white water and through long stretches of placid currents on their various river adventures. Abbey is a good action writer, and his descriptions of the actual rafting and boating episodes are compelling, but he often becomes cranky and opinionated in dealing with environmental politics and land-use policy. As a staunch preservationist, he is unwilling to acknowledge, for example, that national parks might be able to sustain a variety of recreational uses, or that those people not physically fit for the rigors of canoeing or backpacking might also be able to enjoy the beauties of the national parks without despoiling them.

Indeed, the limitations of Abbey's book become apparent whenever he shifts from action to more abstract reflections. He is no profound thinker, as he admits when he remarks disparagingly about his work that he has not had an original thought since World War II. This personal deprecation may be an amusing way to disarm his critics, but in other places, he betrays a belligerent and less admirable anti-intellectualism, as when he attacks such fine science writers as Lewis Thomas, Carl Sagan, and Rene Dubos as "apologists for the glossy technocracy." Abbey's remarks are scarcely fair to the quality of thought of these writers, whose environmental positions are often much more articulate and carefully thought out than his own.

The closest thing Abbey offers to an explicit statement of his own environmental values appears in his essay, "Thus I Reply to Rene Dubos," in which he responds to Dubos' recent book, *The Wooing of the Earth* (1980). In his review, Abbey notes the environmental, social, and psychic costs involved in the agricultural transformations of the European landscape during several millenia. Despite the harmonious beauty of the cultivated agricultural landscape, something important has been lost: the human freedom "inherent in wildness and wilderness." Even if the destruction of the forest liberated the human spirit, that freedom appears to have been short-lived, since people are losing it again to the elaborate social control and organization of the technological state. Abbey obviously prefers the free, egalitarian, adventurous life of the outdoors to the restrictions of "technocratic despotism," but he argues that wilderness also "complements and completes civilization." Moreover, unrestricted technological development threatens the future of all life on earth, even the "gently humanized landscapes so loved by Dubos." The rafting, boating, and hiking adventures that Abbey celebrates in *Down the River* allow people the opportunity briefly to recapture that primeval freedom otherwise denied them by the constraints of modern life. These are valid and important arguments for preserving national parks and wilderness areas for the recreation of the human body and spirit, and Abbey is adamant in their defense.

In other essays, Abbey is also quite eloquent and persuasive in his protest against the potentially adverse environmental consequences of the MX Mobile Defense System and in praising the actions of the nonviolent protestors demonstrating at the Rocky Flats nuclear weapons plant. The policy of Mutual Assured Destruction (MAD) through nuclear warfare is merely the ultimate extension of the policies of environmental destruction practiced by both superpowers. Here his angry, indignant, confrontational style of reporting seems most appropriate in articulating a comprehensive environmental and antinuclear position similar to that of many European environmentalists.

For the most part, however, Abbey is content to let the anger and indignation of his rhetoric carry his arguments rather than offering the kind of close, analytical examination that these complex issues deserve. His arguments are too often simplistic and emotional, consisting of environmental clichés and platitudes, so that one finds oneself responding to the force of his style rather than to the substance of his views. He seems to thrive on controversy, making it plain that he would rather play the environmental provocateur than engage in any genuine discussion with opposing points of view. The letters from angry readers that he quotes with obvious relish indicate his enjoyment of the verbal equivalent of a good brawl with his corporate opponents, slugging it out with words and trading insults in print. Perhaps environmental politics are this rough in the West, but Abbey seems to go out of his way to taunt the opposition.

His simpleminded nostrums can also become irritating, as when he blithely assures his readers, "Be of good cheer, the military-industrial complex will soon collapse." This kind of wishful thinking may make good campfire conversation on a rafting trip, but it scarcely addresses the complexity of the nuclear or enviromental issues. Even if the reader is inclined to agree with the substance of Abbey's positions, he may still find himself put off by Abbey's smugness and superficiality.

Abbey's work is more impressive when he avoids topical issues and concentrates instead on Southwestern regional or local color sketches, such as those found in the section "Places and Rivers." Here, he offers some sharp and perceptive impressions of the Sonora Desert—particularly in its cultural and environmental contrasts north and south of the Mexican border—and of the abandoned mining town of Bodie, California, the history of which gradually becomes a metaphor for the wasteful and exploitative mentality responsible for the present-day environmental impasse. By way of contrast, he then offers his impressions of a Hopi footrace in Old Oraibi, Arizona, in which he and his daughter participated; here, the sketch gradually widens to become a tribute to the resilience and wisdom of the Hopi way of life. "Fool's Treasure" and "Footrace in the Desert" together serve as a parable of the history of the American West and of the choices still confronting Americans today: whether to continue the heedless waste and extravagance of the early white pioneers or to emulate the Native American respect and veneration of the land.

Throughout the esssays in *Down the River*, Abbey offers his descriptions of simple and nondestructive physical activities—running a river, taking part in a footrace, planting a cottonwood tree, watching the birds, tracking a bear, and hiking through canyons—as an alternative to the grasping, polluting, exploitative mentality he condemns as responsible for the destruction of the Southwestern American environment. Together, these essays offer an implicit environmental ethic, one shared with other American naturalists such as Thoreau, John Muir, Aldo Leopold, and Wendell Berry. That ethic might best be summarized by Aldo Leopold's remark in *A Sand County Almanac* (1949): to "think like a mountain." And to think like a river also, Abbey might add, as he invites his readers to share the enjoyments of rafting and floating with him on his Western rivers, "day by day, down to the ultimate sea."

Andrew J. Angyal

Sources for Further Study

American West. XIX, July, 1982, p. 70.
Library Journal. CVII, June 15, 1982, p. 1232.
Los Angeles Times Book Review. May 16, 1982, p. 1.
Nation. CCXXXIV, May 1, 1982, p. 553.
The New York Times Book Review. LXXXVII, May 30, 1982, p. 6.
Progressive. XLVI, September, 1982, p. 59.

DUNCAN'S COLONY

Author: Natalie L. M. Petesch
Publisher: Swallow Press/Ohio University Press (Athens, Ohio). 212 pp. $21.95;
  paperback $9.95
Type of work: Novel
Time: The mid-1960's
Locale: The American Southwest

*A short novel which tells of the establishment and dissolution of a communitarian
society dedicated to surviving a nuclear holocaust and provides a strong sense of the
failings of twentieth century American life*

> *Principal characters:*
> DUNCAN, the organizer of the colony, a former seminarian
> KLARA, a Russian Jew in her sixties, a former labor activist
> MICHELE, a poet whose husband would not accompany her to the
>   colony
> PINOSH, a puppeteer and actor
> MALCOLM, a mycologist and observer of life
> ANDREA, a large, unhappy woman married to Malcolm
> JENNIFER, a student, age fourteen
> CARILLO, a revolutionary, a Vietnam veteran

Between the Southwestern desert and the sea, eight people await nuclear
holocaust. They have not chosen one another but have been chosen by Duncan, the colony's organizer, from among the thousands who replied to newspaper ad. "How odd," one of the colonists muses, "to *advertise* Survival as
though it were a new cereal." Not all have been chosen, for Carillo, a Vietnam
veteran and now a revolutionary, simply wandered in from hiding in the
desert. As Michele writes, the colonists are like the wise men of old; they
watch the stars and dream, "not of the rise of a new kingdom, but of the fall
of the old." They think not of a life to come, but of their lives as they were.

Michele tells the greater part of the story. Duncan has selected Michele,
who is a poet, to tell their collective story ("every apocalypse must have its
scribe"), but Michele has used writing only to kill time while her husband
worked. She had dedicated herself to her husband Mark, who has now willingly allowed her to leave him to go to the colony, where she fears she will
die alone. Free now of her husband, Michele nevertheless finds herself yield-
ing to another man's assertion of "the old order of things": she becomes
Pinosh's lover.

Another of the women in the colony, Andrea, has accompanied her husband
to the colony, though, after twenty-three years of marriage, they had applied
for an annulment and find neither pleasure nor comfort in each other. Andrea,
fat and eager to please, has made no real choices in her life, and she has
failed at the one fulfillment she really sought: to have a child. At the colony,
she plays elaborate charades to avoid being, or appearing to be, rejected.

She can bear the indifference of the men but fears the desire of the women to share their activities with her.

The third woman, Klara Kleist, seems to Michele to be "serene and meditative as a Dalai Lama" and at least eighty, but Klara is in her sixties, and, despite the honors she has won for her social activism, she knows that she has failed: "She saw that she could not uproot this society, she had become a part of it." Born in Russia, Klara and her sister became radicals early. They came to the United States at the end of World War I, and here they continued to study, to work, and to support the unions. A second marriage brought Klara wealth if not happiness; she recognizes that "because we prospered in America we forgot the dream."

Klara wonders at one point if a woman could survive alone. If God had made woman first, would she have needed Adam? "Or would she have connived with the serpent and eaten apples joyously forever?" Like Andrea and Michele, Klara is a victim, at least in part, of her gender: "the weight of wealth and the burden of being a woman were too much." Still, Klara has what these other women do not; she recalls a moment—"only enchantment"—when her teacher in Russia kissed her. Because it was "only enchantment, it need not ever change," and Klara realizes that life has been "too beautiful, too poignant, too mystifying, too painful, too beautiful" and "Another life would be more than we were meant to bear."

Of the females in the colony, only Jennifer, age fourteen, seems able to take hold of her life and live it. Even when Jennifer becomes Carillo's lover and pregnant with his child, she makes her own choices. She resents the idea of the other colonists having a meeting to decide whether she would have to leave the colony to have her baby.

Klara's death, apparently of a heart attack, draws the colonists closer together, although Duncan's perverse and frustrated religiosity has come to be like devil-worship, complete with snakes. Nevertheless, Michele reports that it was "as if by this death we had recorded for history the fact that we were indeed Eden's first family."

The method of presenting *Duncan's Colony* in segments with different points of view enables Petesch to advance her story of the communal society while revealing her concern for the individual and largely isolate human psyches who constitute its social fabric. The book, however, does far more: moving easily from first-person to third-person narrative, Petesch tells, or allows her characters to tell, their entire life stories. So varied are the colonists that their stories provide a virtual social history of the twentieth century. As the characters reveal themselves and one another, they body forth a largely failed culture: the United States during the Vietnam War.

Six sections focus upon Michele, and three upon Jennifer. Although Klara dies at the midway point, two sections focus upon her. Andrea merits one section, and her husband Malcolm none at all. The Vietnam veteran, Carillo, merits two long sections, both told in the third person. By way of contrast, Duncan gets but one section—in the first person—ostensibly for inclusion in the time-capsule Malcolm plans to leave as a record of Duncan's Colony.

Neither Malcolm, the colony's engineer and scientist, nor Pinosh, the colony's entertainer, gets a chapter of his own. From the first page onward, Malcolm defies Duncan by listening to shortwave radio daily, and when Duncan surprises him with the radio on, the two men fight. Malcolm later declares that he would kill all of Duncan's snakes if he had the opportunity. Malcolm is practical and pragmatic; he observes and records. He grows mushrooms and repairs equipment, and shortly after Klara's death, he packs up his costly camera and equipment and abandons the colony.

Pinosh, on the other hand, is whimsical, always playing a role. He picks Michele as his lover and justifies his choice with audacious honesty; he would have to fight Carillo for Jennifer, and Klara is too old, leaving only the obese Andrea and Michele. He does not mention to Michele the possibility of choosing Duncan as his lover, though in his chapter, Duncan admits that Pinosh is his "temptation in the desert."

Sections presenting Malcolm's and Pinosh's points of view would lessen the dramatic impact of the novel. Regardless of what one thinks of Malcolm as a person, he is clearly a strong and contributing member of the colony. Andrea, though she judges him harshly for his sexual failure, his cruelty and indifference to her, nevertheless goes into despair when he leaves. She has followed him to Duncan's Colony and would follow him anywhere. Ironically, the record-keeper, the observer interested in recording the colony's life, disappears, leaving behind only a single, empty notebook.

Similarly, to hear any of the story from Pinosh's point of view would answer questions best left unanswered. The book is sprinkled with evidence of the affinity between him and Duncan. When a snake bites Pinosh, Duncan and Carillo rush him to the hospital, leaving behind Andrea, Michele, and the pregnant Jennifer. As they part, Pinosh assures Michele that he has not been playacting in his relationship with her. Michele wishes to assure him he will be all right and bends over him. He is saying, "not so deep as a well, nor so wide as a church-door; but 'tis enough, 'twill serve." The implication is that Pinosh *is* playacting even in the face of death, and that implication is strengthened by the occurrence here of the word "well."

Although Petesch draws some characters more fully than others, all of them remain individuals while achieving a certain degree of generality. Malcolm and Pinosh, though convincing enough when others speak of them, remain enigmatic, perhaps because neither of them is sufficiently interested in ideas to make them whole. Indeed, Pinosh speaks of himself as the original Pinocchio who turned out to be a real boy, and as she and Duncan go to search for Pinosh, Michele considers taunting Duncan with the idea that Carillo and Pinosh are swimming together and that all of them "can play musical lovers, each one with a chance to make Pinocchio a real boy."

Michele, watching Pinosh and Duncan drawing water from the well, infers from their unison of movement and their seriousness of conversation some-thing of the understanding they share. They spill the water, and Duncan throws himself to the ground, emotionally overcome by what they have shared. At the time of Malcolm's disappearance, Michele writes of Andrea standing at the kitchen window looking out "to where we once stood together watching Duncan try to draw love like water from a well out of the arms of my lover." Shortly before Klara's death, Pinosh joins in Duncan's "'obscene' obsequies" by feeding a "long stringy object" to Duncan's snake. Duncan had written that he regarded the theater as "a well of corruption" and Pinosh as his temptation in the desert, but the snake which bites Pinosh brings them together.

Pinosh and Duncan do not return to the colony. Carillo comes back to find his daughter born and to break up the colony for good. At the end of the book, Pinosh and Duncan remain at the hospital waiting for money to be sent so they can leave together, and Carillo and Jennifer are going away together with their child. Andrea has returned home, and Michele waits in comparative luxury for her husband, Mark, to join her. The serpent has ended the experiment in the garden.

Like all good fiction-writers, Petesch is more interested in her characters than in ideas, but, again like all good fiction-writers, she realizes that human experience includes ideas and thought about ideas—not just thoughtless sen-sation. She has chosen to let the characters most susceptible to reflection and introspection tell the story of Duncan's Colony, and those characters are her women.

Duncan has ideas, but they are mostly muddled by his compulsive and megalomaniacal enactment of the struggle between God and the Devil. The chapter devoted to Duncan's life up to his organization of the colony provides interest as a study in pathology. The boy's adoptive parents mistake his fas-cination with the theater as a tendency toward transvestitism, and the more they punish his "unnatural" behavior, the more he rebels. Chiefly to escape the smell of the chicken house and to repudiate his parents "at their deepest religious level," he turns to the priesthood. He sees things that he interprets as signs—eagles in the sky—and hears voices. He selects Klara for the colony because, after days of fasting, he heard her name "with a K," and he selects Malcolm and Andrea because he saw their names on a petition for annulment under the chancery lamp. Michele, he selects because his venture must have its scribe.

Like Duncan, Carillo is an orphan, but Carillo denies that they have any-thing in common, for "Duncan was adopted." Carillo has made up his own personal myth just as Duncan has, but, despite the horrors of his early life in Texas and later in Vietnam, he emerges as a decent person, gentle and tolerant despite his social anger and his ideology. As a boy, Carillo is subjected to neglect and overwork in various foster homes. When he witnesses the rape of his foster sister and tries to defend her, he too is raped and beaten—and later put in the reformatory. Eventually, he makes friends with a Mexican girl, Elena, who has an illegitimate baby, but Elena is shot at a demonstration for higher wages for migrant workers, and Carillo must choose between prison and Vietnam.

The most painful pages in *Duncan's Colony* detail Carillo's time in Saigon and later in the jungle, where a scarcely human American soldier, Jibaro, undertakes to teach him to kill. Carillo's experiences of social injustice and war parallel events from Klara's life, and in both instances, the characters become social activists. Carillo, however, does not seem likely to suffer from Klara's uneasy conscience, for his convictions assure that he will not prosper in America and lose the dream. Petesch writes that Carillo emerged from the army stockade, where he was thrown for failure to kill, "a different man, . . . a man whose mind has fattened . . . on smuggled books. He emerged what he became, a guerrilla leader, a soldier of the Third World, an officer of the People's Army, a revolutionary."

Duncan's Colony traces, almost incidentally, Duncan's loss of control of his colony and of himself. It traces significantly the development of the colony's youngest member, Jennifer, into a woman and mother, and it also traces Carillo's achievement of the emotional paternity for which he has been striving. Toward the end of the book, Carillo is teaching Jennifer not to call people "queers, zombies, weirdoes," and when she challenges his authority, he identifies himself by saying, "I am the father of . . . I am Bartleby's father," speaking of their unborn child.

The hope Petesch offers from the wreckage of Duncan's Colony may reside in Jennifer and Carillo, or possibly in Michele, or even in Malcolm. Andrea reveals that Malcolm left a note: "Why should I wait for the world to end? I am only fifty-four years old, and have not yet finished my experiment." The novel returns to what seems one of its most basic concerns when Michele discovers that her husband, Mark, no longer wants or needs her. Without Pinosh or Mark, Michele has nothing to do but begin taking charge of her own life. She begins at once.

Too frequent and too facile literary allusions, or worse yet, allusions to films, mar Petesch's otherwise expressive style. Early in Klara's first-person account, she speaks of herself "at the bottom of the great granite steps watching terrified and amazed at the spectacle of the Czar's soldiers firing on the people." The image brings Sergei Eisenstein's *Potemkin* (1925) to mind, but rather than trusting her reader to make the connection, Petesch contrives to allude to "wormy meat for the sailors of the *Potemkin*." Elsewhere, Michele speaks of herself as enjoying her "Last Days as though they were a version of Titticut's Follies," yet Frederick Wiseman's film, which features a scene of criminally insane men and their scarcely saner warden in a chorus line, is no longer even topical. Michele's observation that Duncan sounds "false as Cressid" may be appropriate for a poet, but such obtrusive allusions soon become wearying.

Duncan's Colony is perhaps Natalie L. M. Petesch's best, most richly sustained book to date. Her two collections of short stories (*After the First Death There Is No Other*, 1974, and *Soul Clap Its Hands and Sing*, 1981) have established her as a master of that medium, and the two short novels which make up *Seasons Such as These* (1979) provided a training ground for the longer form. Another novel, *The Odyssey of Katinou Kalakovich*, also appeared in 1979. With five serious books in a decade, Natalie Petesch is regarded as an important voice in contemporary fiction.

Leon V. Driskell

Sources for Further Study

Library Journal. CVII, June 1, 1982, p. 1114.
Publishers Weekly. CCXXI, May 7, 1982, p. 77.
Times Literary Supplement. October 15, 1982, p. 1142.

DUTCH SHEA, JR.

Author: John Gregory Dunne (1932-   )
Publisher: Linden Press (New York). 352 pp. $15.95
Type of work: Novel
Time: 1980's
Locale: A city in Connecticut

A once successful attorney tries to make some sense of the chaos of his life

Principal characters:
JOHN (DUTCH) SHEA, JR., a lawyer
LEE SHEA, his former wife
D. F. CAMPION, his former guardian
HUGH CAMPION, D. F.'s son, a priest
CLARICE CAMPION, D. F.'s daughter, a former nun
JUDGE MARTHA SWEENEY, Dutch's lover
ROSCOE RAINES, a criminal

Failure is a dominant theme in the fiction of John Gregory Dunne. In *Vegas: A Memoir of a Dark Season* (1974), an autobiographical novel, Dunne, on the verge of a nervous breakdown, goes to Las Vegas to cure himself amid the prostitutes and second-rate comedians of the world's most tawdry community, a mecca of failure which turns high rollers into low livers. Tom Spellacy, the Los Angeles homicide cop in *True Confessions* (1977), lives in the shadow of Des, his powerful, esteemed younger brother, a monsignor on his way to becoming a cardinal. Investigating the murder of a prostitute, Tom stumbles upon a network of corruption which he exposes, ruining his brother's career. Similar discoveries drive the protagonist of *Dutch Shea, Jr.* to suicide.

The protagonists of Dunne's first two novels are able to deal with the chaos of their lives and become reconciled to their failures, but Dutch Shea, Jr. feels responsible not only for his own chaos but also for that created by those connected with him. This burden becomes even heavier when a man who thinks he has no illusions about anything finds out that his world makes even less sense than he has thought.

The novel opens with Dutch's thoughts about the death of his adopted daughter Cat, who was killed by an Irish Republican Army bomb in a London restaurant. He blames himself because he recommended the restaurant. All of the crimes in the novel, both violent and nonviolent, seem to point an accusing finger at Dutch or someone he loves.

Dutch, once a promising attorney with a distinguished clientele, now represents pimps, thieves, and murderers. Since his divorce, he has lived in a crime-infested neighborhood where he can better cultivate his failure, which he blames on Cat's death. When a burglar breaks into Dutch's apartment, he ridicules the lawyer for not having anything worth stealing. With the intruder's gun stuck in his mouth, Dutch at first wants to live and then wonders if he really does. The novel consists of his discovery of the evidence against himself and against the world, which leads him to sentence himself to death. He considers his life "a Chinese box full of uninvestigated mysteries" and forces himself to open the series of boxes, knowing that what he will find will increase his guilt and despair.

Dutch would like to find solace in religion but cannot. "In general, he felt about God as he felt about the Kennedy assassination conspiracy theories: he was willing to believe." He occasionally experiences "faith attacks," but they never last very long because of the overwhelming triviality and hypocrisy of Catholicism as practiced in his community. He attends a church where George Patton is depicted in a stained-glass window, where one priest wears Adidas running shoes while conducting mass and another builds a sermon around golf (one of the satirical highlights of an often funny novel). Another priest in the archdiocese steals seven million dollars from a missionary society. (Dutch is attorney for the archdiocese until he is fired for having a prominent pimp as a client.) For Dutch, religion has lost most of its meaning, becoming just one of a handful of ways for him to shut out temporarily the intrusions of his memory, his guilt.

Like religion, law is little more than another way to "anesthetize the memory." He considers court to be restful, a refuge, a "moat against my life." Dutch feels comfortable in a courthouse because everywhere he looks he sees people tainted by guilt. He is cynical about the law, which is as flawed as religion and all of society's other institutions. What is important in a trial, he says, is not the truth, not even the facts, but simply the law itself. His cynicism is such that when he is assigned to defend Roscoe Raines, who turns out to be the burglar who humiliated him, he does so successfully. The law, especially criminal law, fosters a "rancid view of human behavior."

As institutions fail Dutch, so do the people whom he loves. Lee, his former wife, has always seemed distant, somewhat like her father, Judge Fairfax Liggett. Lee hates her imperfect breasts, refuses to admit that she snores, and cannot bear children because of a venereal disease contracted before she met Dutch. When they divorce, she explains that their problem has been that Dutch never believed she loved him. His problem, in part, is that he has always seen himself as unworthy of love and cannot love in return, one of many traits he shares with one or both of the Spellacy brothers in *True Confessions*.

Dutch Shea, Sr., also served his son badly. When Dutch was eleven, his father, a very successful attorney, went to prison for embezzlement and shortly afterward killed himself. Dutch, whose mother died four years earlier, was left not only an orphan but also the inheritor of a public scandal. He has gone on to relive his father's life, first as a lawyer, then as an embezzler, and finally as a victim of suicide. The inevitability of his fate becomes clear as his father's remains wash up on a lawn when rain causes a cemetery hillside to collapse, renewing all Dutch has had to live down.

After his father went to prison, Dutch was taken in by D. F. Campion, a business associate of his father, and he grew up with D. F.'s children, Clarice and Hugh. Clarice, who became a nun, has left the Church to counsel current and former nuns, while Hugh is a priest who has become famous as the host of *Father Hugh's Kitchen* on public television. D. F. is disappointed in his children, and Hugh is slightly ashamed of being a celebrity priest: "Somehow I don't think God had *TV Guide* in mind when he urged the spreading of the Word." Even intelligent, sensitive, honest people become tainted by the triviality or corruption of Dunne's world.

Cat is the only person Dutch has been able to love uncritically, and since her death, he has gone into a severe, despairing decline, becoming more and more like his clients: "I look like something out of *Bleak House*. Not entirely trustworthy." He is not obsessed with despair; he simply wants to understand why his life and the lives of so many he knows have gone sour. Who is responsible? Religion holds no answers; neither does the law. Examining his life, he finds nothing positive about himself other than his ability to talk his way out of difficult situations. His lover, Judge Martha Sweeney, says he is "a conscientious objector to [his] own life."

One of the tenets of Dutch's courtroom philosophy is "Never ask a question without knowing the answer," but he violates his own rule by probing into his past. Like Tom Spellacy, he discovers unexpected connections between people and events. He learns that Cat was pregnant when she died, that she was Hugh's daughter, that D. F. arranged for him to adopt her, that Lee knew who Cat was, that Hugh has never known he has fathered a child. Dutch finds out that his father embezzled to help D. F., who allowed him to take full blame for the crime. (Dutch's embezzlement is similar, since it results from his trying to clear up the tangled financial problems created by Judge Liggett's death.) Opening all of the "Chinese box[es] full of uninvestigated mysteries," Dutch is overwhelmed by a sense of universal guilt.

Although *Dutch Shea, Jr.* is about corruption, guilt, and despair, it is far from being a depressing novel. Dutch uses his wit as a weapon against the world, and Dunne presents a gallery of comic minor characters. A gangster client tells Dutch, "That's the great thing about America, Mr. Shea. A man like me, a gumbah . . . he can have granddaughters with names like that. Ames and Lindsay and Daisy."

Still, the novel is not as funny as *True Confessions* with its tough-talking cops, hookers, and hoodlums, nor is it as insightful. The discoveries Tom Spellacy makes when he opens *his* Chinese boxes are more compelling than Dutch's. However headstrong, the Spellacy brothers are more interesting than Dutch, a rather forlorn creature at the beginning of the novel who does not change significantly throughout the novel. Yet Dunne must be admired for his exploration of the malaise of the age and for his ability to present it in a surprisingly entertaining form. Like Buster Mano, a private detective in *Vegas*, Dunne is a "connoisseur of failure."

Michael Adams

Sources for Further Study

America. CXLVII, July 24, 1982, p. 58.
Library Journal. CVII, April 1, 1982, p. 744.
New Statesman. CIV, September 10, 1982, p. 24.
The New York Times Book Review. LXXXVII, March 28, 1982, p. 1.
Newsweek. XCIX, April 19, 1982, p. 98.
Time. CXIX, March 29, 1982, p. 71.
Times Literary Supplement. September 17, 1982, p. 71.
West Coast Review of Books. VIII, May, 1982, p. 26.

THE EARLY DIARY OF ANAÏS NIN
Volume II: 1920-1923

Author: Anaïs Nin (1903-1977)
Publisher: Harcourt Brace Jovanovich (New York). Illustrated. 541 pp. $19.95
Type of work: Diary
Time: 1920-1923
Locale: Primarily New York City and Cuba

In this second volume of Anaïs Nin's early diaries, the writer emerges from her sheltered adolescence to attend Columbia University, to work as a model, and to fall in love with her future husband

> *Principal personages:*
> ANAÏS NIN, a writer and critic
> ROSA CULMELL DE NIN, her mother
> EDUARDO SÁNCHEZ, Anaïs' cousin and close companion
> FRANCES "DICK" SCHIFF, Anaïs' schoolmate
> HUGH (HUGO) P. GUILER, Anaïs' fiancé

The second volume of Anaïs Nin's *Early Diary* covers the years from 1920 to 1923. A sequel to *Linotte: The Early Diary of Anaïs Nin, 1914-1920* (1978), translated from the French by Jean L. Sherman, this book—written in English—reveals a maturing young woman from the ages of seventeen to twenty. As her journal for 1920 begins, Nin still sees herself as two separate personalities: a frivolous, sometimes moody, impetuous child; and a more serious-minded, responsible adolescent. In a letter to Frances Schiff (affectionately called "Dick") of September 10, 1920—copied dutifully in her diary, as were many other pieces of correspondence that she wanted to retain—she describes the serious person: "You know Miss Nin is the sensible side of me . . . the little housekeeper and sister and obedient (ahem) daughter." Her other self, Linotte, "is the side which must be hidden or else endured—the moody and cranky individual and also the verse scribbler, etc." She signs the letter, still uncertain which part of her is the best, "Anaïs & Linotte." During the three years of her journals that are included in this volume (drawn from books nine to nineteen of Nin's manuscript diary books, usually inexpensive "date books" that allowed for a page a day), the prudent Miss Nin gradually absorbs the childish Linotte. Mademoiselle Linotte (the word literally means "linnet" or, in slang, "featherhead") is still romantic, self-absorbed, fantasizing about an ideal private world; but Miss Nin, her maturing alter ego, comes to control and focus her passions. Yet in one regard, Linotte and Anaïs remain one. In her determination to become a poet, a writer, and a creative talent, the author's purpose never wavers.

At seventeen, Anaïs was a fastidious, sentimental, sometimes moody but generally ebullient adolescent who had been reared in a genteel, old-world matriarchal family environment. Her father, the distinguished Spanish cellist and orchestra conductor Joaquin Nin, had for many years been absent from the family, communicating only occasionally with Nin. From the diary, one learns that he urged Rosa to go through divorce proceedings and demanded custody of the children, but Rosa refused the terms of the proposed divorce, even though Joaquin's financial settlement would have allowed her a measure of security. In Nin's account of the complex, deteriorating relationship between her parents, her sympathies are entirely with her mother. Rosa Culmell de Nin appears as a self-sacrificing, energetic, intelligent, realistic woman, the chief breadwinner of her family, a strong mother whose devotion to her children is steadfast. Anaïs reproaches her father for robbing her childhood and early adolescence of the gifts of affection, security, and parental guidance. Although only occasionally the direct object of her thoughts in the diary, he is nevertheless a menacing presence. Because of him, she feels, her family must suffer deprivation and the acute humiliation of an ambiguous social status within their rigid Spanish class orientation.

Indeed, a theme running throughout the early diaries, as well as throughout those more mature diaries already published—the seven volumes that have since earned for the author a major place in twentieth century literature— is the search for an absent father. In a sense, this second volume of the early diaries, like the first volume, is an extended love letter (which is also an extended letter of reproach, supplication, and self-laceration) to Joaquin Nin. In one stunning entry in the diary, for September 17, 1922, Nin copies a letter that she has written to her "Chèr Papa," one full of recrimination, anguish, and obsessive rancor: "The man who ceases to maintain and serve his home is like a creator who abandons his work . . . and loses it." With icy brevity, she announces her engagement, and concludes: "If I seem hard on you, oh, Papa! think of all the sorrow I have felt in realizing, little by little, the extent of your mistakes against us. Our whole childhood was darkened by you. Our whole youth is difficult, hard, sad, because of you."

Like James Joyce and Thomas Wolfe, among other significant writers of this century, Nin transmuted this search for a "lost" father into art. Indeed, as early as the age of seventeen, Nin regarded herself as an artist. In her diaries, she not only meticulously recorded her impressions of events but also disciplined herself to refine and polish her prose, to expand the range of her sensibilities. She read widely but not always critically. Among her favorite writers were Robert Louis Stevenson and Ralph Waldo Emerson (curious as this conjunction may appear), because, as she wrote in her entry for July 19, 1921, "they are great givers-of-freedom, as it were, givers-of-names to all that is too often mute or inadequately spoken of in other hearts." Even as a novice writer, Nin calculated the moral purposes and effects of art. Indeed, she was attracted to confessional literature precisely because of its moral focus. In a revealing entry from November, 1921, she expresses her youthful artistic credo: "I worship not so much the actions of men but what *moves* them to such actions. I am not satisfied with the actor's behavior. I want to know his soul. I want to know the inner self."

Although passages of psychological introspection can be found throughout the diaries, Nin was not always the serious, self-absorbed writer. Early in this volume, her focus of playful amorous attention is her cousin Eduardo Sánchez, to whom she is drawn by shared experience and similar interests, but above all by his physical attractiveness. In the diary entry for January 11, 1921, she describes the seventeen-year-old Eduardo as "the Prince Charming of all the fairy tales," reserving for herself, however, a critical judgment—"except that he is not old enough to be staunch and true." The true lover whom she was to meet was Hugh (Hugo) Guiler, later to become her husband. As the pages of Nin's diary continue, Hugo occupies more and more of her attention. In an important entry for January 5, 1922, she compares her two admirers, Hugo and Eduardo; both are "impressionable and imaginative." Eduardo's personality is the more responsive, the more personable, but Hugo's is much deeper, much more intense, more "poetical." To the reader it is evident, perhaps some time before the diarist has confided to the page, that Hugo has won her heart.

From the winter of 1922, Hugo clearly occupies most of her feelings and thoughts. Drawn to him because of his fine qualities of mind and character, Nin nevertheless fears the inevitable consequence of their shared passion. Neither Hugo nor she is free of binding responsibilities, so as to act with perfect freedom. Both have family obligations, the need to support relatives, and the need to develop their individual talents. For a while, indeed, Nin considers the odious proposition of marrying a wealthy Cuban, one whom she respects but does not love, for the self-sacrificing purpose of providing financial security for her family. Also, to assist her family in hard circumstances, she works as a model, a position humiliating to her proud nature. Because of her aristocratic beauty, her slender, delicate-boned form, she is popular both as a fashion model and as a painter's and photographer's subject. Most of her jobs are merely annoying, but a few are degrading. Once, while she is telephoning Hugo, a boorish salesman takes advantage of her with a caress. "It is a jungle of leering faces," she writes, "of men waiting to touch me, grasp me." Nin later drew upon these experiences for the erotic story "A Model," reprinted in *Little Birds: Erotica* (1979).

Yet the reader observes at once how little the impulses of eroticism moved Nin at this time, as she emerged from a chaste adolescence to fall deeply in love with Hugo (better known to her readers as the illustrator Ian Hugo). Her reticence in these diaries is not girlish timidity; neither is she constrained solely by the conventions of her strict rearing. Rather, Nin speaks directly of her conscious choice to enjoy a fully satisfying marital relationship which is not wholly sensual but is in equal measure intellectual, moral, and aesthetic. There is no trace here of the writer of erotica; the young woman of these diaries is—even according to the standard of her time—puritanical. In an entry for August, 1922, she asks herself: "Why am I repulsed by talk of sex and mention of whatever is animal in us, when coarsely and frankly dealt with? The animal in man, it seems to me, can be refined and spiritualized."

If readers familiar with Nin's fiction and her later diaries are surprised to discover the author's youthful reticence, they will be no less surprised by her attitudes at this time toward feminism. Although she is unquestionably independent-minded, in these diaries she often approves of a woman's traditional role as wife, mother, and guardian of the household. In the entry for June 5, 1921, she reports her disgust with several young companions who were dressing like jazz-age temptresses, and on several occasions, she assures Eduardo that she is not a flapper but essentially an old-fashioned girl who is uncomfortable with suffragettes. In the entry for October 6, 1921, she writes: "They say a woman who meddles with theories loses her womanliness—whatever that is nowadays. . . . She becomes coarse, she becomes argumentative, strong-headed; she trades her charms for a higher post in the Chamber of Debates."

Yet as Nin matured, she began to abandon her conventional attitudes toward the position of women in a male-dominated society. She left behind the delightful featherhead Linotte and became more firmly the sensible Miss Nin, in control of her destiny as a woman and as an artist. As the second volume of her *Early Diary* concludes, she is preparing for her marriage. In Hugo, she has discovered a man whose poetic sensibility and keen intelligence complements her own. Nevertheless, she has already given up any illusions about the man as perfect. On September 15, 1922, in a thoroughly critical examination of her own faults and of Hugo's, she concludes, quite simply, that "Hugo is *human*. . . . I must learn to fashion my dreams out of clay, to descend in order to rise, because I am repudiating the human, I am repudiating the roots of divinity. What *is* is what I must learn to love." With these words—confessions of a realist who sadly but conscientiously gives up her childish dreams of perfection—Nin becomes a woman. By the conclusion of the second volume of the *Early Diary*, she has already proved that she is an artist.

Leslie Mittleman

Sources for Further Study

Christian Science Monitor. September 10, 1982, p. B4.
Library Journal. CVII, August, 1982, p. 1464.
Los Angeles Times Book Review. September 5, 1982, p. 2.
The New York Times Book Review. LXXXVII, September 5, 1982, p. 6.
Publishers Weekly. CCXXI, June 11, 1982, p. 56.

EMERSON IN HIS JOURNALS

Author: Ralph Waldo Emerson (1803-1882)
Edited by Joel Porte
Publisher: The Belknap Press of Harvard University Press (Cambridge,
　Massachusetts). 588 pp. $25.00
Type of work: Diaries
Time: 1820-1874
Locale: The United States and abroad

A new, one-volume edition of Emerson's journals selected and edited from the Har-
vard edition of Emerson's Journals and Miscellaneous Notebooks

During his lifetime, Ralph Waldo Emerson kept a continuous journal of
more than two hundred miscellaneous diaries, notebooks, and ledgers, beginning when he was a Harvard undergraduate and continuing until late in his
life. This compilation of more than three million words has recently been
made fully available in the sixteen-volume Harvard edition of Emerson's
Journals and Miscellaneous Notebooks (1960-1982). Out of these riches, Harvard English professor Joel Porte has assembled a new one-volume selection,
Emerson in His Journals, which offers a substantially new portrait of the
private Emerson. Editor Porte has judiciously selected and edited passages
from the complete Harvard edition to present a full and balanced view of
Emerson's personality. Porte's new volume quietly incorporates the meticulous scholarship of the Harvard edition without cluttering up his text with
elaborate footnotes or scholarly apparatus. Instead, he simply divides the
journal entries into nine chronological sections, with a brief introduction for
each, and otherwise allows Emerson to speak for himself. The passages Porte
has chosen reveal a candor and frankness not hitherto apparent in previous
selections from *The Journals of Ralph Waldo Emerson* (1909-1914, ten
volumes).

Great minds need to be reappropriated by every generation, and this is
especially true of Emerson, too long mythologized as the "Sage of Concord"
or the transcendental idealist—the disembodied spirit of serenity and self-
reliance. Emerson was much more varied and human than this, as Porte's
selections indicate, and he deserves to be known in all of his moods. For this
reason, *Emerson in His Journals* largely supplants Bliss Perry's earlier collection, *The Heart of Emerson's Journals* (1926). Perry based his text on the
original ten-volume edition of *The Journals of Ralph Waldo Emerson* compiled
by Emerson's son and grandson. The Centenary Edition had followed Victorian editorial standards of taste and delicacy, and as a result largely suppressed many of the most frank and revealing of Emerson's personal comments.
Porte's *Emerson in His Journals* restores these passages and presents Emerson
in the full range of his thoughts and moods.

Emerson's journals were his "Savings Bank" in which he deposited a record of his daily thoughts and experiences. This image of the diary as a spiritual ledger or account book suggests his practice of the Puritan habit of daily examination of one's conscience. Early habits of devotion and reflection that he learned from his mother and his aunt Mary Moody Emerson prepared him to keep a continuous record of his inner life. The value of this exercise for Emerson rests in the candor and frankness of a self-revealed writer who would not deceive himself or be deceived, and whose quest for truth forced him to examine every fact and experience from a variety of perspectives, so that there was never an event that did not suggest more than one interpretation. Porte's edition provides a full and candid account of Emerson's personal life, especially in his doubts and uncertainties, his sharp judgments of contemporaries, and his frank self-assessment. "The dupe of hope," he described himself, yet his optimism was the foundation of his personal philosophy and helped him to bear the loss of his first wife, two of his brothers, and his firstborn son. The personal struggle to attain his serene and tranquil demeanor becomes apparent from these journal entries, since Porte does not censor Emerson's private doubts and struggles, and the private Emerson of the journals is a far more turbulent and passionate personality than the public persona. Through these new selections, one witnesses Emerson's infatuation with a fellow college student, his prolonged grief after Ellen Tucker Emerson's death, his attraction to Margaret Fuller, his despondency after his son Waldo's death, and his occasional exasperation with Henry David Thoreau and Bronson Alcott.

Porte's selections deliberately focus on the personal rather than the literary Emerson, on the autobiographical material rather than on those parts of *The Journals of Ralph Waldo Emerson* that represent a working out of ideas for speeches, essays, or poems. The emphasis is on the man rather than on his works, and the result is a more human and fascinating Emerson than has been seen before, one that complements the portrait in Gay Wilson Allen's recently published biography, *Waldo Emerson* (1981). Indeed the title of Porte's edition, *Emerson in His Journals*, suggests the biographical flavor of his selections. The detailed chronology he includes at the beginning of the text helps to place the entries within the context of Emerson's life. The entries may be read chronologically or randomly, since, despite their sequential arrangement, many passages have an aphoristic, self-contained quality.

Yet *Emerson in His Journals* is not simply a collection of miscellaneous biographical entries. Porte's selections may best be read as a record of the maturing of Emerson's mind. Understandably, the first section, "Prospects," is not as rich as later parts, but the entries show a progressive sharpening of insight and are often startling in their self-assessment. "I have a nasty appetite which I will not gratify," he confesses at one point, and "I am a lover of indolence & of the belly" at another. Emerson chides himself for want of ambition and purpose, comparing his dreamy indolence with the energy and direction of many of his Harvard classmates. His self-understanding is so clear and acute that it often disarms the reader and forestalls criticism by anticipating the worst of what might be said of him. His echoes of the candor of Michel de Montaigne, whom he so much admired, are evident in many of these passages. In short, the private Emerson of the *Journals* possesses a more penetrating and formidable intellect than he is often given credit for, and he proves himself as impressive a critic of his contemporaries and of his general culture as of himself.

In "A Reluctant Priest," one finds Emerson struggling with his lack of prospects and his distaste for schoolteaching or the ministry. He complains of various psychosomatic ailments and of idleness and want of purpose. When he went south for his health in the winter of 1826, he showed a keen awareness of the cultural differences between the North and the South. While he approved of the elaborate manners of the Charlestonians, he lamented the Southerners' primitive religion and their preoccupation with sports and fighting. Later, he would notice these same qualities in Southern students at Harvard, remarking that they ask of a man "How can he fight?" while New Englanders want to know "What can he do?"

The qualities of the entries quite naturally ripen with age and experience as Emerson finds the resources to meet a series of personal misfortunes. One marks the first expressions of his famous self-reliance in his struggle with grief and despondency after his first wife's death, which led him further away from institutional Christianity. "It is the best part of a man," he remarked in January, 1832, "that revolts most against his being the minister." In July of that same year, he observed, "I have sometimes thought that in order to be a good minister it was necessary to leave the ministry." These sentiments led to his resignation as pastor of the Second Church in Boston in September, 1832, after which he embarked on his first European tour. His journals for the next year, during which he traveled through Italy, Switzerland, France, England, and Scotland, bear witness to his enthusiastic response to European art and culture, although he never completely lost his New England shrewdness, judging himself against the men he met and reflecting that the great minds of Europe seemed deficient in a religious sense.

As Emerson struggled to reorient his life after his return to Boston in the fall of 1833, a note of gloom appeared in some entries, even after his second marriage, to Lidian Jackson, in 1835—a gloom that stands at odds with his customary optimism and serenity. "After thirty a man wakes up sad every morning," he lamented, "excepting perhaps five or six until the day of his death." After his move back to Concord in 1834, however, his life gradually settled into a comfortable routine of writing, lecturing, and delivering occasional sermons, and the journal entries thereafter reflect his gradually firming sense of purpose. As he mentions in one 1838 entry, the channel of his life's stream ran more quietly and deeply within its banks and tended to overflow less onto the surrounding meadows. One finds him striving to preserve the freedom and privacy of his reflective life, even at the cost of keeping his family and friends at arm's length. At times, he would tax himself for want of affection, though it was not lack of animal spirits but caution that led him to restrain the emotion that he felt but did not always express. His affection for his children was strong enough, but occasionally a note of coolness or detachment is evident in his references to his wife, Lidian. "I gave you enough to eat & I never beat you," he writes, "what more can the woman ask?" At other times, his affectionate regard for her is evident in the pleasure with which he records her shrewd judgments of their contemporaries. These contradictions in mood did not trouble him. He was practicing the art of individualism that he was to advocate in his essays. Self-reliance and personal growth were his goals, and he needed the freedom and amplitude to achieve them. Life was the art of learning to stand on one's own feet, and he intended to practice it. When George Ripley and Bronson Alcott tried to draw him into their utopian schemes, he resisted, just as he strove to keep the impetuous Margaret Fuller at a respectable distance while they were both editing the transcendentalist journal, *The Dial*.

A series of events in the 1840's tried Emerson's hard-won serenity, especially the death of his beloved son, Waldo, from scarlet fever. This grievous and unexpected loss tested his faith in the doctrine of compensation and left him for a time despondent and bereft of resources. He states in his journals that he could "comprehend nothing of the fact except its bitterness." Political events would also gradually and reluctantly draw him out of his self-imposed isolation. The Mexican War and the Fugitive Slave Law had led him to feel that he had been betrayed by his champion, Daniel Webster, and that he must speak out personally against the manifest evil of the Fugitive Slave Law, which he did increasingly in the 1850's, even if it meant opposing the self-interest of some of the more prosperous New Englanders. "Yankee" and "Dollar" are so close that they ought to rhyme, he complained, and he felt it his duty to defend the ideals of the spirit against the rampant commercialism of his age. Yet even when he spoke out, he never lost the essential moderation, common sense, and stability which are apparent from his journal remarks during these trying times.

Emerson's growing reputation enabled him to embark on a second European tour in 1848, lecturing and collecting impressions on the consequences of English industrialism. There he renewed his friendship with Thomas Carlyle and met other English notables, including Alfred, Lord Tennyson and Charles Dickens. The contrast between English and American culture was very much on his mind, as evident from journal entries which were the genesis of his *English Traits* (1856). After his return home, the Abolitionist agitation and the threat of civil war came to occupy more of his thoughts and energies, along with his reflections on the nature of American culture at midcentury.

At times he feared, prematurely, that his energies were waning, and he showed moments of doubt and apprehension. "America is a vast Know-Nothing Party," he wrote in 1857, in which "we disparage books & cry up intuition." Age and time began to take their toll of his circle, with Margaret Fuller drowning in a shipwreck off Fire Island in 1850, Henry David Thoreau dying of tuberculosis in 1862, and Nathaniel Hawthorne dying two years later, yet Emerson's journal entries show a clarity and vigor through his eighth decade, when the loss of many of his possessions in a house fire in July of 1872 severely shocked his sensibility. Friends sent him on a tour of Europe and the Near East while his house was rebuilt through a subscription campaign, but he seems never to have fully recovered from the shock. Up to that point, he had remained physically vigorous and had undertaken several strenuous lecture tours, though the bulk of his creative work was behind him. Thereafter, his journal entries show a slow but perceptible decline in his mental powers during the last decade of his life. Occasional flashes of brilliance appear alongside the commonplace entries, though Porte's edition ends effectively with Emerson's impressions of his 1872-1873 tour abroad.

The primary value of Joel Porte's new selections in *Emerson in His Journals* is that they provide an essentially fresh portrait of Emerson the man, no longer constrained by Victorian tastes and more accessible to the modern age. One finds a more problematic Emerson here, presented with all of his contradictions, passions, candor, and self-evaluation. There is room in this edition for a substantial reinterpretation of Emerson as more the tough-minded, pragmatic thinker than the vaporous idealist. He understood his age and culture preeminently well, and there is a lesson for modern readers in his clear grasp of his own times. He saw the need for both the scholar and the man of action in America, and by the end of his career, he could count men of both types among his admirers. Above all, he sought to provide for a young nation the self-definition that it sought, and he supplied the contemplative qualities for a heedless age that resisted the balance between action and reflection which he prescribed. Above all, one finds in these extracts from his journals evidence of Emerson's eminent sanity and clear understanding of himself and his contemporaries. That other selections might have been made from the full journals is beside the point: Porte has given contemporary readers an Emerson adequate for their time.

Andrew J. Angyal

Sources for Further Study

American Literature. LIV, December, 1982, p. 607.
Choice. XX, October, 1982, p. 264.

Christian Science Monitor. August 25, 1982, p. 15.
Library Journal. CVII, September 1, 1982, p. 1660.
The New York Times Book Review. LXXXVII, June 20, 1982, p. 14.
The New Yorker. LVIII, May 24, 1982, p. 134.
Times Literary Supplement. August 27, 1982, p. 915.

THE EMPIRE OF SIGNS

Author: Roland Barthes (1915-1980)
Translated from the French by Richard Howard
Publisher: Hill and Wang (New York). Illustrated. 110 pp. $12.95
Type of work: Essays

A series of brief meditations on Japanese culture as a source of sign production

This brief work, as delicate, fragile, and understated as a Japanese floral arrangement, is a translation by Richard Howard of *L'Empire des signes*, published in 1970 by Editions d'Art Albert Skira of Geneva. It is fitting that the words "Japan" or "Japanese" do not appear in the title, for this is not a book "about" Japan in the sense of informative commentary on Japanese culture for Western readers. Nor is it, while undeniably a part of the author's oeuvre, a volume which will serve to introduce previously uninitiated readers to the unique world of Roland Barthes. Instead, *The Empire of Signs* allows readers who have acquired some familiarity with semiological discourse, especially as practiced by Barthes, to observe the ways in which the author's encounters with Japan afford him the opportunity to contemplate the variety of signifying practices generated by that unique culture.

Throughout, Barthes retains his awareness of his own dubious status as a tourist. He remains, in every sense of the word, a "foreigner." It is not his role to serve as a guide, to make Japanese culture intelligible, or to render it familiar. On the contrary, Barthes celebrates the great sense of relief that comes with his own "defamiliarization." His text abounds in passages that suggest the Brechtian ideal of the *Entfremdungseffekt* ("estrangement" or "alienation effect"). For example, Barthes exclaims over his pleasure, as he walks the streets of Tokyo, of being engulfed by an utterly foreign language. He can take pleasure in unfamiliar sounds, rhythms, and cadences of speech without being distracted by the "real meaning" of any of these utterances. "That country I am calling Japan" is the self-conscious phrase that reverberates throughout Barthes's musings, and this refrain reminds the reader that *The Empire of Signs* is neither a window through which to view Japan nor even a glass through which one sees darkly, but, simply, a text. That readers have learned to think of texts themselves as objects rather than as mere vehicles of meaning is part of the legacy of Roland Barthes.

Barthes's enterprise in *The Empire of Signs*, however idiosyncratic, had its roots in his fruitful encounter with the structural linguistics of Ferdinand de Saussure (1857-1913), who proposed that a linguistic "sign" was composed of two elements: the "signifier" and the "signified." While linguistics necessarily had to focus upon the signifiers, the readily available elements of language, Barthes, in taking up from Saussure the development of "semiology" as "the science of signs," extended the search for signs into nonlinguistic areas, even while retaining his own penchant for literary criticism. The book *Mythologies* (1957; English translation, 1972) contains some of his most memorable excursions in this vein.

The first essay of that collection, "The World of Wrestling," is a semiological tour de force in which Barthes explores the levels of signification in the acknowledgedly false world of professional wrestling. What makes these matches satisfying for spectators, Barthes argues, is that the link between signifier and signified within each of wrestling's "signs" is so obvious. Unlike most of life's experiences, wrestling offers a spectacle wherein meanings are easily grasped. One never has to work at "getting the meaning," and this itself gives pleasure. When he turns to the signs within Japanese culture (that includes a very different kind of wrestling), Barthes performs a quite different maneuver. Here, the link between signifier and signified is unnecessary, because the signifiers—that is, the surfaces, the masks, the decorations to be found in "that country I am calling Japan"—are themselves so satisfying. Barthes finds them so completely arresting and diverting that he loses any need to "go beyond" the signifiers (surfaces) to "meanings" (signifieds). The traveler in Japan, then, experiences an altogether different kind of pleasure which is divorced from understanding in the earlier sense of "getting the meaning." Whether this is because "the real meanings" are beyond the reach of the cultural outsider or because Japan's uniqueness lies in the total absence of meanings ("there are only signifiers") is a conundrum with which Barthes teases his readers.

The Empire of Signs thus provides a restatement of the aesthetic concerns and semiological methods of Roland Barthes. The book serves another purpose, though it is one Barthes denies. On the very first page, Barthes writes: "Orient and Occident cannot be taken here as 'realities' to be compared and contrasted historically, philosophically, culturally, politically. I am not lovingly gazing toward an Oriental essence. . . ." Despite this claim, it is easy to show that Barthes proceeds to indict the West in the best French tradition (Diderot, Voltaire, and so on) of writers whose analysis of an alien culture constitutes an oblique condemnation of their own. Barthes finds admirable in Japanese culture precisely what he finds lacking in European culture, and, conversely, when in Japan, he no longer feels oppressed by occidental preoccupations. Only a few pages further in the text, the reader encounters passages which offer a challenge to the disclaimer cited above. Four brief sections are focused upon aspects of Japanese cuisine and dining conventions. In them, Barthes constructs a number of contrasts which make clear where his sentiments lie: clear Japanese broths versus the heavy, greasy soups common to France; the ingenious use of raw elements versus the Western tendency to overcook (read: the violence of culture against nature); or the use of chopsticks to isolate a desired morsel of food and to convey food "harmoniously" to the lips versus Western utensils that enact violent rituals of cutting and piercing. In many ways, Barthes uses his Japanese encounter to declare his alienation from his own culture.

All the same, Barthes resists the temptation to anthropologize these examples in order to explain their significance. His Japan is not a source of "meanings" to be extracted for intensive cultural analysis. To employ a photographic metaphor Barthes was to take up in a later work, "the author has never, in any sense, photographed Japan. Rather, he has done the opposite: Japan has starred him with any number of 'flashes' . . . a shock of meaning lacerated." In Barthes's late reverie on photography, *La Chambre claire: Note sur la photographie* (1980; *Camera Lucida: Reflections on Photography*), he spoke of something in a photograph called the *punctum*, by which he meant the detail within the photographic image that allows the photograph to "speak" to the viewer. This is experienced, according to Barthes, as a moment of laceration, a sharp pricking of the viewer's sensibility that conveys the special power of photographs. From tempura cooking to Bunraku puppet theater to an isolated haiku or the shape of a Japanese eyelid, *The Empire of Signs* documents Barthes's moments of "laceration."

Appropriately for one adept at literary stylistics, what Barthes finds to admire in Japanese culture is the importance of style, of nuance and gesture. Western culture has a marked tendency to think "mere style," and Barthes rebels against this prejudice. Oddly enough, he does not write about the tea ceremony, one of the most stylized of all Japanese cultural expressions, but he makes clear his admiration for the Japanese attention to form, as well as his sense that Western culture suffers from a lack of such emphasis. In "Bowing," he asks:

> Why, in the West, is politeness regarded with suspicion? Why does courtesy pass for a distance (if not an evasion, in fact) or a hypocrisy? Why is an "informal" relation (as we so greedily say) more desirable than a coded one?

In the manner of modern French dramaturges such as Antonin Artaud and Jean Genet, Barthes argues that people need ritual and spectacle, that modern Western culture has too hastily dismissed them.

Barthes surmises that Westerners are suspicious of form, style, and ritual because of a pathological need to decode them in order to get at "the real truth." Western thought is biased in favor of the search for hidden depths and realms of "deeper" meaning, against which form is seen as an obstacle. Barthes contrasts Japanese packages with Western gift wrappings: when Westerners receive gifts, they hurriedly remove the wrapping to claim their prize, but in Japan, the intricate wrappings constitute the real gift, the "contents" being merely trivial. The object within serves as an excuse for the packaging, as opposed to a signifying system within which the package "contains" a treasure.

Why does the West value content over form? Why this quest for plenitude? For Barthes, Japan offers relief from this burden. Significantly, one of the first illustrations included in the book is the ideograph *Mu* ("emptiness"), and this continues throughout to serve as an emblem for Barthes, as when he contrasts the round, deep-set eyes of Westerners to the Japanese eye "inscribed at the very level of the skin." The placement of the Westerner's eye encourages an effort to gaze into meaningful depths, whereas, in the case of the Japanese eye, "meaning" and surface coincide. According to Barthes's "reading" of Japan, meaning is something from which to escape. He argues that the zen moment of satori, conventionally translated as "illumination" or "enlightenment," actually expresses a loss or forgetting of meaning. Similarly, a haiku never means, as Barthes would have it, it simply exists, is present— or, better, its presence constitutes an absence of meaning.

The "de-centering" effect of Structuralist and post-Structuralist discourse has frequently been noted; hence, it comes as no surprise that Barthes esteems what he sees as the lack of a center in key Japanese cultural motifs and activities. A Japanese meal is said to possess no center, no *pièce de résistance*, just as Japanese cities, Tokyo being the prime example, are described as having no real center, out of which the rest of the city and its environs radiate in the fashion of Western cities. There is no core of truth or meaning, and the search for one is a Western affliction. To paraphrase William Butler Yeats, things do not fall apart in Japan because there is no center desperately struggling to hold—or, to paraphrase Friedrich Nietzsche, the truth about Japanese culture is that there is no truth about Japanese culture.

It should be noted that Barthes is predisposed to arrive at these observations in part because of his metaphoric emphasis on writing (*écriture*). Like Jacques Derrida and the Tel Quel theorists with whom Barthes was once associated, he tends to see everything as writing, with society being composed of just so many planes of inscription. The gesture of a Japanese actor is a kind of writing on or within the space of the theater. Haiku represents the "zero degree" of writing, or, to use a word familiar to readers of Derrida, the haiku is a kind of "trace" or impression. Even the slit of a Japanese eyelid becomes for Barthes an inscription. The point is that, within the discourse produced by the intellectual milieu of which Barthes was a conspicuous member, writing itself is a loss of meaning, an absence.

As for Barthes's own writing, it offers pleasure to readers willing to make themselves receptive to his characteristically elliptical mode of phrasing. Naturally, this very characteristic maddens those very readers who associate writing with the "clarity" that Barthes has elsewhere criticized on ideological grounds as a confining bourgeois prejudice. The books that Barthes wrote during the last decade of his life embodied a style that his more patient readers found more graceful, more accessible, less doctrinaire and less theoretical than his earlier texts. *The Empire of Signs* stands at the threshold of that decade, and the writing might best be described in the words that Barthes quotes from Diderot in order to describe a platter of freshly cut, washed Japanese vegetables: "Color, delicacy, touch, effect, harmony, relish—everything can be found here."

Ultimately, then, Barthes's Japan takes its place alongside photography (*Camera Lucida*), fashion-magazine writing (*Le Système de la mode*, 1967), or an obscure novella of Honoré de Balzac (*S/Z*, 1970; English translation, 1974) as another of the systems of signification he found so endlessly fascinating. He ends his book by seeking to justify its title: "Empire of Signs? Yes, if it is understood that these signs are empty and that the ritual is without a god."

James A. Winders

Sources for Further Study

Commonweal. CIX, December 3, 1982, p. 665.
Library Journal. CVII, October 15, 1982, p. 1990.
Los Angeles Times Book Review. September 5, 1982, p. 3.
The New York Times Book Review. LXXXVII, September 12, 1982, p. 1.
Publishers Weekly. CCXXII, September 24, 1982, p. 65.

ETERNAL CURSE ON THE READER OF THESE PAGES

Author: Manuel Puig (1932-   )
Publisher: Random House (New York). 232 pp. $13.50
Type of work: Novel
Time: Winter, 1977-1978
Locale: Greenwich Village, New York

A novel consisting almost entirely of dialogue between two seemingly very different men who come to be related in a kind of mutual dependence that resembles that of self and double

> *Principal characters:*
> JUAN JOSÉ RAMIREZ, a seventy-four-year-old Argentine political prisoner who has been exiled to America and is recovering from amnesia in a Greenwich Village nursing home
> LAWRENCE JOHN (LARRY), an unemployed thirty-six-year-old American and one-time college history instructor who is hired to push Ramirez's wheelchair

Manuel Puig was born and reared in Argentina, studied film direction in Rome and worked as an assistant director there. He has lived in a number of world capitals, and currently resides in New York. *Eternal Curse on the Reader of These Pages* is Puig's fifth novel. Unlike his previous novels, it was written in English, then translated into Spanish and published as *Maldicion eterna a quien lea estas paginas* in 1980. The published English text was based upon both the original, unpublished English version and the Spanish text. In short, Puig represents a new kind of writer: the *international* writer. His fiction owes its distinctive character neither to the materials of his native culture nor to the great tradition of Western literature but rather to an international popular culture exported chiefly from America and flourishing everywhere from Argentina to Japan.

Puig's previous novels—*La tración de Rita Hayworth* (1968; *Betrayed by Rita Hayworth*, 1971); *Boquitas pintadas* (1969; *Heartbreak Tango*, 1973); *The Buenos Aires Affair: Novela policial* (1973; *The Buenos Aires Affair: A Detective Novel*, 1976); and *El beso de la mujer araña* (1976; *The Kiss of the Spider Woman*, 1979)—reveal an almost obsessive preoccupation with certain recurring themes and devices. Thematically, Puig has explored repeatedly the role of popular culture, particularly Hollywood films, in the imaginative life of his characters. All of his novels feature an implicit critique of traditional sexual roles from a homosexual perspective. Essentially an apolitical writer (though several of his books have been banned in Argentina), Puig is inclined to treat political repression as but a manifestation of a more pervasive cultural oppression that is most clearly focused in traditional definitions of masculinity and femininity.

Stylistically, Puig is an exemplary international modernist. From the first, his novels have been collages, comprising such diverse materials as letters, term papers, plot summaries of films and excerpts from film scripts, and (in *The Kiss of the Spider Woman*, long running footnotes discussing various theories concerning homosexuality in particular and sexuality in general. Puig's most distinctive stylistic trait is his preoccupation with speech, with oral as opposed to written language. This trait, evident in his first novel, has become more pronounced as Puig has developed; *The Kiss of the Spider Woman* consists largely of dialogue between the two principal characters.

Both thematically and stylistically, *Eternal Curse on the Reader of These Pages* is a continuation of Puig's previous work. With the exception of several pages of appended "documents" (letters; an informal will; a job application), the novel consists *entirely* of dialogue between two characters. Here it would seem that Puig has reached the logical conclusion of his stylistic development.

An odd author's note on the dust jacket of the novel describes its genesis:

> This novel was born of a crisis I went through. I had returned to New York from a trip, spiritually and morally exhausted. Within a few days I spotted this man, while I was working out in a gym. He was young, healthy, handsome. "I'd like to be like him," I thought. I got to know him and soon discovered he was morally bankrupt. The book is the outcome of a series of interviews I did with him.

Given the dialogic structure of the novel, this author's note is rather ambiguous, perhaps deliberately so, for both of the speakers whose conversations constitute the novel are morally bankrupt. Lawrence John, known throughout the book as "Larry," is an embittered failure at the age of thirty-six. Once a promising student and, by his own account at least, successful college history instructor, he has drifted from one dead-end job to another. A student of Karl Marx and a self-styled "labor organizer," he seems incapable of any sustained commitment.

All this the reader gathers from Larry's conversations with Juan José Ramirez, a seventy-four-year-old Argentine political prisoner exiled to America and now living in a Greenwich Village nursing home. Mr. Ramirez, as Larry addresses him, is confined to a wheelchair and suffers from a strange form of amnesia, apparently as a result of his imprisonment. From his questions to Larry, who, in need of work, has been hired to take him for walks in his wheelchair three times a week, it appears that Ramirez has forgotten not only bits of general knowledge (such as the identity of George Washington) and events in his own life but also what it is like to experience a number of basic human feelings. He attempts to cure this amnesia of the soul by asking Larry to re-create various experiences, chiefly but not exclusively sexual, in obsessive detail.

Larry, in turn, obtains a complex gratification from these memory-sessions (at times, he and Ramirez switch roles, with Larry becoming the aggressive interrogator). Midway through the novel, however, just after Ramirez has been transferred to a hospital room because his health has taken a turn for the worse, Larry discovers something more concrete which he wants from Ramirez. A package has been sent to Ramirez from a human-rights organization in Buenos Aires (perhaps an arm of Human Rights International, the organization funding Ramirez's care). Larry asks what the package contains, and presses Ramirez to open it. It turns out to contain books, French novels, *Les liaisons dangereuses* (1782), *La Princesse de Clèves* (1678), and *Adolphe* (1815), among others.

Puzzling over the incongruity of this "present," as Ramirez calls the package, Larry notices that certain words in the books have numbers written above them, and that the numbered words, rearranged sequentially, form sentences. The first sentence Larry decodes, "Malédiction éternelle à qui lise ces pages," which he quickly translates into English, is the title of the novel: "Eternal curse on the reader of these pages."

Deducing that Ramirez had used this system to encode his reflections while in prison (he identifies the numbers as being in Ramirez's handwriting), Larry is excited at the prospect of reviving his academic career. "It could be an important document about resistance to repression," he says of the memoirs, but it is clear that he is primarily interested in his own future. From that point on, Ramirez uses the books to exercise power over Larry, now offering them, now withdrawing them. In the end, after Ramirez's death, Larry does not get the books. Puig deliberately plants contradictory "clues" which make it difficult to decide whether Ramirez finally intended Larry to have them; Human Rights International, interpreting the "evidence" as it suits them, claims the books on the pretext of respecting Ramirez's last wishes.

Ramirez and Larry are two empty carcasses, parasites feeding on each other in a kind of symbiotic relationship, scarcely existing by projecting borrowed personalities, sometimes pathetic, sometimes disgusting, but always recognizably human. Behind his mask of hardened nonchalance, Larrry conceals the pitiful bankruptcy of moral and emotional aimlessness and the burden of an identity crisis. Mr. Ramirez hides behind his loss of memory—an amnesia never made quite convincing—to pry into other people's feelings in a desperate attempt to retrieve the human fellowship that his commitment to political activism made him forget. Each character is the protagonist of his own story and the antagonist of the other's, both indispensable as complementary facets of the same process. At the same time, each is for the other a means of contact with a wider, deeper reality with which he has lost touch.

In this relationship of permanent deception, role-playing acquires a deep significance. The "as if" that role-playing presupposes is not mere make-believe, as in a childish game: Larry and Ramirez play roles for each other in a pathetic effort to overcome their nullity. Thus, their lies are not lies as such; they are stories that accomplish a double purpose: they enable each character both to know his own chaotic inner reality and to make sense of it—imagination as a mode of perception. Seen in this light, the distinction between "true" stories and make-believe is irrelevant; the stories always add to an understanding of the characters. Their stories spring from a search through different levels of personality, from the need to know who one is beneath the mask and who one can be when other possibilities of being are released—that is, when one escapes from one's repressions.

These two characters do not indulge in fantasies as an easy way out of reality; fantasies for them are an exploration into other levels of reality—evanescent, fluid, shifting. Ramirez's amnesia may be real or fake, and the same can be said of Larry's account of his oppressive relationship with his parents, but whether they are one or the other makes little difference: Ramirez has to retrieve a meaningful past, a past that can justify a life devoted to labor-union agitation and political ideals detrimental to effective relations; Larry gropes in his past for the source of his inadequacy, for the beginning of the failure he is. This inward journey is so essential that even the outer world, the world of objects and of people—which for the reader is never sufficiently concrete—is a projection of their fears and anxieties. Their stories function much in the same way as fiction, or literature in general, does: they modify, determine, and generate meaning, and the relationship between levels of meaning produces the multiplicity characteristic of literary texts.

The strange fantasy Ramirez and Larry invent (or one of them dreams) is illustrative of the quest for selfhood in which both have engaged. An advertisement for a brand of cigarettes serves as a source of inspiration, and Larry finds himself lost in a landscape of "snow-capped mountains and Arctic vegetation," miles away from Ramirez, with whom he nevertheless can communicate. For a man who has lost all memory of feelings, Ramirez detects far too easily Larry's emotions, such as fear, nostalgia, anguish, and loneliness. He finally enters the landscape to offer a final possibility of rescue, and although his use of the word "rescue" is quite ambiguous, it is clear that it refers not so much to Larry as to himself. Larry's plunge into the warm waters of a spring, after stripping himself of "this layer of clothes," resembles the plunge into the unconscious after one has discarded the different levels of superimposed selves. Objective fact or subjective fantasy—whatever it is, it is deeply moving.

Puig is always praised for his skill in keeping the right distance from his characters. In *Eternal Curse on the Reader of These Pages*, the distance is such that the author virtually effaces himself. Reading Puig's novel, one senses a pervasive tone of cross-examination resembling that of a detective story, but the sleuth seems to be absent—until the final realization comes: Larry's decoding of Ramirez's "memoirs" by carefully examining the French novels in which they have been encoded resembles the reader's own efforts to decode the characters from the stories in which they have encoded themselves. The reader is the sleuth and the "recognition scene" is highly ambiguous. Thus

Puig ends by turning the tables on the reader, who is implicitly asked to consider the construction of his own story, his own self.

Olga Liberti de Barrio

Sources for Further Study

Library Journal. CVII, June 1, 1982, p. 1115.
Los Angeles Times Book Review. June 20, 1982, p. 3.
Maclean's. XCV, July 19, 1982, p. 48.
New Leader. LXV, June 28, 1982, p. 19.
The New York Times Book Review. LXXXVII, July 4, 1982, p. 9.
The New Yorker. LVIII, July 26, 1982, p. 95.
Newsweek. XCIX, June 28, 1982, p. 74.
Virginia Quarterly Review. LVIII, Autumn, 1982, p. 131.

FAMILY INSTALLMENTS
Memories of Growing Up Hispanic

Author: Edward Rivera (1944-   )
Publisher: William Morrow and Company (New York). 300 pp. $14.50
Type of work: Novelistic memoir
Time: The 1920's to the 1960's
Locale: Puerto Rico and New York City

An autobiographical account of a young Puerto Rican's youth and education in Spanish Harlem, and of his family and friends

> *Principal characters:*
> SANTOS MALÁNGUEZ, the central character
> TEGO MALÁNGUEZ, his brother
> DONA LILIA "MAMI" MALÁNGUEZ, his mother
> DON GERAN "PAPI" MALÁNGUEZ, his father
> ELIAS and
> MITO, his paternal uncles

What it is like to grow up Hispanic in twentieth century America, whether in the American West or Southwest, in the Spanish-speaking barrios of larger midwestern cities such as Chicago, or in New York's Spanish Harlem, is a story that largely remains to be told. It is becoming more and more apparent that the Hispanic population of the United States (including Puerto Rico) is a significant "minority" which must be listened to, which must be acknowledged. With more than fifteen million Mexican-American, Cuban, Puerto Rican, and Spanish "legal" citizens now living in America, and countless more "illegal alien" immigrants from Mexico, the Hispanic chorus of voices is one with much to say about America and about the ethnic experience.

Certainly, each particular subgroup has its own voice, as does each individual within the Hispanic culture. Nevertheless, Hispanics share many problems and aspirations, whatever their culture of origin, and in the last two decades particularly, the issues of bilingualism—whether to speak English or Spanish or both—go far toward defining the Hispanic experience in America, profoundly determining what it means to "grow up" Hispanic in any region of the country. These issues of language and its relationship with populist and elitist cultures are dramatized and given life in Edward Rivera's excellent memoir—a series of remembrances largely realistic and "factive" but also imaginative and "fictive."

Whether as memoir, novel, or prose suite, *Family Installments* reveals with poignant humor just how a sensitive and intelligent young man carries his Puerto Rican heritage with him during his assimilation into the much-talked-about and sometimes doubted and denigrated "ideal" of the American melting pot. In the process, the author shows that entering the American mainstream, living the American dream, and ascending the socioeconomic ladder is indeed still possible—but at a cost. Although a painful journey, it is by no means an either-or proposition whereby family and ethnicity are hastily abandoned or forgotten. Quite the reverse: one can grow up both Hispanic and American.

Family Installments also provides a wonderful rendering of the effects of language (oral and written) and a compulsive love of words on a special kind of individual—the writer. In this sense, Rivera's memoir is part of a larger, universalized literary tradition: a narrative portrait of the artist as a young man.

Rivera's "family installments" began to appear as early as 1971, when the first chapter of this book, a piece entitled "Antecedentes," was published in the *New American Review*. During the eleven years in which Rivera worked on the book, various other chapters were published in such diverse periodicals as *The Bilingual Review/La Revista Bilingue* and *New York*. As a result, each of the thirteen chapters in the volume stands as a self-contained narrative— whether a story or a vignette. Also, as a result of this kind of protracted composition over a decade of teaching, working, writing, and living, the finished product does not always cohere. There are gaps, and there are repetitions. Nevertheless, the overall chronological framework makes for a relatively unified and satisfying artistic whole.

The two main ingredients which make *Family Installments* so enjoyable are Rivera's earthy, black comedy and his attention to language, its efficacy, power, and beauty. As Rivera's narrator and spokesman, Santos Malánguez, grows up before the reader's eyes and ears, the humorous convergence of Spanish and English in translation, in puns, and in linguistic observations create the very texture and ambience of the speaker's coming of age—his coming to terms with himself, his family, and their shared heritage, which although rooted in Puerto Rico, flowers in that most unlikely of promised lands—Spanish Harlem.

It is no small matter that much of the family history of Santos Malánguez is unknown; at least, much of what past generations experienced in the ancestral village of Bautabarro went unrecorded. Santos' ancestors were peasants who, in their work-weary world, did well to remember the location of the family burial plots. Yet all biography is ultimately a work of the imagination, or so *Family Installments* suggests. Based on the real and imagined memories of his father and mother, Santos marks his beginnings with the story of his grandfather, Xavier F. Alegría, who has the dubious distinction (considering his name) of first attempting to shoot and then starving himself to death. It is thus, with the humble but fantastic and, in its way, heroic life and death of his grandfather, that Santos begins the re-creation of his own family biography, and thus of himself.

Given the scarcity of documentation, the details of Xavier's daily life and world which his grandson is able to reconstruct are truly astounding. Sara Alegría, the narrator's grandmother, was killed by an unknown disease, and it was Sara's father and mother, Papá Santos Malánguez (for whom the narrator was named) and his wife, Josefa, who adopted Geran Malánguez, the narrator's father. Reminiscent of the Buendia family saga in Gabriel García Márquez's *Cien años de soledad* (1967; *One Hundred Years of Solitude*, 1970), Rivera's Malánguez "family tree" soon begins to take shape, stemming from the patriarchial grandfather Malánguez and his insane wife, Josefa, whose death four years before that of her husband, marked the end of four decades of zany family devotion.

Carrying on the family name after the death of grandfather and grand-mother Malánguez are their children—Elias, Geran, and Mito—three brothers who spend much of their time jockeying for family dominance only to wind up selling their land. While a farm worker for the macho, machete-wielding Gigante Hernandez, Geran daringly elopes with Lilia, one of Hernandez's eight daughters, who soon comes to share Geran's grand scheme: to leave the hard life in Bautabarro for the good life up north in "Los Estados Unidos de America." Eventually, the narrator's father marshals the funds to sally forth to that haven for "disrespectful cockroaches," New York City, where, as "Papi" and "Mami," he and his wife are destined to struggle for most of the rest of their lives as the proud but poor parents of two sons, Tego and Santos, each successful in his own way.

Only four chapters of *Family Installments* deal with life in Puerto Rico, and although they are crucial in establishing the moorings of an ancestral home, the heart of the narrative is clearly Spanish Harlem, "El Barrio del Norte." The central family relationship is that of Santos and his brother, Tego, who with their mother leave Puerto Rico for New York when sent for by their father. Alone in his decision, Santos stays in New York and refuses to return to Puerto Rico after the initial installment of his growing up. In the final analysis, Santos remains in New York because of his growing love for language, for literature, for words and writing, and it is his education, another kind of "family" mooring, which points him in this chosen direction.

As in most narratives of initiation and maturation, schooling occupies a central spot in *Family Installments*. For Santos, schooling is a combination of parochial and public education. He begins at Saint Misericordia parochial school, administered by the American Christian Brothers—"Saint Misery," as it is known to Santos and his motley classmates. Not only does he graduate from elementary and secondary school, but also he enrolls in City College, New York, where—both in spite of and because of his bilingualism—he engages in a kind of bittersweet struggle toward graduation. Nowhere is Rivera more successful in rendering what growing up Hispanic in America can be like than in the chapters dealing with his formal schooling and its interplay with the informal lessons learned at home and in the streets of the barrio.

Family member by family member, relative by relative, chapter by chapter, Rivera portrays growing up Hispanic as full of starkly realistic and practical obstacles—linguistic, economic, and simply human—but also as a hilarious, "magic" journey. Santos Malánguez must make it, must persevere in his double worlds of language, geography, and race. In his living and growing, and in the reader's sharing of the small denials and large affirmations, is the joyful sorrow of each individual as an "installment" in life, of each family's mortality.

Robert Gish

Sources for Further Study

Library Journal. CVII, September 1, 1982, p. 1654.
Los Angeles Times Book Review. August 15, 1982, p. 1.
The New York Times Book Review. LXXVII, September 5, 1982, p. 5.
Newsweek. C, August 30, 1982, p. 66.
Publishers Weekly. CCXXI, June 18, 1982, p. 66.

THE FATE OF THE EARTH

Author: Jonathan Schell (1943-   )
Publisher: Alfred A. Knopf (New York). 244 pp. $11.95
Type of work: Journalistic essays

A collection of three long essays that detail the process and consequences of a nuclear holocaust, argues humanity's cause against those who would jeopardize it with nuclear war, and finally offers a plea for a new world order based on total nuclear disarmament

In 1945, fifty-one countries approved the charter of the United Nations Organization at its founding. Today, over 150 states claim membership in the United Nations, and it is certain to grow in the future. Independence movements presently rage in East Timor, Tigre and Eritrea, Puerto Rico, Corsica, Quebec, the Basque region of Spain, Kurdish areas of Turkey and Iran, Namibia, and even in Soviet Armenia. The aim of these struggles is national sovereignty, the main components of which are: a unified system of binding law administered by a unitary structure of authority; the right to raise a standing army and police power for internal and external defense; eminent domain over all national assets; and access to all normal diplomatic channels and institutions.

The first three of these components either imply or entail the monopolistic possession of armed power. Since the rise of the modern nation-state in post-Renaissance Europe, the world has increasingly subscribed to Thomas Hobbes's dogma that, where Leviathan is not the sole master of the instruments of death, there is no Leviathan. Despite having Mahatma Gandhi as its principal founder, India has been a highly militarized state from the start. She is so not only because of palpable threats from her neighbors, but because she is obedient to the requirements of sovereignty. Experiencing no substantial external challenges, Brazil is very heavily armed; indeed, the Brazilians are one of the world's foremost arms suppliers. Regional and worldwide collective security arrangements notwithstanding, modern nations betray few signs of foreswearing sovereignty as a fundamental goal of policy. With the exception of several recent attempts (all failed) by Arab states to submerge sovereignty into higher Islamic unities, there are no cases in modern history of independent states freely surrendering their sovereign status.

Despite these all-too-familiar realities, Jonathan Schell's *The Fate of the Earth* boldly appeals for a sovereignty-free international order. Like a Hebrew prophet preaching destruction and chaos at the high tide of his nation's power, Schell demands that we "lay down our arms, relinquish sovereignty, and found a political system for the peaceful settlement of international disputes." He does not shrink before the magnitude of this transformation: "We are asked to replace the mechanism by which political decisions, whatever they may be, are reached." The task, he recognizes, "is nothing less than to re-invent politics: to re-invent the world."

Such words remind one of those halcyon moments in 1928 when, in their horror of what had happened in World War I, more than a score of nations signed the Kellogg-Briand pact which renounced war "as an instrument of national policy." One must regard the "spirit of Locarno" with suspicion, since it most certainly *invited* the aggressiveness of Hitler, and thus helped create the preconditions of World War II. Is Schell, despite being a seasoned war correspondent of the Vietnam era, simply a reincarnated Locarno optimist, a professional pacifist, naïvely ignorant of the peace-producing function of armed sovereignty?

While "realist" critics mock his counsels, Schell insists that his is the truly realistic position. For something fundamentally new has entered the world since Locarno—something so overwhelmingly new that even though we live and move and have our being in its presence, we refuse to recognize it. That new thing is nuclear weaponry. Schell's jeremiad is meant to awaken us all— and for all time—to the full truth of the Nuclear Age. Under his guidance, we must be fully disabused of the notion that nuclear weapons are simply modernized TNT devices, mere quantitative improvements on traditional ordnance. Most important, he would have us understand that nuclear weapons utterly negate the codes, standards, and structures for whose protection they were invented. It is not too much to say that for Jonathan Schell, history completely turned a corner on July 16, 1945, when the United States detonated the first atomic bomb near Alamogordo, New Mexico. The test site was called Trinity; for Schell, a better name would have been Armageddon.

The Fate of the Earth has quickly become a very famous book. Major newspapers all over the world have printed long excerpts in their magazine sections. In West Germany, a television special dramatized key elements of the book's first chapter. Dr. Helen Caldicott, the ubiquitous nuclear-freeze activist, has proclaimed the book the Bible of the antinuclear movement. On the face of it, this notoriety is a curious development, for what Schell mainly attempts—to picture in the most graphic detail the destruction of a possible nuclear exchange—has been done by other writers and documentarians before him. "Scenario construction" (the clearer the better) has long been a favored method of defense analysts. Novels such as Nevil Shute's *On the Beach* (1957) have shaped and haunted the imagination of millions of readers. Antinuclear proponents have prepared extremely effective tableaux, films, and case studies to make vivid the consequences of a nuclear attack. United States Defense Department footage of major above-ground tests has long been publicly available. There are yearly observances of Hiroshima Day which invariably present potent visual reminders of the attack. Why, then, the commotion about Schell?

Several factors account for the exceptional power of Schell's work. First, he takes pains to acquaint the reader with those principles of nuclear physics that explain the difference between nuclear and non-nuclear explosions. One learns that the violent explosive power of the Hiroshima blast derived from the sudden release of atomic energy resulting from the splitting of nuclei of an extremely stable element such as plutonium or uranium by neutrons in a very rapid chain reaction. Some 12,500 tons of TNT (whose power resides in its unique chemical bond) would have been required to reach the same level of destruction. The first atomic bomb, by contrast, exploded the energy packed in but *one gram* of mass. As a more advanced hydrogen device is exploding, reports Schell, it generates temperatures whose equal can be found only in such cosmic events as supernovae. Schell forces one to confront the full incommensurability of nuclear weapons. They are the sun brought to earth; they are hugely, monstrously, unfathomably disproportionate to the merely terrestrial world they now inhabit.

Second, availing himself of first-rate scientific materials, Schell develops his imaginary accounts of nuclear war on the basis of the *least* controversial data. He has studied the Hiroshima/Nagasaki reports carefully, and continually checks his scenarios against them. His now-famous description of a single-bomb attack on New York City assumes only a one megaton warhead (eighty times more powerful than the Hiroshima device). Since Russia has exploded a *sixty* megaton bomb, Schell can hardly be accused of dealing perniciously in worst cases. One is impressed throughout the book with Schell's willingness to work strictly within the framework of recent research and to indicate the imperfections of that research. *The Fate of the Earth*, therefore, persuades by virtue of its very distance from science-fiction speculation.

At the same time, Schell writes powerfully, and, more important, he relentlessly pursues the implications of our knowledge about the effects of nuclear explosions. The book is stunningly effective because we are forced to survey every dimension of a large-scale nuclear exchange. What might happen to animals? Even those placed at a great distance from the bombs might go blind owing to the predictable depletion of the ozone layer. (If severe enough, this depletion might also subject ocean organisms to lethal doses of ultraviolet radiation.) What of the insects? It seems that this biological class has a very high radiation tolerance level; with most of the birds gone, insects would likely multiply rapidly. This is not good news for human survivors, for some insect species would feed on the millions of available corpses and thus spread cholera and typhoid. What might a limited nuclear war do to the United States economy? Schell argues that the highly technological, interdependent, specialized American production mechanism would be largely destroyed by even a "modest" strike. The typical predicament would be that of the city's bus drivers or the suburban accountants who might suddenly have to grow their own food and make their own clothing. Searching for an uncontaminated refuge, "they would not be worrying about rebuilding the automobile industry or the electronics industry; they would be worrying about how to find nonradioactive berries in the woods, or how to tell which trees had edible bark."

In short, the economy would be that of primitive man, and it would be an economy dominated by the young, for nearly everyone would have cancer.

Schell's insistence on tracing the full range of possible consequences of a nuclear holocaust is thus a key to the book's surprising success. The long first section, grimly entitled "A Republic of Insects and Grass," is now (and, one prays, forever) the definitive image of the unimaginable. Picturing a ten thousand megaton attack on the United States, Schell discusses the destruction meted out by the various types of nuclear lethality—initial radiation, electromagnetic pulse, thermal pulse, blast wave, and local fallout. Each phrase reaps its own terrible harvest. Here is a typical bit of text:

> The thermal pulses could subject . . . one sixth of the total land mass of the nation to a minimum level of forty calories per centimetre squared—a level of heat that chars human beings. (At Hiroshima, charred remains in the rough shape of human beings were a common sight.) Tens of millions of people would go up in smoke. As the attack proceeded, as much as three-quarters of the country could be subjected to incendiary levels of heat, and so, wherever there was inflammable material, could be set ablaze. In the ten seconds or so after each bomb hit, as blast waves swept outward from thousands of ground zeros, the physical plant of the United States would be swept away like leaves in a gust of wind.

Of the five sources of nuclear woe, fallout is easily the most horrifying, so much so that the afflicted survivors would surely envy those millions who died in the first moments of the attack. People coming out of shelters after three months into an area of high fallout would still receive such massive amounts of radiation that over one-third of their future offspring would be mutants.

Schell doubts that "limited" nuclear war is really possible; he is equally sure that a full-scale engagement would mean the extinction of almost every life form. He therefore undertakes to defend life from its nuclear critics. This is the burden of the book's long middle chapter, "The Second Death," a complex philosophical and psychological meditation on what one might call (but does not wish to, so illustrative is the phrase of the deficiency of language) "the problem of human extinction." This might seem an odd and unnecessary excursion—to construct an argument against "omnicide"—unless one recalls that Schell views the world's nuclear arsenal as an expression of man's willingness to risk the life of the entire species. Hence, with utmost seriousness, he sets about to show that "there can be no justification for extinguishing mankind, and therefore no justification for any nation ever to push the world into nuclear hostilities, which, once inaugurated, may lead uncontrollably to a full-scale holocaust and to extinction."

There are several components in Schell's argument. The first is a humanistic rendering of George Berkeley's defense of theism. The physical universe has its being of itself, autonomous from human perception, but its *meaning*, its beauty and worth, derives solely from its status as an object perceived by human subjects. The human species, part of that universe, thus gains its significance by being the object of human perception and appreciation. Mankind is the *only* source of worth in "an otherwise neutral and inhospitable universe." It follows that no value can justify killing off humanity, for humanity is "the inexhaustible source of all the possible forms of worth."

Schell also argues against any theistically grounded justification of nuclear war. Especially concerned with the fundamentalists' identification of nuclear holocaust and the prophesied battle of Armageddon, he insists that the two great commandments—love of God and love of one's neighbor—rule out any Christian resignation in the face of possible nuclear war. When God appeared in human form, he points out, "not only did He not sacrifice a single human being for His sake but He suffered a lonely anguishing, degrading human death so that the world might be saved." Commanded to be reconciled with brother, neighbor, and even enemy, Christians dare not participate in planning the ultimate Final Solution. "Clearly, the corpse of mankind would be the least acceptable of all offerings on the altar of this God," he concludes.

The most impressive part of Schell's philosophical inquiry is his return to Edmund Burke's view of society as a fathomless partnership of the living, the dead, and the unborn. Nuclear weapons are a summary expression of human rationality. That triumphant rationality in our time has engendered a profound numbness in the human psyche. Our instinctual allegiance to the unborn, our desire to be worthy inheritors of what the ancestors have bequeathed us, our sense of the nonhuman species as members in the great partnership—these are now deeply repressed feelings in most people. Nuclear weapons themselves engender a profound and destructive emotional fissure, for they dangle an absurdly massive sword of Damocles above everyday existence, making any pretense of normality mannered, unreal, and fundamentally false. We have arrived at this juncture: in order to recover love for the unborn, ourselves, and our ancestors, we must throw aside our reason-induced willingness to live among weapons of ultimate death. There must be a joyous assertion of our right to *have* future generations to serve and cherish. This may require a new discipline of sensitization and sympathy. "Now reason must sit at the knee of instinct and learn reverence for the miraculous instinctual capacity for creation," Schell proclaims.

Schell, then, rests his case on three premises: first, that nuclear war, even in a limited form, is the equivalent of human extinction; second, that the human community, whether regarded as the source of all value or as the object of God's love, is worth saving; and third, that life lived in the shadow of nuclear weapons is horribly diminished and ultimately impossible. These premises adumbrate a new human task, that of dismantling the mechanism of extinction which vitiates our lives. Once a decision is made to embark on this effort, a new energy will make itself available to us, maintains Schell.

Suddenly we can think and feel again. Even by merely imagining for a moment that the nuclear peril has been lifted and human life has a sure foothold on the earth again, we can feel the beginnings of a boundless relief and calm—a boundless peace.

Invited by this prospect, is there any "realist" willing to continue to insist on the transcendent value of national sovereignty?

Leslie E. Gerber

Sources for Further Study

Choice. XX, November, 1982, p. 504.
Christian Science Monitor. April 9, 1982, p. B1.
Library Journal. CVII, April 15, 1982, p. 799.
Ms. XI, July, 1982, p. 257.
Nature. CCXCVII, June 10, 1982, p. 519.
The New York Times Book Review. LXXXVII, April 11, 1982, p. 3.
Newsweek. XCIX, April 19, 1982, p. 97.
Saturday Review. IX, April, 1982, p. 61.
Sierra. LXVII, July, 1982, p. 77.
Times Literary Supplement. July 16, 1982, p. 757.

THE FEEL OF ROCK
Poems of Three Decades

Author: Reed Whittemore (1919-   )
Publisher: Dryad Press (Washington, D.C.). 119 pp. $10.00; paperback $5.50
Type of work: Poetry

A wry account of how the suburban temperament contends with disorder

Since the late 1940's, Reed Whittemore's poetry has catalogued and satirized both the disorder characteristic of suburban American society and the manner in which its members, especially the poet himself, ignore or accommodate it.

Irony is Whittemore's major technique for expressing his disbelief in the order or perfection that suburban man tries to impose on his life and its setting. In his earliest collection, *An American Takes a Walk* (1956), Whittemore, referring to the self-satisfied American sensibility that is at home in its surroundings, rhetorically asks, "How in that Eden could Adam/ Really be lost?" ("An American Takes a Walk"). Motion-picture characters provide Whittemore with an image for the threat to survival posed by smugness and lethargic hedonism; when these characters are called to action, they simply go on "Drinking their gin and bitters" ("A Day with the Foreign Legion").

The ironic corollaries to this lethargy are the suffering which unravels one's happiness and the rebellion whereby one tries to escape the illusion of order. The ritualized order of "Marriage is designed to route . . . pain . . . through the female to the male and then to the children and the dog" ("The Mother's Breast and the Father's House"). The suburban father in "Bad Daddy," depressed, it seems, by the restrictions of suburban life, visits his irascibility on his children. The poet in "The Girl in the Next Room" has "insomnia," and remarks that the head of the suburban household, suffering his daily round of work, has little to look forward to but "bed" and "an orange Nembutol tablet." The passion for stability, indeed, leads one to vertigo—the sense that stability itself is an illusion ("A Porch Chair"). "Suffering," Whittemore concludes, "is middle class," and in the context of this perception he asks, "Why does one have to be messy, corrupt and old?" ("The Desk"). He says further in "The Seven Days" that, were he to create man, he would create an unhappy and sloppy version of him, which "would sleep poorly at night as he got older/ . . . misquote things, drink too much,/ Rage at women at breakfast, lose keys. . . ."

Though memory may be a partial antidote to suffering, it is also a source of it, for what one loves and remembers crumbles, even from memory itself. Unhappiness becomes the rule, and finally forces a man to "Despair" in "the kingdom of the 10% joy the 15% satisfaction the 20% love" ("The Mother's Breast and the Father's House"), where "The waking is always . . ./ To sickness and loneliness and loss and emptiness" ("Rocks").

Civilized man in a suburban setting may end up negotiating a compromise with disorder, but he sometimes rebels against the forms of order in which the compromise takes place. As the suffering which he experiences in the confinement of custom is enervating, so the rebellion he enacts is useless. Rebellious memory itself may refuse to "be tamed, chafed, defined" ("The Past, the Future, the Present"), but it can neither recoup a life restricted by its choices nor save it from its pain. "Honest" people may have "a duty to blaspheme" ("Wordsworth and the Woman"), but they remain disgruntled and stuck in their customary agendas. The children who rebel, running away from their middle-class lives, return "broke and broken to suffer properly in the home" ("The Mother's Breast and the Father's House"). The ironic best that can be said for the rebellious sensibility is that it refuses to grow up ("The Farmhouse").

Rebellion, to be sure, is an agent of the disorder which permeates a person's soul. Thus, Whittemore cancels the distinction between the disorder which afflicts man from without and the disorder which defines him from within. As for exterior disorder, it surrounds one: not only is "The oven . . . sticky with grease," and not only do "the bulbs blacken,/ The dishes pile up in the sink" ("Variations on Being Thirty"), but chaos reigns in the world outside the library overseen by "Miss Prunewhip" ("The Mind"), nature is "largely locust and no God" ("Meditative Stomp on the State of Something"), and being is only an "and" in the nothingness preceding origin ("Genesis Revised"). As for interior disorder, the essence of man himself, including his desire for order, is ineffable, disorderly. The soul, as Whittemore notes in "Genesis Revised," "is not logical . . . not metrical."

The ultimate form of disorder for a human, besides the collapse of his houses and furniture and mementoes, is his own death. Whittemore is alert to death in its abstract as well as concrete modes. If the past is dead and exists in the present as that fact, then "the present is death," Whittemore facetiously but cogently argues in "A Treasure." Death is also "The teacher, killing all one loves, remembers" ("Dead-Walk"). Alluding to his personal death, Whittemore quips that it is "45, alcoholic, rational" ("What It Was Like"), and that "They won't find much but some undone verse, some old smokes,/ And an empty chair by a desk in an empty room" ("The Seven Days"). In his most recent collection (1975-1981), he presents a satirical, albeit almost comfortable, scene of himself in his coffin, "Alone at last," where he reminisces about his adolescence and muses, "What is my state?/ So hard to know sometimes. And so I am smiling" ("Smiling Through").

This ironic tone seems to be a significant aspect of what Whittemore means by accommodation—at least his own—to decay. He joins his fellow suburbanites in pretending that all is quite satisfactory rather than falling apart, as he ridicules them and himself: "Our lives are rich and full at the shore/

Because our kind are sports" ("Song: The Summer People"). With similar irony, he calls attention to the suburban housewife: "All the pastoral landscape that she chose/ She tacked to parlor walls" ("The Self-Made Man"), reducing thus her perception of nature, which overwhelms everything in its way, "Shutting the heavens out" ("Inventory").

For the most part, Whittemore uses himself as an example of how a self-mocking suburban temperament accommodates disorder. "I build a modest martini and sip it here/ By my pencil," he says in "The Past, the Future, the Present." Beyond "Making few affirmations," he assents to his own urge to be disorderly, "favoring lines/ Of odd lengths and irony" ("Poem to Jackson"). When he is at an artists' colony in "The Seven Days," he acknowledges that nature pays no attention to his effort to re-create it in poetry, and he goes "to breakfast" instead. The "god" in the poem is the poet, and he concludes by being content with having "made what he could."

The notion of loyalty is behind Whittemore's ethic of accommodation. What else but this virtue, worthy of satire as it may be in a suburban setting, would make the father "work hard and make money and pay his taxes/ . . . and love women/ And take children to zoos and wear tweeds" ("The Seven Days")? From such a life, supported by a memory which would be "wholly trivial if it were not ours" ("Writer and Reader"), Whittemore derives the essential and "inexhaustible fact" about the "self": its persistence ("The Mother's Breast and the Father's House"). This stubbornness applies itself to reducing the disorders of life to a manageable size, breaking them "into smaller and smaller rocks," as the poet says in "Rocks."

As John Cheever has embodied in his fiction the frayed expectations and nerves and the ironic doggedness of suburban American society, so has Reed Whittemore embodied them in his poetry—his prosody deliberately and elegantly seedy, and his tone at once self-deflating, biting, and jocular.

Mark McCloskey

Sources for Further Study

Library Journal. CVII, September 15, 1982, p. 1758.
Publishers Weekly. CCXXII, July 23, 1982, p. 131.

FICTION AND REPETITION
Seven English Novels

Author: J. Hillis Miller (1928-   )
Publisher: Harvard University Press (Cambridge, Massachusetts). 250 pp. $15.00
Type of work: Literary criticism

Miller's collection of insightful studies on a selection of nineteenth and twentieth century novels is a useful introduction to Deconstructive analysis, illustrating some of the advantages and limitations of this important modern critical methodology

Perhaps the maturity of a particular style or system of criticism may be measured by its level of comprehensibility. A critical approach need not always be lucid or simple, but to be a vital intellectual force it must nevertheless, at least sometimes, show itself as explicable and useful to more than a tiny band of true believers. Like many others before it, the most recent critical rage, loosely called "Deconstruction," has aroused a tremendous amount of hostility in the traditional literary-critical establishment, in part because of its apparently willful opacity and disinterest in clarifying its major premises, intentions, and modes. If J. Hillis Miller's new study, *Fiction and Repetition: Seven English Novels*, is any indication, this work of self-clarification is under way. Miller's essays contained herein are Deconstructive, yet reasonably accessible and provocative even to those who are not well versed in the writings of Jacques Derrida, the father of Deconstruction, or who cannot— or perhaps choose not to—follow the nuances of interminable critical debate in such journals as *New Literary History*, *Critical Inquiry*, and *Diacritics*.

Miller acknowledges from the beginning that his book "is not a work of theory as such, but a series of readings of important nineteenth- and twentieth-century English novels." Indeed, the individual chapters on *Lord Jim* (1900), *Wuthering Heights* (1847), *Henry Esmond* (1852), *Tess of the D'Urbervilles* (1891), *The Well-Beloved* (1897), *Mrs. Dalloway* (1925), and *Between the Acts* (1941)—a curious mixture of classic and neglected novels—give his work a much-welcomed specificity and focus. As disarming as this may be, Miller is nevertheless an extremely sophisticated critic, and *Fiction and Repetition* elaborates a number of sustained theoretical arguments regarding the nature of the text and the responsibilities of the critic and/or reader in arriving at meaning (or, as he might insist, meanings). Summarizing a few of these arguments inevitably disrupts the balance and blend of theoretical and practical criticism that is one of the great achievements of this book, but may also help outline Miller's debt to and graceful restatement of basic principles of Deconstructive analysis.

First and foremost, as the title suggests, Miller is concerned with showing how various modes of repetition function in the novel. There is nothing at all startling in his preliminary suggestion that the "identification of recurrences and of meanings generated through recurrences" forms an important part of the reader's work, as he traces throughout a novel repeated verbal elements, events or scenes, images, motifs from one character appearing also in another, and so on. It soon becomes clear, however, that Miller's definition of repetition is meant to be somewhat unsettling. In addition to the familiar kind of "Platonic" repetition, in which an original model is copied by other examples similar to it, Miller describes "Nietzschean" repetition, paradoxically based not on similarity but on difference. Nietzschean repetitions involve "ungrounded doublings," in which "It seems that X repeats Y, but in fact it does not, or at least not in the firmly anchored way of the first sort of repetition." Platonic repetitions seem to establish a "figure in the carpet" of the novel, a general ordering structure; Nietzschean repetitions, on the other hand, complicate or "unravel" simple patterns of order. Though he stops just short of making a sweeping generalization about all novels, Miller states quite boldly that at least all of the novels he will discuss are characterized by the simultaneous presence of Platonic and Nietzschean modes of repetition.

The consequences of this premise are everywhere visible in the way a text is defined, approached, and interpreted in *Fiction and Repetition*. In the very least, as Miller points out about each novel he treats in his study, a text invites a reader to decipher its meaning, and at the same time continually frustrates any attempt to arrive at one unified but still comprehensive meaning. Perhaps the most distinctive and telling quality of a literary work for Miller is that "the text is over-rich," filled with details that may support a great number of interpretations, not all of which may be logically compatible. The responsibility of the reader, then, is not to fuss over reducing a novel to a homogeneous unity, but rather to confront its "strangeness," a term frequently used by Miller to emphasize the ambiguity and the challenge of a text. This requires what may turn out to be a radical reorientation on the part of a reader who, for whatever reasons—shrewdly theoretical or naïvely conventional—expects a novel to be a puzzle with an intelligible solution, but it is a reorientation well worth undertaking. Deconstructive analysis such as Miller proposes raises a great deal of anxiety, suggesting that texts, and perhaps the "reality" behind them, are unstable and filled with simultaneously "true" yet contradictory meanings. At the same time, though, the strain of Miller's approach to literature can be exhilarating as close, attentive reading reminds one of the richness and perpetual newness of a text.

Fiction and Repetition is filled with fine examples of close reading, and while it is extremely important to understand the theoretical foundation from which he proceeds, most readers will of course be interested primarily in what happens as Miller takes particular novels into his hands. As might be expected from a critic who treats texts as texture, the chapters here are so subtle and finely argued that they resist quick summary. At the same time, though, each chapter has a precisely defined focus which orients the reader in the midst of

Miller's often dazzling critical displays.

After a short introduction defining what he means by repetition, Miller begins with *Lord Jim*, a novel particularly suited to his understanding of the novel as an open form, complicated rather than clarified by structures of repetition. Joseph Conrad's intuition that a mystery, not a coherent revelation, lies at the heart of a character or an event is a premise elaborated not only in this chapter but also throughout *Fiction and Repetition*. Miller reads *Wuthering Heights*, for example, as a novel that, like *Lord Jim*, promises but never delivers a unified explanation of its many mysteries, either to its readers or to the characters within the novel who are similarly trying to "interpret" the story. William Makepeace Thackeray's *Henry Esmond* uses repetition not for the ghostly, "uncanny" effects of Conrad and Emily Brontë but rather in league with a corrosive irony which first constructs and then dismantles a character: the self-portrait of an ironic man, Miller argues, can only be ironic and therefore untrustworthy. Thomas Hardy's acknowledged masterpiece *Tess of the D'Urbervilles*, much like his less well-known work *The Well-Beloved*, which Miller takes up separately, is approached as a novel in which the reader's experience duplicates that of the fictional characters: all are trapped in a pattern of repetition that has no discernible beginning or end. Finally, Miller concludes with two particularly interesting and moving essays on Virginia Woolf. The many levels of repetition in *Mrs. Dalloway*, he suggests, trace out a fragile web of continuity, between past and present, between one character and another, that gives one the courage to continue living. This problem of Clarissa's life proves to be the problem of Miss La Trobe's art in *Between the Acts*, and it is fitting that Miller closes his volume with an analysis of Woolf's not completely successful dramatization of how one can keep "the human story from disintegrating into unconnected fragments."

Though his book lacks a formal conclusion, Miller uses his last paragraph to note somewhat coyly that the relationship between fiction and repetition still remains an open question. Many readers and critics will no doubt be quick to respond to Miller's implicit invitation to a continuing debate by objecting to certain aspects of his approach. Perhaps most noticeably, though Miller takes great pains to define the various modes and uses of repetition precisely, from the very beginning the term picks up more and more momentum, until it finally includes more than should be allowed. So much of his argument hinges on his distinction between "Platonic" and "Nietzschean" repetition that one should expect a much more developed discussion, particularly of this latter mode. Once one accepts the notion that there can be a repetition based on "difference"—and Miller "clarifies" this concept by referring to an almost impenetrable but nevertheless evocative illustration from the writings of Walter Benjamin—the door is open to admit almost any kind of connection, allusion, or association as a kind of repetition. Furthermore, despite his discovery of new layers of meaning in the novel, Miller's descriptions of the reading and interpreting process may strike some as rather disheartening: most frequently, he uses such phrases as the "weaving movement of advance and retreat," "the senseless movement toward a light which always remains hidden in the dark," and the "lateral dance of interpretation," leading the reader to believe that if there is such a thing at all as "the pleasure of the text," it may well be only a cerebral affair. No wonder *Fiction and Repetition* does not include mention of novels by James Joyce or D. H. Lawrence.

Ultimately, though, Miller does not restrict the pleasure of the text to a sophisticated, intellectual reverie, and in this respect he steps beyond one of the major limitations of Deconstructive analysis. He provides glimpses of Deconstruction with a human face. For all his emphasis on the text as an interminable puzzle, and on the human character, both inside and outside the novel, as perhaps primarily a maker, manipulator, and interpreter of signs, Miller nevertheless approaches the novel as a form that is not only open but also warm, that engages one's emotions as well as one's intellect. He distinguishes his critical method from that of the reader-response theorists, who believe that meaning is located not in the text but in the affective transaction between reader and text; yet each one of his chapters in some way or another suggests that readers feel a powerful pull toward the novels they read and explicate. *Tess of the D'Urbervilles*, for example, is an intricately woven fabric of repetitions that challenges, teases, and mystifies, but also deeply moves every good reader. For Miller, the "emotional experience of following through the novel" provides a crucial shared background even for those who disagree radically about the novel's meaning. Diehard Deconstructionists may object to any such attention paid to the emotional involvement of a reader with a text, but others may find it to be a subtle link between *Fiction and Repetition* and Miller's earlier work on fiction, as well as an indication that Deconstructive analysis need not always take the antihumanistic form that many traditional critics fear is the way of the future.

Sidney Gottlieb

Sources for Further Study

Antioch Review. XL, Summer, 1982, p. 361.
Choice. XIX, May, 1982, p. 1242.
Library Journal. CVII, June 1, 1982, p. 1098.
New Statesman. CIV, December 31, 1982, p. 24.
The New York Times Book Review. LXXXVII, April 18, 1982, p. 15.
Times Literary Supplement. September 10, 1982, p. 975.

FLAWS IN THE GLASS
A Self-Portrait

Author: Patrick White (1912-   )
Publisher: The Viking Press (New York). 260 pp. $14.95
Type of work: Literary memoir
Time: 1912-1982
Locale: Australia, England, Europe, Palestine, and North Africa

These candid sketches of times and places and people in the life of the Nobel Prize-winning novelist are suffused with a depth of emotion and intellectual honesty that elevates them to the level of literature

> *Principal personages:*
> PATRICK WHITE, an Australian novelist
> MANOLY LASCARIS, his lover and companion
> RICHARD (DICK) WHITE, White's Victorian father
> RUTH WHITE, White's domineering mother

Some human beings are "doomed" to become artists, writes Patrick White in this memoir—or, as he calls it, a collection of sketches—and these chosen individuals are seldom also blessed with equanimity. Part of the artist's burden is to be tossed to drunken heights one minute and then brought down to despair the next. Similarly, the creative artist can move from arrogance to humiliation and uncertainty, from confidence to timidity. None of this makes an artist easy to be around—or even easy to *be*.

White compares the creative artist's extremes of emotion and attitude to the playacting of children and the grown-up playacting of the theater. He speculates that he may well have turned to writing as a means of coming to terms with the frustrated actor in himself: writing was a way to harness the swings of temperament inherent in his nature. Nevertheless, he adds, the magic of art remains unexplained and unexplainable. These themes—the sense of doom, the quality of "theater," the aura of magic—run through all of Nobel Prize-winner White's fiction, and through this informally constructed but fascinating and well-written autobiography.

Because he lacked the flamboyance and confidence of the professional actor, White writes, and because he was cursed with an instinctive and sometimes crippling reserve, he chose fiction—or was compelled toward fiction—as a means of introducing to the world "the cast of contradictory characters" of which he was composed. In the pages of White's chatty but honest memoir, the reader discovers the curious contradictions of fate that thrust an essentially domestic individual into the midst of some of the more dynamic events of the twentieth century, from the development of a raw continent to the greatest war yet seen by mankind. Although a man with strong geographical and national roots, White nevertheless has spent much of his life caught up in the storms of history, far from his own continent. Yet his artistic vision, his "magic," has remained true to his own rugged Australian world, and to the remarkable cast of characters who have journeyed from that unique land— through his genius—to the immortality of the printed page.

Not that White has always felt at one with his countrymen. On the contrary, he often has been at odds with the rough, proud, and often intolerant and insecure people of Australia. The land itself, however—that vast, unconquered, and unpredictable island continent—he loved and always found consoling. During his various periods of exile over the seven decades of his life, White has found that he was inevitably drawn back to Australia, to the wild, ruthless landscape, even more than to the people, and perhaps this is why his novels—despite their many vivid characterizations—leave the reader primarily with a sense of the land.

White was—and is—he confesses, an "obsessive" writer. He could not *not* write. From adolescence, he tried to make sense of the contradictory, often violent world by capturing it on paper as filtered through his own consciousness. A suggestion of the uncontrollable nature of existence runs through these memoirs. White speculates, without really coming to any conclusion, about the alternate directions his life might have taken: *could* his life and career have turned out any differently than they did? He seems to look back at his successes with awe and wonder, as if to say, "Fancy, *my* words causing all this fuss!"

Although his novels are filled with a violence appropriate to such a rough, dynamic, still-evolving land, Patrick White himself emerges from this book as a gentle, quiet man of enormous sensitivity. He suggests that when he writes, some unknown power takes command, driving him until the work is complete. Looking back at his novels, he is amazed by what he discovers in their pages. On one level, he remarks, he does find in the books a recognizable collage of his personal experiences, but on another level, he does not recognize the personality who seems to be revealed in his works. It is, paradoxically, that unknown man whom the critics and interviewers want to know: it is this literary magician who creates huge landscapes from unknown and hitherto uncharted territories of the soul and who fascinates the world.

Yet, White says, the masks he wears in his fictions are not those that other people expect him to wear in actual life. He is composed of many characters, but not all of them have been revealed to him or, through him, to the world. Entering his eighth decade, he still is embarking on voyages of exploration from which he may yet learn some fragments of truth about himself. It is this humility and this disarming openness that infuses all of his writing and that charges his work with the dynamic of a youthful, vigorous society. It is, he suspects, as if fragments of some universal truth rise continually from the black, bubbling pool that is his essential self, but not all of them are recognized, or even recognizable—even by himself. All he can do is continue to probe and write and discover, until his voyage of exploration crashes against the shores of mortality.

Perhaps the power of this memoir chiefly resides in White's ability to capture the universal in the particular. Casually, he slips in and out of his own past, not always in chronological sequence, and meanders through the gardens of his memories. Yet at the same time, he seems to be carefully assessing the human condition and the pain and beauty of life on earth for every man and woman. In his discussions of his art and craft, White tenderly explores the agonies—and the occasionally sublime joys and triumphs—of the creative artist everywhere.

As a child, White was overwhelmed by his eccentric parents, the relentlessly upper-middle-class Dick and Ruth White, who had no notion of the kind of human being their son was (since they could not conceive of any human being different from themselves), and who later were horrified by his inclinations toward the arts and literature. They never understood Patrick and did not feel obligated to try. *Their* world was the *correct* world; *their* ideas were the *correct* ideas. Patrick's obligation was to conform, or, at least, to put up a front of conformity. Indeed, White came to realize that all his parents cared about was the *appearance* of respectability. They never did understand how he could be indifferent to "appearances."

In some respects, White's personal story is the classic one of the sickly, sensitive youth who never fits in with the bourgeois world of his parents and who eventually flees it to embark on his own quest for personal salvation through art. Yet, when he writes about it, he does so with a touching honesty that raises the story above the familiar. The cast of supporting players, the aunts and uncles and cousins, the godparents and neighbors, are sketched in with the deftness of a Charles Dickens.

One of the primary events of White's life was World War II. He served in the Air Force Intelligence in the Middle East and in London, and his experiences in Egypt, Palestine, and Greece profoundly affected him, changing his perception of the world and altering his future life. He was in London during the Blitz, seeing with his own eyes the horrors of war turned on innocent civilians. The decadent and chaotic life of Alexandria, Egypt, during those years might have provoked White to produce fictions of surrealistic sensuality and stylistic ornateness, in the manner of Lawrence Durrell, but in fact, his time there made him focus ever more firmly on the world he had left behind. As a censor, he discovered in the private letters of the men a new breadth of understanding about the human condition. Every experience added to White's perception and to his determination to reveal his own vision through his writing. As he says, seeds were planted during those violent, drawn-out war years that lay buried in the dark, moist recesses of his heart and mind, seeds that years later bore fruit in the vast garden of his literary work.

It was during the war that White became concerned with the philosophical and moral rationale behind human actions. How do human beings, as individuals and as nations, emerge as they finally do? What forces shape them? What unconscious drives propel them? What torments and fears warp or twist them? He came to have little doubt that entire countries or civilizations can be twisted and corrupted as easily as individuals, yet part of him always retained a belief in the healing power of the land, especially that of the wild homeland he had left behind.

White knew very well that many of his own problems derived from his relationship with his mother, Ruth. Imperious, quick to quarrel, snobbish and essentially shallow, she devoted her life to the pursuit of impossible social goals. Eventually, she gave up her battle to achieve status and respectability— beyond that of the family's nouveau-riche position—in Australian society and fled to England for her last days. Even when he was separated from her, when he was abroad or when she was gone, White found her shadow extending over his life. Even in his seventies, he found it difficult to write objectively of her power over him.

During World War II, while stationed in Palestine, Patrick White met the man who was to become his closest friend and lifelong companion, Manoly Lascaris, a young Egyptian-born Greek. Although sometimes separated by war or other circumstances, White and Lascaris remained partners from the time of their meeting in July, 1941.

Lascaris proved to be a calming influence on White's often impetuous nature. With his encouragement and support, White was able to devote himself to his writing with a renewed dedication. Nevertheless, when White was invited to lunch on the British royal yacht *Britannia* with Queen Elizabeth and Prince Philip, Lascaris was not invited.

Although White threw off the restraints of conventional, organized religion while in his late teens, he embraced art and writing as a different kind of religion. His inklings of God's presence, he writes, must necessarily be interwoven with his love of individual human beings and his love of his art. Perhaps, he adds, that is why he does not extend his love to human beings in general. Yet, no one who reads his novels could doubt his love of humanity, as expressed in the compassionate (although sometimes angry) portraits of his countrymen.

The teachings of Carl G. Jung also profoundly influenced White. He was particularly moved by his first reading of Jung's *Psychologie and Alchemie* (1944; *Psychology and Alchemy*), which had a direct influence on his masterpiece *The Solid Mandala* (1966). During the time when he was composing this novel, White reexamined his spiritual values and realized that for better or worse, his spiritual roots were indeed in the soil of Australia.

"Doomed" to be an artist, the aging White surveys the world around him and realizes that very little beyond his work remains of value to him. Possessions are meaningless, unless one has someone to whom to leave them, and White is childless. His memories, except for those he puts on paper, will die with him. He has had everything, he writes, and nothing. Only love, in the end, redeems; and it was with love that this man, doomed to be an artist, created his "children," his works of art. It is with love that he bequeaths them to the world and to posterity. He tries his best, in this memoir, to be a crabby old man, but his essential humanity triumphs, just as it triumphs in his novels.

Bruce D. Reeves

Sources for Further Study

The Atlantic. CCXLIX, March, 1982, p. 83.
Library Journal. CVII, January 15, 1982, p. 179.
The New Republic. CLXXXVI, March 31, 1982, p. 40.
New Statesman. CII, October 30, 1981, p. 30.
The New York Times Book Review. LXXXVII, February 7, 1982, p. 9.
Newsweek. XCIX, March 1, 1982, p. 71.
Saturday Review. IX, February, 1982, p. 62.
Times Literary Supplement. November 20, 1981, p. 1373.
World Literature Today. LVI, Summer, 1982, p. 569.

FLOOD
Poems

Author: William Matthews (1942-   )
Publisher: Atlantic Monthly Press/Little, Brown and Company (Boston). 72 pp.
$10.00; paperback $6.95
Type of work: Poetry

This new collection of verse marks a major advance in the development of an increasingly major talent

Several years ago (in the *American Scholar*, Summer, 1978), Paul Breslin delivered a powerful attack on a group of poets, including William Matthews, whom he called "the new surrealists." In Breslin's view, these poets are imprisoned in a rigidly Jungian view of the poem as an interior journey, by a Jungian predisposition to refer poetic symbols to archetypes prior to the context of a particular poem and to the personal history of a particular poet, and by a stock poetic diction. Breslin's lexicon of the new poetic diction should sound distressingly familiar to inveterate readers of contemporary American poetry; words such as *stones*, *silence*, *water*, *light*, *absence*, *sleep*, and *darkness* are the stock of much of the going trade. The favorite word of these poets is *stone*; for stone, Breslin argues, is a symbol of the collective unconscious. Breslin's new surrealists reject, implicitly, the ego of Freudian psychology, and participate in a solipsistic, dehumanizing irrationalism, treating the unconscious as a mysterious god.

Although Breslin's essay is brilliant and challenging, many of his generalizations will not stand up when applied to the work of the poets he censures. Such is certainly the case with William Matthews. Matthews' poems from the first have been uncommonly good; since *Broken Syllables* (1969), he has been a good poet getting better, with a variety of tones and subjects at his command. Some of his poems are interior journeys, to be sure, but—others, dramatic, narrative, descriptive, lyric—are public, outward gestures. To reread his earlier books is a pleasure, and one will find in them only a few poems that accommodate Breslin's thesis: for example, "Goodbye Again" (in the 1975 collection *Sticks & Stones*), a poem typified by lines such as these:

> In one pocket the stones
> are laying their eggs.
> I throw my breath
> over my shoulder.

In any case, *Flood* shows that Matthews has emerged as a major poet whose work transcends (and to some extent contradicts) the terms of Breslin's argument.

A specifically personal past, implicitly—and at times explicitly— under-

stood from a Freudian perspective, has always been important in Matthews'
poetry. In an early poem, "Psychoanalysis" (in the 1970 collection *Ruining
the New Road*), Matthews trolls the surface of the past in a "glass- bottomed
boat . . . letting down/ the line" to where the "parents and siblings lurk/
among the coral with thick eyes" in the hope that "it will come up slick/ with
significance, laden/ with the sweet guilt you can name." Much of *Flood* is
reminiscence; one memorable poem, "Housework," describes the poet's boyhood room. There "the tiniest socks ever knit/ are crumpled on a chair." The
boy the poet was sleeps "like a cat in a drawer,/ in this house memory is
always dusting." The poem itself is the act of dusting, a saving act because
reminiscence is a "lie of memory unless it be made clean." Far from fleeing
from the ego and its guilts, as Breslin describes the central impulse of his
"new contemporary poets," Matthews seeks to encounter a historical self and
to understand the predicaments that make such an encounter difficult to
achieve. Thus, he remarks in "Our Strange and Lovable Weather,"

> anyplace lies about its weather,
> just as we lie about our childhoods,
> and for the same reason: we can't
> say surely what we've undergone,
> and need to know, and need to know.

Perhaps there is something self-consciously Frostian in Matthews' repetition
of "need to know," an imitation of Frost's repetition of "and miles to go
before I sleep." As he emerges as a major poet, Matthews' connection with
strong poetic precursors becomes increasingly clear. Undoubtedly the father
of Matthews' poetic style—and of that of innumerable other contemporary
poets—is William Carlos Williams, with Walt Whitman as a shadowy grand-
sire, but there are two poets, stronger than Williams, who together establish
the best context in which to read Matthews: Robert Frost and A. R. Ammons.
Matthews' allegiance to Frost is openly proclaimed in *Flood*, for Frost is the
sort of major predecessor who can be openly acknowledged. Matthews' relationship to Ammons, on the other hand, is covert, for Ammons is too powerful
and contemporary a figure to acknowledge publicly without feeling the autonomy of one's own poetic style threatened.

In the last poem in *Flood*, "On the Porch of the Frost Place, Franconia,
NH," the poet reflects on Frost:

> For cash crops he had sweat and doubt
> and moralizing rage, those staples
> of the barter system. And these swift
> and aching summers, like the blackberries
> I've been poaching down the road
> from the house where no one's home—

In that last line especially, Matthews assumes Frost's voice, and one reenters with him the lost upland world of Frost's "Directive." Contemplating the view from Frost's porch, the poet thinks he sees

> the parts—haze, dusk, light
> broken into grains, fatigue,
> the mineral dark of the White Mountains,
> the wavering shadows steadying themselves—
> separate, then joined, then seamless:
> the way, in fact, Frost's great poems,
> like all great poems, conceal
> what they merely know, to be
> predicaments.

In one of the finest poems in *Flood*, "Bystanders," the fourth in the volume, Matthews writes a blank verse reminiscence strikingly similar to Frost's monologues, recalling especially poems such as "Out, Out":

> Over the hillbrow one mile up the road
> came two pale headlights and the whine
> of a car doing fifty downhill through
> four tufted inches of snow atop a thin
> sheet of new ice. That shut us up,
> and we turned in thrall, like grass
> in wind, to watch the car and all
> its people die. Their only chance
> would be never to brake, but to let
> the force of their folly carry them, as if
> it were a law of physics. . . .

The car crashes over a "boulder-and-stump-/ strewn meadow"; the driver, who turns out to be its only occupant, is killed; and the poem concludes:

> So we began to ravel from the stunned
> calm single thing we had become
> by not dying, and the county cleared
> the turn and everyone went home, and, while
> the plow dragged up the slick hill the staunch
> clank of its chains, the county cleared the field.

Thus alluded to near the beginning of *Flood* and referred to by name in the concluding poem, Frost is an inalienable presence throughout the book.

The presence of Ammons is, by contrast, covert. *Flood* is divided into three numbered sections. The first is devoted to poems that revolve around the idea of time, past, present, and future ("we disappear into the past/ and into the future at once"); the second is apparently a miscellany of meditative, lyric, confessional, and occasional poems; while the third section is the most obviously coherent. All of the poems in it refer, literally or figuratively, to water and to flooding. In "The Waters," there is a beautiful description of a "bright day when the wind is down/ and the waters move only to groom/ themselves," which leads into a statement about the impulse to poetry:

> you'll rise
> to the sacraments of memory and lie down
> unable to forget what you can't name,
> and the wine in your glass will be ink.

In "Taken at the Flood," rain is the occasion for thinking of "loving your children wrongly":

> and all
> your fatal habits will see
> you through, though you
> rant against them:
> lordly as the froth
> on the lip of the waterfall,
> you urge them to carry you
> over, and they do.

"Record Flood" seems to be literal in its description of rain that "pumped snakes from their holes," but bracketed by "The Waters" and "Taken at the Flood," the waters of "Record Flood" are infused with symbolism. In "Unrelenting Flood," the water is purely metaphoric; the unrelenting flood is the impulse of joy that underlies the creative act. In "Flood Time," by contrast, the water is the solvent of tears, "ready when we are" to give vent to grief. When Matthews sums up in the closing poem of the section, "Everywhere," the Ammonsian tone is unmistakable:

> By the way its every
> event is local and exact,
> and by the reluctance of water
> to rise and the way it climbs
> its reluctance, so shall you know
> flood, and by the way it compiles
> the erasure of its parts
> and takes to itself the local
> until all but sky is water.
> On this huge page no breath
> will write. The text is already
> there, restless, revising itself.

Like Ammons, Matthews is more playful and more dryly metaphysical than the kind of poet Breslin seems bent on caricaturing.

Matthews is a witty poet. Better yet, he is an often funny one, a skilled

manager of comic effects. The deepest current of humor running through his
poetry turns against himself. In "Descriptive Passages," he imagines how
someday his middle-aged children will remember him and his perennially
"drunk hair":

> I give them good wine to talk by,
> I've lit them a fire if it's cold.
> I can't leave them alone, I think
> from the grave: a father's work
> is never done.

In "Pissing off the Back of the Boat into the Nivernais Canal," the poet shakes

> my shriveled nozzle and three drops lurk
> out like syllables
> from before there were languages. Snug
> in my pants it will leak a whole sentence
> in Latin

In the end he thinks,

>   as I drizzle
> to sleep . . . how much
> the imagination makes
> of its body of work
> a place to recover itself."

Matthews' humor is the leavening in the work of an imagination that "knows
itself/ to be tragic and thereby silly."

Humor and the Ammonsian idea of the poem as a sanctuary where the
imagination repairs and cleanses itself—these are the buoyant foundations of
a body of work that, with *Flood*, Matthews is more than ever building large
and clean and high, a spacious house that "memory is always dusting."

Daniel Mark Fogel

Sources for Further Study

Choice. XX, September, 1982, p. 86.
Georgia Review. XXXVI, Fall, 1982, p. 675.
Library Journal. CVII, April 1, 1982, p. 733.
Publishers Weekly. CCXXI, March 12, 1982, p. 82.

THE FOUR WISE MEN

Author: Michel Tournier (1924-   )
Translated from the French by Ralph Manheim
Publisher: Doubleday & Company (Garden City, New York). 255 pp. $14.95
Type of work: Novel
Time: The birth of Christ
Locale: Meroë, Nippur, Palmyra, Mangalore, and Palestine

Each of the three wise men tells the story of his journey to pay tribute to the Christ-child, but the longer story of a legendary fourth wise man enriches the mythic significance of the event

> *Principal characters:*
> GASPAR, the King of Meroë
> BALTHASAR, the King of Nippur
> MELCHIOR, the Prince of Palmyra
> HEROD THE GREAT, the King of the Jews
> TAOR, the Prince of Mangalore

In less than twenty years, Michel Tournier has come to be regarded internationally as a major writer. His novels are best-sellers in France and have been translated into eighteen languages. All four of his novels have been published in the United States and a collection of short stories, *Le Coq de bruyère* (1978), is scheduled to appear in 1984. Among his works of nonfiction are *Canada: Journal de voyage* (1977) and two volumes of essays, *Le Vent paraclet* (1977) and *Des Clefs et des serrures* (1979). He is not as well-known in the United States as the quality of his work merits.

Some knowledge of Tournier's background illuminates his fiction. Born in Paris of parents who were German scholars, he studied at the universities of Paris and of Tübingen. A student of Claude Lévi-Strauss, he earned master's degrees in law and in philosophy. He produced programs on photography for French television, for which he was also a cultural consultant; he was a newspaperman for several years; and for a decade, he was literary director at Éditions Plon. A bachelor, he lives in an old vicarage twenty-five miles from Paris in the Chèvreuse Valley.

Mythological conceptions that lend a transcendent quality to documentary facts govern all Tournier's fiction. All of his central characters share Tournier's obsession with processes of metamorphosis, transfiguration, and inversion, terms that characterize his style. "There's a secret collusion, deep down, connecting what happens to me with what happens in general," says Abel Tiffauges in Tournier's second novel, *Le Roi des aulnes* (1970; *The Ogre*, 1972). For Tournier's characters, everyday life becomes filled with signs and symbols that have mythological significance. Abel sees "experience as an inversion of values"; he is "alert to changes in signs, from benign to malign, from malign to benign." His vocation is "not only to decipher essences but also to exalt them, to bring all their qualities to the point of incandescence."

In *Vendredi: Ou, Les Limbes du Pacifique* (1967; *Friday*, 1969), a close retelling of Daniel Defoe's *Robinson Crusoe* (1719), Tournier implies analogies between a classic work of literature and contemporary everyday life. An example of this rare genre in American literature is John Seelye's "adult" version of Mark Twain's *The Adventures of Huckleberry Finn* (1884). The point of view of Tournier's novel is not first person, as is Defoe's, but third person omniscient, with journal entries in first person as contrast. Seen as inverted twins, Robinson and Friday anticipate the theme of Tournier's third novel, *Les Météores* (1975; *Gemini*, 1981); and racial concepts of black and white become even more important in *The Four Wise Men*. *Friday* won the Grand Prix du Roman of the Académie Française, and the *Chicago Tribune* listed it as one of the outstanding books of the year. Tournier also wrote a children's version, *Vendredi: Ou, La Vie sauvage* (1971; *Friday and Robinson: Life on Esperanza Island*, 1972).

In *The Ogre*, Abel the giant, a benign ogre, like St. Christopher the Christ-bearer, pursues his destiny as a childbearer. Tournier sees mythic patterns in World War II and the Holocaust. *The Ogre* was the first unanimous winner of the Prix Goncourt, and Janet Flanner called it "the most important book to come out in France since Proust." It is one of the most intellectually demanding novels of recent years; it is also one of the most sensuous. One thinks of William Gaddis' *The Recognitions* (1955).

In *Gemini*, Tournier explores numerous facets of the concept of twins to project a vision of life. Similarly, in his fourth novel, a major myth of Christian civilization, enhanced by an apocryphal dimension, provides Tournier with another way of conceptualizing all human experience in symbolic terms. The French title is *Gaspar, Melchior, and Balthazar* (1980). The American title, *The Four Wise Men*, simplifies, perhaps distorts by overemphasis, Tournier's unique approach.

In a sense, three of the Evangelists, like Taor, the fourth wise man, missed the adoration of the Magi. The basis for Tournier's novel is found only in the Gospel of Matthew (2:1-16). Tournier imagines everything else. Many writers have been attracted to the "What if. . . ?" possibilities inherent in famous legends, myths, and historical events. Old and New Testament possibilities have attracted Thomas Mann (*Joseph und seine Brüder*, 1933-1942; *Joseph and His Brothers*, 1934-1944), Paul Claudel (*L'Annonce faile à Marie*, 1912; *The Tidings Brought to Mary*, 1916), André Gide (*Le Retour de l'enfant prodigue*, 1907; *Return of the Prodigal Son*, 1953, in which a new character is introduced), and, more recently, in America, William Goyen (*A Book of Jesus*, 1973) and Romulus Linney (*Jesus Tales*, 1980).

There are seven facets to Tournier's vision of the legend of the Magi, with a different character focus for each. Tournier has Gaspar, King of Meroë, tell his story first to set up several of the ironic paradoxes, inversions, affinities, and parallels for which he has a kind of obsession. "I am black, but I am a king," Gaspar begins. He bought and fell in love with a white slave, whom he imagines saying, "I am a slave but I am blond!" In his kingdom, whites are despised, but his blonde slave takes possession of his life, causing him to hate his negritude. She spurns Gaspar for her fellow-slave, a blond who she implies is her brother. Hoping to forget her, Gaspar travels, following the path of a golden comet, "a head dragging a train of flowing hair behind it." He is told that a "journey . . . is a series of irrevocable disappearances." The gait of his she-camel "favors metaphysical speculation." The sight of the two colossi of Memnon moves him to meditations that anticipate the Virgin Mother and the Christ-child. In Hebron, he meets Balthasar, King of Nippur; they talk in the cave of Machpelah, "which harbors the tombs of Adam and Eve." "Legends live on our substance," he meditates, suggesting the response which Tournier seeks to the testimonials of all of his characters: "If we cannot recognize our own story in them, they are dead wood and dry straw." There in the cave, Balthasar meditates on the biblical notion that "God made man in his image and likeness" and sets in motion a line of thought that makes Gaspar conclude that Adam was black, as he is, but that Eve, like his beloved blonde slave, was white. "Is it not conceivable that the aim of our journey is the exaltation of negritude?"

Balthasar begins his briefer story with an account of his meeting with Gaspar, then flashes back to the reasons for his journey. His own obsession has always been with art: "The one passion of my youth was the love of pure, simple beauty." Tournier offers an awesome image of the butterfly as the incarnation of pure beauty; Balthasar's meditation on butterflies, which he collects, extends over ten pages. "Can you conceive of any more sublime transfiguration than that which starts with a gray, crawling caterpillar and ends with a butterfly?" asks a man who is teaching him the complexities of butterflies. Like most of Tournier's symbols, the butterfly is polyvalent, standing for several things equally well.

When he was a young man, Balthasar found in Greece the nourishment the soul of an aesthete craves; travel became an aspect of his aesthetic vocation. He collects various works of art, "all those figurations of life which exhort us to rise above ourselves." He falls in love with the portrait of a pale, blue-eyed girl and marries a girl who resembles it; their daughter becomes an even clearer likeness. With his pages, he travels again to Greece, where this time he finds not gods, but men. He builds a "Balthasareum," in which to display an eclectic collection of the world's art, "mirabilia," as he calls them; he organizes his pages into a secret society of Narcissi. To the priests, his treasures are sacrilegious images and idols; they incite a mob to destroy the Balthesareum. Seeing the comet as a fiery butterfly, the portent of a "benign revolution," the oldest of the four wise men sets out on a journey that is "an unbroken celebration." His story ends as he meets Gaspar in the cave.

The shortest and least interesting of the journey narratives is told by young Melchior, Prince of Palmyra, a pink city built by King Solomon. In an attempt to usurp the throne, Melchior's uncle kills his father and holds his mother hostage. To save his mother, he flees, accompanied by his old preceptor who thus saves his life. To elude his uncle's hired assassins, they walk as beggars through the country. Just as the two other kings, with different intentions, arrive, Melchior's secret wanderings bring him accidentally to Jerusalem. Like Mary and Joseph, he spends the night at a third-rate inn. To prove his identity as heir-apparent, he carries a gold coin bearing the image of his father. His ideal is a new social order in which there will be no kings, bandits, or beggars (Christ is to become a beggar king). Almost half of Melchior's story is devoted to a description of Herod and his reign. Melchior, Gaspar, and Balthasar finally meet Herod when he gives a feast in their honor.

After the three wise men have told their own personal stories, with acute consciousness of mythic and symbolic implications, Tournier has a professional, Oriental storyteller present an emblematic fable at the insistence of King Herod. The fourth section is given over to "King Goldbeard, or the Problem of Succession." For some readers, this fable may mystify more than it elucidates.

Within each narrative, a pattern takes shape and is developed further in successive sections. Numerous signs and symbols overtly point the way along the narrative thrusts. It may seem to some readers, about halfway through, that this novel is merely an exercise in symbolism with a few brilliant flashes. For readers of Tournier's first three novels, the author's obsession with pattern-making may be wearying at first, but Herod's monologue and the ninety-page story of Taor, the fourth wise man, are as exhilarating as any of Tournier's previous work.

The thirty pages of Herod's dramatic monologue, set in an omniscient frame, have a powerful narrative thrust, enhanced by meditative moments. He speaks to each of the three wise men, criticizing their ways of dealing with their problems, then tells them how he has dealt treacherously with problems of his own that parallel theirs. "I am a king but I'm dying." Having experienced almost everything, "I'm the unhappiest man in the whole world, the most betrayed friend, the most flouted husband, the most defied father, and the most hated despot in history." For him, the star is the white bird in the golden egg that was spoken of in "King Goldbeard." He implores the three kings to visit the Babe in Bethlehem and, as an act of fidelity and good faith, report to him. They are "borne by a tenderly jubilant intimation that a new era might be opening before them." Each meditates on parallels between his own life and Herod's, "and all three, each in his own way, tried to imagine the little King of the Jews," a paradoxical King of transformation and benign inversions.

"The Ass and the Ox" is a brief interlude. Tournier gives, very briefly, in the third person, the attitude of the ox, who represents the old order. Standing in the manger, he is unimpressed "by a god born in a stable to a maiden and the Holy Ghost!" Tethered next to the ox is an ass who has a horror of oxen. "I am a poor man's ass." White-haired, with a star on his forehead, he speaks in a sarcastic tone. He overhears a satirical dialogue between the Angel Gabriel and a shepherd about Abraham's near-sacrifice of Isaac "a failed revolution." Gabriel promises that there will be no more sacrificial lambs now that The Lamb of God is born. Nor will the asses be forgotten this time. The new king will ride into Jerusalem on an ass. "The rich are insatiable. They want to own everything, even poverty." They even steal Christmas.

The longest of the seven narratives is the story of Taor, told appropriately from the omniscient point of view. Taor, the twenty-year-old Indian Prince of Mangalore, is a hedonist, an epicurean. A gift comes to him from the Occident: pistachio "Turkish delight." It is so delectable, he must find the secret recipe. Rather than send his cold, intelligent, ambitious slave, Siri, to find it, Taor, who has seldom gone outside the palace gardens, never beyond the boundaries of his kingdom, sets out to "elucidate the mystery of the little Levantine sweetmeat." "The imminent invention of a transcendent food" is predicted. The Divine Confectioner, some think, will be born in Bethlehem. Taor demands "concrete proof, material evidence, something one could see, touch, or better still, eat." He, too, tries to find the Babe, but he arrives too late. His subsequent journey takes him out of an "Age of Sugar" into thirty years of "Salt Hell" in a Roman mine.

One may feel that Tournier's imaginative conception of the nature and tribulations of the fourth wise man is a clever contrivance, and it is; but the ending of his story lends it and all that has gone before a magnificence rare in contemporary fiction. An impressive and moving narrative that could stand alone, it is full of surprises with profound significance that no review should reveal.

In Tournier's fiction, the literalness and the temperament of the photographer is extended into the realm of myth and symbolic concepts. Tournier the mythmaker has the journalist's mania for documentation. One suspects him of plundering encyclopedias. His style, the same for all the narrators in *The Four Wise Men*, except for the ass's monologue, has the formal, rhetorical qualities of the old-fashioned omniscient narrator. He is garrulously philosophical. He seldom employs the modern writer's device of implication; his brilliant conceptions stun and stir the reader but deny him the participation in the creative process that implication would provide. These seemingly negative observations point, however, to the peculiar joys of reading Tournier. The most distinctive pleasure the reader experiences comes as he watches

Tournier self-consciously develop several patterns simultaneously. No other writer approaches Tournier in what is most distinctive about his art: his overt use of symbolic conceptualization. He has the rare power of being able to change a reader's way of looking at all living creatures and their acts.

David Madden

Sources for Further Study

America. CXLVII, November 13, 1982, p. 297.
The Atlantic. CCL, October, 1982, p. 105.
Library Journal. CVII, October 15, 1982, p. 2006.
National Review. XXXIV, October 15, 1982, p. 1290.
New Statesman. CIV, November 19, 1982, p. 27.
The New York Times Book Review. LXXXVII, October 24, 1982, p. 14.
Publishers Weekly. CCXXII, August 13, 1982, p. 66.

GEORGE MILLS

Author: Stanley Elkin (1930-   )
Publisher: E. P. Dutton (New York). 508 pp. $15.95
Type of work: Novel
Time: The eleventh, nineteenth, and twentieth centuries
Locale: England; Poland; Constantinople; Cassadaga, Florida; St. Louis, Missouri;
and Juárez, Mexico

Written in five parts and set in various locales and historical periods, the novel traces
the misadventures of a long line of George Millses, who claim to be fated to lead second-
rate lives but who in fact doom themselves because they prefer their extraordinary fate
to ordinary human life

> *Principal characters:*
> GEORGE MILLS, the last of the Mills line
> LOUISE, his wife
> NANCY, his mother
> GEORGE MILLS, SR., his father
> LAGLICHIO, his employer
> GREATEST GRANDFATHER, the first George Mills
> GEORGE XLIII, the Mills who was sent to Constantinople by
>   King George IV of England
> CORNELL MESSENGER, a second-rate writer
> JUDITH GLAZER, a dying woman who hires Mills to accompany her
>   to Mexico
> HARRY CLAUNCH, Judith's brother
> REVEREND WICKLAND, a spiritualist

Stanley Elkin, the author of six novels and two collections of shorter fiction, is a maddeningly elusive writer whose work defies easy classification. His novels are, page-by-page, brilliantly and inventively composed, but they are also plotless, digressive, and therefore, say some reviewers, badly flawed. Yet his shorter fictions, excepting the novella *The Bailbondsman* (1973), are for all their unity less satisfying than his novels. Chronicler of the most outrageous vulgarities of American popular culture, he nevertheless treats them sympathetically, even lovingly, as if he were a combination Walt Whitman-Jewish comedian. Yet to call Elkin a chronicler of his times is to overlook the dense texture of his prose, which, unlike Theodore Dreiser or Sinclair Lewis, he produces at the painstaking rate of a page a day. (*George Mills*, for example, took seven years to complete.) This emphasis on narrative disruption and pyrotechnic style suggests Elkin's affinity to post-Modernist writers such as his close friend, William Gass; while Elkin's fiction has all of Gass's artifice and precision, however, it has neither Gass's cold detachment nor Thomas Pynchon's academic trappings. In the recent debate over the purpose of fiction begun by John Gardner in *On Moral Fiction* (1978) and argued more forcefully by Gerald Graff in *Literature Against Itself* (1979), Elkin is one writer who uses his extravagant style in the service of human values rather than literary hermeticism—a position that keeps him outside both the avant-garde and the traditionalist camps and inimitably on his own.

Winner of the National Book Critics Circle Award for Best Fiction of 1982, *George Mills* is, with *The Franchiser* (1976), the most successful of Elkin's characteristically odd novels. Part family saga, part confession, and part picaresque, *George Mills* has a beginning and an end but a wildly jumbled middle filled with seeming digressions (one of which is 113 pages long), lurching shifts in time, place, and point of view, and interpolated passages set off from the "main" story by parentheses and brackets. Instead of using plot, Elkin organizes his novel around his central personality, following the logical consequences that flow from placing this character in certain situations. In *George Mills*, this character is the last in a long (some fifty generations) and distinctly pedestrian line of George Millses. The lengthy sections devoted to the misadventures of Greatest Grandfather at the time of the First Crusade (1097), of George XLIII in the early nineteenth century, and of George's father shortly before and during the Depression are not extraneous to the novel; they are integral parts of the Mills legacy and serve to establish the current George's Millsness.

In many ways, George is a typical Elkin protagonist. He is obsessed, powerless, isolated, unkind, and prone to self-pity; most important, he has a compulsive need to tell his story, to explain himself to everyone and anyone, including the dispossessed blacks whose furniture he carts away for his employer, Laglichio. In other ways, however, Mills is atypical among Elkin's protagonists. He is too humorless, too passive, too satisfied with his unsatisfying life; he has no aspirations, no quest, no energy, no desire for community; also, he lacks some of the verbal flashiness and virtually all of the "*heroic* extravagance" that Elkin bestows on his favored characters. Moreover, George feels "saved, lifted from life," his "will and soul idling like a car at a stoplight," sure that nothing will happen to him. His salvation is, as one expects in Elkin, ironic. In the scene in which the saved Mills indifferently, even mechanically, masturbates his wife—a scene that is, like so much of Elkin's fiction, precariously balanced between comedy and horror—the reader understands that in trying to protect himself from life's pains, Mills has withdrawn not only from others, including his wife, but also from whatever would make him human. Unlike Elkin, who agrees with the William Faulkner character who says, "Between grief and nothing I will take grief," Mills unwisely chooses nothing.

The cause of George's predicament is his Millsness. Although a number of other Elkin characters are affected by their past—Feldman's salesman father in *A Bad Man* (1967), for example, or Ben Flesh and the inheritance from his godfather in *The Franchiser*—only Mills carries the burden of a nine-hundred-year family history that began when Gillalume, "a sissy sir," "doomed" his servant, the first George Mills, and "cursed" his race: "Learn this Mills.

There are distinctions between men, humanity is dealt out like a deck of cards. There is natural suzereignty like the face value on coins. Men have their place. . . . It isn't luck of the draw but the brick walls of some secret, sovereign Architecture that makes us so." It is neither curse nor fate, however, that dooms the Millses; it is the Mills *story* which they take so seriously, so humorlessly. Passed down orally from father to son, always assumed to be true but never verified, the Mills history has no status other than as fiction, as family myth. Thus, the Millses are doomed by their own credulity, their failure to imagine for themselves any other than a cursed life, and their choosing, albeit unknowingly, to perpetuate the Mills myth by telling and retelling their stale story and by naming the son George in generation after generation.

George nearly comes to understand this simple fact when, in his youth, a spiritualist named Wickland tells George about his parents. As Wickland explains, any George Mills could have broken the chain; none did "Because people are suckers for fate, for all the scars to which they think they're entitled." Seeing themselves as victims—history has thwarted them, tied their hands, controlled their destiny—even gives a certain tragic dignity to their self-inflicted sufferings and shortcomings and at the same time effectively excuses them from responsibility for their lives. Elkin, whose muse is "Serendipity," believes not in fate but in an arbitrary world ruled by "whim." Whim, however, including the "controlled whim" of art, is one thing the George Millses have never accepted. George's Oedipus-like attempt to escape his fate (by fleeing from the spiritualist camp at Cassadaga, Florida, and from his parents) cannot succeed because even in his flight, he continues to believe the Mills myth. Instead of abdicating his role as myth-victim in the Millses' nine-hundred-year slapstick history, George carries his self-imposed burden with him.

Among those whom George meets by chance during the course of his whimsical odyssey, two are of special importance both for the light they shed on Mills and for the way their vibrant characters and stories outstrip Mills and his family saga. For all their differences, Mills and Cornell Messenger, a well-to-do university writer, are similar in many ways. Both are middle-aged, passive, burdened with family problems, burned-out, conscious of being second-rate, and submissive to fate; both are heirs (George of his Millsness, Messenger of his aunt's wealth), both are storytellers (one by compulsion, the other by profession), and finally, both are go-betweens. It is through Messenger that George meets Judith Glazer, who, although dying of pancreatic cancer, is the novel's most vital character. A compulsive mischief-maker, she takes pleasure in humiliating her family and friends, betraying their secrets and trivializing what they hold important. Herself betrayed and humiliated by cancer, Judith responds with all the bitterness that Elkin's powerless characters can muster. She is, in Elkin's view, the human situation in extremis, and because she fights back, her bitterness is rendered in nearly heroic terms as she translates her pain and humiliation into the language of the impotent—sarcasm: "God is good," she tells Mills in Mexico. "He really is. He's a genius. He creates the poor and homeless and gives them a warm climate to sleep it off in."

Although Mills travels to Mexico as Judith's employee, her paid companion and chauffeur, the relationship soon deepens. As her condition worsens, he becomes her sole visitor, her friend, nurse, brother, and, of course, her audience. When in her pain, the hallucinating woman screams "Marco," it is Mills who plays her deadly serious child's game, soothing her with his answering "Polo," and it is Mills who, having heard her litany of quotidian losses and complaints, the "I never had's" which end with "and I never had all the shrimp I could eat," brings her a large bag of boiled shrimp—a comic yet utterly moving gesture. These understated signs of affection and compassion contrast with the reader's earlier view of Mills as a man unable or unwilling to love. (The "nonreciprocity of desire," as one character calls it, is one of Elkin's recurrent themes.) For a time, George breaks free of his Millsness and is not indifferent to any despair but his own, but if Judith's dying brings out the best in Mills, then her death brings out the worst. The *inter vivos* trust Judith leaves her husband and daughters results in a legal contest (as she maliciously planned), and for a time, Mills has a measure of power: both sides want his affidavit. Mills discovers that the wealthy and powerful are dependent on the Millses of the world and always have been dependent on them. The reader discovers something more: that the difference between the powerful Claunches and the lowly Millses is less important than the anguish, suffering, and death that bind them together. There is a certain poetic justice in Harry Claunch's refusal to help the man who helped his sister; as Claunch explains, "You're a guy gets a kick out of other men's power." Claunch is right, for George does envy power, but it is also true that George has come to understand the depth of his loneliness and to grieve, not entirely selfishly, for the love he has never received or given.

For a while, the world does seem to conform to George's Mills-induced preference for unhappy endings—lost jobs, disinherited husbands, psychologically disturbed and brain-damaged children, marriages ending either in death or divorce—but then suddenly, queerly, "things work out," as Messenger, "the epilogue man," says. Having neither confidence nor hope, George is isolated from that vision of community, of reciprocated love, for which so many of Elkin's characters yearn. Not having fathered a son, George has finally broken the Mills chain, but in the worst possible way, for now he has no one to whom he can tell his story. *George Mills* does not end, however, on this ironic note: in a lay sermon delivered to a Baptist congregation, reminiscent of Fred Clumly's sermon at the end of John Gardner's *The Sunlight Dialogues* (1972), George finds his talk turning into a confession, and along the way, he makes a number of important discoveries: that he is not saved; that he has been "stuck in his grace like a ship sunk in the sea"; that there never was a curse; that life is not a curse; that he is not all alone—all people are his brothers and sisters; that his desires are theirs as well—that desire is universal, not personal; and, finally, that "I ain't saved. I spent my life like there was a hole in my pocket, and the meaning of life is to live long enough to find something out or to do something well. It ain't just to put up with it." George's discoveries are rather unstartling, even trite, but that is exactly Elkin's point: the clichés *are* true, the ordinary *is* extraordinary. That, not nine hundred years of fate, is George's serendipitous discovery.

Robert A. Morace

Sources for Further Study

Christian Science Monitor. February 9, 1983, p. 15.
Harper's Magazine. CCLXV, November, 1982, p. 74.
Library Journal. CVII, September 1, 1982, p. 1675.
Los Angeles Times Book Review. October 31, 1982, p. 3.
The New Republic. CLXXXVII, December 27, 1982, p. 37.
The New York Times Book Review. LXXXVII, October 31, 1982, p. 11.
Newsweek. C, October 25, 1982, p. 117.
Publishers Weekly. CCXXII, August 20, 1982, p. 58.
Time. CXX, November 1, 1982, p. 79.

THE GIFT

Author: H. D. (Hilda Doolittle, 1886-1961)
Edited, with an introduction, by Perdita Schaffner
Publisher: New Directions (New York). 142 pp. $14.95; paperback $5.95
Type of work: Memoir
Time: The 1890's and 1941-1943
Locale: Bethlehem and suburban Philadelphia, Pennsylvania; and London, England

A distinguished poet's recollections of her childhood seen from the perspective of war-ravaged London during the Blitz

> *Principal personages:*
> HILDA DOOLITTLE, the author
> CHARLES DOOLITTLE, her father
> HELEN DOOLITTLE, her mother
> GILBERT DOOLITTLE, her older brother
> HAROLD DOOLITTLE, her younger brother
> FRANCIS WOLLE, her grandfather
> ELIZABETH WOLLE, her grandmother

Imagist poet H. D. spent much of World War II in her London apartment, where, with her longtime friend, the novelist Bryher, she endured many nights of German bombings. The events of these years sent her back into the memories of her childhood in search of answers to the questions raised by the senseless horrors that surrounded her. The result of this quest into the past was *The Gift*, now edited and published in full for the first time by the author's daughter, Perdita Schaffner, who has also contributed a moving introduction to the work describing the circumstances of its composition.

The book is one that works on several levels. It is first, and most obviously, a vivid memoir of a Pennsylvania childhood during the 1890's, a reflection of life in the Moravian town of Bethlehem, Pennsylvania, and in a village outside Philadelphia, where the author's family settled in 1895. The details of this period in her life, however, are carefully chosen and linked by H. D. to incorporate many of the themes that preoccupied her for much of her career— time and eternity, the nature of reality, religion, and mythology.

Young Hilda Doolittle's life, as it is depicted here, was in most ways a happy one, filled with creative activities, memorable excursions, and the companionship of a large and affectionate family that extended beyond parents and grandparents to include aunts, uncles, and cousins. She was the only surviving daughter of Charles and Helen Doolittle, a fact that assumed considerable significance for her later. Her father was a distinguished astronomer, a professor at Lehigh University and then at the University of Pennsylvania. Her mother, the descendant of generations of devout Moravians, centered her life on her husband and children. She seemed fulfilled as wife and mother, but she somehow conveyed to her daughter her sense of regret that she had given up the music that was once her special gift.

The other most important figures in Hilda's life at this time were the two brothers nearest her in age—Gilbert, two years older, and Harold, a year younger—and her maternal grandparents, whom she called Mamalie and Papalie. Her grandfather, principal of a Moravian seminary in Bethlehem and a scientist like her father, introduced her to the wonders of life in a drop of water under a microscope and contributed to the magical feeling of the Moravian Christmas by modeling tiny clay sheep for the children's manger scene. Though he died before the family moved to Philadelphia, when Hilda was about nine, he remained vivid in her memory. His wife survived, her mind clouded by age, long enough to share with her granddaughter her vision of an early spiritual pact between a group of Moravians and Indians, an episode that was to be crucial to the author's understanding of her world.

The Gift brilliantly conveys the thought-patterns of the child, whose mind absorbs detail without analyzing and moves rapidly from one subject to another by a process of association. Using the same skills that allowed her to distill experience with perfect clarity in her Imagist poems, the author makes her memories live for the reader. Most striking, perhaps, is her re-creation of the Moravian Christmas, more an overwhelming sensation of happiness than an annual event, a feeling composed of the scent of the dried pine needles left in the paper wrappings around the glass Christmas tree ornaments, of the stumps of beeswax candles and Papalie's clay sheep, of a treasured collection of wooden animals—polar bear, deer, lynx, camel. These animals became symbols both of the author's love for her father and of the permanence of special moments in life. She returns throughout the book to the wintry evening, just before Christmas, when her father took her with Gilbert and Harold on an unprecedented shopping trip to a toy store and instructed them to choose a gift they could enjoy together. The happiness of this excursion crystallized for the author in a picture of snow swirling around a lamppost, one of the major images in the book.

H. D. conveys her childhood emotions equally effectively in her recounting of a far more traumatic episode, again one involving her father. Returning on the streetcar from Philadelphia one night, he had an accident of some kind and reached his home in a stupor, bleeding and unresponsive to his daughter when she went out to meet him. She led him to his study and began to wipe his bloody face with a wet towel, baffled and terrified by his blank expression. Her shock is evident in every line of this section, in her dissociation from her actions, her mechanical wringing out of the bloodstained towel, her awareness of isolated objects in the room, her sense that nothing was quite real: "The clock stood there and ticked and it was a clock that belonged to a story." After what seemed to her an interminable time, adults came to help; what she later remembered was that no one praised her for her presence of mind or attempted to reassure the children about what had happened. Their father had had a concussion, someone finally told them. Hilda asked what "concussion" meant but received no satisfactory answer. The scars of this incident went so deep into her memory that this was the event that rose up in her mind in connection with the concussion of the bombs and heavy guns in London during the Blitz—the senseless, unexplained horror.

The third crucial incident described in detail is a conversation Hilda had with her grandmother on a summer evening when she had heard her parents and friends discussing shooting stars. Frightened by the thought of stars that might "fall on us and fall on the house and burn us all to death," she asked her grandmother where shooting stars got their name. Her question aroused a train of reflections in the older woman's mind, and she began to speak, half to herself, half to the child. Hilda found herself with a series of new identities as her grandmother remembered different stages of her past and called the child Helen, Aggie, Lucy—the names of her daughters and an old friend. Hilda carefully put herself into each role, responding as she thought her mother or aunt would have done, so that she would not interrupt the fascinating story that was coming to her in bits and pieces. It took years for her to put together the fragments, but even as she listened she was entranced by the story of a mid-eighteenth century meeting between Indian Chief Shooting Star, Princess Morning Star, and a group of Moravians which included a woman named Anna von Pahlen and her husband, John Christopher Frederick Cammerhof. They met at a place called *Wunden Eiland*, the Isle of Wounds, to celebrate together a liturgy honoring the spirit they worshiped under different names.

A century after this meeting, Hilda's grandmother and her first husband read a parchment describing the ritual and apparently had a visionary experience in which they relived this moment of unity and exaltation with the original group. Hilda, listening, was fascinated by the German words that punctuated the story and by the new insight into her grandmother. She could hardly believe what she was hearing, yet she worked hard to say the right things to keep Mamalie talking, to avoid jarring her back into the present, when she might realize that she was speaking to Hilda, not Helen or Lucy, and send the child to bed. The story of *Wunden Eiland* remained in the child's memory, intertwined with a shadowy tale of an Indian massacre, her father's bleeding face, and eventually with the *"Storm of Death"* beating down on London as she wrote.

There are other significant but less fully developed incidents woven into the memoir: the burning of a girl in the school where Papalie was principal; a performance of Harriet Beecher Stowe's *Uncle Tom's Cabin* (1852) by a touring company; a visit to the home of an old gentleman whose young gardener gave her a lily; the loss of a treasured edition of *Grimm's Fairy Tales*. H. D. elaborates upon these and other memories and brings them together to give meaning to both past and present. The book begins with an apparently random reference to the girl who was burned to death at the seminary. The significance of the episode becomes clear in the last chapter, when the adult H. D. reflects in the midst of a bombing raid, "Now I would be burnt and it did not matter what happened any more, only I did not want to be burnt." Other apparently disconnected references in the early sections become relevant in this perspective as well, especially the emphasis on the death of women and girls—Charles Doolittle's first wife and their young daughter, Hilda's own sister who died before the author's birth, her aunt's baby, photographed in her coffin in a long white dress. The child Hilda appeared to take some comfort in the fact that Little Eva, seen on her first trip to the theater, did not really die during the performance but appeared for a curtain call.

The fear of death, then, is mitigated by the author's belief that moments can have their own kind of permanence. There are, she suggests, two kinds of time. Clock time, measured by the ticking of the grandfather clock in the hall throughout the book, is the kind of time her father meant when he said, "*Tempus fugit*," and she "wondered if Papa remembered how he had bought the box of animals." The event had, perhaps, faded completely into the past for him; for her it was eternal. A game of anagrams with her family, a sleigh ride (she later decided it must have been a vision or a dream) with her mother, her brothers, and the young gardener who gave her the lily—each experience, like the trip to the toy shop, could be seen as "a drop of living and eternal life, perfected there; it was living, complete, not to be dried up in memory like pressed moss." These moments are seen not as times to be remembered but experiences to be relived. Linear time, H. D. seems to feel, can be obliterated. The shabby procession of the cast of *Uncle Tom's Cabin* through the street was a recapitulation of moments throughout history:

> I know it was only Little Eva in a jerry-built, gold chariot, and yet it was the very dawn of art, it was the sun, the drama, the theater, it was poetry. . . . It was Alexandria, it was a Roman Triumph, it was a Medieval miracle-play procession with a devil, who was Simon Legree, and the poor dark shades of purgatory, who were the negroes chained together, and it was Pallas Athenè, in her chariot with the Winged Victory poised with the olive crown, who was coming to save us all.

The "gift" of the title refers at least in part to this ability to live in several dimensions at once. The word appears first, however, in a more ordinary context. Friends wonder why so brilliant a man as Charles Doolittle does not have "gifted" children. Then H. D. recounts a fortune-teller's promise to her mother that she would have a child with a gift. Young Hilda, hearing the story, is not quite sure what a "gift" is. Her mother, she reflects, had a gift for music, but she gave it to her brother, Hilda's Uncle Fred, who was so dedicated to his art that he hid under the counter of the drugstore where he worked to study sheets of church music. Another uncle told the child that writers were people with a gift; the author could, in that sense, see her own career as the fulfillment of the prophecy. There is another more significant manifestation of the gift, however, the one that allowed her grandmother to experience the joy and laughter of Anna von Pahlen and Princess Morning Star, so that "she herself became one with the *Wunden Eiland* initiates and herself spoke with tongues—hymns of the spirits in the air—of spirits at sunrise and sunsetting, of the deer and the wild squirrel, the beaver, the otter, the kingfisher, and the hawk and eagle."

This is the other gift H. D. believed she inherited, the gift that she recognized as she sat in a chair in her London apartment, feeling the vibrations of the antiaircraft guns and listening to the enemy bombers overhead: "The Gift was a Gift of Vision . . . of the Holy Spirit." It carried H. D., as it had carried her grandmother, back in time to the Ritual of the Wounds shared by the Moravians and the Indians, and she felt herself in the presence of Anna and Morning Star, even as she sat with Bryher in London. The Isle of Wounds was not only an island in the Monocacy River; it was also beleaguered England—and more: "Our earth is a wounded island as we swing round the sun." For the author, the journey into the past is a kind of baptismal experience, a death and resurrection: "I was not drowning though in a sense, I had drowned; I had gone down, been submerged by the wave of memories and terrors repressed since the age of ten and long before, but with the terrors, I had found the joys, too."

The Gift is far more than a beautifully written distillation of the experiences of a writer's childhood. It is a moving statement of H. D.'s view of life, one in which she draws together her interest in Freudian psychology, her exploration of the nature of men and women, her sense of the relationship of the temporal and the eternal, and her belief that all religions are, in essence, one religion. The author's extraordinary memory, her ability to convey feeling through meticulous description, and her remarkable sense of structure, which enabled her to unify the disparate strains of her narrative—all these elements combine to make *The Gift* a work that seems likely to become a minor classic.

Elizabeth Johnston Lipscomb

Sources for Further Study

Booklist. LXXIX, September 1, 1982, p. 28.
Library Journal. CVII, September 1, 1982, p. 1660.
Publishers Weekly. CCXXII, September 3, 1982, p. 56.

GISSING
A Life in Books

Author: John Halperin (1941-   )
Publisher: Oxford University Press (New York). Illustrated. 426 pp. $29.95
Type of work: Literary biography
Time: 1870-1903
Locale: England and France

A carefully detailed biography, emphasizing the connections between George Gissing's life and the characters, opinions, attitudes, and events in his novels

> *Principal personages:*
> GEORGE GISSING, a British novelist, 1857-1903
> NELL HARRISON, a prostitute, Gissing's first wife
> EDITH UNDERWOOD, the daughter of a stonemason, Gissing's second wife
> GABRIELLE FLEURY, a French translator, who lived with Gissing in pseudomarriage
> EDUARD BERTZ, a German intellectual; Gissing's closest friend and lifelong correspondent
> H. G. WELLS, a novelist

The novels of George Gissing have perhaps always been more respected than enjoyed: readers generally find his books depressing. Though he published twenty-three novels, more than one hundred short stories, and assorted pieces of nonfiction, poverty generally forced him to sell copyrights outright, and for much less than his more popular contemporaries were paid. His reputation as a feminist and as a novelist of the working class is confounded by the misogyny and social conservatism embedded in his fiction. Similarly, his reputation for "modernism" is hardly borne out in the books—except for one striking twentieth century trait: to a far greater extent than most Victorians, Gissing used his own life as the substance of fiction.

John Halperin makes sense out of this mass of contradictions by treating Gissing's life and the books together in minute chronological detail, using Gissing's journal and letters, discussing his short fiction in sequence with the novels, noting the public response provided by reviews, and minutely analyzing Gissing's fictionalized reflections of the life he had lived—and, more astonishingly, was yet to live: Gissing had the disconcerting habit of prefiguring, in fiction, steps (often disastrous ones) that he was about to take in life. Gissing's novels are always about the interaction of sex, class, and money. His pervasive theme is exile; in particular, he writes about men of intellect and taste who are forced by circumstances to live unhappily among inferiors.

Gissing's own class outlook was ambiguous from the start. He did not have the working-class background sometimes imputed to him. His father was a chemist, an amateur botanist, and the author of several volumes of poetry.

Although active in local Liberal politics, he was apparently something of a snob and he would not allow his children to associate with the children of other tradesmen. After his father died (when Gissing was thirteen), the community raised a subscription to send his sons to a rigorously academic boarding school. In 1883, Gissing entered Owens College, Manchester, on a tuition-free scholarship. He worked hard, took the matriculation examination for London University, won national prizes for English, Latin, and history, and seemed destined for a brilliant academic career, perhaps as a university professor of classics. Then, in May, 1876, he was caught stealing money from other students at Owens College—and worse yet, admitted that he was giving the money to a young prostitute, Nell Harrison. He was stripped of his prizes, denied an academic future, sent to jail for a month, and burdened with a guilty secret which he apparently believed barred him forever from the company of ladies and gentlemen. After a brief exile in the United States, during which he sold some stories to Chicago newspapers, he returned to London, earned a minimal income by writing and tutoring, and lived with Harrison. In October, 1879, he married her.

The marriage was a disaster before it even began, and by 1881, the couple separated. Gissing paid for Nell's keep at various boardinghouses and invalid homes and quixotically refused to file for divorce even after she had been arrested as a common prostitute. In 1888, she died of alcoholism and syphilis. Gissing sold more novels, took a trip to Italy, and struggled with loneliness. His only close friend was Eduard Bertz, a German exile who made Gissing's acquaintance by placing a newspaper advertisement seeking intellectual companionship. Gissing felt uncomfortable with everybody but especially with middle-class women. In 1890, feeling that only a "decent work-girl" would be willing to provide domestic comfort and some companionship on slender means, he picked up Edith Underwood at a music hall. They were married in 1891, had two sons, and separated in 1897. In 1902—after abusing their younger child—Edith was declared insane and committed to an asylum. In the meantime, Gissing had already begun a relationship with Gabrielle Fleury, who translated his *New Grub Street* (1891) into French. In 1899, they began living together. Gabrielle's relatives in France were told that they were married; Gissing's relatives (and particularly his legal wife) were told nothing at all. He recorded his infatuation with Gabrielle in *The Crown of Life* (1899). Although Gissing perpetually felt an exile in his own land, exile in France made him truly miserable. He became convinced that Gabrielle's mother and French cuisine were conspiring to starve him to death. He died in 1903, before the relationship had completely disintegrated.

Halperin's treatment emphasizes both the conscious and unconscious self-revelations in Gissing's work. He traces Gissing's personae in virtually every novel; he searches even the least autobiographical books for indications of Gissing's response to his private experiences. *Born in Exile* (1892) is archetypal. The protagonist, Godwin Peak, shares nearly every detail of Gissing's early life—except that one significant alteration makes him undeserving of the humiliation that forces him to leave college. The novel is satiric—even vicious—in revealing the extent of Peak's hypocrisy as he tries to make a good marriage, but the marriage he wants is, surely, with the woman who embodies Gissing's ideal. Peak's views, Halperin argues, are Gissing's own even when they are satirized: he despises vulgarity; he attacks the working class (rather than the system that degrades its workers); and, because he needs to feel superior in order to love, he hates (or fears) emancipated women.

New Grub Street, by far Gissing's best-known and most widely read novel, is a self-dramatizing protest against the commercialism that degrades literature and prevents the novelist from fulfilling his artistic genius. Edwin Reardon is transparently a Gissing persona, a classical scholar frustrated by the need to produce work that will sell. Reardon's descriptions of Italy are taken almost verbatim from Gissing's diary, and even his impractical self-destructiveness is romanticized as the inevitable consequence (even hallmark) of his aesthetic sensitivity. Halperin shows that the novel's other literary men—who also have problems with money, class, and sex—are further aspects of Gissing. Biffen's grubby realism (he wants to take down verbatim the speech of grocers) satirizes Gissing's early "proletarian" phase. Whelpdale shares Gissing's American experience and his propensity for wooing the wrong women. By marrying a woman too inferior to take with him in public, Alfred Yule destroys his chance to make the social contacts that would gain him an editorship. Jasper Milvain, according to Halperin, is a fantasy-persona composed equally of wish-fulfillment and self-justification, who shows what Gissing could achieve if he were willing to sacrifice his idealism for affluence.

The most startling aspect of Gissing's autobiographical method is that it often worked in reverse: his life took a course he had already written. To a certain extent, this may be commonplace. Fantasy often precedes action; people daydream, try out certain plans, come to see themselves as a particular kind of person, and then take the steps that realize some part of the dream. That seems a likely explanation for Gissing's relationship with Nell; he may have already embroidered a rescue fantasy (one of the commonest of adolescent power-dreams) which set him up to fall for a pitiable woman. He may also have used fiction deliberately to try things out: *In the Year of Jubilee* (1894) contains the plan he used, three years later, to provide a safe home for his eldest son before leaving Edith. It is appalling, however, that he could contemplate an action, imagine its fatal consequences—and then go ahead despite them. His first published novel, *Workers in the Dawn* (1880), details the misery that grows from Arthur Golding's inability to reform the alcoholic, promiscuous, lower-class girl whom he marries out of pity and idealism. Yet almost as soon as he had written the novel's bitter conclusion, Gissing married Nell Harrison. *New Grub Street*, written immediately after he met Edith

Underwood, shows Alfred Yule unable to get ahead as a free-lance scholar and critic because he has married a London workgirl, a woman he patronizes, keeps shut up, and makes generally miserable, just as Gissing was to do with Edith in the next few years. *Denzil Quarrier* (1892) has a couple living together as husband and wife, though one of them is married to someone else, and Alma Rolfe, in *The Whirlpool* (1897), is cultured, educated, housewifely, and an able musician. One would guess, in this case, that Gissing had already fallen in love with his own creation; when Gabrielle Fleury showed up a year later, she was a near enough match to fall instantly into the role as beloved.

One feature of the recent Gissing revival is the new popularity of *The Old Women* (1893), which many feminist critics see as a moving study of women who lack money, status, and mates but are nevertheless compassionate and strong, in contrast to the desperately unhappy women who marry simply for lack of an alternative. Halperin's approach is somewhat different. He quotes Gissing's letter to Bertz at the time that he began the novel:

> It will present those people who, congenitally incapable of true education, have yet been taught to consider themselves too good for manual, or any humble, work. As yet I have chiefly dealt with types expressing the struggle of natures endowed *above* their stations; now I turn to those who are *below* it. The story will be a study of vulgarism—the all but triumphant force of our time. Women will be the chief characters.

These remarks are tied to the attacks on emancipated women that appear in many of his less frequently read novels and short stories. Gissing idealized the perfect housewife, pilloried women whose ambitions led them to deny their true vocation within the family, and believed that the education of females ruined good housekeeping. As Halperin's close chronological recording makes clear, a good deal of the anger which fueled Gissing's fictional attacks on women arose from domestic discord with Edith—but, after all, he chose to marry her.

Tracing the correspondences between life and books thus illuminates Gissing's biography but, to some extent, makes it harder to read the novels as literary texts. Despite Gissing's misogyny, his wretched treatment of the women with whom he lived, and his exasperating tendency to alternate between idealization and condescension, women characters are important in most of his novels. They are often as full, as flawed, and as complex as the male characters. As Gillian Tindall points out in *The Born Exile* (1974), a novelist who felt exiled from his true station by material circumstances put a good deal of himself into women characters who faced comparable barriers.

Gissing argued in an essay entitled "The Place of Realism in Fiction" (1895) that "the spirit of truthfulness" is the central value in literature: "every novelist beholds a world of his own, and the supreme endeavour of his art must be to body forth that world as it exists for him. The novelist works, and must work, subjectively." Halperin demonstrably operates on the same standard of values: he gives highest praise to the novels that exhibit greatest biographical accuracy. His enthusiasm leads him to overvalue works such as *Sleeping Fires* (1895), which he praises for its exuberance (not a noted Gissing characteristic); the biographer, involved with his subject, is glad to see Gissing happy for once. This species of criticism raises significant questions about the relationship between life and art. After all, a writer who produced twenty-three novels in twenty-four years must indeed have lived much of his life in his books. Gissing's difficult relationship with H. G. Wells (whose similar class background led to a certain congeniality—but who was a commercially successful writer) is a reminder of the even more difficult link between Wells and Dorothy Richardson, a writer for whom life and fiction became virtually inextricable.

Since 1960, publishers have brought out seven volumes of Gissing's correspondence and private writings and more than fifteen bibliographical, biographical, and critical studies. Many of the novels are again in print, several in inexpensive editions. *Gissing: A Life in Books* is a rich, detailed, and meticulous synthesis of the available materials, revealing both the strength and the limitations of biographical criticism.

Sally Mitchell

Sources for Further Study

Economist. CCLXXXV, October 2, 1982, p. 101.
New Statesman. CIV, October 15, 1982, p. 24.
Spectator. CCXLIX, September 18, 1982, p. 20.
Times Literary Supplement. December 31, 1982, p. 1447.

A GLASS FACE IN THE RAIN

Author: William Stafford (1914-   )
Publisher: Harper & Row, Publishers (New York). 126 pp. $12.45
Type of work: Poetry

A volume of almost a hundred poems appearing for the first time in book form

Five years earlier than the publication of *A Glass Face in the Rain*, a collected edition of William Stafford's poems appeared. That publication, in 1977, did not mark for Stafford, as collected editions have for some poets, the end of his writing career. Steadily, in the intervening years, Stafford has continued to publish poems in a host of periodicals, including *American Poetry Review*, *Cimarron Review*, *Harvard Magazine*, *Iowa Review*, *The New Yorker*, *Poetry*, *Spectrum*, *The Virginia Quarterly Review*, and *Wallace Stevens Journal*. The range of readership of the sixty-two periodicals in which the poems have appeared is impressive. The range of periodicals also illustrates how solidly Stafford has established himself in the realm of American poetry, surviving through several decades when the future of poetry was in doubt, especially the 1950's, when the poetic situation in America was torn by widely disparate points of view with the practice of the Beat Generation on the one hand and the academic poets on the other. Stafford's poetry, which critics have suggested has caught the best of both sides, continues to demonstrate the poet's vigor, although he is well along in life and in his career.

William Stafford is a poet who celebrates life, who finds in life veritable wonder, joyous at times, awestruck at times, and always curious. Although he is a quietly friendly man himself, his poetry, including the poems collected for the first time in this volume, shows him to be something of a loner, a person who is not afraid of solitude, who is not afraid of facing himself as his only companion. He comes through to his readers as a man who, at least figuratively, can and does stride through life vigorously and independently, but well aware of other people and their independence. In the dedication of *A Glass Face in the Rain*, the poet remarks of the people who travel on parallel ways, known to one another only by smoke signals, and he says that his present volume is intended especially for those people. The poet looks to them because they have accepted their lives and the world about them. We must, suggests Stafford, each go through the world leaving unmistakable, yet unobtrusive smoke signals for one another, recognizing one another's existence without placing obligation on one another, sharing independence and respecting one another.

Little incidents in life are important; that is one of the messages Stafford's poetry frequently suggests, even insists, to the reader. For example, in the first poem of the collection, "How It Began," he portrays carefully, vividly, in ten lines of controlled verse, the taking into his care and to a friend's home of a litter of black, white, and gray puppies, blind and hungry, after their mother had died. He rejoices in the living quality of the puppies and passes that enthusiasm for life on to the reader. Part 1 of the volume is entitled "A Touch on Your Sleeve" and includes an individual poem by that title. This poem also illustrates the poet's use of the small but important experience. In the poem, a dandelion puff, carried by the air from afar, brushes a sleeve as it descends to earth, falling like snow and suggesting, writes Stafford, that life has become important again just through that tiny happening.

In part 2 of the volume, entitled "Things That Come," Stafford has included poems that reflect the hardness of life, the cruelty that can occur in the human experience. One such poem, "Murder Bridge," seems to reflect an incident that happened in the poet's home state of Oregon some years ago, when a young woman and her lover dashed the woman's children to death on the rocks of the steep, deep canyon of the Crooked River. Recollecting the place he once visited, the persona of the poem reflects on how life requires luck and cannot be considered easy, though later at the site of the crimes, all is quiet while the rocks seem to dream in the sun. In a somewhat similar fashion, he suggests of occurrences in "Seeing and Perceiving" that we must learn to appreciate what life presents to us to perceive through the sense of sight. He mentions the pattern of a crooked tree branch, the way of a knotted string, the wing of a bird flying home. We learn, he suggests, by clinging to these sights as bits of form, as bits of light reflected by the sympathy of our sight.

Part 3 of the collection celebrates William Stafford's belief in the connections among human beings, the ways in which communication is established between poet and reader, for which there is no accounting in an ordinary sense. The first poem in this grouping is "Glass Face in the Rain," the title poem of the volume. The short set of three stanzas gives the poet room enough to suggest how, when we are gone from the earth in some future time, for those who remember us we may return, somehow, invisibly, but still there and real, as glass faces in the rain.

The poet also celebrates the meaning of communication, suggesting that everything, ourselves included, is a message through the universe, as in the poem "A Message from Space." He writes that we know by living, even though we may not know how to live. He suggests that we human beings build huge antennas aimed at the stars beyond our solar system, not realizing that we, human beings, are the message: "Everything counts. The message is the world." Related to this theme is "A Course in Creative Writing," a poem stemming from the poet's experience of many years as a teacher of creative writing, most of them at Lewis and Clark College in Oregon. He notes the irony of the students' wish to have a wilderness in which to work, a new world to explore, but that at the same time they wish to have a map of that wilderness, to have the teacher explain and show them the way. As Stafford says, however, it cannot be that way. Rather, the writer must sing a song, whistle a little tune, walk along with the new experience, finding a world beginning under the map of the work one creates.

Part 4 of this collection is called "Troubleshooting." This is a series of poems which have some basis in the poet's past, some memory or group of memories which he brings to life for himself and to his readers. In one of the poems, he utilizes a memory of accompanying his father on trips to repair rural telephone lines; in another poem, he recalls hitchhiking one wintry night in Montana during the 1940's; in a third poem, he recollects himself as a young man in 1935, standing at dusk in traffic with his bike on a street named Lakeside Drive; a fourth example recalls his chiding of a younger brother for crying while waiting one cold afternoon for the older boy to finish playing hockey with his friends.

In the last series of poems in this volume the poet begins by tentatively welcoming his readers, saying that he offers his poems with no claims for them beyond his acknowledgement of their being his own. He tells the reader that he has found some trancelike events which he has turned into things to tell. He comments, "If you like them, fine. If not, farewell." In one of the poems he recalls some of the little things that he did during a stay on a fire lookout within sight of Mt. Shasta: eating breakfasts of animal crackers and milk out of a blue bowl, sitting on the deck of the lookout reading Leo Tolstoy's *Voina i mir* (1868-1869, *War and Peace*), Charles Dickens' *David Copperfield* (1849-1850) and Thomas Mann's *Der Zauberberg* (1924; *The Magic Mountain*, 1927). He sums it up, in a Thoreau-like way, by saying that he balanced his life there in the wilderness for a year, then washed the breakfast bowl and returned to life in civilization once again. Taking a longer look at life, he tells the reader that life is faint and that little is done, but he adds that he wants us to be easy when he is gone and let the stars go on.

William Stafford has continued the poetic way that he began years ago, a strict way for a poet, disciplining himself to write in a careful manner. His metrics are seldom obvious, his word pictures are carefully delineated in spare, even lean, language, with each word and phrase well-chosen to carry its share of literal and metaphorical meaning. It is the way he chose early in his career and has continued into the present volume, which is the work of a professional in the truest and best sense of the term.

Gordon W. Clarke

Sources for Further Study

Christian Century. C, March 23, 1983, p. 279.
Georgia Review. XXXVI, Winter, 1982, p. 911.
The New York Times Book Review. LXXXVIII, March 13, 1983, p. 6.
Publishers Weekly. CCXXII, August 27, 1982, p. 351.

GOD'S GRACE

Author: Bernard Malamud (1914-   )
Publisher: Farrar, Straus and Giroux (New York). 223 pp. $13.50
Type of work: Novel
Time: The late twentieth century, immediately after a nuclear holocaust
Locale: Cohn's Island, an imaginary spot in the tropical zone

An ironic post-Armageddon history of God's new chosen people, told from the point of view of the last surviving human

> *Principal characters:*
> CALVIN COHN, a rabbinical Robinson Crusoe, the last man on earth
> BUZ (GOTTLOB), the chimp Cohn loves as a son
> MARY MADELYN, the chimp Cohn loves as a wife
> GOD

A brief but dispositive thermonuclear war defaces and depopulates the earth. An enormous flood follows. God enters, behind a black cloud. He addresses Calvin Cohn, a short, balding paleologist in his late thirties who is horrified to find that he is the sole surviving human. "I regret to say," says God, "that it was through a minuscule error that you escaped destruction." He admonishes Cohn to live quickly, to take "a few deep breaths. . . . Beyond that lies nothing for you." Cohn, a dropout from the rabbinate, tries to negotiate with God but gains no advantage. God exits, snapping shut the crack in the cloud. When Cohn raises his fist to the heavens in anger, he is bombarded with a shower of rocks.

An aptly perverse modern version of the Genesis account of creation, this opening episode sets the tone of *God's Grace*, a tone which is at once delightfully irreverent and frighteningly ominous. As the story develops, the irreverence remains but loses its lightness and becomes a daring confrontation with the terrifying developments which God's anger promises. This opening episode also introduces the novel's principal literary technique, which is biblical irony. Bernard Malamud is clearly secure in his knowledge of the Bible stories. He deftly inverts one after another, as he does with the creation story, to show how, when their central message is misunderstood or ignored, they become stories of God's punishment rather than God's mercy.

The inverted Bible stories are lived out, in a sort of accelerated Jewish history, by the small society which Cohn founds and over which he presides until his death. Given Malamud's masterful narrative skills, it is scarcely remarkable that the society consists of a band of chimpanzees, a lone gorilla, and a few baboons, all of whom have escaped to the idyllic island on which Cohn finds himself after the floodwaters recede. Nor is it very odd that the chimps speak, albeit in a somewhat precious dialect; that they have biblical names; and that each is, if not a well-developed character, at least a well-developed character-type.

The educated chimp is Buz, who was taught speech and the tenets of Christianity by Cohn's scientist colleague Walther Bünder, a "round-faced man with a rectilinear view of life." Finding the young male chimp affectionate and alert, Cohn undertakes to educate him and to treat him like a son. Discomforted to hear Buz insist that Jesus preached to the chimps, Cohn reflects, as he begins life on his new island home, that "if one of them was a Christian and the other a Jew, Cohn's Island would never be Paradise." The attractive chimp is Mary Madelyn, the only young female on the island, and the object of the desires of Buz, of his competitor the brutish Esau, and eventually of Cohn himself. The other chimps are an assemblage of senior citizens and children. George the gorilla is a silent but omnipresent gloomy observer, evidently meant to be a reincarnation of Cohn's rabbi father. The baboons are the clan inhabiting the other end of the island, latecomers without speech, who become the inevitable magnet for the chimps' violence.

In the hope that he can elevate the new society to a level where they, too, can make a covenant with God, Cohn begins to deliver his store of human knowledge and values to the primates (not monkeys, Cohn corrects the memory of his rabbi father, who responds that "To me it's all the same, a monkey is a monkey"). Humorously drawing on familiar biblical images, Malamud has Cohn give his lectures from a stool set on a teaching platform under the eucalyptus tree into which the chimps climb each day to listen,

> sitting alone or in two's, chewing leaves and spitting them out; or cracking nuts they had brought along, and eating them out of their palms as they listened to Calvin Cohn lecture; or groomed themselves and their partners as he droned on. When the lectures got to be boring they would shake branches and throw nuts at him.

As they founder in obedience to ethical norms, Cohn gives the chimps his twentieth century version of the Ten Commandments, suitably adapted to primate society ("Blessed are those who divide the fruit equally"). He calls his moral rules the Seven Admonitions, reads them aloud to the chimps in the schooltree, and leads a cheer for each. Two figure prominently in Cohn's eventual demise:

> Note: God is not love, God is God. Remember Him.

> Love thy neighbor. If you can't love, serve—others, thy community. Remember the willing obligation.

Cohn recognizes that he is teaching the chimps and leading their moral formation in an attempt to justify himself to an angry God, but he loses his clarity of perception when he begins to desire Mary Madelyn and plans to perpetuate his line through her. Ignoring God's instructions, Cohn reasons:

> In sum, a worthy primate evolution demanded, besides a few macroevolutionary lucky

breaks, a basis of brainpower; and commencing with a combination of man-chimp child, the two most intelligent of God's creatures might produce this new species—ultimately of Cohn's invention—an eon or two ahead on the molecular clock.

When Cohn takes Mary Madelyn, with her permission but against the will of Buz and Esau, the prosperity and harmony of the island begin to disintegrate. Cohn's hubris leads inevitably to the biblical episode that concludes the book, the episode of Abraham's sacrifice of his son Isaac.

The two principal concepts that Malamud explores in this telescoped Jewish history are love and obedience. He explores them, with varying degrees of success, on several levels and in a variety of relationships with each other. Malamud appears to be on the firmest artistic and religious footing when he gives the concepts of love and obedience their Old Testament meanings. Obedience, in this sense, is obedience to the Law, those small and large precepts addressed to the violence of human nature, whose observance humanizes the follower, tempers his relationship with his fellow man, and constitutes the fine print of his pact with God. Malamud draws Cohn as a religious man, one who follows the Law despite his divorce from a culture which would encourage his fidelity. Cohn loses track of time but nevertheless treats one day in seven as the Sabbath. He celebrates auspicious occasions with the Seder meal. Grieving for those destroyed in the nuclear holocaust, he says Kaddish for "one hundred souls whose names he had picked at random in a heavily thumbed copy of a Manhattan telephone directory. . . . He kept it for company in the cave as a sort of 'Book of the Dead.'" As a religious man, Cohn should anticipate the necessary consequence of his transgression of the Second Admonition (" . . . God is God. Remember Him"). Blinded by his pride, Cohn violates God's direction to live and then die and attempts to supplant God in the universal scheme by creating a new race in the image of Cohn. His punishment is swift and terrible.

Love, in the sense of the willing obligation, is the virtue which binds the members of society, permitting all to grow and prosper in a way that no one could do on his own. The abandonment of love, by the chimps and by Cohn, spells the abandonment of their civilization and their descent back into alienation and violence.

Malamud becomes less surefooted, however, when he uses the concepts of love and obedience in a double and treble sense and attempts to oppose them to each other. One such play is Malamud's use of obedience as the dominant religious characteristic of Judaism and love as the dominant religious characteristic of Christianity. The two religions come into confrontation when Buz revises the Second Admonition to read "God is   love, God is God." After this assertion of religious independence, the relationship between Buz and Cohn becomes symbolic of the relationship between Christian and Jew at its historical worst. The significance of this conflict between obedience and love becomes even more complex with the conversion of the other chimps to Christianity and the fruition of God's plan that Cohn's life and his influence over the chimps end.

Malamud does not limit his exploration of the concepts of love and obedience to creating complex disputes between them. He also poses questions which he suggests can be answered by a proper understanding of love and law. What does it mean to be, like Abraham and Job, servants of God, and how did they earn the right, one which Cohn never earned, to contend with God? How must one who rails against the injustice of society be disposed within himself before he is a prophet? What truth is revealed by the statement that God is the Word and that creation lies in naming? What role does the persecution of the Jews play in the plan of God? These are magnificent and enticing questions. Unfortunately, Malamud gives them little attention after he first poses them.

Like all religious novels, *God's Grace* is artistically vulnerable to the religious vision which informs it. Such novels are likely to suffer in artistic merit in direct proportion to the number of religious questions they raise. This may be because the novel's point of view is dictated by the author's religious perspective; the more diffuse the author's religious vision seems to be, the less orientation he provides his readers.

Two novels which invite comparison with *God's Grace* are Walter M. Miller's *A Canticle for Leibowitz* (1959) and Russell Hoban's *Riddley Walker* (1981). Both, like *God's Grace*, are set in a postapocalyptic landscape, where the only issues which deserve discussion are those important enough to have survived a nuclear holocaust. Both, like *God's Grace*, are unhampered thematically by societal conventions, because the authors are at liberty to make up any post-holocaust world they like. All three novels treat of sin and its consequences and examine the role of God's witness in a sinful world. What distinguishes the other two novels from *God's Grace* is that they address from a single perspective the problem of how to break the circle of sin which will result time and again in violent destruction. *A Canticle for Leibowitz* preaches the redemptive nature of love for God and mankind, while *Riddley Walker* dramatizes a pilgrimage toward self-knowledge. Such a unified perspective, regardless of whether it is true, at a minimum permits the reader to see the world as one person of faith sees it.

God's Grace, by contrast, in what may be an attempt to ensure the truth of the vision by omitting none of its complexities, presents so many worldviews that, at its conclusion, it has failed to identify precisely wherein lies God's grace.

Angelika Kuehn

Sources for Further Study

America. CXLVII, October 9, 1982, p. 195.
Christian Science Monitor. September 10, 1982, p. B3.
Library Journal. CVII, July, 1982, p. 1345.
Los Angeles Times Book Review. September 12, 1982, p. 1.
The New York Times Book Review. LXXXVII, August 29, 1982, p. 1.
The New Yorker. LVIII, November 8, 1982, p. 167.
Newsweek. C, September 6, 1982, p. 70.
Times Literary Supplement. October 29, 1982, p. 1188.

GRACE ABOUNDING

Author: Maureen Howard (1930-   )
Publisher: Little, Brown and Company (Boston). 175 pp. $13.95
Type of work: Novel
Time: The early 1980's
Locale: The United States

A four-part novel which chronicles the intellectual and emotional development of Maude Lasser, a widow with a teenage daughter

> *Principal characters:*
> MAUDE LASSER (NÉE DOWD), the protagonist, a widow who remarries and pursues a successful career
> ELIZABETH, her daughter
> GILBERT (BERT) LASSER, Maude's second husband
> TED LASSER, his son from a former marriage

Grace Abounding, Maureen Howard's most recent novel, is the story of Maude Dowd, who, as the work opens, is a widow with a teenage daughter, Elizabeth. The dust jacket proclaims that Maude "comes of age" after her first husband's death, but this work is more than a novel about a woman's psychic development. It is also about mankind and what, for lack of a less pretentious term, can be called "the human condition."

The book is divided into four sections, the last being a kind of epilogue. The first shows Maude making weekly visits to her senile mother and attempting to communicate with her withdrawn daughter. Maude's first husband has already died before the novel opens, and, in spite of her attempts to redecorate her house and thus establish a new identity, her disorientation is apparent. She has constant sexual fantasies about men she meets in casual encounters and even seems to court death on the dangerous winter drives to her mother's house. She purposely neglects to repair a leaking tire, lets her gas tank run nearly empty, and refuses to drive during daylight, preferring night and back roads "where if my tire blows, I will be stranded."

By the time the second section opens, Maude has remarried and earned a degree in counseling. In flashbacks, the reader learns that a school production of *West Side Story* revealed a hitherto unknown singing talent in Elizabeth and that, while Maude pursued her degree, Elizabeth prepared for a career in music, a career she abandoned when she married. In the second section, she is expecting her first child. In the third part, all the major characters face some type of crisis. Elizabeth takes her infant son to visit the house where she grew up and, encountering a violent storm, is unable to return home. She seeks shelter with a former neighbor—a fat, ill-kempt, bawdy woman whose deceased sister had been the town poet. Ironically, Elizabeth discovers that Mattie, the living sister, was actually the town's "Emily Dickinson" and merely passed the poems off as her sister's. Mattie threatens her physically, but Elizabeth and her child escape.

The section then explores the relationship of Bert Lasser, Maude's second husband, with his minister son from a former marriage. Stopping to see him on impulse on the way back from a business conference, Bert eavesdrops on his son and can only conclude that "He's a limp clergyman, empty." He leaves without even seeing his son. Maude, meanwhile, has been having office surgery for a small cyst—the minor chalazion of this section's title—and as she makes her way home after the surgery, bandaged and unsteady on her feet, she is consumed by self-pity. This section ends with Bert's return home and his lovemaking with Maude.

The small epilogue, "Grace Note," is not about any of the main characters and, as a rounding-out of the novel, is problematic at best. It opens with the woman who inherited Mattie's house after her death throwing out all of Mattie's manuscript poems. It then switches to Bert Lasser's son as he dines with his rich parishioners and later visits the poorer people in the neighborhood, even though they are "not on the calendar." It is hard to know what Howard is saying about this young man. His visits bearing clothes to the poor seem to imply a hitherto unrevealed compassion in him; one also learns, however, that he sometimes parodies sermons for their entertainment, certainly a cynical act. It is perhaps unwise on Howard's part to allow a minor character—and one introduced so late in the novel—to have, as it were, the last word. The reader simply does not know how to take this oblique conclusion.

This rather long plot summary should give some idea of the texture of the novel, although it leaves out a lot: Maude's affair with and betrayal by a man who runs a religious gift shop; her work with a seemingly autistic child who later jumps from his bedroom window to his death; Elizabeth's relationship with her husband, who is accepted only halfheartedly by her family. In fact, it may be that Howard goes into too much detail about too many people—detail extraneous to her main plot.

There are also anomalies in the development of the central character. As the second section opens, the reader is confronted by a Maude so radically different from the one in the beginning as to seem the same in name only. Puzzled, the reader continues reading but is not told how this change came about until late into the section, a bit of clumsy pacing on Howard's part. Furthermore, the explanation of the mother's transformation is not really clear; the discovery of Elizabeth's fine voice might turn Maude into a stage mother, but it is problematical whether it would motivate her to take a graduate degree in psychology. The reader cannot help feeling that some important link is missing.

Similar problems mar Howard's treatment of Elizabeth's relationship with her husband. When Elizabeth gives up her career to marry, Maude blames her daughter's husband, even though Elizabeth makes it clear that he did not ask her for this sacrifice. Yet, when she tells Maude in the third section that she is going to resume singing, she sounds as if she is doing this furtively: although her husband is a successful corporation lawyer, she is taking singing lessons with the "household money and her money for Christmas" but will soon have to "confess" because she is scheduled to perform in a local church. Her secrecy seems out of keeping with what has previously been revealed of her marriage. Although merely a small slip on Howard's part, it seems to indicate that she is not in total control of her novel.

Pacing is also an occasional problem in the novel. The delayed revelation in the second section of the reasons for Maude's transformation has already been mentioned. A similar lapse occurs at the end of this section when Maude's young patient jumps to his death. His mother calls and leaves a message on Maude's recorder that seems to promise complications to be developed in the next section: "You killed him. He should have been in an institution. He'd be alive but you treated him normal. You killed a three-year-old child . . . I am going to sue for every dollar. . . ." Yet when the next part opens, there is no mention of a lawsuit, and the child himself is not mentioned until the very end of "Minor Chalazion," when Maude laments his death in her general despair over life and its difficulties. One feels that Howard introduces the child to make a thematic point and then simply leaves him until he is needed again. His death works on a thematic level, but Howard's treatment is clumsy on the basic level of plot.

In fact, the novel works best in pieces, even if they do not add up to a satisfying whole. Her portraits of the minor characters are striking indeed. Bell Petry, Maude's mother's nurse—who paints her toenails, calls Maude "kiddo," and faces a potentially fatal operation with a stoic "What the hell"— is memorably drawn. Similarly, Howard is wonderful when she gets into the senile mother's mind and records her thoughts, living as she does partly in the past, partly in the present, and partly in some fantastic amalgam of the two. Howard also excels at picking out the striking or ludicrous detail. When Elizabeth comes to care for Maude after her surgery, she reads her articles from *House and Garden* that are so full of ridiculous decorating jargon as to reduce Maude to helpless laughter: "Working from a neutral palette, Mr. Pear floated the entire room in biscuit and beige."

For all this talent, however, the novel is fragmented—a weakness emphasized by Howard's shifts in narrative focus. Half the time, the characters are revealing their feelings in the first person; half the time, Howard is describing them in the third person as the omniscient narrator explores their thoughts. Although both points of view reveal the perceptions of the characters, the sometimes creaky shifts from "I" to "she" are distracting. Furthermore, some events in the novel seem contrived, mere excuses for Maude's own perceptions. When she has the small cyst removed and leaves the doctor's office, for example, people respond to her with her bandaged eye as though she were an apparition from a horror movie: "A mother shielded her child from the sight of me." Surely this is overwriting on Howard's part in order simply to account for Maude's later flood of self-pity; yet her situation by itself would account for this. Facing surgery alone, her husband away at a business conference and her daughter comfortably ensconced in affluent suburbia, Maude would naturally feel abandoned. Howard's portrayal of Maude would be more convincing here if she allowed the intrinsic inner drama of her character's situation to develop naturally, without recourse to melodramatic gesturing. In fact, this section improves enormously when she returns to her main characters and writes about Elizabeth's loving attempts to nurse her mother: "Here was my girl fetching aspirin though there was not a moment's pain."

Any overview of this novel must take into account the religious references, which form a network linking together the book's four sections. The title recalls John Bunyan's *Grace Abounding* (1666), a work written while he was in prison, with the purpose, as its subtitle indicates, of showing "the exceeding mercy of God in Christ, to his poor servant John Bunyan." Howard further develops this idea of mercy through her epigraph from St. Augustine: "Do not despair; one of the thieves was saved. Do not presume; one of the thieves was damned." When the reader actually gets into the novel, however, he finds only small references to formalized religion: Maude and her first husband both lost their religious faith before the novel opens; the owner of the Regina Caeli Gift Shop sells religious articles but, as the reader later learns, also kills his wife.

Yet several of the titles of the novel's four sections—"Sin," "Sorrow," "Grace Note"—seem to denote religious concerns, and the one major section—"Minor Chalazion"—which, at first, seems out of place in this scheme is actually an integral part of it. The cyst on Maude's eye comes to be a secular emblem of a fallen world, which Maude can only partially restore. Even after she has received her degree, pursued a successful career, and remarried happily, she still has to come to terms in "Minor Chalazion" with the unhappiness of her past and the failures of her present. As she thinks sorrowfully of her three-year-old patient who jumped to his death, her husband can only offer the consolation that "Poor Warren was predictable."

Yet, if the epigraph tells the reader that "one of the thieves was damned," it also reminds him "not [to] despair," and Maude and Bert's lovemaking at the end of the third section seems to be an affirmation in the face of a chaotic world. One wishes that Howard had not tacked on the jarring final section— jarring because it switches to minor characters and develops them ambiguously. In fact, given the excellence of the pieces of this novel, one wishes Howard had more control over the whole.

Carole Moses

Sources for Further Study

America. CXLVIII, February 19, 1983, p. 137.
Library Journal. CVII, November 15, 1982, p. 2189.
National Review. XXXIV, September 17, 1982, p. 1156.
The New Republic. CLXXXVII, October 4, 1982, p. 35.
The New York Review of Books. XXIX, December 2, 1982, p. 46.
The New York Times Book Review. LXXXVII, September 26, 1982, p. 7.
The New Yorker. LVIII, October 18, 1982, p. 179.
Newsweek. C, October 11, 1982, p. 109.
Publishers Weekly. CCXXII, August 27, 1982, p. 346.

GRAMMATICAL MAN
Information, Entropy, Language, and Life

Author: Jeremy Campbell (1931-   )
Publisher: Simon and Schuster (New York). 319 pp. $16.50
Type of work: Intellectual history

A history of the development of information theory and an analysis of its relationship with and contribution to contemporary physics, biology, linguistics, philosophy, and psychology

Regardless of what the jacket blurb says, *Grammatical Man* is not the first book to tell the story of information theory from its beginnings during World War II. It is, however, the first book to try to tell the story in layman's language without requiring any mathematical knowledge on the part of the reader—no small feat considering that information science had its basis in a complex set of theorems first published by Claude E. Shannon in the *Bell System Technical Journal* in 1948, entitled "A Mathematical Theory of Communication." Probably the first history of information theory was *Symbols, Signals and Noise: The Nature and Process of Communication* (1961), written by J. R. Pierce, an electrical engineer who knew Shannon, and who began his own book by admitting that although his account was less mathematical than Shannon's, it could not be nonmathematical. The advantage of Jeremy Campbell's book, because it leaves out the math, is its increase in readability and its currency in comparison to Pierce's 1961 history. Its concomitant disadvantage lies in the fact that this new account was written by a journalist rather than a specialist. What Campbell, a Washington correspondent for the *London Standard*, offers here is a popularized history of the development of the new science of information, which at the same time attempts to show how information theory has synthesized research and theory in most of the hard and soft sciences.

The first part of *Grammatical Man* focuses on the background of information theory in the nineteenth century study of the science of probability and the principle of entropy. Campbell charts the progress of scientists and mathematicians as they attempted to come to terms with the crucial tension between the predictable and the unpredictable in any given system. System, or structure, as researchers in the so-called "soft sciences" of psychology and sociology would call it, is the crucial word in information theory, for information is defined in terms of its relationship to other possibilities within a system, rather than atomistically in isolation. After establishing that the relationship between the predictable and the unpredictable could be determined by laws of mathematical probability, the next step for scientists of the twentieth century was the discovery of the rules that govern a system. The history of this search in various areas of study dominates the remainder of *Grammatical Man*.

The basic premise on which Campell proceeds, and which he continually repeats, is that the metaphor for all life processes is the sentence of a language, a model itself for the complex mix of predictability and unpredictability that makes information possible. Metaphor is another key concept in Campbell's discussion, for he often suggests that certain processes are "like" a language, or that "in a metaphoric sense" certain processes must be understood as one understands language. For example, he notes that, in a metaphoric sense, when a thermodynamic system is in a state of low entropy, it is like a message, whereas when it is in a state of high entropy, it is like noise. Moreover, Campbell, in order to avoid the use of mathematical notation, also must make use of his own metaphors or analogies, such as illustrating the principle of entropy by discussing the arrangement of molecules in a glass of ice water or by postulating the arrangement of books in a hypothetical library.

Grammatical Man is filled with references to essays, books, and monographs written by the primary researchers in the field, but the documentation is unobtrusively tucked away at the end of the book with page references so that the text is not cluttered with notes. Campbell summarizes with admirable clarity the salient points of the work of Claude Shannon, the originator of information theory; Norbert Wiener, the founder of cybernetics; Noam Chomsky, the great innovative linguist; and many others. Moreover, he charts the development of the basic principles of these thinkers whose discoveries have become household words. For example, few people are now unaware that "bit," which Shannon postulated as a basic measure of information, is short for "binary digit," which, in a remarkable series of yes/no patterns, is able to perform the high-speed word processing and number-crunching in countless 8-bit home computers across the country.

Shannon's work began with the basic problem of trying to find ways to separate message from noise (or order from disorder) in a communication system. Noise always adds itself to messages and by randomizing and distorting messages makes them less reliable. Thus, an extra ration of predictability is necessary in messages to reduce the randomizing; this extra ration is called redundancy, one of the most important concepts in information theory. Rules of language are a form of redundancy, for these rules make certain groups of letters and sequences of words more probable than others; for example, the fact that a "u" usually follows a "q" in an English text is a predictable rule. By making use of binary digits and the rules of redundancy, Shannon was able to show that in a communication system, one could send a relatively error-free message even through a noisy channel if one coded it in the proper way. Campbell says that Shannon's discovery had universal application, for it indicated that reliable information was possible in an unreliable world.

After Shannon, Campbell cites Noam Chomsky as perhaps the most influential contributor to modern information theory, for Chomsky has searched for the basis of the structures of information in the inherent structures pro-grammed genetically in the mind itself. The issue has become increasingly circular as researchers have indicated that the genes themselves are like a language system—linear, onc-dimensional symbols for proteins in a complex, symbolic relationship of codes—even as language competence itself is genet-ically bound and inherent. Language, or grammar, is a central metaphor in information theory and linguistics for processes by which surface performance is always generated by the deep structure of basic competence and governed by rules of transformation. Since Chomsky's *Syntactic Structures* was pub-lished in 1957, linguistics has become the model for the search for the elusive source of knowledge and reality itself, as thinkers in various fields have sought to understand the self-regulating complexity not only of language but also of all living systems, a complexity made possible by the principle of redundancy and generated by very simple rules which can produce exceedingly complex structures.

Grammatical Man attempts to show how thinkers and researchers now understand language to be the mirror of mind, which, by its syntax, reflects basic innate principles similar, Campbell says, to Carl Jung's theory of arche-types a generation ago. For if the syntax of the language reflects mind, then larger structures of language also reflect mind. For example, the great struc-turalist-anthropologist Claude Lévi-Strauss (whom Campbell does not men-tion), has tried to show that myths or stories also reflect structures which even in their diversity indicate their generation by basic rules of transfor-mation. Similarly, the structuralist psychoanalysis of the late Jacques Lacan treats the unconscious in terms of structure to reveal its language-like nature. Campbell does not mention Lacan either, nor does he refer to the most influential and seminal thinker in modern philosophy, Jacques Derrida. Such a lack of references to the most important structuralist thinkers is hard to understand in a book which attempts to show the significance of information theory in all fields of human thought from aesthetics to sociology.

Such an omission can be forgiven, however, when one understands that information theory encompassess so many fields of study that to mention the theorists who have been influential in all of them would be to undertake an enormous task. As it is, Campbell manages to range from Aristotle to Albert Einstein and from Sigmund Freud to E. M. Gombrich. Moreover, he manages to include in his fields of coverage thermodynamics, psychoanalysis, neurol-ogy, sociology, and art criticism. Chapters in the book deal with the efforts of scientists to crack the code of DNA, to understand the nature of evolution, to clarify the basis for human development, and to understand the sophisti-cation of primitive man. Campbell also focuses on scientists' attempts to understand the language-like structure of the brain, the selective nature of perception, the basic structure of memory, and the information of dreams.

Campbell is more reliable when dealing with the immediate sources of information theory than he is in the related fields of psychology, philosophy, and aesthetics. If there is one weakness in Campbell's book, it is that while he mentions the possible relevance of information theory to the study of art and dreams—that is, to the products and processes largely of the unconscious—he does not deal with them in sufficient and suggestive detail. For example, the most contemporary literary critic whom he cites is T. S. Eliot, and while Eliot's discussion of the relationship between the structured and the original in "Tradition and the Individual Talent" may very well be in line with the more recent theories of information, what Eliot began has become highly sophisticated in recent years. Similarly, Campbell's discussion of the studies of the British art historian E. M. Gombrich, who has developed a complex theory dealing with the relationship between originality and tradition, is only cursory. Nevertheless, these are merely quibbles with a book that marks out an extremely large territory to cover and then does it admirably.

The most basic and widely valuable result of information theory, says Campbell, is that it corrects the older notion of the entropy principle—that order is an exception within the general rule of disorder—to suggest instead that order and complexity are natural. Information theory proposes that structure is natural to the world and to human beings. The crucial tension is that if there is too much structure, the creative impulse is cramped, whereas if there is too little, then art, music, and literature become disordered and meaningless noise. The realization made possible by information theory is that structure and freedom are not opposites, but rather are complementary forces essential to life and the productions of life. The result, Campbell says, is the realization that grammatical man inhabits a grammatical universe.

The most basic assumption of information theory, an assumption that underlies many of its corollaries in philosophy, psychology, and sociology, is that reality can only be known as a symbolic system and never directly. The result, which can be seen in so much of modern art, is that creative productions become increasingly reflexive—that is, the previously tacitly held rules that govern structure are foregrounded and laid bare in works of art which are ultimately "about themselves." Lest the educated lay reader begin to think that such studies are only so much intellectual narcissism, it is well to be reminded that the so-called computer age, which allows the average person to manage information and process it in highly efficient ways, has been made possible by such narcissistic analyses of the means by which human beings create and know the symbolic reality that they have previously taken so much for granted. Even the most sophisticated computer program, with the most elaborate patterns of bits of information, still cannot equal the basic competence of the human brain to create and understand the highly complex structure that constitutes information and therefore reality. Although the concepts of information theory may be puzzling to many, once understood, they should be reassuring, for they remind the reader that there is order, or grammar, both within the mind and without.

There is little doubt that information theory and such related fields as transformational linguistics and structuralism have revolutionized theoretical research in all fields of human endeavor in recent years, for they have provided a new paradigm of symbolic thought to replace the old empiricism. The complete story of information theory has yet to be told, for it is constantly developing, but in *Grammatical Man*, Jeremy Campbell has provided for the educated layman a most helpful introduction to the new world of information.

Charles E. May

Sources for Further Study

Choice. XX, December, 1982, p. 611.
Library Journal. CVII, August, 1982, p. 1471.
Los Angeles Times Book Review. September 26, 1982, p. 2.
The New Yorker. LVIII, August 9, 1982, p. 95.
Publishers Weekly. CCXXI, June 11, 1982, p. 55.

THE GREAT CODE
The Bible and Literature

Author: Northrop Frye (1912-   )
Publisher: Harcourt Brace Jovanovich (New York). 261 pp. $14.95
Type of work: Literary criticism

In this first of two projected volumes, Northrop Frye analyzes the Bible as the most important influence in the imaginative tradition of Western art and literature

Northrop Frye is recognized as one of the world's greatest living scholars, and his body of work one of the most impressive in the recent history of criticism. More than thirty years ago, when he was a junior instructor at the University of Toronto, where he still is on staff, the chairman of his department suggested that he teach a course in the English Bible. The reasons were obvious: professors could no longer anticipate that many of their students would have a working familiarity with the Bible, the cornerstone of Western culture, a principal contributor to man's visionary account of the universe and of himself within it. Without some such familiarity, one simply cannot understand English literature or appreciate the West's imaginative heritage. *The Great Code* is based on a series of courses given by Frye at his university and on lectures given at various universities throughout North America.

Being the holder of a degree in theology and an ordained minister as well as one of the world's leading literary theorists, Frye is in a unique position to approach the Bible. In this book, his "own personal encounter with the Bible," Frye suggests principles around which the Bible becomes intelligible to those who have studied it as well as to those who have never read it. He takes his title from an aphorism by William Blake—"The Old and New Testaments are the Great Code of Art." Frye's book may be read as a long meditation on that remark.

The Great Code is divided into two parts: "The Order of Words" and "The Order of Types." Part 1 is an inquiry into the language of the Bible; Part 2 is an inquiry into its structure, narrative, and imagery. It is a schematic book, in which the first section—"Language I," "Myth I," "Metaphor I," and "Typology I"—is mirrored in the second section—"Typology II," "Metaphor II," "Myth II," and "Language II."

No book could have had so specific and concrete a literary influence without possessing literary greatness. Part of the Bible's greatness lies in the fact that it has traditionally been read as a unit, and this is the way it has influenced Western culture. Its narrative begins where time begins, with the creation of the world, and ends where time ends, with the Apocalypse. In between, it surveys human history under the names of Adam and Israel. Thus, while the material contained within its pages is remarkably diverse in subject matter, style, and viewpoint, it still has an underlying unity.

A second remarkable feature of the Bible is its translatability. How is it that the Scriptures have retained such force in their transformation from Hebrew and Greek (sometimes via Latin) into countless vernaculars? This question in particular attracts Frye's interest, and his approach to it combines his longstanding attention to archetypes with some of the principles of Structuralist hermeneutics. Frye adopts the French distinction between "the *langue* that separates English and French and German" and "a *langage* that makes it possible to express similar things in all three languages." The greatest value of a study of the Bible such as he has undertaken, Frye suggests, is that it provides a starting point for "the history of language as *langage.*" Such a history would treat "a sequence of modes of more or less translatable structures in words, cutting across the variety of *langues* employed, affected and conditioned but not wholly determined by them."

The implications of this hermeneutic in Frye's hands, only gradually apparent, are radical indeed. In Frye's view, the translatability of the Bible is not a function of its essential realism, its claim to be telling the truth both about a specific series of historical events (above all, the events in the life of Christ) and about the condition of man in all cultures and all times. On the contrary, Frye asserts that the Bible is the supreme paradigmatic work of Western literature precisely because it is a self-contained artifact, an extraordinarily complex linguistic structure almost infinitely capable of translation because it is absolutely free of any claims to historical or "literal" truth. As Frye remarks, "When the book of Jonah says that the Lord prepared a great fish to swallow Jonah, there are no great fish outside the Book of Jonah that come into the story."

Frye argues that the self-referential structure of the Bible is reflected in the use of typology, a device whereby earlier events and people foreshadow later ones. Frye thinks that biblical typology is a likely source of man's common secular belief that history has a meaning, that if he does not understand current events immediately, their purposes will be revealed in time. Christianity teaches that the Old Testament becomes fully comprehensible only in the New Testament. The type of deliverance, the liberation from bondage in Exodus, for example, is followed by the antitype of deliverance, the liberation from death by resurrection.

Typology is a rhetorical device, a means of bringing coherence to scriptural writings. Above all, it is a way of understanding events. Frye says that the authors of bibilical narrative intended their types and antitypes to be understood spiritually and not as literal reincarnation. Poetic typology therefore can make for a more rewarding understanding of the Bible as a sequential unfolding of seven stages of revelation: Creation, Revolution, Law, Wisdom, Prophecy, Gospels, and Apocalypse. Each phase provides a wider perspective than does its predecessor, to which it is related as type and antitype.

Frye's poetic insight into the Bible through typology also involves the identification of key clusters of recurring poetic images. The paradisal, pastoral, agricultural, urban, and human metaphorical clusters have both an ideal or apocalyptic and an evil or demoniac counterpart. In this context, the reader can use the term "myth."

Myth does not mean fable or fairy story, but rather the embodiment of truth in poetic imagery. For example, a myth in the Bible is liberation from bondage through a leader, with the example being the definitive deliverance and type of all the rest. The death and resurrection of Jesus Christ is the New Testament antitype, and the pattern is carried on in the individual Christian's struggle for liberation from a world of sin into a new way of life, which is the spiritual freedom of God.

Thus, in the best sense, "the Bible is a gigantic myth, a narrative extending over the whole of time from creation to apocalypse," that proclaims a revelation of liberation. As sacred stories, myths have a power and significance transcending that of profane stories that are told for sheer entertainment. It is precisely the Bible's typology and poetic imagery—not primarily the historicity of the events it recounts, or the doctrines that can be deduced from it, or even the spiritual teachings—that constitutes its perennial and literal meaning, for the myth is the inexhaustible reservoir of stories and images from which everything else flows.

Thus, what Frye tries to teach the modern reader is to read the Bible poetically, to read it as, for example, William Blake or John Milton or even Dante would have read it. What remains clear is that the Bible has several sorts of languages, and these languages transcend the spoken or written word. For this reason, to look at the Bible with the inner eye of the poet may be richly rewarding, intensely stimulating, and spiritually edifying. The power of the Bible over man's imagination has profoundly affected his view of himself, of the universe, and of God. Moreover, it has colored the Western world's art and literature throughout the ages.

Dale Salwak

Sources for Further Study

America. CXLVII, August 21, 1982, p. 96.
Chronicle of Higher Education. XXV, October 27, 1982, p. 19.
Georgia Review. XXXVI, Winter, 1982, p. 900.
Library Journal. CVII, June 1, 1982, p. 1097.
The New Republic. CLXXXVI, June 9, 1982, p. 30.
The New York Times Book Review. LXXXVII, April 11, 1982, p. 10.
The New Yorker. LVIII, May 31, 1982, p. 104.
Times Literary Supplement. July 2, 1982, p. 712.

THE GREETING
New & Selected Poems

Author: R. H. W. Dillard (1937-   )
Publisher: University of Utah Press (Salt Lake City). 165 pp. $20.00
Type of work: Poetry

An analysis of the nature of dreams and imagination and of their relationship to art and human sexuality

To focus attention on the posture his poetry has assumed since his first collection, *The Day I Stopped Dreaming About Barbara Steele* (1966)—which begins the evolution of his commitment to the power of dreams and the nature of imagination—R. H. W. Dillard has placed his most recent work at the head of *The Greeting: New & Selected Poems.* In the poem "The Greeting," he asserts himself as an epistemologist of the nonrational mind who has "always known the dream/ How it . . . flares . . . fades" and reminds his readers that female characters and the theme of linkage remain important to his poetry.

The poem "Walking with Young Women" suggests that the poet's fascination with women derives from his tentative perception of them: "Walking with young women as in a dream,/ As in memory, as in fact," he says, adding the world at large to this mode of comprehension in "Dream-Land, Landscape like a Dream." The richly textured nature of his mental experience also moves Dillard to treat objects not simply in and for themselves but also as analogies for states of feeling—a habit which gives rise to his favorite prosodic mannerism, the simile.

As an example of this technique, Dillard makes extensive use of private symbols in "January: A Screenplay." Based on the separation of two lovers and their eventual reunion, this long poem—framed throughout by the directional tactics of a screenplay—invests personal objects and features of setting with the emotions of the main characters. The hands of the separated lovers, along with other significant images, constantly recur, even in such allusions as the hands which "frame/ . . . the camera's eye." There are, for example, "gloved hands," and dreams that "touch here,/ . . . hold like hands," and "Her hands holding yellow roses." The roses themselves, the "silver ring ... on her finger," the "silver chain around his neck," the "silver and enamel/ sun," the "tiny golden heart . . . the pin with its two clasped hands," as well as works such as plays, dances, and novels, and occurrences such as rain and light, function as talismans in and touchstones for the lovers' fantasies.

Crucial to the plot of this poem is the separation of the lovers; it allows them to unite in memory (which seems to be a function of imagination) and ignites their obsessive thoughts. As the woman in the poem says, "'To be with you I have to journey,'" and when the lovers reunite at the end of the poem, Dillard emphasizes their responsibility to each other, foreshadowing this by references to Advent and the Angel of the Annunciation, and suggesting that love has a moral significance when it engages the imagination.

The effect—one might say the moral flavor—women give to the energies and fantasies of men occupies an important part of Dillard's poetry up to his collection *After Borges* (1972). Women may cause a sort of delicious confusion in the male mind. In the poem "The Day I Stopped Dreaming About Barbara Steele," the poet wonders if "In the last dream before waking," a woman is "More flesh than real,/ More real than the dark before?" Moreover, in "Inside Sally," a woman's name is given to a play in football, a man's game. In "The Black Finger," a vampire (one of Dillard's recurrent tropes) looms over a sleeping woman with "golden hair," and the "dancer, small child, girl" in "Tanjong Malim: 1934" lures her male attacker who waits "Outside in the rain . . . his knife easy on his fingers."

Indulging his taste for deriving such women from movies—that is, from an art form which, in his mind, seems to project archetypes—Dillard continues to place women at the center of male power and violence. As "Inside Sally" alludes to the sexual aspect of the female in the competition men engage in with one another, so "Desert Fox" alludes to it in the most violent of male enterprises—war. The character Miranda is not only Erwin Rommel's lover but an English spy; she distracts him from the efficient pursuit of his profession and thus helps to defeat him. Conversely, the woman in "Out of Sight, Out of Mind" is Christopher Columbus' victim; she remains "In a pout" as he—perhaps having drawn nourishment from her like a vampire—deserts her to indulge in his male adventure.

In "Night of the Undead," the movie-vampire is attracted by his female victim, and appears "Hunched over her small bed" to "lick her veins dry." "The topless go-go girls" in "Downtown Roanoke: 1967" "dance/ In the dark beyond the light"—in that dream-world where women often exert their power over men. The main thrust in this collection, however, is its concern with the nature of thinking, by which Dillard seems to mean the ability to dream or imagine. "There are things I have seen/ Although I have not been/ To where they are," he says in "Travelogue," attesting to the mind's power over space; he attests to its power during time in "News of the Nile" in that the mind transforms the past (the Nile River and ancient Egypt) into the present. The movie-mummy "disguised as Ardath Bey/ Attempts" to resurrect his ancient lover in the present. Dillard uses analogies in the form of similes in "Travelogue," moreover, to specify the effect of the exotic on the imagination: "My eyes spin," he says, "Like firework wheels, crackle/ Like Frankenstein's machines." Dillard's ultimate assertion, as described in "Mobilization," is that the "mind pays no mind to fact"—that is, imagination turns the rational aspects of perception to its own uses.

The mind's ability to re-create the objective world in images and dreams is the major focus of *After Borges*. In "The Other Tiger," "thought" itself is regarded as the "fiction" upon which ones notion of the real depends. "The tiger/ To whom you just spoke in this poem/ Is only symbols and shadows," and maps—abstractions themselves—trigger in the mind places more real than the ones they represent ("Maps"). On the other hand, in "Rain," the real "rain" evokes in the mind that rain which fell in the past, until the distinction between the past and present disappears. Imagination also evokes the tones and feelings attached to the images it perceives. Thus, the tiger in "A Tiger You May Have Missed" is "practical and sure . . . hermetic, secret . . . deadly, silent . . . familiar." Furthermore, imagination realizes its own limits—that it cannot ultimately control or replace the exterior objects of its attention.

Dillard expresses his epistemology of the imagination most clearly and fully in his poems about well-known painters. Like Borges himself (whose art Dillard overlays with his own in the form of adaptations intended to convey the multilayered texture of imagining), these artists become Dillard's spokesmen. "'Nature . . . is only an hypothesis,'" Raoul Dufy is made to say in "Three Friends," and "'It is necessary . . . to create/ A world of things that one does not see,'" whereas Fernand Léger claims that the very precision of the factual serves the imagined, and Joseph Turner that "'the shape of the world/ Is the shape of the eye.'" In "Homage to Henry Green," reality "is all in a manner of seeing," and in "Three More Friends," imagination endows nature with an uncommon resonance.

Some of Dillard's final pronouncements about imagination convey the enthusiasm it produces in those who believe in and use it. "You are everything that you could ever wish to be," he writes in "Things to Look At," and further in "Emerson, Poe and Borges," "You, too, have made marvels,/ Written words that will last," and, "You are in a world of forms/ . . . They glow like new coins."

R. H. W. Dillard is less a poet of place in the regional sense favored by much current American poetry than he is a poet of place made exotic and archetypal by the human presence infusing it. In this framework, he is at pains to examine desire as it is mediated by dreams and imagination, and to fabricate the tones of this process in analogies commensurate with his own experience of it.

Mark McCloskey

Source for Further Study

Virginia Quarterly Review. LVII, Summer, 1982, p. 94.

GROUP PORTRAIT
Joseph Conrad, Stephen Crane, Ford Madox Ford, Henry James, and H. G. Wells

Author: Nicholas Delbanco (1942-   )
Publisher: William Morrow and Company (New York). Illustrated. 224 pp. $11.50
Type of work: Literary biography
Time: 1900-1914
Locale: Kent and East Sussex, England

An exploration of the relationships among five important writers who lived in south-eastern England at the turn of the century

> *Principal personages:*
> JOSEPH CONRAD, a novelist
> STEPHEN CRANE, a novelist
> FORD MADOX FORD, a novelist and a man of letters
> HENRY JAMES, a novelist
> H. G. WELLS, a novelist

In this interesting study, Nicholas Delbanco argues that five major novelists who lived within walking distance of one another in 1900 constituted a distinct literary group as significant as that in Bloomsbury. His candidates for this hypothetical community are Joseph Conrad, Stephen Crane, Ford Madox Ford, Henry James, and H. G. Wells. Although his evidence does not support his thesis, Delbanco provides a number of insights into five diverse personalities and the ways in which these personalities interacted. Crane and James were Americans, Conrad a Pole; James and Conrad were practitioners of the novel as a comprehensive, in-depth examination of life; Crane and Wells represented a new generation of writers and fresh approaches to fiction. Ford was a man of generous impulses, indefatigable and optimistic, a highly talented writer whose work has only recently been given the recognition it deserves. These men knew and liked one another; they were convivial and met for social occasions. Otherwise, there are few indications of the shared activity characteristic of a literary "group."

Delbanco begins with Crane, who had moved to England in 1897 and later, drawn by admiration for Conrad, relocated near the latter at Brede House in Kent. The initial discussion centers around a play put on by the Cranes at Brede schoolhouse, for the amusement of their friends and the local residents, on December 28, 1899. This play, entitled *The Ghost*, was a farce written by ten popular novelists of the time. It was of no literary significance and was written purely for fun, but the list of those who contributed to it is interesting. In addition to Crane, James, Conrad, and Wells, other authors included George Gissing, a novelist and exponent of naturalism; Robert Barr, a Scottish editor and novelist who later completed Crane's unfinished novel *The O'Ruddy* (1903); A. E. W. Mason, best remembered for his novel of contemporary life, *The Four Feathers* (1902); and H. Rider Haggard, prolific and enormously popular writer of romantic adventure novels, among them *King Solomon's Mines* (1885), *She* (1887), and *Allan Quatermain* (1887). Delbanco does not mention some of these authors again, and there are those among his readers who will wonder what associations may have existed between his chosen five and the others. Rudyard Kipling, who lived nearby, also receives scant attention. Delbanco states at the outset that he has been selective; his selectivity leaves many dangling questions.

Brede House was a fourteenth century manor, reputed to be a place of dampness and primitive sanitation, less than ideal for a man dying of consumption. Nevertheless, the Cranes hosted many parties there, and Crane seems to have been resigned to the certainty that his days were numbered. He and Conrad shared a genuine affection for each other, and it appears that this was the only really close friendship among the five.

Despite his affection for Crane and his appreciation of Crane's genuine gifts, Conrad expressed reservations concerning the younger man's ability to realize his potential as a writer. Delbanco, who shares Conrad's estimate, notes in passing that Crane's writing declined in quality after his arrival in England and suggests that American writers often fail to improve with recognition. The point may be well taken—Jack London, F. Scott Fitzgerald, and Dashiell Hammett are examples of American writers destroyed by success—but it may be less appropriate in the case of Crane, whose rapidly accelerating physical decline could easily have impaired his creative abilities. Be this as it may, Crane's brief career would seem to fit the implied pattern. Delbanco does not document any close relationship between Crane and James, although he notes that James was said to have been deeply distressed by Crane's death.

More central to the writer's craft is a collaborative effort between Conrad and Ford, to which Delbanco shifts in his next chapter. This partnership was one of convenience, with the hope of financial profit. The two men were essentially opposites. Conrad wrote painfully and with difficulty, distilling works of great depth from his experiences and internal conflicts; Ford was an extrovert who wrote easily, fluently, and well. Their collaboration, although it produced no major works, was not unproductive. *The Inheritors* (1901), *Romance* (1903), and *The Nature of a Crime* (1924) were published under their joint authorship. Ford's other contributions to the work of Conrad are less well-known. There seems to be no question that he supplied a chapter for *Nostromo* (1904) when the exhausted Conrad could not bring himself to meet a deadline; by drawing out Conrad and acting as amanuensis and editor, he evidently made *The Mirror of the Sea* (1906) and *A Personal Record* (1912) possible. He supplied plots for three stories, the idea for another, and he may have assisted with other works.

Conrad acknowledged Ford's help and was grateful for it. There is some evidence nevertheless that the persistent Ford, who was unfailingly energetic and helpful, was at times considered a nuisance. Conrad's wife, Jessie, resented him, and he often wearied Conrad. No doubt there were times when Ford felt frustrated by his obligations to Conrad.

The other relationship explored by Delbanco is that between James and Wells. Once again, the two personalities were dissimilar. James, the acknowledged master of prose, took a fatherly interest in younger writers and was not averse to giving them advice and counsel. He wrote to Wells on more than one occasion, offering to take one of the latter's novels and turn it into a work of art. Wells respectfully but firmly declined these offers. Delbanco does not comment on the tone of James's letters, but they are frankly patronizing, and a recipient might well have considered them brazen effrontery. If Wells felt any resentment, however, he did not allow it to appear in his correspondence. James was no doubt captivated by the force and freshness of Wells's writing and by the brilliance of his imagination, but in his view, Wells's work was crude and unfinished.

Wells always wrote with drive and conviction, and he produced prose of high quality. He was interested in history, social issues, science as it affects society, and the future of civilization. He is remembered today for several acknowledged classics of science fiction which speculate upon the effect that science or technology might have on people and institutions. Even his eerie forecast of atomic warfare in *The World Set Free* (1914) is more an imaginative assessment of social outcomes than a sensational account of devastation.

Much is made, by Delbanco and others, of the break between Wells and James that occurred when Wells and Rebecca West attacked, in print, the master's formidable and universally respected prose style. The importance of this rupture is perhaps exaggerated. Wells belonged to a new generation, a new century, and a new kind of writing. He repudiated the nineteenth century by rejecting one of its most prominent literary figures—a man who had also been his friend. In so doing, he severed his link with the past and proclaimed his own independence; he was merely acting out the familiar ritual of emancipation. That James's stature has not diminished, and that his own has faded, would not have dismayed him.

James was deeply hurt, and it is probable that he never understood why Wells had attacked him. In fact, it is likely that he did not understand either Wells or Crane. He was the soul of discretion and propriety; their unconventional life-styles must have appalled him. He recognized their gifts but had little sympathy with the purposes to which they turned them.

It is curious that Delbanco did not include a chapter on the relationship between James and Conrad; certainly, the two had much in common. Perhaps there was no relationship to explore. The two treated each other with respectful courtesy, and it may be that their association was limited to polite exchanges.

Delbanco provides no insights.

It must be concluded that, in spite of Delbanco's argument, these five men would constitute a group only in terms of acquaintance, propinquity, and a commitment to the novel. Each was a strong individualist who lived in the country because he preferred to work alone and required some degree of solitude. There is no evidence of cohesion within the group, no shared sense of mission, no effort to create a movement, school of thought, or collective style. They impinged upon one another; two maintained, off and on, a literary partnership; one of the partners, Ford, may have improved his own craft as a consequence. There is no indication of influence by a particular writer upon any of the others, and the single effort to exert influence failed. This arbitrarily designated group was in no sense the kind of closed corporation that was Bloomsbury.

Nicholas Delbanco is a British-born American novelist whose writing has received critical recognition for its elegance, poetic qualities, and mastery of contemporary forms. He has provided a distinctive framework for this study, an introduction and epilogue written by Delbanco the novelist rather than Delbanco the scholar; there is a startling but enjoyable contrast between the two elements. There are eight pages of appropriate illustrations, including two maps; the maps, however, require the use of a strong magnifier, and their legibility, even with such assistance, is minimal. The book is provided with adequate notes and a good index.

Delbanco's epilogue is a digressive but admirable celebration of writers and writing, but its final statement, "The best things come, as a general thing, from the talents that are members of a group," cannot be allowed to go unchallenged. It is true to the extent that no artist labors within a vacuum and that individuals learn from others. Beyond this point, there is little to substantiate the theory that group influence is either desirable or necessary for creative development. All major works are the result of individual talent; the greatest works are created by determined individuals who possess the strength of their own convictions and go their own ways, whether these lead to renown or to oblivion. Works that emerge from an artistic community are all too often those of the group leader, who has shaped or manipulated the talents of pliant members. They may be significant, but they are often derivative, the potential they represent distorted or unrealized. Group-inspired masterpieces, if they exist at all, are exceedingly rare.

In spite of its uneven qualities, *Group Portrait* is an enjoyable and challenging book. It can be expected to fulfill the ambitions of its author, who says that he wrote it primarily to interest others in the authors of books that he loves to read.

John W. Evans

Sources for Further Study

The Atlantic. CCXLIX, May, 1982, p. 106.
Boston Review. VII, August, 1982, p. 25.
Christian Science Monitor. July 21, 1982, p. 17.
Harper's Magazine. CCLXIV, April, 1982, p. 108.
Library Journal. CVII, April 1, 1982, p. 730.
Listener. CVIII, October 28, 1982, p. 20.
New Statesman. CIV, October 8, 1982, p. 26.
The New York Times Book Review. LXXXVII, May 30, 1982, p. 26.
The New Yorker. LVIII, June 21, 1982, p. 122.
Times Literary Supplement. October 22, 1982, p. 1148.

GROWING UP

Author: Russell Baker (1925-   )
Publisher: Congdon & Weed (New York). Illustrated. 278 pp. $15.00
Type of work: Autobiography
Time: 1925-1949
Locale: Northern Virginia, New Jersey, and Baltimore

Winning the 1983 Pulitzer Prize for Autobiography, this is the story of the early life of a prizewinning columnist

Principal personages:
RUSSELL BAKER, a young boy growing up during the Depression who eventually becomes a columnist for *The New York Times*
LUCY ELIZABETH ROBINSON BAKER, his mother
DORIS BAKER and
AUDREY BAKER, his younger sisters

As a columnist for *The New York Times*, Russell Baker is public property. According to literary critic R. Z. Sheppard, Baker's regular readers "wade expectantly toward him through bloated accounts of disaster, inhumanity, avarice and hypocrisy," seeking in his "Observer" column respite from the news. During the two decades that Baker has been writing the column, this respite has taken varied forms, but in general, Baker follows the tradition of the Horatian satirist, whose urbane and humorous voice points out weaknesses in humans and their institutions and gently insists that they mend their ways. Coming as he does out of this long-established literary tradition, and writing as he does in the most witty of journalistic styles, Baker has earned a devoted following and has won several prizes for commentary, among them, in 1979, a Pulitzer Prize. This prominence alone would seem to justify publication of an autobiography. Baker's readers may legitimately feel entitled to know something about the development of his wonderfully distinctive voice. Such readers will certainly find in *Growing Up* a portrait of the columnist as a young man, from his childhood in rural Virginia and, after his father's death, in New Jersey, to his early adulthood in Baltimore, but *Growing Up* is more than a personal chronicle. Taken as a whole, the book is an elegiac meditation on time, on the relation of the past to the present and to the future, not only in an individual life but also in the common life that eventually becomes the historical record of a people.

Baker's concern for connecting past and present arises in part from his conviction that "There has been an important change in the nature of society. Nothing seems to make sense any longer; there is no sequence to anything." As a child, he knew old men who could remember Lincoln's presidency; he also knew a black woman, Annie Grigsby, whose chief distinction was that she had been "born in slavery." "Living so close to Annie, who had been freed by Lincoln himself," he writes, "made me feel in touch with the historic past." Young people in the 1980's, Baker believes, do not have this same clear sense of the past. In both social and personal terms, the young are disconnected from what has gone before; they see themselves as isolated individuals, and they are—understandably—oriented toward the future. Still, Baker writes, "We all come from the past, and children ought . . . to know that life is a braided cord of humanity stretching up from time long gone, and that it cannot be defined by the span of a single journey from diaper to shroud." In one sense, then, *Growing Up* is written for people the age of Baker's own children—people who are young adults—in an effort to explain the circumstances that made their parents who they are. A child of the Depression, Baker writes on behalf of all who were young in that time, illuminating their values for those who grew up in a more affluent era.

He also writes in homage to his mother, Lucy Elizabeth Robinson Baker. The book is framed by visits to Lucy Elizabeth, for whom historical sequence has irretrievably broken down: she is in a nursing home where, under the power of advanced senility, she makes "free-wheeling excursions back through time." *Growing Up* is as much a reconstruction of Lucy Elizabeth's history and motivations as it is of Baker's own. Retrospect allows Baker to see that his mother was more than a fierce and opinionated individual; she embodied a tension between two conflicting views of women's position: "Her modern feminist passion for equality was at war with her nineteenth century idea of women as the purifying, ennobling element of society." Thus, while recording his mother's unending insistence that he make something of himself—"For God's sake, Russell, show a little gumption for once in your life"—Baker never lets the reader forget that in addition to possessing enormous personal strength, Lucy Elizabeth was a product of her times.

He also sympathizes with his mother's need for a man on whom she could depend economically. Widowed with three small children at the onset of the Depression, she was thrown on the mercy of her brothers, who were themselves struggling to survive. Despite her family's generosity, Lucy Elizabeth was never comfortable as their dependent, so, armed with a "bottomless supply of maxims," she set out to rear a son who could eventually protect and support her. Her goal imposed a heavy burden on the young Baker, but reading *Growing Up* gives one a sense less of the burden's heaviness than of the good humor with which Baker bore it. On the whole, he treats his mother with the affectionate tolerance afforded by hindsight; at the same time, he implies that he was "subdued . . . by too much melancholy striving to satisfy [his] mother's notions of manhood." It is a cruel irony that the family's entire supply of gumption was allotted to Baker's younger sister Doris, to whom *Growing Up* is dedicated. High-spirited and courageous, Doris might have satisfied Lucy Elizabeth's highest ambitions but for the "defect" of being a girl.

Besides Doris and Lucy Elizabeth, there are other strong women in this delightful book: Baker's paternal grandmother, Ida Rebecca, who stood six feet tall and between whom and Lucy Elizabeth there flourished a lively antagonism; the beautiful Mimi Nash, who ended Baker's hilariously unsuccessful attempts to lose his virginity and whom he eventually married. Baker was also blessed with colorful uncles on both sides of his family. Uncle Lewis, a perfumed and dandified barber, was the child's "first vision of what male elegance could be"; Uncle Tom's house boasted a mysterious flush toilet. Uncle Hal was forever putting together business deals that would not stay put together. Uncle Charlie, who spent his days indoors rereading *The Auto-biography of Benjamin Franklin* because he had once been frightened on the street, gave Baker his first experience with Republicanism. "For the longest time," Baker writes, "I thought of Republicans as people who rose from twelve-hour stretches in bed to denounce idlers and then lie down with a good book." Uncle Harold's legacy was especially important. Harold was a liar, and Baker was fascinated by him: "It was his intuitive refusal to spoil a good story by slavish adherence to fact that enchanted me. Although poorly educated, Uncle Harold somehow knew that the possibility of creating art lies not in reporting but in fiction."

It is in statements such as these that a reader can trace the beginnings of many of Baker's adult predilections. His father's death, when Baker was five, caused him "to sense that any happiness that came [his] way might be the prelude to some grim cosmic joke." At age seven, he "discovered the joys of politics" when the upstairs landlady nailed a Herbert Hoover campaign poster on the front door, throwing the Democratic household below into an uproar. President Hoover's insistence, against all the evidence, that prosperity was just around the corner generated in Baker a deep distrust of politicians and a sensitivity to the emptiness of political rhetoric. A college teacher's observation that the aspiring writer had a talent for dialogue inspired him to explore that talent; Baker's readers should be eternally grateful.

Even Baker's characterization of himself as an observer is consistent with his early inclinations. More than simply a watcher, he was a listener. In a lyrical passage describing "the luxuries of a rustic nineteenth-century boyhood," Baker recalls "majestic depths of silences, silences so immense I could hear the corn growing," and then catalogs sounds "no city child would ever hear." In the evenings, when his aunts and uncles sat on his grandmother's porch and talked about the weather, the day's work, and the adversities of rural life, Baker listened "to a conversation that had been going on for generations."

Later, after the family had moved to New Jersey, he would wake in the middle of the night to the sound of his relatives "down in the kitchen, talking, talking, talking." Baker's gift for dialogue is apparent in these records of domestic conversation; he uses repetition to richly humorous effect, showing how proverbs and clichés both deaden and enliven everyday speech. Eating sugar, Uncle Hal would say, was "like digging your grave with your own teeth"; Aunt Pat was always giving somebody "a piece of her mind." Valuing highly the "sense of family warmth that radiated through these long kitchen nights of talk," Baker writes: "What I absorbed most deeply was not information but attitudes, ways of looking at the world. . . . Sometimes their talk about the Depression was shaded with anger, but its dominant tones were good humor and civility. The anger was never edged with bitterness or self-pity. Most often it was expressed as genial contempt"—a label that describes very well the tone Baker frequently adopts in his columns.

This habit of observation, of watching and listening, was related to another trait which became evident early in Baker's life: his restraint. "Bred to repress the emotional expressions of love," he admired emotional engagement and openness, but he rarely participated in such displays. His Irish Aunt Pat was a case in point. Aunt Pat was "big, noisy, and relished messy human combat." While Baker appreciated Aunt Pat's gusto, he did so from a distance. Throughout *Growing Up*, he portrays himself as reserved, somewhat shy, and so self-conscious that when he accidentally discovered a Christmas present his mother had hidden, he practiced exclamations and expressions of surprise so as not to disappoint her—observing himself in advance. These tendencies—to draw apart, to watch and listen, to reflect—are fundamental to the craft of writing as Baker practices it. His mother never seems to have realized that the lack of gumption, which she so vigorously deplored, was in fact the wellspring of her son's ability to write.

Not that she failed to encourage Baker in his literary efforts. In fact, Lucy Elizabeth ghostwrote his first published work, entitled "Wheat." She continually held up to him the model of Cousin Edwin, a columnist for *The New York Times*, and she shared Baker's "pure ecstasy" when an essay he had written made his classmates laugh "with openhearted enjoyment." She urged her son not to give up on the idea of going to college, even when there was no money to send him. "Something will come along," she repeated, until something did—a scholarship to The Johns Hopkins University. When Baker opened the letter informing him that he had won the scholarship, Lucy Elizabeth reacted characteristically: she fixed him some iced tea. Baker explains that in his family, both major and minor events tended to prompt the preparation of food. Cooking was a "ritual response to death" in the Virginia village where he spent his earliest years; later, in New Jersey, "making a pot of coffee was the automatic reaction to every event." In one of the book's most moving passages, Baker recounts that immediately following the death of Baker's father, Lucy Elizabeth, practically destitute, decided to send her ten-month-old daughter Audrey to be reared by a brother-in-law and sister-in-law. Baker describes the scene and the aftermath of Audrey's departure with absolute restraint. After kissing the baby goodbye, he writes, Lucy Elizabeth "sat staring at the stove and rocking for the longest while. I went back out into the road, but she came out right behind me and touched my shoulder. 'Do you want me to fix you a piece of jelly bread?' she asked." Such passages show Baker's style at its most powerfully austere: simple syntax, concrete physical details, and not a Latinate polysyllable in sight.

This scene does more than display Baker's stylistic elegance; it shatters that monolith, the Great Depression, breaking it into small and intimate pieces. Baker achieves a similar effect with his reflections on the bombing of Hiroshima, set against the background of an exchange of mundane letters with his mother: "Doors were closing forever on our past. . . . Soon the world we had known and the values we had lived by in that world would become so obsolete that we would seem to Americans of the new age as quaint as travelers from an antique land." *Growing Up* is filled with such passages, some painful, many humorous. In them, Baker insists on the interconnectedness of the historical and the personal, creating as he does so an elegy for a world, and for people, he will never see again.

Carolyn Wilkerson Bell

Sources for Further Study

Christian Century. XCIX, November 17, 1982, p. 1155.
Los Angeles Times Book Review. October 10, 1982, p. 1.
National Review. XXXIV, September 17, 1982, p. 1156.
The New York Times Book Review. LXXXVII, October 17, 1982, p. 13.
Newsweek. C, November 8, 1982, p. 88.
Publishers Weekly. CCXXII, August 27, 1982, p. 350.
Social Education. XLVI, November, 1982, p. 470.
Time. CXX, November 1, 1982, p. 80.
The Washington Monthly. XIV, October, 1982, p. 57.

HANNAH ARENDT
For Love of the World

Author: Elizabeth Young-Bruehl (1946-   )
Publisher: Yale University Press (New Haven, Connecticut). Illustrated. 563 pp.
$25.00
Type of work: Biography
Time: 1906-1975
Locale: Germany, France, and the United States

A biography of one of the foremost political philosophers of the twentieth century, a woman as fascinating as she was brilliant, a thinker as controversial as she was profound

> *Principal personages:*
> HANNAH ARENDT, political philosopher and controversial reporter
> on the Eichmann trial
> HEINRICH BLÜCHER, her husband and intellectual companion
> MARTIN HEIDEGGER, existentialist philosopher, Arendt's teacher
> and an early influence on her thought
> KARL JASPERS, existentialist philosopher, Arendt's teacher and life-
> long friend

Elizabeth Young-Bruehl, a former student of Hannah Arendt, begins her biography of her eminent teacher with a study of Arendt's family and educational background (1906-1933), proceeds to a description of her life in Europe as a refugee (1933-1941), and concludes with a series of chapters concerning her life in the United States (1941-1975). Young-Bruehl's stated intention is to produce a work of "philosophical biography," a work which shows the "historical bases for [Arendt's] generalizations, the particular experiences that launched her thought, the friendships and loves that nourished her, and—if possible—her thinking manner or thinking style."

Inevitably, the result of such an ambitious enterprise is a book of considerable length, well over five hundred pages. Young-Bruehl is at her best when she analyzes Hannah Arendt's philosophical theories, the assumptions underlying those theories, and her style of presentation. Her examination of the controversy which arose over Arendt's articles on the Eichmann trial is impressive because of the kinds of questions she considers. Instead of arguing simplistically for or against Arendt's positions, she examines the reasons why her articles on the Eichmann trial became so controversial.

In spite of its obvious strengths, however, Young-Bruehl's biography is marred by a number of significant weaknesses. There are times when the book seems too heavily psychological, veering into psychohistory. It is problematical to find a biographer explaining Arendt, a Jew who was very critical of Zionism for political reasons, and who psychologically identified with Rahel Varnhagen. If in fact Arendt did identify with Varnhagen, it was probably because the latter represented certain abstract ideas which interested Arendt as a philosopher. As Young-Bruehl acknowledges, Arendt herself resisted psychological explanations of political events and causes.

Frequently, Young-Bruehl seems to lack a clear sense of her audience. Those who are interested in Arendt's thought will find the painstaking attention to the stories of her infancy related in Martha Arendt's diary, *Unser Kind*, merely boring. Those who are interested in Arendt's early intellectual development will be surprised by certain omissions. "Die Schatten," the poem which Young-Bruehl mentions as a particularly important revelation of Arendt's psychology, is discussed or referred to on pages xix, 26, 50, 51-56, 87-88, 90, and 308. Without any explanation, however, the original German version is omitted from the appendix which contains the original German texts of Arendt's poetry.

Young-Bruehl's account of Arendt's early love affair with Martin Heidegger seems to have been dredged up from correspondence, sometimes from letters written to third parties by Arendt. The source, for example, of Heidegger's reported revelation to his wife that Arendt was the "passion of his life and the inspiration of his work" is a letter from Arendt to Hilde Fränkel. Young-Bruehl should have either resisted the desire to include such a quote or invited the reader to approach it with some skepticism.

The biographical details of Arendt's life are interesting, but the social context of her thought, particularly the intellectual and literary circles to which she belonged, receives less attention in this study than many readers might wish. For example, Hannah Arendt reportedly described Rosalie Colie, her colleague at Wesleyan University, as the most erudite woman she had ever met, but the reader learns almost nothing here of the interaction between the two women. Young-Bruehl does give an account of Arendt's long friendship with Mary McCarthy, who became her literary executor.

Many readers interested in Arendt's life will be disappointed at the degree to which Young-Bruehl depends upon written sources, upon letters rather than the anecdotes of Arendt's acquaintances and friends. Arendt's correspondence will one day be edited and published, but personal recollections are easily lost. This study might have had more lasting value if it had been written from the perspective of Young-Bruehl as Hannah Arendt's student, as a young scholar investigating the sources of her mentor's thought.

Young-Bruehl may indeed be covering ground that must be covered when she attempts to provide a social history of the Jewish reaction to Nazi persecution; on the other hand, her ostensible subject is the intellectual development of Hannah Arendt. The strains of social history, intellectual history, and personal history are very difficult to separate in presenting the life of this formidable woman. Still, Young-Bruehl's analysis of the origins of World War II and of the Nazi persecution of the Jews becomes at times merely a list of friends and acquaintances of Arendt and her husband. Her description of Arendt's last years is far more successful than her attempt to deal with the "sources" of persecution.

Young-Bruehl's book is not without merit, but her subject matter, as she defined it, required a complete mastery of the social and literary history of the mid-twentieth century, the background and experience of an Edmund Wilson. Not surprisingly, she seems most reliable when she discusses Arendt's contributions to political philosophy and less informative concerning the literary context of her work.

Young-Bruehl adroitly handles the controversy over Arendt's report on the Eichmann trial, adopting a tone which is critical as well as sympathetic; this section combines impressive scholarship with a readable style. Young-Bruehl indicates ways in which Arendt's *Eichmann in Jerusalem: A Report on the Banality of Evil* (1963) was unnecessarily inflammatory to a Jewish audience, particularly in beginning with a negative portrait of David Ben-Gurion, but also in criticizing the actions of Jewish leaders, even suggesting that they organized the Holocaust for the Nazis. According to Young-Bruehl, these insensitive comments inspired the furious reaction of Jewish intellectuals. The controversy which ensued obscured Arendt's important analysis of the banality of evil.

Typically, Arendt was skeptical about the women's liberation movement. Young-Bruehl summarizes her view as one which supported the pursuit of concrete political goals which were coordinated with those of other political groups. The analysis of "psychological" oppression, whether it was of Jews, blacks, or women, disturbed Arendt because, as Young-Bruehl rightly emphasizes, Arendt insisted upon a division between social and political questions. No society, Arendt claimed, could enforce legislation ensuring social equality, and no society must ever be allowed to pass legislation enforcing political inequality.

More personally, Arendt understood the danger of allowing herself to be labeled as an exceptional woman. With a full understanding of the irony and its sources, Young-Bruehl quotes Arendt's comment: "I am not disturbed at all about being a woman professor, because I am quite used to being a woman." Young-Bruehl deftly parallels Arendt's unwillingness to treat women's issues apart from the demands of all groups for equality with her unwillingness to treat the "Jewish question" in isolation from other issues. Arendt herself refused to be treated as what she called an "exception" as a woman because she understood the historical consequences of being treated as an "exception" as a Jew.

Young-Bruehl took her subtitle for Arendt's biography, "For Love of the World," from the title which Arendt wanted to use for *The Human Condition* (1958), when that book was still in manuscript. *The Human Condition* attempts to take the traditional questioning of "philosophy" and apply that questioning to the world of human affairs. It is an attempt to take the active life seriously, to give it the same attention that philosophy has traditionally given to the contemplative life. For this reason, the European title of *The Human Condition* was *Vita activa oder von tätigen Leben* (1960). In *The Human Condition*, the book which she first wanted to call *Amor mundi*, Arendt intended to provide an alternative to *contemptus mundi*, the contempt for the world which has repeatedly surfaced in traditional Western philosophy.

Young-Bruehl has presented a complex portrait of a fascinating woman of great intellectual complexity. It is interesting, for example, to learn of Arendt's associations with Rainer Maria Rilke and W. H. Auden, and especially with Isak Dinesen. It is also valuable to learn of the depth of her concern with American social and political issues, ranging from the integration of Little Rock, Arkansas, to the election of President John F. Kennedy, to the antiwar protests of the 1960's. Arendt's positions on American political issues are not very thoroughly discussed in Young-Bruehl's biography, but even these glimpses suggest how deeply Arendt loved the new world of which she had become a citizen.

This biography, detailed as it is, should be assessed as a pioneering work, a first step in the careful examination of the life of a remarkable woman, her friends, enemies, acquaintances, and students.

Jeanie R. Brink

Sources for Further Study

Choice. XX, September, 1982, p. 182.
Christian Science Monitor. June 2, 1982, p. 17.
Library Journal. CVII, May 1, 1982, p. 883.
Los Angeles Times Book Review. May 30, 1982, p. 10.
Ms. X, June, 1982, p. 80.
The New York Times Book Review. LXXXVII, April 25, 1982, p. 1.
Newsweek. XCIX, May 3, 1982, p. 75.
Saturday Review. IX, May, 1982, p. 66.
Time. CXIX, April 1, 1982, p. 77.
Times Literary Supplement. August 6, 1982, p. 843.

HAPPY TO BE HERE

Author: Garrison Keillor (1942-   )
Publisher: Atheneum Publishers (New York). 210 pp. $11.95
Type of work: Short stories

Five stories dealing with the arts and media, baseball, political phenomena, and contemporary styles

Garrison Keillor is best known as the host of "A Prairie Home Companion," a weekly two-hour radio show that originated in 1974 in St. Paul, Minnesota, and is now available on many National Public Radio affiliates. This broadcast has brought Keillor's humor to a national audience, which delights in his weekly stories of past and present in his mythical hometown of Lake Wobegon, Minnesota, "the town that time forgot." His other popular creations include advertisements for mythical products and businesses, such as Powdermilk Biscuits, which "give shy persons the strength to get up and do what needs to be done," the Fearmonger's Shoppe, "serving your phobia needs," and Bertha's Kitty Boutique "In the Dales." These and other inventions, including poems of Margaret Haskins Durber, "the poet laureate of Lake Wobegon," can be heard on two long-playing recordings: *A Prairie Home Companion Anniversary Album* (1980) and *The Family Radio* (1982). Keillor's radio humor depends to a great extent on his voice and his delivery. For the reader conditioned by Keillor's homey, sincere, almost nostalgic radio voice, it is difficult and somewhat unnerving to enter into the many-voiced stories of *Happy to Be Here*, a collection of pieces which first appeared in *The New Yorker* and elsewhere between 1969 and 1981. Once the transition is made, however, the reader will be delighted.

In his introduction and in many of the pieces, Keillor pays homage to *The New Yorker* and its writers, especially James Thurber and S. J. Perelman. Like these and other of *The New Yorker* humorists, Keillor enjoys playing with language. He is not above including a letter in disguised verse among those in the mailbag in his parody of military action stories, "Mission to Mandala," nor is he above naming a character "Gloria Mundi" in "Your Transit Commission," or using a "multipun" title such as "The Lowliest Bush a Purple Sage Would Be."

Keillor most resembles Thurber when he reminisces, perhaps about his own childhood, as in "Drowning 1954," a first-person story of a man who, as a boy, pretended to attend swimming lessons, felt damned because he had deceived his parents, and then felt saved when he learned to swim by himself. "Nana Hami Ba Reba" may remind readers of "The Secret Life of Walter Mitty" when the apparent parody of "high-tech" science fiction ends with the narrator "materializing" in a present-day middle-class home in time to dine with his family. "The Drunkard's Sunday" recalls Thurber's more melancholy pieces, such as "The Evening's at Seven": the drunkard moves from a despairing vision of his ruin to a manic hope that he will fully realize the life he seems already to have, only to return again to despair and the fear that he will lose everything.

Keillor pays his respects to Perelman most clearly when he parodies verbal styles, especially those of advertising and popularized social science. In "Your Transit Commission," he parodies the rhetoric of "friendly" bureaucracies as they appeal to selected markets. Joggers can ride a bus with seats in the center aisle and a track around them. Those who wish to escape the "old linear idea that has imprisoned transit" may find themselves someday on the Freedom Bus, which when it is "almost there," becomes a surprise all-day excursion to some local attraction. In this way, the transit commission becomes "more than just a transit commission. It is a total urban transit delivery system." Keillor repeatedly pricks such jargon. In "Around the Horne," baseball-coach-turned-sportswriter Ed Farr applies self-awareness therapy, not very successfully, to his losing baseball team. In "The New Baseball," holistic jargon and futurology meet to transform baseball: "In time . . . the entire stadium setup will become useless as spectators are drawn into the playing area. . . . This will lead to the disappearance of ballplayers as a performing elite." In "Plainfolks," Tom Wolfe and Studs Terkel are echoed, if not parodied, when high schoolers apply oral history and folklore techniques to the popular culture of the 1950's and 1960's. The language of popular anthropology suffers in "Oya Life These Days," the account of a "tribe" which sets at naught most of the tools of social science by behaving like participant-observers. Parody of verbal styles is perhaps Keillor's comic tool of choice. Some other targets include the rhetoric of minority liberation movements in "Shy Rights: Why Not Pretty Soon?" of military-industrial-complex lobbyists in "Re the Tower Project," of pollster reports in "How It Was in America a Week Ago Tuesday," of food faddists in "The People's Shopper" (which ends with a visionary conversion to junk food) and of country and western music lyrics as an advertising gimmick in "The Slim Graves Show."

While virtually every piece in the collection is good for a laugh, no mean accomplishment, several pieces stand out because of their extended development or because they offer some substance which adds significance to their humor. "Don: The True Story of a Young Person," recounts the difficulties of seventeen-year-old Don Beeman, who is trying to become a man while playing with Trash, his punk-rock band. The band is a small-town imitation of "real punk," confining their outrageousness to words and gestures the Rolling Stones made old, until they achieve notoriety by attacking a chicken at the President's Day County 4-H Poultry Show Dance. Even though the chicken is not seriously hurt, the boys earn sensationalized condemnation in the *Gazette*, and Don's participation exacerbates the usual father-versus-teenage-son conflicts in the Beeman home. Don is, in fact, a fairly typical

Midwestern adolescent who loves his family, who does well in school, and who can devote great energy to something that interests him. He is also typical in being more distant from his father than he wants to be because his father is unable to talk with him about feelings and dreams. As local sentiment against them organizes, the band members work out their resentment in their rehearsals and gradually fall into the childish rebellion which the story suggests is implicit in punk rock: "They tell lies about us—O.K., we're going to make those lies come true!" As attacking a surrogate chicken becomes a ritualized rebellion in their rehearsals, Don begins to wonder whether the band is "going off the deep end." When another band member asks, "If it feels good, then what's wrong?" Don wonders, "How can you feel good if you don't know it's right. . . . And how do you know if something is right?"

Don comes to believe that he must make an adult moral decision about whether to stay with the band. This need presses upon him as his parents, in an understanding attempt to give him another chance, schedule another dance. As Don wavers, the national media complicate the scene, for Green Phillips of *Falling Rocks* will give the band national coverage if they eat a chicken at their next performance. They attack the chicken (the same one with its now bandaged neck) and, within forty-eight hours, are asked to perform in Omaha and Tampa. Having become rock stars, they *have* to eat chicken, and they find they do not particularly care for it. Don's moral decision remains unmade except by default. In Tampa, it falls to him to bite the chicken: "While he waited, he thought to himself that perhaps by doing it and feeling sick about doing it he would do some good, perhaps by showing any kids that might be in the audience that they should not try to do this, and that maybe it would be an example to them about violence." Don is cut loose from his moral moorings in home and family, hoping absurdly that what he does will not cut others loose from their moorings. In this comic treatment of the morally bewildered, Keillor may remind readers of Jean Shepherd or John Updike.

"My North Dakota Railroad Days" is the bitterly humorous first-person narration of a former conductor on the North Dakota State Railroad, a man who has gradually lost the symbols of honor belonging to his profession: his train, his job, his pension, and his union hall. He is split between love of the Prairie Queen (his train) and anger about the shenanigans which ruined the line. The Prairie Queen was an American dream train. In its best years, the tracks were so smooth that the Queen carried a billiard table, and the train was so fast that it could make unscheduled pleasure stops for the passengers to take photographs, to accept invitations to small-town celebrations, or even to do a little hunting. There was a dance car with good music, and there was a special sleeper on which one could ride from Fargo to Grand Forks *and back* overnight if he needed a rest. Everything about the train was rich, friendly, and pleasant. Behind it all was R. G. Houtek, the state-appointed President and General Manager of the line, whose lawyers authored the charter by which the state railroad was established, who got rich when the line did well and who bled it when it began to decline. Houtek warned the narrator not to invest in the North Dakota State Railroad, but the narrator's investment was in pride and love, "commodities" which Houtek did not value. When Houtek's shady dealings were about to be exposed, he went mad and sent the train on a runaway race which ended deep in the Red River. The narrator's final curse on Houtek includes the provisions that dogs dig up his bones and drag them through the streets of Minneapolis and that all of his money be given to the bankrupt union pension fund. In the tall-tale tradition, but with a wealth of realistic detail which makes one wonder if it is not fictionalized history, this story realizes the clash of the common man's dreams and the financier's ambitions, a conflict not unlike what one might expect in an episode of John Dos Passos' *U.S.A.* (1937).

"WLT (The Edgar Era)" is the account of the early years of a radio station which grows out of Edgar Elmore's desire to bring the first families of Minneapolis into his sandwich palace. He and his brother, Roy, hope to attract a more distinguished clientele by broadcasting from their restaurant programs which will show what a respectable place they operate. Within a short time, however, the radio station comes to dominate the restaurant. As the brothers gradually discover what radio can do, they stumble across the popular format of interviewing members of the audience. This discovery so increases their popularity that the restaurant ceases to be fun. They are beseiged by customers and by eager talent. Edgar comes to fear the spontaneity of live radio, to fear that sometime someone will say "something so repulsive, crude, and vile as to make his name Mud in thousands of homes. . . ." He becomes a prisoner of his medium, taking no pleasure in listening to the show, but feeling uncomfortable when he does not listen. He realizes that there is really nothing he can do to prevent this disaster. He is lucky enough to die before it actually occurs, when the announcer in the children's story hour discovers that his script is a racy melodrama. This story is one of several to which Keillor's characteristic radio voice and delivery are appropriate. Like his Lake Wobegon stories, it follows a central thread, but attaches semi-digressive ribbons and bows. For example, there is the fanciful account of exotic sound effects used in one program, including the parting of the Red Sea, conveyed with the aid of "ten quarts of motor oil and an upright vacuum cleaner."

Though it may not be obvious, one strength of Keillor's stories is the moral seriousness which informs them. Though his parodies are usually gentle attacks on misuses of language, their cumulative effect is serious. Keillor asks that people not tell lies to one another; he urges his readers to avoid being caught in forms of discourse which make it easy for them to hide from themselves. In "Attitude," he argues that even amateur baseball players ought to regret their dumb plays and leave it to others to forgive. Anyone who pays attention to the language of contemporary culture realizes that the ideas behind this sort of parody are important, perhaps crucial to the survival of democracy. To succumb unconsciously to a "dialect" is to lose a degree of freedom to think. It may be Keillor's central accomplishment that, while delighting his readers, he also contributes to liberating them from some of the more insidious traps which American culture lays for them.

Terry Heller

Sources for Further Study

Christian Century. XCIX, July 21, 1982, p. 793.
Library Journal. CVII, January 15, 1982, p. 195.
National Review. XXXIII, December 11, 1981, p. 1492.
The New York Times Book Review. LXXXVII, February 28, 1982, p. 12.
Time. CXIX, February 1, 1982, p. 74.
Virginia Quarterly Review. LVIII, July 2, 1982, p. 793.

H. D.
The Life and Work of an American Poet

Author: Janice S. Robinson
Publisher: Houghton Mifflin Company (Boston). Illustrated. 490 pp. $17.95
Type of work: Literary biography
Time: 1886-1961
Locale: Pennsylvania, England, and Continental Europe

An analysis of the interrelationship between the life and work of an American poet and novelist

> *Principal personages:*
> HILDA DOOLITTLE, the writer, better known as H. D.
> EZRA POUND, the poet to whom she was engaged
> RICHARD ALDINGTON, H. D.'s husband
> D. H. LAWRENCE, the novelist
> FRIEDA LAWRENCE, his wife
> BRYHER, an English writer, born Winifred Ellerman
> SIGMUND FREUD, the psychoanalyst
> PERDITA SCHAFFNER, H. D.'s daughter

American writer Hilda Doolittle made her reputation in the years during and immediately after World War I as the Imagist poet H. D., author of beautiful, crystalline lyrics and friend of Ezra Pound, Amy Lowell, D. H. Lawrence, and other well-known literary figures. By the time of her death in 1961, however, her name had almost faded from public view, except for a sentence or two in literary histories and an occasional poem in an anthology. Recently there has been a resurgence of interest in her work. *End to Torment*, her memoir of Pound, was published in 1979; *HERmione*, a novel, in 1981; *The Gift*, recollections of her childhood, in 1982. Several volumes of her poetry, including her World War II poems collected in *Trilogy* (1973) and her epic, *Helen in Egypt* (1961), were reprinted during the 1970's. Scholars have paid increasing attention to her work in the last decade, and feminist critics have begun to examine her career as a model of the struggle of the woman artist in a patriarchal environment.

Janice S. Robinson's book draws on this feminist approach to H. D.'s life and work, but it is much more than an account of a writer's attempt to achieve independence in the face of attacks from oppressive men. Robinson has read the work of H. D. and her contemporaries extensively; the book is the product of twelve years of research. It is neither a conventional biography nor a survey of H. D.'s literary career, though it contains elements of both. What Robinson has done is to explore the interrelationship between H. D.'s poems and novels and the significant events in her life. In the process, she makes considerable demands on her readers. Much of this book consists of close analysis of passages of prose and poetry, and Robinson's style can be opaque at times.

This is not a volume for a reader interested in a little literary gossip, pleasantly presented.

Robinson's approach to H. D. rests on the assumption that there is in all her work "a buried level of experience coming through the surface writing." She uses H. D.'s own image to illuminate this concept: the palimpsest, the piece of parchment that is used, erased, and used again. It may thus contain several stories, even though only the top one is visible. Throughout the book, Robinson tries to search out and explain, in the light of her knowledge of H. D.'s life, the hidden meanings of her work. Then, in turn, she uses the submerged messages she has found in the work to expand her understanding of the life.

Robinson suggests that H. D.'s use of this kind of symbolism was a natural outgrowth of her upbringing in the Moravian church, which provided her with "a mystical love language as well as a form of religion, social and familial organization . . . a community of shared experience, of shared symbolism, of a common language about the experience of life." Having grown up within a tradition that stressed truths hidden beneath symbolic words, H. D. found this a congenial technique for writing about the most significant experiences in her life.

The critical years for H. D. as woman and artist were, in Robinson's view, those between 1905 and 1920. The poet was eighteen in 1905, the year in which she became engaged to Ezra Pound, then a student and an aspiring poet at the University of Pennsylvania, where her father taught. Their engagement continued, somewhat tenuously, for the next six years, with H. D. living at home, reading and writing under Pound's guidance. He, meanwhile, began to travel in Europe and form close friendships with several other women as he developed his own career. H. D. finally joined him in England in 1911, expecting to be married, but she found that he was also engaged to Dorothy Shakespear, who eventually became his wife. H. D. stayed on in London, maintaining her friendship with him, and began to concentrate on her writing— the first of many times she would find in her art a way of fighting back against masculine desertion and betrayal.

Her professional career as a poet began in August, 1912, in the British Museum Tea Room, where Pound took one of her poems, crossed out a few phrases, signed it "H. D. Imagiste," and sent it off to Harriet Monroe, the editor of *Poetry*. H. D. was also working at this time with Richard Aldington, a young English poet who was also a member of the group who called themselves Imagists. The two were married in 1913. Their marriage foundered within three years, perhaps as a result of basic incompatibility, but also because of the stillbirth of their child in 1915 and H. D.'s fear of another pregnancy. Aldington's experiences as a soldier and his wife's lack of understanding of them also apparently contributed to their difficulties. Although they stayed together for a time, both turned to others. H. D. entered into a relationship with the man Robinson is convinced was the single most important influence on her life, D. H. Lawrence. The Aldingtons separated in 1919, when H. D. became pregnant with someone else's child. She never identified the father, even to her daughter, Perdita.

At this point in her life, H. D. was virtually abandoned by the men to whom she had been close. Aldington, Lawrence, and Cecil Gray, whom some scholars have identified as her lover, removed themselves from her life; Pound offered sympathy but no concrete help. She was rescued by a wealthy young Englishwoman, Winifred Ellerman, who called herself by her pen name, Bryher. She and her father, shipping magnate Sir John Ellerman, took in both mother and child and provided financial support for many years afterward.

Robinson's account of the remaining forty years of H. D.'s life is much less detailed than her discussion of the preceding decade. She devotes surprisingly little attention to H. D.'s relationship with Bryher, apparently because she believes it had a less significant effect on her work than her friendships with others. The critical encounter of the second half of H. D.'s life, in Robinson's view, was that with Sigmund Freud, who helped her to come to terms with her past in many sessions of psychoanalysis in 1933 and 1934. Freud's appreciation of her as an artist compensated for the earlier betrayals; Robinson says that he "restored her . . . as friend and teacher, he was in touch with the whole secret of the mystery." Building on the strength he gave her, H. D. produced much of her finest work during the 1940's and 1950's: the war poems, *The Walls Do Not Fall* (1944), *Tribute to the Angels* (1945), and *The Flowering of the Rod* (1946); the autobiographical novel *Bid Me to Live* (1960); and the long poem on a little known variant of the Helen of Troy legend, *Helen in Egypt*. She continued to write almost to the end of her life. One of her last works was *End to Torment*, her memoir of Pound, with whom she kept in touch through all his political and mental problems during and after the war.

Inevitably, the aspect of Robinson's book that has attracted the most attention is her assertion about H. D.'s relationship with Lawrence. Her thesis is not altogether new. *Bid Me to Live* was widely recognized to be a *roman à clef* about H. D., Aldington, Lawrence, and his wife, Frieda, but scholars have generally assumed that the unconsummated, broken romance depicted in the novel was the full account of the H. D.-Lawrence relationship. Robinson is convinced that it was not. She devotes approximately one-quarter of her book to detailed analysis of works by the two writers to show that they were in fact lovers, and to suggest strongly that it was Lawrence, not Gray, who was the father of H. D.'s child.

Robinson finds the strongest support for her thesis in Lawrence's *The First Lady Chatterley* (1944), *John Thomas and Lady Jane* (1972), and *Lady Chatterley's Lover* (1928), three versions of the same novel. She believes that Lady Chatterley, her impotent, insensitive husband Sir Clifford, and her game-keeper lover, are portraits of H. D., Aldington, and Lawrence, and that Lady

Chatterley's pregnancy by a man not her husband is based on H. D.'s situation. Lawrence accepted in his fiction, she implies, the responsibility he denied in life.

She also points out striking similarities between H. D.'s unpublished novel, "Paint It Today," written in 1921, and the Lady Chatterley stories. The heroine of H. D.'s work, clearly autobiographical, meets her lover in a "little house in the woods," a place very much like the trysting place of the lovers in *John Thomas and Lady Jane*. In both works, the woman sits on the porch of the hut, seeking peace and calm; in both, she stands nude and examines herself in a mirror; in both, the couple make love on an old blanket. There seems to have been no possibility that either writer saw the other's manuscript; if the details are as close as Robinson says they are, the works must have derived either from a common experience or from remarkably close imaginative processes.

Robinson also makes an exhaustive comparison of images and themes in two other works to illustrate her point. H. D.'s "Pilate's Wife," another unpublished novel, was written between 1924 and 1929 and revised in 1934. Lawrence's *The Escaped Cock* began as a short story published in 1928. The complete novel was printed in Paris in 1929 and reissued as *The Man Who Died* in 1931. In this case, it is possible that the final version of H. D.'s work was influenced by her reading of Lawrence's story, but Robinson is certain that the two writers began independently. Both novels deal with a Jesus who did not die after the Crucifixion but recovered from his wounds to enter a new life. Lawrence's Christ figure becomes the lover of a priestess of Isis; H. D.'s, of Pontius Pilate's wife Veronica, a devotee of the cult of Isis. Robinson finds many common images as well as similar details of plot in the two works, demonstrating fairly conclusively that whatever the two writers' personal relationship may have been, they certainly shared artistic insights.

Robinson analyzes a number of H. D.'s later works in the light of the Lawrence relationship, showing how she told the same story again and again, in different settings, with characters of different names. It is most richly interpreted in *Helen in Egypt*, Robinson suggests, with the poet characterized as Helen, Aldington as Paris, Lawrence as Achilles, Pound as Odysseus, and Freud, now incorporated into H. D.'s private mythology, as the wise teacher Theseus. Once again, the H. D. persona and the Lawrence persona are brought together to conceive a child.

Robinson's argument is, on the whole, persuasive, but because it is based almost entirely on interpretation of literary texts, most readers will want to reserve final judgment. As she recognizes, the absence of corroborative evidence is a weakness in her case. For this lack, she blames Aldington, whom she discusses with considerable hostility throughout the book. She accuses him of deliberately suppressing evidence of H. D.'s relationship with Lawrence, not to protect her privacy as he claimed, but out of jealousy and resentment. Robinson may be right, but the passages from his letters and H. D.'s that she quotes to justify her accusation generally seem open to a kinder interpretation than she gives. It is clear that H. D. had many opportunities to reveal whatever details she chose in the thirty years she survived Lawrence; perhaps Aldington was following her wishes in asking Lawrence's biographers to minimize her role in his life. Is it, in the last analysis, really necessary to answer the question Robinson raises at the end of the section on H. D. and Lawrence: "To what extent did the realities described in these works occur somewhere, somehow, in historical time at a particular place or location, and to what extent was the H. D.-D. H. Lawrence vision conceived and born within the temple of twin minds?"

Whatever the validity of Robinson's theory, her book should be an indispensable tool for all future students of H. D.'s work and perhaps for Lawrence scholars as well. It does not satisfy all needs. A less thesis-dominated, more comprehensive biography of H. D., directed to a wider audience, would still be welcome. There is also room for more detached, evaluative discussion of the works Robinson treats with such intensity. Her immersion in her subject seems at times to limit her ability to stand back from the works and assess them objectively, but her book adds much that is new and important to an understanding of H. D.'s life and work. Her provocative interpretations and the quality of the writings from which she quotes copiously should do much to confirm H. D.'s reputation as an important figure in the history of twentieth century poetry.

Elizabeth Johnston Lipscomb

Sources for Further Study

American Literature. L, October, 1982, p. 457.
Choice. XIX, May, 1982, p. 1244.
Library Journal. CVII, March 1, 1982, p. 551.
Los Angeles Times Book Review. May 30, 1982, p. 12.
National Review. XXXIV, May 14, 1982, p. 577.
New Leader. LXV, April 5, 1982, p. 18.
The New York Times Book Review. LXXXVII, February 14, 1982, p. 3.
Publishers Weekly. CCXXI, January 8, 1982, p. 78.

HEADBIRTHS
Or, The Germans Are Dying Out

Author: Günter Grass (1927-   )
Translated from the German by Ralph Manheim
Publisher: Harcourt Brace Jovanovich (New York). 144 pp. $9.95; paperback $2.95
Type of work: Novel
Time: 1979-1980
Locale: Germany, India, Bali, and China

On a Third World lecture tour, Günter Grass develops ideas for a screenplay about a touring German couple

Principal characters:
GÜNTER GRASS, the author
HARM PETERS, Grass's typical liberal German
DÖRTE PETERS, Harm's wife
UTE GRASS, Grass's wife
VOLKER SCHLÖNDORFF, the director of the film *The Tin Drum*

The "headbirths" of the title refers to the way Harm and Dörte Peters spring from Günter Grass's head, comparable to the way Athena sprang from the head of Zeus. Grass creates these people, in part, to counteract the decline in German population. He speculates on the gains and losses if the Germans were multiplying like the Chinese and the Chinese declining like the Germans. Grass, recalling the notorious Nazi demand for "living space," argues that, since the Germans see themselves as overcrowded, they might as well let the myth become reality.

Within the novel (first published in German as *Kopfgeburten: Oder, Die Deutschen Sterben Aus*, 1981), Grass anticipates criticism of it on the grounds that this is one of his contemporary, political books, rather than one of his more popular "historical" ones. That argument is more than a little disingenuous. *Die Blechtrommel* (1959; *The Tin Drum*, 1962) and *Der Butt* (1977; *The Flounder*, 1978) are by no means apolitical. They are highly regarded because they have been formed with great care and contain plenty of "living space" where large issues can develop. The real problem with *Headbirths* is not the ephemeral nature of 1979 German politics and world issues, but the ephemeral nature of Grass's treatment of characters and themes.

Grass cannot resist an imaginative historical trip with himself cast as a German ten years older than he actually was during World War II, pandering to the Nazis in order to get publication, serving in the army, becoming disillusioned at Stalingrad. Although a promising idea, it is not developed to the point of telling readers anything about Grass that they were not given in depth in earlier works, nor does it contribute anything to the basic themes of this novel. Current relations between East and West German writers and Grass's "modest proposals" for governing a unified Germany are very much to the point of 1979 liberal malaise, but Grass's criticism of the Nazi he might have been is merely awkward base-touching, with World War II as a *pro forma* prelude to Germany in 1979.

Grass views the division between the two Germanies as an arbitrary piece of foolishness perpetrated by the Soviet Union and the United States. He proposes a Germany united by a cultural history museum at the Berlin Wall, with a switch of economic systems between the two Germanies every ten years to relax the East and burn fat off the West. He proposes an end to compulsory education, the civil service, and all German births, while at the same time advocating the establishment of a tax on Church property and of a citizen's militia to allow Germany to take control of its own gloomy destiny. In the death of his friend, novelist Nicholas Born, and of a radical-gone-tame, Rudi Dutschke, Grass sees signs of the passing of German artistic and politically liberal leadership.

While the cumulative effect of these whimsical set-pieces contributes to the shapelessness of this novel, it also pushes Grass forward as the central character. By presenting Harm Peters' reactions to Grass's own "modest proposals," the novelist emphasizes Peters' lesser role in the novel. Interestingly, Grass's wife, Ute Grass, does not overshadow the fictional Dörte Peters. Harm Peters is a foil for both Grass and Dörte; Ute Grass does not participate in the action in any vital way.

Volker Schlöndorff, director of the film *The Tin Drum*, is another foil for Grass. Grass has a good grasp of the relationship between filmmaking and writing. A short book full of striking images makes a better film than a long book full of authorial narration and verbosity, but the vision of an author self-consciously writing a novel in which his primary expressed concern is roughing out a film scenario cannot be wholly satisfying to readers, especially since this book does not even do that wholeheartedly, but relies heavily on the very kind of authorial asides that are least filmable.

A summary of this brief novel would whet appetites for something that is not there, something not developed much beyond the summary stage. Harm and Dörte's central struggle is whether or not to have a baby. The familiar liberal arguments for and against are made poignant by the background of world hunger and overpopulation. Indian slum dwellers do not understand what the Peterses mean when they explain that each of them sometimes wants to have a child but never both at the same time. Balinese fertility rites make this kind of liberalism seem all the more stiff and German. Objective correlatives are provided by the pregnant cat, whose kittens the Peterses feel obligated to drown, and by the liver sausage sweating inside its safe wrappings but becoming dubiously edible as the Peterses drag it through the tropics with them. Grass considers and rejects building a spy thriller around the sausage, but he likes the symbolism of a snake suddenly coming from beneath Dörte's skirt in Bali and a bat seemingly seeking Dörte wherever she goes.

More indirectly, the Peterses' indecision about having a baby is a symptom of liberal inertia. Nuclear power is both good and bad; mechanized farming in China would be efficient but would create unemployment. The most vivid, thematically unifying scene occurs when Dörte has an extended hallucination in which Harm "goes native" before her eyes, defecating in the street and squatting to chew betel nut, thus becoming indistinguishable from the Indian slum dwellers.

The most ineffective scene occurs when Harm and Dörte project themselves as the stars of a John Wayne film they see on their plane, and Grass laments the prohibitive costs of reshooting. The most casual inquiries on Grass's part would have revealed advances in dubbing that are more effective for fantasy purposes than reshooting. This passage casts doubt on Grass's insistence that he is doing a scenario.

The final scene is effective: Harm nearly runs over a Turkish boy but is able to stop the car in time, thus affirming his desire to let other societies increase as Germany decreases. The development of the population motif is obscured throughout the novel, however, by Grass's presentation of his views on the state of literature. These are worth knowing in themselves, but they diffuse the energy of the narrative. The inability of postwar writers to measure up to Thomas Mann and Bertolt Brecht is slipped in as the subject of Grass's lectures to the Chinese. A Chinese writer responds to that notion with what, to him (and, apparently, to Grass), is the analogous difficulty of writing about normal experiences of love and sex in a China that represses and outlaws normal experience.

Further on, Grass compares the role of Nazi-era writers, as being precursors to that of postwar writers, with the Chinese acceptance of a favorite playwright of the "Gang of Four" as a major writer. These superficial notions are not pursued with a view toward deeper insights into Germany or China.

If the basic notion that this book is a novel is abandoned, then the Peterses can be viewed as merely a collective device that enables Grass to present scenes from his real trip and the accompanying reflections. In that case, however, there would be no reason for Grass to single out as he does certain experiences of the Peterses, insisting that these are "real" and based on his own experience. The reader is left with a mixed body of real and false information about serious issues.

Were Bombay slums leveled to provide recreation facilities for nuclear plant workers? Are there really "Sisyphus Tours" for those who wish to see the real world and spend a night with slum-dwellers? Is the gulf between non-traveling Germans worried about street lights and bicycle prices and traveling Germans worried about Indonesia more or less as depicted? Is this information put forward primarily to provide entertainment, to provoke indignation, or to evoke some other response?

It is not a question of "trivializing" world hunger: any writer who provides a mix of serious issues and entertainment can be so charged by knee-jerk readers. Yet by allowing his book space, Angus Wilson in *As If by Magic* (1973), for example, did a more convincing job both of entertainment and instruction on world hunger than Grass does here.

Every writer has only so much sand in his hourglass. Writer-teacher-critic-citizen-traveler-celebrity will never be in balance. Many writers dread the thought that a book will carry some subtle aura of having been begun on planes and in hotels. Grass disingenuously flaunts the obviously "off the top" nature of this book, and that is a disappointment.

T. G. Shults

Sources for Further Study

The Atlantic. CCXLIX, April, 1982, p. 110.
Commonweal. CIX, July 16, 1982, p. 409.
Library Journal. March 15, 1982, p. 650.
Nation. CCXXXIV, April 24, 1982, p. 502.
The New York Times Book Review. LXXXVII, March 14, 1982, p. 11.
The New Yorker. LVIII, June 14, 1982, p. 129.
Saturday Review. IX, March, 1982, p. 57.
Times Literary Supplement. April 23, 1982, p. 455.
West Coast Review of Books. VIII, May, 1982, p. 25.

HER VICTORY

Author: Alan Sillitoe (1928-   )
Publisher: Watts (New York). 590 pp. $15.95
Type of work: Novel
Time: Primarily the present, though there are many flashbacks
Locale: Nottingham, London, Brighton, and Europe

A psychological novel which deals with the quest for liberation of three principal characters by focusing on their separate histories, their current interrelationships, and their attempts to achieve victory over the forces that have determined and shaped their present situations of emptiness and loneliness

> Principal characters:
> PAM, a middle-aged woman who leaves her brutal husband after twenty years
> TOM, a middle-aged former officer in the merchant navy who discovers his Jewish heritage at age fifty; Pam's lover
> JUDY, a middle-aged single parent with two children and with Lesbian predilections; lover of both Pam and Tom

Alan Sillitoe made his mark on the literary establishment with the publication of *Saturday Night and Sunday Morning* (1958) and *The Loneliness of the Long-Distance Runner* (1959). In these early works, the author's style is taut and lean; the stories amply display what Henry James calls solidity of specification, for Sillitoe's representations of life in a working-class district of Nottingham are concretely realized and densely textured. His ear for speech is unerring, and he adroitly captures the quotidian rhythms of his native idiom. These works have a raw anger that is barely kept under aesthetic control, and Sillitoe gives his robustly anarchistic view of society memorable spokesmen: Arthur Seaton, the working-class hero of *Saturday Night and Sunday Morning* whose rebellious temperament, sensuous vitality, and intellectual cunning allow him to define himself uniquely against the ubiquity of the "they" who have power and to beat the system to the degree that it is beatable; and the delinquent Smith, a long-distance runner in the eponymous short story, a rebel who refuses to play the game, to win the race for the governor of the prison. The verbal energy and brute realism of these early works are, paradoxically, the vintage Sillitoe. The writings of the so-called angry young men seem pallid in comparison. Thus, if one has only intermittently kept track of what Sillitoe has been doing for the last twenty years, *Her Victory* will come as a surprise.

It is hard to imagine a slower-moving novel. The reader is subjected to nearly six hundred pages of laborious, stilted, and repetitive prose. At points, Sillitoe is overly solemn, puritanical, and pontifical. The two most important characters in *Her Victory*, Pam and Tom, attitudinize philosophically and speculate endlessly, especially Tom. Moreover, the ideological posturing of the narrative as a whole is predictable. The causes of feminism, lesbianism, and Zionism are blandly espoused without any attempt to consider the complexities of the issues involved; hence, the implied liberalism seems facile. Sillitoe's early work expresses a healthy skepticism toward all ideological posturing. This is not the case in *Her Victory*. What weakens the book is not the inclusion of ideological sentiments and philosophical observations but the spurious rhetoric and self-indulgence which attend them. As D. H. Lawrence points out in his "Study of Thomas Hardy" found in *Phoenix: Posthumous Papers* (1936), "it is the novelists and dramatists who have the hardest task in reconciling their metaphysic, their theory of being and knowing, with their living sense of being." *Her Victory* has much discussion about being and knowing but rarely evokes any living sense of being. As Lawrence notes in the same study, "every work of art adheres to some system of morality. But if it really be a work of art, it must contain the essential criticism on the morality to which it adheres." *Her Victory* is devoid of this essential criticism; it takes itself very seriously.

If the ideological posturing of the narrative is predictable, the plot development is even more so. The "significant" and "unexpected" climax of the book, as advertised by the dust jacket, is neither significant nor unexpected. Once the reader discovers halfway through the novel that Tom is Jewish, his eventual voyage to Israel is inevitable. The idea of redemption through Israel is hardly "unexpected." Sillitoe establishes early in the novel that Tom is a rootless wanderer in search of an identity. He has clumsily planted incongruous references to Judaism—in part 1, a long quotation from the book of Isaiah (part of a sermon which Pam just happens to hear) and, in part 3, the unusual beliefs of a wireless operator on Tom's ship, who subscribes to the view that the British people are one of the Lost Tribes of Israel. These and other references cannot help but strike the reader as "significant" since they are otherwise unmotivated.

The thematic content of the novel falls somewhere between Ayn Rand's "virtue of selfishness" and D. H. Lawrence's "star-equilibrium." The narrative unfolds a dialectic of self and other, identity and communion, loneliness and dependence, free will and determinism. In order to achieve victory over the present, the characters must absorb and transcend the past, conquering the forces of environment and heredity that have determined and shaped their present state of inanition. They must become victors of consciousness rather than the victims of circumstance. The first step is to become self-determining rather than other-determined. This is the virtue of selfishness. Only with a solid sense of one's own identity can one develop a significant relationship with another, a relationship that depends on neither dominance nor dependence and that does not consume the individuality of either participant. This is Lawrence's "star-equilibrium," "an equilibrium, a pure balance of two single beings, as the stars balance each other," "a mutual unison in separateness."

The essential movement of the novel, as typified by the development of Pam (whose victory is designated by the title), is from dependence to loneliness to love, though it is a love that preserves the integrity and independence of each consciousness. Pam and Tom progress toward this desideratum; they do not entirely achieve it. The novel is in some measure open-ended. Though it is almost a certainty that she and their child will join him in Israel—it is even suggested that Judy (their mutual lover) and her two children will later emigrate—the idea of redemption through Israel is strategically ambiguous. As in Lawrence's works, the nuclear family does not suffice; what does suffice is not altogether clear. The important point is that the characters have seized control of their destinies and thus possess the existential potential to move toward a better life. This is their victory.

In the first part of the novel, Pam's quest for liberation begins when she breaks away from a loveless and stultifying marriage, fleeing from Nottingham to London in order to discover her own clean, well-lighted place and to cultivate a sense of her own identity. The naturalistic premises are laid out explicitly. The narrative moves back and forth through time present and time past, the retrospective technique giving the reader a detailed account of her marriage to a brutal and insensitive husband. In accordance with the conventions of naturalism—the idea that human motivation and behavior are determined by heredity and environment—the fact that neither is to blame for the unhappy marriage is constantly reiterated. Nevertheless, *Her Victory* is not a naturalistic novel. Pam must understand the determining factors in order to transcend them. Her taking a room in London is the first step. In the building, she meets Judy, a single parent with two children, feminist attitudes, and Lesbian predilections. Moreover, it turns out that Tom also has a room in the building, though he is presently away.

The second part of the novel chronicles the history of Tom, a merchant navy officer who had been reared in a Christian orphanage and whose only remaining familial connection is his dead mother's spinster sister, Clara. Despite his dedication to work, duty, responsibility, and survival, Tom is essentially purposeless, a rootless, middle-aged wanderer without a cause. The death of Aunt Clara propels the narrative back into time present. She bequeaths to him her Brighton home, rendering him financially secure for life. In these quasi-Laurentian novels of self-discovery and intimate contact, chararacters cannot be saddled with the responsibilities of having to work for a living. When Tom returns to London to pack his belongings, he rescues Pam from her attempted suicide. Eventually, she goes to Brighton with him.

The fourth part devotes itself to the exhumation of Tom's family history, heretofore unknown to him. Sifting through Aunt Clara's papers, Pam and Tom discover that his mother was Jewish. Lack of identity is transformed into a sense of roots, and he proudly wears the Star of David heirloom they uncover and decides to learn Hebrew. That a fifty-year-old man should instantly become a Zionist may strike some readers as improbable.

The ménage-à-trois becomes stabilized in the fifth part. Pam and Tom have become intimately involved, and Judy and her two children are now living with them. Pam and Judy become lovers, and Tom and Judy also encounter each other occasionally. The relationship between Pam and Tom, however, is far from being perfect: she must constantly reaffirm her separate identity; he still feels a lack of purpose in his life.

In the sixth part, Pam and Tom cut themselves adrift from domesticity and journey to the Continent, planning to wander until they find the place that announces itself as home. Pam's pregnancy and a car crash terminate their wanderings, necessitating a return to Brighton, where Judy and her children are still ensconced. A healthy baby is born, Tom finds his purpose by going to Israel, and Pam and the child are to join him in the near future.

Her Victory is the kind of novel that a brief discussion necessarily trivializes, for the gradual evolution of the characters and the changing texture of their relationships are the salient concern of the book; this the reader must himself experience. The process is thus more important than the product, and Sillitoe's solemn sense of moral purpose compels, at great length, grudging assent. The assent is grudging because the process is laborious and parts of the novel are almost unreadable.

Greig E. Henderson

Sources for Further Study

Library Journal. CVII, October 15, 1982, p. 2005.
Los Angeles Times Book Review. November 21, 1982, p. 6.
New Statesman. CIV, October 1, 1982, p. 27.
The New York Times Book Review. LXXXVII, December 12, 1982, p. 15.
Observer. September 26, 1982, p. 34.
Publishers Weekly. CCXXII, August 27, 1982, p. 346.
Spectator. CCXLIX, November 6, 1982, p. 29.
Times Literary Supplement. October 15, 1982, p. 1122.

HOMETOWN

Author: Peter Davis (1937-   )
Publisher: Simon and Schuster (New York). 331 pp. $14.95
Type of work: Narrative sociology
Time: Late 1970's
Locale: Hamilton, Ohio

A subjective portrait of the social tensions facing several families and individuals in Hamilton, Ohio, detailing their lives in the contexts of work, education, play, crime, and politics, and climaxing in the trial of a popular teacher charged with public indecency

Peter Davis is well-known as a writer and producer of fine documentary films, including his Academy Award-winning *Hearts and Minds* (1974), about the Vietnam War; the television documentary "The Selling of the Pentagon" (1971); and his six-part public television series "Middletown" (1982). Although *Hometown* is Davis' literary debut, he is on familiar ground, presenting the residents of Hamilton, Ohio, with almost television-like immediacy. *Hometown* is not a strictly sociological study, such as Robert and Helen Lynd's study of Muncie, Indiana, in *Middletown* (1929), although Davis does use the sociologist's framework to paint the life of Hamilton: family, religion, work, play, crime, and politics. Nor is it the fiction of Sherwood Anderson's *Winesburg, Ohio* (1919), for in *Hometown*, the reader is conscious of the marriage of the storyteller and the documentary filmmaker, a fusion that prompts questions about Davis' control over his material—questions which are not easily resolved—and earns the work the designation of "creative nonfiction," a term that warns a reader to differentiate fact from fiction in this apparently documentary work.

In the opening chapter, Davis explains how Hamilton was selected. Davis wanted "to understand America by going into one community and penetrating its society as deeply and widely as possible." This may be asking the impossible, overlooking, as it does, the sheer size and variety of America. Nevertheless, a statistician at the Census Bureau gives him a sensible answer: Hamilton, a city of sixty-three thousand people, is "northern enough to be industrial, southern enough to have a gently rural aspect, western enough to have once been on the frontier, eastern enough to have a past." With this answer in mind, Davis spent two and a half years living in Hamilton, recording the life there as it presented itself to him, yet without a camera or microphone.

The town's mayor, Frank Witt, describes Hamilton as a community "deeply fragmented" within itself. The mayor's description rings true throughout the book, beginning with the ironic account of a wedding ceremony in which Bobby Jackson, a carpenter, marries Nancy Sloneker, a young teacher from the wrong side of an illustrious Hamilton family. The marriage ceremony in the small Presbyterian church proceeds with formal precision, uniting not only Nancy and Bobby but also the Slonekers and Jacksons; the scene that follows at the reception is illuminated with a cold, harsh light. Here, Davis draws on his documentary experience, allowing the reader to eavesdrop on each family's complaints and using flashbacks to provide background on the families and on life in Hamilton. What is presented is no surprise to the reader: although the marriage ceremony unites two members of the community, it serves only to heighten the fragmentary nature of the community as a whole. Here, in describing the reception, Davis gives the reader an inkling of the social barriers separating two families of similar economic standing yet of different social backgrounds. "The Wedding," in spite of its promise for a bright future, ends pessimistically with the hinted-at future portrait of Nancy as a bride who will be happy "most of the time."

"The Game" more clearly and completely defines the social boundaries in this community. Remarkable for its vividness and drama, this chapter recounts the crosstown rivalry between Taft and Garfield schools. Taft's students are from prominent families and affluent neighborhoods, while Garfield's student body comprises mainly blacks and Appalachian whites. Like the families from which Garfield's students are drawn, its basketball team is an underdog to the very successful Taft team. The action of the game plays like an adventure film, with the underdog Garfield team barely missing a come-from-behind victory. For a moment at the game's end, the score and the social barriers are forgotten as representatives of both sides hoist the star Garfield player to their shoulders, but the unity is part of the frenzy of the moment, and it is clear that after the game, Hamilton will again fragment along clearly defined lines.

The next two sections, "Deliverance" and "In Court," provide a contrast to each other as well as a suitable introduction to the later sections dealing with the murderer Ned Wortees. In "Deliverance," Pastor Alexander adjudicates a charge of wife abuse made by the sobbing Rowena Clegg against her husband Jack. Pastor Alexander's judgment embraces them both as he recognizes the frustration of their lot, representative of the fate of the poor from Kentucky and Tennessee. In cold contrast, Judge Wendell Parks deals with similar problems in the courtroom. Among his many cases is another one of wife-beating, and his judgment is impersonal if impartial, in marked contrast to Pastor Alexander's impassioned driving out of the devil in the Clegg marriage. The wife-abuse case before Judge Parks brings only a quick, small fine and Davis implies that Judge Parks's justice is that which is meted out when the subculture of the poor can no longer care for its own. Pastor Alexander's failures, then, are destined to become the subject of the impersonal machinery of Judge Parks's courtroom.

The largest section of *Hometown* presents the story of the murderer Ned Wortees, who, in a fit of anger, shoots his brother-in-law, an act prompted by what the police report would call a domestic dispute. The events leading up to the murder are detailed, particularly the misfit status of Ned Wortees and his victim, Billy Krug, who shared a need for violent confrontation. Whereas other sections of the book illuminate the broad social differences which fragment Hamilton, Davis' account of the murder and the subsequent trial focuses primarily on the family members involved and especially on the murderer, Ned Wortees, in flight from the police. The account of Wortees' flight is fascinating, if only for the curious detail Davis provides. Davis maps out Wortees' route along the interstate highways and backroads of the South and back to Ohio, where he returned to give himself up. Davis also lists virtually every item Wortees charged on his credit card. Certainly this touch provides realism, but it also suggests the sociologist's refuge in data rather than the storyteller's imperative to be selective, to make sense of his narrative. If *Hometown* is about a community in pieces, this section, though compelling reading, loses sight of this governing theme, except to introduce the obvious contrast between the defendant and the lawyers, both those representing him and those prosecuting him.

The most compelling section in the book provides its climax. In "Hamilton Divided," a popular high-school music teacher, Samuel Shie, is accused, on the basis of flimsy evidence, of exposing himself in a department store men's room. To avoid any publicity, Shie pleads no contest to the charge of disorderly conduct. His pleading no contest is interpreted as an admission of guilt by the board of education, and Shie is fired. In order to retain his job, Shie asks for a public hearing, believing that since he is innocent and therefore has nothing to hide, a public hearing can do him no harm. Shie is sadly wrong, in spite of all the support he receives from friends and colleagues.

"Hamilton Divided" invites comparisons with "Hands" in Anderson's *Winesburg, Ohio*, the story of Old Wing Biddlebaum, one of the few teachers in his town to understand young people, who is accused of homosexuality. Like Biddlebaum, Shie is an excellent teacher and is popular with students and other teachers. Also like Biddlebaum, Shie is falsely accused. While poor Biddlebaum is physically beaten and threatened with lynching by some of the townspeople, Shie is subjected to a far more painful psychic beating when his behavior is questioned during a lengthy public hearing. Shie's expulsion— he is forced to leave town—is the result of a community's inability to understand itself, or perhaps of a community refusing to think about itself. At one point in the hearing, Shie is asked by the lawyers for the school board whether he thinks he could teach in the same school again, even if he is innocent. Although Shie answers affirmatively, the school board does not share his view. What must strike the sensitive reader is that in this trial, the wrong party is being prosecuted: the community should be asking the school-board members whether they can continue to serve in that capacity after what they have done to Samuel Shie. That question is never asked at the hearing, but it is asked by implication in Davis' full treatment of this case and in the pains he takes to show the variety and depth of the support behind Shie.

"Hamilton Divided" provides a fitting climax to *Hometown*, since the divisions described and drawn elsewhere in the book are exacerbated by Shie's crisis. In addition, the courtroom drama—including an expert witness' failure to identify Shie—makes for compelling reading.

It is at times like these that the reader can overlook the awkward fusion of storytelling and documentary which too often mars *Hometown*. Davis' technique as storyteller forces the reader to ask what he has witnessed directly and what he has reconstructed or simply imagined. The opening sections build the reader's confidence in Davis as a direct witness, but with the transition from "Cops," where Davis is writing as a direct witness, to "Murder," where he reconstructs the action, the reader begins to wonder how Davis received his information, a question that interferes with the narrative process. Given Davis' background as a documentary filmmaker, and given his proclaimed intention of observing in the manner of the Lynds and telling his story in the manner of Sherwood Anderson, the attentive reader looks for the weld between directly witnessed fact and reconstructed fact. A related problem is Davis' effect, as an observer, upon the very events which he is supposed to be rendering with great objectivity. Indeed, Davis' presence as an observer is heavy throughout, and in "Strike," he becomes part of the action as he pursues a worker picketing a local tool factory who does not want to speak to Davis, since Davis is dressed suspiciously like an office worker rather than like a union member.

Despite such flaws, *Hometown* is successful in depicting the fragmentation of an American community. In Davis' vision of America, the social lines are clearly drawn and permanent.

Paul A. Bateman

Sources for Further Study

Christian Science Monitor. May 14, 1982, p. B3.
Commonweal. CIX, October 22, 1982, p. 573.
Library Journal. CVII, May 1, 1982, p. 899.
The New Republic. CLXXXVII, July 5, 1982, p. 39.
The New York Times Book Review. LXXXVII, April 18, 1982, p. 9.
Psychology Today. XVI, April, 1982, p. 86.
Saturday Review. IX, April, 1982, p. 63.
Virginia Quarterly Review. LVIII, Summer, 1982, p. 91.

HUNDREDS OF FIREFLIES

Author: Brad Leithauser (1953-   )
Publisher: Alfred A. Knopf (New York). 71 pp. $11.50; paperback $5.95
Type of work: Poetry

Strength of perception and ease of formal control characterize this first collection by a young poet

The reigning poetics of the 1960's and 1970's, aided and abetted by poetry workshops that dotted every major campus in the United States, heavily stressed the virtues of free verse, personal utterance, the "deep-image," and what poet Stanley Kunitz has referred to as "cornfed Surrealism." In keeping with the spirit of that apparent cultural democracy, poetry was widely demoted from the status of an art to that of a craft; anybody with an image and a pen could do it. Formality was eschewed as "academic," and larger cultural themes were put to bed as poets withdrew to establish their personal authenticity. Now that the youthful cultural ethos of that time has largely faded, along with long hair, student protests, and blotter acid, so too the confession-oriented poetry of that time seems to have exhausted its mandate. It is clear now that a return to formalism is in the air and with it, a new generation of poets working under values of strict form, clarity of discourse, and objective treatment of subject matter.

With his first collection, *Hundreds of Fireflies*, Brad Leithauser announces his allegiance to the (old) new poetic values without trying to galvanize the tired, still-available corpse of academic verse. In the strict meters of these poems (most are rhymed, too), one finds an observer so astute that his perceptions break into vision—not unlike what one experiences in the poems of Elizabeth Bishop. Leithauser builds a handsome dialectic between the seen and revealed world, between the desire for light and light itself, between biological life and transcendent being by setting out his themes early in the book, later doubling back to retrieve earlier connections, pushing them in new settings to reveal further meaning. As the poems overlap, glossing, developing, and elaborating one another, the web of significance grows, catching more than merely the sum of discrete poems. Such a high sense of architecture is rare in a book of poems; in a first book, it is extraordinarily so.

The first of the book's three sections spells out the poet's main concerns: the urban sensibility returned to nature, the giving way of surfaces to reveal new reality, and the unseasonal need of all life to seek what is brighter than itself. The opening poem, "An Expanded Want Ad," fleshes out in great imaginative detail an advertisement for a summer cottage in Michigan. Here the setting is all, and the poet's loving descriptions overturn the imagined hesitations of a city-dweller. Despite the rustic atmosphere—the ramshackle house, the dirt roads, the weird, nocturnal voices of the bullfrogs—the poet concludes that daybreak itself ("the morning's flashy gift") mends all that is wrong, all that one wished to vacate in the first place.

The book's next three poems take up the theme of landscape as a basis of perception and knowledge. In "Alternate Landscape," the poet watches from the window of a jet plane while his minutes-before reality becomes lost in a surge of clouds. At this height, mountains "roll slowly downhill" in a terra firma description of clouds, which suggests an endurance one knows they do not possess. Meanwhile, patches of earth slip by; these are "another life," mentioned thus casually to suggest the ease with which one clings to the given perspective. "Miniature" depicts an anthill shone upon by a sun-yellow dandelion and a white dandelion ("a dainty crumb-/ came of a moon"), but the tiny, work-obsessed insects "erect a temple to this sun and moon," although the moon floats away to germinate elsewhere. In the frenzy of their task, they are paradoxically "unmindful/ of all suns and moons." Yet their lack of "mind" is perhaps the reason for their unrelenting energy and the cohesion of their community. In "Between Leaps," the animal and plant worlds are suspended in equilibrium until a frog, spotted "like an elderly hand" yet green as "new leafage," arbitrarily disrupts the tenuous balance by hopping from his place of "green languor" into the water, at which point "the place's spell/ is lifted."

If these poems test the surfaces of our given reality, they also suggest that the urge—some would say the necessity—to test them results from a desire to experience greater relevance from the natural world, a relevance that will yield itself up only to the unromanticizing eye. This desire finds a clear expression in the title poem. Here, fireflies in their brief, seasonal mating bring even the oblique heavens, of which they are a substitute and symbol, closer, though they are "nearer than the heavens/ will ever be." The desire of the mute fireflies is reflected in the urge vacationers feel to experience them, for they, too, feel that "Merely/ to watch, and say nothing,/ gratefully,/ is what is best." Seasonal animals themselves, they realize that they will be "drawn too by the light,/ of another firefly season."

The second section consists of a poem that stands in perhaps ironic contrast to the book's more serious concerns. A longish narrative poem called "Two Summer Jobs," it involves two turning points in the poet's life. The first ("Tennis Instructor, 1971") took place during the summer before the poet entered college; the other ("Law Clerk, 1979") seeks to justify, with some hesitation, the poet's profession, law. The poem departs in style and intention from everything else in the book, and perhaps because it occupies the center of the collection, it provides the book's only disappointing moments. Unlike the exquisitely crafted poems found elsewhere in the volume, this poem suffers from slackness and self-indulgence. The rite of passage of the first narrative involves the poet's coming-of-age in the presence of a group of middle-class, worldly-wise young women, his students. There is much mock-innocence here, combined with a yearning for social position that reminds one of the F. Scott Fitzgerald of "Winter Dreams." By the end of the summer, these intuitive women have found out his "secret wish"—to be a poet—and during a farewell party, they introduce the subject. The fact that the wish had remained a secret is perhaps an embarrassing indication of the respect paid in this world to country clubs and privilege. The maternal line with which his going forth to Harvard is christened ("Never forget: the world is yours"), well-meaning as it is, cuts two ways, as one learns in the second poem of the pair.

Here, the poet is at last launched into a legal career, but he wavers between self-congratulation and doubts about his choice of profession. After all, here is the young poet from the Midwest hobnobbing and lunching sumptuously with a pedigreed member of the Establishment, a partner no less, atop a Manhattan skyscraper. Is this cause for guilt? Yet, the poet keeps the narrative going, rimmed with this vacillation toward commitment. He devotes his after-hours at the office to wrestling with a writer's block he intends to break by engaging in imitations and parodies of school poetry texts. Next, one sees him running into an old Harvard poetry buddy who now "throws pots" but is, in a more parodic way, really as ambivalent about the artistic calling as the poet wants the reader to believe he is, or might be, or was (but surely, surrounded by the many splendid pieces in this book, the very thought is absurd). Nevertheless, responding to the version of the Reality Principle outlined here, the friend will indulge in his pots only "a summer or two before going on for [an M.B.A.], just as the parents planned." The final tableau reveals the poet once more in his office musing over the city skyline. Having been asked to join the firm, he concludes that he will leave: "I know/ 'for good' is for the better in some way, and know/ I'll be ready to leave. Or nearly so." This last hesitation, so lacking in earnestness, fails to establish a sense of regret, as it is intended to do; the conclusion typifies the poem's grating, precocious-schoolboy tone, directed with special pleading toward a subject for which there is little resonance. This centerpiece is a regrettable, but understandable, lapse in taste.

The book's final section, however, brings the themes of the first section to final fruition and contains at least one poem that ought to become well known. In "Duckweed," a pond's surface presents what seems to be a solid floor, but dipping one's hand into the water reveals "a room . . . nobody's/ Entered for years." This poem, nicely placed, alludes both to the earlier "Alternate Land-scape," where clouds seen from a plane share with the pond a "false firmness," and to "Between Leaps," where the frog's "reflection-/ shattering *plop*" is now the questioning insertion of human hands.

Just as these previous poems are revivified by allusion, so too "Along Lake Michigan" brings the volume's opening poem, "An Expanded Want Ad," to mind, where roads shrink to paths and paths roughen to nature against the lakeshore. In this natural setting, the wild creatures so faithfully coincide with their surroundings that they are invisible until they move. Masters of camouflage, flocks of ducks skip across the lake-top like stones, and snakes repose like sticks among logs. In this landscape of necessary deception, the poet and his companion are almost deceived into thinking that a doe, lying mysteriously dead along the shore, might return to life. And why not? After all, they had just seen more unlikely metamorphoses. As this wish overtakes them, however, another "heartbeat"—a wave—breaks against the doe's breast. As a timely image for natural process, it is greater and more inexplicable than the doe's lost life.

More compelling and spookily well-timed is the poem "The Ghost of a Ghost." Here, a perfectly ordinary man, situated in a perfectly ordinary family, descends, first abruptly then by degrees, into sheer otherness. The man's ghost speaks throughout, moving in perfect modulation as he remembers his simple family life, through the melancholy limbo-talk of ghosts, until, atomized and bereft of the need to remember, he becomes only a frontier of outward-moving words and "misses nothing at all." How Leithauser accomplishes this marvelous descent reveals again the finely tuned eye and ear with which he can register minute shifts in perception. The poem begins in the domestic mundane as the speaker delivers a series of autobiographical one-liners intended to establish him as without exceptional talent, imagination, or vices. "The pleasures I took from life," the speaker begins, "were simple things," though he admits, "Sometimes I liked to drink too much/ but not too often." In the course of this bland résumé, one also learns that he liked to horse around with his son, watch television, and tease his daughter. As for his relations with his wife ("Emily"), he discloses the fact that "we had our problems, of course," but the spats were only "ploys, harmless because love ran/ through every word we spoke." Just as this soliloquy begins sidling up to bathos, the section ends, "and then, an accident, I died."

The poem's second part chronicles the ghost's presence in the house, where memory of him keeps him "alive." As time begins to reestablish a new order, however, his existence is threatened by a second death, forgetfulness. At first, a predictable grief takes hold: his wife weeps and looks "ruined"; his children suffer from nightmares. Then, before the year is out, a "stranger" moves in. It is his arrival that begins to render the ghost superfluous in his own mind, for he has spent the intervening time trying, in the manner of ghosts, to communicate with the living. What is affecting here is the way Leithauser makes the ghost's point of view believable ("Where did they think I'd gone?") by making the ghost a consistent being hinged to the only piece of earthly reality available to him, his family. In time, because he cannot be heard, he resorts to the "vicious trick" of breathing icily upon their necks ("anything to show them who was near!"). Ultimately, through their healing and forgetting, the ghost dies, as the living father died.

The final section of the poem adopts the eerie tone of a radically dispossessed being for whom there are no ties whatever. The dissolution of even his tenuous ghostly being finds him unable to recall "the downy scrape of a peach skin/ . . . the smell of the sea." Finely punning, he adds, "By turns I have grown other-wise." This wisdom, this letting-go, sets him free to roam "not toward sleep but a clarity of broadened linkages." Such clarity could never have been in the possession of the narrow man when alive and tethered to his domestic rounds; neither could it have come to the remorseful ghost. Only a "ghost of a ghost," the final gift of time to consciousness, enables him to see the "course which homes outward." The choice of the word "home" here, set against the changeableness of his earthly home, is one of the many verbal felicities that makes this poem knowing and right.

Hundreds of Fireflies is, in all, a satisfying and well-developed performance by a young poet of considerable range, ease, and precision who ought to find even finer strands of articulation falling within his grasp. This is not only to give high praise to the promise evidenced in a first book. The promise is there, but within the dialectic the poet has set, the book is there, too. It delivers, and makes a marriage of rich skill and a wonderful eye.

David Rigsbee

Sources for Further Study

Hudson Review. XXXV, Autumn, 1982, p. 479.
Library Journal. CVII, January 1, 1982, p. 96.
The New Republic. CLXXXVI, April 14, 1982, p. 37.
The New York Review of Books. XXIX, September 23, 1982, p. 41.
The New York Times Book Review. LXXXVII, March 14, 1982, p. 12.
Poetry. CXLI, December, 1982, p. 170.
Time. CXIX, March 15, 1982, p. 84.
Virginia Quarterly Review. LVIII, Autumn, 1982, p. 133.

IMAGINARY CRIMES

Author: Sheila Ballantyne (1936-   )
Publisher: The Viking Press (New York). 265 pp. $13.95
Type of work: Novel
Time: 1936-1975
Locale: Seattle and San Francisco

A woman comes to terms with her difficult childhood

> *Principal characters:*
> SONYA WEILER, the protagonist; a woman attempting to come to terms with her past
> RAY WEILER, her father
> VALERY WEILER, Sonya's mother
> GRETA WEILER, Sonya's sister

Sheila Ballantyne's first novel, *Norma Jean the Termite Queen* (1975), deals with liberation from the confining roles of wife and mother. Her second novel, *Imaginary Crimes*, deals with liberation from painful relationships with parents. In both books, the female protagonists are nearly overwhelmed by the past before they gain strength enough to move beyond it. In fact, each of Ballantyne's books tells a different segment of the same story, the one which fascinates so many contemporary women writers: the story of coming to terms with the past, of becoming a creator, a "woman of my own. . . . alive, and separate, and moving on." What distinguishes Ballantyne's work from that of her colleagues is the archaeological quality of her characters' examination of the past. In *Norma Jean the Termite Queen*, Ballantyne draws heavily on anthropology and ancient history to inform her protagonist's struggle toward a new self-definition. In *Imaginary Crimes*, Ballantyne's central character, Sonya Weiler, is an archaeologist of her own emotions, sifting through layers of experience to reach the complicated truth of her feelings toward her parents. Sonya's "artifacts," collected in albums and manila envelopes and cardboard boxes, are family pictures—data which are, by themselves, inconclusive, but which Sonya eventually assembles into a coherent and moving whole.

Sonya's history begins in a tiny basement apartment in Seattle in the late 1930's. Her mother, Valery, stays at home while her father, Ray, tries to earn a living by a variety of enterprises of dubious legality: restoring shiny suits to their original fuzziness, selling a knitting device called a pik-loom, and, eventually, conning investors to sink capital into fraudulent mining schemes. Sometimes Ray drinks too much. Valery's heart's desire is to have a home of her own. Deprived of that home by Ray's ineptitude as a provider, she spends most of her time smoking Lucky Strikes, reading mystery novels, and fantasizing about movie stars. The couple's second daughter, Greta, is born when Sonya is eight. Soon thereafter, Valery contracts breast cancer, but because she and Ray are Christian Scientists, they reject the surgery which would save her and decide instead to rely on God's perfect love. The family moves to a rented dream house, with a bedroom for each daughter and a maple tree in the front yard; here Sonya witnesses her mother's slow death from the untreated cancer. After Valery is gone, Sonya and Greta are cared for by a succession of nasty housekeepers, and Ray, sinking deeper and deeper into alcoholism, continues his unsuccessful efforts to make the deal of a lifetime. The family moves frequently, leaving behind treasured possessions; the housekeepers become more malevolent, Ray more unpredictable and abusive. Given these circumstances, Sonya's adolescence is a humiliating ordeal. Her escape comes when she has a chance to go to college; she works her way through, graduates, gets a job, assumes responsibility for Greta, marries, and has two children. It is not until Ray's death, shortly after the birth of her second child, that Sonya is forced to come to terms with her suppressed feelings toward her parents.

The problem of presenting these unhappy events, along with the changes in Sonya's understanding of her feelings toward them, is a complex one, and Ballantyne's solution is ingenious. She tells Sonya's story in a series of vignettes, or narrative snapshots, using these "artifacts" to structure the novel. Some of the short narratives have titles, like the captions in a photograph album; in these titled sections, Sonya herself narrates, in the first person and, usually, in the past tense. Interspersed among these titled sections are untitled passages, more omniscient and expository in tone; most of these are written in the present tense, though they sometimes range into past and future. In the beginning, the apparently disconnected sections disorient the reader, but it is soon evident that the novel's basic arrangement is chronological and that Ballantyne is shifting the angle of narration to achieve two effects. First, the changes in tense help to assert the impact of past events on Sonya's present life. Second, Ballantyne's narrative method allows the reader to understand the events of Sonya's childhood when Sonya herself cannot, without sacrificing Sonya's youthful impressions to her adult insights.

Even as a child, though, Sonya is not without perspective on her own story. From the outset, she emphasizes "firsts" and discoveries, almost as if she were a doting parent keeping a baby book: her first memory of snow, her "first words spoken as a free person," the turning point in her understanding of her parents' religion. Soon after receiving her first "A" on a story for an English class, she becomes aware that she has an eye for detail, and she dreams of becoming a writer. With the support of a sensitive teacher, she begins to discover the "thrill of creation, to know that it was possible to turn the misery of life into some form of art. And strangely enough, being able to do that also became a means of enduring life itself." A college writing professor teaches her the value of remaining true to her own vision, and, although her belief in her creative power wanes after she graduates and marries, still, she senses that her vision has "retreated to the darkest center of me . . . waiting out its cycle, invisibly coiled for rebirth." When Sonya marries, she turns her creative energy in a new direction, believing she can make a family that "will bear none of the scars of the past," a family that will be "pure, undamaged, her own creation." She is, of course, wrong. Her husband, a psychiatrist, tells her that "we carry our own chaos within us"; eventually, with the guidance of a therapist, Sonya enters this chaos, experiences it, and, in the process, re-creates herself.

In the case of her relationship with her mother, Valery, Sonya must explore a complicated mixture of sympathy and anger. Even as a little girl, Sonya rejects Valery's confinement and dependence. When Ray cannot provide for her and hocks her few valuable possessions, Valery develops a depressive addiction to movies and murder mysteries that, Sonya sees, enables her mother to "swallow her disappointment, contain her sense of loss; she must believe and endure." It is only during the war, and during summer visits to her native Canada, that the mother's depression lifts. Singled out to serve as an air-raid warden, she begins to feel a sense of purpose; she wears her scarf upside down and considers going to work as a riveter, but Ray insists that she stay at home to care for their daughter. By the time Sonya is five, she knows that she does not want to be like her mother. By the time she is ten, her mother is dead. Sonya has seen Valery's bleeding, wasted body: she has brushed her smelly hair, knowing that "there is no way out of this labor of love and revulsion"; she has watched her father cradle her mother's corpse in his arms. Worst of all, she has become convinced that the helplessness and anger and despair she feels toward her mother for being ill, for dying, for abandoning her, are crimes that only a truly evil person could commit.

Sonya's crimes against Ray are equally reprehensible, the major one being her rejection of him for his drunkenness, his dishonesty, his manipulative use of his poor motherless babies to get what he wants without paying for it. Ballantyne perceptively explores the role of rebellion in the formation of taste and opinion, as she shows how Ray's hatred of "kikes" and "commies" leads Sonya to develop "a lifelong pattern: whoever Daddy called a kike, I made my best friend." His failure to pay money he owes—for rent, for tuition, for the piano lessons he insists Sonya take—causes profound embarrassment. Unable to discuss with her music teacher the reasons Ray has not paid for her lessons, Sonya is paralyzed by the impossibility of her position: "I didn't know which was worse: to betray him by telling, or to betray myself by keeping still." Ray's tirades against her looks, her interests, and her friends erode her self-esteem and, in adolescence, send her out of the house for long drives, one of them a near-suicidal excursion into the blackness of her own soul. At college, Sonya takes a psychology course which gives her labels for Ray's behavior: he is delusional, paranoid, psychopathic. At this time, she also learns that Ray's fraudulent mining deals have landed him in jail for grand larceny. Ray's crimes are real, but he believes himself innocent; Sonya's crimes are imaginary, but she believes herself guilty. The fact that her father is a criminal makes her a criminal too, and though the psychological labels allow her some measure of understanding and control, they do not account for Ray's loving moments: his bedtime stories, his nursing Sonya through glandular fever, his characteristic gesture of rubbing her cheek with the backs of his fingers. The complex character of Ray Weiler elicits from the reader, as from Sonya herself, both sympathy and anger: she is torn between the "wish to love" and the "need to hate" this drunken con man who cares so deeply for her.

Sonya cannot resolve her feelings toward her father until the night terrors that follow his death make resolution a necessity. In a series of sessions with her therapist, she struggles with her conviction that to speak of her parents "is to enter the land of the dead. And that requires you to die, yourself." Then, alone, she travels back to Seattle, the scene of her crimes, and, finally, of her acquittal. In structural terms, this symbolic journey is a recapitulation of characters and incidents introduced earlier; what has at first seemed disorientingly haphazard makes a pattern at the end, when Sonya frees herself of the "old ghosts" of her parents, ghosts that have kept her from experiencing her strength and value as an adult. The novel's conclusion moves and satisfies because it does not try to deny Sonya's pain, even as it bears witness to her hard-won transcendence.

Despite its distressing content, *Imaginary Crimes* is a pleasure to read because of the combination of subtlety and vigor in Ballantyne's style. Brilliant similes and metaphors illuminate the intricacies of Sonya's character. For example, during a tense interview with the school principal, Sonya notes that "my fingers twitched involuntarily from their sweaty nest in my lap." Describing her first date with an eager young man, she recounts, "He started French kissing me, right there in the street; his mouth, like a tender mollusk, attached itself and settled over mine." Other metaphors, those that inform the book as a whole, are presented less explicitly, so as to support the narrative without being obtrusive; there are recurring allusions to climbing mountains, losing consciousness and "coming to," and dying at Easter time, as well as the attention, already discussed, to the important motifs of crime, guilt, and acquittal. Ballantyne controls all this potentially inconsistent material with a firm hand. Even when she is dealing with mental chaos, she does so with intelligence and compassion, using the dexterity of a skilled archaeologist to explore the mysterious recesses of the human psyche.

Carolyn Wilkerson Bell

Sources for Further Study

Library Journal. CVII, February 15, 1982, p. 471.
Ms. X, May, 1982, p. 71.

Nation. CCXXXIV, February 27, 1982, p. 249.
The New York Times Book Review. LXXXVII, February 21, 1982, p. 1.
The New Yorker. LVIII, April 5, 1982, p. 197.
Newsweek. XCIX, February 22, 1982, p. 74.

ISAK DINESEN
The Life of a Storyteller

Author: Judith Thurman (1946-   )
Publisher: St. Martin's Press (New York). 455 pp. $19.95
Type of work: Literary biography

A complete and very readable biography of the great Danish writer Isak Dinesen, based on previously unavailable sources, outlining Dinesen's life and personal difficulties and discussing the tales for which she is best known

> *Principal personages:*
> KAREN (TANNE) DINESEN BLIXEN-FINECKE, the noted Danish author
> WILHELM DINESEN, her father, who committed suicide when she was ten
> INGEBORG DINESEN, her conservative mother
> BROR VON BLIXEN-FINECKE, her husband and partner in a coffee plantation
> THOMAS DINESEN, her brother and confidant
> DENYS FINCH-HATTON, her lover

Isak Dinesen was born Karen Christentze Dinesen on April 17, 1885, and died as Baroness Karen Blixen-Finecke on September 7, 1962. Her long life was filled with a bizarre mixture of family problems, illness, world travel, and the sort of fame that causes one's name to become a household word. For all of her fame, however, Karen Blixen lived an unenviable life, although anyone might covet the talent and determination that she possessed.

Dinesen was the second child (the second daughter) of a well-to-do Danish family, and throughout her life she was known by the childhood nickname "Tanne," which came from her mispronunciation of her given name. From earliest childhood, Tanne thought of herself as a very special person, particularly in contrast to her mother's family—proper, bourgeois, Unitarian, and politically conservative. Because of the staid maternal atmosphere that surrounded her, Tanne's favorite was her father Wilhelm. This lively, witty man would spend hours in the company of Tanne, talking and laughing. He told his daughter stories of his life as a soldier, and his adventures as a trapper among the Chippewa Indians of America. He even encouraged Tanne's literary efforts, admiring the tales she wrote and the pictures she drew to illustrate them.

Tanne enjoyed too few years as her father's confidante. When she was ten, her father, then newly elected to the Danish Parliament, hanged himself in his apartment in Copenhagen. The shock of his death was increased by its unexpectedness: he had shown no sign of depression. In fact, the children were not told until years later that his death had been a suicide. Even so, they felt deserted, especially Tanne, who was devastated. She felt rejected, and her choice of a husband many years afterward may have been influenced by the suitor's resemblance to her father.

As Tanne grew older, she continued to write little stories, but she preferred drawing. Her desire to study art drew objections from her mother, who thought the world of art too bohemian for her young daughter. The expected happened. Rebelling against the maternal injunction, Tanne chose art for a career. She studied at the Danish Royal Academy of Fine Arts in Copenhagen and later in Paris, where she won respect for her talent.

Tanne found more than art in Paris: she fell in love for the first time, with Hans von Blixen-Finecke. Hans and his brother Bror were Swedish, blond, athletic, and expert hunters. (Bror especially became famous as a hunter in Africa, where he served as the model for Robert Wilson in Hemingway's "The Short Happy Life of Francis Macomber.") Although Tanne fell in love with Hans, she married Bror, for reasons that none of her friends could understand. Later, she herself said that the choice had been governed by her desire to be Baroness Blixen (Bror was the elder brother), but many of her friends at the time thought that Bror's resemblance to Wilhelm Dinesen was the key.

Despite his physical likeness to Wilhelm Dinesen, Bror absolutely lacked Wilhelm's appreciation of literature. Tanne's father had shared her love of writing, and their likemindedness in this respect was one reason for their closeness. Bror, with all his bravado and outdoorsmanship, could never hope to match the type of love that Tanne dimly remembered and treasured from her life with her father.

The couple's engagement was announced in 1912, and Bror, who left afterward for an African safari, was joined by Tanne and they married in 1914. They had collected money from their friends and relations to buy a coffee plantation in Kenya. The choice was a strange one: both were such novices that they did not realize for several years that they were doomed to fail as coffee planters. Their land was too acidic and the region too dry ever to produce an adequate crop, and for many years they picked only a fraction of the tonnage they had expected.

Their move to Kenya in 1914 began a period of more difficulties than just agricultural ones. The Blixens found themselves in the middle when World War I began: Kenya, as a British protectorate, joined the hostilities against the German colonies. Tanne and Bror were technically neutrals, but they decided to aid their host country. Bror joined a regiment with other foreigners in Kenya, leaving Tanne with the job of managing the farm and overseeing the African field hands and house servants.

Tanne describes the adventures of those years in *Out of Africa* (1937). For example, she tells how she once led a supply train through Masai country to bring supplies to her husband's unit. One of Bror's adventures was to have serious consequences: to visit his wife, he walked eighty-six miles in two days. He arrived at her camp with dysentery, contracted during a night he had spent in a Masai encampment. Although Tanne feared for his life, he recovered and rejoined his unit the next day.

The next few months were nightmarish: besides the conscription of most of the field hands and the requisitioning of most of the farm animals, Tanne became seriously ill with what she thought was malaria. The doctor she saw ordered her home to Europe. Before sailing home, Tanne took a two-month African vacation and then returned home to doctors who diagnosed her illness as syphilis. Her symptoms were such that the doctors were able to pinpoint the start of the disease: it had most probably been during Bror's visit at home after he had stayed with the Masai.

To a certain degree, this conclusion was not unexpected. Syphilis was rampant among the Masai then; many of the women were sterile from it. This could have been the source from which the Blixens had been infected. Bror made no secret of his cohabitation with native women, but he never suffered outwardly from the illness. Tanne, on the other hand, paid the price of his unfaithfulness. In the early years of the disease's progress, she suffered pain in her joints, fever, headaches, and loss of appetite. Her later years were still worse: the disease settled in the nerves of her spine and caused almost unendurable pain in her abdomen. She had never been a big eater, but the abdominal pain and the loss of appetite diminished her eating still further. She grew progressively thinner, and when she finally died, it was from malnutrition.

In addition to the physical suffering it produced, syphilis also made Tanne more conscious than ever of her "difference" from others. She saw a mark of the devil in her illness, and syphilis, Satan, and art became strangely bound together in her thoughts. She often said that the disease was the price that she paid for her art, even glorying in her pain and in the sacrifice of a sexual life when the disease was in a contagious stage. Her stories she saw as outgrowths of her pain and terror; she claimed to have promised her soul to the devil so that everything she experienced would become part of her tales. According to Tanne, the promise was sealed when she first discovered her disease and could no longer hope for a normal sexual life.

If sex was sometimes impossible, love was not. The great love of her life was an Englishman, Denys Finch-Hatton. Finch-Hatton, the son of an earl, had found England too small for his taste and had come to Kenya to raise flax and cattle. Like Tanne, he loved the veldt, and together they would take many safaris, spending weeks in the wilderness and returning with their affection increased. Tanne hoped someday to marry Finch-Hatton; after her discovery of her syphilis and with Bror's continuing infidelities, divorce seemed to be the only course possible. In January of 1921, the decree of divorce became final, freeing her, she thought, for Finch-Hatton. He was not, however, the marrying kind. Essentially a loner, he repeatedly refused to tie himself down with a wife. In 1931, Finch-Hatton died in a plane crash, and Tanne returned to Denmark, forty-six years old and sick.

In the rubble of her personal life, Tanne's mind turned once again to the stories that she had enjoyed writing as a child. (She had, in fact, already published stories when she was twenty-two years old.) She collected them into a book, but she must have thought of herself as a vastly different person from the Tanne Blixen who had written them. She chose a new name: *Isak*, for its meaning in Hebrew, "the laughing one," and *Dinesen*, for her beloved father, Wilhelm. The tales that followed she wrote in English, the language she had shared with Finch-Hatton, and she looked forward to publishing them in Great Britain as a kind of memorial to her lost love.

Tanne, or now Isak, took great pride in her craftsmanship. She said that her first inspiration for a tale might be a place, a landscape, or a house. Then she carried the tale with her mentally, creating characters and reworking the parts, until it emerged fully grown on paper. She called her first collection *Seven Gothic Tales* (1934); the term "Gothic" she chose for the period in which the tales were set, between the time of the poet Lord Byron and 1871. She felt that setting the stories in the past rather than making them contemporaneous gave her a greater freedom.

Dinesen maintained that she wrote tales instead of novels because she felt a tie to the great tradition of oral storytelling from which the Norse sagas came. Like the writers of those sagas, she was often more interested in atmosphere and psychology than in realistic details. She gave the name "nemesis" (evoking almost a Greek sense of destiny) to the process by which she plotted the events in a tale—events determined, she said, by the psychology of the characters.

Dinesen finished the manuscript of *Seven Gothic Tales* in 1933, but at first had difficulty in finding a publisher. After trying several English firms unsuccessfully, she sent the work to Robert Haas in New York. Haas agreed to publish it, without any real hope of profit. To his surprise, the book was an immediate commercial and literary success. Newspapers vied to be the first to discover the person behind the pseudonym "Isak Dinesen." Finally, *Politiken*, a Danish newspaper, tracked her down. In her home country, publishers bid for the rights to a Danish edition. Rather than trust the work to a translator, she reworked the tales herself for a Danish edition. Another English-language edition, in Great Britain, soon followed.

In 1935, at age fifty, Dinesen began to reassess her life. The result was *Out of Africa*, a delicate retelling of her life as if it were a tale. The work is not autobiographical in every detail, though, for Dinesen tries to evoke moods in her descriptions and anecdotes, even when the raw material is her own experience. She wrote off and on during 1936, spending some time in the hospital being treated for syphilis, by then in its tertiary stage.

Out of Africa was well-received, and the happiness of that time was marred only by the death of Dinesen's mother at the age of eighty-five. Even though their relationship had often been troubled, in later years Dinesen and her mother had worked out a placid and friendly routine. With her mother's death, she was alone.

Winter's Tales (1942) was composed during the dark years of the Nazi occupation of Denmark. Dinesen desperately needed the money because the war had disrupted the payment of her foreign royalties. She turned, therefore, to publishing *Winter's Tales* in a Danish edition, and its appearance in 1942 enabled her to survive. The same Nazi occupation, with its hardships and its inhumanities—such as the rounding up of Danish Jews—caused her to break a vow she had often made: never to write a novel. The result was certainly not one of her best works; it was a silly little story of two Danish sisters caught by white slavers, their eventual escape, and their marriage to handsome noblemen. Reviewers dismissed it as lightweight trash.

In later life, Dinesen had many literary friendships, with people such as Ole Wivel, Bjorn Poulson, and the poet Thorkild Bjornvig, who was her protégé. She was twice nominated for the Nobel Prize in Literature; she was financially secure with royalties coming from many translations; and she even made peace with the most stodgy members of her mother's family. Physically, however, she grew weaker and thinner. Finally, in 1962, she died at home, of malnutrition brought on by syphilis.

Since her death, Dinesen's reputation has remained constant; her tales are still read and enjoyed. She remains a mystery, although the relationship between her life and her work has been richly illuminated in this biography by Judith Thurman.

Walter E. Meyers

Sources for Further Study

Commonweal. CIX, December 3, 1982, p. 663.
Library Journal. CVII, October 15, 1982, p. 1990.
Ms. XI, November, 1982, p. 26.
Nation. CCXXXVI, February 19, 1983, p. 212.
National Review. XXXIV, September 17, 1982, p. 1156.
The New York Times Book Review. LXXXVII, November 14, 1982, p. 1.
Publishers Weekly. CCXXII, August 27, 1982, p. 352.
Time. CXX, November 15, 1982, p. 90.

THE JOKE

Author: Milan Kundera (1929-   )
Translated from the Czech by Michael Henry Heim
Publisher: Harper & Row, Publishers (New York). 267 pp. $14.95
Type of work: Novel
Time: 1948-1963
Locale: Czechoslovakia

A narrative fugue on the futility of man's attempt to use sex to avenge a wrong done him fifteen years earlier and, in general, on the frailty of man's strongest emotions and most compelling illusions

Principal characters:
>LUDVIK JAHN, a researcher living in Prague who returns to his Moravian hometown
>PAVEL ZEMANEK, a Marxist professor who, as a student, was responsible for Ludvik's expulsion from the university and the Communist Party
>HELENA ZEMANEK, his wife and a radio journalist
>JINDRA, a young radio sound technician, assistant to Helena
>LUCIE SEBETKA, a hairdresser with whom Ludvik has an affair while in Ostrava
>JAROSLAV, a musician and champion of Moravian folklore
>MARKETA, a humorless Communist student on whom Ludvik had a fateful crush
>KOSTKA, a virologist who attempts to reconcile his Christianity with his Communism

First published in Prague as *Žert* in 1967 and then made available to English readers in 1969 in a mutilated, simplified British rendering, *The Joke*, Milan Kundera's first novel, is now republished in a translation more faithful to the original Czech text. The novel was initially received with enthusiasm in Czechoslovakia, where, in the aftermath of the Soviet invasion, it was soon suppressed. Kundera subsequently emigrated to France and has since published *Směšné lásky* (1963; *Laughable Loves*, 1974), *La Vie est ailleurs* (first published in French in 1973; *Life Is Elsewhere*, 1974), *The Farewell Party* (translated from the Czech manuscript in 1976; *Valčík na rozloučenou*, 1979), and *Le Livre du rire et de l'oubli* (first published in French in 1979; *The Book of Laughter and Forgetting*, 1980). Despite a tendency by many critics to see Kundera's work in exclusively political terms, all five of his books share musical forms, a sophisticated and demanding concern for perspective, and an attempt to prove the mysteries of individual existence.

The Joke is a tale of accident, inadvertence, and the perversities of fate. When Ludvik Jahn, a brilliant young university student and Communist Party member, determines to twit his sanguine sweetheart Marketa for abandoning him during the summer in order to attend an indoctrination session on Communist ideology, he sends her a postcard declaring: "Optimism is the opium of the people! A healthy atmosphere stinks of stupidity! Long live Trotsky!" The attempt at rambunctious wit proves a joke only *sub specie aeternitatis*. The authorities read Ludvik's correspondence and become incensed at his subversive irony. In a humiliating public ceremony and at the instigation of Pavel Zemanek, a former friend, Ludvik is expelled from both the university and the Communist Party. He leaves Prague and is forced to become a mine laborer in a penal battalion near Ostrava. During rare furloughs from his dismal barracks existence, Ludvik befriends a lonely young woman named Lucie Sebetka. The relationship develops into love, but Lucie runs away when Ludvik becomes sexually demanding.

The Joke focuses on one summer weekend in the present tense when, fifteen years later, Ludvik, now thirty-seven years old, visits the small town in Moravia where he was reared. He has become a scientist in Prague, and his purpose in returning after a very lengthy absence is to wreak belated revenge, to have the last joke on his student prosecutor, Zemanek. Zemanek's wife Helena, a radio journalist, had become enamored of Ludvik while interviewing him about his research. They plan to tryst in that same Moravian town, where Helena is to report on a local folk ritual, the Ride of the Kings. Ludvik does not reciprocate Helena's affection, but callously intends to appropriate her body in retribution against her husband.

Like his others, Kundera's first novel is organized into seven parts. Four characters—Ludvik, Helena, Ludvik's genial childhood friend Jaroslav, and Kostka, a pensive Christian Communist who lends Ludvik his apartment for the weekend—provide overlapping perspectives on what is happening and on its roots in the past. Ludvik narrates parts 1, 3, and 5, Helena part 2, Jaroslav part 4, and Kostka part 6; the nineteen sections of part 7 interweave the points of view of Ludvik, Jaroslav, and Helena. The kaleidoscopic effect is to magnify the inadequacy of any single account and to dramatize the pathos of misapprehensions, failed intentions, and cross-purposes. Jaroslav is an accomplished fiddler, and the detailed disquisition on folk music contained within his narrative suggests a formal analogy between the structure of the novel and the spirited harmony of the local ensemble in which he plays. Ludvik, its former clarinetist, abandoned the group long ago when he deserted his native Moravia. The narrative design of *The Joke*, like the exuberant scene in which Ludvik rejoins the ensemble after grim years in Prague and Ostrava, embodies the truth that genuine music of the spheres is a chorus, not an aggregate of soloists.

The novel's eponymous joke (Ludvik's postcard to Marketa) begets other jests, and a complex network of cosmic irony occurs. Ludvik decides to play a retaliatory joke on Zemanek by seducing his wife, but the trickster himself is once more tricked when he discovers that Zemanek has been a husband in name only and that he is quite grateful to Ludvik for absolving him of any guilt for running off with a much younger lover. The abducted Helena of

Prague now proves an embarrassingly passionate limpet, and Ludvik desperately seeks to rid himself of the woman he had regarded merely as an instrument of his will. Helena's response, attempted suicide, proves as inept a joke as any of the others. She swallows an entire jar of pills belonging to Jindra, the adolescent sound technician who is infatuated with her, but all that is mortified is her pride, for the pills—laxatives—are merely diarrhetic not deadly. Perpetuating the joke, Jindra vows revenge on Ludvik.

The Joke is a drama about the illusions of control in a universe governed by drift. While mocking the arrogance of ideology, it also makes a mockery of mockery; both the politician and the court jester naïvely believe they can shape the world, whereas in Kundera's fiction, reality is fundamentally amorphous. Fifteen years after the original incident, Ludvik cannot avenge himself on Zemanek, because Ludvik is no longer Ludvik, Zemanek no longer Zemanek, and even anguish is ephemeral. Similarly, the experience of Jaroslav demonstrates that collective memory is no less deceptive and insubstantial than the individual kind. Jaroslav dedicates his life to the perpetuation of folk culture but finds himself and the vanishing traditions he cherishes derided as antiquated jokes. *The Joke* concludes with Jaroslav, the only kindhearted character in its cast, performing his beloved Moravian music before bored and boorish restaurant patrons—and suffering a heart attack. Jaroslav has been the principal organizer of the annual Ride of the Kings ceremony, an ancient ritual reenacted despite the fact that its significance has been lost to time. His own son scorns these unintelligible rites and dupes his father into believing he is an active participant when he has in fact sneaked off to the motorcycle races. According to Kundera, entropy makes a mockery both of history—man's attempts to arrest and comprehend a patterned past—and of man's faith in his ability to direct what has not yet occurred. Ludvik comes to the plaintive realization that "everything will be forgotten and nothing will be rectified. All rectification (both vengeance and forgiveness) will be taken over by oblivion."

Kundera's first novel is sardonically jocular only to the detached perspective of the reader. Ludvik's original sin is to be a humorist in a world where dogmas are held in earnest and earnestness is dogma. Yet, though ironic detachment is liberating, it is also portrayed as debilitating. Each of the novel's multiple perspectives is in itself deficient, but the inadequacy of any one point of view is evident only to those who, like the reader, are able to integrate each fragment of the story into a global vision. Formally complex, *The Joke* demands a reader willing to undertake a project of restoration and reintegration. In its energetic play between the humor of fission and the comedy of fusion, Kundera's engagingly grim novel tells many a vital truth under the guise of jest.

Steven G. Kellman

Sources for Further Study

The Atlantic. CCLI, January, 1983, p. 104.
Library Journal. CVII, November 1, 1982, p. 2109.
National Review. XXXV, January 21, 1983, p. 59.
The New Republic. CLXXXVIII, February 14, 1983, p. 30.
The New York Times Book Review. LXXXVII, October 24, 1982, p. 3.
The New Yorker. LIX, February 21, 1983, p. 126.
Newsweek. C, November 8, 1982, p. 87.
Publishers Weekly. CCXXII, September 10, 1982, p. 66.

THE JOURNALS OF SYLVIA PLATH

Author: Sylvia Plath (1932-1963)
Edited by Frances McCullough and Ted Hughes
Publisher: The Dial Press (New York). 370 pp. $16.95
Type of work: Journal
Time: 1950-1962

Selected journal entries which include Sylvia Plath's thoughts on her prose and poetry

> *Principal personages:*
> SYLVIA PLATH, a lyrical poet troubled by a lack of self-identity
> TED HUGHES, her husband

The Journals of Sylvia Plath, which includes excerpts from the writer's notebooks during a twelve-year period, gives readers an opportunity to hear Sylvia Plath's honest and distinct voice speaking out from the welter of critical and psychological analysis that has built up around her work. Here are her observations about herself and others, her goals and obsessions, her particular delights, furies, and demons. The individual who emerges is wise, funny, introspective, and self-aware. Most important, seeds of her poetry and prose can be located and traced to fruition with the aid of these journal entries: especially when read as a companion piece to the recently published volume, *The Collected Poems* (1981), the journals will provide scholars with a valuable primary source where links can be discovered between Plath's life and her work in order to piece together a portrait of the artist as a young woman, self-drawn, rather than the mythic fresco she has become. In an entry dated May 20, 1959, Plath asks about her poetry, "Will I ever be liked for anything other than the wrong reasons?" These journals may provide some of the right reasons.

In the first section of the journals, dated 1950 to 1955, it is clear that Plath's urge to write sprang not only from her driving ambition but also from her need to justify her life, to confirm her identity even as she searched for it. She asks repeatedly who she is and answers with lists of achievements or tentative identifications: "'a passionate, fragmentary girl,' maybe?" In the midst of adolescent rites of courtship and stirrings of passion, as she perfects herself as "the American virgin, dressed to seduce," she states that her "happiness streams from having wrenched a piece out of [her] life, a piece of hurt and beauty, and transformed it to typewritten words on paper."

She worries about future conflicts between her role as writer and wife, wondering if she can preserve her identity as a writer while scrambling eggs for a man. By her sophomore year at Smith College, she sets her goal: a symbiotic relationship between husband and wife in which each can work to realize potential. She expresses the desire to deliver babies, both human and poetic; she wants a husband and family, but firmly rejects the traditional

1950's concept of a woman's place. This ambition to achieve personal and career goals is perhaps one reason that she has been labeled a protofeminist.

Plath set high standards for herself academically, professionally, and socially. In May of 1952, she writes: "I will still whip myself onward and upward . . . toward Fulbrights, prizes, Europe, publication, males." At the same time, however, she doubted her ability to live up to the ideals she erected: "I have the choice of being constantly active and happy or introspectively passive and sad. Or I can go mad by ricocheting in between." This difficulty would beset her throughout her life, and although the early journals evince a surprising degree of self-awareness, she is often unable to thwart her negative, self-destructive impulses.

Plath's writing shows promise during this early period. While she is capable of adolescent gush, she is also capable of writing a lyrically erotic entry about feeling sexually aroused by the sun's heat on a rock, being purified by the sea, and emerging "clean" from "dwelling among primal things." Her attention to sound is apparent in such phrases as "swatch of winking stars" and "numb dumb snow-daubed lattice of crystal." Moreover, echoes of much later poems can be discovered in such phrases as "Cats have nine lives . . . You have one," a variation of which becomes a line in "Lady Lazarus." In one entry, Plath discusses one use of the moon as an image. She elucidates clearly the progression of the metaphor of moon as plant bulb, demonstrating an ability to analyze her own work, and also a keen eye for imagistic progression, a progression that culminates in such poems as "Fever 103°" and "Cut."

One primary theme that runs through the early journals and is also an identifiable current in Plath's poetry and prose is the theme of rebirth. After a bout of depression during the fall of her junior year, she characterizes her rehabilitation as rolling "the stone of inertia away from the tomb." She sees herself as "The girl who dies. And was resurrected." Often sounding like Norman Vincent Peale, she credits her rebirth to mental magic, a belief that attitude can change everything. She attributes achievements—poems in *Harper's Magazine*, a summer guest editorship at *Mademoiselle*—to the conscious choice she has made, that of transforming wish to reality through hard work.

The three entries drawn from the summer of 1953, however, prior to her suicide attempt, belie Plath's ability to choose between dark or light, death or life. The first entry parallels the opening of her novel, *The Bell Jar* (1963), as she speaks of her physical sickness at the imminent electrocution of the Rosenbergs. She longs to crawl back to the womb, to avoid choice, to abdicate responsibility. She labels one entry "Letter to an Over-grown, Over-protected, Scared, Spoiled Baby," while trying to exhort herself to think, to take action. The final entry ends with a pathetic plea: "please, think—snap out of this. *Believe* in some beneficent force beyond your own limited self. God, god, god: where are you? I want you, need you: the belief in you and love and mankind. You must not seek escape like this. You must think." Perhaps this plea can be seen as a longing for the father/authority she does not have, a theme that appears more frequently in her journals as she matures.

At the end of this section, the editors have appended a note stating that journals no longer exist (if they ever did) for the two years following Plath's suicide attempt, so that while the dates given are 1950 to 1955, the final entry is dated July 14, 1953. This two-year gap is the first that readers will bemoan, since ideas for *The Bell Jar* and many poems originated from this time.

The second section of *The Journals of Sylvia Plath* covers the two years Plath spent as a Fulbright Scholar at Cambridge University and her year as a teacher at Smith College, a time of transition and change. By the end of this period, 1955 to 1958, she had committed herself to a life of writing rather than to academia, as well as to marriage. Plath's infatuation with Ted Hughes was immediate; they married four months after meeting. In her journal, she characterizes him as a panther, a Neptune, a god, taking clear delight in marriage and in performing such duties as typing his poems. While she feels fortunate to have found domestic happiness with her poet husband, she is concerned about losing her writing self in the world of domesticity, and while she wishes to have a child, she wants first to produce a book. In one entry, she worries, prophetically, that she is too bound to Hughes, that if anything happened to him "I would either go mad, or kill myself." Her capacity for rage is revealed in an entry made on May 19, 1958, which describes her husband walking with a young Smith student when he was supposed to be meeting her. Months later, she was able to link this rage to her feelings of abandonment by her dead father.

Indeed, the search for a father assumes major proportions in this section. Pleas abound for "some man, who is a father." In a particularly enlightening entry written on Mother's Day, 1958, Plath discusses the possibility of using "Full Fathom Five," the title of one of her poems, as a book title because of the importance of the sea as a central metaphor in her work, the father as "buried male muse and god—creator risen to be my mate in Ted, to the sea-father Neptune." She continues, "so the river flows to the paternal source of godhead."

Aspects of the resurrection theme appear also, sometimes linked to the search for father, and, more often, in reference to herself. She recollects her electroshock therapy as "waking to a new world, with no name, being born again, and not of woman." In fact, she speaks directly about her fascination with the Lazarus story, paralleling it with her own rising again after her suicide attempt. Her appreciation of "the mere sensation value of being suicidal" resonates in the dramatic tone of "Lady Lazarus."

Both direct and indirect references to Plath's work appear often in this section. Notes and observations can be traced to subsequent poems, including "Spider," "Hardcastle Crags," and "Mussel Hunter at Rock Harbor," to name only a few. The poems, "Whiteness I Remember" and "Ariel" seem to derive in part from the following entry: "Then there was the time . . . when the horse galloped into the street-crossing and the stirrups came off leaving me hanging around his neck, jarred breathless, thinking in an ecstasy: is this the way the end will be?" Plath describes the completion of several poems, as well as her plans for a novel which include ideas that were incorporated eventually into *The Bell Jar.* Her system of imagery and correspondence begins to emerge as she sprinkles her journal entries with references to colors (red and black, colors she often wore), to fire and electricity (tied to passion and to destruction), to the moon, frogs, sea, rock—a fascinating mine for Plath scholars. Here, too, she discusses several writers she wishes to emulate in her prose. She makes particular reference to Henry James and D. H. Lawrence and draws artistic and personal parallels between herself and Virginia Woolf. With her other hand, she makes plans to write commercial stories for the "slicks" under a pseudonym: Sylvan Hughes.

Throughout this period, Plath's two-headed demon of self-doubt and ambitious perfectionism never leaves her: "*Again, I feel the gulf between my desire and ambition and my naked abilities.*" The phrase "a life is passing" forms a motif, and she puts great pressure on herself to write, thereby re-creating her life. Such re-creation makes her feel godlike, gives her the aura of immortality and control. In this period of transition, she wants to succeed in the adult literary world, not in the adolescent markets where she has experienced what she now characterizes as facile success. At the same time, she admits that she depends too much on having poems published in *The New Yorker.* She is often frankly envious of and acidly humorous about more successful writers. Nevertheless, Plath continues to fight her demon, the one who "wants me to think I'm so good I must be perfect. Or nothing."

The final section of the journals contains entries from the summer of 1958 through the fall of 1959, when Plath lived in Boston. The last real entry is dated November 15, 1959, from Yaddo, prior to Plath and Hughes's return to England to await the birth of their first child. The last years of her life are represented by a piece titled "The Inmate," written between February 27 and March 6, 1961, when Plath was in the hospital having her appendix removed, and by a series of sketches of her Devon neighbors dated February through July, 1962.

During her time in Boston, Plath was faced with having only to write, an immense task that initially overwhelmed her, but again, she set goals: "I must slowly set my lands in order: make my dream of self with poems, breast-sucking babies, a Wife-of-Bath calm, humor and resilience." Two poems were accepted by *The New Yorker*, yet she remained dissatisfied with her work, feeling that she was still searching for her "true deep voice." In her journal, she even wonders if her poetry is simply an escape from prose, from the novel and stories she longs to write.

The entries from December 12, 1958, through June 20, 1959, are filled with penetrating questions, self-analyses, and remarkable insights, during a period in which Plath underwent therapy with the psychiatrist who treated her after her suicide attempt in 1953. These entries weave a tapestry in which readers can discern the pattern of recurring conflicts and problems: the issues of father-search, mother-guilt, hostility, and manipulation, as well as Plath's concern with rebirth, a desire to remake herself as a strong woman and writer. Apparent is her urge to become independent, both from Hughes—to show him none of her poems—and from her mother—to avoid confiding in her.

Plath's search for identity paralleled her search for voice, and in the fall of 1959 at Yaddo, as if released, she began to write poems which hinted at the power of her later work, including "The Manor Garden," "The Colossus," "Medallion," "Poem for a Birthday," "The Burnt-out Spa," and "Mushrooms." As she comments: "I wonder about the poems I am doing. They seem moving, interesting, but I wonder how deep they are. The absence of a tightly reasoned and rhythmed logic bothers me. Yet frees me. . . ."

Throughout this section, Plath discusses many poems, stories, and ideas for a novel, an invaluable source for research. Unfortunately, the final two notebooks from late 1959 until her death in February, 1963, are not available—the last one destroyed by Hughes, the other missing. It is regrettable that scholars do not have these journals, since Plath wrote the body of her work during this turbulent, but most creative, period. It must be noted also that *The Journals of Sylvia Plath* are edited selections, encompassing only one-third of Plath's notebook entries. The editors state that they have cut lists of characters, prospective poems and stories, descriptions, and commentary, as well as particularly devastating remarks. The remaining unedited journals are available, however, at The Neilson Library at Smith College. It is there that readers can find a more complete self-portrait of Sylvia Plath, the complex woman and artist that this book so tantalizingly sketches.

Lynne Davis Spies

Sources for Further Study

The Atlantic. CCXLIX, May, 1982, p. 102.
Choice. XX, September, 1982, p. 87.
Christian Science Monitor. September, 1982, p. 17.
Los Angeles Times Book Review. May 30, 1982, p. 6.
Macleans. XCV, May 17, 1982, p. 57.
Ms. X, June, 1982, p. 76.
The New York Times Book Review. LXXXVII, May 2, 1982, p. 1.
Newsweek. XCIX, May 3, 1982, p. 77.
Saturday Review. IX, May, 1982, p. 62.

KAFKA
A Biography

Author: Ronald Hayman (1932-   )
Publisher: Oxford University Press (New York). 349 pp. $19.95
Type of work: Literary biography
Time: 1883-1924
Locale: Primarily Czechoslovakia and briefly, Berlin, Germany

A brief but sharply detailed and persuasive biography of Franz Kafka that illuminates the social background of his writing

Principal personages:
FRANZ KAFKA, a novelist and writer of short fiction
HERMANN KAFKA, his father
FELICE BAUER, twice engaged to Kafka
DORA DYMANT, Kafka's final love

Originally published in Great Britain under the title *K: A Biography* (1981), Ronald Hayman's concise, artistically restrained, and moving study offers many pleasures and at least two surprises: that the author's knowledge of Franz Kafka is far more detailed, more exhaustive than one would have believed possible; and that his interpretation of the life, not at all ambiguous or tentative, is unified and wholly convincing. For those whose recollections of biographical evidence are limited to the early studies, primarily by Max Brod, Kafka's friend and literary executor, Hayman's book is a revelation. To be sure, since Brod's biographical and critical studies were published, much more information has become available concerning Felice Bauer, Grete Bloch, Dora Dymant, and Milena Jesenská-Polaková, the love interests in Kafka's life—mostly through correspondence. The general reader, however, would have little reason to expect the wealth of information that Hayman has patiently gathered. Even though Kafka was not, at the time of his death in 1924, entirely obscure as a literary figure, he was assuredly not the subject of considerable attention, either. Given the historical circumstances—the invasion of Czechoslovakia in 1939 by German armies, the resulting Holocaust, and the eventual establishment of a Communist satellite government—one might doubt the survival of any archives or additional scraps of information concerning Kafka's family background, his childhood, his schooling, his young manhood, his circle of friends, or his literary connections.

These pessimistic expectations, however, have been proven wrong. Through the publication of memoirs and specialized scholarship, a great deal of information has become available concerning Kafka's Prague, his Jewish roots and the influences upon him from Hasidic and Yiddish literature, and the significant romantic involvements in his life. From these sources and others, Hayman has reconstructed Kafka's life. With compassion, intelligence, and tact, he has selected a pattern of details to place the man in his time, and to remove from Kafka's life an aura of strangeness that had previously defined him.

For although Kafka's fiction is, for many readers, an investigation into strange quarters of human imagination, his life-pattern no longer seems outside the grasp of understanding. Hayman reveals a neurotic personality, to be sure, but Kafka's neurosis had fairly clear origins. Moreover, Kafka was well aware of these origins, transmuting the crude suffering and anxieties of his early childhood years and his adolescence into the stuff of fiction. Chief among the shapers of his character was his father. Mostly for ill, but not entirely so—as Hayman points out—Hermann Kafka dominated his son, along with others in his family, demanding from the frail, sensitive boy a resolute, vigorous, decisive temperament that Franz manifestly lacked.

Beginning at age fourteen as a merchant in small items such as buttons, threads and shoelaces, Hermann gradually progressed, eventually opening a fancy-goods shop in Prague. In the Zeltergasse, near the center of the old city, he earned a modest livelihood. A robust, energetic, ambitious businessman who was at home an autocratic, demanding, but not entirely selfish husband and father, he could not understand the needs of his quiet, timid, delicate first-born son. Because the family moved frequently during Franz's early childhood, the boy had little parental supervision; when his mother was not pregnant with his siblings or preoccupied with household duties, she worked with her husband to advance the business. Deprived of close affection, young Kafka withdrew into himself, with a deepening sense of inferiority and depression.

At school, these qualities were, for the most part, made permanent elements of his personality. Because of his slight physique, he rarely participated in children's games, and because his academic achievements—generally above average but not superior—were not high enough to satisfy his father, his childhood sense of ineptness was augmented by a consciousness of guilt and failure. Although Kafka's later recollections of school at the Alstädter Deutsches Gymnasium were sketchy, Hayman provides richly detailed information about the boy's schoolmates, his teachers, and his course of study. These years, on the whole, helped to fashion in the adolescent Kafka some assurance in language and literary skills, but the atmosphere within and outside the classroom was oppressive. As a secularized Jew, Kafka was torn between contrary allegiances: to become a good Czech or to become a good German. Attracted to German culture, at least partly because of Czech anti-Semitism, he was also moved by patriotic impulses. Yet, he was comfortable with neither group. Treated by both Czechs and Germans as an alien, indifferent to Jewish values but repulsed by Gentile hostility, he was a youth estranged from his roots: family, community, country.

As Hayman makes clear, the etiology of Kafka's neurosis was neither unique nor pathological. Thousands of young Jews living in pre-World War I Prague— or Budapest or Bucharest or Warsaw—must have considered themselves alienated from societies that would not accept them as ordinary citizens. Culturally assimilated into the Gentile world but deprived of their full rights to education, to the professions, or to the sociopolitical structure, they had at the same time loosened their ties with traditional Judaism. As a result, they were like displaced persons in a threatening environment, with the peculiar neurosis that springs from deracination. Like many of his Jewish friends, Kafka vacillated between acceptance of his Judaism to the point of advancing Zionism and the opposite urge toward complete assimilation. As a young man, Kafka had been generally ignorant of Jewish religion and philosophy, but by the end of his life he was undertaking a serious study of the Hebrew language, was reading selections from Talmudic and Hasidic literature, and was advocating Zionism. Having overcome at least one source of his neurosis—cultural estrangement—he was making progress toward becoming an integrated person who could function with "normal" competency.

Other elements of his neurosis were more difficult to control. Because of his ambivalent feelings toward his father, he suffered a lifelong inferiority complex. Nevertheless, Kafka was making some slight progress in asserting his independence from his family, and by the end of his life he was able to enjoy a brief but mature love relationship with Dora Dymant. Indeed, in all of his relationships with women, no matter how incomplete, he made significant progress in freeing himself from the isolation and self-hatred of his youth. Although unable to marry Felice Bauer, mainly for reasons of his poor health but also because of financial concerns, he had at least discovered passion, and from his affectionate friendships with Julie Wohryzek, Grete Bloch, and Milena Jesenská-Poláková—all three women of refinement—he enjoyed some moments of laughter, some consolation.

Just as Hayman discovers in Kafka's biography a pattern that allows the reader to perceive a psychology tormented but not warped, so he also shows that pattern as an artistic unity. Kafka no longer appears to be a remote, strange being. Indeed, Kafka understood his own condition very well. Through his art, he succeeded in turning his private neurosis into universal symbols of twentieth century malaise. Hayman shows how Kafka made of his loneliness, his anxiety, and his physical suffering the fables of a modern Sisyphus.

Hayman begins his study with a chapter entitled "The Turning Point: 1912." That particular occasion was ten o'clock in the evening of September 22, 1912. Kafka, then twenty-nine years old, had just sat down to write his story "Das Urteil" (1913, "The Judgment"). He worked without pause until six o'clock the next morning. He completed the manuscript with a sense of having discovered "how everything can be said, how for everything, for the strangest fancies, a great fire is ready"; he had discovered his unique voice as a creative artist. The "great fire" that could consume and transform his suffering into a higher form of consciousness, that could change the "strangest fancies" of a neurotic into fables of the human spirit, permitted him to "complete an opening of body and soul." By focusing upon this point in Kafka's life as a revelation of his calling, Hayman allows the reader an insight into the creative process that fired Kafka's imagination.

In many respects, Hayman's biography is also a work of intense creative imagination. Although the author is not particularly concerned with Kafka's writing from the standpoint of critical exegesis, he shows how Kafka's work developed inexorably from his life. For example, in a brilliant chapter entitled "Captive Insect," he relates Gregor Samsa's transformation into a giant insect in the story "Die Verwandlung" (1915, "Metamorphosis") to Kafka's suffering at the time of his engagement to Felice. Hayman traces, moreover, Kafka's identification with rodents and insects, and shows how his experiences provided the startling symbolism of many of his tales. By the time that the reader completes the last chapter, "Hunger Artist," he has come to identify Kafka with his writings. Kafka can be understood as a "hunger artist," gaunt, tubercular, obsessive—but not mad, not strange, not odious. With the sureness and trenchancy of Kafka's own lean prose, Hayman describes a life that seems as wonderful and unsettling as the artist's fables of the absurd.

Leslie Mittleman

Sources for Further Study

Choice. XIX, May, 1982, p. 1246.
Christian Science Monitor. April 9, 1982, p. B6.
German Quarterly. LVI, January, 1983, p. 168.
Library Journal. CVII, March 15, 1982, p. 631.
The New York Times Book Review. LXXXVII, January 17, 1982, p. 1.
Newsweek. XCIX, February 1, 1982, p. 65.
The Sewanee Review. XC, October, 1982, p. 583.
Times Literary Supplement. February 5, 1982, p. 139.
World Literature Today. LVI, Summer, 1982, p. 510.

KATHERINE ANNE PORTER
A Life

Author: Joan Givner (1936-   )
Publisher: Simon and Schuster (New York). 572 pp. $19.95
Type of work: Literary biography
Time: 1890-1980
Locale: The United States, Mexico, Germany, France, Spain, Italy, and Belgium

Katherine Anne Porter's chosen biographer has provided a well-balanced account of the life of one of America's finest artists in fiction

> *Principal personages:*
> KATHERINE ANNE (CALLIE RUSSELL) PORTER
> HARRISON BOONE PORTER, her father
> CATHERINE ANNE SKAGGS PORTER, her grandmother
> ANNA GAY HOLLOWAY HEINTZE, her niece
> GLENWAY WESCOTT, her longtime friend and confidant
> JOSEPHINE HERBST, her writer friend and confidante
> JOHN HENRY KOONTZ,
> EUGENE DOVE PRESSLY, JR.,
> ERNEST STOCK, and
> ALBERT RUSSELL ERSKINE, Porter's husbands

One of the chief obstacles facing a biographer of Katherine Anne Porter is separating fact from fiction. Porter had a lifelong tendency to romanticize, to fantasize, to transfer experiences or circumstances of other people to herself, to mislead, to falsify, and sometimes even to lie outright. Perhaps, as the years passed, she may have forgotten what *was* the truth about many events in her earlier life.

Joan Givner, Porter's chosen biographer, remarks, "She edited the story of her life as she might have shaped one of her short stories." She became angry when critics erred about "facts" and even more so when she was confronted with the actual record which proved her own distortion. Yet, astonishingly, says Givner, Porter was eager to "achieve immortality by having the story of her life told," and she carefully preserved many of the materials that her future biographer would need.

Givner's portrait of Porter includes blemishes that might have infuriated the living subject. However, Givner has balanced objectively Porter's charm with her faults, her genius with her pettiness, and her accomplishments with her failures in this story of the long life of one of America's most gifted writers of fiction. Although Givner devotes some critical attention to Porter's writings, the emphasis is properly on the character and the life. Since the life contributed so much to the writings, though, Givner frequently cites and discusses characters, places, and incidents that were transformed or transmuted from reality to fiction.

Porter was born in Indian Creek, Texas, in 1890 (not 1894, the year given in many reference books). She shed her given names, Callie Russell, which she disliked, and appropriated, with a slight spelling change, the given names of her beloved grandmother, Catherine Anne Skaggs Porter. The new names she considered better suited to a daughter of the aristocratic Southern family she created to replace the undistinguished one to which she actually belonged. Having lost her mother at two, she was cared for by her grandmother until she too died seven years later. This double loss so early in life had a profound and lasting effect: Porter frequently believed, whether with justification or not, that she had been abandoned or rejected by people she had trusted or on whom she had depended.

At sixteen, to escape from her difficult father, she married the first of her four husbands, John Henry Koontz, whose name she would refuse to reveal in later life. They were temperamentally unsuited to each other, and the marriage ended after nine years, including two of separation. Porter said the marriage was never consummated, but Givner disbelieves this. Miranda, Porter's alter ego in "Old Mortality," one of her Texas stories, asserts her independence in the same way that Porter did, by leaving her husband and striking out on her own.

Dreaming of motion-picture stardom, Porter headed for Chicago at the age of twenty-three and did a little acting but soon returned, disillusioned, to Texas. Yet, says Givner, there was a long-term benefit from the experience, since Porter developed the "ability to dramatize the psychological, internal action of her stories" and learned to read dramatically.

Before beginning to write for a Fort Worth newspaper, Porter was treated for tuberculosis in a Dallas sanatorium and at another in West Texas. Later in life, she developed frequent bronchial troubles, which were further aggravated by her smoking. A near brush with death came in Denver when she was struck down by influenza during the epidemic of 1918. This experience led her, years later, to write her remarkable short novel *Pale Horse, Pale Rider: Three Short Novels* (1939), in which Adam, the soldier friend who has helped the frail Miranda survive the disease, dies of it himself. Typically, Porter gave on different occasions several versions of the "facts" on which she had based this story.

Unhappy with her writing for the *Rocky Mountain News* in Denver and wishing to get away from Parke French, to whom she had become engaged, Porter moved east. She settled in the Bohemian atmosphere of New York's Greenwich Village, and soon became acquainted with a number of writers and artists there. When she received an offer to write for the *Magazine of Mexico*, she moved to Mexico City. Here and in the surrounding countryside, she found the inspiration for such later stories as "Maria Concepción," "Hacienda," and the symbolic "Flowering Judas."

In childhood, Porter suffered from a short attention span, and for much of her mature life she was easily distracted from her writing by her love of entertaining and socializing. The poet Marianne Moore called her the world's worst procrastinator. Givner suggests that Porter's delays and evasions relative to her work were also the result of an "uneasy balance between confidence and self-doubt." Certainly, Porter was late developing as an author. She was thirty-two when she published what she referred to as her first story, "Maria Concepción." There had been several earlier children's stories, but she chose to forget these. At her death, she left as her contribution to literature one collection of short stories (including several short novels), one long novel, and a collection of essays and occasional writings. The total is small for an important author who lived to be ninety years old.

Distractions from Porter's writing also included her four marriages, which brought her much quarreling and misery, and a series of love affairs extending even into her old age. She once told the critic Malcolm Cowley that she had had four husbands and thirty-seven lovers. One should allow for the characteristic exaggeration, but Givner names a dozen of the lovers, who included artists and writers, as well as less-notable men. The theme of rejection, which appears so often in Porter's fiction, relates closely to her own experience, since she felt herself rejected by her lovers. Yet there seems at times to have been a perversity in Porter's nature. Though a highly intelligent woman, she was impulsive, and she plunged into situations or involvements that were almost certain to bring her pain. She was pretty, vivacious, and an entertaining talker, but when drinking, she could become noisily quarrelsome. Narcissistic, she desired masculine adoration, but there were limits to her lovers' capacity for devotion. Though she thought she might have been happy married to one of her lovers, who already had a wife, the probability is that she could never have achieved a long, happy marriage with anyone.

For several years, Porter engaged in varied activities or projects in Mexico and the United States, mingling with Mexican revolutionaries, with expatriate Americans, and with New York Bohemians. She earned pesos in Mexico by teaching and translating, and she earned dollars in New York by ghostwriting and reviewing books. During the Sacco-Vanzetti troubles in Boston, she was jailed briefly on several occasions for picketing. Among the friends she made in New York were the writers Caroline Gordon and her husband, Allen Tate. Through them, she was introduced to several members of the Fugitive Group, who were prominent in the Southern literary renaissance of the 1930's. Porter came to appreciate the value of using her own Southern experience in developing her art, and several of the best stories she later wrote used Texas locales, incidents, and characters drawn from her past.

Attracted to the life and character of the fanatic Puritan minister Cotton Mather, Porter planned to write his biography, and she moved to Salem, Massachusetts, for several months to gather material. Suffering from one of her many periods of ill-health, though, she next sailed for Bermuda, where she remained for five months to recuperate and to continue work on the

Mather book. Blocked in this project (which she never completed), she returned to Mexico to work on a novel which she tentatively called "Thieves' Market." It was never published, but excerpts from it appeared as the Mexican stories in *Flowering Judas and Other Stories* (1930).

In Mexico, as so often in Porter's life, the temptations of socializing seriously interfered with her writing. Also, she fell in love with Eugene Dove Pressly, Jr., whom she would marry three years later. An award of a two-thousand-dollar Guggenheim fellowship offered her the opportunity to escape a welter of unpleasant complications in Mexico and to make a long-desired trip to Europe. Pressly accompanied her as they set sail in 1931 for France on the German ship *S. S. Werra* (which would become the *Vera* of her novel, *Ship of Fools*, 1962, still many years away from publication; she and Pressly would become Jenny Brown and David Scott in the novel). They were not permitted to land in France; they debarked at Bremen and went on to Berlin.

Irritation, anger, and malicious accusations against various persons marked Porter's unhappy months in Germany. From this point on in the biography, Porter's travels or moves from one country or one city to another become so numerous that one wonders how a woman subject so often to spells of ill-health managed to survive to old age: Paris, Madrid, Paris, Basle, Paris, New York, Texas, Paris, Washington, Pennsylvania, New Orleans, Saratoga Springs, California, Georgetown—Porter was always on the move.

With the publication of *Pale Horse, Pale Rider: Three Short Novels*, Porter began to receive increasing attention and praise from critics. Her writing was not of the sort to attract a large following, though, and in order to increase her income, she began to accept speaking and reading engagements on college and university campuses. A lucrative offer from a Hollywood motion picture studio led to nearly four years of life in California, though less than one year was spent as a screenwriter. Admittedly prodigal in nature, she squandered much of the movie money after paying off her accumulated debts.

Ship of Fools was finally published in 1962 after more than twenty years of delays. Though it had a mixed critical reception, it immediately became a best-seller and was sold for $400,000 to United Artists for filming. Porter, then seventy-two, was freed finally of the burden of supplementing her writer's income through university teaching and speaking and anticipated a "new life of peace and ease" in her remaining years. For a time, however, she was besieged by a multitude of writers, publishers, autograph-seekers, columnists, and photographers. Her novelist friend Glenway Wescott gave her sound financial advice, but she spent twenty thousand dollars for a diamond-set emerald ring and set out on a trip to Europe with her niece Anna. She later bought a large Maryland home and hired a secretary and three servants. Porter in her last years declined to senility, became increasingly paranoid, and was put into a nursing home, where she died in her ninety-first year. She was buried in Texas, next to her mother's grave, in a wooden coffin which she had ordered by mail several years earlier and had kept standing in a closet, reserved for future use.

Givner's well-written biography is a fine memorial to an author whose stories such as "The Circus," "The Grave," "Noon Wine," and "Pale Horse, Pale Rider" are classics of modern fiction.

Henderson Kincheloe

Sources for Further Study

America. CXLVIII, February 19, 1983.
The Atlantic. CCL, December, 1982, p. 105.
Library Journal. CVII, November 15, 1982, p. 2177.
Ms. XI, November, 1982, p. 32.
National Review. XXXIV, December 10, 1982, p. 1559.
The New Republic. CLXXXVII, November 22, 1982, p. 30.
New York Review of Books. XXIX, January 20, 1983, p. 13.
The New York Times Book Review. LXXXVII, November 7, 1982, p. 3.
Time. CXX, December 6, 1982, p. 92.

THE KILLING GROUND

Author: Mary Lee Settle (1918-   )
Publisher: Farrar, Straus and Giroux (New York). 385 pp. $14.95
Type of work: Novel
Time: 1960-1980
Locale: Canona, West Virginia

A search for a pattern of death that ends in a discovery of life

> *Principal characters:*
> HANNAH MCKARKLE
> JOHNNY MCKARKLE, her brother
> SALLY BRANDON NEILL MCKARKLE, her mother
> MOONEY MCKARKLE, her father
> MELINDA MCKARKLE CUTRIGHT, her sister
> UNCLE EPHRAIM MCKARKLE, her uncle
> AUNT ROSE MCKARKLE and
> AUNT ALTHEA, daughters of Beverley Lacey
> TEL LEFTWICH, Johnny's mistress

The Killing Ground is the fifth and concluding volume of Mary Lee Settle's magisterial Beulah Quintet, a series of novels published over a period of twenty-six years and spanning some three centuries of English and American history. The internal chronology of the quintet differs from the sequence of publication. *Prisons* (1973) is set in England in 1649; it tells the story of Johnny Church, about to be executed, who as a sixteen-year-old boy had set out in 1645 to join the forces of Oliver Cromwell. *O Beulah Land* (1956), set in what is now West Virginia, covers the twenty years from 1754 to 1774 and tells the story of Johnny Church's descendant, Johnny Lacey, who founds a great estate called "Beulah." *Know Nothing* (1960), set in the same region in 1837-1861, concerns the downfall of the estate, which has become a slave-owning enterprise. *The Scapegoat* (1980), again set in West Virginia, is centered on a bitter coal-mining strike in 1912 which pits descendants of the Church-Lacey line against one another.

To complicate matters, the final volume of the quintet, *The Killing Ground*, set in the present but including many flashbacks, is itself a significantly expanded version of an earlier Settle novel, *Fight Night on a Sweet Saturday* (1964). Dissatisfied with her editor's cutting of the original work, Settle claimed that the cuts destroyed its crucial connection to the other books. The protagonist of *The Killing Ground*, Hannah McKarkle, is a novelist: at the literary luncheon which opens the novel, Hannah is identified as the author of *Prisons*, *O Beulah Land*, *Know Nothing*, and *The Scapegoat*—the very titles of Settle's books. Hannah identifies herself with her ancestor Hannah Bridewell, Johnny Church's heir who emigrated to America. This complex sense of history that is still powerfully at work, of the present informed by the past, is Settle's great achievement in the quintet, and though the five novels can be read independently of one another, they can be appreciated fully only when seen as a whole.

One problem with reading only one book of the quintet is especially prominent in *The Killing Ground* and the character of Hannah McKarkle. The book centers on the event of Johnny McKarkle's murder, but beyond that, there is no plot in the sense that a book's plot is usually constructed. Hannah discovers who killed Johnny very early, and the story from then on is Hannah's own personal search for the real Johnny and, more important, for herself. Hannah, searching superficially for her brother's killer, but actually finding a deeper understanding of her family's roots and connections, and finally of herself, refers to the "first Hannah" throughout the book. The relationship between the two Hannahs is necessary to a full understanding of the current Hannah. Unless one knows that the first Hannah was Hannah Bridewell, born in a London prison and expelled from London as a thief and a whore, the same Hannah in *O Beulah Land* who escaped from an Indian massacre at Fort Duquesne and, alone in the wilderness, stumbled upon the cabin of Jeremiah Catlett and thus became the "grand matriarch" of the aristocratic families delineated in the three later books, one misses the close connection between the first Hannah, her character and prostitution, and the prostitution, although of a different nature, of the Hannah in *The Killing Ground*. Even though Settle touches on past family and regional history in *The Killing Ground*, and gives a sense of "how we got to where we are," the present family progeny come more fully to life if the earlier stories have been followed. Reading only one book of the quintet handicaps the reader in the same way that the characters in each book are handicapped by not seeing the grand design, by not being in touch with life closely enough to see themselves in the broader sense. All the characters are suspended in their own place and time; it is only in each succeeding novel that their true importance is established.

To eliminate another element of confusion likely to arise with the publication of *The Killing Ground*, one must return to Settle's early dissatisfaction with *Fight Night on a Sweet Saturday*. *The Killing Ground* is a revision, or, in a technical sense, an expansion of the earlier novel. After the first 165 pages of the new novel, the remainder is almost identical, word-for-word, with *Fight Night on a Sweet Saturday*. A few paragraphs have been added, a few deleted, and some characters have different names. In each of the novels, Settle carefully researched not only the period, but the language, and chose a tongue appropriate to the time and characters. *The Killing Ground* is more sophisticated in style than *Fight Night on a Sweet Saturday* and more contemporary in tone. The change in title and the revision were necessary to Settle's new vision of what she wanted this last book to be and do. When she wrote *Fight Night on a Sweet Saturday*, neither *Prisons* nor *The Scapegoat* had been written, but once they were completed, Settle's vision changed and solidified in *The Killing Ground*, allowing her to expand her horizon even beyond the first Hannah, beyond Johnnny Church—"If a city consists, not of old camp-sites, old fires, but of shelters, tombs, sacred forms, and places for murder, with the illusion of permanency so that in a lifetime it can be left and returned to, as I have done, then this city is three thousand years old"—to the mythic story of sacrifice on the "killing ground" where now stands the spire of All Saints, the Episcopal church, in place of the stone stela that once marked the spot.

This kind of revision is not unprecedented: William Faulkner changed both *Flags in the Dust* (*Sartoris*, 1929) and *Sanctuary* (1931) to satisfy his publisher, but both books have recently been published in the form Faulkner intended. Gore Vidal rewrote *The City and the Pillar* (1948; revised edition, 1965) and John Fowles, *The Magus* (1966; revised edition, 1978). Nevertheless, Settle's situation is unique. By the deliberate, nearly word-for-word reprinting of *Fight Night on a Sweet Saturday*, she evidences satisfaction with the central event of that book, but by building around and into the original work, material that ties the book closely with the first four books, and to some extent, sums up the previous works, *and* reveals *its* own story, Settle assuages her dissat-isfaction with its lost connection with the other four novels in the quintet.

Whatever classification these novels may receive, they are definitely not "historical escape novels." Settle demands as much of her reader as she has of herself in her research and writing. *The Killing Ground*, like *O Beulah Land* and *The Scapegoat*, is divided and marked by time periods: "The Return, June 1978"; "Before the Revolution, 1960"; "The Beginning, 1960-1980"; and "Epilogue, 1980." Within each section, the reflections of the characters and sometimes the omniscient narrator transport the reader either back in time or ahead. This technique is effective in allowing the reader to see a broader pattern, an evolving heritage, a repeated tradition, that—sometimes blessedly—the characters do not see.

In his introduction to the Ballantine paperback editions of the first four novels in the quintet, Roger Shattuck says: "We may not be able to notice everything, but Miss Settle, patiently and convincingly weaving history into her *roman fleuve*, reveals that nothing has to be lost for good." Compelled to leave no stone unturned, Settle shifts the point of view frequently from one character to another. For example, in the opening of *The Killing Ground*, Hannah McKarkle, an accomplished author, returning from New York to Canona in 1978 to speak at a fund-raising event for a new art gallery, is being driven to the function by several of her former friends. Beginning with Han-nah's observations that "They are, in one of the bloodiest centuries of the Christian era, women to whom nothing has happened that is not personal. . . . They exist on sufferance and rule kingdoms too small, clubs, gardens, their imitators. They are the prisoners of the welfare of their parents, their hus-bands, the habits of their privileges," Settle shifts the point of view to each of the women and their private thoughts. While *Fight Night on a Sweet Saturday* is narrated in the first person, *The Killing Ground* is narrated from multiple points of view, and this change is appropriate to Settle's intention to illuminate the complexity of the relationships; as each character is revealed, another is veiled, a question surfaces. Hannah's search finally removes all the veils, and she, like the reader, sees the complete design. Hannah, who searched as much for her brother—"Brother Jonathan, Johnny Rebel, Johnny Dalton, Johnny the Kid, Johnny run the streets . . ."—as for his killer in 1960, in her speech reiterates the pattern of genealogical and historical Johnnies—"Brother Jonathan, Johnny Reb, Johnny Appleseed, a character once as familiar as Uncle Sam, fades in and out of our history. . . ."

In this section, it may be noted that Settle inserts an autobiographical element by referring to Hannah McKarkle as the author of the previous books of the quintet. But while she has used elements of her experience in the area where she lived a portion of her life, in 1983, Settle states that the books are not autobiographical. How else could Hannah McKarkle know the things she knows about the past if she had not done research on her past generations for a purpose larger than her own curiosity, and how else could she link herself to the first Hannah?

By the device of indirection, the search for her brother Johnny, Hannah finds herself. As she explores intimately the relation of Mrs. McKarkle to both Johnny and to herself, coming to realize that the mother has rendered both Johnny and herself sexless, she also realizes that her relation, as well as her mother's, to Johnny has been mentally incestuous:

> For if obsession, siege, the hovering of a spirit demanding a central place, all the way into a darkness where I have not yet gone, is love, then I am in thrall, sunk in love, as I have always been in whatever guise I found him, with my brother Johnny. . . .

While Johnny has escaped this mental anguish in death, Hannah must escape in life.

The paranoia of her search for Johnny—"For he, my brother, Johnny, deep within me, has run away from the little old woman and has run away from the little old man, and run away from me too, he can, he can"—changes to panic as Hannah realizes her own possible fate after Johnny's death—"Run run as fast as you can, you can't catch me, I'm the Gingerbread Man. Come on, Johnny, come on Gingerbread Man, let's get out of here."

Mary Lee Settle is reminiscent of Thomas Wolfe in her language, her detailed description, her passion for family. Certainly, "you can't go home again" is one of the themes of *The Killing Ground*.

> Five years after Johnny's death I had come back, carrying with me some hope, as we all have, that 'things would be different.' I see now that it was the kind of nostalgia that soldiers have, that things will be the same, but only the same as the simple dream of calm

they carry with them for a place that has never been on any earth but the landscape of their hope. . . .

In her grand design, however, Settle surpasses Wolfe, escapes the criticism that has been his for sentimentality and overblown phrases, and transcends the personal, subjective style.

As one lifts with Hannah in the silver plane that carries her away from the Canona Valley, as Hannah gives up Johnny, gives up "all the people that I had conjured up and brought to life again," and the land, one shares the nostalgia that will forever be a part of Hannah, and identifies with her independence as she realizes ". . . I knew that I had joined the wanderers, from Johnny Church, through the old Hannah, lost in the woods below, Jonathan Lacey, who had brought us there, Johnny Catlett, Carlo Michele, Eduardo Pagano, and Lily; all of those who have set out alone, perhaps self-deluded by necessity."

As a final touch and a quintet signature, Settle, who began *Prisons* with Johnny Church saying "I am twenty today. There is only Thankful Perkins to tell it to, but Thankful is asleep," ends *The Killing Ground* with Hannah, dreaming, saying, ". . .And I was twenty and there was only Thankful Perkins to tell it to."

One hopes that, now that Settle has completed her quintet, a publisher might release all the books together. To date, this has not happened; Ballantine has published the first four books in paperback, while *The Killing Ground* will be published in paperback by Bantam Books. The Beulah Quintet is a notable accomplishment in the world of fiction and deserves proper recognition.

Peggy Bach

Sources for Further Study

Christian Science Monitor. August 13, 1982, p. B3.
Library Journal. CVII, July, 1982, p. 1346.
Los Angeles Times Book Review. July 11, 1982, p. 1.
Nation. CCXXXV, August 21, 1982, p. 150.
The New Republic. CLXXXVI, June 16, 1982, p. 30.
The New York Times Book Review. LXXXVII, July 11, 1982, p. 1.
Publishers Weekly. CCXXI, April 30, 1982, p. 47.
Saturday Review. IX, June, 1982, p. 71.
West Coast Review of Books. VIII, November, 1982, p. 33.

LAST STANDS
Notes from Memory

Author: Hilary Masters (1928-   )
Publisher: David R. Godine, (Boston). 210 pp. $14.95
Type of work: Memoir
Time: c. 1860-1980
Locale: The Midwest and the East Coast of the United States

A search for identity, place, and meaning through memories

Memoirs often are published because they have been written by someone famous or by someone related to a famous person. Hilary Masters, while not famous, is known for *The Common Pasture* (1967), *An American Marriage* (1969), and *Palace of Strangers* (1971). He also is the son of Edgar Lee Masters, who attained his place in American literature with *Spoon River Anthology* (1915). Masters' memoir, however, is not dominated by himself or by his famous father. As the younger Masters writes, "It's not about me, but about how I was used by my grandparents and parents as a hollow log in which they left messages for each other. . . ." While *Last Stands* does contain many elements of the conventional memoir, it must be seen in its own unique perspective.

While Masters' style appears plain and rather plodding, it is the structure of Masters' memoir that holds the most interest for the reader, a structure that is uniquely analogous to the lives he is describing. Young Hilary's life was divided between the Midwest and the East. He spent the school year in Kansas City with his grandparents so that his mother might pursue her studies toward a teaching career, and he spent his summers in the East, sometimes with his father, sometimes with his mother, sometimes with both. Consequently, Hilary and his mother made many trips back and forth across the country. Very early, he establishes that the pattern of his memoir was inspired by the pattern of his life. Back and forth is the way Masters tells his story. He goes from grandfather to mother to father to grandmother to grandfather, back and forth, from one to the other, from one time to another, from one place to another, and from one event to another. Masters does provide points of reference along the way, such as his age at a particular time in the narrative or the particular year it is, but his mind takes abrupt leaps from early boyhood days and memories to the last days of his grandfather, his grandmother, and his father, and the later life of his mother.

The title, *Last Stands*, alludes to Custer's Last Stand, playing on Grand-father Thomas F. Coyne's cavalry days at Fort Custer. In extending *stand* to the plural *stands*, Masters lends the title multiple implications, as the memoir deals with the last years of each of the four persons with whom Masters' life was so entwined.

Masters begins the memoir with the funeral of his beloved grandfather, known as Gee Gee, in Arlington Cemetery in 1954. In the next pages, he relives scenes of childhood in which he sits on Gee Gee's bed while his grandfather performs his nightly cleansing rituals in water a few degrees below boiling to accommodate the lingering symptoms of yellow fever and malaria. Hilary listened as Gee Gee told him stories of his cavalry days, of fighting the Indians, and of his life as a railroad builder in central America after he left the Army.

Later, Masters shifts to the funeral in Petersburg of his father whose death occurred four years prior to that of his grandfather. With such dramatic shifts, Masters reveals the peculiar character of not only the people themselves but also of their interaction with one another and with Masters himself.

Gee Gee is a fiery, strong, and exceptionally stubborn man who relives his past through the stories he tells Hilary and by a pilgrimage he makes in 1932 to Fort Custer. As an Irish immigrant, Gee Gee joined the United States Army illegally and did not attain his United States citizenship until 1885, through a civil court in Kansas City. As Hilary talks with him in the soldiers' home, Gee Gee bemoans the fact that he is one of the last men still alive from the days he holds dearest, the only survivor of the Indian Wars still living in the home. He awakens every morning hoping that death will come soon. He had tried to commit suicide by slashing his wrists in the lavatory, but he was discovered and was taken to the hospital where he recovered from the suicide attempt but fell victim to pneumonia. His act of despair led Hilary's mother, Ellen Masters, to obtain permission for him to be buried in Arlington Cemetery, thereby honoring his wishes. He was laid to rest on a hill to the firing of the six-gun salute and taps. As the flag that covered his coffin was presented to Ellen, she nodded toward Hilary, and he received the honor.

Masters describes his father in brief phrases that reveal a man of great talent and great complexity. He was a successful lawyer and a secret poet, a devoted family man and a womanizer, a man of property and the defender of union causes. He is best remembered as the author of *The Spoon River Anthology*.

Gradually, Masters illuminates each of the descriptive phrases until there emerges a detailed portrait of an aging, cantankerous man, driven after receiving critical attention later in life than most writers, "to create an *oeuvre* by a terrible urgency that pushed like an unseasonable tide into the caves of his imagination to flush out material that should have had more time to develop." With the years slipping away and with the continued resentment he felt because his sister Madeline had been sent to Knox College to study drawing and French while he had to study law and work in his father's office, Edgar Lee Masters produced masses of work. At sixty, he was still trying to make up for the neglect he suffered thirty years earlier.

The female influences in Hilary Masters' early life lend a twist to the superficially male-dominated environment in which he lived. His grandmother and his mother fought against chauvinistic attitudes in their husbands. Both women were expected to reflect passively the men to whom they were married; but each woman exerted her influence in a definite, though different manner. Grandmother Mollie Coyne, tall and beautiful, with an agreeable mien and graceful expression, appeared to follow the dictates of her husband, trying to keep a normal household, trying to prevent her prize pieces of china and crystal from disappearing as they moved from one house to another. Many times the thought of leaving Gee Gee crossed her mind, but she withdrew quietly into work with the church, and especially into an involvement with Tom Pendergast's Democratic Party, as a means of escape. After an accident in which she was hit by a truck, breaking her arm, she was cruelly taunted by her husband. She began to withdraw from life, taking to her bed and turning her face to the wall. The woman Masters remembers as having a "residue of Evening in Paris" upon her body and who held him in her arms with "no obligation to hold me save for the dumb, unknowing turn of her heart, the selfless surrender that would bring her to destruction but for now presses me to her forever," finally turned away even from Hilary "like one of James's misunderstood heroines, her doom setting around her on Robert Street with the certainty of cement."

Ellen Masters, Hilary's mother, inherited Mollie Coyne's strength, but she used this inner will differently, and it is she who was the strong force that held the family together. In fact, ultimately *Last Stands* becomes a tribute to Ellen Masters as Hilary Masters finally realizes that "what appeared to my grandfather, to all of us sometimes, to be an all-out assault, an interference with our lives, was really the manifestations of my mother's frantic efforts to keep those lives going on a day-to-day basis." Because she was born female and suffered the shame of being unable to attend West Point, she persuaded her father to send her to the University of Chicago; she was given orders to study either law or medicine. Dark-haired, with luminous eyes, explosive laughter, and dramatic gestures, Ellen aspired to be an actress, and she did tour with small companies for a time. After her marriage and the birth of her child, she knew that someday four people would depend on her economically. She began to teach and to work toward a further degree, much to the chagrin of her father and her husband. She met with so much opposition from Edgar Lee Masters that she left the Chelsea Hotel where they lived and moved into a small apartment alone. Ellen was constantly torn between her duties to her parents and her duties to her husband and son. H. L. Mencken—having no understanding of an independent woman who refused to keep her proper place in a world in which men were superior—commented that she was a "stupid woman," exemplifying her husband's attitude; both were unpleasantly surprised when she proved that she could take care of herself.

It was Ellen who insisted that her parents install a telephone and buy an electric refrigerator; it was she who planned Hilary's schooling, who supported Edgar Lee Masters, encouraging him, and making his last days more comfortable. After her father's confinement to the soldiers' home, her mother's depression grew steadily worse and Ellen brought her East. It was Ellen Masters who so carefully tended the memory of Edgar Lee Masters, making corrections in the family history whenever she returned to Petersburg, recounting repeatedly her life with her husband.

In contrast to the search he conducts in *Last Stands*, Hilary Masters accepted passively the nature of his life. By his own admission, the only time he tried to establish an identity separate from the receptacle he had been for the residue from his parents' and grandparents' lives was during the time he went to school in New Hampshire after his grandparents could no longer care for him. There he tried for the term of each school year to create his own identity. During this period, he began to compare his own life to that of the boys with whom he attended school. "The arrangement gave me the best of two worlds, for a time; moreover, no one told me it was unusual."

As Masters relates the stories told to him by his grandfather, the memories of his grandmother as the stable point of contact with the real world, the trials and tribulations of his father's writing career and the everyday life he led, and the role his mother played in the scheme of all their lives and as the continued keeper of the Masters family history, it is evident that the people he talks about and lived among lived in a present dominated by the past. It was inevitable that such a preoccupation would affect his own life.

Masters has, in a sense, created his own *Spoon River Anthology* in *Last Stands*, as he juxtaposes bits and pieces much as his father did. He was never expected to contribute to the lives of those who took care of him, but this book is his contribution. Perhaps he realized, while talking with Gee Gee before he died, "that there are certain things that can never be spoken of directly, or described as they happen, but if one is lucky, the attempt can be made later to talk about them, or even write about them."

Peggy Bach

Sources for Further Study

The Atlantic. CCL, December, 1982, p. 106.
Booklist. LXXIX, October 1, 1982, p. 146.
Publishers Weekly. CCXXII, October 1, 1982, p. 119.
Smithsonian. XIII, February, 1983, p. 144.
Time. CXX, November 29, 1982, p. 95.

THE LEFT BANK
Writers, Artists, and Politics
from the Popular Front to the Cold War

Author: Herbert R. Lottman (1927-   )
Publisher: Houghton Mifflin Company (Boston). 319 pp. $14.95
Type of work: Political and literary history
Time: 1930-1950
Locale: Paris

A study of the rise and fall of the "engaged" French writers of the period between 1930 and 1950 against the background of political movements which shaped their work and gave their ideas prominence

> *Principal personages:*
> SIMONE DE BEAUVOIR, a writer in the Existentialist movement; a close associate and companion of Jean-Paul Sartre
> ALBERT CAMUS, a French-Algerian writer associated with the Existentialist movement in Paris; an editor of the underground publication, *Combat*, during World War II
> PIERRE DRIEU LA ROCHELLE, an author and a Nazi collaborator who avoided standing trial after the liberation of France by committing suicide
> ILYA EHRENBURG, a Soviet writer and Paris correspondent for *Isvestia*, who was instrumental in establishing an International Writer's Congress for the Defense of Culture and otherwise served as a liaison between Western intellectuals and the Soviet Union
> GASTON GALLIMARD, a publisher of books and of *La Nouvelle Revue Française*, which continued publication during the German occupation of France
> ANDRÉ GIDE, an elder statesman among French writers of this period, generally sympathetic to left-wing causes
> ANDRÉ MALRAUX, a novelist of ideas, very active in anti-Fascist activities during the occupation of France, joined the Resistance near the end of the occupation, and ultimately became President Charles de Gaulle's Minister of Education
> JEAN-PAUL SARTRE, an Existentialist philosopher, novelist, and dramatist

The neighborhood surrounding the church and square at Place Saint-Germain des Près on the left bank of the Seine occupies a unique niche in the intellectual and cultural history not only of France, but also of the world. This small community was the center of French intellectual life during a period in which a number of the most influential literary and philosophical works of the twentieth century were produced in France. This period, from about 1930 to 1950, was the heyday of the "engaged" artist whose commitment to political action took precedence over art for its own sake. The subordination of aesthetic considerations to political expedience all too often came at the expense of artistic quality, and Lottman points out that "the international impact of many of these writers is disproportionate to their artistic achievement," perhaps because "to produce enduring art one had to be a loner." Lottman characterizes *The Left Bank* as "more of a political history than a literary one," however, and the matter of aesthetic quality does not arise, except tangentially, as a topic for consideration here. Above all, the engaged writer was a political animal, and Lottman's subject is the politics of the French literary community.

The movement of French writers toward political engagement began in the 1930's, spurred by the rise of Fascism throughout Europe. The major organized resistance to Fascism in the early days was provided by international Communism, and attachments between Communist organizations and other individuals and groups dedicated to anti-Fascism developed almost from the beginning. In fact, so ubiquitous were these relationships that Lottman is compelled to ask some vexing questions:

> Was it because the Soviet Union, acting through the Comintern, had devised a strategy for enlisting support from individuals and groups beyond Soviet borders that the anti-Fascist movements of the 1930s developed as they did? Or was it because sincere men and women, Communist sympathizers or not, threw themselves into the anti-Fascist struggle, seeing it as a legitimate effort regardless of its origins?

Whatever the causes, one of the characteristics of political commitment of the period was its internationalization, as involved individuals looked outside their own national borders to respond to events in Germany, Spain, Italy, and, eventually, the Soviet Union itself. At the very least, the Communists proved adept at exploiting anti-Fascism to bring together activists and radicals of a variety of political stripes and hues in a united front sympathetic to the Communist position.

One of the figures most responsible for the emergence of such anti-Fascist coalitions was the Soviet journalist Ilya Ehrenburg, a familiar figure in Parisian cultural and intellectual circles in the days prior to World War II. According to Lottman, it was Ehrenburg who first suggested to his supervisors in Moscow that an anti-Fascist writers' group be created to encourage support for the Communist position. The proposal apparently caught the attention of Stalin himself, who summoned Ehrenburg back to the Soviet Union for consultation. Although the meeting never took place, Ehrenburg was ordered to submit to his superiors a detailed proposal for the establishment of an international organization of writers. Ehrenburg's proposal led to the landmark International Writers' Congress for the Defense of Culture in July, 1935, the first such coalition. It not only marked the beginning of close cooperation between Communists and the non-Communist literary Left, but also was a key event in the internationalization of an important segment of the literary establishment of the time. Attracting such luminaries as Aldous Huxley, E. M. Forster, Bertolt Brecht, and Maxim Gorky (the United States was represented by such minor figures as Waldo Frank and Michael Gold), the Writers' Congress set a precedent for future political activism.

An even more significant event in the evolution of political activism in the French literary community followed the outbreak of anti-government rioting in Paris by groups of both the Right and the Left. The Communists, realizing how near the Rightists had come to a coup, suspended their quarrels with non-Communist intellectuals and joined in the "Popular Front" movement, which, within two years, would elect a government with Communist support. Those events, Lottman writes, "were to change not only French politics but French hearts, the way Communists and Socialists perceived each other, the way they faced up to the Fascists, from then until the German occupation of France and perhaps beyond."

Clearly the most interesting section of *The Left Bank* is that which covers the war years—particularly the years of the German occupation. If ever the opportunity for "engagement" existed, it was during this dangerous time, yet for the intellectual community of the Left Bank, it was to a surprising extent a time of business as usual. Lottman notes "the remarkable loyalty between men and women whom opinions and sometimes wars should have separated once and for all. They went to the same schools and then taught in the same universities, or worked on the same magazines and in the same publishing houses, took coffee in the same salons, sat side by side in restaurants and cafés." Indeed, Lottman observes that shifts in political affiliation did not necessarily require the severing of old friendships: "The resulting confusion in the order of battle is sometimes enough to make the head spin. It may suggest that commitments were not always taken seriously, especially when the committed wore the fancy dress of *La Nouvelle Revue Française*."

The takeover of *La Nouvelle Revue Française* (*NRF*) is represented by Lottman as a paradigm of the cultural life of Paris in the occupation years. As the premier journal of contemporary literature and thought, the *NRF* was a potentially valuable propaganda tool. Prior to the occupation, the journal was edited by Paul Paulhan, whose sympathies lay with the Left. Pierre Drieu La Rochelle was "virtually the house Fascist," representing the extreme Right in the stable of regulars writing for the journal. Through a series of negotiations involving Otto Abetz, the German Ambassador to France, Gaston Gallimard, whose publishing firm owned the *NRF*, and Drieu, the Germans gained effective control of the journal. Drieu became its editor, and Gallimard was able to convince most of the *NRF* writers, including the anti-Fascist ones, to continue publishing in the journal. Paulhan retained an office in the Gallimard building, from which he participated in a variety of Resistance activities under the noses of Drieu, his collaborationist staff, and the Germans. When Paulhan was eventually arrested, Drieu interceded with the Germans on his behalf and probably saved him from execution. As a result of his compromise concerning the *NRF*, Gallimard was able to continue publishing books, including such landmark works as Albert Camus' *L'Étranger* (1942; *The Stranger*, 1946), a translation of James Joyce's *Ulysses* (1922), Sartre's *L'Être et le néant* (1943; *Being and Nothingness*, 1956), and a variety of other works, including several which "could hardly have been appreciated by the Germans."

During his editorship of *NRF*, Drieu wrote that "The Germans were there and it was necessary to work things out with the Germans. . . . We are collaborating, and that is a guarantee of survival. . . . Those in the government, those in business, intellectuals, are all collaborating. . . ." While this may be a self-serving overstatement, Lottman makes it clear that the politics of collaboration were complex indeed. Some would claim that even the publishing of nonpolitical works with the tacit consent of the Germans was a form of collaboration, and this occurred with enough regularity to give credence to Drieu's charge of widespread collaboration. Even Sartre, whose anti-Nazi play, *Les Mouches* (1942; *The Flies*, 1947), was first produced during the occupation, is not exempt from the charge. Ironically, as Lottman points out, there was actually a good deal more intellectual freedom in German-occupied Paris than under the Vichy regime in unoccupied France.

Lottman's account of the individual comings and goings, alliances and animosities involving such major figures as Gide, Malraux, Camus, Sartre, and others, though too complex to permit a brief summary, is one of the most fascinating aspects of *The Left Bank*. These individual histories give credence to the author's suggestion that, to some degree, "everybody collaborated." The literary world of occupied Paris was politically complex and morally ambiguous—a world of few heroes and even fewer saints.

Lottman concludes with Alain Robbe-Grillet's obituary of "engagement":

> How can we forget the successive submissions and resignations, the explosive ruptures, the excommunications, the imprisonments, the suicides? . . . Let us give the notion of commitment the only meaning it can have for us. . . . Instead of being political, commitment for the writer is the full consciousness of the current problems of his own language, the conviction of their importance, the will to resolve them from the inside.

Perhaps so, but one cannot help but note that today, only those writers who live in democracies can afford the luxury of art for its own sake. In less favored states and communities, the committed writer remains an outspoken force against oppression, and we are richer for his testimony, in human spirit if not in art.

William E. Grant

Sources for Further Study

Choice. XIX, July/August, 1982, p. 1623.
Commentary. LXXIII, January, 1982, p. 72.

Economist. CCLXXXIV, August 28, 1982, p. 70.
Library Journal. CVII, May 1, 1982, p. 887.
National Review. XXXIV, May 14, 1982, p. 567.
New Statesman. CIII, May 28, 1982, p. 21.
The New York Times Book Review. LXXXVII, April 18, 1982, p. 3.
The New Yorker. LVIII, July 5, 1982, p. 98.
Times Literary Supplement. October 1, 1982, p. 1057.

THE LETTERS OF GUSTAVE FLAUBERT
1857-1880

Author: Gustave Flaubert (1821-1880)
Selected, edited, and translated from the French by Francis Steegmuller
Publisher: The Belknap Press/Harvard University Press (Cambridge,
   Massachusetts). 309 pp. $15.00
Type of work: Letters
Time: 1857-1880
Locale: Paris and Croisset, France

*The second of two volumes which includes representative correspondence by one of
the world's greatest novelists and letter-writers*

> *Principal personages:*
> GUSTAVE FLAUBERT, one of the most fastidious and deliberate of
>   major writers
> MME. FLAUBERT, his mother, in whose house he lived most of his
>   life
> CAROLINE COMMANVILLE, his niece, who contracted an unhappy
>   marriage with a corrupt businessman
> GEORGE SAND, a novelist and feminist with whom Flaubert had a
>   firm, platonic friendship
> CHARLES-AUGUSTIN SAINTE-BEUVE, a leading French critic of this
>   period
> IVAN TURGENEV, a Russian novelist, and a friend of Flaubert
> ÉMILE ZOLA, a French novelist, and a friend of Flaubert

The Letters of Gustave Flaubert: 1857-1880 is the second of two volumes
of Gustave Flaubert's correspondence in a selection drawing on the recently
issued Pléiade edition of Jean Bruneau. Francis Steegmuller, who has selected,
edited, and translated these letters for the Belknap Press, is the leading
American Flaubertian; his previous books include a fine translation of *Madame Bovary* (revised Modern Library edition, 1982); a double biography,
Flaubert and Madame Bovary (1939), analyzing both the genesis of the novel
and the accompanying course of its creator's difficult liaison with Louise Colet;
an earlier selection of Flaubert's letters (1953); *Flaubert in Egypt* (1972), a
narrative of Flaubert's travels there from 1849 to 1851; and the first volume
of the Belknap Press edition of Flaubert's letters (1980), covering Flaubert's
life up to the age of thirty-six, when the novelist achieved fame at one bound
with the publication of *Madame Bovary* (1857) and his subsequent trial for
alleged obscenity.

After the popular and literary success of *Madame Bovary*, Flaubert continued his cloistered life in his mother's country house in Croisset, Normandy.
He increased the number of his friends, acquaintances, and admirers, yet
refused to become a public figure in the conventional way by starring in
Parisian literary salons. Although he occasionally spent a week or two in a

leased apartment in Paris, he preferred to pursue his unremitting aestheticism in his country retreat, with no guiding stars save for his own judgment and the advice of a few carefully chosen friends.

None of Flaubert's later works approached the popularity or influence of *Madame Bovary*, yet his reputation as a writer of enormous integrity and magnificent talent shone steadily. Steegmuller points out that "a curious and growing public sympathy was extended to this uncompromising artist who held himself aloof." His melancholia and misanthropy—a generalized disgust with what he regarded as humanity's dominant stupidity and vulgarity—intensified in his later years, encouraged his literary and social seclusion, and led to such splenetic texts as *Bouvard et Pécuchet* (1881) and *Le Dictionnaire des idées reçues* (1913; *Flaubert's Dictionary of Accepted Ideas*).

Flaubert suffered, sometimes stoically but more often cholerically, a number of severe disappointments and trials. His sparse literary production was often misunderstood; his attempts to write for the stage failed miserably; the deaths of his closest friend, Louis Bouilhet (1869), and of his beloved mother (1872) left him inconsolable; the Franco-Prussian War of 1870 to 1871 and subsequent harsh struggles between radicals and reactionaries embittered him; worst of all, he helped to ruin the life of his beloved niece, Caroline, by pushing her into a loveless marriage with an apparently respectable bourgeois whose business failures cost Flaubert considerable sums. No wonder his letters are replete with such exclamations as, "Everything moves me, everything lacerates and ravages me."

The main course of this edition is a generous helping from the celebrated correspondence between Flaubert and George Sand, which contrasts in its mellow sensitivity and mutual respect with the sensual turmoil of the Flaubert-Louise Colet letters in the first volume of Steegmuller's edition. (The entire corpus of Flaubert-Sand letters was published in 1981 in Paris, edited by Alphonse Jacobs, but has not yet been issued in English.)

The friendship between Flaubert and Sand began in February, 1866, at a brilliantly attended dinner where she found him "more sympathetic" than the other guests. It developed rapidly, so that by May, she dedicated her newest novel to him, and in August, he had her visit his Croisset home for several days. From then on, they regularly exchanged letters between her home in Nohant, his in Normandy, and their respective apartments in Paris. His customary salutation to her was "chère maître," combining the feminine form of the adjective ("dear") with the masculine noun ("master")—because, he told her, he admired the man in her.

Interestingly enough, their aesthetic ideals were at considerable variance, and their political and social views were wholly at odds. Yet they respected each other's devotion to their craft and capacity for hard labor at it. More significantly, they were deeply fond of each other. He admired her candor, directness, and good temper, and the high level of her intelligence: "She has insights that evince very keen good sense, provided she doesn't get on to her socialist hobby horse." Additionally, both agreed on the desirability of leading intense, risk-taking lives. Wrote Flaubert in one of his most eloquent passages:

> Everything has its price! Large natures (and those are the good ones) are above all prodigal, and don't keep such strict account of how they expend themselves. We must laugh and weep, love, work, enjoy and suffer—vibrate as much as possible, to the whole extent of our being. Thus it is, I believe, to be truly human.

Flaubert complained mildly to Sand that her writing was too confessional and rhapsodic, too infused with her own experiences, ideas, and temperament. A novelist, he admonished her, *"hasn't the right to express his opinion* on anything whatsoever. Has God ever expressed his opinion?" Instead, he preached insistently the doctrine of art's impersonality, of the writer's need to transport himself inside and into his characters, effacing his own identity.

In 1869, Flaubert's ambitious novel, *L'Éducation sentimentale* (1869; *A Sentimental Education*), received largely negative reviews (although the twenty-nine-year-old Émile Zola praised it highly in a periodical article). "No one is coming to my defense," Flaubert complained to Sand, and shyly asked her to champion the book. She dashed off an enthusiastic newspaper review within twenty-four hours, then wrote a small stream of supportive letters to him during the next month, ranking him above Victor Hugo and Honoré de Balzac. She also tactfully indicated that young readers, naturally idealistic and optimistic, found his novel too melancholy and depressing for their tastes.

When Sand occasionally encouraged him to overcome his isolation by romantic attachments, Flaubert sounded his insistent note of asceticism for the sake of his art:

> As for ladies, there are none available here abouts, and even if there were! . . . I have never been able to accommodate Venus with Apollo. For me it has always been the one or the other—being as I am, a creature of excess, given over entirely to whatever I'm engaged in.

Flaubert's tendency to excess took the form of fiercely apolitical statements when German-French tensions erupted into the Franco-Prussian War of 1870: "Art is our country: a curse on those who have any other." He favored what he sometimes called a *mandarinat*; France would be run by men who, after appropriate examinations and competitions, would be recognized as her brightest and therefore best. In his exasperation about the state of society at large, he cried out: "Give me a tyrant of genius who will protect arts and letters and lead us out of the mediocrity we are wallowing in!" His ideal civilization was that of the classic Athenians, who "in the time of Pericles devoted themselves to Art without knowing where their next day's bread would come from. Let us be Greek!" When he went so far as to launch a tirade against universal suffrage, Sand replied that, instead of encouraging stupidity, it would be

> the universal safety of the future. This is a machine gun that must resolve, peacefully, all questions awaiting their answer in days of tumult and terror—let us not forget it! The day it begins to function properly, errors of Power, whatever they may be, will become impossible.

Steegmuller provides illuminating information about the conflicts within the National Assembly during the crisis of 1870 to 1871, leading up to the "Bloody Week" of May, 1871, when perhaps as many as twenty-thousand Left-wing Communards were killed by French soldiers in one of French history's most tragic chapters. The Prussians had meanwhile dealt the French military a humiliating defeat, leading Flaubert to turn suddenly patriotic and excoriate the conquerers:

> I didn't consider myself a believer in progress or a humanitarian. No matter! I did have illusions! What Barbarism! What retrogression! I resent my contemporaries for having inspired me with the feelings of a brute of the twelfth century. I am choking on gall. These officers who smash your mirrors with white-gloved hands, who know Sanskrit and fling themseves on your champagne, who steal your watch and then send you their visiting-card, this war for money, these savages for all their civilization—they horrify me more than Cannibals.

George Sand was saddened by the excesses of cruelty committed by all sides, to the point of exclaiming to Flaubert that she was awakening from her Utopian meliorism "to find a generation divided between idiocy and delirium tremens!" This encouraged Flaubert in his obsessive misanthropy: "Mankind is displaying nothing new. Its irremediable wretchedness has embittered me ever since my youth." He urges Sand to hate the world instead of seeing it through a golden haze of idealism: "Cry out! Thunder! Take your great lyre and touch the brazen string."

Sand's reply to Flaubert's invitation was a five-thousand-word article, published in a newspaper on October 3, 1871, which Steegmuller reprints as an appendix. This long public response is one of Sand's most humane and impassioned statements. Its first paragraph represents its tone and content:

> What! You want me to stop loving? You want me to say that I have been mistaken all my life, that mankind is contemptible, hateful, has always been so and always will be? And you reproach me for my anguish, calling it weakness, childish regret for a lost illusion? You say that the populace has always been savage, the priest always a hypocrite, the bourgeois always craven, the soldier always a brigand, the peasant always stupid? You say you have known all this since youth, and you rejoice in never having doubted it because that has spared you disillusionment in later life. You have never been young, then. Ah! You and I are very different, for I have never stopped being young—if to persist in loving is a sign of youth.

Despite these sharp differences, their tender friendship continued. Again, Sand urged him to seek out women, even to marry: "Isn't there some woman you love, and who would find joy in loving you? . . . Being alone is odious, it's deadly." His answer was a series of explanations why he found her suggestion "fantastic": he had never enjoyed female company on more than an occasional basis; he lacked the income for a couple; he was too old (fifty-one when he wrote this on October 29, 1872); he had too much decency to inflict his depressed personality on another. "Deep down, there is something of the priest in me that no one senses."

By the end of 1872, Flaubert was suffering from a problem that was to beset him the remaining eight years of his life: he had to beg his niece Caroline Commanville several times to have her husband send him money for household expenses—money which rightfully belonged to Flaubert, but which he had given to Commanville to "manage" for him. In another appendix, Steegmuller details the involved, sordid tale of Commanville's misappropriation of money. Flaubert felt responsible for his niece's mismatch, since he had discouraged her from marrying her true love, a struggling young artist. Despite his inveterate apostleship of the religion of art and detestation of the bourgeoisie, Flaubert wrote Caroline in December, 1863, when she was seventeen:

> . . . Yes, my darling, I declare I'd rather see you marry a millionaire philistine than an indigent genius. For the genius wouldn't be merely poor; he would be brutal and tyrannical, and make you suffer to the point of madness or idiocy.

Ernest Commanville's lumber business suffered badly from the Franco-Prussian War. In 1872, Caroline's capital came to include the house at Croisset, which Flaubert's mother had bequeathed to her with the proviso that Gustave be permitted to spend his remaining years in it. Caroline's husband mismanaged this property as well as his own business, with the result of splitting his wife's loyalties between her husband and her uncle. She usually sided with Ernest, pleading with Flaubert to obtain more and more credit for the Commanville estate. He remained devoted to Caroline despite her increasing harshness to him, but only a small government pension saved him from penury, while the creditors with whom Ernest Commanville had involved him hounded him to his last days.

The paradox is an excruciating one: Flaubert the aesthete/artist found his final years soured as a result of having, for once, yielded to the bourgeois beneath his skin by having helped bully his impressionable niece into an uncongenial marriage with a merchant who was to prove incompetent at the very activity Flaubert loathed—the making and management of money. A final irony can be found in Flaubert's story: after her uncle's death in 1880, Caroline sold the Croisset estate, supervised publication of Flaubert's general correspondence (being careful to expunge most passages unfavorable to her or her husband), and enjoyed a comfortable income from the worldwide sale of Flaubert's works.

Gerhard Brand

Sources for Further Study

The Atlantic. CCL, November, 1982, p. 167.
Library Journal. CVII, September 15, 1982, p. 1756.
National Review. XXXIV, October 1, 1982, p. 1226.
The New York Review of Books. XXIX, December 16, 1982, p. 26.
The New York Times Book Review. LXXXVII, October 17, 1982, p. 3.
The New Yorker. LVIII, November 22, 1982, p. 196.
Publishers Weekly. CCXXII, September 17, 1982, p. 103.

LETTERS TO OTTLA AND THE FAMILY

Author: Franz Kafka (1883-1924)
Translated from the German by Richard and Clara Winston
Edited by N. N. Glatzer
Publisher: Schocken Books (New York). Illustrated. 128 pp. $15.95
Type of work: Letters

A collection of letters written largely to Kafka's favorite sister, Ottla; all but a handful of the letters were written between 1917, when Kafka suffered the first hemorrhage in his lungs, and 1921

Since Franz Kafka's death in 1924, several volumes of his correspondence have been published; with these volumes and his diaries, it is possible to construct a more or less continuous narrative of Kafka's adult life. Indeed, Ronald Hayman's *Kafka: A Biography* (1982; first published in England in 1981 under the title *K: A Biography*), the first full-scale biography of its subject since Max Brod's in 1937, is largely stitched together from references to the diaries and letters; despite pretentions to the contrary, very little of Hayman's narrative depends on interviews and unpublished materials.

The first volume of Kafka's letters to be published was *Briefe an Milena* (1952; *Letters to Milena*, 1953). This correspondence began when Milena Jesenská-Polaková (1896-1944) wrote a letter to Kafka in October, 1919, asking for permission to translate some of his stories into Czech. Not long before this request, Kafka had broken his engagement to Julie Wohryzek, a young woman whom he had met a few months earlier in a sanatorium where they were both convalescing. In a short time, Kafka had begun an intense correspondence with Milena. They met only a handful of times—their first meeting was a passionate interlude of four days in Vienna in the summer of 1920—before breaking off their relationship. Milena did not want to leave her husband, despite his infidelities and cruelties, and Kafka was ambivalent, as always, about commiting himself to a romantic relationship. Still, his last letters to her, extraordinarily moving, were written shortly before his death. Milena died in the concentration camp at Ravensbruck; an odd but fascinating memoir by her daughter, the late Jana Černá, appeared in *Cross Currents: A Yearbook of Central European Culture* (1982).

Kafka's *Letters to Milena* reads like a Modernist epistolary novel, brilliant, neurotically self-conscious, charming, tragic, full of uncanny insight. Equally compelling is *Briefe an Felice* (1967; *Letters to Felice*, 1973), a massive volume which documents Kafka's inner life from 1912 to 1917, a period during which he was twice engaged to marry the recipient of these letters and twice broke off their engagement. Felice Bauer (1887-1960) was by all accounts Kafka's opposite in temperament; Kafka himself described her as "a happy, healthy, self-confident girl." In 1919, she married a prosperous Berlin businessman, by whom she had two children; she spent the last twenty-five years of her life in the United States. What Felice made of Kafka's letters is not known. Excruciating passages of self-analysis—these recall the inexorable logic of *Der Prozess* (1925; *The Trial*, 1937) and *Das Schloss* (1926; *The Castle*, 1930)—mingle with endearments; invaluable reflections on writing mingle with endless calculations concerning letters received, letters sent, and letters in transit.

Letters to Felice is among the memorable books of the century; it has a unity which distinguishes it from the typical collection of letters. By contrast, *Briefe 1902-24* (1958; *Letters to Friends, Family, and Editors*, 1977) is a miscellany, with a majority of the letters addressed to Kafka's friend and literary executor, Max Brod. Though it lacks the intensity of *Letters to Milena* and *Letters to Felice*, this collection is extremely valuable. Aside from many passages of individual interest, the volume provokes a reassessment of Kafka's relationship to his work. The Kafka depicted in many critical and biographical accounts is largely indifferent to publication; his final instructions to Max Brod—to burn his manuscripts—are notorious. Yet the Kafka of these letters frequently corresponds with his publishers, even taking an active interest in the typeface and design of his books ("If it were possible to give the book a dark cardboard binding with tinted paper somewhat like the Kleist *Anecdotes*. . . .").

Now, finally, there is *Letters to Ottla and the Family* (first published in 1975 as *Briefe an Ottla und die Familie*). Kafka was the first child born to his parents, Hermann and Julie Kafka (née Löwy), who had married in 1882. In 1885, when Kafka was about two years old, a baby brother, George, was born. George died before his second birthday, and several months later, in 1887, another boy was born, Heinrich, who lived only six months. In Hayman's account, the young Kafka's resentment at his displacement by these siblings and subsequent guilt at their deaths had a decisive impact on his psyche, marking him as an outsider before he even started school. It seems not to have occurred to Hayman that the average family in the 1880's lost more than one child in infancy.

After the death of Heinrich, three girls were born in quick succession: Gabriele, known as Elli, in 1889; Valerie, known as Valli, in 1890; and Ottilie, known as Ottla, in 1892. All three girls lived into adulthood; all three were to die in concentration camps.

Ottla was Kafka's favorite, the only one of his sisters with whom he was close; thoughtful, unselfish, yet independent, she suffered a particularly poignant fate. In 1920, against the wishes of her family, she had married Josef David, a Czech Christian. In 1942, with the Nuremberg laws extended to Nazi-occupied Czechoslovakia, Ottla persuaded her husband to divorce her to protect himself and, primarily, their two daughters. After registering as a Jew, she was sent to the concentration camp at Theresienstadt. In 1943, she volunteered to accompany a transport of children to Auschwitz.

There are two essential points to be made about this collection of letters to Ottla (with a few to other family members, including Ottla's husband). First, it is by far the slightest of the volumes of Kafka's correspondence which have appeared to date. The letters take up fewer than one hundred pages of text, and they lack the intrinsic interest of the letters to Milena and Felice and of many of the letters to Max Brod and others in the previous volumes. When writing to his sister, Kafka is much less introspective, much less given to self-analysis. He says little about his own writing or about literature in general. Many of the letters show him preoccupied with practical matters; Kafka is constantly asking Ottla to do little "errands" for him, requesting the purchase of certain stamps, for example, for the stamp-collecting brother of the proprietress of the chest clinic at Matliary.

On the other hand, this collection is valuable precisely because it is so mundane—the more so because almost all of the letters were written after Kafka's first hemorrhage in 1917. The urge to romanticize is incurable and takes an infinite variety of forms. In the brilliant studies by Walter Benjamin, Elias Canetti, and many others, Kafka becomes larger than life, a legendary figure. His writings are treated as sacred books; critics become high priests and exegetes of "the Word." The necessary corrective to such studies, indispensable as they are, is not to be found in the banal and reductive Freudianism of Hayman's biography (Hayman romanticizes his own role as demythologizer), but rather in the recognition that Kafka was after all simply a man.

There are some complaints to register concerning the production of this volume. The notes—greatly reduced, editor N. N. Glatzer explains, from the German edition—are inadequate and contain several inaccuracies; for example, the Czech writer Božena Němcová, remembered for her fiction, is identified as a "popular Czech poet." The translation, the work of the distinguished team of Richard and Clara Winston and the last translation Richard Winston completed before his death in 1979, is occasionally unidiomatic, not at all up to the Winstons' standard. Finally, the publisher chose not to continue with the beautiful uniform binding which was used for the two previous volumes of Kafka's letters. On the positive side, *Letters to Ottla and the Family* includes some fine photographs, and the mere publication of the volume is testimony to Schocken's enduring commitment to Kafka's works.

Reflecting on the centenary of James Joyce (born February 2, 1882), Hugh Kenner, in *The New York Times Book Review*, did not hesitate to establish Joyce's claim upon our attention: "Writing as we know it is unthinkable without him; imagine physics without Einstein." Franz Kafka is the one other modern writer for whom such a claim can be made, and his centenary in 1983 is an invitation to reflect on his influence, for indeed it is no hyperbole to say that "writing as we know it is unthinkable without him."

John Wilson

Sources for Further Study

Choice. XX, October, 1982, p. 272.
Christian Science Monitor. April 9, 1982, p. B6.
German Quarterly. LVI, January, 1983, p. 168.
Library Journal. CVII, March 15, 1982, p. 632.
The New York Review of Books. XXIX, February 4, 1982, p. 6.
The New York Times Book Review. LXXXVII, January 17, 1982, p. 1.
The New Yorker. LVII, February 1, 1982, p. 132.
Newsweek. XCIX, February 1, 1982, p. 65.

LEVITATION
Five Fictions

Author: Cynthia Ozick (1928-   )
Publisher: Alfred A. Knopf (New York). 158 pp. $11.50
Type of work: Short fiction
Time: The early 1980's
Locale: New York City

A collection of three novellas and two short stories, each involving a departure from reality into pure fantasy or an altered past

To readers acquainted with Cynthia Ozick's power to create charmingly humorous and sophisticated fictional worlds, *Levitation* will represent an extension of her distinctive talents. The subtitle, "Five Fictions" is a warning to the uninitiated reader who may expect a cautious regard for the coherence of facts and ordinary reality. These are purely literary documents: each story is a "construction," a work of make-believe, spun out and guided by the intelligence, affection, and beauty of the creative mind behind these often wry and lyrical tales.

Like *The Pagan Rabbit and Other Stories* (1971) and *Bloodshed and Three Novellas* (1976), Ozick's earlier collections of short fiction, *Levitation* is not designed around a single theme or character. With the exception of the title story, all of the pieces collected here have previously appeared in magazines or literary journals. The stories are nevertheless a unity, held in suspension by the power of dramatic voice and narrative order. In this new book, all that was best in Ozick's previous work is intensified with charm and style.

"Levitation" returns to a persistent theme in Ozick's writing: the nature and function of the artist. In a limited sense, this self-conscious examination of the writer draws in the highly touted concerns of metafiction—who is the writer and for whom is he writing? An eternal student of Henry James, Ozick shares his fascination with the art of fiction. Like James, she sees the writer as storyteller, the creator of worlds within worlds. "Levitation" offers no dry philosophical musings about the state of the art today. With flair and irony, Ozick portrays a pair of novelists, husband and wife, as they give a rare literary party.

The disturbance about the State of the Novel had escaped their attention. They wrote "as naturally as birds" and were devoted to accuracy, psychological realism, and earnest truthfulness, also virtue and wit. Lucy and Feingold were literary friends and lovers, "like George Elisa and George Henry Lewes." Both agreed on a single and fundamental principle: "the importance of never writing about writers." It was the "wrong tack, solipsism, the Forbidden Thing." The protagonist must always be someone *real*, with real work-in-the-world. They were both devoted to omniscience, but they were not acute enough to see what they meant by it. Addicted to counterfeit pity and absorbed by the notion of "power," they were attracted to the bitter side of life. They joked about their own lives: they were "secondary-level" people, living in a secondary-level house, working at a secondary-level job.

Thus, Feingold and Lucy bumped along, dreaming of the day when power and celebrity would descend upon them. Living in the Forbidden City, they were lured by circular routes to write (Lucy especially) about writers. Aware of the dangers—solipsism, narcissism, tedium, lack of appeal to the common reader—they nevertheless fell into the baited trap. They were always looking "inward," seeking the secret which would make life luminous.

Feingold and Lucy had invited a long list of famous names to their literary party, but none of these people came. Nevertheless the apartment filled up— mounds of rainboots and closets packed tight with raincoats and fur coats: "The party washed and turned like a sluggish tub; it lapped at the walls of all the rooms." Bravely, Lucy and Feingold pretend the party is a success, but privately and grimly, they realize "no one" came. Their heady concern for the power of this world blurs in Lucy's mind, and with magical insight, her spirit "levitates" from the earth. Experiencing an illumination, Lucy sees dancers dancing and children playing. Everything is a miracle, and Lucy sees that she has abandoned nature. She understands her loss of the true religion of life for the oddities, pretensions, and affectations of the "literary" life. "Levitation" thus advocates acceptance of earthly reality without hopeless regrets for a more heightened, "romantic" other world—the land of vain hopes and useless dreams.

Two interrelated stories, "Puttermesser: Her Work History, Her Ancestry, Her Afterlife" and "Puttermesser and Xanthippe," are showcases for Ozick's affection for a Jewish subject. The first of these stories is, as its title indicates, a fractured biography of Puttermesser, a thirty-four-year-old lawyer from the Bronx. As a young woman, she did not want to become a legend, but merely "a lawyer among lawyers." Her teachers described her as "highly motivated" and "achievement oriented," but her "scholastic drive" has not paid off as she hoped: she is and will always remain a Jewish girl from the Bronx. As a bright young attorney, Puttermesser is accepted into a posh law firm, but she is not advanced. She sees and understands the falsity of social gestures and the necessity of blue eyes and an aquiline nose. She does not shake her fist at the world or clutch in great anger at cultural injustice. She contentedly studies Hebrew with her great Uncle Zindel and accepts a new job in the Department of Receipts and Disbursements. An example of the muddy sub-speech on which bureaucracy relies, her new title—"Assistant Corporation Counsel"—is meaningless. Loyal to certain environments, Puttermesser will always be a victim to the acuteness of her own perceptions.

Puttermesser's biography does not proceed romantically. The rich young Commissioner of the Department of Receipts and Disbursements does not fall in love with her, and she does not end her work history in a suburban bower of bliss. Indeed this is not "an optimistic portrait," as the narrator explicitly tells the reader. Ozick brilliantly breaks the flow of time and moves the reader with the direct phrase: "Puttermesser . . . had a luxuriant dream, a dream of *gan eydn*." In this reconstituted Garden of Eden, Puttermesser spends her celestial days sitting in the greenness of July, reading, reading, reading: "Her eyes in Paradise are unfatigued." The daily uncertainty of the present world dissolves, and Puttermesser lovingly studies Hebrew.

In the "dream" section, Puttermesser has been transplanted "upward," and her mind and life take unexpected turns. Finally, the author can no longer accept the tale and implores the narrator to stop: "Though it is true that biographies are invented, here you invent too much." Puttermesser is not to be examined as an artifact but as an essence; her symbolic complexity is linked with a spiritual state. Here Ozick is working in a rich Hebrew tradition: trapped in the banal ordinariness of life, man yearns for the fulfillment of the eternal.

"Puttermesser and Xanthippe," a sequel to the previous story, is a much longer and more complex work. Divided into twelve sections, this novella extends the biographical portrait of its protagonist, now forty-six, as she tries to control and extend her power over a world which has lost the excitement of invention and discovery. For Puttermesser, life has settled into the humdrum of bureaucracy and the endlessly familiar. Her lover, Morris Rappoport, has left her because she read in bed too much. She has developed periodontal disease, and her old apartment complex on the Grand Concourse in the Bronx has been burned to cinders by arsonists: Puttermesser's childhood vanished in the flames. Finally, in the swirling change of administrations, Puttermesser is "relieved" of her duties after years of faithful service.

In her lonely apartment, distracted from the many cares of the municipal world, Puttermesser finds a white clay body in her bed. The creature is Puttermesser's imagined lost daughter, created by her mother from the earth of potted plants. Deprived of speech, the girl has written on a tablet: "This is a holy place. I did not enter. I was formed. Here you spoke the Name of the Giver of Life. You blew in my nostril and encouraged my soul. You circled my clay seven times. . . . You pronounced the Name and brought me to myself. Therefore I call you mother." The creature wishes to be known as Xanthippe. At some unknown hour in the night, Puttermesser has created a golem.

Puttermesser pores over the historical literature on golem-making; as a rationalist, she is satisfied that her creation of Xanthippe is true to tradition and legend. The golem becomes a useful companion in Puttermesser's life; she takes over the duties of cooking, cleaning, and shopping. Xanthippe expands her usefulness as secretary and planner of a great new scheme for reorganizing the entire city of New York. As is the nature of a golem, Xanthippe grows until she is bloated and immobile, but through her great plan, Puttermesser has become mayor of the city. She is ready to implement the great plan, to make the city a wondrous Eden, but excesses follow excesses, and the ripeness turns to rot: "Too much Paradise is greed. Eden disintegrates from too much Eden. Eden sinks from a surfeit of itself." Ultimately, the golem returns to earth, and her remains are interred under the red geraniums of City Hall Park.

"Puttermesser and Xanthippe" can never be reduced to its narrative line; the story resonates with the subtlety of its own myth and the power of style. For Ozick, fiction is the playground of mysticism and magical notions. The story is filled with comic charm and irony in the contrast between the intellectual/bureaucratic mind and world of Puttermesser in the real city and the redemption-seeking golem.

Two very minor stories in this collection remain to be discussed: "Shots" and "From a Refugee's Notebook." The former is an ingenious study of the concept of time as it is applied both to the distant past and to the limitless present. The unnamed protagonist is a professional photographer who has come to her trade not by way of special talent but because she is obsessed with taking pictures. Her fascination began with the discovery of a discarded old photograph of a girl whom she calls "the Brown girl": "a grave girl; a sepia girl; a girl as brown as the ground. She must have had her sorrows." The picture itself is evidence of life at a particular moment never to be effaced. Caught in a special instant on paper, the Brown Girl is time. "And not time on the move, either, the illusions of stories and movies. What I had seen," the protagonist tells the reader, "was time as stasis, time at the standstill, time at the fix; the time of Keats's Grecian urn. Time itself is death the changer; death the bleacher, blancher."

From the description of the Brown Girl, the narrator moves the center of events to recount her own involvement with Sam, a tenured professor of South American history. They spend their days walking in the rain under Sam's big blue umbrella. Sam's wife is both a shrew and a paragon, a woman whose range of talents and virtues extend beyond belief. Clearly, there is no hope for the protagonist to remove Sam from his loving home, in spite of his endless complaints of misunderstanding. "They are a virtuous and wholesome family. . . . They are sweeter than the whole world outside. When Sam is absent, the mother and her daughter climb like kittens into a knitted muff." In capturing this picture of the infinite contentment of Sam's family, the protagonist realizes that she has become like the Brown Girl, a figure trapped in a moment of time, reeking of history. Of herself, she says: "I am grave; I have no smile. My face is mysteriously shut. I'm suffering. Lovesick and dreamsick, I'm dreaming of my desire." Her face is the face of the Brown Girl, a static portrait before the changes of time.

"From a Refugee's Notebook" combines two separate and previously published short stories. "Freud's Room," offered only as a fragment, is a meditation on the primitive and subterranean dreams of man. These newly discovered notes reflect upon Freud's desire to become a god. "Is the doctor of the Unconscious not likely to be devoured by his own creation, like the rabbi of Prague who constructed a golem?"

The second piece, "The Sewing Harems," is pure fantasy. The tale opens with the following sentence: "It was for a time the fashion on the planet Acirema for the more sophisticated females to form themselves into Sewing Harems." An elliptical parable on the state of women, the story is too oblique and unclear in its intentions to be satisfying.

From the beginning of her career, Cynthia Ozick has had the reputation of being a writer's writer—a writer with extremely limited commercial appeal on the one hand, and, on the other, an intelligence too quirky to win the widespread critical attention accorded to a select number of "serious" contemporary writers. There are signs, however, that Ozick may be gaining the wider recognition she deserves. *Levitation* has been followed in short order by a brilliant collection of essays, *Art and Ardor* (1983), and a novel, *The Cannibal Galaxy*, is also forthcoming in 1983. Recently, Ozick and the short-story writer Raymond Carver were recipients of the first, generous Strauss Living Awards from the American Academy and Institute of Arts and Letters. As the stories in *Levitation* confirm, Ozick is a writer whose strangeness is not mere artistic caprice: it is worth the trouble to see the world through her eyes.

Daniel J. Cahill

Sources for Further Study

Library Journal. CVI, January 1, 1981, p. 75.
Ms. X, April, 1982, p. 94.
The New York Review of Books. XXIX, May 13, 1982, p. 22.
The New York Times Book Review. LXXXVII, February 14, 1982, p. 11.
Newsweek. XCIX, February 15, 1982, p. 85.
Saturday Review. IX, February, 1982, p. 58.
Time. CXIX, February 15, 1982, p. 74.
Times Literary Supplement. April 23, 1982, p. 456.

THE LIFE OF JOHN BERRYMAN

Author: John Haffenden
Publisher: Routledge & Kegan Paul (Boston). 415 pp. $22.50
Type of work: Literary biography
Time: 1914-1972
Locale: The United States and England

An account of the difficult and often painful life of one of America's most important recent poets and men of letters

The romantic myth of the poet holds that the production of art requires intense self-sacrifice on the part of the writer, who must be willing to accept personal suffering as the cost of his art. John Haffenden's account of the life of John Berryman is a chronicle of personal suffering, often intense and costly to Berryman and to those close to him, which ultimately ended in suicide. An alcoholic haunted by the suicide of his own father, Berryman, who married three times, was also a chronic adulterer. Yet, he produced a body of poetry recognized for its excellence by his contemporaries, who gave him the Pulitzer Prize as well as a host of lesser awards, and by his fellow poets, who found in his work a model for the "confessional" style of verse.

Such a career begs for examination in the light of the romantic myth. Was Berryman's art dependent on his self-destructive behavior? Certainly, as Haffenden points out, Berryman at times believed that he could write poetry only when drinking. He first achieved his intensely personal poetic voice when he turned the experience of a troubled love affair into a long series of sonnets. Yet, such beliefs can also be self-justifying, functioning as an excuse for personal excesses. As Haffenden notes, Berryman was extremely ambitious; he sought fame and treasured recognition as much as he feared bad reviews. One must wonder to what extent his own acceptance of the romantic myth prevented him from changing behavior he himself was able to recognize as self-destructive.

Another matter related to this myth is the poetic self whom the poet creates. Berryman assigned the name "Henry" to the persona of his works; readers may want to know the relationship between such a fictional self and the real self of the poet. Such a persona can serve as a distancing device, to separate art from life, or it can serve as a complicating factor, to lead the reader into endless speculation about the extent of autobiography in a poem. In Berryman's case, it is necessary to know what role he assigned to his poetic alter ego.

Such questions have a great deal of merit in the light of recent trends in American poetry, for the "confessional" school marked a major departure in literary history. T. S. Eliot, for example, sought the elimination of self from art and pursued a level of anonymity, a hiding behind masks and adopted roles, that gives his work much of its flavor. In contrast, the confessional mode seeks to bring the self into art, to ground art in the experiences of the artist's life, which gives it an immediacy and power not available in the cooler and more distant older mode. With that power, however, comes a vulnerability and a making-public of the poetic self which, in the case at least of Berryman and Robert Lowell, seems to have contributed to their personal difficulties and self-inflicted deaths.

While *The Life of John Berryman* provides much of the raw material for pursuing such questions, it rarely pursues or draws conclusions based on that material. Haffenden has carefully compiled most of what readers need to know about Berryman's life. He has read extensively in the Berryman files of letters and unpublished manuscripts, interviewed vast numbers of people, checked references for traces of personal memory failure or evasion, and put the mass of material together into a coherent narrative that is fascinating and compelling. There is much that is unpleasant in this book, for it honestly portrays Berryman's difficult relationship with his mother and his several wives, and his chronic struggles to overcome emotional difficulties and alcohol dependency.

Yet, by the very nature of the genre, the book presents difficulties for the reader. It fails to provide the reader, as such biographies often do, with Berryman's perception of the relationship between his art and his life. Never is this more crucially requisite than in the case of Berryman, for whom art was to a great extent a confession of life, a revealing of experience. Here, Haffenden constantly raises the issue by, for example, pointing to Berryman's having written *Berryman's Sonnets* (1967) during the course of the affair they chronicle, but he never presses the issue to any conclusion. At some point, he does concede that art prevailed; Berryman continued the affair and perhaps shaped it to meet the demands of writing poems to follow a narrative that such a sequence of poems might be said to demand. Yet the implications one might draw from such an observation are not pursued.

Nor does Haffenden pursue the issue of "Henry" to help readers know how Berryman's fictional voice differs from the actual experiences and reflections of his creator. In other words, he makes little use of Berryman's art to reveal his life. Perhaps the most valuable quality of this "life" is that it reveals aspects of the art that readers might otherwise have missed. It sends them back to the art seeking answers to a new host of questions.

Berryman's experience will stimulate readers to ask numerous questions about the role of the artist in contemporary society. His seeming acceptance of the value of art over life raises the issue of the relationship between the arts and the healing professions, whose practioners sought periodically during Berryman's tortured life to help him curb his self-destructiveness. It also raises questions about whether the rewards that society gives poets and other artists are adequate, or whether *any* reward would be enough to assuage the consuming self-doubt of an approval-seeking artist such as Berryman.

In reading Haffenden's biography of Berryman, one should anticipate that many questions were merely raised and not answered. To supply the answers was clearly not Haffenden's intention. However, Haffenden has certainly made available the material we need to begin.

John N. Wall, Jr.

Sources for Further Study

Encounter. LX, February, 1983, p. 71.
Los Angeles Times Book Review. October 10, 1982, p. 2.
Nation. LXXXV, October 23, 1982, p. 406.
The New Republic. CLXXXVII, November 15, 1982, p. 35.
The New York Times Book Review. LXXXVII, October 24, 1982, p. 9.
Publishers Weekly. CCXXII, August 13, 1982, p. 63.
Times Literary Supplement. October 29, 1982, p. 1181.

LIVING BY FICTION

Author: Annie Dillard (1945-   )
Publisher: Harper & Row, Publishers (New York). 192 pp. $12.45
Type of work: Literary criticism

An idiosyncratic, conversational analysis of the metaphysics of modern fiction

Annie Dillard first made a name for herself as a mystical nature writer in 1974 with her Pulitzer Prize-winning personal narrative *Pilgrim at Tinker Creek* and has since furthered her reputation as a latter-day female Thoreau with such books as *Holy the Firm* (1977) and *Teaching a Stone to Talk* (1982), which is also reviewed in this set. Here she applies her personal Platonic and religious views in an attempt "to do unlicensed metaphysics in a teacup." Her ultimate subject, she says, is the meaning of the world, approached via the microcosm of contemporary fiction.

In this three-part book, sections of which have appeared earlier in such magazines as *Harper's Magazine*, Dillard sets out in part 1 to draw distinctions between such Modernist writers as William Faulkner, James Joyce, and Thomas Mann and such "contemporary Modernists" as John Barth, Robert Coover, and Jorges Luis Borges. In part 2 she attempts to deal with general issues concerning the status of contemporary fiction; and in part 3 to "raise the roof on fiction" and take on the world at large. Made up of what she herself calls "free speculation, blind assertion, dumb joking, and diatribe," Dillard's book is not intended for the professional literary critic, but rather for the general reader. Critics and scholars familiar with European literary thought from the Russian Formalists to the French Structuralists will find nothing new here. Dillard does manage, however, to put together many of the implications of contemporary phenomenological thought in a popular (although at times cloying) style, posing such basic questions as "What is (gasp) the relationship between the world and the mind?"

Much of part 1 of *Living by Fiction* focuses on such familiar conventions of modern fiction as the shattering of narrative time and the breakup of traditional cause-and-effect relationships, the flattening of character and the notion that the fictional world is self-contained, the intrusion of the authorial voice and the interruption of narrative flow and verisimilitude, and the foregrounding of point of view toward fictional reflexivity. Dillard also approaches here the bothersome problem of the integrity of the art work itself. Confronting the common misgiving about contemporary fiction—that is, when is a work *about* meaninglessness, and when is it simply meaningless?—Dillard delves into the metaphysical problem of metaphor itself. Because she is still firmly entrenched in the now outmoded "New Critical" approach to literature, however, her only real solution is that the integrity of an art work lies in its unity, although she never actually defines the term "artistic unity." She suggests, for example, that the image of an egg in a cage is a more unified metaphor than that of a shoe in a cage. However, she persists in her own mystical belief that the integrity of a metaphor depends on the things being compared; she ignores the fact that the human mind can perceive a revelatory meaning in the juxtaposition of any two objects.

In fact, what Dillard intellectually knows often seems at odds with what she intuitively believes. For even as she tenaciously holds to her Platonic views, she willingly nods to the theories that have evolved from Albert Einstein to Werner Heisenberg to Kurt Gödel, that the world is more likely to be mind stuff than thing stuff. Moreover, she seems to endorse the studies of phenomenological thinkers in various fields, such as Gregory Bateson, Claude Lévi-Strauss, Jean Piaget, and Roman Jakobson, and admits that any penetrating interest in anything leads ultimately not to ontology but to epistemology. No matter where you start, says Dillard, "you end up agog in the lap of Kant." Her main point in part 1 is to suggest that the significance of such Modernist writers as James Joyce and Franz Kafka is that they expanded fictional techniques to achieve traditional ends, whereas contemporary Modernists have, she claims, lost sight of those ends. For example, she suggests that whereas Kafka wrote profound cultural criticism and along the way had a character turn into a cockroach, some contemporary writers throw away the rest and keep the cockroach for a laugh.

The concept that traditional fiction is a container and an embodiment of cultural and philosophic ideas is still in the mainstream, she says. Although Dillard is not as radical in her reaction to so-called "post-Modernist" fiction as John Gardner was a few years ago in his diatribe *Moral Fiction* (1979), she still waxes nostalgic for the good old days when a story was a story and was weighted with moral meaning. Some critical readers more professionally concerned with the nature of narrative in the twentieth century may feel that Dillard underestimates Kafka's self-conscious awareness of the metaphysics of his metamorphosis and that she is oblivious to the deeper cultural meaning in the works of writers such as John Barth and Donald Barthelme.

Dillard begins part 2 of her meditation with the basic question of whether the material of the writer is the phenomenal world in its entirety or whether it is made up of only words and linguistic techniques. Admitting that the post-Modernist view doubts that words correspond to anything, she says that she wants to treat this idea with some respect before she discards it. There is little evidence, however, that she gives it the respect that it deserves. For example, she suggests that Charles Dickens drew the materials for *Bleak House* (1852-1853) from London society and British legal usage; "it were madness, or quibbling, to say he drew them from a dictionary." Such reasoning is both equivocal and sophistical. One might indeed admit that Dickens drew the material stimulus for his novel from his perceptions of such phenomenal sources, but that is not to say that what he created is merely a representation of such sources. Moreover, the dictionary is surely not the core of contemporary linguistic thinking. By suggesting that the materials of fiction are "bits of the world," Dillard completely ignores the process of defamiliarization by metaphor developed by the Russian Formalists, with whom she claims to be familiar.

Another argument which Dillard holds up to support more traditional functions of narrative is that fiction only keeps its audience by holding tenaciously to the world as its subject matter. "When the arts abandon the world as their subject matter, people abandon the arts." Because fiction is not the prerogative of specialists (as poetry is more likely to be), Dillard suggests that fiction is by its very nature a basically conservative mode; the nonspecialist prefers content to abstraction. If one considers fiction an essentially inferior art form— as it was indeed regarded until the end of the nineteenth century—then perhaps Dillard's point here is well taken, but surely Henry James settled this question at the turn of the century when he made his case for the art of fiction precisely on the basis of its technique and abstract surfaces.

Dillard is also troubled by the possibility that contemporary Modernist fiction is essentially a creature of criticism and of the academic study of literature. It stands to reason, she says, that the critical approaches which dominate the graduate schools will also dominate undergraduate thinking about fiction and will thus affect what those undergraduates will eventually write. She suggests that as a result of this relationship between fiction and criticism, the works of such writers as Barth and Samuel Beckett "tremble with the sense of being read critically." Again, it seems that this bias against a relationship between criticism and fiction is really a bias against fiction as an art form. Surely, Dillard would not complain about the relationship between poetry and criticism since the two have gone hand in hand since Aristotle, each in turn inspiring the other. It is difficult to think of the poetry of William Wordsworth without the criticism of Samuel Taylor Coleridge or the poetry of Alfred, Lord Tennyson without the criticism of Matthew Arnold. Furthermore, one would certainly hope that all literary works of art tremble with the sense of being read critically.

Dillard is obviously concerned here with the relative readability of fiction, a mode which, unlike poetry, she feels, should, or must if it is to be read at all, remain rooted to the world. As Raymond Federman (one of the post-Modernist writers who, Dillard would say, has thrown the baby out with the bathwater) has recently suggested, the term "readability" describes that which "guides us back from the text to the world, to the security of the world, and therefore gives us comfort—the pleasure of easy recognition." If the writer cuts off the referential paths to reality, or if he examines his relations with language within the text, he is declared "unreadable," and to be unreadable these days, says Federman, is to be immoral.

After what amounts to a long digression on prose style, a digression which suggests a moral difference between the "fine" writing of such writers as William H. Gass and the plain prose of Jorge Luis Borges, Dillard finally presents her most basic questions: Can art have meaning? Can criticism know art? In the beginning of this final section, where she attempts to deal with the problem of whether it is ultimately possible to discover meaning, her style is a bit precious: she urges readers, "Bear with me, please, for a few difficult points before the shooting starts," and advises those who are not interested in the complex internal problems of literary criticism to skip several pages to the point where "this chapter and the book as a whole, begin to take off at last." At last indeed, with only fifty pages remaining! While the reader is waiting for the book to "take off," Dillard attempts to describe Deconstructionist criticism, which she understands primarily to hold that the art object cannot be known, that criticism itself is prose poetry. Although Dillard does not believe that the truth of criticism can be validated, she is confident that, by consensus, readers can say when criticism is probable, workable, or fruitful; thus, although she does not say who shall constitute that consensus, she does maintain her underlying Platonic view that art works are unified because the world is, and thus that criticism is unified because of the unity of all world-inspired work.

True to her New Critical background, Dillard, like Philip Wheelwright and William Wimsatt before her, suggests that art, like religion, probes those difficult areas where blurred and powerful symbols are the only language and where their arrangement into works of art are the only grammar. The problem is that, although artists are interpreters of the world, they prize originality rather than fidelity; thus, although they interpret the world, they hide the true significance of their discoveries and thus require interpretation by critics. Basically, then, says Dillard, since art interprets nature and culture, criticism of the arts is perhaps the best of the interpretative disciplines for interpreting the world at large. In this last section of her book, Dillard also reveals most emphatically her own fence-sitting position between the traditional conception of criticism as the New Critics saw it (that is, as a means to lay bare meaning) and criticism as it is understood by a number of contemporary critical schools (that is, as the means to lay bare process).

On the one hand, Dillard claims that art presents objects for contemplation, and that art objects interpret the world itself. On the other hand, however, she notes that it is the manner of the art work's representation—that is, its surface structure rather than its content—that is a form of knowledge. Works of art symbolize the juncture between spirit and matter and matter and ideas, says Dillard, and she sums up her Janus-faced position in one crucial sentence: "Any art object is essentially a model in which the creative process is frozen with its product in its arms." This is true as far as it goes, but it evades the issue: What is the art object, and how should one approach it—via its process, or via its product? It is just at this point that the old New Critics and the

Deconstructionists, for example, either part company or uneasily hold hands, for the issue is between interpretation, which attempts to uncover the product to reveal its latent meaning, and criticism, which is concerned with the nature of artifice and the process of the mind encountering the problematical world.

Dillard's response to this juncture, what she calls her own "timid" solution, is a Platonic one, finally laid bare on the penultimate page of a book saturated throughout with its assumptions: that if any coherent order is true in the art work, and thus if any coherent order is true in the world, it is because it partakes of a universal order, an order that does not exist solely in the symbol-making mind of man, but that somehow exists out there in the world itself. Yet even after tentatively asserting her idealistic dictum, Dillard, coy to the last, ends her book with the following: "Do art's complex and balanced relationships among all parts, its purpose, significance, and harmony, exist in nature? Is nature whole, like a completed thought? Is history purposeful? Is the universe of matter significant? I am sorry; I do not know."

There is clearly a need for a book aimed at the educated lay reader which would clarify the complex issues of epistemology in which literature, especially fiction, now finds itself entangled, relating those issues to the larger concerns of the reader and demonstrating the relevance of literature and criticism to contemporary life. In *Living by Fiction*, Annie Dillard goes a long way toward performing such a service, but her mystical intuition too often interferes with her capacity for analysis. Dillard is a great friend to literature and literary criticism; it is simply that she is not a fine enough critic to be the friend that literature and criticism need.

Charles E. May

Sources for Further Study

Choice. XX, September, 1982, p. 76.
Christian Science Monitor. April 9, 1982, p. B6.
Library Journal. CVII, March 15, 1982, p. 638.
Los Angeles Times Book Review. October 31, 1982, p. 2.
The New York Times Book Review. LXXXVII, May 9, 1982, p. 10.
The New Yorker. LVIII, May 9, 1982, p. 140.
Progressive. XLVI, June, 1982, p. 61.
Saturday Review. IX, March, 1982, p. 64.

LORD BYRON
Selected Letters and Journals

Author: George Gordon Byron, Baron Byron (1788-1824)
Edited, with an introduction, by Leslie A. Marchand
Publisher: The Belknap Press of Harvard University Press (Cambridge,
Massachusetts). 400 pp. $17.50
Type of work: Letters and journals
Time: 1805-1824
Locale: England, Continental Europe, and Asia Minor

A one-volume collection of letters and journal excerpts drawn from Marchand's
twelve-volume Murray-Harvard edition of Byron's letters and journals

One of the great literary events of the past decade was Leslie Marchand's
award-winning edition of the letters and journals of Lord Byron. Published
in Great Britain by John Murray Ltd. (the house which originally published
most of Byron's works) and in America by Harvard University Press, this
eleven-volume series plus its volume-long cumulative index enabled readers
to gauge, with a precision not before possible, Byron's epistolary achievements. The collected letters, many of which appeared in print or in unbowdler-
ized form for the first time in Marchand's edition, demonstrated that Byron,
famous as poet and public figure, deserves equal stature among letter writers.
This vast and challenging project on which a full career of Byron scholarship
was brought to bear has won Marchand a place of distinction among twentieth
century editors.

Still, multivolume editions, however fine, tend to find their way almost
exclusively to the shelves of libraries and the collections of specialists, so a
one-volume selection from Byron's engaging and articulate letters and journals is especially welcome, for it is likely to help win Byron's prose and the
Marchand edition thereof the wide attention they deserve. In preparing this
volume, Marchand's strategy has been to choose the best and most generally
interesting of Byron's letters and to quote them in entirety. Likewise, he
offers self-contained passages that are the highlights of the 1813 to 1814
Journal, the Ravenna Journal (1821), and "Detached Thoughts" (1821-1822),
while he presents in full the shorter Alpine Journal (1816), and Journal in
Cephalonia (1823). Because this decision to respect the integrity of the individual letter and journal entry excluded many memorable passages from the
book, Marchand has compiled a topically organized "Anthology of Memorable Passages" which his audience would otherwise miss. These eloquent
extracts are well-calculated to please and dazzle the first-time reader of Byron,
though they strike the confirmed Byronist much as a concert of cadenza upon
cadenza would a music lover. To guide his reader through Byron's prose,
Marchand supplies, along with spare but careful footnotes, a concise life of
Byron, biographical sketches of his principal correspondents, and a list of the

letters and journals included. The volume is, in short, easy to use and easy to enjoy.

What sort of person emerges from the letters here presented? Not a man whose full range of feelings is given voice or whose complete life story is readily apparent. The introspective gloom and enigmatic misanthropy so characteristic of the heroes of Byron's poems, traits the reading public has come to identify as "Byronic," are notably absent. Instead, one finds man-of-the-world raillery, nonchalance and the artfully contrived pose of nonchalance, a lusty appetite for a wide range of experiences, people, and ideas, the occasional lapse into ennui, outrageous exaggeration and love of teasing or shocking combined with an unusual degree of honesty, and complete freedom from cant (the quality Byron detested above all others). Inconsistent from moment to moment but open and candid about what he feels or thinks at a particular time, the Byron of the letters is, like the poet of his masterpiece *Don Juan* (1819-1824), a man of mobility—occasionally given to deep-seated melancholy, passionately devoted to liberty and truth, but nevertheless a laughing philosopher inclined to take things from "the absurd point of view."

The first major group of letters included in Marchand's selection are those which Byron, traveling in the Mediterranean between 1809 and 1811, dispatched to friends and relations back home in England. These adventures in Spain, Greece, Albania, and Asia Minor were elevated to high-flown poetry in the cantos of *Childe Harold's Pilgrimage* (1812, 1816, 1818), but Byron's letters from abroad create an entirely different impression. Neither gloomily self-obsessed nor caught up in mere description as so many writers of travel letters are, Byron dispatches witty and amusing accounts of sights and societies, and his responses to them. He strikes a pose calculated to amuse, or sometimes annoy, his reader. For example, to Mrs. Byron, the mother he loved but sometimes disliked, he sends descriptions of Seville enriched with talk of defending his British virtue against the onslaught of a predatory señorita. Henry Drury, his former tutor at Harrow, at length receives a promised letter, not because of what Byron has seen but because of what he has done. "This morning I *swam* from *Sestos* to *Abydos*," writes Byron. "The immediate distance is not above a mile but the current renders it hazardous, so much so, that I doubt whether Leander's conjugal powers must not have been exhausted in his passage to Paradise."

This aquatic accomplishment proved so satisfying to Byron that he wrote about it years later in other letters to other correspondents. Here, however, having given his news, Byron proceeds to speak of his travels in what can be seen as his characteristic manner. Disavowing description, he goes on to describe in such a way that his observation of the environment, natural and human, becomes a means of expressing his own personality. He reveals in his assessments of the delights and tedium of "tourifying" a sharp eye, common sense, and dandiacal self-consciousness. Throughout his letters, Byron sustains a remarkable mobility—a talent not so much for adapting to new settings as for appropriating the unfamiliar and making it reflect or complement him.

Never is this Byronic versatility more evident than in the letters written to ladies during the "years of fame" from 1812 to 1816, when Byron, having returned to England, published *Childe Harold's Pilgrimage* and became the literary lion of Whig society, a habitué of London's most glittering salons, and a pale, handsome fascinator to debutantes and matrons alike. There are intense if sometimes insincere missives to his "little volcano" Lady Caroline Lamb, just the sort of clever, capricious married woman to please him—for a time. To Annabella Milbanke, the rich, spoiled, priggish miss he would marry, go abstract and abstruse letters almost as convoluted as are hers to him. Byron is more direct with Lady Melbourne. Mother-in-law to Caroline, aunt to Annabella, and an urbanely intelligent woman of great charm in her own right, she receives his comments on both of these ladies and his confessions of supplementary amours, most notably the "platonic" flirtation with Lady Frances Wedderburn Webster. This two-month adventure, conducted in billiard rooms and passageways of country houses, reads like the best sort of Restoration comedy. Byron casts himself as the rakish protagonist, Lady Frances as the pliant but unpredictable heroine. Her husband, the stupid, complacent, philandering Sir James, completes the artfully drawn triangle. Byron's letters of this period are so full of romantic intrigue that it is a relief to turn to the journal and find that he had other pastimes: "To-day I have boxed one hour—written an ode to Napoleon Buonaparte—copied it—eaten six biscuits—drunk four bottles of soda water—redde away the rest of the time—besides giving poor * * a world of advice about this mistress of his. . . . I am a pretty fellow truly to lecture about 'the sect'"

Ill-suited to offer advice on women, Byron was all too soon to need it. Having married Annabella Milbanke in January, 1815, and having been not the most even-tempered or domestically inclined of husbands to her, Byron, who despite his moods loved this "Princess of Parallelograms" in his fashion, was stunned when a visit that she and their month-old daughter, Ada, paid to the Milbankes turned into a separation. His confused, then bitter, dispatches to Lady Byron and her father are the last letters from England included among Marchand's selections. The legal separation Annabella insisted upon took effect on April 25, 1816, and Byron left England to embark on Continental travels that were to become a permanent self-exile.

In the earliest of the expatriate letters and the Alpine Journal (a record Byron kept for his half-sister Augusta of his journey in September, 1816, through the Bernese Alps with John Cam Hobhouse), one finds what seems to be a valiant attempt at avoiding self-scrutiny by means of immersion in new surroundings. The outside world never absorbs Byron, though; it speaks to him of his own inner condition. A withered and lifeless pine wood, for example, reminds him of his family, similarly laid waste by a single winter. Once the "metaphysics and mountains" of Switzerland have been left behind, though, Byron demonstrates himself able to accept and enjoy what life has to offer.

Settled comfortably in Italy and situated in a subtle, hedonistic society quite unlike the "tight little island" left behind, Byron writes some of his finest letters to those congenial souls—notably Hobhouse, Douglas Kinnaird, Thomas Moore, and his publisher John Murray—whom he could depend upon to appreciate and circulate his comments on Italian manners and morals, to execute his personal and literary commissions, and to pass on gossip of the "Great World" he had quitted. Marchand's volume contains a particularly generous sample of letters from this period. One is privileged to enjoy frank and spontaneous accounts of Byron's Italian adventures, whether they be social (he was as welcome at the *conversazioni* of Italian ladies as he had been at the crushes of English ones), romantic (the catalog of mistresses who received Byron's attentions before he settled down as *cavalier servente* to Theresa Guiccioli is truly epic), literary (during this exceptionally fertile period, Byron concluded *Childe Harold's Pilgrimage* and wrote *Beppo*, 1818, *Don Juan*, and his dramatic pieces), or political (along with Theresa Guiccioli's kinsmen, Byron was a member of the Italian revolutionary society of Car- bonari). Supplementing the splendid letters from Italy are portions of the Ravenna Journal, which details Byron's daily life, and the "Detached Thoughts," a retrospective account showing that, though Byron had shaken the dust of England from his boots, he had not obliterated his former asso- ciations there from his mind and heart.

Byron's life in Italy must have been gratifying. He had found a congenial, not to say ideal, society, a woman for whom he could feel greater attachment than he had deemed possible, and a poetical project (*Don Juan*) both perfectly suited to his distinctive talents and infinitely expandable. All this was not enough, though, and when he left his easy and agreeable existence to embark upon a frustrating and uncomfortable one assisting the Greeks in their cam- paign for independence from the Ottoman Empire, a new side of Byron emerged and found voice in his prose. The facetious, self-indulgent poet-peer now shows aptitude for being a practical, efficient man of business, and his letters lose the dramatic quality previously so characteristic. Like many other men who have allied themselves with a cause, Byron is relieved of the need to play parts by having found something real to do.

The letters from Greece and "Journal in Cephalonia" (an 1823 memoir which he broke off on account of its frankness) indicate his total engagement in the Greek cause. Never, though, does he lapse into the blind fervor of the true believer. Byron sees the Greeks objectively, as a long-enslaved people possessing all the vices endemic to their subjugated condition. In spite of— perhaps in part because of—this insight, he works hard on their behalf. "I shall continue to pursue my former plan of stating to the Committee things as they *really* are—" Byron writes to John Bowring, secretary of the London Greek Committee. "I am an enemy to Cant of all kinds—but it will be seen in time—who are or are not the firmest friends of the Greek Cause—or who will stick by them longest—the Lempriere dictionary quotation Gentlemen— or those who neither dissemble their faults nor their virtues." Byron was to stick by the Greeks to death. Avoiding the naïve extremes of the idealist and the cynic, Byron demonstrates in this passage the sincerity of the humane broadmindedness so often to be glimpsed in the letters and journal passages judiciously selected by Marchand. Readers of this volume will be doubly rewarded: it both delights and edifies, as Byron wished his best poems to do.

Peter W. Graham

Sources for Further Study

Choice. XX, February, 1983, p. 827.
Christian Science Monitor. December 29, 1982, p. 14.
History Today. XXXII, December, 1982, p. 60.
The New Republic. CLXXXIII, December 31, 1982, p. 32.
New Statesman. CIV, December 10, 1982, p. 28.
The New York Times Book Review. LXXXVII, November 7, 1982, p. 9.
Publishers Weekly. CCXXII, September 3, 1982, p. 49.
Smithsonian. XIII, February, 1983, p. 142.

THE LOSER

Author: George Konrád (1933-   )
Translated from the Hungarian by Ivan Sanders
Publisher: Harcourt Brace Jovanovich (New York). 315 pp. $14.95; paperback
$7.95
Type of work: Novel
Time: World War II to the present
Locale: Primarily Hungary

The work of a deeply reflective historical consciousness which explores a wide range of both personal and political experience in postwar Hungary

Principal characters:
    T, the novel's narrator and principal character
    DANI, his brother, alter ego, and the only character, besides T, who
        figures throughout the narrative fabric

The "loser" of the title of George Konrád's latest novel (first published in Hungarian as *Cinkos* in 1980) is its nameless narrator, identified only as "T," and what he loses is any sure sense of the course of his country's history, a history in which he has participated since the beginning of World War II. T is also a loser in the sense of being one who has failed—in his case, he has disappointed himself, his lovers, his brother, and his comrades and just as many of them have disappointed, even betrayed, him. There is, however, no self-pity in T. He does not ask for sympathy and does not engage in special pleading. His brutal honesty has been taken by some reviewers as aloofness, and that aloofness has been attributed to T's status as a "composite figure" embodying the experiences of several individuals in postwar Hungary. The somewhat disjointed, fragmentary quality of the novel may indeed be the result of Konrád's attempt to capture the spirit of his time, for each phase of modern Eastern European history has been marked by the violent disruption of social norms and has required a reinvention of the self. If some readers of the novel miss the presence of a complete identity, of a person with whom they can identify, they may wish to reconsider, as T does, the nature of the human psyche. One questions whether T, a survivor of so many struggles for and against himself, can integrate his life, which has often been caught between cross-purposes, into the single story of a well-developed self. T seems to have taken it upon himself, instead, to become the emblematic self of Eastern Europe.

The novel's first sentence aptly defines T's state of mind: "I talk all day, I keep hearing things; moments out of the past, like honeycomb cells during extraction, burst open—riffraff overrun my dreams." He is in an asylum, because—as one learns in part 5—to others he appears catatonic; he has ceased to function as a normal human being. In his mind, history erupts, as though every crevice in his brain were charged with memories of family, war, and politics, all condensed in a dreamlike confusion in which he is one of the "conspirators" looking for "the informer." He can hardly recognize his brother, Dani, with whom he grapples in his dream for a place on a cot: "We get tired of fighting, he points upward: we see the face of a huge clock on the ceiling, the hands moving around so fast they make us dizzy." History has moved so rapidly that it has been transformed into phantasmagoria, a mixing of images from private and public life that cannot be easily sorted out. For as one learns later, T has conspired to change history; his brother has informed against him; and both of them will tire of fighting over the cot, an appointed but illusory place of rest in their competitive efforts to secure themselves a place in history.

As an alternative to the nightmares of history, T expresses a preference to "live for a while in the city of my childhood," but even there, history follows him in the form of a circus, where a clown violinist has his instrument confiscated by "a beet-nosed policeman," "an authority figure, clearly an enemy of art." T watches the violinist become his own instrument: "His slight, sardonic tune can be heard, now through his teeth, now from his nostrils." T urges the clown violinist to teach him his tricks, but the clown refuses and remarks that his is an act he has been practicing for decades: "if you are patient, by the time you are an old man you'll perfect your own." Indeed, T eventually, in his mid-fifties, adopts what he calls an aesthetic view of history, an attitude formed by his reading of great novels, while his comrades, the most august ideologists and historians, retain their faith in history as an objective form that is knowable by scientific procedures. For T, history is the art of survival, an art that is predicated on an appreciation of the roles people play, the tricks they have learned in order to surmount the state's confiscation of personality. The clown violinist's advice is a lesson T has learned the hard way and then superimposed on his memory of childhood.

T recalls that "each station of my life was an error," and he governs all of the history presented in this novel by the superimposition of his memory. He recounts how he fought with the underground against the Nazis, served in their forced labor corps, served as an officer in the Soviet occupying army after the war, and worked as a "party functionary of a satellite state." He has been locked up twice by the very government he helped to establish, interrogated by the young people in state security whom he had trained to be revolutionaries, and is constantly under official surveillance. The director of the asylum is a childhood companion who argues against T's stubborn independence and therefore against fighting the reversals of history that have thwarted T: freedom is "the obsession of paranoiacs," the director asserts. He simply wants to find his place in the world, not to change it. He will have independence, but not at too great a price, and he believes that "whenever we have to make a stand we get beaten, but when we lie low we come out ahead." The director tells T to wait for "a thaw and you'll again become the person you always were." T cannot take the director's advice, however, so long as he is in possession of his formidable consciousness which, he remarks, names, frames, and kills its objects, which "reverts to itself" and regulates and records the world, as the novel's first sentence suggests.

No doubt the director feels that T leads the life of a loser. In part 2, which deals with T's family, Dani, who is an extreme version of T, affirms that "one day I'll rescue the losers inside me." He is even more frenetic than T in trying to involve himself in the currents of history. He claims to pass on T's ideas in wittier form, to sense the changes in the currents more quickly than his brother, and to document those changes more assiduously, even though his writing—indeed all of his schemes—comes to nothing. Dani is, in short, a parody of T whom T cannot completely trust or love, especially since, mixed with Dani's imitation of his brother, is hatred, envy, and ridicule. Dani seems unconsciously bent on proving the absurdity of T's efforts to master history and on fulfilling their grandfather's dire words: "Like drunkards, we live in a fog of self-love, and, confusing good and evil, we grope our way in the darkness and laugh when our neighbor falls."

The brothers, and the family from which they emerge, are not without great fellow-feeling, but as part 3 demonstrates, it is impossible for them not to become part of "the machinery of violence." T invokes this phrase as something dies in him while he is watching the torture of his beloved Sophie, with whom he worked in the Communist underground against the Nazis. At first he does not speak to save her because he will not betray the other members of the underground, but as her torture continues, he realizes that he is "willing to sacrifice his love and would do the same to his own son, just so that he shouldn't have to say anything." His momentary catatonia here foreshadows the longer silence that will estrange him from his wife and the world many years after the war. There is a numbing of fellow-feeling, even a vindictive arousal of the sense of self-preservation when T quiets himself, in the horrible prolongation of Sophie's agony, by saying: "Do it out of spite."

Shortly thereafter, T's memory reverts to his "first killing [that] was as ugly as only a killing can be," followed in part 4 by his first "real murder" in 1945 as he reenters Budapest with the Soviet army. As one reviewer notes, Konrád gives very little space to the idealism that motivated T to such inhumanity. In a rare passage of self-justification, T does acknowledge that "Communism for me was a metaphysical future, a second creation, the work of man replacing God . . . the thing we would accomplish together, correcting our errors as we went along, an open alternative to familiar oppression." One who is not conversant with the history of Hungary and of Eastern Europe may not fully value Communism's appeal to human solidarity and rebirth invoked in these few phrases. One may fault the novel for making T's idealism excessively abstract. T's sardonic persona, like that of the clown violinist's, perhaps makes it difficult for him to revive his very early dedication to the Communist cause.

He never fully shared in their kind of humorless togetherness of purpose, as one can glimpse in his first meeting with Sophie. At the same time, T's insatiable consciousness fastens on the discrepancies between ideology and reality and seems to have predestined him for dissent, so that, like his grandfather, he strays from the orthodoxy of belief to express his peculiar sense of the world.

By October 23, 1956, T finds that he would rather read history than make it, and yet he reveals some satisfaction in another reversal of history of the kind he has failed to achieve. He observes people in the streets rebelling against their satellite state and trying to govern themselves: "The regime's own slogans turn against the system. During the years of oppression we had to greet our neighbors with the word 'Freedom.' Now we give the word a little meaning." Dani is frantically trying to organize the chaos of revolt even as his frenetic efforts expose his want of self-control. T is "some sort of minister at the moment"—this is his suggestive appellation for his tenuous hold on power. He advises against confronting the Soviets in the name of freedom, yet he accepts responsibility for the futile act of delivering the message that asks them to leave the country. This "last political act" liberates T, and he declares "this moment a holiday of the spirit," perhaps because of his public acknowledgement that his long alignment with the Soviets is finally destroyed. A house search in 1973 comes just after T has confessed that "I am glad I am no longer a soldier, an activist, a political prisoner, a social scientist, or a dissident leader . . . I have fought my way out of my lies but not yet hit upon my truths." The search itself and T's interrogation are not nearly so brutal as previous examples of the state's invasion of privacy, but the principle, T sees, is the same: to worry the state's subjects into complete conformity.

Part 5 continues with T's weariness, which develops into catatonia. This grim last section of the novel is relieved only by T's restless consciousness— a consciousness that cannot conform and cannot relinquish its own measurement of reality to the state. Dani has committed the brutal, nonsensical murder of his girlfriend. T can choose to help the authorities track down his suicidal brother, or he can elude surveillance and confront Dani alone once more. T's dilemma is exacerbated by his fatigued withdrawal from history, by his desire to make no impression at all on his times, and by his feeling that he is a "fragment" that should return to the asylum, but he knows that he has "never paid enough attention to Dani." In their final dialogue, each accuses the other of being the bigger loser, and T wryly comments "Two Eastern European brothers, true to form." There is humor here in the grimmest of situations that lifts T's spirit into self-knowledge, for he accepts his brother's failure as part of his own. What keeps T from suicide is his awareness that history may be cyclic, even somewhat repetitive, but it is not redundant or reductive. T's consciousness will persist, if not prevail, since in this novel, dense with images of life, T admits that "All things considered, it's more interesting to live than not to live."

Carl E. Rollyson, Jr.

Sources for Further Study

Library Journal. CVII, September 15, 1982, p. 1769.
Los Angeles Times Book Review. October 17, 1982, p. 1.
The New Republic. CLXXXVIII, February 14, 1983, p. 28.
The New York Times Book Review. LXXXVII, September 26, 1982, p. 1.
Publishers Weekly. CCXXII, August 6, 1982, p. 58.
Time. CXXI, January 17, 1983, p. 70.
West Coast Review of Books. VIII, November, 1982, p. 43.

MAILER
A Biography

Author: Hilary Mills
Publisher: Empire Books (New York). 477 pp. $14.95
Type of work: Literary biography
Time: 1923-1982
Locale: Primarily the United States

This is the first work to investigate thoroughly the career of Norman Mailer, an American novelist, and while it will serve very well as the basis for further explorations of his life and work, it devotes insufficient attention to the significance of his writing and thereby obscures the central importance of his place in American literature

This valuable biography of Norman Mailer is the first attempt to capture his life and career together as a whole. After so many years of having Mailer's activities reported piecemeal, it is particularly instructive to have Hilary Mills's careful reconstruction of the phases of Mailer's still-evolving personality. She has interviewed a great number of his friends, family, and business associates and dutifully conveys their impressions of an unusually complex man. She has warily but firmly followed all of the controversies through which he has engaged the public's attention and has shown how his notoriety has fed his work. Although she does not offer a truly critical biography that provides deep insight into his writing, she has at least described some of the important conditions out of which his significant books have emerged. Finally, she has managed to maintain an even-tempered voice no matter how outrageous and ridiculous her subject seems to get, for she thoroughly respects his genius without becoming partisan, and in her last pages, she praises his enormous talent without ultimately committing herself to a judgment of its lasting value. This is an understandable if arguable position to take, given that Mailer has, as Mills says, "a career with time still to run and with works to be written."

Although Mills's narrative is chiefly chronological, she begins her biography with the drama of Mailer's much-condemned defense of Jack Abbott, a prison writer whose release on parole Mailer was instrumental in securing. Shortly after his release, Abbott stabbed and killed a young waiter, Richard Adan, on July 18, 1981. At the murder trial, Mailer spoke for Abbott and at a subsequent press conference expressed the hope that Abbott would receive a "light sentence" of about ten years. The press attacked Mailer not only for his seeming insensitivity to Adan's brutal death but also because he appeared to be making a special case for writers, since he was particularly worried about the death of Abbott's talent during a long prison term. Mills suggests that the press was also responding negatively to Mailer's reputation for a fascination with violence, both in his life and his work. He had stabbed his second wife, Adele Morales, about twenty-one years before his involvement with Abbott, and he had been in the news several times since then for his fights and disorderly conduct. Indeed, for many years he had flaunted a pugnacious, truculent persona. Although Mailer is later quoted in the biography as pointing out that Mailer the author, the creator of himself as a character in his work, is not the same as the everyday man, his self-promotion has made it seem otherwise. This is one of the paradoxes of Norman Mailer that Mills is anxious to explore. Mailer, the modest, middle-class Jewish son, very much the product of his strong mother, has transformed himself into a rough contender for the literary honor of becoming America's greatest novelist. Defending himself in a press conference after testifying for Abbott, Mailer adopted at different times Southern and Irish accents, slipped in and out of different personas, and gave the press a condensed version of the many selves he has tried on in the course of his life. Mills shifts from this quintessential media event to Mailer's quiet, serious, and well-received reading of his magnum opus, *Ancient Evenings* (1982), at the Young Men's Hebrew Association in Manhattan, where twenty years earlier he had given a controversial reading shortly after stabbing his wife. Thus, Mills dramatizes the paradigm of Mailer's career: "Moving from the depths of rejection to the summit of appreciation in one day has not been unusual in the life of Norman Mailer."

Throughout his career, as Mills shows, it has been Mailer's strategy to court disaster in order to win success. Some of his most powerful prose has been provoked by his effort to get out of a jam—as E. L. Doctorow, one of Mailer's editors, remarks to Mills. Mailer told the judge at the hearing, held to determine the charges against him for stabbing his wife, that it was his ambition to explore the most dangerous areas of existence—the forbidden territory that other writers evade. This was said not to relieve himself of responsibility for the stabbing but to argue for his freedom to explore any human subject at a time when his mental stability was in question. In order to create great literature, Mailer has felt the need to break rules, to flout literary conventions and genres. He began as a fairly conventional writer from an unremarkable social background, but at an early age, he apparently determined that he would have to reinvent himself, to become iconoclastic, eccentric, and—when he finally made up his mind to it in the mid-1950's—subversive of both societal and literary niceties. Mills's biography is the story of Mailer's incredible quest to dominate an age through the incessant making over of himself, so that his many styles mimic and prophesy the development of postwar America.

Mailer began writing at Harvard during World War II, and his first major achievement, the war novel *The Naked and the Dead*, appeared in 1948. Hailed as one of the first writers of a new age, he was only twenty-five and unprepared for the fame he had so assiduously sought. Enjoying the instantaneous celebrity that came with the publication of *The Naked and the Dead*, Mailer nevertheless felt that he no longer had a personal connection with any big subject, and for him, big books had to have big subjects. He disdained the idea of becoming a Jewish writer who would simply mine memories of the past. Mailer spent the late 1940's and the 1950's, as Mills carefully documents, in a restless search to involve himself with major events, places, and trends of his time. He traveled to France to study at the Sorbonne; he participated in the Henry Wallace presidential campaign in 1948; he went to Hollywood to write for the movies and to gather inspiration for a novel; he took various drugs and consorted with various "hip" elements—all in his search for raw material. He changed wives—from the extremely intelligent Beatrice Silverman, whose life was similar in its Jewish background to Mailer's—to Adele Morales, who seemed to provide a hot-tempered Latin combativeness, an artistic vitality and volatility that he appropriated for himself. At the same time, however, he was floundering with his novels. *Barbary Shore* (1951) almost universally received negative reviews, and the reception of *The Deer Park* (1955) was mixed. Mailer was struggling to find an original voice.

The turning point for Mailer, as for the United States, was the Kennedy election of 1960. In covering the Democratic convention, Mailer discovered a way to filter politics through his own poetic sensibility and to respond, quite early, to the movie-star aura of presidential candidate John F. Kennedy, whose charisma was of the kind Mailer himself had sought. The brilliant title of his essay on Kennedy, "Superman Comes to the Supermarket," summed up the mass appeal that this singular political figure would come to have. Still, as Mills correctly observes, it was not until his piece in 1963 on the Sonny Liston-Floyd Patterson heavyweight fight that Mailer was able to make the shift from observer of a national drama to the center of consciousness in which a country's conflict was definitively shaped and articulated.

By this time, Mailer had been married for a third time, to Lady Jeanne Campbell—seemingly an improbable match for America's literary tough guy but actually appropriate, Mills demonstrates, when one considers that his pose as "psychic outlaw" masked, at least in part, an insecurity about being accepted by the Establishment, an insecurity that partially disappeared after his stabbing of Adele, when he seemed to have experienced, in Mills's word, a "catharsis." At any rate, he apparently faced the worst in himself and "felt better," as he himself later said.

Mailer's life and career from the 1960's—his most prolific period to date—to the 1980's had a frenetic, protean quality. Mills's descriptions of Mailer's six wives, his six novels, and all of the writing, loving, politicking, and filming reveal Mailer's relentless quest for achievement and recognition, his influence on the New Left of the 1960's, and his increasing stature as a literary and public figure. Mills handles all of these different aspects of Mailer deftly and fairly but without much conviction about exactly which parts of his work will last. She seems to have no doubt about major works such as *The Naked and the Dead*, *The Armies of the Night* (1968), and *The Executioner's Song* (1979), but these are books which most critics praise highly. Mills's commentary on most of Mailer's other work seems critically timid, and she is content to pass along summaries of reviewers' opinions.

For a biographer who is primarily intent on recording a controversial writer's life and career as objectively as possible, it may seem safest and fairest to withhold critical judgment and to give the history of each book's reception. Reviews—first impressions of books—can be extremely perceptive. Mills, however, makes no mention at all of the considerable body of thoughtful commentary on Mailer that has been produced in recent years. This failure to assess the full range of Mailer's work seriously weakens Mills's biography, for Mailer's life cannot be clearly discerned until one can ascertain the development of his work. One gets no sense in Mills's book, for example, of the great theme which Mailer discovered in *An American Dream* (1965)—that what is called "reality" is actually explosively problematic, a notion violently opposed to the complacent conceptions of realism that limited the reach of *The Naked and the Dead*. Just as Mailer has not been content to be one self, so his writing has not been confined to one literary mode, a fact that Mills realizes but does not fully explore. In the midst of recounting Mailer's paradoxical life, Mills manages to grasp its principle of coherence: Mailer's ability to live with opposites in himself, a knack he has attributed to Marilyn Monroe. Nevertheless, Mills's biography is somewhat diminished by her unwillingness to commit all of her resources—her impressive organizational skill, keen intelligence, and economical style—to a full judgment of Mailer's writing. As a result, this is a biography that leaves its subject still something of a mystery even as it astutely opens up and readies the ground on which later biographers will have to stand in order to measure Mailer.

Carl E. Rollyson, Jr.

Sources for Further Study

Booklist. LXXIX, November 15, 1982, p. 410.
Commentary. LXXV, March, 1983, p. 84.
Los Angeles Times Book Review. November 28, 1982, p. 1.
Newsweek. CI, January 24, 1983, p. 68.

THE MAKING OF THE
REPRESENTATIVE FOR PLANET 8

Author: Doris Lessing (1919-   )
Publisher: Alfred A. Knopf (New York). 160 pp. $11.95
Type of work: Novel
Time: An unspecified period of time anywhere from years to millennia in the past
Locale: Planet 8

Unspecified but natural causes bring about climatic changes that render an alien planet uninhabitable, dooming all who live there

> *Principal characters:*
> DOEG, the narrator, chief of the storytellers on Planet 8
> JOHOR, agent of the Canopan Colonial Service and overseer of life
>   on Planet 8
> MARL,
> KLIN,
> ALSI, and
> NONNI, various representatives and inhabitants of Planet 8

The Making of the Representative for Planet 8 is the fourth book in a series collectively entitled Canopus in Argos: Archives. It was preceded by *Re: Colonized Planet 5, Shikasta* (1979); *The Marriages Between Zones Three, Four, and Five: As Narrated by the Chronicles of Zone Three* (1980); and *The Sirian Experiments: The Report by Ambien II of the Five* (1980). A note in the front matter classifies these books as a "novel-sequence" (a generic term many will find new), but to call all of these works "novels" makes the word useless as a literary term; they are not all the same kind of work, nor, despite their common series title, do they all tell the same story.

Re: Colonized Planet 5, Shikasta, the first book of the series, is marginally science fiction, differing from the pulp variety chiefly in that it offers less characterization and science, and more preaching and high seriousness. Had H. G. Wells had to label it, he would arguably have called it a scientific romance. It is certainly not a novel, if one means by "novel" what Sir Walter Scott meant—a long prose work set in the present and telling of ordinary people and events.

The second, *The Marriages Between Zones Three, Four, and Five*, is neither novel nor scientific romance. One is tempted to call it a parable or fable, except that parables seldom run to 245 pages. The first book of the series was set on Earth: Earth's history and geography are there pictured, although the evolutionary history of the fictional planet departs considerably from that of the familiar world. "Shikasta" is the name that the Canopans give to Earth. Although the setting of *The Marriages Between Zones Three, Four, and Five* is also called Shikasta, its setting is nothing like that of the first book. There is no more connection between the Shikastas of the first two books than, for example, between New York City and the Emerald City of Oz.

The third work, *The Sirian Experiments*, is a fantasy continuing the story of *Re: Colonized Planet 5, Shikasta*. Both take place on Earth; in both, the pliable humans are being gently urged toward goodness by the benevolent Canopans; being dispassionately studied by the uninvolved Sirians; or being secretly corrupted by the despicable Puttiorans. Again, one may describe the book as a scientific romance.

The most recent work in the series, *The Making of the Representative for Planet 8*, is still another kind altogether, a member of a species rare in the twentieth century—the allegory. Like such works as John Bunyan's *The Pilgrim's Progress* (1678, 1684), *The Making of the Representative for Planet 8* supplies only the sketchiest of characterization (perhaps intentionally: the people of Planet 8—let them be called "Planetarians"—have so little imagination that they call their world "Planet 8," and they have so little personality that instead of personal names, they have labels that derive from their jobs; indeed, if two switch jobs, they swap names as well). As in Edmund Spenser's *The Faerie Queene* (1590, 1596), at least some of the characters have names that stand for or suggest some noteworthy function of the character: Masson (drop an S) is the aptly named Chief Representative for Buildings and Sheltering, while the chief of the teachers is Pedug—for pedagogue, no doubt. Not all the names are so obvious, but enough so that they seem more like titles than personal names, sending up unmistakable signals of allegory.

One genre into which the work certainly does not fit is science fiction, which, at the minimum, requires what Wells described as "an ingenious use of scientific patter." That is, the science in the work need not *be* possible, only sound possible. The science in *The Making of the Representative for Planet 8*, by contrast, is simply unbelievable.

The Canopans planned the world as a paradise; like the Earth before the fall in John Milton's *Paradise Lost* (1667, 1674), Planet 8 has no tilt to its rotation, its axis is perfectly perpendicular to the plane of its orbit, producing an unvaryingly mild climate over almost the whole of its surface. Then something happens to what Lessing calls the "alignments." In *Re: Colonized Planet 5, Shikasta*, the start of the Earth's troubles had been marked by the tilting of its axis about twenty degrees, producing seasons and interrupting the interplanetary flow of Canopan niceness. One wonders initially, therefore, if Planet 8's axis of rotation has shifted, too, but more radically, but Lessing's narrator, Doeg, explains that the change in alignment (whatever it may be) is not a physical change that occurs on or to Planet 8.

As the weather grows colder, plans are made to evacuate the towns near the poles, because these will soon be uninhabitable. After this event, early in the book, either one pole mysteriously and inexplicably gets warmer, or the author forgets what she has said, because from this time on, one hears about the "cold pole" and the "warm pole." Temperatures drop, and the immediate danger to life on the planet is the rapid growth of the polar ice cap (but around the "cold pole" only). To protect the Planetarians, Johor, an emissary from Canopus, orders the people *to build a wall around the entire planet to hold back the ice*—which they promptly do.

Doeg mentions that the wall is fifty times the height of their tallest building. The Planetarians have multi-story buildings, but even if one assumes that their highest building is only a modest ten feet, then the height of the wall is five hundred feet, or just a little shorter than the Washington Monument. Whatever its height, after the wall's completion, the chief representatives of the planet are instructed to survey the situation by walking around the globe on top of the wall. This they do, walking "into, not with, the revolving of the planet so that the sun always rose ahead of us. . . ." The innocent-looking prepositional phrase just quoted is either a misprint (which is unlikely) or a physical impossibility: the sun appears to rise in the east because the earth is rotating to the east; to have the sun rise ahead of one, one must walk with, not into, the revolving of the planet. This requirement holds for either hemisphere of any planet with its axis anything like perpendicular to the plane of its orbit.

Like *The Marriages Between Zones Three, Four, and Five*, then, *The Making of the Representative for Planet 8* is an allegorical fantasy—a work which requires the reader to suspend his disbelief. It is also by far the shortest of the four in the series, leading its American publisher to ask Lessing for some comments to pad the work. In a lengthy afterword, Lessing says that both *The Making of the Representative for Planet 8* and *The Sirian Experiments* grew out of her fifty-year interest in polar expeditions and were specifically influenced by the 1910 to 1913 journey of Robert Falcon Scott to the Antarctic. She notes that Scott's career and especially his tragic last voyage are now being reassessed: whereas he was almost sanctified in his own generation, today his competence is being questioned. Scott's story is certainly fascinating, and the question Lessing raises about "the atmosphere of the times" and how it changes is interesting, but it is hard to see what these themes have to do with *The Making of the Representative for Planet 8*.

Certainly, the behavior of the poor Planetarians changes under the impact of their ice age. As they become crowded, underfed, restricted in their activities, threatened by cold, and depressed by unbroken winter, they become touchier, prone to violence at first and to lassitude later. This behavior, however, was not that of the polar explorers; if the Planetarians are supposed to be symbolic of the downtrodden of Earth, then the comparison seems pointless, because the Planetarians suffer from conditions over which they have no control, not from poor distribution of goods or poor government or human greed.

One last set of examples illustrates a further problem with the work. When the existence of every form of life on Planet 8 is threatened, the Canopans, creators and civilizers of the Planetarians, do not abandon them. They intend to move the people of Planet 8 to another world, Rohanda, another name for Earth. Johor tells Doeg that the Canopans must first ready the natives of Rohanda so that they will accept the Planetarians. While their vigil continues, and as Planet 8 becomes more frigid each day, the Puttiorans begin their 631. subversion of Earth: beautiful Rohanda becomes nasty Shikasta, and the Canopans conclude that they cannot move the Planetarians to Earth. Johor must bring this terrible news to Planet 8, and to show the depth of his commitment, he remains on the planet, with the suffering people, as every living thing (himself included) freezes to death.

Yet Johor's sacrifice, if intended as a model, is actually no sacrifice. A digression into the events of *The Sirian Experiments* will show why. In that book, the Sirian woman Ambien admires the Canopans' willingness to lay down their lives for others—in one instance, a slave named Rhodia, a Canopan in disguise, sacrifices herself to set Ambien free. Ambien later realizes, however, that she had known Rhodia before, when Rhodia inhabited another body. Likewise, Johor has appeared before, as a character in *Shikasta*. In that book, he has had a lifespan stretching from prehistoric times to the present and beyond. The events of *The Making of the Representative for Planet 8* occur at the same time as the Puttioran corruption of the human race, an occurrence far in the past. Canopans enspirit various bodies as they choose; what happens to those bodies does not seem to affect them much. Johor "dies" with the Planetarians but shows up none the worse for wear in the chronologically later *Shikasta*, ready to possess the body of the Earthman, George Sherban. For a Canopan, suffering the death of a particular body is notsthe all-or-nothing choice that faces ordinary mortals. It is hard to be moved by someone's gift of something so easily replaced.

The Canopus in Argos series seems strangely undirected; perhaps the intended fifth work will reveal the common theme that these four so earnestly yet so confusingly struggle toward.

Walter E. Meyers

Sources for Further Study

Library Journal. CVII, February 1, 1982, p. 273.
Nation. CCXXXIV, March 6, 1982, p. 278.
National Review. XXXIV, February 5, 1982, p. 116.
New Statesman. CIII, March 26, 1982, p. 21.
The New York Times Book Review. LXXXVII, February 7, 1982, p. 1.
Observer. March 28, 1982, p. 31.
Times Literary Supplement. April 2, 1982, p. 370.

MALGUDI DAYS

Author: R. K. Narayan (1906-   )
Publisher: The Viking Press (New York). 246 pp. $14.95
Type of work: Short stories
Time: Primarily the 1940's to the 1980's
Locale: The imaginary city of Malgudi in southern India

Thirty-two stories, most of which have been culled from two previous collections, that create a gentle, often satirical, but loving portrait of the populace of Malgudi— ranging from holy men to businessmen, from beggars to students, from housewives to saints, and including several very distinctive animals

Malgudi Days is a very special book, but it also may well be a book for special tastes. A collection of thirty-two stories, most of which have been selected from two previously published collections, *An Astrologer's Day and Other Stories* (1947) and *Lawley Road* (1956), *Malgudi Days* offers a mosaic of a life that seems to belong to a lost time. The tone of the stories belongs to the nineteenth century, to the world of Rudyard Kipling and O. Henry, to the days when stories were expected to have neat little plots, a touch of irony, and a surprise ending. R. K. Narayan has long ago mastered his form and techniques, but the result is a body of work that is not for everyone's taste.

Narayan, over several productive decades, has written eleven novels, several collections of stories, a memoir, and new versions of several classic Indian epics. He is, without question, what used to be called "a man of letters." The recipient of many awards for his writing—both individual prizes for specific works and awards acknowledging the merit of his entire body of work— Narayan is considered one of India's most distinguished authors. Although approaching eighty, he continues to write, still adding to his monumental picture of Indian life during the twentieth century.

In some respects, Narayan might be compared to William Faulkner, Honoré de Balzac, or to other writers who carried in their imagination the vast landscape of an entire culture, and who re-created that culture in volume after volume. Many of Narayan's stories possess a folktale quality, a sense of collective memory being shared with the reader much as an elderly relative might tell old stories to children around a fire at night—or as a visitor might regale a friend against his will with story after story. Most of the brief tales in *Malgudi Days* are remembered from previous times, ranging from not long ago to decades earlier. The result is a patchwork-quilt effect, with splashes of color and subtle vignettes working together to create an often dazzling tapestry of real and imagined life. Sometimes the stories may not be strictly true. Occasionally, they are blatant tall tales, with little pretense at veracity. The truth inherent in these tales, however, goes beyond the mere plausibility of the facts of the narrative. The tiger in "The Tiger's Claw" may or may not have behaved as the author says, but it does not really matter. The reader does not know if the story is true, but it *might* be, especially if one is willing to suspend disbelief and enjoy the tale on its own merits.

One cannot bring the prejudices of modern literary criticism to the tales of Narayan. In a literary world in which stories of psychological violence and formal experimentation prevail, Narayan's little stories seem naïve and simple. Here, however, is where their strength may lie. They do not pretend to be anything other than what they are. In their clean prose and simple attitudes, they may well achieve a power and a truth that many more fashionable works miss.

Often, it appears that there is little point to a story beyond an intent to picture the way the villagers look at their lives. Sometimes Narayan relies too heavily on an O. Henry twist at the end of a story to provide an ironic commentary on what has gone before. This mannerism mars "Such Perfection" and "Father's Help," stories which one would like to see carried further, elaborated and explored, rather than cut off so skillfully.

Frequently, Narayan touches on moral or philosophical questions. In "Such Perfection," for example, he explores the question of perfection in art. Is the artist like a god—or even a competitor of the gods? Does the artist, in his effort to create a work of absolute perfection, step over the proper boundaries and challenge the authority of the divine? It is clear in this story that Soma, the sculptor, in his genius and his pride, does create a work that is too perfect, a work that challenges the immortals. This is a fascinating concept, and one that could have been explored at greater length, with more than the pat ironic conclusion that it rates in this tale.

These stories, despite their overemphasis on tricks of plot, do convey a vivid and sometimes gritty sense of life in twentieth century India. The loss of a job can be both demoralizing and terrifying to a man and his family, propelling him to foolish gambling in the hope of a miracle that will set them back on their feet again. A gardener can take pride in a lifetime spent in caring for the garden of a once-grand estate, failing to understand that times change and that his wonderful garden is now seen as an impediment to progress. The city officers can deny their responsibility for the diseases and poverty that pervade Malgudi, yet their pretenses benefit no one—not even themselves. These are human beings that one might find—in different clothes and with different mannerisms, but essentially the same—in any small city anywhere in the world, and their concerns are essentially universal.

Fortunes rise and fall in Malgudi, often with little provocation or warning. In "The Martyr's Corner," "Out of Business," and other tales in the collection, one feels the precariousness of life in India. In this world, an innocent mistake can be fatal—or not, depending on the luck of the individual. Luck is still an important part of life in Malgudi. Chance becomes increasingly important as individual effort crashes against the unfairness of life. The men and women and even the children in Malgudi hope for the best, but do not dare to expect it. They are never surprised by a bad turn of events, but good fortune amazes and delights them. Narayan captures with subtlety and dexterity the wistful fatalism of his characters. He makes the reader *care* about the citizens of Malgudi, perhaps more than the slender story lines warrant.

Narayan's prose is, for the most part, simple, with a flavor of the poetic, but without excessive ornament. Always, however, a tension exists in the narration, a sense that the story may suddenly veer off in an unexpected direction. The tone is that of a sovereign storyteller, unconstrained by aesthetic or formal considerations. Often false clues are dropped along the way, and promises to the reader are easily cast aside, as the story doublecrosses both the characters and the "listener" of the tale.

The newest stories in the collection are slightly more complex in plot and narrative structure than the earlier ones, but their focus is essentially the same as the others. Pop music and hippies make an appearance—among other phenomena of the modern world—but they are involved in stories not so different from the tales previously told. Narayan seems to be implying that while the surface of life changes the essential core remains the same. Certainly, the stories in this collection are admirable testimony to this belief.

Narayan has been asked many times to pinpoint precisely where Malgudi is on the map of India. Literary scholars have tried to locate this now mythical city and the region surrounding it, even going to the length of creating maps based on internal evidence from the stories. Narayan himself insists, however, that Malgudi is strictly imaginary, the fruit of his imagination colliding with the real world. He can, he claims, find inhabitants of Malgudi anyplace in the world, even in New York City. People are people, he says, characters are characters, wherever one finds them. It is this conviction, this love of the human race in all of its imperfections and small glories, that gives these stories their lasting value.

Bruce D. Reeves

Sources for Further Study

The Atlantic. CCXLIX, April, 1982, p. 106.
Christian Science Monitor. May 14, 1982, p. B2.
Library Journal. CVII, April 1, 1982, p. 746.
Nation. CCXXXIV, April 24, 1982, p. 499.
The New York Review of Books. XXIX, April 1, 1982, p. 21.
The New York Times Book Review. LXXXVII, March 7, 1982, p. 1.
The New Yorker. LVIII, August 2, 1982, p. 84.
Saturday Review. IX, March, 1982, p. 62.

THE MAN IN THE BLACK COAT TURNS

Author: Robert Bly (1926-   )
Publisher: The Dial Press (New York). 62 pp. $18.95
Type of work: Poetry

A new collection of poems from one of America's most prolific poets, who continues to make public his mystic, visionary world

Since the 1960's, Robert Bly has been one of America's more influential poets. As an editor, translator, and poet, he has done much to shape a generation's expectations of what the poet should be writing about and how the poem should look on the page. Critics have called him America's most imitated poet, but they have not agreed that his leadership has been positive— too easily imitated, some have said. Since first publishing *Silence in the Snowy Fields* in 1962, Bly has published ten volumes of poetry, translated and edited many more, and founded a small press and a literary magazine. He was also a founder of "American Writers Against the Vietnam War" and one of its leading spokesmen, giving numerous readings on college campuses across the country. When his highly political *The Light Around the Body* (1967) received the National Book Award in 1968, Bly donated the prize money to aid young Americans resisting the draft. Prolific, visible, and in tune with a violent period, Robert Bly became something of a hero to the generation of the 1960's.

In 1971, before the feminist movement had reached national visibility, Bly was advocating the female principle as a viable alternative to male-dominated consciousness. His poetry argued that the feminine consciousness—natural, mythic, creative, and irrational—had once ruled in matriarchies and would rule again. If nothing else, Bly has caught the temper of his times, changing his emphases well before the man of the street. In this sense, he has been prophetic—just what one expects from poets in the Romantic tradition.

Readers of *The Man in the Black Coat Turns* will be somewhat disappointed if they expect a similar prophetic vision for the 1980's. Bly is now fifty-seven, and it is hard to be an old romantic. In these poems, one finds him no less mystical, no less romantic, but more and more, one sees him turning back to Wordsworthian "spots of time," to visionary moments of times past. The political anger that fueled his verse in the 1960's has largely cooled, and the Great Mother of the 1970's is in the background. The images he has long employed—dust, dark, death, water, night, animals—remain staples, but their focus is almost entirely personal. Bly is not speaking here for the generation of punk rockers and game freaks; there is nothing in this volume that speaks directly to nuclear disaster, terrorism, or unemployment. These poems are meditative—the poet grown older, setting his house in order. They are death-ridden, but the darkness that awaits the poet is not that of worldwide apocalypse; it is rather his own death.

For those who have followed Bly's career, the most noticeable change in this volume is his use of recognizable if idiosyncratic metrical structures. It is almost as if he were responding to critics who have claimed that his verse is too easily imitated because it plays by no rules. In "Visiting the Farallones," he writes, for example:

> The wagon behind bouncing,
> breaking on boulders, back
> and forth, slowly
> smashed to pieces. This crumb-
>
> ling darkness is a reality
> too, the feather
> on the snow, the rooster's
> half-eaten body nearby.

The metrics, effectively uneven, are consistent; the stanza form, while imitating no traditional pattern, seems generated by the subject matter, just as Ralph Waldo Emerson said it should be. Bly does not repeat this particular stanza, but he does carve most of this collection into stanzas controlled by the musical beat. After all these years of consciously avoiding his American heritage, it is as if Bly had only just discovered Ezra Pound's Imagist manifesto. Sometimes his poetics work quite effectively; sometimes they are a little rough. If this volume is at all prophetic, perhaps its prophecy lies in its poetics. Perhaps Bly is telling his reader that poetry must return to technique. Perhaps it is time for poetry to be as well-written as it once was. If that is his subtextual message, there are critics who would say that it arrives not a moment too soon.

Coming to his mysticism via William Blake, D. H. Lawrence, Rainer Maria Rilke, and Pablo Neruda, Bly insists on the primacy of the flesh, the holiness of sensory perception. He has said, "Whoever wants to see the invisible must penetrate more deeply into the visible." Bly enters his visionary world not by denying the physical world, as a Christian mystic might, but by going deeper into the world of sense-perception. In some of the poems, he takes the reader along with him. In "Kennedy's Inauguration," one of the two overtly political poems in the collection, a dried gumball leads the seer into metaphors: "Dry spikes, beaklike/ splinters—hen/ beaks widening in fear." The metaphors expand and, in doing so, become visionary; the poet "sees" Nazis leading women off to "breeding hotels," "sees" Marilyn Monroe drugged to death, "sees" coming out of her back "the Marine's/ cry for the medic." In what seems more like free association than vision, Bly leads the reader through the dark images, and the reader believes. Here, Bly is looking back at cathartic moments—indeed, violence is at the heart of this collection.

Sometimes, in fact too frequently, the image leads to vision altogether too private. The reader is left behind with lines such as

> How difficult it is,
> bending the head, looking into the water.
> Under the water there's a door the pigs
> have gone through.

Wherever those pigs go, only the poet accompanies them. The reader is left high and dry.

Bly's metaphors are not particularly difficult, but they are at times too private and sometimes simply silly. In "Written at Mule Hollow, Utah," one of his more unfortunate titles (Mule Hollow may have associations for Bly, but they never enter the poem), Bly says that the scaly bark of the pine tree is "like someone constantly waking up at night." Grammatically, that makes sense, but the reader will struggle in vain to find the metaphoric connection. The poet may know, but he does not make it clear. On other occasions, as he does with the water comparison in "Mourning Pablo Neruda," Bly will so overload his metaphor that it collapses under the weight.

This overloading of metaphor is nowhere clearer than in the prose poems that occupy the center section of this volume. In "The Ship's Captain Looking over the Rail," Bly writes that it sometimes seems to a man "that he has lived his whole life to create something dark. What he has created is the wine in the hold of the ship." This is a fine passage, but it leads into a tangle in which one is never sure if the captain is the poet or whoever is in charge of this universe. The confusion is dreamlike; dreams have always been likened to the visionary experience. Just when one is sure that the captain is the poet, and that the wine stored below decks is his poetry, Bly explicitly rejects this reading. The individual images of the poem all work beautifully; it is the governing metaphor which breaks down. One feels as if he has read something quite profound, or perhaps quite silly.

The book's dust jacket says that "Some of the poems . . . began as prose poems, then were recast into continuous lines, then recast a third time into stanzas." Indeed, some of the poems read as if they might have been composed in this way. The Romantic cry for spontaneous verse is no longer Bly's. The idea of prose poems interlarded with poetry, the idea of casting and recasting the form, recalls Robert Lowell and his innovative *Life Studies* (1959). Bly, in fact, has taken many of his cues from Lowell's generation, those poets who came to prominence in the 1950's—Lowell, John Berryman, Theodore Roethke, Randall Jarrell—poets who broke the ground for "confessional" poetry. Bly has outlived his masters and come into his own, but much of what he writes still sounds derivative.

As one has come to expect from Bly, the world of these poems depends heavily upon the poet himself. It is his ego that focuses the phenomena; it is his response that gives the world its validity. The "other world" within that links man to Nature is the poet's business. It is Bly's own capacity to open this "inner-eye" that assures the reader that *he* is capable of the same kind of inner vision. In "Four Ways to Knowledge," Bly maintains that what is given man to know, he will know. It is unavoidable and everywhere. If one resists the knowledge of "otherness," the godhead will turn to

> . . . accidents,
> disease, suffering,
> lost letters, torpid sleeps,
> disasters, catatonia.

Of the four ways to awareness, dreams are the least painful conveyors, if only people would listen. Walt Whitman said this in "The Sleepers," as did Emerson in his essays. From whatever direction one comes to the mystic tradition, the message invariably is the same. All that is required is a leap of faith from the rational to the spontaneous.

"The man in the black coat," who turns, may be the poet turning toward new vistas; he may be death who turns to wait for the poet. This book is a five-finger transition piece. It looks back to some of Bly's most effective work, doing well what he has always done well. It reaffirms his visionary stance, but it breaks no new ground. What comes next will be crucial for Bly. Either he will pause and watch his fields go back to pine, or he will begin to clear new ones. It would not be surprising to find him beginning a poem of book-length or longer, a work to take him through to the dark. Pound and William Carlos Williams, to name but two, found that to be the romantic's answer to growing older.

Michael S. Reynolds

Sources for Further Study

Christian Century. XCIX, March 24, 1982, p. 348.
Library Journal. CVI, October 15, 1981, p. 2032.
Nation. CCXXXIII, October 31, 1981, p. 447.
The New York Times Book Review. LXXXVII, February 14, 1982, p. 15.
Western American Literature. XVII, November, 1982, p. 282.

MANTISSA

Author: John Fowles (1926-   )
Publisher: Little, Brown and Company (Boston). 196 pp. $13.95
Type of work: Novel

A playful attempt to articulate the complex relationship between a writer and his muse

Principal characters:
    MILES GREEN, an author
    ERATO/DR. DELFIE/NURSE CORY, his muse

According to ancient Greek mythology, the Muses were a group of nine sisters, daughters of Zeus and Mnemosyne (memory), who inspired those proficient in the arts. From Homer forward, the Muses served as a source of appeal for creative and artistic genius. The great epic poets always began their works with invocations of their heavenly muse to supply them with both the substance of their tale and the artistic skill to get it told. Because of this dependency, the muse-figure could serve as both an object of praise for artistic success and an object of blame for artistic failure. Because the Muses were female, courtship of them by male writers could take on aspects of male/ female relationships among humans.

John Fowles's *Mantissa* derives its dramatic situation and its narrative from the writer/muse relationship. The action of this work consists of the inter- actions and conversations between an author and a series of women, all of whom finally appear to be his muse in different guises and roles. Fowles reminds the reader at one point of the meaning of the word "mantissa": "an addition of comparatively small importance, especially to a literary effort or discourse." In light of his other novels and writings, this book may appear to have just that character, for it is deliberately playful and lighthearted, in contrast to Fowles's serious novels, such as *The Magus* (1966) and *Daniel Martin* (1977). Here, the relationship between writer and muse is depicted as a play of wits, a drama of sexual combat coquettishly engaged in, a con- stantly shifting array of roles and relationships, none of which is taken too seriously by either participant.

Yet, one suspects, Fowles has larger issues in mind. One subtheme in this work is a series of references to Structuralist and post-Structuralist literary theorists who would seem to deny the connection between art and life and the authority of the author in relationship to his work. Such critics suggest that art is self-enclosed and self-referential; Fowles's *Mantissa* is a book about its own writing which makes constant reference to other writers and their work. Recent critical theory also suggests that authorial intention and control in a work are false issues, for a writer is not really in control of the language he employs nor is he able to manipulate the reader toward desired ends; here, Fowles raises, through the convention of the muse, the question of the sources and the purposes of art. If, for example, the writer is a mouthpiece for his muse, then he cannot be said to be in control of the workings and ends of his writing.

More central, however, is the issue of humanity itself; is one's conception of the importance and dignity of human beings undercut by the kinds of issues raised by the Structuralist and post-Structuralist critics? Michel Foucault, for example, has written that the concept of "man" is a recent invention and one that will soon pass away. One may suspect that Fowles's *Mantissa* is a kind of answer to that claim, an answer which poses a different concept of "man" from the one Foucault is rejecting, while seeking to hold onto the central affirmation of the human self-image.

The stage for the action of *Mantissa* is a small room, apparently in a hospital, although the walls of the room have a strange habit of changing shape and, occasionally, of disappearing. In the opening chapter, the reader meets Miles Green, who is apparently waking up from a period of unconsciousness and who seems to be suffering from amnesia. In mythology, the Muses could take away memory; occasionally, they gave artistic gifts to the amnesiac as a kind of recompense. Here, the reader is introduced to Dr. Delfie and her assistant, Nurse Cory, who claim to be trying to restore Green's memory. Their therapeutic technique, however, is one based on the value of sexual arousal. Green resists; both women become involved. Their technique is successful, at least in producing orgasm in Green. Nurse Cory then congratulates him on his efforts, which turn out to be the very pages of the novel at hand.

Fowles has thus sketched out an erotics of writing, to go with Roland Barthes's erotics of reading. Quickly, one learns that Dr. Delfie has become Erato, the Muse herself, and much of the rest of the novel consists of a lengthy conversation between Green and Erato. Green attacks her for not helping him more; she says that she may not be the most satisfactory Muse, but she is the only one he has. Erato reminisces a bit about her past, including her former relationships with Vergil, Ovid, and William Shakespeare, among other major writers. As the author is a seducer of the muse, so the muse plays a variety of traditional female roles—coquette, seductress, mother, friend—each of which dramatizes part of the creative process.

For that seems to be Fowles's intent in this novel—to suggest at once how dependent the artist is on a process of inspiration over which he has no control and how completely his art is at the beck and call of his playful creativity. From time to time, Fowles suggests that *he* is Green, for example having Green claim authorship of a novel with three endings, which must be Fowles's *The French Lieutenant's Woman* (1969). At other times, one is reminded that Green and his muse and the whole narrative of the novel are under Fowles's control. At yet other times, one finds that Green does not have control of his muse, who often acts independently of his desires; presumably, Fowles has had a similar kind of experience. In these cases, the muse becomes a difficult taskmaster, insisting that Green meet demands and pass tests in return for her continued work on his behalf.

At one point, in a complete reversal of roles, Erato says that her participation in the creative process is merely one of spreading seeds of ideas, which the writer must develop; sexually, Erato becomes the male, and Green becomes the female who must nurture and bring to birth the ideas Erato has planted. As should already be clear, this is but one instance in which *Mantissa* plays tricks on the reader. Reading this book is like entering a hall of mirrors in which things, and characters, are constantly reflecting one another, changing places, reversing the process of narrative.

If play is integral to the image of writing which this book presents, that fact perhaps suggests the source of its central character's name. Falstaff, the *miles gloriosus* or braggart soldier of Shakespeare's history plays, "babbled of green fields" on his deathbed, a line echoed on the last page of *Mantissa*. Thus, "Miles Green" is perhaps a fictional construct, one who comes into being through language, like Falstaff, who is one of the most fully human of Shakespeare's characters. Through the use of words that delight and excite and promote living, Green is a "soldier green," a fighter for the humanity, the productivity, the greenness, of human life. Perhaps one cannot point with clarity to where the author ends and his words begin, any more than one can point to where a writer's own invention ends and inspiration from a muse or other uncontrollable source begins. What one can do is point to the work itself, and experience that work, letting the fictional constructs of author or muse or whatever become part of the delight of reading as well as writing.

In this light, *Mantissa* becomes a kind of answer to modern literary theorists, joining their game in a way that juxtaposes its own playfulness to their high seriousness, its rejuvenation of ancient fictions about art against their own often difficult concepts. In that regard, *Mantissa*'s weakness as a fiction becomes part of Fowles's answer; the lightness with which one is invited to view this work stands in contrast to the heavy seriousness of the critics to which it would respond. Fowles perhaps would not want this book to attain the enduring significance of some of his earlier work, for that would give more credence to those theorists to whose work it is a kind of rejoinder. Instead, it serves as an exercise in the playful and re-creative resources of human language.

John N. Wall, Jr.

Sources for Further Study

The Atlantic. CCL, November, 1982, p. 170.
Los Angeles Times Book Review. August 29, 1982, p. 10.
The New Republic. CLXXXVII, October 18, 1982, p. 34.

New Statesman. CIV, October 8, 1982, p. 26.
The New York Times Book Review. LXXXVII, August 29, 1982, p. 3.
Newsweek. C, September 27, 1982, p. 72.
Time. CXX, September 6, 1982, p. 74.
Times Literary Supplement. October 8, 1982, p. 1091.

MARCO POLO, IF YOU CAN

Author: William F. Buckley, Jr. (1925-   )
Publisher: Doubleday & Company (Garden City, New York). 233 pp. $13.95
Type of work: Novel
Time: 1939-1960
Locale: Russia, Washington, D.C., and Berlin

In the fourth of Buckley's espionage novels, Blackford Oakes returns as the pilot of a U-2 which lands in Russia just before the Paris peace talks between Dwight D. Eisenhower and Nikita Khrushchev in 1960

> *Principal characters:*
> BLACKFORD OAKES, a thirty-four-year-old retired CIA agent, recalled into service
> MICHAEL BOLGIANO, his best friend, also a CIA agent
> BENNI BOLGIANO, Michael's father, a leader in the Italian resistance to Hitler
> DWIGHT D. EISENHOWER, thirty-fourth President of the United States
> NIKITA KHRUSHCHEV, the Premier of the Soviet Union
> ALLEN DULLES, the Director of the CIA
> J. EDGAR HOOVER, the Director of the FBI
> AMANDA GAITHER, a CIA agent and secretary to Dulles' deputy
> SALLY PARTRIDGE, Oakes's girlfriend

In *Marco Polo, If You Can*, William F. Buckley, Jr., includes all of the elements necessary for a good espionage novel—an engaging CIA agent, a beautiful traitor, an elaborate plot, fast-paced action, and the familiar confrontation between American and Soviet intelligence operatives, but the key to the novel's appeal is Buckley's use of the U-2 incident of 1960 as the basis for his plot. Instead of Francis Gary Powers, it is the fictional Blackford Oakes who crash-lands in the Soviet Union, but Nikita Khrushchev, President Dwight D. Eisenhower, Allen Dulles, and other well-known figures are brought back to life in disconcerting detail. By the end of the book, one cannot help wondering how much of Buckley's plot is pure fiction. As an ex-CIA agent with many prominent connections, he has access to information not available to the public. In any case, *Marco Polo, If You Can* is a witty and thought-provoking blend of fiction and nonfiction. Between the lines, Buckley raises some serious questions about the ethics of politically motivated intelligence operations.

The structure of *Marco Polo, If You Can* is more complex than that of Buckley's previous spy novels. The story begins with Oakes being tried in Soviet Court for "a squalid career of espionage and other forms of hateful work against the Soviet state." From there, the scene shifts to Washington, New York, and Berlin, from present to near past to distant past with sometimes confusing rapidity. In chapter 3, two characters are introduced whose behavior is obviously suspicious but whose allegiances and actions are unclear, and little clarification is provided until chapter 9. To follow the maze, one must pay close attention, above all, to the dates. It is clear from the epigraph, if the reader has forgotten, that the events leading to the U-2 incident began in 1959 with Khrushchev's American visit, and clear from the first chapter that Oakes plays the part of Powers. From that point, Buckley depends on chronological markers to maintain the order of his narrative, but they are often not enough to keep bewilderment at bay. Buckley uses flashbacks to provide pieces to the puzzle of Oakes in Soviet Court, but his approach is so convoluted that a systematic analysis is nearly impossible for the reader.

One of the great pleasures of the novel is its gallery of amusing portraits of familiar political figures. Eisenhower appears early, decisive and commanding, but also occasionally impatient and vainglorious. The Director of the FBI, renowned for his thoroughness, takes months to locate the Soviet "mole" who leaks the minutes of the National Security Council—a humorous swipe at J. Edgar Hoover. Buckley even takes a stab at Nixon, who appears near the end of the book in a situation foreshadowing Watergate. Khrushchev—irrational, loud, rude, dangerous, and, in the end, foolish—is an entertaining stereotype. Whether Buckley's interpretations of these public figures are wholly accurate is not the point; it is intrinsically pleasing to be taken behind the scenes, and Buckley's characterizations are executed with supreme confidence.

Buckley's fictional characters, within the limits of the novel, are not merely the black and white agents of good and evil. Anyone who has read any of the three earlier novels (*Saving the Queen*, 1976; *Stained Glass*, 1978; *Who's on First*, 1980) will know that Blackford Oakes and Rufus are old friends. Rufus, the somewhat mysterious and paternal sage, comes out of retirement as the only intelligence creative and sophisticated enough to solve the problem at hand. He is a little larger than life, plausible because one wants to believe that a beneficent brilliance such as his exists. (In a flashback, Eisenhower refuses to go ahead with the Normandy invasion until Rufus has assured him that it is safe.) Oakes is more human, perhaps because Buckley draws on his own experiences in the CIA for his convincing details. Once asked to resign for "giving way to sentimentality" by saving the life of a Soviet scientist (not in the best interests of the Agency), Oakes returns to service as a favor to Rufus. As he becomes more involved in the mission, he must question his loyalty to his country, to the CIA, and to his friends. On the darker side, Benni Bolgiano is a pathetic traitor whose political idealism causes him to betray his family. He is not without redeeming qualities, but in the end, those virtues cannot save him from his own beliefs.

It would be a mistake to regard Buckley's novel as an exercise in ideology, but to disregard the novel's ideological thrust would also be misleading. Buckley is, after all, a conservative spokesman with strong political views. The world he creates in *Marco Polo, If You Can* is not, in many ways, the world with which most readers are familiar. The man on the street does not deal with matters of national security on a daily basis, and does not often socialize with Soviet or American intelligence agents. In another way, however, the novel's world is familiar enough, for everyone is threatened in some way by death or disloyalty, fear or disillusionment. From beginning to end, Oakes must defend his relationship with Sally, his lover of many years. To this point, the two have assumed that Oakes's involvement in the CIA precludes their marriage, but by the end of the novel, they relinquish superficial rationalizations. Sally agrees to accept Oakes's profession; more important, she finally submits to commitment: "She sensed that this next mission was distinctively dangerous, but her energies were for the first time given to convincing him that if in his judgment it was right to go forward, in her judgment, derivatively, it was right to go forward." Both acknowledge the necessity for trust and commitment in a relationship, and at the same time are aware of the tangible and intangible dangers that will threaten them.

On a larger scale, the betrayal of trust is what ultimately causes the U-2 incident. It involves Benni, whose secret Communist allegiance eventually kills his son, a CIA agent working unwittingly against his father. It involves Amanda Gaither, a CIA agent, the trusted secretary of Allen Dulles' deputy, and occasional lover of Oakes. The small betrayals lead inevitably to the larger, until Oakes must risk his life to justify the death of his best friend and to complete the mission successfully. As he waits in Lubyanka, sentenced to death with no word of American intervention, he succumbs to the doubt and fear which confront everyone at some time: "How clamorous, he thought, must have been the prayers from this building, over the years. Did God shroud the Lubyanka with a silencer, so that nothing could reach His ears from this encephalophonic misery hole?" It is, for that moment, a sobering thought, one that echoes the reader's own private fears. Faced with death, with no one at all to care, how important are the ideals of friendship or love or patriotism?

In the end, that momentary doubt is lost in the triumph of success. Oakes uses his ingenuity, reason prevails, and, through careful political manipulation, Khrushchev looks more like the culprit than Eisenhower in the U-2 incident. Nevertheless, one should pause to wonder briefly about the implications of Buckley's generally lighthearted fiction. As plausible as it is, one can be certain that *Marco Polo, If You Can* is, after all, just a good story, but it is convincing because every detail, every person, every action seems utterly logical and possible. One must wonder, as Buckley surely intends, how many such "incidents" actually occur, only to be covered up by the government and forgotten by the public.

Terry Teachout said of the book (*National Review*, January 22, 1982) that "anyone with lingering doubts about the wisdom of allowing Western intelligence agencies to launch covert operations ought to read it closely and think twice." Unless one shares Buckley's conservative views, however, it is difficult to disregard the ethical and political ramifications of such "covert operations." Political implications notwithstanding, *Marco Polo, If You Can* is a refreshing departure from typical thriller fare. The blend of fiction with nonfiction gives Buckley more freedom to seduce his readers with suspense and humor. One knows that Eisenhower and his coterie are trustworthy, and one is certain that somehow Oakes will survive to be reunited with Sally, but Buckley avoids trite explanations and resolutions. Part of the pleasure of this book is found in trying to determine how the pieces will fit together to make a logical whole, and part is found in the sheer joy of the language. If Oakes and his machinations are occasionally difficult to follow, one is too busy admiring Buckley's style to worry about it.

Melinda W. West

Sources for Further Study

Christian Science Monitor. April 7, 1982, p. 17.
Human Events. XLII, April 17, 1982, p. 11.
Library Journal. CVII, January 1, 1982, p. 110.
National Review. XXXIV, January 22, 1982, p. 56.
New Statesman. CIII, May 28, 1982, p. 25.
The New York Times Book Review. LXXXVII, January 24, 1982, p. 12.
Policy Review. Summer, 1982, p. 183.
Saturday Review. IX, January, 1982, p. 62.
Time. CXIX, January 18, 1982, p. 81.
West Coast Review of Books. VIII, April, 1982, p. 38.

A MARGIN OF HOPE
An Intellectual Autobiography

Author: Irving Howe (1920-   )
Publisher: Harcourt Brace Jovanovich (New York). 368 pp. $14.95
Type of work: Intellectual autobiography
Time: The 1930's to 1982
Locale: Primarily New York City

Recollections of Irving Howe's years as a Trotskyist radical, his rise to prominence as a New York intellectual, his work as an interpreter of Yiddish culture, and his battles as an advocate of democratic socialism

To escape the totalitarian gaze of Big Brother, the hero of George Orwell's *Nineteen Eighty-Four* (1949) rents an upper room in an obscure proletarian neighborhood. In this private haven, Winston Smith savors relics from an authentic past (not the mutable past defined by the Party), revels in the liberating power of unpoliticized sexuality, and contemplates an exquisite piece of coral enclosed in a globe of lead crystal. Room, relationship, and glass all awaken in Winston a vision of "the Golden Country." Here nature runs clean and free, the antique past mingles richly with the present, mechanism and urban giganticism are banished, the rowdy vitality of traditional folk culture is everywhere in evidence. The Golden Country has no politics; not even the "participatory democracy" of classical Athens is evoked. Recoiling from massive and omnipresent psychocentric tyranny, Winston naturally seeks comfort in a fully apolitical, private utopia.

In the last chapter of his intellectual autobiography, *A Margin of Hope*, Irving Howe confesses to an uncritical, passionate love for ballet. He feels guilty about it and imagines Leo Tolstoy sitting beside him in the theater, chastizing him for succumbing to the arch frivolity of "this elegant prancing." Like his research on Thomas Hardy and William Faulkner, this enchantment with ballet is a quest for "the Golden Country," for a world set far apart from politics—but who is the Big Brother from whose eyes Howe seeks relief? There is not one, but many: the imagination of a possible Stalinist tyranny in America (brought into being by the likes of Tom Hayden in whom, in the early 1960's, "one could already see the beginnings of a commissar"); the equally abhorrent face of American Fascism as defined by Joseph McCarthy; the visages of Weathermen terrorists, shrill feminist ideologues, sectarian Maoists and elitist Leninists of all types. Like the Orwell he so much admires, Howe has fought against these various instantiations of Big Brother. Like Orwell, Howe has grown a bit weary of endlessly defending his conservative socialism from attacks by Right and Left. As Socialists willingly permit Orwell and Winston Smith their private space and vision, so will they perhaps not begrudge Howe his ballet.

Since Howe has embraced Orwell as one of his models (along with Norman

Thomas, Ignazio Silone, and Max Shachtman) it is not surprising that their ideas and careers are so similar, yet the completeness of this similarity is genuinely remarkable. Both are moderate Socialists, committed to a life of Socialist letters. Both polemicize against the totalitarian Left to such an extent that, though remaining Socialists, they can licitly be identified as Conservatives. (It is certainly a fine irony that Orwell should have provided the American Right with its most cherished symbol—Big Brother.) Howe, like Orwell, struggled mightily to find, claim, and justify his identity as Socialist litterateur—though he did not see fit to change his name as a way of proclaiming that identity. ("George Orwell," it will be recalled, was the pseudonym of Eric Blair.) Both men took up spiritual residence outside their inherited religious tradition, but they were simultaneously drawn to these traditions— Orwell to Christianity and Howe to Judaism.

It is Howe's Jewishness, however, that most clearly sets him apart from his English mentor. Orwell always bore the stamp of his "shabby genteel" colonial upbringing and his Eton education. For Howe, the molding force was the immigrant Jewish community of the East Bronx. An only child of Ukrainian-born, Yiddish-speaking parents, he saw his family descend from the lower-middle class to the jobless proletariat in the early years of the Depression. Eventually both parents found work in the dress trade, joined the International Ladies Garment Workers Union, and participated in the great (and successful) strike of 1933. While in high school, Howe fell in with Socialist sons of ILGWU officials and began working in the Socialist Party.

At this point, the predominantly Jewish character of Howe's milieu began to change. He encountered Norman Thomas and the heritage of indigenous American radicalism. In 1936, several hundred Trotskyists entered the Party, eventually causing a split in the ranks. Led by James Burnham, James P. Cannon, and Max Shachtman (with directives coming from "the Old Man" himself in Mexico), the Trotskyists led a sizable number of former Socialists into the Socialist Workers Party—a sect trying to become a mass political party. Howe went with this anti-Stalinist faction—"for two or three years," he reports, "I was an almost total believer." By then in college at City College, New York, he devoted little time to his studies. His energies went into meetings, demonstrations, the study of Marxist doctrine, and debates about the history of Trotsky's struggles with Stalin and his minions: "our main task in life seemed at times to be 'the taking of positions.' In the radical world a 'position' is a very serious matter, accorded a value similar to that which mystics give to revelation." The center of Howe's world became Alcove 1, along the edge of City College's lunchroom. "Here gathered Trotskyist, Socialist, Lovestonite students with their books, pamphlets, ragged overcoats and cheese sandwiches." Day and night, the sectarian positions were debated and refined: on the New Deal, the Spanish Civil War, the French Popular Front, applications of the concept of surplus value, the idea of permanent revolution. In Alcove 2, the more powerful and fanatical Young Communist League headquartered itself. As Howe recalls it, the battle for the heart and mind of the campus (twenty thousand) waged by Alcoves 1 and 2 was both a rigorous training in sectarian political combat and a high farce. He likens it to the education of seminarians before their encounter with the flawed reality of the Church.

Trotsky, a skillful literary critic himself, encouraged his disciples to embrace the high literary heritage of the West as well as the great Modernist writers such as T. S. Eliot, James Joyce, and Marcel Proust. Howe, always responsive to literature, began increasingly to be drawn to literary investigations. At the same time, a split with the Trotskyist ranks occurred, with Howe leading the more liberal, "social democratic" faithful into the Independent Socialist League. By then he had been graduated with a degree in English, and in 1941 he became the editor of *Labor Action*, commencing a long and distinguished career in political journalism. A draft notice soon brought one of the happiest periods in Howe's life to an end. Ironically, in his four years in the military, Howe would not be permitted to take up arms against Fascism. During a long, lonely posting to Alaska, he found the leisure to read more than four hundred books. The United States Army was his "graduate school," his *entrepôt* into the world of criticism and literary studies in which he earned his livelihood for forty years.

By the mid-1950's, Howe had fully established himself in the New York intellectual scene. His reviews, critical articles, polemics, and books secured for him a teaching position at newly founded Brandeis University. By 1961, when he left New York for what would be a two-year stay as professor of English at Stanford University, he had published books on the United Auto Workers and Walter Reuther, Sherwood Anderson, William Faulkner, the political novel, and the American Communist Party. Perhaps more important, he was the editor of *Dissent*, the cultural voice of democratic socialism in the United States. Politically, Howe had repudiated Marxist-Trotskyist ideology, although his Socialist advocacy continued to draw inspiration from a Marxist analytic framework.

Parallel to these activities, Howe was engaged in an effort which has since come to bear a rich fruit for American letters: the translation of Yiddish literature into American English. Working first with Eliezer Greenberg, Howe brought to public view a rich series of anthologies and collections of poetry and fiction. He is one of the "discoverers" of Isaac Bashevis Singer, who has since earned the Nobel Prize for Literature. The culmination of Howe's Yiddish research was his much-lauded *World of Our Fathers* (1976), an account of the struggles of Eastern European Jews to fashion a new existence for themselves in the bewildering world of early twentieth century America.

That Irving Howe importantly sustains an interlocking series of American cultural institutions—one is tempted to say "establishments"—is evident.

Academia continues to enjoy his presence, as he now holds a professorship at City University of New York. He is a major interpreter of the Jewish experience in America; a public television series based on *World of Our Fathers* has been produced. To Howe's legacy of literary criticism there will soon be added books on Orwell and Rudyard Kipling. Although he now shares the editorship of *Dissent* with political theorist Michael Walzer, Howe's dedication to this thirty-year-old organ of Left-liberalism and democratic socialism remains untempered. Howe recently edited *Beyond the Welfare State* (1982), a collection of writings by such *Dissent* stalwarts as Michael Harrington, Robert Heilbroner, Philip Green, and Kenneth Arrow.

The source of coherence for Howe's disparate activities is geographic. Preeminently, he is a New York City figure. All his ventures outside its confines have been notably brief (Princeton, Stanford, Israel) and always undertaken with an eye trained on the New York scene. Niched firmly in the dense, tradition-ridden, polemical, and marvelously sophisticated world of the Manhattan intelligentsia, Howe's natural home—either as speaker or object of attack—is between the covers of *The Nation*, *Partisan Review*, *The New Republic*, *The New York Review of Books*, *Commentary*, and of course *Dissent*. Not surprisingly then, his intellectual autobiography provides an unusually vivid portrait of the forces, personalities, and issues which have shaped this milieu in the postwar era.

So riveted on the New York intellectual scene is *A Margin of Hope* that some would question its pretensions to autobiography. Howe says nothing about his early childhood. While his father's death is treated in the book's final chapter, one learns little about the man's character; his mother is hardly mentioned. Indeed, although Howe intimates that he has remained excessively dependent on women throughout his life, he can barely manage a single sentence about them. One would assume from reading the book that Howe's only marriage failed in the early 1960's. Actually, he has been married three times. About his daughter Nina, a clinical psychologist, he says nothing. One learns of his son Nicholas' existence in a passing reference in the book's final chapter. It is as if Howe's real parents were Max Shachtman and Philip Rahv or Edmund Wilson and Lionel Trilling—the looming figures on the Leftist literary horizon in New York. By this reading, Howe's true children are the likes of Michael Walzer and John Rawls, who have been vitally touched by Howe's teaching and writing.

Howe's omissions might be justified by noting that he intends the book to be an *intellectual* autobiography only, but from the start, it is far richer than that. "In the Movement" and "Life in a Sect," the first two chapters, not only trace the development of Howe's Trotskyist faith but also depict vividly the scenery, characters, and concrete action of these years in which Howe "lived at so high, so intense a pitch." Similarly, "Literary Life: New York" and "Loose-Fish, Still Flapping" invite the reader to consider much more than

Howe's evolving ideas and positions. The entire socioeconomic reality of the New York intelligentsia (especially its Jewish component) is Howe's concern.

One learns that Harold Rosenberg, the great art critic, once supported himself by a job at the Advertising Council, where he created Smokey the Bear. Howe recounts the bitter dispute that erupted when Ezra Pound's *The Pisan Cantos* (1948), containing explicit pro-Fascist and anti-Semitic material, received the Bollingen Award in 1949. There are portraiture studies of Delmore Schwartz, John Berryman, Richard Blackmur, Hannah Arendt, and C. Wright Mills. In discussing the ideas and influence of the New Critics, Howe is also concerned to show how the personalities and sensibilities of Allen Tate, John Crowe Ransom, and Robert Penn Warren meshed with those of the New York critics. Here he observes interestingly that a certain similarity of situation bound the Southerners to their New York counterparts: "both groups were semioutsiders starting to break into the central spaces of American culture, yet unwilling to succumb to its slackness, its small optimisms."

Thus, *A Margin of Hope* transcends the narrow category of intellectual autobiography. It offers cultural history and an analysis of the *Zeitgeist*; it is also a sustained apologia for Howe's mature political philosophy. Socialist he remains, but the accents are all on liberty and democracy and the concrete traditions and structures which sustain them. Howe is now a conservative Socialist and a Socialist Conservative (in the Burkean sense). There is no Marxism in his claim that "the case for socialism must be made increasingly on moral grounds: democracy in the work place as fulfillment of political freedom; an end to extreme inequalities of socioeconomic condition; the vision of a humane society as one that requires a setting of cooperativeness and fraternity." Howe's analysis of the New Left is especially revealing. Its members neglected to study the failures of earlier radical movements in America, and so evolved into competing sectarian factions. Increasingly influenced by Marcusean notions (abhorrent to Howe), they became all too willing to withdraw tolerance and liberty from their "oppressor" opponents. Howe reads the Weathermen phenomenon as a recrudescence of Russian nihilism and a fulfillment of the implicit authoritarianism which entered SDS (Students for a Democratic Society) in the mid-1960's. Howe's credo is nicely captured in these lines:

> My own idea of socialism rests on unbreakable liberal values, and if at any point a socialist proposal were to conflict with the fundamental values of liberalism, I would unhesitatingly opt for the latter. With liberty you can struggle for greater equality; equality without liberty is a new mode of enslavement.

From a strictly literary viewpoint, however, *A Margin of Hope* is less than fully satisfying. The quality of Howe's prose varies according to his engagement with the incident or topic under consideration. When he writes of his father's final months or of his own sojourn as editor-printer of *Labor Action*, a refreshing intensity transforms the book. One then realizes that the other material has been slightly tiresome, delivered too dispassionately. Joseph Sobran, in a predictably hostile review for the *National Review*, complains of the book's boring, literary-society quality. Caustically he observes of Howe: "When he speaks of death, you aren't quite sure whether he expects to be buried or remaindered."

The problem here is partly one of Howe's fuzzy intention. While the book is much more than an intellectual autobiography, it is not quite a fully realized "life and times." Howe supplies enough purely autobiographical detail to arouse one's interest, but he then withdraws under the cover of the adjective "intellectual." At one point, he begins to recollect a shattering mid-life crisis (complete with divorce, psychotherapy, and self-imposed exile from New York), but he abruptly closes this line of narrative with a wise anecdote about his psychiatrist. He is concerned to portray key figures of the literary Left, yet these always end up as mere sketches. One wants to know about Howe's sustaining relationships, about loves, fears, joys, and losses. Without such detail, the reader is left with the impression that what matters most to Howe are his acquaintanceships with the likes of Norman Mailer, Saul Bellow, and Richard Hofstader. In the worst light, Howe's book seems little more than the autobiography of a name-dropper.

It can be argued that the book's flaws derive not so much from its ambiguous intention but from the intellectual poverty from which this ambiguity arises. Howe's unifying theme is that of marginality. He adheres to a Socialist credo which has been banished to the borderlands of American intellectual life. No theist, he is a "partial Jew," operating as a vague fellow-traveler at the edges of American Judaism. Neither New Critic nor Deconstructionist, Howe cultivates a side-garden of historical criticism. To his accusers, Howe is a symbol of failure of nerve. If socialism is too problematic, why not "convert" to a vigorous defense of capitalism (as have many of Howe's old associates)? If the other religious options do not work, why not resolutely embrace that Judaism which sustained "the world of our fathers"? Midge Decter faults Howe for reducing himself to the defense of a mere "socialist ethic," which is however less an ethic than a vague posture. "From this posture," she writes, "no failure of policy ever need be confronted, no error need be confessed. Most of all, no choices need by made." (*Commentary*, December, 1982). In the case of Howe's autobiography, this failure to make (literary) choices is too much in evidence; it deprives the book of any claim to greatness.

Leslie E. Gerber

Sources for Further Study

America. CXLVII, February 5, 1982, p. 97.
Human Events. XLII, October 23, 1982, p. 9.

National Review. XXXIV, October 1, 1982, p. 1226.
The New Republic. CLXXXVII, November 1, 1982, p. 32.
The New York Review of Books. XXX, February 3, 1983, p. 5.
The New York Times Book Review. LXXXVII, October 31, 1982, p. 1.
Progressive. XLVII, February, 1983, p. 57.
Publishers Weekly. CCXXII, September 24, 1982, p. 68.

ME AGAIN
Uncollected Writings of Stevie Smith

Author: Stevie Smith (1902-1971)
Edited by Jack Barbera and William McBrien
Preface by James MacGibbon
Publisher: Farrar, Straus and Giroux (New York). Illustrated by Stevie Smith.
  360 pp. $15.95; paperback $6.95
Type of work: Anthology of writings

A diverse collection of poems, essays, reviews, stories, letters, and a radio play, including many previously unpublished pieces, emphasizing Stevie Smith's barbed humor and intelligent skepticism

Stevie Smith's critics, even those who acknowledge her as a major British poet of the twentieth century, have found it impossible to place her work within any literary movement. Smith herself recognized that she could not be lumped with T. S. Eliot, or Stephen Spender, or Dylan Thomas. This volume of poems, essays, reviews, stories, and letters portrays a quirky, individual writer who traced an unconventional literary path into delightful tangles and cut through clichés with terrible, swift words. Smith's literary executor, James MacGibbon, in his brief preface, disagrees graciously with the editors, Jack Barbera and William McBrien, about Smith's attitude toward death, but he praises their diligent research. In their persuasive introductory essay, following the preface, Barbera and McBrien offer a lively biographical interpretation of Smith's writings, touching on her sharp judgment of children as neither innocent nor guileless, on her interweaving personal friendships with her literary creations, on her loneliness, on her delight in intelligent discourse, and on her affectionate regard for death. A reading of this anthology supports Barbera and McBrien's portrait of Smith: unromantic, whimsical, at times morbid, but always entertaining.

The splendidly funny line drawings included throughout this collection suggest both the speed of Smith's insights and the mature, complex personality giving rise to her sharp judgments on human society. These drawings have not been published previously, and, although her collections of poetry are all illustrated, those drawings rarely have accompanied her poems included in anthologies. At first glance, Stevie Smith's line drawings remind one of James Thurber's cartoons; their strength derives, however, not from ridicule or a familiar contempt, but rather from sympathetic mockery and sharp-witted observation. As Smith herself notes, in a review of Thurber's cartoons, the monotony of his work betrays a schoolboy's obsession with pursuing, devouring women; her images reveal more tolerance for diversity. The eyes in her figures capture the viewer's attention and create the attitude which gives each sketch its zest. One lowered eyebrow defines a British bulldog's skepticism. The rolled-back glance of a woman in a feathered hat combines with her half-smirk to suggest that, though she hears the words being spoken from on high by a fellow bus-rider, she does not take them to heart. Within a bewildering world, contentment miraculously appears in the upwardly slanting eyes of a woman standing in the rain, amid leafless trees and evergreens, backed by slanting, tall urban buildings, under a sky in which the sun, a star, and the crescent moon shine together. The rounded oval eyes of the girl on the title page convey both innocence and a sort of stunned despair. These various attitudes also characterize Smith's collected writings.

Stevie Smith's achievement as a poet should not be judged on the evidence of the sixty-three poems included in this anthology. Perhaps eight of these succeed; the others display her affection for playful doggerel and quick, caustic summary. Fortunately, her nine volumes of poems stand on their own merit. The poems reprinted in *Me Again* do offer a diverse sampling of her verbal facility, her fascination with the morality of human relations, and her keen ear for colloquial speech, which she hears as unconsciously funny and revealing too much.

In many of her poems, the reader eavesdrops, with a narrative persona, on the speeches of characters who, by their omissions and by their unconscious transferals, invite one into their most intimate lives. The earliest poem reprinted here, "Goodnight," brutally exposes the unpleasant, unsatisfactory sexual intimacy between a man and a woman. Three perspectives remain distinct: the voyeuristic narrator, the passively suffering female, and the contemptuously nasty male. Their three voices comment coldly on sexual arousal. In a letter about this poem, Smith, after toying with the term "obscenity," does not, finally, accept the label. In "Goodnight," the voices convey no titillation, no pleasure; each voice barely conceals pain, frustration, and weariness.

In "On the Dressing Gown Lent Me by My Hostess the Brazilian Consul in Milan, 1958," Smith again reveals the dissatisfactions of marital intimacy by juxtaposing a third person and an unhappy couple, but she adds, in effect, a fourth persona, by having the third person retrospectively meditate on their encounter. The narrator, a British woman, recalls her fling with the husband by remembering the wife's dressing gown, and her sympathetic memory today distances her from the careless, irresponsible, childish role she once played with the husband. The snatches of conversation that she now recalls combine with her contemporary reflection on herself as a stranger, speaking with a British accent, intruding on the Portuguese and the Italian spoken by her hostess and by the natives of Milan. As this narrator confesses her offenses, however, the rhythm of her lines captures the frivolity of her escapade, in a quickstep and glide.

Platitudes become dangerously self-fulfilling prophecy in "Marriage I Think," as an overly intellectual woman articulates her dismay that her thoughts frighten away a potential mate. Her loneliness and self-pity begin to seem excessively indulgent in the final lines, as her tragic fate is mourned by the narrator's flat voice. Smith echoes the conversations and monologues of ordinary social discourse, but her poetic imagination, by creating an unconventional listener, forces one to hear the tension behind the words spoken.

A skeptical listener annotates her BBC feature program on prostitution. She begins by sardonically recording the artistic motives claimed by a promoter of pornographic films, then she notes that he never mentions his monetary gains. Her drama develops as she replays voices of the women who perform in those shows and who sell their bodies, protesting that there is no sin in their business. Finally, one hears the women reveal their dream of one day earning enough money to retire.

"Beautiful," written when Smith was fifty-five, and four years after a suicide attempt, gently articulates a philosophical defense of human life's rising and fading. The beauty she perceives is not sensual, nor is her imagery ornate; rather, after an opening quatrain in contemporary colloquial style, rhyming "wasnt" with "isnt" and employing the usually humorous tetrameter-trimeter alternation, she then shifts into free-flowing lines, deliberately echoing the rhythmic phrases and familiar, archaic verb forms ("riseth") of Ecclesiastes. This poetic sermon, advocating acceptance of death as a beautiful, appropriate end to life, charms by its unexpected simplicity.

Smith develops a slightly different, more threatening portrayal of the approach to death in her radio play, "A Turn Outside." A character named "Stevie Smith" is interviewed by a character designated as "Interlocutor." Although the play begins as a conventional interview of a famous writer, the dialogue becomes a competitive struggle for power, with each participant seeking to manipulate the other and to control the topics under discussion. As long as their conversation continues, the audience has the illusion that "Stevie Smith" is alive, but Interlocutor's insidious and repeated suggestions that the two of them take a turn outside creates dramatic tension by the inference that he is inviting her to die. In the final words of the play, she agrees to accept his invitation, in a sentence that remains incomplete.

Readers familiar with Smith's poetic voices will recognize some of the same personae in her prose, and her essays and stories reprinted here offer to American readers fresh samples of her insight and mordant wit. Her reviews of biographies on Ethel Smyth, Radclyffe Hall, and Algernon Charles Swinburne demonstrate Smith's tolerance for loving relationships, no matter how socially unconventional, and her rejection of intolerance in any form is evident in her reviews of books on political, ecclesiastical, and feminist debates. Her delightful literary reviews and her autobiographical essays demonstrate that Smith's own individuality as a poet and fiction-writer did not arise from any ignorance of contemporary or classical literary movements.

Smith recalls loving to recite memorized poetry in school, especially the ballads and other story-poems with regular rhythms. While stressing the importance of a classical, traditional education to form a poet's judgment, however, she also admits her pleasure in reading a miscellany of good and bad literature. Even as a child, her interpretations could be eccentric: Gertrude and Claudius, the much-maligned lovers, attracted her more than the morbidly self-reflecting Hamlet. Her memoir-essay on the strict but unconventional school she attended combines affection with a defense of her teachers' educational philosophy, and she echoes the same views expressed in her earlier review of a biography of two schoolteachers, Miss Frances Mary Buss and Miss Dorothea Beale, who championed the right of girls to study the same curriculum as boys. In her review of an anthology limited to poetry by women, she expresses dismay at the awkwardness of the editors' justifications for a collection based on gender, rather than on the quality of the work; she does recognize that women writers work under different constraints than men in her culture. As a working woman, she looks on children, spouses, and animals as impediments which she is thankful not to have.

In a brilliant essay, the cliché "too tired for words" becomes an exact expression of Smith's frustration when she cannot force herself to write. She also reveals her sensitivity to the easily crossed line between serious verse and nonsense, and between inconsequential phrases and witty turns. Her judgment, in excluding some of her poems from her selected anthologies, discriminated wisely. Her muse, sketched as a long-legged, bull-horned moose, is a strong angel, whose heartiness the poet sometimes feels as fear. Struggling to grasp her muse, Smith calls upon the classical image of a hero wrestling with Proteus, the god who could assume different shapes. Expressing her awe at poetry's power, however, Smith calls upon an image of the atomic age: the terrible mushroom cloud in the sky, casting down radiation that spreads and spreads.

Smith's awareness of contemporary history, and her strong responses to her age, are evident in these letters, essays, and stories. In her letter of April 18, 1941, to her friend Rachel Marshall, she mentions the effect of an aerial bombing raid on a visitor to London, but her description reveals also the effect those raids were having on her:

> That was a blitz, and London looks very knocked about now I can tell you, Piccadilly's a treat, so is the Strand. Yesterday morning we paddled to our offices through piles of broken glass, in the sunshine the streets sparkled like diamonds and frost. There is a large bomb crater in the London clay and with fountains of water cascading down into it from broken mains; smells of gas and burning everywhere, but all that has been dealt with by now, I mean the gas, water, and burning. It's bloody silly knocking each other's cities to bits like this, I'm sure these air terror tactics are futile. . . . The effect it has on us seems to be fury. . . .

Smith's exploitation of cliché, her unexpected grasp of strange beauty in the devastation, her exasperation, and, finally, her purposeful analysis provide a glimpse of her complex, creative intelligence at work.

Smith's stories on contemporary political themes include "In the Beginning of the War," in which two terribly earnest German political refugees fail to shake members of the Inter-University Peace Aims Group out of their various eccentric postures (this story was originally part of Smith's novel, *The Holiday*, 1949), and "To School in Germany," which sketches the character of a young German university student before the war, a man who passionately argued his anti-Semitic theories before the indifferent audience of a sixteen-year-old English girl who was then determinedly apolitical.

Neville Chamberlain's 1938 flight to meet with Adolph Hitler at Berchtesgaden is the point of departure for her essay "Mosaic," in which she offers a composite portrait of English tempers as World War II approaches. She herself seems to believe, in 1939, that war with Germany, though terrible, is inevitable. Her aunt, much more bellicose, considers Germany England's natural enemy. Her neighbor, absentmindedly matching colors for her woolwork while not quite listening to the radio announcement of Chamberlain's flight, does not understand why England should be involved with Czechoslovakia. In a blustering voice, Smith, as if carrying on a debate under her breath, classes ignorance about Czechoslovakia with ignorance about Trafalgar and Waterloo. She tries, unsuccessfully, to engage her neighbor by mentioning that her neighbor's sons are old enough to serve in a war, but her neighbor contentedly replies that they have signed the Peace Pledge. Smith's persona in this essay, exaggerated for emphasis, bitterly regrets the sad, ridiculous response of her ignorant neighbor, who represents England's calm in the face of the approaching storm. The voice Smith adopts for this essay rants and poses rhetorical questions, mocking the overblown style of contemporary speeches, and yet she conveys genuine concern over England's apparent indifference to the necessary, if terrible, choice of battle against a national ideology she viewed as essentially evil.

One of the most illuminating essays in this collection sets Smith apart from another poet, one who was famous for his dogmatism. Smith judged T. S. Eliot by her own criteria, and she found him lacking in both compassion and intellectual integrity. Her harsh evaluation of Eliot's *Murder in the Cathedral* (1935) in an essay entitled "History or Poetic Drama?" articulates her distinction between her own work and Eliot's. Interpreting his play in the context of England's fearful and guilty frivolity of the interwar years, she identifies his nostalgic appeal to an earlier, better age. Focusing on the effect Eliot intended to produce on his audience, she introduces a brilliant comparison: "This play comes like Hamlet's portrait of his father which he shows to Gertrude. Look on this, it says, and reform yourself." Smith asserts that Eliot, who is not a Hamlet, means to be equivocal. Through the villainous, lying voices of the knights justifying their murder, Eliot, in Smith's judgment, deliberately relies on two contradictory and false generalizations: "as if he thought that men did not sometimes have to govern, as if he thought that by the act of governing they became at once not men but monsters. It is a disingenuous and not uncommon thought, it is one aspect of the arrogance of art and the arrogance of highmindedness divorced from power, it is something one should not put up with." As she develops her critique, she asserts that the poet, unlike the historian, is not required to be impartial, but she does require the poet to recognize "the truths of humanity." She expects Eliot to acknowledge fear, not to conceal it or distort it into some "neurosis of the invasion of uncleanliness." Her lucid critique reveals her own clearly defined purpose, as a writer who battled against dishonest voices and evasive language.

Reading through this anthology, one discovers the uncompromising values underlying Smith's flippant tone and satire of insipid social forms. She frequently displayed her exasperation and anger at the cowardice of those who evaded necessary choices, whether in personal relations, or in the political arena, or in theological debate, or in literature. Beneath the idiosyncratic surface of her art, one discovers a powerful analytical intelligence and a strong moral vision.

Judith L. Johnston

Sources for Further Study

Choice. XX, September, 1982, p. 89.
Christian Science Monitor. September 10, 1982, p. B5.
Los Angeles Times Book Review. July 18, 1982, p. 7.
Ms. XI, September, 1982, p. 94.
The New York Times Book Review. LXXXVII, May 16, 1982, p. 7.
The New Yorker. LVIII, August 2, 1982, p. 87.
Saturday Review. IX, June, 1982, p. 76.
Time. CXX, July 5, 1982, p. 69.

A MEDITATION

Author: Juan Benet (1927-   )
Translated from the Spanish by Gregory Rabassa
Publisher: Persea Books (New York). 366 pp. $15.95
Type of work: Novel
Time: 1920-1965
Locale: Región, a fictional place in Spain

A novel which re-creates, through a series of disparate remembrances, the fate of two families in post-Civil War Spain

Principal characters:
NARRATOR, whose recollections of his family and its associates form the novel
GRANDFATHER, the patriarch of one of the two important families of Región
MISS MARY, the narrator's cousin
JULIAN, the tutor of the Ruan family, who marries Miss Mary
CRISTINA HOCHNER, the narrator's cousin
JORGE RUAN, the poet whose death and memorial service is the occasion for the narrator's return to Región
CAYETANO CORRAL, a friend of the Ruan family, obsessed with making a clock
LEO (LAURA), a woman who returns to Región to rebuild her family's home and becomes the lover of Cayetano
CARLOS BONAVAL, a friend of Cayetano, who has an affair with Miss Mary and with Leo
EMILIO RUIZ, the manager of the mine in Región, engaged to Miss Mary's older sister
RUFINO, the foreman of the mine workers
THE INDIAN, a mysterious hermit who follows a family tradition by killing his father
THE PENITENT, a visionary who frequents the mine
ANTONIO AND CAMILA ABRANTES, an orphaned brother and sister who become engaged in an incestuous relationship
ROSA DE LLANTES, a woman who acts as the guardian of Antonio and Camila
ANTORAX, a strange, sickly young man kept by Rosa as her lover
MUERTE, the proprietess of the inn in which various characters have intimate liaisons

In a series of novels begun in 1967 with the publication of *Volverás a Región* and continued in *Una meditacion* (1970; *A Meditation*, 1982), *Un viaje de invierno* (1972), and *La otra casa de Mazón* (1973), Juan Benet has created the chronicle of a mythical area of Spain to which he has given the name Región. Critics have frequently compared Benet to William Faulkner, not only for his invention of a fictional place as the locale of his several novels, but also for his dazzling stylistic innovation and linguistic complexity.

Critics have also noted the similarity between Región and the Macondo of

Gabriel García Márquez's *Cien años de soledad* (1967; *One Hundred Years of Solitude*, 1970). In *A Meditation*, as in García Márquez's novel, there is an indefinable narrative attitude that seeks a mythic base to the collective identity of a people—the Spaniards of Benet's novel and the Colombians of *One Hundred Years of Solitude*. Stylistically, however, the two works are as different as one could possibly imagine, and to that difference is attributable the extraordinary popular success of García Márquez and the very limited appeal of Benet. Because it is a mythic interpretation of the origins of the present generation of the Colombian urban middle class, *One Hundred Years of Solitude* has an enormous appeal to the general reading public in Latin America as a kind of cultural history. *A Meditation* is also a search for the mythic origins of the present generation in Spain. It does not, however, have the accessibility of its Colombian counterpart because of its esoteric, convoluted style. Although Benet's novel attracted the attention of the literary establishment and received the prestigious Biblioteca Breve literary prize, it will only appeal to the serious, dedicated reader of fiction. It is one of those rare works that contribute to the evolution of the novel as an art form, but it is a book that will be read by very few.

In *A Meditation*, Benet creates an experience of the Spanish society that is the heir to the trauma of the Civil War of 1936 to 1939. The unnamed narrator is an exile who returns home to attend a memorial service for Jorge Ruan, a young poet and son of the family that has always been the rival of the narrator's family in the struggle for dominance in Región. The narrator's return becomes a pretext for reconstructing through memory the intricate relationship between the two families.

The similarity of this basic premise of the novel to that of Juan Goytisolo's *Señas de identidad* (1966; *Marks of Identity*, 1969) is striking. The theme is the same but the techniques are quite different. *Marks of Identity* is a novel of transition, still in the tradition of realistic narrative, although there is a tendency toward the innovation of the later novels of Goytisolo's exile trilogy—*Reivindicacion del Conde Don Julián* (1970; *Count Julian*, 1974) and *Juan sin tierra* (1975; *Juan the Landless,* 1977). When Goytisolo becomes more experimental, he tends to create a fantasized representation of reality which becomes an extensive metaphorical expression of his reaction to the Spanish experience. Benet creates a world much more in accord with the historical reality that his narrative reflects. The narrator of *A Meditation* tells a story that, for the most part, is plausible, however convoluted and fragmentary.

In Benet's novel, the reconstruction of the past takes the form of a meditation, in which the narrator allows each memory to conjure up other recollections, which lead in turn to philosophical observations on the meaning of the recollected experiences, which return him to other remembrances of other events and other characters. As the reader slowly and gradually accumulates details about the complex relationships of the characters, much of the mystery of this enigmatic reality is clarified, yet there is also much that remains confused and contradictory.

Benet has been compared to Marcel Proust, and the similarities are striking at those points in Benet's novel in which the narrator is stimulated to a remembrance of the past by the things of present experience. There is a moment in *A Meditation* that is reminiscent of the famous Proustian madeleine scene. The narrator stoops to tie his shoe, looks at three of the friends attending the service for Jorge, and—frozen in that instant of concentration on his own posture in adjusting the shoelace and the posture of the three friends—draws together the various threads of the remembrance, explaining a complex web of relationships that summarizes the novel. As he sees Cayetano Corral and Carlos Bonaval talking to Mary, he realizes that Bonaval is the man with whom Mary ran away for an amorous adventure on the eve of her marriage; the man with whom she spent nights in the inn from which she called for Jorge's brother Enrique, who summoned Julian to marry her; the man who had returned primarily to find the posthumous papers of the poet Jorge. These same papers are those which Mary's son would put in her coffin right before her burial a year later, after which Carlos Bonaval and Leo (Laura) would go off to the mountains for a lovers' tryst, where they would be seen by Emilio Ruiz, who had been waiting for Mary to die so that he could marry her older sister. These illicit affairs occurred in the same inn to which Jorge fled from the sanatorium and, finding Muerte, the proprietess, in bed, nearly bit off her earlobe while having coitus with her, because he had seen Rufino, the foreman of the mine run by Emilio Ruiz, bite the jugular vein of a rat to kill it, a rat like the ones that Camila Abrantes persuaded him to burn alive before she sent him to the Indian's hut, where he was found by two Civil Guards, near the spot where he was later found murdered.

It is not until the last pages of the novel that it becomes obvious that the meditation is constructed around the trip that Bonaval and Leo take to the mountains, a trip that touches the lives of many of the characters in a direct or an oblique way. As Bonaval brings Leo home and deposits her, immobile in her ecstasy, on her bed, the narrator recapitulates all of the events and relationships of the novel, as if everything were concentrated on that moment of Bonaval's realization that the sexual adventure with Leo has left him in despair. In the enigmatic condensation of the experiences of all of the characters in that moment—enigmatic because the reader does not understand why that episode is the distillation of everything else—the meditation ends with Bonaval rubbing his face with the black earth of the ruins of the factory where Cayetano Corral had worked on his clock, the very place where Bonaval had first met Leo.

The enigma of this narrative is unresolved, and the reader is left with an intense uncertainty about the characters and their relationships. Although the narrative is so obscure that it often becomes irritating, the novel creates an extraordinary representation of the process of meditative reconstruction of the past through memory. The narrative is indeed a meditation, a series of references to events in the lives of the characters, references that are repeated continually, at times clearly and at times obscurely. The accumulation of remembered reality gradually reveals a truth—albeit a partial truth—both to the narrator and to the reader.

That partial truth has something to do with the intermingling of the two rival families—the narrator's and the family of Ruan. Carlos Bonaval, locked in a struggle with the narrator's grandfather, has his liaison with Mary, marries her to Julian, the Ruans' tutor, then runs away with Leo, the lover of Cayetano and an intimate friend of the Ruans, while Emilio Ruiz, a distant relative of Cayetano, marries Mary's older sister. The truth of this reality is also related to Cayetano's clock, an extraordinary pendulum timepiece that symbolizes to these characters their own anxieties; it is also related to the inn over which presides the mysterious Muerte (death), and in which occur the events that seem to be the most significant of the novel.

That *A Meditation* creates only a partial truth which is not entirely accessible through rational cognition is evidence of Benet's departure from the postwar tradition of the Spanish novel. As Jorge Rodríguez Padrón has observed in a review of Benet's work in the literary magazine *Insula* (November-December, 1979), Benet's novelistic theory rests on the concept that fiction is a mythographic activity that configures its own world according to its own laws, that creates with words not a reality which can be fully known by the intellect, but a potentiality—a suggestion of an uncertain reality. In *A Meditation*, Benet creates a representation of the process of memory, which restores the past through recall, analysis of the remembered facts, evaluation of the evidence, and a positing of a possible truth.

Reading Benet's *A Meditation* can be frustrating but is also enriching and rewarding. Gregory Rabassa's translation is a monumental achievement, for the structures of English are not as suitable to Benet's continuous narrative as are the structures of Spanish. There are no traditional divisions in the text, no paragraphs, no chapters. The punctuation is chaotic, and there are sentences that go on for pages, with parentheses inside of parentheses inside of other parentheses. It is significant that Benet wrote this novel not on sheets of paper but on a long, continuous roll. It is unfortunate that it could not be published in the same format, for the narrative is continuous, with no breaks and no pauses. This is Benet's most significant achievement, that he has been able to re-create that process of memory, that flow of consciousness which many novelists have attempted, but he has mastered.

Gilbert Smith

Sources for Further Study

Choice. XX, September, 1982, p. 90.
Christian Science Monitor. XCIX, July 9, 1982, p. 14.
Library Journal. CVII, May 1, 1982, p. 902.
Los Angeles Times Book Review. October 24, 1982, p. 7.
The New York Times Book Review. LXXXVII, May 23, 1982, p. 13.
Publishers Weekly. CCXXI, March 19, 1982, p. 55.